BUSINESS INSURANCE
Fourth Edition

BUSINESS INSURANCE

Fourth Edition

Edwin H. White, J.D., J.S.D., C.L.U.
Member of the New York Bar

and

Herbert Chasman, J.D., C.L.U.

Member of the New York Bar;
Dean, School of Advanced Career Studies
American College of Life Underwriters

PRENTICE-HALL, INC.   Englewood Cliffs, N.J.

Prentice-Hall International, Inc., *London*
Prentice-Hall of Australia, Pty. Ltd., *Sydney*
Prentice-Hall of Canada, Ltd., *Toronto*
Prentice-Hall of India Private Ltd., *New Delhi*
Prentice-Hall of Japan, Inc., *Tokyo*

Fourth Printing . . . . . July, 1976

Library of Congress Cataloging in Publication Data

White, Edwin Harold,
    Business insurance.

    1. Insurance, Business life--United States.
2. Insurance, Business--United States. I. Chasman,
Herbert, joint author. II. Title.
KF1180.B8W47 1974   346'.73'086   74-5286
ISBN 0-13-100859-5

Printed in the United States of America

PREFACE TO FOURTH EDITION

At the time the third edition of this text was published, it was appropriate for a book titled *Business Insurance* to be limited generally to the uses of life insurance to fund the purchase of a business interest. However, the term "business insurance" encompasses much more. It is used to identify any life and health insurance policies that are owned by and payable to a business. In addition to life insurance used to fund the purchase of a business interest, this includes disability insurance used for that purpose. The terminology also applies to disability insurance used to fund a salary continuation plan, life and health insurance used to indemnify a business for the economic loss caused by the death or disability of the insured, life insurance used to fund a nonqualified deferred compensation plan, and life insurance arranged under a split-dollar plan to provide a fringe benefit to valued employees.

The fourth edition of this encompasses the expanded definition of "business insurance" by including entirely new chapters. These chapters are grouped under the title "Other Uses of Life and Health Insurance to Benefit the Business Organization, Its Owners and Employees." The first chapter is "Disability Buy-Sell Agreements and Salary Continuation Plans." It puts the finishing touch on buy-sell agreements by adding to the earlier coverage on the uses of life insurance to fund a business purchase. This chapter highlights the twin problems that disability of a closely held business owner can cause: the need to provide salary continuation and the need to purchase the interest of a disabled owner. This section of the book presents information on the tax treatment of disability income plans, including a study of cases dealing with the requirement that such plans benefit a "class of employees." This chapter also provides some unique insights into the design of a disability buy-sell agreement. It covers such important questions as when the buy-out should become effective, who the

3

purchaser should be, how the business interest should be valued and how disability income insurance can be used to fund the plan.

The second new chapter is "Key Man Insurance." It is aimed at the uses of key man life and health insurance to indemnify a business or business owner for the economic loss that will be suffered in the event of the death or permanent disability of a key man. The material presented identifies the persons who are key men in a business as well as the types of businesses that have a need for key man insurance. There are data concerning the effect on key man insurance of the income and estate tax laws. Specific attention is paid to the income tax treatment of premiums and proceeds. The effects of the transfer-for-value rule and the accumulated earnings tax on key man insurance are also featured. On the estate tax side, there is an up-to-date account of the position of the Internal Revenue Service concerning key man insurance on the life of a majority stockholder. Placing a dollar value on a key man has long been a difficult task. The chapter offers suggestions on how to accomplish this, including a detailed example of the use of a formula to arrive at an answer.

The third new chapter is "Nonqualified Deferred Compensation Plans." Such plans are explored in depth, with emphasis on the uses of life insurance to aid an employer in meeting its obligation to pay deferred compensation benefits. This chapter develops two roads to a nonqualified deferred compensation plan. One is traveled by the employee who voluntarily defers a portion of his present compensation in order to maximize the benefit from each dollar deferred by minimizing the amount to be paid in income taxes. The second road is the one an employer will take when he wants to tie a key employee closer to the firm. Under this "inducement to stay" deferred compensation plan, the employee is not given the option of receiving additional current compensation. The employer chooses deferred compensation for him. The chapter unfolds the necessary steps to defer taxation of income for an unfunded and a funded plan. There is coverage of the problem facing the employer who is considering a deferred compensation plan but hesitates because of the loss of a current income tax deduction. An arrangement for overcoming this objection—illustrated with a numerical example—is found in this chapter.

The income and estate tax treatment associated with death benefits included in deferred compensation plans represent an important part of the chapter. The chapter also addresses itself to the most difficult task associated with a deferred compensation plan: designing it to meet the needs and expectations of the parties involved. It is for this reason that a detailed explanation of the important provisions of a deferred compensation plan are included. Specific attention is given to the various arrangements available for the payment of benefits and the use of life insurance to fund those benefits.

The final new chapter covers Split-Dollar Insurance Plans. A split-dollar insurance plan allows a person who needs insurance protection, for whatever reason, to secure it at a cost that is less than if he simply purchased the insurance on his own. In a case where the person in need of insurance protection is a key man in a business, the premium expense can be split between the key man and the business. An explanation of how a split-dollar plan works, using both the endorsement system and the collateral assignment system, is presented. There are data on the factors that bear on which split-dollar system is preferable in a specific instance.

Since the tax consequences of a split-dollar plan are extremely important, detailed explanations of the income tax treatment of premiums, proceeds, and policy dividends are included. In addition, the importance of the estate tax treatment of any life insurance plan has been recognized by an in-depth study of the estate tax consequences associated with a split-dollar plan. Included is a discussion of the plans that can be utilized in an attempt to avoid the payment of estate taxes. A number of variations of the basic split-dollar plan have been devised. An explanation of the most popular ones, such as the level contribution method and the noncontributory method, will be found in this chapter. In the typical employer-employee split-dollar plan, insurance is purchased on the life of the employee. However, where an employee is in need of insurance protection, not on his life, but on the life of someone else, the employer may nevertheless help to provide the insurance protection through the use of a split-dollar plan. The chapter tells how this may be accomplished to fund the purchase of a sole proprietorship or the purchase of an interest in a partnership or corporation under a cross-purchase buy-sell agreement.

In addition to the new material, there is a fresh look given to the materials on buy-sell agreements funded with life insurance in a sole proprietorship, partnership, and corporation. References are made to many new cases that deal with business purchase agreements. Expanded coverage is provided on such topics as business purchase agreements in a Subchapter S corporation, the effect of the accumulated earnings tax on stock redemptions, Section 303 stock redemptions, and the distinctive characteristics of a buy-sell agreement in a professional partnership. Despite these additions, the number of pages overall has not been increased from the previous edition. This has been accomplished by deleting references to many cases that are no longer considered necessary and by dovetailing coverage of certain concepts which are the same regardless of whether they are applied to a sole proprietorship, partnership, or corporation.

The material on Proprietorships is grouped into three parts. Part I sets forth the fundamental facts about proprietorships and the economic losses attendant upon their discontinuance and liquidation at the death of the proprietor. Part II deals with the various plans that have been attempted to avoid closing out the sole proprietorship upon the owner's death, in order to avoid these losses. Part III provides detailed information on an ideal business continuation plan: the insured buy-sell agreement between the proprietor and a key employee. Emphasis is placed on the specific benefits of the insured buy-sell agreement, its content, and tax consequences.

The material on Partnerships is divided into three parts. Part I deals with the fundamental facts about partnerships. Particular emphasis is placed upon the fact that the surviving partner will be held to the highest standards of duty and accountability in liquidating the partnership's affairs and that any "bargaining" with the heirs of the deceased partner will not be countenanced by the court. Part II discusses the plans that have been used in an attempt to avoid liquidation upon the death of a partner. The text highlights the adverse consequences that result in the absence of a plan and those that lurk in any plan improvised after the death of a partner. By the process of examining and eliminating defective schemes, the discussion leads to the one workable plan by which the partnership business may be continued. Part III deals with the details of this plan—the buy-sell agreement among the partners themselves, or with the partnership, funded by life insurance.

The problems that can exist at the death of a partner and the soundness of the insured buy-sell solution are illustrated by reference to the actual facts found in many leading cases on the subject.

The material on Corporations is also divided into three parts. Part I deals with the fundamental facts about corporations, including the characteristics of a close corporation and the consequences of the death of a close corporation stockholder. Part II discusses the various plans that have been used in attempts to avoid the deleterious effects ordinarily following upon the death of a close corporation stockholder. Part III explains how the buy-sell agreement funded with insurance can function to eliminate the problems attendant upon the death of a close corporation stockholder. A different set of problems can arise when a close corporation stockholder wants to pass his business interest to a family member who is or will become active in the business. Discussed in some detail are the factors that must be evaluated to determine if this is a wise course of action. Where retention of close corporation stock for a family member is advisable, the chapter discusses the possibility of a partial sale funded with life insurance to provide cash with which to meet death costs while retaining control of the corporation for the family.

In sum, the Fourth Edition represents a major revision of areas previously covered, along with the addition of significant new material. These changes enable the text to keep pace with the expanded definition of the term "business insurance."

The book should be a valuable learning tool and reference source for those persons concerned with estate planning for business owners and interested in the uses of life and health insurance to meet the cash needs of a business and its employees.

Edwin H. White
Herbert Chasman

Contents

9

continued

Part III: THE PROPRIETORSHIP INSURED
BUY-SELL AGREEMENT

PARTNERSHIPS

Part I: FUNDAMENTAL FACTS ABOUT PARTNERSHIPS

Part II: PLANS ATTEMPTED TO AVOID LIQUIDATION
ON DEATH OF A PARTNER

continued

Part III: THE PARTNERSHIP BUY-SELL AGREEMENT
FINANCED WITH LIFE INSURANCE

CORPORATIONS

Part I: FUNDAMENTAL FACTS ABOUT CORPORATIONS

OTHER USES OF LIFE AND HEALTH INSURANCE TO BENEFIT
THE BUSINESS ORGANIZATION

continued

continued

PROPRIETORSHIPS

Part I

FUNDAMENTAL FACTS
ABOUT PROPRIETORSHIPS

Chapter 1

GENERAL INFORMATION
ABOUT SOLE PROPRIETORSHIPS

A proper understanding and appreciation of the most efficient plans that have been developed for the continuation of the one-man unincorporated business after the death of the proprietor must rest upon an adequate knowledge of the problems involved. An awareness of these problems and their implications, in turn, calls for a clear conception of the nature of the sole proprietorship.

Sole proprietorship defined. A sole proprietorship may be defined as a business or professional enterprise owned by one individual, who is usually its manager as well. Our concern here, however, is with business proprietorships, of which there are approximately nine million in the United States. We can characterize a sole proprietorship business as follows:

1. It is a business enterprise owned entirely by one person in his individual capacity, as distinguished from ownership by a partnership or by a corporation.
2. It is customarily conducted by the owner—the sole proprietor—its business being transacted by him alone, or with the assistance of any agents or employees that he may hire.

HOW SOLE PROPRIETORSHIPS ARE FORMED

A sole proprietorship is created simply by the bringing together of those components necessary to carry on the particular enterprise and then opening shop. It is thus distinguished from the creation of a partnership, brought

23

about by the voluntary agreement of the members, or the creation by law of a corporation upon completion of the necessary legal steps and the granting of the corporate charter by the appropriate state or Federal government.

Joe King notices a vacant store space at the corner of Main and Elm. Around the corner on Elm Street is a prosperous residential neighborhood, the inhabitants of which must go two blocks farther down Main Street for their groceries. Joe obtains a long-term lease on the store, stocks up, places a freshly painted sign over the door bearing the legend JOE KING, GRO-CERIES, and opens for business. As simply as that, a new sole proprietorship has been born. No special documents are required and no special legal procedure is necessary.

True, if Joe had desired to do business as the ACME GROCERY STORE he would probably have had to file with the proper authorities a certificate of doing business under an assumed name. True also, if he had intended to open up a business peculiarly affecting the health, safety, or morals of the community, such as, for example, a restaurant or a liquor store, a special license to do so would no doubt have been a prerequisite. But aside from meeting the necessary requirements of regulatory laws of this type (laws which apply equally whether the business is to be conducted as a proprietor-ship, partnership, or corporation), the birth of a sole proprietorship is legally unhampered.

PROPERTY RIGHTS IN A SOLE PROPRIETORSHIP

Before he opened his grocery store, Joe King owned various kinds of property. These he could keep, use, destroy, or otherwise dispose of as he chose, subject only to the general laws restricting uses of property that would encroach upon the rights of others. Happily, among these items was a sturdy bank account, part of which he has now expended in the purchase of store fixtures, stocks of merchandise, and other needed business property—the property for his sole proprietorship.

What changes have been wrought by this substitution of business property for that which was personal? Legally, none of any consequence. Joe has, in general, the same rights of dominion and control over the business assets that he has over his personal assets. Subject to the rights of others and subject to any voluntary restricting agreements that he may make, his legal property rights are still entire. Changes have taken place with respect to his property, but they are economic and financial in nature rather than legal. On the economic front, there has been recorded a new business unit: a sole proprietorship possessing valuable "place utility" because of its accessibility and convenience to the housewives of Elm Street. On the financial front, Joe has received, or shortly will receive, a credit rating as a proprietor. He has opened up a set of business books, and at the end of the year will be required to complete a special schedule in his income tax forms exhibiting the income, expenses and net profits of his business enterprise.

In spite of these economic and financial changes however, the establishment of the sole proprietorship business has wrought no new pattern of property rights, as would have been the case had a partnership or a corporation been formed. The assets of the business remain Joe's personal assets in the legal sense, and they will, in the event of his death and in the absence of a special statute or of special will provisions specifically dealing with them, be distinguishable only by description from the other items in his estate.

LIABILITIES IN A SOLE PROPRIETORSHIP

Before the establishment of JOE KING, GROCERIES, Joe had from time to time entered into various obligations for himself and his family. A small outstanding account at his family's favorite department store is not unusual, his last car was purchased on the installment plan, and only a few months ago he signed a new lease on his residence. For all these obligations Joe always knew, of course, that he was fully liable.

But what about his liability for the new obligations he is now assuming as proprietor of the corner grocery store? He is as completely liable under his store lease as he has been, and is, under his house lease. If he buys a delivery truck on the installment plan, he will be as personally liable for any unpaid balance as was the case when he bought his family automobile. In short, there is no legal distinction between his so-called personal liabilities and the liabilities that he creates as a proprietor. In each case he is fully liable and his liability is unlimited and unshared.

Nor would any distinction be made between his "business" and his "personal" liabilities in the event of Joe's death—as contrasted with the case were he a partner in a partnership or a stockholder in a corporation. Subject to the prior payment of such items as funeral and administration expenses, subject to the statutory order in which personal and real property and property generally and specifically bequeathed is applicable to the payment of debts, and subject to any outstanding mortgages and pledges, all of his property not expressly exempt by special statute would ultimately be liable for the payment of all his debts. Proprietorship debts would have no preferential right to be paid out of his proprietorship property, nor would personal debts have any priority of payment out of his other property. Naturally, a proprietor may make special provisions in his will with reference to his business or personal obligations, but in the absence of any such special will provisions, his debts would not be separated into the categories of "business" and "personal" in his estate; they would be treated indiscriminately.

ADVANTAGES OF PROPRIETORSHIP AS A MODE
OF CONDUCTING BUSINESS

The advantages of the individual proprietorship as a method of carrying on a business stem largely from its simplicity, the outstanding characteristic of this form of business enterprise. An undertaking owned and operated by one man who hires all his other help, it may be established without any formal organizational procedures. No special legal requirements must be met, unless the venture is to be conducted under an assumed name or unless the business is to be of a type requiring a state or local license as a prerequisite to its operation. The former is readily complied with and the latter is a requirement unrelated to the form of business organization.

Once established, the pattern of operation of the individual proprietorship is flexible. The single owner and "boss" has the distinct advantage of being able to make decisions regarding its conduct as the exigencies of the business may demand, unhampered by a board of directors or any other impediment to swift and decisive action. Thus, new opportunities may be quickly grasped, new fields of business entered, or old ones abandoned with a freedom of choice and celerity of execution granted only to the sole proprietor.

Owning all of the business, the sole proprietor is entitled to all the profits of his enterprise. This is in direct contrast with the situation in a partnership or in a corporation. In a partnership, each partner receives his agreed share of the earnings of the firm. In a corporation, the profits are corporation profits, and ultimately go to the individual stockholders in proportion to their dividend-paying stock. Thus, except where a corporation is entirely owned by one person—a status in many respects more analogous to a proprietorship than to the ordinary corporation, in spite of the corporate legal structure— other forms of business organization call for the sharing of profits between at least two individuals; often, among several. In the case of the sole proprietor, the profits are his alone.

DISADVANTAGES INHERENT IN A SOLE
PROPRIETORSHIP

Simplicity of structure not only accounts for the advantages of the sole proprietorship as a mode of conducting business, but conversely is the source of its chief disadvantages.

Foremost among these disadvantages is the complete liability of the proprietor for all the obligations of the enterprise. As we shall see later, this outstanding handicap is also present in the partnership form of organization but not in the corporation, where the stockholders enjoy limited liability. In a partnership, a partner who has discharged more than his share of the firm's ordinary obligations has—for whatever it may be worth in the particular case—either a right of contribution from the other partners of their respective shares of the total obligations, or the right to be reimbursed or indemnified by the partnership itself. The sole proprietor shoulders alone the obligations that he can so freely create. His liability is entire and unshared.

This complete liability is accompanied by the full responsibility which the individual proprietor must assume at all times for the conduct of the business. Being the sole boss, he is in a position to "call the shots," but by the same token he cannot avoid bearing the burden of all weighty decisions. True, he can delegate many minor responsibilities to his employees (and if he is a capable executive he will do so whenever possible), but the "yoke" must be borne ultimately by the proprietor himself. Unlike a partner, there is no one on his own plane of responsibility with whom to share the mental load. Unlike the corporate executive, there are no fellow-officers or directors with whom he can divide the responsibility for the management of the enterprise.

A third disadvantage of the proprietorship is that whereas the owner is entitled to all the profits, he must also bear all the losses. There are few businesses that can show net profits year in and year out, and when a poor year does come, the sole proprietor must stand the loss alone.

A disadvantage which circumscribes the field of operations of sole proprietorships generally is the limited capital funds usually available to them. Ordinarily, such an enterprise must be conducted with the money which the owner can personally put into it, supplemented only by the money he can borrow and the credit he can obtain. Consequently he must usually forego opportunities requiring considerable investments of capital. But many of these same opportunities might be grasped by a partnership, since the resources of all the partners may be made available, or by a corporation, in which the funds of numerous individual investors are pooled to form the capital of a single corporate enterprise.

We now take up that disadvantage of the sole proprietorship which most concerns us: the fact that the proprietorship ends with the death of the proprietor. This follows from the circumstance that such a business has no legal entity apart from the owner. Immediately upon his death, the assets and liabilities of the business become assets and liabilities of his estate along with—and in the absence of special statute, special agreement, or special will provisions, not distinguishable from—all of his other assets and liabilities. In any event, the old proprietorship is gone and unless effective plans have been made in advance by the proprietor, the once profitable and valuable going business will go out of existence with substantial losses to his family and to the community as a whole. These losses will be discussed in some detail in the following chapter.

Chapter 2

TERMINATION OF A
SOLE PROPRIETORSHIP

CAUSES OF TERMINATION

Termination of a sole proprietorship may be brought about either by the voluntary act of the proprietor or from causes beyond his control such as, for example, bankruptcy or death.

Voluntary termination. Since he owns and directs the business entirely by himself, the individual proprietor may conclude at any time to cease operations. In such event, he would first fulfill outstanding commitments and then liquidate the assets of the proprietorship in whatever manner he believed was to his best advantage; or he might sell the business as a going concern to a partnership or to a corporation. Again, he might decide to continue the business, but not as a proprietorship. This he could accomplish by taking in a partner or by incorporating the enterprise. Voluntary changes such as these are, of course, a commonplace sight in the daily kaleidoscope of the nation's business.

Death of proprietor. In the previous chapter it was pointed out that, at the death of the proprietor, the proprietorship is terminated because it has no legal entity distinct from that of the proprietor as an individual. When a proprietor dies the assets and liabilities constituting the proprietorship immediately become assets and liabilities of his estate along with his so-called personal assets and liabilities.

But his death generates a problem peculiar to a proprietorship business: until an executor or administrator is appointed by the probate court, the

28

business operations must cease entirely since no one possesses legal authority to act. This sudden and immediate interruption of business continuity will persist until a personal representative qualifies in the probate court. In one representative case,[1] the executor did not qualify until one month after the proprietor's death; in another,[2] the executor qualified two months after the proprietor's death. In both of these cases, rents accrued for stores idled during the interregnum. Obviously, this period may be a costly one. This being so, some probate courts have used the technique of promptly appointing a temporary administrator and giving him authority to keep the proprietorship business in operation during the interim until the regular personal representative qualifies.[3]

If the proprietor has left a valid and subsisting will, his property and obligations will be administered by his executor in accordance with its terms. If there is no will, an administrator will be appointed to wind up his affairs in conformity with the applicable probate and intestate laws. Briefly sketched— and consequently over-simplified—the administration of his estate in either event will require his personal representative (executor or administrator, as the case may be) to take possession and to inventory all of the deceased proprietor's property, conserve it, convert it into cash (excepting real property, property specifically bequeathed by will, and items agreed to be accepted by the heirs in kind unless these items are required for the payment of debts or preferred legacies), pay the expenses of administration and the obligations of the deceased, and distribute the remainder to those properly entitled to it.

The procedure as to the proprietorship assets and liabilities is particularly rigid and costly, but departure from it may be made under certain exceptional circumstances. Some such circumstances are the existence of special will provisions relating to the business, the existence of special statutes authorizing a limited continuation of the business beyond the owner's death, or the existence of some form of special business continuation agreement. Each of these special situations will be discussed in detail in later chapters. Here we are concerned with the situation which prevails in the absence of any such special alleviating or remedial circumstances, on the death of a proprietor and its effect in requiring prompt termination and liquidation of the proprietorship business.

ECONOMIC EFFECTS OF TERMINATION OF PROPRIETORSHIP BUSINESS

The deleterious economic effects of terminating the proprietorship busi-

---

[1]*Re Stewart's Will*, 109 N.Y.S.2d 609 (1951).

[2]*Re Kitzes' Estate*, 109 N.Y.S.2d 673 (1951).

[3]This technique was used in *Graybar Electric Company, Inc. v. McClave*, 91 Ariz. 223, 371 P.2d 350 (1962), discussed in the following chapter.

ness on the death of the proprietor are five-fold. The first relates to the general economy and the others relate to the economic status of those immediately concerned.

Effect on the general economy. The sustenance of our economic life consists of the innumerable commercial transactions occurring continually within the nation. The "blood corpuscles" that carry this nourishment into every community are its business units—its proprietorships, partnerships and corporations. When one of these units goes out of existence and its business is terminated, whether it be a large, nationally known corporation or a small, local proprietorship, the economic might of the country is to that extent weakened.

Careers of employees interrupted. Most proprietorships have in their employ one or more employees whose livelihoods and those of their dependents are derived from the business. Termination of the enterprise, of course, destroys these jobs, usually with financial loss to the employee and to the community. To the newer and younger employees, the set-back will be temporary, but to those old in years and service, the loss often will be permanent.

Stoppage of income to the family from the business. During the lifetime of the proprietor, his income consists of the profits made from the business transactions of his proprietorship. He and his family live on this income. But on his death, these transactions cease abruptly, except for the completion of any contractual obligations which may have to be carried out by his executor or administrator. With their generating source rendered impotent, profits are no longer made and the flow of sustaining funds to the family is arrested. This loss of income can be substantial. In the *Dennis* case,[4] for example, the probate court refused to authorize the Temporary Administrator to continue, except for the purpose of liquidation, an excavating business that was grossing $10,000 monthly.

Possible delay in administration of the estate. Among the duties of the executor or administrator is the carrying through to completion of the unfinished contractual obligations of the deceased proprietor, excepting, however, those contracts that were to have been performed only by him personally. The law on this subject is well stated in a 1956 Pennsylvania case,[5] as follows:

> The general rule is that to the extent of the assets that come into his possession, the personal representative of a decedent is responsible on all contracts incurred by decedent in his lifetime. . . . An exception to this rule is: "* * * Where the agreement is for services which involve the peculiar skill of an expert,

---

[4]*Matter of Dennis' Estate*, 136 N.Y.S.2d 84 (1954).

[5]*Re Stormer's Estate*, 385 Pa. 382 (1956).

by whom alone the particular work in contemplation of the parties can be performed, or more generally, where distinctly personal considerations are at the foundation of the contract, the relation of the parties is dissolved by the death of him whose personal qualities constituted the particular inducement to the contract. . . ." *Billings' Appeal,* 106 Pa. 558.

To illustrate, Joe King, the corner grocer, may have contracted with the local American Legion Post to supply it with certain canned goods during the next year. In anticipation of this, Joe has scheduled certain purchases of the requisite goods from his wholesaler. Neither contract would be discharged upon Joe's death and his personal representative would be called upon to perform. On the other hand, had Joe been contractually engaged by the Legion post to supervise personally the food purchases of the post canteen, this contract, requiring personal performance on his part, would be discharged upon Joe's death.

Little imagination is required to visualize many instances where, upon the death of a proprietor, delay in the settlement of his estate will be caused by the necessary performance of obligations that the proprietor has entered into and that have outlived him. Such delays invariably result in increased administration costs, and create vexations, if not hardships, for the heirs.

Shrinkage of assets upon liquidation. As stated by Henderson, Surrogate: "It is the duty of the administrator to convert the assets of the estate into money within a reasonable time after his appointment."[6] In the event the deceased proprietor leaves a will, it is the duty of his executor to convert all personal property into cash except that specifically bequeathed or that permitted by the will or consented to among the heirs to be distributed "in kind." Delivery of specific items of property, however, even though directed or permitted, can be accomplished only to a limited degree in many cases, because a substantial amount of cash may be required to pay the costs of last illness and funeral, taxes, executor's fees, legal fees, probate charges, and all outstanding personal and business debts. Normally, delivery in kind of the assets of a proprietorship is utterly impracticable, not only because of the need for cash to pay the above items (which on the average will absorb approximately one-third of the gross estate value), but also because the unsuitable nature of such assets makes them unacceptable to the heirs as bequests "in kind." Therefore, in the absence of specially designed plans for the disposal of a proprietorship business, it will be incumbent upon the personal representative, whether executor or administrator, to liquidate the assets of the business for cash.

It is common knowledge that the liquidation of the assets of an enterprise usually results in severe losses. Accounts receivable will be impossible to

---

[6]*In re Lazer's Estate,* 247 N.Y.S. 230 (1930).

collect in full. The forced sale of inventories must often be made at fractional prices and equipment frequently is sold at great sacrifice. Moreover, good will, an asset that accounts for a significant percentage of the profits in many an active business, evaporates upon the closing out of the enterprise by the personal representative; its value is totally lost. Only on those rare and fortuitous occasions when a single buyer can be found who will purchase the proprietorship business "in bulk" as a going concern will these sacrificial losses be materially reduced. And only when the proprietor, during his lifetime, has set up an effective plan for the continuation of his business—a plan to prevent the normal processes of estate liquidation from running their costly course—will this destruction of values be surely averted.

The ruinous economic effects of the termination of the proprietorship business on the death of the owner are such that every proprietor should search diligently for a business continuation plan that will enable him to pass along to his heirs the true "going" value of his enterprise.

Part II

PLANS USED IN ATTEMPTS TO AVOID LIQUIDATION AT THE DEATH OF THE PROPRIETOR[1]

Chapter 3

CONTINUATION OF THE BUSINESS WITHOUT PROPER AUTHORITY

The heavy financial losses that are precipitated when a proprietorship business is liquidated on the death of the proprietor clearly demonstrate the need for some plan that will avoid such liquidation. In the hope of avoiding a sacrifice of values, many schemes have been attempted to keep such business operating. In this and the following chapter, we shall examine various plans that have been improvised after the proprietor's death.

CONTINUATION OF BUSINESS WITH NO AUTHORITY

Continuation by the personal representative. Upon the death of a proprietor, one of the duties of his personal representative is to take possession immediately of the assets of the proprietorship. Frequently these assets represent a thriving, profitable business, and the executor or administrator, well aware of this fact but ignorant of the legal perils involved, may decide on his own initiative, without authority, to continue operations for the benefit of those interested in the estate. This happened in the *Moran* case.[2]

In that case, where Mrs. Moran as administratrix sustained a loss in continuing her deceased husband's hotel business without authority, Pennsylvania's highest court held her liable. It stated that under such

---

[1]In Part II, Chapters 3 and 4 deal with alternatives to liquidation improvised after the proprietor's death; Chapter 5 treats of alternatives to liquidation set up prior to the death of the proprietor.

[2]*Re Moran's Estate*, 261 Pa. 269, 104 Atl. 585 (1918).

circumstances the general rule was that "the gain, if any, belongs to the estate, while the loss falls upon" the personal representative.

Another of the legion of cases illustrating that rule is the *Wenzlaff* case.[3] There, the widow as administratrix was held personally liable for over $3,000 she had lost in less than three months in continuing without authority her deceased husband's small jewelry shop.

A larger surcharge was meted out in a 1957 New York case.[4] Arthur R. Mack had conducted a grocery store in Lyons, New York, for some time prior to his death in 1955. His widow renounced her right to administer the estate in favor of her daughter and son. It was decided that the business should be continued for the purpose of obtaining the best possible price as a going business. It was also decided that the daughter should continue the business since the son lived in a city some distance away. Apparently, no effort was made to get a court order authorizing such continuation. There were numerous accounts payable and accounts receivable outstanding, and the daughter extended further credit and incurred additional accounts payable in operating the store during the succeeding ten months until it was sold. The daughter lacked experience in business and in estate administration, with the result that "the operation of the store did not prove successful and at the time of the sale, there were insufficient assets to pay the claims of all the creditors." Ultimately, the family residence was sold for the purpose of paying the decedent's debts.

The probate court imposed on the daughter surcharges of $11,730.87 in connection with her operation of the business. Further, the court disallowed a merchant's claim against the estate to the extent it represented merchandise supplied the store after the proprietor's death, the opinion stating: "Since the representatives of this company were well aware of the conditions and were presumed to know that the administratrix had no legal authority to carry on the business, they must look for payment of this amount to the administratrix, Rosemary D. Mack, individually."

As the foregoing cases clearly show, the unauthorized continuation of a proprietorship business by an inexperienced personal representative, instead of avoiding sacrifice of estate values, usually results only in sustaining additional losses, for which the imprudent executor or administrator is personally liable.

Before leaving this discussion of a personal representative's unauthorized continuation of a proprietorship business, something should be said of the difficulty in determining, under certain circumstances, whether or not a continuation is authorized. On the one hand, the personal representative has the duty to conserve the estate assets; on the other, he is penalized if he

---

[3]*Estate of Wenzlaff*, 55 Ill. App.2d 92, 204 N.E.2d 148 (1964).

[4]*Re Mack's Estate*, 168 N.Y.S.2d 859 (1957).

continues the business without authority. Where is the dividing line, in the absence of authority by will, court order, or statute? In the absence of such authority, the personal representative must at his peril guess where the line will be drawn. The courts still draw a strict line. But, having become increasingly aware of the disastrous losses that follow piecemeal liquidation of a business, some recent cases show a tendency to approve continuation for a reasonable period in order to sell the business as a going concern—particularly when in fact the business has been sold advantageously and was operated profitably in the interim. This tendency is apparent in the *Ridosh* case.[5]

Nicholas Ridosh was operating a retail liquor store at the time of his death. Having left no will, his widow was appointed administratrix. Soon after she qualified, one of the distributees offered to purchase the business for the price at which it was sold to a stranger about eighteen months later. Because the price was less than the attorneys for the estate and the distributees considered adequate at the time, and because the offer required acceptance within two days, it was declined and the administratrix continued to operate the store until sold. She worked more than twelve hours a day, six days a week, had her meals in the store, and retained for herself wages at seventy-five cents an hour. All during the period of operations, which were profitable, active efforts were made to dispose of the business. The distributees did not consent to the continuation of the business, and they challenged the administratrix' final account. The probate court surcharged her $2,836 as business profits unaccounted for, and $4,412 as wages retained by her. She appealed to the New York Supreme Court, Appellate Division.

The Appellate Division upheld the surcharge for profits unaccounted for, but remanded the case for further consideration as to whether the surcharge for wages was justified. On this, the opinion stated in part:

> Her retention of wages can be justified, if at all, only for such period as was reasonably required to liquidate the business and then only to the extent, if any, that her services were of a nonexecutorial nature. The general and well recognized rule is that a decedent's business may not be continued unless authorized by his will or by the beneficiaries affected, except temporarily for the purpose of liquidation. . . . There is some recognition of a right to continue a business for a short time for the advantage of obtaining a better price on the sale of a going concern, and as to this it has been said: "In continuing a business for such a purpose, however, care must be used. No definite rules have been established by the courts. Each case will be decided

---

[5]*Re Ridosh*, 5 App. Div. 2d, 67, 169 N.Y.S.2d 54 (1957); 7 App. Div. 2d 534, 185 N.Y.S.2d 80 (1959).

upon its own facts and circumstances." (3 Warren's Heaton on Surrogate's Courts [6th ed.] 266.)

On remand, the Surrogate decided that one year was sufficient time to allow for disposal of the business, and that $26.25 per week for one year was sufficient compensation for nonexecutorial services.

The Appellate Division disagreed with the finding that $26.25 per week for one year was sufficient compensation for the administratrix' nonexecutorial services, and decided that $60 per week for fifty-four weeks should be allowed.

This case shows clearly the recent trend to allow a deceased proprietor's personal representative a reasonable time during which to sell his business as a going concern. Even here, however, continuation of the business, though profitable to the distributees, resulted in surcharges against the administratrix of $2,836 for business profits unaccounted for, and $1,172 for wages retained for the period beyond which it was reasonably necessary to operate the business.

Later we shall resume our discussion of the plight of the personal representative.

Continuation by an heir. Sometimes the business of a deceased proprietor is carried on without authority, not by the personal representative himself, but by an heir. This was the situation in a South Dakota case.[6] J. Peterson was engaged in the mercantile business in Newark, South Dakota at the time of his death in March, 1909, and Bjorn B. Gislason, who lived in Minnesota, was named in the will and qualified as executor. At the time of Peterson's death, his son Emil was in charge of and conducting the business for his father, and without authority to do so in the will, the executor allowed Emil to continue it in the name of the J. Peterson Estate. During the continuance of the business, Martin Bros. Co. had sold goods to Emil, who was unable to pay for them because of financial difficulties. Martin Bros. Co. brought suit against Emil and also against Gislason, suing the latter both as an individual and as executor of the estate. The executor denied any liability on the ground that he had had nothing to do with the continuation of the business. South Dakota's highest court, however, affirmed a lower court's decision dismissing the action against the executor as such, but holding both the executor and the son personally liable for the debt as individuals. The opinion quoted the following from 11 R.C.L. *Executors and Administrators,* section 142:

> An executor or administrator ordinarily has no power to continue the business in which the decedent was engaged at the time of his death; and this is true although he acts in the utmost good faith and believes that he is proceeding for the best interests

---

[6]*Martin Bros. Co. v. Peterson,* 38 S.D. 494, 162 N.W. 154 (1917).

of the estate. The penalty for continuing a business of the decedent without authority is the imposition of a personal liability on the executor or administrator so doing for all the debts of the business.

The last sentence quoted is somewhat misleading without further explanation. In the absence of a special agreement or special statute, an executor or administrator is personally liable for the debts of a business which he continues, whether or not its continuance has been authorized. This is well stated in 31 American Jurisprudence 2d §221 as follows:

> The executor is personally liable for torts committed by him, or his employee, incident to the continuation of the decedent's business under authority of the will. And except insofar as the carrying on of business is incident to winding it up and converting its assets to cash, the executor or administrator is personally obligated for debts contracted in continuing the business of the decedent, whether he is authorized to continue the business or not. The reasoning is that the representative need not carry on the business and that by doing so he voluntarily assumes personal responsibility for all contracts incident to the business operation. (Footnote 17 cites *Willis* v. *Sharp*, 113 N.Y. 586, among other authorities.) Such debts, if properly incurred, may be allowed by the court as an expense against the estate even though the business resulted in a loss.

The important distinction, therefore, is the personal representative's right of indemnity when authorized, and his lack of such right when not authorized, to continue a decedent's business; in either case he assumes personal liability unless ruled out by special agreement or special statutory provision. (Where the continuance is pursuant to the 1964 New York statute, for example, the court may rule out personal liability except for wrongful acts or negligence). The absence of this right to be indemnified when an administrator continues a decedent's business without authority was brought out in an important Michigan case.[7] In this case, the administrator, in continuing the business of deceased, had purchased merchandise from Marshall Field & Co. on credit, and, failing to pay the account when due, he was sued personally. The court held that he alone was liable for the debt, Michigan's highest court saying in part:

> In the instant case, defendant has no authority to continue the business. It was a personal undertaking altogether outside of his duties as administrator. He was not acting for his estate. He could not bind it by any of his contracts. His creditors could not sue him in his representative capacity. Their only remedy would be in

---

[7]*Marshall Field & Co. v. Himelstein*, 253 Mich. 344, 235 N.W. 181 (1931).

an action against him personally. . . . His creditors could not look to the estate for payment of his debts. He alone was liable and, if he paid for goods received while conducting the business, the probate court could not reimburse him out of the assets of the estate.

We saw this rule applied in the 1957 case of *In re Mack's Estate* where the probate court disallowed a merchant's claim against the estate to the extent it represented merchandise supplied the decedent's grocery store after his death, the store business having been continued without authority.

Trade creditor may also lose. However, assuming the collectability of judgments obtained against personal representatives as individuals, it would be incorrect to conclude that the trade creditor of a business continued without proper sanction never himself sustains the loss. In the following case it appears that the creditor "sat down between two chairs" with respect to part of the debt owed him, neither the estate nor the representative individually being liable for it.

In a New Hampshire case,[8] the brother of the deceased, who had been appointed administrator, continued the decedent's saloon business without authority, running up a bill for ale purchased from the brewing company. He gave two promissory notes to the company for part of this debt, the balance being on open-book account. Both parties were acquainted with the facts; defendant Flaherty had considered that he was acting for the estate and apparently had come to an oral agreement with the brewing company to look to the estate for payment. The notes not being honored, the company sued to recover on them and also on the open account owed. On the trial it was found that the administrator's agreement with the brewing company provided for exclusion of personal liability on his part. However, a rule of evidence that forbids the introduction of parol evidence to vary or control a written contract excluded testimony on this agreement with respect to the notes, and the brewing company obtained judgment on them. As for the open account, however, the testimony, accredited by the jury and affirmed on appeal to New Hampshire's highest court, was admitted to absolve the administrator of any liability. While the court did not have before it the question of the liability of the estate, it is obvious that since the administrator had no authority to act for it, he could not create any liability against it. Hence it appears that under the special agreement made, the brewing company was left without legal recourse with respect to the open account. In arriving at its decision in favor of the defendant, on the open account, the court stated in part:

> The question is not whether the estate is bound, but whether defendant is. If he fully disclosed the situation to the plaintiff,

---

[8] *True W. Jones Brewing Co. v. Flaherty,* 80 N.H. 571, 120 Atl. 432 (1923).

and the plaintiff chose to make a sale, or an attempted sale, to
the estate, he is not made liable personally because it appears that
the principal for whom he assumed to act was not bound.

... The complement to the general rule that the administrator
is liable is that—

"He might have made a special contract, excluding any
personal liability on his part, if he had chosen to do so."
Livermore v. Rand, 26 N.H. 85, 90.

The evidence offered by the defendant tended to prove that this
is what was done in the present instance.

Thus we find a trade creditor absorbing a substantial portion of the cost of
this unauthorized business continuation.

Estate may profit, but not personal representative. In most of the
foregoing cases, the proprietorship businesses were continued with consequent losses. Because of the inexperience of the executor or administrator
in the particular business involved and often because of his lack of vital
concern, "red ink" results are usually to be expected, but there are some
exceptions. One of these is well illustrated in the case of *Matter of Peck.*[9]

George Banker, at the time of his death, was engaged in the business of
selling certain merchandise under patents owned by himself. His will left all
of his property to his wife, Henrietta, and nominated Peck as executor.
Although no authority was given in the will to continue the business, Peck
and the widow immediately entered into a partnership agreement to do so.
The widow, however, died twelve days after the death of her husband, and
since her will had named her husband as executor and Peck as contingent
executor, the latter took charge of all the assets. He then decided to continue
the business himself, despite the advice of his lawyer that Peck as executor
would be personally liable to the widow's estate and legatees for any losses
incurred, and that whatever profits he might make would be deemed the
property of the estate.

Peck continued the decedent's business for over a year and made out very
well, finally selling the business on satisfactory terms. In his accounting, he
showed a profit of $2,764.31 after he had deducted $2,371.53 paid to his son
for services rendered as his assistant in running the store, and also the sum of
$3,071.95 as compensation to himself in conducting the business. The final
decision in the case held him liable not only for the profits as shown in his
account, but also for the additional sum of $3,071.95 he had credited to
himself as salary. The opinion stated as follows:

It is a well-settled rule of equity that a trustee is not permitted
to deal with the trust property so as to gain any advantage,
directly or indirectly, for himself, beyond his lawful compensa-

[9] 79 App. Div. 296 (1903), affirmed, 177 N.Y. 538.

tion. He may not use it in his own private business. He may not make any incidental profits for himself in its management, and he may not acquire any *pecuniary gains* from his fiduciary position. The beneficiary is entitled to claim all advantages actually gained, and to hold the trustee chargeable for all losses, if any, happening from *a violation of his duty.* (Pom. Eq. Juris. s. 1075.) Within this rule I am unable to see upon what theory Peck may withhold from the estate of which he is executor any portion of such earnings to his own use or benefit. . . . The estate owes him nothing for his services, but may, under the rules of equity, demand from him everything that *he*—that is, his labor and skill—has succeeded in clearing up out of the business. And such demand is imposed against him for his wrongful act in using the funds of the estate in a manner forbidden by law.

At first glance, the result in this case seems to conflict with that in *Re Ridosh*, discussed earlier in this chapter. Both, however, reflect the rule that a personal representative may not receive compensation for nonexecutorial work done during the period of unauthorized continuation of the decedent's business. There, the business was held properly continued for a period of fifty-four weeks; here—as the last-quoted sentence reveals—the entire period of business continuation was considered unjustified.

Summary. The following short but sufficiently explanatory quotation from the surrogate's opinion in *In re Archer,*[10] succinctly sums up the liability of the personal representative to the heirs if he continues a proprietorship without authority:

> The executors, not having authority under the will to either continue the brick-manufacturing business of the testator or to engage as executors in a new brick-manufacturing business, were bound to account for the net profit derived from these businesses, or, at the option of those entitled thereto (who herein elected to accept the net profits), to refund the amount of the property diverted, with 6 per cent interest. *Matter of Peck . . .* [Other cases also cited] .

Clearly, the position of the estate in the law of unauthorized continuance of businesses in relation to the personal representative is "heads, I win—tails, you lose." In carrying on a business without authority the representative violates his fiduciary duty. Moreover, he risks his own savings because of the personal liability he alone must assume without the right of indemnity for obligations created in continuing the enterprise. And if his business ventures prove successful, he is told, as were the executors in the *Archer* case, that "the court will not permit them [him] to profit by their own misconduct."

---

[10]77 Misc. 288, 137 N.Y.S. 770, 774 (1912).

The estate, on the other hand, is protected to the best ability of the courts. If, perchance, profits are made, they go to the lucky heirs; and if profits are not made, the personal representative is surcharged for the losses. But it must never be forgotten that a judgment is only as good as its collectability. Obviously, unauthorized continuance as an alternative to the liquidation of the business, spawned from a breach of trust, and nurtured solely by the personal liability of the executor or administrator as an individual, is the antithesis of a solution to the problem.

CONTINUATION OF A PROPRIETORSHIP BUSINESS ON CONSENT OF THE HEIRS

Occasionally, upon the death of a proprietor, his heirs will request the personal representative to continue the proprietorship business or, if they are importuned by such representative, will give their consent to it (although such continuation has not been authorized), in the hope that the enterprise will ultimately be disposed of as a going concern and forced liquidation of its assets will be avoided. The effect of such consent on the parties concerned will now be examined.

Minor heirs cannot consent. This improvisation is in the first instance confined to those situations in which all of the heirs are adults, minor heirs being legally incapable of giving their sanction. This limitation is clearly brought out in the case of *Gilligan v. Daly,*[11] in which the court stated:

> In carrying on the business, the executor clearly acted without authority, not only because of the general rule relating to the administration of estates, but also because all of the legatees were infants, incapable of consenting to the continuance, and one of them is still an infant.

Personal representative not liable to consenting heirs for losses. Even if all heirs are competent adults, the personal representative has a difficult if not impossible task to obtain their unanimous consent to keep the business running, for usually some of them are inaccessible or they are unwilling to expose their inheritance to the risks involved. But if all of the heirs are of age, are within reach, and are competent and willing to consent, their unanimous sanction to the continuation of the business by the executor or administrator usually gives him a modicum of protection, at the expense of the heirs. If, under such circumstances, profits result, the obligation of the personal representative to turn the increment over to the heirs remains unchanged. But if the personal representative sustains losses, the consenting heirs will find that they have surrendered their right to hold him liable. The rule is well stated in the case of *In re Ennis' Estate* (Wash.),[12] in which the court said:

---

[11] 79 N.J. Eq. 36, 80 Atl. 994 (1911).

[12] Page 124 of 165 Pac.

The weight of authority undoubtedly is that the consent of the adult heirs that the administrator may carry on the business conducted by the decedent will estop them from enforcing any personal liability against the administrator for losses incurred by him in such business. *Swaine v. Hemphill,* 165 Mich. 561, 131 N.W. 68, 40 L.R.A. (NS) 201.

This rule is stated even more clearly in *Mathews v. Sheehan,*[13] as follows:

Where an administrator or executor, acting in good faith and with ordinary care and prudence for the good of the beneficiaries of the estate, deviates, with their consent and approbation, from the strict line of his duty, and loss results therefrom—as for instance by continuing the property in business without authority—the consenting beneficiaries cannot charge the representative of the estate with such loss. *Poole v. Munday,* 103 Mass. 174; *Duffield v. Brainerd,* 45 Conn. 424.

The facts of this last case show an interesting application of the principle. At first all the heirs had consented to a continuance of the decedent's business activities by the administrators, but some months later one of them withdrew her consent. The administrators were held liable to her for any losses to her distributive share of the estate occurring after she withdrew her consent.

Personal representative nevertheless liable to creditors. Although the personal representative is relieved of liability to the consenting heirs for losses incurred in continuing a decedent's business, he remains in financial jeopardy nevertheless. It has been noted earlier that an executor or administrator who continues the business of a deceased becomes personally liable for the obligations entered into on behalf of such business. If the assets of the business are sufficient for the purpose, he can retire these obligations therefrom, and even if the final result of such operations constitutes a loss, he cannot be held responsible by the consenting heirs for the depletion in assets. If, however, the assets of the business become exhausted, any unsatisfied trade creditors may hold him to his personal liability to them. Compelled thus to pay such debts out of his own pocket, he ordinarily would have no recourse against other estate assets or against the heirs individually.

Creditors of the *deceased,* however, constitute a far greater financial hazard to the personal representative than do the new creditors of the continuing business. The effect on the personal representative of failure to obtain the consent of the decedent's creditors is dramatically illustrated by the decision of Pennsylvania's highest court in the case of *In re Shinn's Estate.*[14]

---

[13] 76 Conn. 654, 56 Atl. 694 (1904).

[14] 166 Pa. St. 121, 30 Atl. 1026, 1030 (1895).

Before his death, William P. Shinn, a resident of the state of Pennsylvania, had taken a twenty-year lease on a tract of iron-ore land in Westchester County, New York, that granted him the right to mine and remove the ore at an annual minimum royalty of $5,000. During his lifetime, Shinn had expended more than $100,000 in improvements and patents, and when he died there was a chattel mortgage on the leasehold and other charges of about $40,000. At Shinn's death, his next of kin, after examining the leasehold, advised the administrator of the estate to continue the operation. This was done, but without his consulting the estate's creditors. The administrator then expended $44,736.36 of general estate funds in an effort to make the iron-ore mining project successful. However, as stated in the court's opinion, "The business proved a most disastrous failure." On his accounting, the administrator claimed credit for the expenditure of this money. The decision of the court surcharged the administrator for the $44,736.36.

Summary. The plan of continuing a proprietorship business by the personal representative on consent of the heirs has now been examined in sufficient detail to make evident the conclusion that it is at best a financially dangerous expedient. The heirs, by their own consent, forfeit their most valuable legal right: the right to hold the personal representative to account. The executor or administrator is nevertheless personally liable to any new creditors, and remains primarily liable to the present creditors of the estate to the extent he is charged with estate assets. For these obvious reasons the plan is totally undesirable if there are unsatisfied estate creditors who have not consented to the continuance of the business.

We shall next look at the situation presented when all parties interested in an estate, including the estate creditors, consent to the continuance of a decedent's business.

CONTINUATION OF A PROPRIETORSHIP BUSINESS ON CONSENT OF ALL PARTIES INTERESTED IN THE ESTATE

From what we have already seen, no well-informed personal representative unauthorized to continue the business of his decedent would do so without first obtaining the consent of all interested parties, both the heirs of the estate and its creditors. Now, let us see what happens when such consents, in fact or in effect, have been given.

Personal representative not liable to consenting heirs for losses. One of the leading cases on the subject is *Swaine v. Hemphill.*[15] Frederick J. Swaine had conducted a proprietorship in Ypsilanti, Michigan, consisting of a small malting business. At his death, his personal estate amounted to $16,261.01. His liabilities amounted to $16,132.14. His heirs were his widow and two

---

[15] 165 Mich. 561, 131 N.W. 68 (1911).

daughters, the youngest about nineteen years old. The widow turned over to the administrator $5,650, consisting of life insurance which she had received on her husband's life together with a legacy from a brother, this fund to be applied against the debts of the estate. With the consent of all interested parties and fortified with a waiver of notice of hearing on his final account and a power of attorney from the heirs, the personal representative continued the malting business for eight years. During this time, the administrator paid $9,493.88 to the heirs, heated their home from the plant, paid for real estate improvements amounted to $1,578.66, and from time to time even sent a man from the plant to do work about their residence. Profits were realized in each of the first three years (during which the minor daughter became of age), but of the next five years only two showed a profit.

When the administrator submitted his final account, showing a net loss of $1,685.65 in the operation of the business, his account was approved by the court of probate. The widow and daughters then filed a bill of complaint, asserting that they had consented to the continuance of the business for only so long as it proved profitable, that the administrator had continued it at a loss without informing them, and that he had fraduently secured their consent to his discharge as administrator. They petitioned that he be held liable for the loss and be ordered to reimburse them for it. Michigan's highest court held, however, that where all the persons interested in an estate had agreed that the continuation of the decedent's business was for the best interests of the estate, and had advised its continuance by the administrator, he could not be held personally liable for any resulting losses in the business. The court said in part:

> We are of opinion that it was the conviction of all the complainants . . . that it was best to continue the business in the hope that it might be disposed of as a going concern. Changes and improvements in the method of manufacturing malt and large combinations of malting interests made it impossible to realize this hope. It would be unjust and unequitable to now compel this defendant to bear the loss occasioned by this course of action.
>
> The duty of administrators generally to liquidate estates without undue delay is not questioned, nor can it be doubted that they cannot leave estates at the risk of business disaster by continuing without authority to operate business ventures in which the estates are invested when they come into their hands. The authorities cited by complainants clearly establish this doctrine and executors or administrators who violate the rule, even if acting in the utmost good faith, are held strictly liable for all losses incurred, and are not even permitted to offset the profits against the losses [citing several cases].
>
> There seems to be no doubt, however, that, when all those interested in an estate agree that a certain course should be

followed, the executor or administrator will be relieved from personal liability if disaster follows. Schouler on Executors, p. 422, lays down the rule as follows: "We may presume that the personal representative can never be strictly justified in deviating from the line of bailment or fiduciary duty. But in case of doubt as to his proper course he may protect himself by prudently pursuing in advance one of two courses: (1) He may procure the advice and consent of all the parties in interest; or (2) he may take the direction of the court. * * * He may prosecute or defend suits, compromise claims upon the estate, or deal with the estate in a particular way, not usual or strictly legal, as by continuing the property in business, and those parties in interest by whose request or consent it has been done, will not be permitted to impute it as maladministration."[16]

With reference to the daughter who was a minor at the time of Swaine's death, the court said:

It is noted that no complaint is made of the continuation of the business during the first three years while it was making a profit. During those years the youngest daughter attained her majority, and had then a right as well as her mother and elder sister to demand discontinuance. This neither she nor they did.

Creditors of continued business preferred over consenting estate creditors as to assets embarked in trade. In the ordinary process of administering an estate, the personal representative's first duty is to conserve the decedent's assets and to apply them so far as necessary to the payment of the claims of the estate creditors. When, however, these creditors consent to the continuance of a proprietorship after the proprietor's death, they are in effect consenting also to the creation of new debts and new creditors. The estate creditors are allowing their claims to assets of the estate to be subordinated to those of the new trade creditors. This was the primary holding in another leading case.[17]

A.C. Ennis had operated a dry-goods store in Elma, Washington. He died in January, 1911, without having made a will and leaving a widow and four adult children. The widow was appointed administratrix. The assets of the estate consisted of $4,000 of merchandise in his store and real estate appraised at $11,250. He owed $800 on the merchandise, $400 to a son, Mark, and $2,000 on a note given his bankers. Patently, the estate was solvent. Prior to his death Ennis had expressed a wish that his son Donald be entrusted with the carrying on of the business, and that, on settlement of his

---

[16]Citing *Poole v. Munday*, 103 Mass. 174; *Perry v. Wooten*, 5 Humph. (Tenn.) 524; and *Watkins v. Stewart*, 78 Va. 111.

[17]*In re Ennis' Estate* 96 Wash. 352, 165 Pac. 119 (1917).

estate, Donald be paid $1,000 over and above his distributive share. Upon Ennis' death, all the heirs entered into an agreement to carry out this oral wish.

The store was conducted by Donald for more than a year, but the venture was not successful, and the heirs petitioned under the Washington statute for an order of private sale of the stock of goods. This was granted, but it was not strictly complied with. The store at Elma was closed out and a new one opened at Centralia, the administratrix assisting Donald at the new location. Several months later, after $3,824.82 of debts had been incurred at Centralia, Donald died. The following month the heirs procured another court order authorizing a private sale of the stock. From this sale the administratrix reported net proceeds of $879.90.

All of the estate creditors except the bank had been paid promptly. But the bank, although it knew the store business was being continued, had neither expressly consented nor pressed for payment of its claim. Thus, the question was whether the administratrix should apply the $879.90 net sale proceeds against the trade debts owed the store creditors, or against the estate debt owed the bank.

Washington's highest court held that the creditors of the continued business were entitled to have the proceeds of the store sale applied against their claims. But it added that such creditors had no rights against assets of the estate not embarked in the business. Regarding the decedent's wish that his son Donald carry on the business, the court, said:

> Such a parol direction prior to death is not, however, recognized in law as a sufficient justification for a personal representative to continue the business for the benefit of the family or estate. *Raynes v. Raynes,* 54 N.H. 201; *In re McCollum,* 80 App. Div. 362, 80 N.Y.S. 755. The general rule is that a personal representative has no power to continue the business of a decedent unless expressly authorized by will, by statute, or by an order of the court.

In holding that the store creditors could not get the balance of their claims paid from the general assets of the estate, the court held that the trade creditors "stand on a different footing from that of the heirs and creditors of the decedent, in that they never had an interest in the general assets." Therefore the trade creditors could not take advantage of the principle of estoppel against the heirs and the general creditors to reach such assets. The court also held that "while the fact that the business was carried on with the consent of the heirs and the administratrix was sufficient to estop them from disputing the prior rights of appellants in the trade assets, it does not estop them [the heirs and administratrix] from denying liability as to the general assets." The court further explained its judgment that the store creditors had no right against general estate assets not used in the continued business with the following statement:

> Trade Creditors have no right to be placed on an equality with those existing at the date of decedent's death, and who are entitled to share in the estate as it then existed.
>
> They contract with the personal representative, chargeable with notice as to any limitations on his powers to bind the estate. They are not in any sense creditors of the decedent. They deal with the administrator on his personal credit and on the credit of the business conducted by him. The primary idea of administration is to preserve the estate for the benefit of those interested in it at the time of the owner's death, and courts should be slow to adopt a rule involving departure from that idea.

In closing, the court referred to the personal liability of the administratrix for the store debts:

> Whatever rights the appellants may have against the administratrix, while raised in the briefs of counsel, are not properly before us for consideration, and hence will not be passed upon at this time.

Had this question been before the court, however, there could have been but one answer. As above quoted, the trade creditors "deal with the administrator on his personal credit." The court had held that Donald acted as her agent and that she was clearly estopped to assert that she was not bound by his acts; undoubtedly it follows that the widow was personally liable and there could have been a personal judgment rendered against her if the case had been handled differently. The leading case of *Willis v. Sharp*, 113 N.Y. 586, at page 591 states as follows: "It is the settled doctrine of the courts of common law that a debt contracted by an executor after the death of his testator, binds him individually, and does not bind the estate which he represents, notwithstanding it may have been contracted for the benefit of the estate."

Creditors of continued business sometimes reach assets not embarked in the business. It was noted in the *Ennis* case that although the trade creditors were successful in reaching the assets of the continued business, they were unable to reach the other assets of the estate and have them applied against the unpaid balance of their claims. This holding appears to be sound law, but sometimes the courts, in dealing with exceptional circumstances, have allowed such creditors access to the assets not embarked in the continued business. This is illustrated in the case that follows.[18]

Abraham Damsky had conducted a radio store in Brooklyn. He died in 1934 without a will, leaving adult heirs, and his son Bernard was appointed

---

[18]*Philco Radio & Television Corporation of New York v. Damsky*, 250 App. Div. 485, 294 N.Y.S. 776 (1937).

administrator. With the consent of all the heirs, the administrator continued the operation of the store. At this time it was not certain whether there were any unsatisfied estate creditors. The Philco Radio Corporation sold the continuing business large quantitites of merchandise, but when the administrator was alleged to be insolvent, the corporation brought suit in equity against the administrator and all heirs to recover out of the assets of the general estate for an unpaid bill of $3,627.57. On a motion by the defendants to dismiss the complaint, the court held that the action could be brought on the facts alleged. The court held in effect that a creditor of a continued business may recover in equity out of the general assets of the estate when, although no authority existed to continue the decedent's business, all the heirs, being of age, have consented to such continuance and when the personal representative is insolvent. This recovery is subject, however, to the rights of creditors of the decedent, if any. The basis of the court's decision is contained in the following excerpt from the opinion:

> The situation here disclosed constitutes a species of fraud which, combined with the financial inability of the parties, individually, to meet the obligation, entitles the plaintiff to payment out of the assets of the estate, subject, of course, to the rights of creditors of the intestate, if any there be.

Summary. Although the foregoing cases do not deal with all of the ramifications of the situation created when, without legal authority but with the consent of all the parties interested in the estate, a deceased proprietor's enterprise is carried on after his death, they do afford a sufficient background against which to summarize the ultimate effect on the various interests of the parties involved.

First, the personal representative cannot be held liable to the consenting heirs and creditors of the proprietor's estate for any losses incurred by him in conducting the business, excepting, of course, such losses as are the result of his own negligence or dishonesty. He continues to be accountable for any profits made. Although he remains personally liable for the obligations created in continuing the proprietorship business, he may, in so far as possible, retire these obligations out of the trade assets and any net loss will be allowed on his accounting, as in the case of *Swaine v. Hemphill.* However, because his right to be reimbursed, that is, his right of indemnity, would ordinarily be limited to the trade assets, he may find himself ultimately absorbing some of the trade debts, if the trade assets are insufficient, as they were in the *Ennis* case. In spite of this possibility, however, the consent of the parties interested in the estate to the continuance of the business largely transfers the hazards involved from the personal representative to the persons consenting to such continuance.

Second, the creditors of the continued business, the trade creditors, who are in fact individual creditors of the personal representative, may sue him individually. Moreover, through the personal representative's right of indemnity, the trade creditors are entitled to be paid out of the trade assets of the continued business, and they are entitled to be paid before the consenting creditors of the deceased proprietor's estate and ahead of any interest in such assets of the consenting heirs. But the trade creditors ordinarily possess no right to have their claims paid out of the general estate assets, that is, the property of the decedent not embarked in the continuing business.

This last rule is the holding in the *Ennis* case and appears to be sound, especially where there remain unpaid estate creditors. As stated in *Frey v. Eisenhardt,*[19] and quoted in the *Ennis* case: "We understand the rule is that where an administrator or executor, instead of closing out the business, continues it, even when authorized by will to do so, the trade debts will reach only the trade assets; that is, the property that was employed in the business or that was the result of doing business. *Laible v. Ferry,* 32 N.J. Eq. 791. See also *Altheimer v. Hunter,* 56 Ark. 159; *Lucht v. Behrens,* 28 Ohio St. 231." *Lucht v. Behrens* specifically held that the creditor of a business continued without authority could not subject general estate assets that were not embarked in the business to the judgment of his claim.

Of course, a decedent may, by specific terms in his will, put his entire estate at risk in continuing a business, but as Justice Story of the United States Supreme Court said in *Burwell v. Cawood,*[20] "nothing but the most clear and unambiguous language, demonstrating in the most positive manner that the testator intends to make his general assets liable for all debts contracted in the continued trade after his death, and not merely to limit it to the funds embarked in that trade, would justify the court in arriving at such a conclusion from the manifest inconvenience thereof." And of course, the consent of the heirs and estate creditors in a specific case could be couched in such language as to risk the entire estate. But "the most clear and unambiguous language" should be required before trade creditors, who "contract with the personal representative, chargeable with notice as to any limitations on his powers to bind the estate," are allowed access to the general estate assets for the payment of their claims. The holding in the *Philco* case, therefore, was extreme, and it would have been interesting to have seen whether New York's highest court would have affirmed it, had the case reached the Court of Appeals.

Whether or not, however, the trade creditors in a particular case can reach the assets of the general estate, we find them still unpaid in the *Ennis* case and in the other cases reviewed, in two of which the personal representatives had allegedly become insolvent. Nevertheless, the consent of the parties

---

[19] 116 Mich. 160, 74 N.W. 511.

[20] 43 U.S. 560.

interested in the estate to the continuance of the business has definitely improved the position of the trade creditors by giving them ultimate access to the trade assets in payment of their claims.

Third, the estate creditors of the deceased proprietor, by their own consent, give up the right to have the assets embarked in the proprietorship business promptly applied to the payment of their claims. In the absence of consent, "they have the power and the means of calling forth after the decedent's death the whole of his property in discharge of their demands."[21] Furthermore, the estate creditors, by their consent, allow the trade creditors priority of access against the assets of the continued proprietorship. These estate creditors therefore subject their claims to the hazards involved in the continuance. In the *Swaine* case, one estate creditor was still owed $4,000 when the continued proprietorship business was closed out because of overpowering competition. In the *Ennis* case, the decedent's bankers were still unpaid, although the estate assets had been, at time of Ennis' death, ample for the discharge of all estate obligations. And in a case not previously referred to, the consenting estate creditors with unpaid claims of $21,587.41 failed to recover from the administratrix, who continued the decedent's nursery business, or from her surety.[22] The facts showed no estate assets left from which to pay the claims, although the opinion stated that "originally the estate was regarded as a comparatively large one and abundantly solvent." We can only conclude that if the estate creditor can obtain his money at time of death, he will be well advised to do so.

Fourth and last, come the heirs of the deceased proprietor, who are the natural objects of his bounty. By their consent, they gamble the possibility of the profits to be made in the continuing business against the possibility of the loss of the property embarked in it. Against that property, trade creditors have first claim. If any such assets are left (there proved to be a deficiency in the *Ennis* case), the consenting estate creditors are next in line with their unpaid claims. Finally, if any proprietorship property remains, the heirs may have it. In the vast majority of cases, the heirs would be far better off, in the absence of a suitable continuation plan, to allow the personal representative to carry through a prompt liquidation of the proprietorship upon the death of the proprietor, in spite of the substantial liquidation losses likely to be suffered.

---

[21]Lord Chancellor Eldon, in *Ex parte Garland,* 10 Ves. Jr. 110.

[22]*Hicks v. Purvis,* 208 N.C. 657 (1935).

Chapter 4

CONTINUATION OF PROPRIETORSHIP BUSINESS BY COURT ORDER

Previously, we have considered situations in which executors or administrators have continued proprietorship businesses without the proper authority to do so, and have noted in detail the generally disastrous results that followed. We now come to the one clear avenue of authority available after the death of the proprietor to the personal representative who lacks proper sanction under the decedent's will to continue the business: the order of a probate court.

NARROW SCOPE OF COURT ORDERS AT COMMON LAW

Originally, all such court orders were based upon the principles of common law. However, as each state has developed its own interpretation of common law principles, there has been considerable disagreement as to the existence and extent of the power of a court of probate to authorize continuation of a decedent's business. A few states have held that their courts had no power to grant such orders. The majority of states, however, have held that authority could be granted to the personal representative to carry on a business temporarily but only for the purpose of winding it up.

The restricted scope of the majority of such orders is apparent in the case of *Gordon-Tiger Mining & Reduction Co. v. Loomer.*[1] There, the order of the county court authorized the administrator to continue the decedent's second-hand business and replenish stock as necessity might require to make the entire stock of goods more salable in closing it out. The administrator, however, went to the extent of borrowing funds to use in the business. Under the local probate statute, expenses incurred in settling an estate were proper claims against the estate. When the lender attempted to collect the amount of his loan, contending that it was an administration expense, the court disallowed it on the basis that the administrator had not been granted authority to borrow the money. The narrow scope of such orders is apparent from the following quotation from the court's opinion:

> Generally speaking, an administrator may not continue the business of the decedent, nor use the assets of the estate for business purposes. To this rule, however, there are exceptions, as, where the decedent was engaged in the mercantile or manufacturing business, his representative may, under order of court, carry on the business for a sufficient time to close it up. The administrator, if properly authorized, could continue the business for the purpose of disposing of the stock to advantage, and might purchase necessary merchandise to make the property more salable. . . .
>
> There is a great difference between buying goods for the purpose of replenishing short stock while closing out, and borrowing money to put into the business. . . . The county court gave him no authority to borrow money to put into the business; it would have been a remarkable exercise of power.

Although the lender was thus unable to procure repayment from the assets of the estate, he would be able to pursue the administrator individually, based upon the latter's personal liability for obligations created after the death of the proprietor. That this can be done is clearly shown in *Miller v. Didisheim & Brother.*[2]

On the death of Miller, his widow, Mary Miller, qualified as executrix under his will and she continued her deceased husband's mercantile business under order of the Probate Court of Cook County. The court order had stated, "that said executrix have leave to carry on the business formerly conducted by said deceased in his lifetime, at 102 Madison Street, Chicago, Illinois, as long as the same is conducted with a profit to the estate of said decedent; and it is further ordered by the court that said executrix have leave to sell the said business at not less than the appraised value thereof at private

---

[1] 50 Colo. 409, 115 Pac. 717 (1911).

[2] 95 Ill. App. 321 (1900).

sale." While the business was being conducted by the widow, she incurred a trade obligation in favor of Didisheim & Brother. The continuation of the business by the widow, however, resulted in a loss. The widow made up the loss in her accounting by paying over that amount to her successor from her own resources. The business was afterwards closed out by the administrator, who paid 59 percent of the debt owed to Didisheim & Brother. Didisheim & Brother then brought action against the widow for the 41 percent of their claim remaining unpaid. The court held the widow liable for this debt, ruling that a personal representative is personally liable for debts of a continuing business, despite the fact that such business is operated under the authority of the court.

Thus we find that the widow, who had continued his business under a proper court order and who had already paid from her own funds the amount of losses suffered, was nevertheless required to pay the balance of a debt owed an unsatisfied creditor of the continued business.

A few states have held under the common law that their courts may authorize continuation of a business for sale as a going concern during the usual period of administration. We saw that common-law rule applied by the intermediate court in *Re Ridosh.* In that case, however, the rule did not save the personal representative from surcharge for taking too much time to sell the business. Where the decedent's business has a going-concern value, this rule offers the best chance of salvaging that value in the absence of better statutory authority or special arrangements made by the decedent.

COURT ORDERS UNDER STATUTORY AUTHORITY

Because of the uncertainty and confusion regarding the authority that could be granted to the personal representative by court order at common law, and because the common law has failed to evolve a satisfactory method of dealing with the business of a decedent, a majority of the states have enacted statutes on the subject. Some of these laws are of many years' standing, but in general they are a recent development, as shown by the fact that the number of such statutes has more than doubled since 1937. Space does not permit of a complete analysis of these various enactments, but something should be said of their scope and general effect.

As might be expected, no two of these statutes are identical (although the Connecticut and Rhode Island sections are nearly so). The same may be said of the more recent Indiana and Missouri statutes, being based on the Proposed Model Probate Code provision. Many of them consist of a single short sentence; others, such as the Michigan law, comprise several pages. A goodly number of them function merely to put an end to any uncertainty that may have existed at common law in their respective jurisdictions; they grant the personal representative the authority by court order—when the decedent's will has failed to do so—to continue a business for a reasonable time for the purpose of permitting the sale of the stock of merchandise in the ordinary course of business. This avoids forcing the business to close its doors and causing the assets to be sold piecemeal along with other estate assets.

Statutes of this type provide for a more prolonged and more orderly liquidation, by which the losses on a forced sale may be circumvented. Nevertheless, they fail to provide a satisfactory solution. While the business is being liquidated, the ordinary overhead expenses continue and may offset any profits gained in selling the goods in the regular course of trade. But most important, the continuation of a business merely to close it must ultimately result in a total loss of the good will and going-concern value of the enterprise. Furthermore, the personal representative often is left in the same precarious position that he is under the common law: Under many of the statutes, he is not relieved of personal liability for debts contracted in continuing the business under the court orders issued. This is clearly brought out in *Anglo-American Direct Tea Trading Co. v. Seward.*[3]

William T. Abbott had conducted a proprietorship under the name of William T. Abbott and Company. At his death, his estate was insolvent, but on petition of the executors and beneficiaries of the estate, the probate court, by authority of the Massachusetts statute, authorized continuation of the business by the personal representatives. During such continuance, the plaintiff tea company sold tea to the executors. Subsequently Ide, one of the executors, died and the tea company brought an action against Seward and others, Ide's personal representatives, to recover the price of the tea. The tea company won the case, the court holding that an executor carrying on a business under the authority of a decree of the probate court is nevertheless liable personally on his contracts in furtherance of such business, in the absence of any agreement with the other contracting parties excluding personal liability.

Most of the statutes that permit a personal representative to continue the decedent's business "for a reasonable time, to provide a better opportunity of liquidation," for example, authorize court orders that go further than those usually issued under common law. The quoted phrase is from the Colorado statute which—possibly with the result in the *Gordon-Tiger Mining* case in mind—also provides specifically that if it is necessary for the personal representative to borrow money to continue operations, the court may so order, upon notice to all persons interested. This borrowing provision protected the personal representative in *Re Smith's Estate.*[4]

Smith, who died intestate in August 1954, had conducted a roofing business. The business had been prosperous at various times, but there were numerous claims against the estate. Most of the claims were secured, leaving

---

[3]294 Mass. 349, 2 N.E. 2d 448 (1936).

[4]145 Colo. 406, 359 P.2d 1020 (1961).

doubt whether much would be available to pay the general creditors. The widow was appointed administratrix. She was familiar with the business, and obtained a court order permitting her to continue operating the business for a reasonable time to assist in liquidating it and ultimately close the estate. Soon learning that she could not continue the business without acquiring some working capital, and having received a substantial amount of proceeds from the decedent's life insurance, the widow obtained a court order allowing her, as administratrix, to borrow $10,000 from herself individually.

It appeared for a while that the administratrix could restore solvency to the estate. She discovered, however, that the decedent has received part payment for jobs which had been started, and for which no material had been secured. "Finally the inevitable happened," says the court, "the business collapsed and the estate wound up with insufficient assets to pay creditors, notwithstanding the $10,000 loaned by Mrs. Smith that went into the business. In the meantime the U.S. filed claims for taxes, for unpaid withholding taxes related to Social Security accounts of employees, and for damages for an alleged faulty or incomplete roofing job done by decedent at Lowry Air Force base in Denver."

When the administratrix claimed reimbursement for the money she loaned the estate as an expense of administration, the Government objected to its allowances since it would then take precedence over the Government's claim. The Government's position was that it had received no notice of the court order authorizing the loan, that the statute authorized a loan only on notice and for a short period for the purpose of liquidation, and that the administratrix' continuation of the business for approximately three years was in excess of a reasonable time. The Government relied on the *Gordon-Tiger Mining* case.

The county court allowed the administratrix' claim as a cost of administration. There was no working capital in the business at the decedent's death, and yet the business had approximately six months' work which it was committed to do; therefore, it was to the best interest of the estate that the $10,000 be borrowed by the administratrix. Events occurring subsequent to the date of authorization cannot change the classification of a claim as a cost of administration.

Colorado's highest court affirmed the judgment. It noted that the Government had not filed any claim against the estate when the loan authorization was granted, but did not decide whether a creditor who had not yet filed his claim was a person interested in the estate. The court also noted that the estate creditors had full knowledge of the loan, and had made no complaint during the time the business was continued.

Statutes allowing continuance for sale as a going concern. A second group of statutes goes a step further, allowing continuation of a business in the ordinary course for the purpose of its sale as a going concern during the normal period of estate administration. In the hands of an efficient personal representative, and under propitious circumstances, a satisfactory disposal of the business of the decedent can be effected. But under these statutes, too much depends upon the general business conditions prevailing in the months immediately following the proprietor's death. The period of permissible continuance is too short to grant any assurance that an advantageous sale of the business can be negotiated. And in this connection it should be noted that if the personal representative should take it upon himself to conduct the business beyond the term provided by the statute, or by the court order under which the continuance is authorized, he will become a person carrying on a business without authority and will then be responsible, without right of indemnity, for any losses thereafter incurred. On the other hand, if the personal representative properly keeps within his authority, the presence of unfavorable economic conditions during the period of administration will nevertheless result in heavy losses to the persons interested in the estate. We must conclude, therefore, that statutes falling into this category still leave much to be desired.

Broad statutory authority. Approximately a dozen states have enacted statutes sufficiently broad to authorize continuation of a decedent's business in the regular course until a sale of the enterprise as a going concern can be made, even though such a sale cannot be made during the usual period of estate administration. Given favorable business conditions and given an alert and capable personal representative who is familiar with the problems and duties involved in running the business, these statutes provide as satisfactory a method of disposing of a proprietor's business as can be improvised in the absence of any plan worked out and implemented by the proprietor himself during his lifetime.

Under approximately half of the statutes mentioned in the broad group above, authority may be granted to carry on a decedent's business with a view to making a profit for those interested in the estate, instead of merely to allow its continuance until it can be sold as a going concern. In these particular states, the personal representative, on proper court order, is allowed to exceed the function of an executorship, which is to close out the estate, and to take on the function of a trusteeship. This last allows him to continue the business for a definite or an indefinite period for the purpose of deriving income from it. Some of these statutes, including the 1964 New York Statute, provide for relieving the personal representative from personal liability except for his own wrongful acts or negligence. Whether under these laws the periphery of permissible continuance by an executor or administrator has not been extended too far is open to question. How far a personal representative will be authorized to go in a particular case, however, is left to the discretion of the court having supervision of the administration of the particular estate. Furthermore, most of these statutes wisely permit anyone interested in the estate, on showing proper cause, to petition for a discontinuance of the business.

Statutes permitting incorporation of decedent's business. The longstanding Pennsylvania law and the later Hawaii, Indiana, Missouri and New York statutes specifically permit incorporation of a decedent's business, in which event the new creditors will be creditors of the corporation rather than of the personal representative. But relieving the executor or administrator who continues a decedent's business from personal liability can be a two-edged sword. While it facilitates the problem of inducing the personal representative to act in this capacity, at the same time it renders his task of carrying on the enterprise far more difficult, and sometimes impossible. Individuals and concerns are inclined to deal rather freely with a personal representative who possesses the requisite authority when they know that his personal liability for his obligations makes him their primary debtor and that, should he prove financially unable to respond, they can reach the assets engaged in the business through his right of indemnity. The elimination of the personal liability of the executor or administrator, therefore, takes away from the potential new creditor of the continuing business his primary debtor, with the inevitable result that such potential creditors will refuse to do business unless the continuing enterprise is left by the decedent in a strong financial position, a requirement which, unfortunately, is only too often lacking.

Summary. The broader statutes provide, insofar as it is possible to do by legislative enactment, that the discretion of the court fill in the gap left by the failure of the proprietor to leave a subsisting plan for the disposal of his enterprise. In the light of the fact that great numbers of proprietors will continue to neglect to plan adequately for the disposal of their businesses, such statutes deserve both our highest commendation and the emulation of other states still following the antiquated and costly procedure, regardless of circumstances, of requiring forced liquidation of a business on the death of the owner.

Nevertheless, the best drawn statutes fall short of providing an ideal solution of the problems involved when a proprietor dies. Almost every small business is built by the sweat and toil of its proprietor over a substantial period of time. He knows intimately every facet of its operation, every pillar and every frailty in its economic structure. As a going concern, it reflects the ability, industry and personality of one man—its owner. Consequently, he and he alone has the knowledge, experience and keen personal interest requisite to plan effectively for its disposal upon his death. The ideal solution must come from him.

Chapter 5

CONTINUATION PLANS MADE BY
THE PROPRIETOR ACTING ALONE

In the two previous chapters a reasonably close examination has been made of the alternatives to the immediate liquidation of a proprietorship business on the death of the owner who has left no subsisting plan for the disposal of his enterprise. This investigation has demonstrated both the need for, and the value of, up-to-date statutory provisions that will give the personal representative a limited opportunity to continue the business, in order that he may avoid disastrous losses on a forced sale and that he may have some chance of selling the enterprise as a going concern. Obviously, however, a general statute, coming into play after the death of the proprietor and in the absence of provisions made by him, cannot be expected to function as effectively as a plan drawn up and implemented by the proprietor himself. In our search for the most desirable plans for the continuation of proprietorship businesses, we shall now turn our attention to those plans set up by the owners in advance of the emergency calling for their use.

PROPRIETOR'S ORAL DIRECTIONS FOR
CONTINUANCE

Sometimes a proprietor will sit down with the members of his family and come to an oral agreement with them regarding the continuation of his enterprise after his death. In fact, this is what A.C. Ennis did with respect to his dry-goods store in Elma, Washington, arranging verbally for his son Donald to continue it. On page 47, we saw that such a provision was held to be totally ineffective in point of law and hence provided no authority whatever for the continuation of the proprietorship business after death. Such a plan, therefore, may be discarded without further consideration.

PROVISION IN PROPRIETOR'S WILL FOR CONTINUANCE OF BUSINESS

General principles. Nowhere are the general principles governing the continuance of a business under authority of a decedent's will more clearly and concisely stated than by Surrogate Wingate in *Matter of Gorra.*[1] Although this case summarizes the New York law, these rules apply in most jurisdictions. They are as follows:

> *First.* "A testator may authorize or direct his executor to continue a trade * * * or business." (*Willis v. Sharp,* 113 N.Y. 586, 589.)
>
> *Second.* "The intention of a testator to confer upon an executor power to continue a trade must be found in the direct, explicit and unequivocal language of the will or else it will not be deemed to have been conferred." (*Willis v. Sharp, supra,* p. 590); [other New York cases also cited].
>
> *Third.* Such authority, if found, authorizes the conduct of the business in the usual manner unless otherwise expressly directed or limited. (*Matter of Rosenberg,* 213 App. Div. 167.)
>
> *Fourth.* A power "to carry on the testator's trade, or to continue his business in a firm of which he was a partner, without anything more, will be construed as an authority simply to carry on the trade or business with the fund already invested in it at the time of the testator's death, and to subject that fund only to the hazards of the trade and not the general assets of the estate." (*Willis v. Sharp, supra,* p. 590); [other N.Y. cases cited].
>
> *Fifth.* The trade fund which may thus be employed embraces the general property employed by testator in the business including accounts receivable. (*Boulle v. Tompkins,* 5 Redf. 472, 478.)
>
> *Sixth.* The ordinary expenses of the conduct of the business are chargeable to income. (*Dannat v. Jones,* 2 Dem. Sur. 602, affd. *sub nom, Matter of Jones,* 103 N.Y. 621).
>
> *Seventh.* Since "the creditors of the testator * * * are entitled to have the assets collected in and applied upon their debts * * * a direction of the testator that his business should be continued would not be allowed to interfere with this right of

---

[1]135 Misc. 93, 236 N.Y.S. 709 (1929).

existing creditors, or put to hazard the property of the testator applicable to the payment of their debts." (*Willis v. Sharp, supra* p. 590.)

Eighth. An executor who continues testator's business pursuant to powers granted by the will is not entitled to extra compensation for so doing in the absence of agreement by all persons interested in the estate. (*Matter of Popp*, 123 App. Div. 2 modifying s.c. *sub nom Matter of Kempf*, 53 Misc. 200).[2]

Ninth. "An authority or direction" for continuance of the business, "if strictly pursued, will protect the executor from responsibility to those claiming under the will, in case of loss happening without his fault or negligence." (*Willis v. Sharp, supra*, p. 590); [other N.Y. cases cited].

Tenth. "An executor, carrying on a trade under the authority of the will, binds himself individually by his contracts in the trade. He is not bound to carry on the trade and incur this hazard, although authorized or directed to do so; but if he does carry it on, the contracts of the business are his individual contracts." (*Willis v. Sharp, supra*, p. 591; . . . *Austin v. Munro*, 47 N.Y. 360.) As is said in the last cited case at page 366: "The principle is, that an executor may disburse and use the funds of the estate for purposes authorized by law, but may not bind the estate by an executory contract, and thus create a liability not founded upon a contract or obligation of the testator."[3]

Eleventh. "An authority or direction" for continuance of the business will entitle the executor "to indemnity out of the estate, for any liability lawfully incurred within the scope of the power." (*Willis v. Sharp, supra* p. 590); [other New York cases cited].

Twelfth. Those having claims resulting from the continuance of the business may, in the ordinary case, proceed only against the executor in his individual capacity (*Austin v. Munro, supra* p. 366; [other N.Y. cases cited]), although there is some authority for the position that where the trade conducted is a partnership, or the executor is insolvent they may go against trade assets. (Cf. *Willis v. Sharp, supra* p. 591); [other N.Y. cases cited].

Thirteenth. But where the testator has expressed in his will an intention to "bind his general assets for all the debts of a business to be carried on after his death * * * then, in case of the insolvency of the executor * * * in equity, the general assets become liable for the debts of the business." (*Willis v. Sharp, supra* p. 591); [other N.Y. cases cited].

---

[2]Often, however, provisions for extra compensation are contained in the decedent's will.

[3]The terms of the will may provide that the fiduciary shall not be personally liable, but the efficacy of the provision may depend upon the particular jurisdiction or the particular actions of the fiduciary.

POSSIBLE PURPOSES OF WILL PROVISIONS

A proprietor in his will may authorize the continuance of his enterprise for any of the following purposes: (1) to enable the stock of goods on hand to be sold in the ordinary course of trade instead of piecemeal; (2) to afford his personal representative an opportunity for selling the business as a going concern during the normal period of estate administration; (3) to enable his business to be sold as a going concern, whether or not an advantageous sale can be made in due course of administration; (4) to keep the enterprise intact until a later time when some member of his family can take it over; (5) to provide a more or less permanent source of income to his family; and (6) to allow his personal representative to use his discretion for the disposal of the business in the light of the circumstances encountered.

CONTINUANCE OF BUSINESS UNTIL STOCK
SOLD OUT

A provision in the proprietor's will authorizing continuation of the business until the stock of merchandise on hand can be disposed of in the ordinary course of trade is necessary only in those states where the prevailing law is exceedingly narrow. It will avoid the tremendous losses that usually follow the immediate closing of a business and the piecemeal selling of its assets along with the other assets of the estate. It is nevertheless an undesirable provision because both the good will and going concern value of the enterprise will be totally lost.

CONTINUANCE OF BUSINESS FOR SALE AS A
GOING CONCERN DURING ADMINISTRATION

A clause in the will directing the personal representative to continue the business until he can sell it as a going concern during the normal period of administration of his estate is an improvement on the foregoing provision, but it too must be rated as generally unsatisfactory. This has been clearly demonstrated by the experience gained under a parallel provision contained in the Massachusetts statute that, until recently amended, gave the probate court authority to "authorize an executor or administrator to continue the business of the deceased for the benefit of the estate for a period not exceeding one year from the date of his appointment." Several cases had occurred in which the personal representatives, unable to dispose satisfactorily of businesses during the time limit, had taken it upon themselves to continue the enterprises beyond the year and had subsequently made creditable disposals of the businesses as going concerns. When some of these cases came before Massachusetts' highest court, the court refused to penalize the personal representatives for losses and expenses during the periods of unauthorized continuance, on the ground that by ultimately selling the enterprises as going concerns they had actually saved money for the estates involved. Based upon these experiences, the Massachusetts statute was amended in 1945 to provide that "The court, for cause shown, may extend such authority beyond one year."

CONTINUANCE OF BUSINESS UNTIL SOLD AS A GOING CONCERN

A will provision for a business to be continued until it can be disposed of as a going concern is similar to the statutory provision found necessary in the Commonwealth of Massachusetts for the satisfactory sale of an enterprise as an operating commercial unit. Hence we may conclude that if, under the circumstances of a particular proprietorship, no better purpose can be served, the proprietor should provide in his will for the continuation of his business by his personal representative "until it can be advantageously sold as a going concern." This plan cannot be followed, however, unless the proprietor has made sufficient cash available to his executor with which to pay all taxes, administration expenses and personal and business debts, together with sufficient cash capital so that the proprietorship operations may be continued. Life insurance is, of course, the most certain and most practical method of providing this cash. However, such a plan should not be followed unless the proprietor is satisfied that there is no superior plan available to him. Nor should such provision be made unless he has appointed in his will an executor who is both willing and competent to take over the business and conduct it until such time as it can be advantageously sold. This point cannot be overemphasized. It is necessary that the executor be willing to run the business, for as we have already seen under the tenth rule given in *Matter of Gorra,* "He is not bound to carry on the trade and incur this hazard, although authorized or directed to do so." And it is, of course, equally necessary that the executor be competent if the continuance is to be successful.

The task of procuring a competent executor is unusually difficult. The personal representative must step in on a moment's notice and successfully carry on an enterprise that is largely the result of the peculiar abilities and personality of the decedent. As Francis W. Jacob states in 18 Iowa Law Review, pages 44, 45: "Experience gives no great assurance that a new hand, taking over the business under these circumstances, will administer it successfully. There is a substantial risk, except in abnormal times, that the business will be continued at a loss."

The risk involved has been legislatively recognized in Arkansas. That state has a statute which provides that, unless the will directs otherwise, the personal representative may continue a business for one month without a court order, and may, as authorized thereafter by the probate court, continue it for successive periods of three months each. The last sentence of the statute reads: "It is specifically recognized that the operation of any business undertaking involves hazard, chance, and danger of loss; and in recognition of this condition, it is declared herein to be the legislative intent that no executor or administrator shall be held personally liable for loss resulting from mere lack of familiarity with the business operations, mistakes of judgment made in good faith, or like causes."

But experience and familiarity with the business operations do not eliminate the risk under adverse conditions. *Conant v. Blount*[4] illustrates the difficulties that may be encountered under depression conditions in carrying out will provisions authorizing limited continuation of a business, even though the person is exceedingly well qualified. In this case it was the key employee of the proprietor who remained in active charge of operations for six years following the proprietor's death. The case also shows how far a simple will provision is sometimes "stretched" by exigencies and by the injection of the personal ideas of the executor with respect to the ultimate destination of the business.

Marcus Conant had for many years conducted a proprietorship, a mortuary, in Jacksonville, Florida under the trade name of Marcus Conant Company. He died in 1926, leaving a will in which his sixteen-year-old son and his daughter were the surviving legatees, under which Blount was the surviving executor, and which contained the following provision:

> I do authorize my executors and trustees to carry on my business after my death for the necessary length of time to wind same up without unnecessary sacrifice or loss to my estate.

The will also allowed the executors full authority to sell any estate property at public or private sale on terms satisfactory to the executors. Conant's estate totaled approximately $80,000, of which about $17,000 represented assets of the proprietorship. The real property on which the business was located was heavily mortgaged, and the executor sought to devise some plan to defray the expense of this mortgage and also to preserve the business until the son reached an age when he could succeed to the business. Accordingly, the executor organized a corporation under the same name, and the assets of the proprietorship were turned over to it in return for 151 shares of the total 300 shares of $30,000 par value. The remaining 149 shares were bought by one A.W. Ruus, who had been in the employ of the deceased proprietor for many years and had enjoyed his confidence, and who gave the executor in payment a note for $15,000 payable $200 monthly.

Ruus, who had operated the business for the one month from Conant's death until the corporation was organized, continued in charge until it went into bankruptcy in 1932. The cause of the bankruptcy was neither poor judgment, lack of attention, nor inexperience; it resulted from an inability to

---

[4]141 Fla. 27, 192 S. 481 (1939).

realize upon accounts receivable during the universal economic depression, complicated by increasingly keen competition.

The executor had rented to the corporation the premises occupied by it. He had received in payment for the account of the estate about $11,550, but $4,600 rent was still due him. He then bought the assets of the corporation for $4,500 at forced sale, releasing as a credit the amount of unpaid rent, and proceeded to organize a new corporation, Conant Funeral Home, which continued the business without interruption. The executor turned over the assets purchased from the bankrupt corporation to the new corporation and received back 73 of its 100 shares of stock, 23 shares being sold for $2,000 to one E.C. Long, who paid $1,000 to the estate and $1,000 to the corporation.

After April, 1933, the son, who had at all times been advised about the condition of the business and who had become of age two years before, was made a director. During the same year the executor, with the son's written consent, sold the estate's stock in the new corporation to Long for $500 cash and took Long's personal note for $1,800 rent then due the estate from the corporation. This corporation lasted until December, 1933, at which time the executor, under distress proceedings for unpaid rent of $1,375, again obtained the assets. These assets, or what was left of them, were finally sold to the Florida Funeral Home by the executor, who then rented the old premises to the successor of the Conant Funeral Home, which was called Long and Ruus and in which the estate had no interest.

In 1935 the son purchased his sister's interest in the estate and subsequently brought action against the executor for an accounting and reimbursement for losses occasioned by the executor's alleged misconduct in continuing the business. The executor had already made ten annual accountings, all of which had been approved by the county judge.

Florida's highest court affirmed the decision in favor of the executor. It held first, that the period of time "necessary" to wind up the business without unnecessary loss was a matter depending upon the circumstances to be determined by the executor; and second, that where the son had participated in the business, was acquainted with its various phases and had acted as a director in one of the corporations, he had thereby ratified the executor's acts and could not complain of them. Regarding the economic difficulties faced by the executor, the court said:

> The difficulty of liquidation in the economic conditions which have persisted since the year nineteen twenty-nine, or even following the year nineteen twenty-six, when financial depression descended on the state of Florida, is easily understood. The impediments were all the more serious because the property attempted to be sold was adaptable to but one kind of business. Certainly hearses, caskets and the like could be disposed of only to one following the vocation of undertaker.

The facts of this case have been given in some detail for two reasons: to show the ramifications that can follow from a simple will provision; and to raise the pertinent question of whether the proprietor's plan, as he wrote it in the will, or as it was developed by his executor, was the best plan available to him. Here was a valuable key employee, Ruus, who finally set up an undertaking firm of his own despite the failure of the decedent's enterprise. Was there a plan which the proprietor could have entered into with him that would have worked out better for all the parties concerned? We shall return to this question later.

CONTINUANCE OF BUSINESS UNTIL RELATIVE TAKES OVER

Occasionally, a proprietor will have a young son, nephew or other minor relative to whom he desires to leave his proprietorship. In this circumstance he may provide in his will that the enterprise be continued by his personal representative until such time as it can be turned over to the person designated. The hazards involved in such a provision, however, are many. In order to give the personal representative a sporting chance to hold the business assets inviolate during the period of administration of the estate and to carry on the enterprise successfully, he must be provided with ample cash from other sources (e.g., life insurance proceeds) for the payment of taxes, administration expenses, and all business and personal debts, as well as cash capital for the operation of the business. This last item is imperative, because the death of the proprietor will cut off the primary source of credit for the business: his integrity, ability and industry.

The depression hazard. Here again the proprietor must select a competent personal representative, one who is willing to stay on the job in the capacity of an operating trustee over a period of years. Furthermore, he must select a contingent trustee, equally competent, willing to step in and continue the business in the event of the death, disqualification, or renunciation of the representative originally nominated. In most of these situations there is a probable gap of several years' duration between the death of the proprietor and the time when the business can be turned over to the legatee. This means that the continued enterprise will have to run the course of the business cycle successfully, or there will be nothing left to be turned over. A comparison of the dates of past business depressions with the dates of failure of businesses set out in the various cases cited herein shows that this is a great hazard. This was just seen in the case of *Conant v. Blount,* for example.

The hazard of business changes. Another risk which must be contemplated in providing for the continuation of a business over a period of years by a personal representative lies in the possibility that the business changes which are constantly taking place will render the product, service, or method of doing business inefficient, or obsolete. In *Swaine v. Hemphill,* the decedent's brewing concern was closed down after three years because of losses brought about by the cut-throat competition of large manufacturers of malt, who had come into the field with the then current development of "big business."

The case of *In re Doelger's Estate*[5] is of equal interest in this connection. Peter Doelger died in 1912, leaving a will in which he directed his executors to continue his brewing business—a mammoth proprietorship which at his death had assets approximating $7,000,000—in trust, and for that purpose to form a corporation under the name of Peter Doelger Brewing Company. The corporation was formed and was operated successfully for many years, until the Eighteenth Amendment was enacted. Prohibition, of course, changed the entire business picture for the corporation. Some years later the brewing business was sold, the name of the corporation changed to Peter Doelger, Incorporated, and its business confined to the management and operation of its extensive real estate holdings and other investments.

The hazard of widow's inheritance rights. The proprietor who desires to make provision in his will whereby his business will be continued and will ultimately be turned over to a relative often has another serious problem. Under the decedent estate laws of most states, a widow is entitled to a specified minimum share of the decedent's estate, and if a lesser portion is given to her in her husband's will, she has the right to elect against the will and thus receive her full share of the estate despite the will provisions. This right cannot be denied her unless she has waived it in a formal manner usually prescribed by statute.

Therefore, where a proprietorship constitutes the major portion of a testator's property—which is frequently the case—such a plan, standing alone, is not practicable if the proprietor's wife is living. And even where this legal obstacle can be surmounted, the plan alone may not be feasible because of the inequality it works among the heirs. For example, a proprietor with a family consisting of his wife, a son, and a daughter would certainly not want to leave the bulk of his estate to his son at the expense of his wife and daughter, even though the arrangement might meet the minimum requirements of the decedent estate law. Under such circumstances, if this plan for the continuation of a proprietorship otherwise appears to be the best one available, and if the proprietor is insurable, he may purchase additional property in the form of life insurance sufficient to equalize, or at least to bring into suitable ratio, the shares going to the various members of his family.[6]

In this connection, however, it must be kept in mind that in most jurisdictions life insurance proceeds going directly to a widow as named beneficiary are not counted in calculating the minimum share of her

---

[5]4 N.Y.S. 2d 334 (1937), affirmed 279 N.Y. 646.

[6]See the example, involving corporate stock, at page 413.

husband's property to which she is legally entitled. Therefore, either her waiver of statutory rights should be made a part of the plan, or the insurance proceeds destined for her should be made payable to the proprietor's estate—unless a more elaborate arrangement is added to the plan, including the creation of a living insurance trust.

The insurance trust arrangement. Under this arrangement an insurance trust would be executed immediately, with the amount of life insurance payable to the trustee equal to the value of the proprietorship. The will would provide for the continuation of the business by the designated personal representative under a testamentary trust until the son is ready to take over the business. In the meantime, the net income from the business and from the insurance trust would be paid to the members of the family in suitable shares or to the widow, as may be desired. And when the son is ready to take over the business, the trustee, following instructions contained in the insurance trust, will purchase the proprietorship business from the personal representative under the will, turn it over to the son, and pay the corpus of the insurance trust to the personal representative in payment for the business. The testamentary trust also may be terminated at this point and the funds divided between widow and daughter, or it may be continued for their benefit, in accordance with the testator's wishes. Of course, the instruments will have to be carefully drawn to include alternative provisions for the disposal of the business in the event that it cannot be operated profitably, or in the event that the son never takes over the business, either because of death or because of a desire to pursue a different career.

The above arrangement will enable a proprietor with a wife and two children to leave each of them one-third of his property provided his proprietorship constitutes one-half of his net estate. If the value of his business amounts to less than one-half, he can equalize the share going to his son, if he wishes to do so, by an additional bequest to the son in the will. Where the value of the business amounts to more than one-half, he can equalize the shares going to his widow and daughter by the purchase of additional life insurance made payable to his estate in an amount that, together with his property other than the proprietorship, will equal the value of his business. Thus it is clear that in any ordinary family situation, an insurable proprietor, by suitable will provisions and by the purchase of the prescribed amount of life insurance, can work out equal shares for each member of the family and at the same time preserve his proprietorship as a unit for one member.

Ability of personal representative of prime importance. Before leaving the discussion of plans by a proprietor for the continuation of his business until a son or other relative is ready to take it over, it should be further emphasized that the carrying through of such a plan depends ultimately upon the ability of the personal representative to conduct the business successfully during the period intervening between the death of the proprietor and the time when the heir can assume the responsibility. Only too frequently, the proprietor delegates this difficult task to an individual lacking the necessary aptitude or experience—often his widow.

This was the situation in the great leading English case of *Ex parte Garland*,[7] in which Henry Ballman left his property in trust under his will and directed his widow, Margaret, to carry on his trade as miller until such time as the trustees should think proper to establish his sons, or either of them, in the business. In addition to the milling business assets of about £-1351, Ballman directed in his will that his trustees advance to his widow up to £600 to enable her to carry it on. After his death, the widow continued the enterprise for several years, being advanced the £600 and an additional £768 from the trust estate. She then became bankrupt. The creditors of the continued business tried to reach the other assets of Ballman's estate, but Lord Eldon held, in a decision which has been a landmark of the law since 1804, that where a testator directs a business to be carried on and designates a limited fund to be used for that purpose, the general assets beyond that fund are not liable for the debts of the continued business. For our purpose here, however, the case is one of the oldest that illustrates the dangers inherent in the selecting of an "amateur" to continue a decedent's proprietorship.

Sometimes, however, it is a widower who proves to be the "amateur" at continuing a decedent's business, as is shown in the leading New York case of *Willis v. Sharp*,[8] a case cited as authority for so many of the rules collated in *Matter of Gorra*. Fida C. Sharp had for many years conducted a merchant-tailoring busines in New York City. On her death she left a will directing that all of her property should be placed in trust for the education, maintenance and support of her son Harry until he became 25, and that some legitimate business should be carried on for his benefit until that time, with her husband retained as its manager at a salary of $1,500 a year. The will also provided that her executors could "sell or make such other disposition of my real and personal estate as the safe conduct of such business shall seem to require." The surviving husband alone qualified as executor and continued the merchant-tailoring business, but within six months after the death of his wife he had run up a bill with Willis amounting to $1,380. Willis, who could collect only $65 in payment from the husband and executor, sued in equity to reach the general assets of the estate on the ground that the executor was irresponsible individually. Willis won the case; the court opinion stated that the wording in the will of Mrs. Sharp "indicates, we think, unmistakably, an intention on her part to subject her general assets to the debts of the business

---

[7]10 Ves. 110 (1804).

[8]113 N.Y. 586 (1889).

and to authorize the executor to contract debts therein binding her general estate."

Corporate trustee preferred. The books are full of cases which could be cited to emphasize further the fact that any plan for the continuation of a business until an heir can take over can be no better than the ability of the personal representative selected to conduct the enterprise in the interim. By now it should be apparent that such an undertaking should be entrusted only to a professional trustee or to an individual who possesses outstanding qualifications for operating the particular proprietorship in question, and who is willing to do so. And even though such an individual is available, he is subject to the personal hazards of death and disability. For this reason a professional corporate trustee is recommended whenever such an institution is willing to undertake the trust and to resist the well-known tendency to be overly conservative in operating the continued business.

CONTINUANCE OF BUSINESS FOR INCOME TO FAMILY

A proprietor may direct in his will that his executor continue his enterprise for the purpose of providing a more or less permanent source of income to his family. Under such a provision, as under the plan of continuance until a relative can take over the business, the personal representative will be called upon to accomplish two distinct and difficult tasks. As executor, he must keep the business intact and operating efficiently; and at the same time he must perform the regular duties of his office with respect to the other assets of the proprietor's estate, including their possession, appraisal, liquidation (if required), the payment of taxes, debts, and administration expenses, and the distribution of the remainder in accordance with the terms of the will. As trustee, he will be called upon to continue the operation of the business successfully during a substantial period of years for the benefit of the members of the deceased proprietor's family.

It should not be necessary at this point to recite again in detail the hazards involved in this plan. Nevertheless, some of the potential dangers need further underscoring. In settling the estate, the personal representative, as executor, can keep clear of personal liability for the obligations created by the proprietor if he acts prudently and without fault or negligence. In continuing the business, the personal representative, as trustee, is personally bound by the contracts he makes. He is, however, entitled to indemnity out of the assets embarked in the continuing business (or out of the assets of the entire estate if the will unequivocally devotes the whole estate to the carrying on of the enterprise), providing he acts prudently. If, on the other hand, the executor and trustee is guilty of misconduct, bad faith, negligence or imprudence in settling the estate or in continuing the business, the right to be indemnified will be withheld by the court, with the result that the money paid to discharge the obligations involved in any breach of duty must ultimately come out of the personal representative's own pocket.

Undesirability of naming proprietor's widow as personal representative. That the personal representative be held liable obviously is essential, but its application may bring about unforeseen and undesirable consequences from the standpoint of the proprietor if he has designated a member of his family as personal representative to continue his business. An outstanding example showing such undesirable results has already been given in the case *Miller v. Didisheim & Brother,*[9] in which the proprietor's widow and executrix continued his business under a court order authorizing its continuation "as long as the same is conducted with a profit to the estate of the decedent." After suffering losses, she resigned and paid the amount of the losses to the successor from her own funds. However, because of her personal liability for obligations incurred, she was subsequently required to pay the balance of a debt owed an unsatisfied creditor of the continued business. The result would have been no different had she continued the business under a will provision similar to the court order granted her—but had that been the case, the deceased proprietor Miller could have been criticized for putting his widow in such a predicament.

When will provisions that designate the proprietor's widow as personal representative are coupled, not with positive directions to continue the decedent's business, but with broad discretionary authority to do so, they are particularly susceptible to undesirable results. There is an added danger that if the widow suffers losses, the court will refuse to allow her to be indemnified on the ground that she was imprudent or negligent in not discontinuing the business at the time when the court may think it should have been done.

This and other points are well illustrated by the case of *In re Onstad.*[10] P.C. Onstad conducted a general store in Cambridge, Wisconsin, during which time one Robert N. Nelson had become an accommodation maker of a note with him for $800. Onstad died August 24, 1929, before the note became due; and when it did fall due, the bank demanded and received payment from Nelson. Onstad's will gave his estate to his widow for the duration of her life and thereafter to his children, appointed her executrix, and stated that it was his desire that his wife, Jennie, should use her discretion in continuing the general merchandise business for the benefit of his estate. In addition, the widow procured a court order authorizing her to continue the business as "special administratrix" and as expense to pay herself $75 per month, her son $100 per month and a woman clerk at $60 per month. She failed to inform the court, however, that at the time of the proprietor's death the business was

---

[9](See pages 53–54.)

[10]224 Wis. 332, 271 N.W. 652, 109 A.L.R. 630 (1937).

only paying expenses and that there had been a decided decrease in business since his death and before her appointment as executrix.

Armed with this authority, but without filing proper inventories, keeping segregated records of estate property, or closing out the estate, the widow continued the business until April, 1932. The original inventory of merchandise was $9,206.45 and of fixtures was $1,221.50. When she discontinued operations, the merchandise inventory was $3,348.93 and the fixtures $900. Shortly thereafter the merchandise was sold for $1,200 and the fixtures for $300. (The last two sets of figures illustrate the amount of shrinkage in value suffered on forced sale—approximately two-thirds.) When the widow filed her final account, it showed a balance on hand for distribution of $434.47, which was sufficient to pay the creditors only 7 percent of their claims. The account was approved as containing the following items of credit: loss by depreciation through operation of the business, $7,953.29; loss by depreciation of fixtures, $811.50; loss on sale of stock of goods below inventory, $2,148.93; loss on accounts, $1,314.86.

All of the creditors except Nelson accepted 7 percent of their claims and released the estate. Nelson, however, filed objections and moved for an order requiring the widow to pay his claim in full. The lower court allowed his claim but denied his motion, which left him still in the position of being able to collect only 7 percent, and he appealed. Wisconsin's highest court reversed the judgment of the lower court that had approved the widow's final account, and remanded the case with direction to order her to pay Nelson's claim in full. While the opinion cannot be taken as a model of pellucidly expressed judicial reasoning, it nevertheless contains several points of interest. First, it shows clearly that provisions for the continuation of a decedent's business must be predicated upon provisions for settlement of the obligations of the deceased. On this point the court said:

> The rule in *Willis v. Sharp*, supra, that creditors of a testator
> are not bound by the provisions of his will for continuance of his
> business, follows from the statutory provisions that a decedent's
> estate less exemptions, preferred claims, widow's allowance
> during settlement, etc., must be devoted so far as necessary to the
> payment of the testator's debts. [Wisconsin statutes cited.] This
> is also implied from the conditions of the statutory bond of an
> executor, that he will "pay and discharge all debts" out of the
> personal property of the estate.

The estate at the time of Onstad's death had ample funds with which to pay Nelson, and failure to do so was held a breach of duty on the part of the executrix. Of course, Nelson might have expressly consented to the continuance, or might have been estopped by conduct that would imply consent, as were the bankers in the *Ennis* case, but the court found to the contrary.

Second, the will provision authorizing the widow to use her discretion as to continuing the business was interpreted impliedly to mean her "prudent" discretion. The court held that under the circumstances she had been imprudent in continuing the business and in failing to settle the estate within a year, in the absence of an extension of her original court order beyond that time. On this point, the court says in part:

> It appears clear that the loss sustained by reason of the imprudent continuation of the business by the executrix and the conduct of the business by her after the time when under the statute the estate, in absence of an extension for cause by the court, should have been closed, exceeded the amount of appellant's claim.

Third, it is clear that, had the executrix failed to make settlement and to get releases from the other creditors, her ultimate liability would have been several thousand dollars instead of several hundred. It is evident from the opinion that the court would have ordered a new accounting had there been any creditors then interested in the funds other than Nelson.

Fourth, the case is another example of the disaster that may result if an inexperienced personal representative attempts to continue a proprietorship during a business depression.

Extraordinary personal representative may produce extraordinary results. It was stated previously that the continuation of a business should be undertaken only by a professional trustee or by an individual trustee who possesses outstanding qualifications for operating the particular proprietorship, and who is willing to do so. The businesses placed in the testamentary trust involved in *Holmes v. Hrobon,*[11] had the benefit of such an individual.

Starting with only $3,000 of capital in 1920, the decedent had built up a laundry and linen supply business out of earnings to the point that yearly profits in 1936 and 1937 exceeded $30,000. His wife had worked with him full time until 1931. About 1935, he had also begun a real estate development operation. In 1931, Harry B. Holmes had become the decedent's attorney and was particularly active in the real estate operation.

A few days before his death in 1938, the decedent, by codicil to his will, had authorized Holmes as testamentary trustee in his discretion to carry on any business for such time as "shall be for the best interest of my estate," and had added that "it is my wish that the said trustee continue my linen and laundry business as long as the same may be profitable." Broad powers and discretion were given the trustee. The decedent's widow was life beneficiary of the trust. Since the trustee was given no working capital with which to operate the business, he used portions of current profits as capital in successfully maintaining and expanding the business. Up to September 1946, the trustee had paid the widow over $263,000 as trust income, but had

---

[11] 158 Oh. St. 508, 110 N.E.2d 574 (1953).

devoted a somewhat larger amount to operating and expanding the business. Among other things, the trustee had purchased several small competing businesses, and on approval of the probate court had insured his life for $75,000 for the benefit of the trust.

Ohio's highest court held that the trustee had properly used part of the business income as business capital; this must have been the decedent's intent, since otherwise it would have been impossible to continue operations. The widow's ultimate right to the income so used, however, must be preserved. The court also approved the trustee's purchase of life insurance for the trust's benefit, and the expenditure as an operating expense although, unfortunately, the policy had been cancelled due to objections made in lower-court proceedings.

Here, we witness a business being continued in trust with extraordinary success. Not to be overlooked, however, is the cause of that success: the extraordinary business ability of the trustee selected by the proprietor to continue his business operations. Few proprietors have the opportunity to make so fortunate a choice.

Provision in will for incorporation of business. Before leaving the subject of will provisions that direct the continuance of a proprietorship for the purpose of providing a more or less permanent income to the proprietor's family, further reference should be made to plans that call for incorporation of the enterprise after the proprietor's death and that place all or part of the stock in trust for the benefit of the family. One such scheme has already been alluded to: the provision for the incorporation and holding in trust of the Peter Doelger Brewing Company. With such an immense proprietorship establishment to deal with, Peter Doelger no doubt selected the best plan for his will that was available to him, even though the trustees found it advisable some years later, as a result of changed conditions, to dispose of the brewing business and to direct their operations into other channels. Another plan of this nature, the plan set out in the case of *Matter of Noll,* will now be discussed.[12]

Rudolph R. Noll was the sole proprietor of a granite memorial business, employing William Heinz as manager. Noll died in September, 1933, survived by his wife and his daughter, a minor. His will, executed a few months before his death, directed the payment of "all my just debts, and funeral expenses," made certain specific bequests and directed as follows with respect to his business:

> *Fourth.* I authorize and empower my executors to continue my business . . . and I direct that as soon as convenient after my death said business be incorporated under the laws of the State of New York . . . in such sum as my executors may deem desirable,

---

[12]273 N.Y. 219, 7 N.E. 2d 108 (1937).

and that my said executors transfer to said corporation all the assets of said business in exchange for an equivalent amount of the capital stock of said corporation, and that the total expense for incorporating said business shall be charged against my estate.

(a) I direct that Twenty Five percent of the capital stock of said corporation be given to my friend and manager William Heinz; and it is my wish that he be retained as the manager of said business, as incorporated, and adequately compensated for his services as such manager, irrespective of his ownership of the said Twenty Five percent of the capital stock of said corporation.

(b) I direct that Seventy Five percent of the capital stock of said corporation, be held by my executors, as hereinafter further provided [in trust, one-half for the benefit of his wife and one-half for the benefit of his daughter].

Noll's gross estate was appraised at $152,000. The value of the business was fixed at $42,925.31, of which $16,000 represented good will and over $19,000 merchandise. There was a cash balance on the books of $2,274.78 and business debts owed in the amount of $5,470.15. His other debts were $1,225.52. The two individual executors and trustees paid all the debts out of the general funds of the estate, organized the corporation with a capital stock of $44,000, and transferred to it all of the assets of the business free from the liabilities. Trouble brewed on the accounting, however, when the Surrogate decided that the business debts should have been paid out of the business assets, and surcharged the personal representatives for that amount. This decision was affirmed by the intermediate appellate court, but was reversed by New York's highest court. Chief Judge Crane pointed out in the opinion that there was no distinction between the business debts of a proprietor and his other debts, that the personal representatives were called upon first to pay "all" of the debts of the testator, and that they could not deal with the assets for incorporation purposes or any other purpose until the creditors were satisfied. With respect to the plan of continuing the business, which is our primary concern here, the opinion states in part:

> William Heinz was his manager. The business presumably could not continue after Noll's death without Heinz. This the testator recognized, and by his will made it an inducement for him to continue, so that his wife and daughter might have the income from the business, or such portion of it as was not given to Heinz. The business had been running down, from a profitable one, to one without profit. The annual income of approximately $14,000 in 1929 and 1930 dwindled each year and, in the first eight months of 1933, the business was operating at a loss. It was during this last year that the will was drawn. The merchandise was of a kind not easily salable, yet no doubt the testator had

hopes that with the improvement in financial conditions the
business would improve. He counted on Heinz. The criticism,
therefore, of the gift of stock to William Heinz, no relative, is
unjustifiable. The income, as the testator knew, for his relatives
would depend upon Heinz, the manager, after he, the owner, had
passed away. . . .

The testator knew his circumstances; his will indicates a desire
to provide solely for his wife and daughter, and no doubt he used
the best means to accomplish the purpose by keeping Heinz in
the business.

Notwithstanding the highest respect for the dictum of the learned judge,
the question might still be raised as to whether Noll *did* use the best means to
provide for his wife and daughter. Under the plan they are dependent upon
three-fourths of the net income of a small business which, over the five-year
period immediately prior to the proprietor's death, had varied from an annual
profit of $14,000 to a net loss. Consequently, similar fluctuations might have
been expected to occur in the future; hence the beneficiaries of the plan
could never be certain of the amount of their income in any year or that
there would be any income at all for them. Their interest in the business,
therefore, must be classed as speculative. Heinz, in spite of his legacy of
one-fourth of the business, had heavy responsibilities. His future salary was
dependent upon the board of directors of the corporation, which was
controlled by the trustees who held the majority stock. Stock dividends were
dependent almost entirely on his own efforts, yet three-fourths of the total
amount would go to others. On his shoulders rested the task of carrying on
the enterprise and of producing profits satisfactory to the widow and
daughter. Criticism of the gift of stock to him was made in the probate
proceedings and he could expect a resurgence of criticism at any time profits
were not made. At the time Noll acted—just a few months prior to his
death—the plan may well have been the best expedient available to him at
that late date, but its hazards are so apparent that it cannot be accepted
generally as a suitable business continuation plan.

The *Noll* case illustrates the general rule that business debts and other
debts of a decedent are not treated separately in administering his estate.
They will be treated separately, however, if the decedent so directs in his will
and his estate is solvent. In *Re Chertow's Estate*,[13] the decedent had directed
in his will that "all my just debts, funeral and testamentary expenses be paid
by my Executrix," and had specifically bequeathed his luggage business
"subject to all debts and claims connected with said business." The latter
phrase was held to separate the two varieties of obligations so as to charge the

---

[13]109 N.Y.S.2d 567 (1951).

business debts against the business assets, and the other debts against the general estate.

Widow's right to elect against will may defeat trust plan. We have already mentioned the hazard to a proprietor's will plan represented by the widow's right to elect against his will and to take her intestate share of his estate. The exercise of this right may sometimes entirely disrupt the proprietor's plan to have his business continued in trust. This was the result in *Mayhew v. Atkinson*.[14] The decedent had left his service store, and the real property on which it was located, in trust, with fixed amounts to be paid to his widow for life or until she remarried, and with remainders to two employees. Upon the widow's renunciation of her interest under the will, the court held that the interests of the remaindermen became accelerated into immediate specific legacies so that the intended testamentary trust never came into being. This hazard must not be overlooked.

SPECIFIC BEQUEST OF PROPRIETORSHIP

There remains one other distinct type of will provision to review: the will provision that bequeaths the business to a legatee immediately upon the death of the proprietor. If the legatee is an adult son or a brother of the owner, and someone who is capable and desirous of carrying on the enterprise, this plan is "a natural." The testator must, of course, describe most carefully what assets are embraced in the bequest, and state whether the legatee is to pay the business debts. Preferably, there should be insurance on the testator's life sufficient to pay them, along with the other obligations of the estate. Certain precautions, however, must be taken.

First, it is essential that the proprietor make sure that his will provisions cannot be upset by other legatees. This possiblity will exist if there is a surviving widow who has not been given her legal share in the estate, or who for other reasons may elect against her husband's will, and may be overcome by securing from her in advance a proper waiver of her right to elect against the will; but such procedure is feasible only where she has an ample fortune of her own. Ordinarily, if other property is lacking, the proprietor should be advised to procure, as a minimum, sufficient additional life insurance to be received by his widow in such manner as to satisfy the legal requirements. The same method is, of course, available to do equity to other members of the family if the assets of the proprietorship make up the bulk of the estate.

If the use of this method would require the proprietor to purchase more life insurance than he could maintain conveniently, a modified plan may be used whereby the son (or other potential legatee of the proprietorship) will agree to purchase part of the business at the proprietor's death. The son would then obtain insurance on the proprietor's life to cover the purchase

---

[14] 93 F. Supp. 753 (1950).

price, and would pay that price into the estate for distribution under the proprietor's will to the other members of the family. The son would receive the remaining part of the business as legatee. Under this modified plan, used alone or in conjunction with additional life insurance purchased by the proprietor, considerably less insurance is required in order to achieve an equitable distribution of the proprietor's estate among his family.[15]

Second, it is equally essential that the proprietor make sure that his provisions will not be upset after his death by his own creditors. Examination of the cases shows that this precaution is too often neglected, to the embarrassment of the legatees. However, it is also of interest to note that specific legatees (legatees of particular items of property) occupy a preferred position with respect to the creditors of the proprietor. In the first place, such legatees are beneficiaries of the well-nigh universal rule that general assets of the estate must be exhausted in payment of estate debts before resort can be had to property specifically bequeathed. In the second place, if resort must be had to property specifically bequeathed, its legatees are usually liable only to the extent of its value at the time of the testator's death.

The case of *Bowen v. Lewis*[16] shows the effect of some of these rules in the estate of a proprietress who had not provided for the cash needs of her estate. The decedent, Mrs. Ward, had inherited full ownership of a 100-room hotel in Kansas upon her husband's death. She made a gift of the hotel furnishings to a son and daughter and her son operated the hotel as her agent until her death in 1955. Her will devised the hotel to these children equally and named the son as executor. Her estate, however, was insolvent because of a $93,000 claim for income taxes she had failed to discharge. Under the Kansas statute, the son was authorized to continue operating the hotel as executor for successive six-month periods until December 1962, when it was sold to outsiders at public auction to close out the insolvent estate. The son had resigned as executor to bid at the auction, but his bid fell far short of that made by the successful bidders. Thus, Mrs. Ward's plan to keep the hotel in the family failed because of inadequate provisions for paying off estate creditors. Insurance on her life sufficient to wipe out her debts would have made her plan a success.

DETERMINING WHAT CONSTITUTES THE PROPRIETORSHIP

Before leaving the subject of continuation plans under the proprietor's will, something should be said of another problem the personal representative may encounter: determining exactly what items of property belong to the

---

[15] See an example at page 413, where corporate stock is involved.

[16] 198 Kan. 706, 426 P.2d 244 (1967).

proprietorship business. This problem is likely to be faced in its most difficult form where the business is specifically bequeathed or placed in trust, with other estate property bequeathed to certain beneficiaries. Since the business is not a separate legal entity, the solution of the problem depends largely upon how carefully the proprietor was in segregating his business from his personal affairs. Even then, however, a court may have to solve the problem.

This was the solution required in *Shaw v. Shaw.*[17] There, the proprietor of a successful proprietorship bequeathed it, "including stock, equipment, furniture and fixtures, cash, accounts receivable and any other assets (but subject to bills payable) . . ." in trust for his widow and two daughters by a former marriage. He bequeathed all his personal property "not connected with the business," to one of his daughters. Despite the fact that the proprietor had an established place of business, and had an employee keep not only strictly business records but individual records for himself, the problem of whether twelve certain items of personal property worth over $7,000 belonged to the business, or to the daughter, had to be settled by Arkansas' highest court. Even then, the decision was not unanimous as to one bank account and a station wagon. Obviously, this is a difficult problem at best, and one that must not be neglected by the proprietor or his attorney.

SUMMARY OF WILL PLANS

In summary, it may be said that because of the tremendous number of existing proprietorships, situations will be found in which each type of will provision has its place.

In a very few cases, a will provision directing the sale in the ordinary course of the stock on hand in a mercantile business will be called for. It should never be used, however, except as a last resort; heavy losses always may be expected from the liquidation of the business assets. Furthermore, the business enterprise goes out of existence, and its good will value and its value as a going concern are then totally lost to the heirs and to the community. Whenever such a provision must be used, life insurance should be purchased by the proprietor, and paid for out of the profits of the business, in an amount that will offset these losses and transmit the full value of the business to his heirs.

A provision for the continuance of a proprietorship business as a going concern until it can be sold as such by the personal representative involves danger of substantial losses and should be restricted to those cases in which a competent and experienced personal representative is available who can be furnished with ample cash capital, and to those cases in which the proprietor, during his lifetime, has been unable to arrange for a satisfactory sale of his business to be effective at his death.

A provision directing the continuance of a business until a son or other

---

[17] 224 Ark. 833, 276 S.W.2d 699 (1955).

relative can take over has its logical place. Because of the hazards involved, it should not be used if there is a very young son or other relative whose future vocational qualifications, aptitudes and desires are entirely problematical. When used, it calls for an able and willing personal representative who has sufficient funds at his disposal, an equitably balanced will so that other members of the family are suitably provided for without recourse to the proprietorship assets, and a well-established business that, if properly managed, can weather economic recessions and changes in business trends.

A will direction for the continuance of a proprietorship business in order to provide a more or less permanent source of income to the proprietor's family should seldom be used. Experience teaches that it should, in general, be restricted to gargantuan proprietorships such as, for example, the Peter Doelger Brewing Company. In the ordinary situation, the enterprise is largely a one-man affair and it is too much to expect that an outsider will be either able or willing to operate it for the benefit of others besides himself with any like degree of success over a substantial period of years. Therefore, such a provision usually leaves the estate funds for the support of the widow and children unsuitably "invested" in a speculative venture.

A provision specifically bequeathing the proprietorship business to an adult son or other adult relative is desirable if such a legatee has the qualifications, experience and aspiration to continue the enterprise. This provision, however, must be accompanied by provisions for the equitable balancing of property given to other members of the proprietor's family, with particular reference to the minimum share of the estate that must be given to his widow. The legatee of the business should also be furnished with additional business capital to offset the loss of the credit and key-man value of the proprietor.

This plan would fail, and probably the business would have to be liquidated at the proprietor's death, if the potential legatee of the business dies first. To hedge against this possibility, the proprietor would be well advised to insure the potential legatee for the difference between the going-concern value of the business and its liquidation value.

And finally, collateral to any and all of these provisions, the proprietor should provide cash for the payment of debts outstanding at time of death, for it should always be remembered that directions for the continuance of a business will not be allowed to interfere with the right of existing creditors to receive their money.

Thus, we find that in certain well-defined situations special will provisions are suitable to solve the problem of continuing a proprietorship business, but that in the absence of such special situations, provisions available through a proprietor's will are generally unsatisfactory.

In our search for a better solution of the remaining situations, we shall now examine plans available to the proprietor that he may enter into with others during his lifetime.

Part III

THE PROPRIETORSHIP
INSURED BUY-SELL
AGREEMENT

Chapter 6

AGREEMENTS BETWEEN PROPRIETOR AND OTHERS FOR CONTINUATION OF BUSINESS

TWO TYPES OF AGREEMENTS AVAILABLE

Two general types of agreements looking to the continuation of his business after his death are available during the lifetime of the proprietor: a living trust agreement and an agreement to buy and sell.

A revocable living trust agreement is commended to those proprietors who have minor sons or other relatives to whom it is desired to leave the business but who would not be ready to take over immediately upon the proprietor's death. Such a present trust of the business has the outstanding advantage, over a corresponding will provision, of allowing the owner during his lifetime to familiarize the trustee with the intricacies of operating the business successfully and of testing out the trustee's ability to do so. Among other advantages, it currently relieves the proprietor of some of the burdens of sole management, and after his death it largely disengages the business from any will complications that might otherwise arise.

A living trust of the business, however, presents certain difficult problems if the business is to be carried on for a substantial period after the proprietor's death. Foremost is the problem of obtaining a trustee willing and capable of administering such a trust. While a corporate trustee usually is preferable, many refuse to take on this exacting task, and those willing to do so usually require that the proprietorship business be incorporated. Then, of course, there is the added expense of trustee's fees to consider. Furthermore, most such trustees will insist on broad powers of control after the proprietor's death, including the power to sell or liquidate the business if necessary to preserve the trust corpus. And such trustees undoubtedly will require the trust instrument to include as broad an exculpatory clause as local trust law will permit. Provided these and similar problems can be solved satisfactorily, situations present themselves in which a revocable living trust of the business is to be recommended.

The second type of agreement, an agreement to buy and sell the proprietorship, effective upon the proprietor's death, is commended to the vast number of proprietors who have no sons or other relatives as logical successors. This form of agreement will now be discussed.

WHY A BUY-SELL AGREEMENT IS DESIRABLE

Often a proprietor has devoted the best years of his life to building up a substantial business that, under his ownership and management, affords him and his family a satisfactory livelihood. For many reasons, he does not want to have the enterprise crumble upon his death. But he knows, or should know, that without some pre-arranged plan, the business will close its doors when he passes away and the assets will be sold, in due course of the administration of his estate, for a fraction of their former worth as assets of a profitable going concern. He also knows that the business, if he provides in his will for its continuance until it can be sold as a going concern, may well run into serious difficulties before a likely buyer can be located; and that such a plan is, therefore, fraught with uncertainty and risk. He knows further that he is leaving a speculative source of income for the maintenance and support of those dearest to him if he provides in his will for the continuance of the business by his personal representative in order to provide income more or less permanently for his family.

What, then, should he do? It is submitted that he should at once look for a logical successor to his proprietorship business, and when such a person is found, enter into a binding agreement with him for the purchase of the enterprise as a going concern, to be carried out upon the proprietor's death. The buyer of the business under such an agreement will acquire it as an actively operating unit; hence he can well afford to pay its going-concern value, and the proprietor's estate will suffer no liquidation losses. With proper arrangements for financing the purchase price, the proprietor's family will receive the full value of the business in cash, which can be placed in investments suitable for the widow and children. Under such a plan, the proprietorship business will continue uninterrupted, to the benefit of the buyer and the community, and as a monument to the ability and foresight of the proprietor who founded and perpetuated the establishment.

THE PARTIES TO THE BUY-SELL AGREEMENT

Where will a proprietor find his prospective buyer? In most instances, he need not go afield; he should look among his own employees. There he will usually find one or more individuals of ability and ambition, familiar with the business, who may already have wondered what would happen to their jobs and future business careers should the proprietor suddenly pass away and who would gratefully and enthusiastically respond to the opportunity of becoming successors to the business.

For an apt example, let us turn back for a moment to the case of *Conant v. Blount* (page 64, et seq.). Marcus Conant, proprietor of the undertaking business, had associated with him one A.W. Ruus, "who had been in the employ of the testator for many years and enjoyed his confidence." Ruus, you may remember, bought approximately one-half of the stock of the first corporation organized by the executor after the proprietor's death, Ruus delivering notes calling for payments of $200 a month. Then at the end, on the failure of the second corporation, the executor rented the old premises to the successors of the Conant Funeral Home, Long and Ruus. Clearly, here was a key employee who logically would have welcomed the opportunity during Marcus Conant's lifetime of entering into an agreement with him to purchase the proprietorship business upon his death. As we shall see later, he could have financed the purchase in advance and owned the entire business outright on Conant's death with smaller monthly payments than he obligated himself to pay on the notes, after death, for a half-interest. With the business free and clear, Ruus would then have been in an enviable position to ride out the depression. The executor would have received cash in payment for the sale of the business and could have applied it against the mortgages which caused him so much trouble. Can it be doubted that everyone concerned would have been far better off had such an agreement been entered into between proprietor Conant and key-man Ruus?

Let us turn to another case, *Matter of Noll* (page 74 et seq.). Here again we find a proprietor, Rudolph Noll, and a key employee, William Heinz, who would have been logical parties to an agreement of purchase and sale of the granite memorial business. Indubitably both Heinz and the proprietor's family would have been better served had such a plan been set up. Had this been done, Heinz would now own the business instead of holding only a one-fourth interest; and the widow and daughter would have had cash to place in suitable investments instead of being dependent upon a portion of the fluctuating earnings of a small enterprise.

These cases are typical of thousands of existing proprietorships, among whose employees will be found a "Ruus" or a "Heinz," eager for the chance to enter into an agreement that will assure his future and will someday make him the proprietor of his own business.

There are, however, many proprietorships that do not have in their employ men of the calibre of Heinz and Ruus. In those situations, it will pay the proprietor well during his lifetime and his estate after his death to search out such an employee and bring him into the business. As the proprietor grows older, he will then have able shoulders on which to shift some of the burdens of management while he enjoys his later years, and he will be afforded the opportunity of ideally solving the problem of the disposal of the business upon his death.

There are, of course, many strictly one-man proprietorships, businesses run without a need for employees. Proprietors of these establishments, so long as their establishments remain such, will have to fall back upon other solutions.

FINANCING THE BUY-SELL AGREEMENT

A buy-sell agreement between a proprietor and one or more of his key employees for the purchase of the business upon the proprietor's death sets up a pre-arranged market for the business. Such an agreement, to be valid, must of course contain a stipulated purchase price or a definite valuation formula that may be applied at the time of death to produce a price. The plan must go further, however; it must assure that the purchaser has the money with which to pay over such price in full, or nearly in full, promptly on the proprietor's death. Life insurance carried on the proprietor by the purchaser in the amount of the purchase price, exactly matching the purchaser's obligation both as to time and amount payable, obviously is the most satisfactory method of financing such an agreement. Life insurance owned by the purchasing employee on the life of the proprietor in the amount of the purchase price not only assures all parties to the agreement that the cash with which to carry out the transaction will be forthcoming when needed, it also constitutes the most convenient and practical method of financing the purchase.

Non-insurance financing methods impractical. It would be a rare case indeed, in which an employee of a proprietor had sufficient wealth to enable him to pay cash for the business on the proprietor's death. Eliminating this possibility because of its rarity, there remain three possible methods open to the employee other than the life insurance method: to stint and thereby save the purchase price; to pay the purchase price in installments after the proprietor's death; and to borrow the money at the time of the death.

The method of saving the purchase price is entirely impractical. Years of stinting would be required to build up the necessary fund; yet the full amount might be required in a few years or even in a few months—when, no one can possibly foresee.

The method of paying the purchase price in installments over a period of years after his death would be unsatisfactory to the proprietor because the payments which should go to his family would be dependent upon the future fortunes of the business, one of the major hazards he is attempting to avoid. It would be equally unsatisfactory to the employee for it would be a drain on the future income of the business for many years to come.

The method of borrowing can hardly be considered more than a mere hope or expectancy. Because the credit standing and borrowing ability of the purchasing employee at the unknown future time when the money will be needed cannot be foretold, there would subsist only a hope that he could then obtain the funds somehow in order to carry through the purchase. Not only does this uncertainty condemn this alternative in the eyes of both parties but, if perchance such a loan were made, the required payments of loan interest, together with repayment of the loan principal, would be twin millstones grinding down upon the purchasing employee.

The life insurance method of financing the purchase. The only completely satisfactory method of financing an agreement by which one or more key employees of a proprietorship will purchase the business on the death of the proprietor is by means of life insurance carried by these employees on the life of the proprietor. The effect of such a financing arrangement is to set up an advance installment plan for the payment of the purchase price. The amount of each annual installment is small—for example, approximately 2 percent if the proprietor is age 37, 3 percent if he is age 47, 4 percent if age 55, 5 percent if age 59, *et cetera*—and may be broken down into semi-annual, quarterly, and even monthly payments, if desired. And these installment payments cease at the death of the proprietor, when the financing plan automatically become self-completing. (See further discussion of premium payments at page 177.)

By this advance method of financing the purchase price, compound interest is put to work immediately in favor of the purchaser, with the result that only in exceedingly rare instances do the total payments equal the purchase price; in contrast, under a purchase arrangement calling for installments after the death, compound interest works against the purchaser and must be paid in addition to the full purchase price.

From the standpoint of the proprietor, this plan of financing guarantees that his estate will receive the full going value of the business at once, in cash. For him, an immensely difficult estate problem is solved perfectly. From the standpoint of the purchasing employee, the event that causes the purchase price to be due and payable will automatically cancel all future installment payments and will place in his hands the full purchase price. For him, a going, profitable, familiar business is his, "free and clear."

VALIDITY OF THE BUY-SELL AGREEMENT

No case has yet come to our attention in which the validity of an agreement of the exact type being discussed has been challenged. The legal principles involved, however, are similar to those involved in agreements for the purchase and sale of close corporation stock on the death of a stockholder. Many cases are cited later, in the sections dealing with partnerships and corporations, upholding these last two types of agreements.

Courts will compel specific performance of agreement. The courts will require the parties or their representatives to carry through the exact transaction of the purchase and sale of the business that is the subject matter of the agreement, rather than to require the recalcitrant party to pay a judgment for money damages for breach of contract.

Thus, we find Maryland's top court granting specific performance of a contract for the resale of a burial vault business with underlying lease, in *Wolbert v. Rief*[1] and stating: "It has been held that where the sale of personal property is incidental to the sale of a going business, equity may afford relief. See Pomeroy, Specific Performance, 3d Ed., s 16(e), p. 46, and cases cited in the note 152 A.L.R. 4, 61."

This is especially important to the purchasing employee, because his future business career naturally will be planned around the contemplated acquisition of the particular proprietorship business with which he is familiar and which he has agreed to buy.

These points are well illustrated by *Garber v. Siegel.*[2] There, the proprietor of a carbonated route and beverage business had left the business to his widow. She immediately employed her brother to manage the business under a five-year contract that also gave him an option to purchase the business for $11,000 during the contract term. After three years of successful operation, he exercised his option to buy. When the owner refused to carry out the sale, the employee sued for specific performance. In granting this remedy, the Court stated:

> Plaintiff is entitled to relief by way of specific performance for this is a business which he was associated with for a period of years and which he personally helped to develop. It involves specific customers and cannot readily be duplicated or obtained in the market, and it is apparent that his damages and loss of profits over an indefinite period of years cannot be readily ascertained and would, in no event, furnish a complete and adequate remedy. *Butler v. Wright*, 186 N.Y. 259, 262, 78 N.E. 1002, 1003, motion for reargument denied, 187 N.Y. 526, 79 N.E. 1102; *Waddle v. Cabana*, 220 N.Y. 18, 114 N.E. 1054 . . .

---

[1] 194 Md, 642, 71 A.2d 761 (1950).

[2] 194 Misc. 966, 87 N.Y.S. 2d 597 (1948), modified and affirmed, 274 App. Div. 1068 (1949).

Chapter 7

SPECIFIC BENEFITS OF THE INSURED BUY-SELL AGREEMENT

An agreement between the proprietor and one or more of his key employees, financed with life insurance, by which the key employee will purchase the proprietorship assets and business for cash on the death of the proprietor, is of immense benefit to all concerned.

BENEFITS TO THE PURCHASING EMPLOYEE

Business future assured. Without such an agreement, the applicable law would normally force the closing out of the business on the death of the proprietor and with it, the closing out of the employee's job. However, with such an agreement, the employee will not only have a job, he will be the new proprietor of a going business, with all of its assets, customers and good will intact. And because he is familiar with the operations of the enterprise, the new proprietor will have every opportunity to continue it successfully. His business future is assured.

BENEFITS TO THE DECEASED PROPRIETOR'S ESTATE AND HEIRS

Estate receives payment in full, in cash, at once. In case after case, we have contemplated the difficulties and disasters that have overtaken estates trying to salvage the true value of a proprietorship in the absence of a practical plan for the disposal of a business on the death of the owner. With a subsisting insured buy-sell agreement, regardless of vicissitudes of other estates, the proprietor's estate will receive the full going-concern value of his proprietorship immediately, in cash.

Proprietors's estate can be settled promptly and efficiently. In many of the cases, we have seen estates kept open for long periods of years because of the difficulties encountered in the disposal of a business. To review a few at random: In the *Ennis* case, the various creditors were litigating the proceeds of a closing-out sale six years after the death of proprietor Ennis; in the *Conant* case, the executor was being sued for an accounting of the continued funeral home thirteen years after proprietor Conant's death. If the proprietors had only arranged their affairs with more foresight, these difficulties could never have arisen. With an insured buy-sell agreement, the proprietorship business is disposed of for its full value as soon as the transaction can be consummated; and when the proprietorship business has been transferred to the purchasing employee for cash, the personal representative can administer the proprietor's estate efficiently, economically, and with dispatch.

Proprietor's widow relieved of business worries. A backward glance shows that the widow of the proprietor has often fared badly. In the case of *Swaine v. Hemphill*, Mrs. Swaine's consent to continue her husband's malting business cost her approximately $1,700, besides the almost $6,000 of her own funds used to pay estate debts because of lack of cash. In the *Ennis* case, approximately $13,000 was lost when the widow allowed her son, Donald, to continue the business. In the case of *Miller v. Didisheim & Brother*, the widow of the proprietor Miller was apparently required to pay twice for certain debts incurred by the continued proprietorship. In the *Onstad* case, Mrs. Onstad was fortunate that only one estate creditor refused to settle at seven cents on the dollar. And to go back to the year 1804, Mrs. Ballman, in the case of *Ex parte Garland*, went bankrupt trying to carry on Ballman's proprietorship until his sons were able to take over.

How different the picture is for the proprietor's widow who is protected under an insured buy-sell agreement. She is entirely relieved of future responsibilities in connection with the business; she need not face the insuperable task of attempting to dispose of her husband's proprietorship for its full value, or, without proper training, to cope with highly competitive business operations. Under a pre-arranged plan, the proprietorship is disposed of for its full going-concern value in cash, which may be invested in securities suitable for the widow and children. For her, business burdens, worries, liabilities, and financial hazards have been eliminated.

BENEFITS DURING THE PROPRIETOR'S LIFETIME

The business is profitably stabilized. Although the primary objectives of an insured buy-sell agreement are realized upon the death of the proprietor, very important advantages accrue from such an agreement during the proprietor's lifetime. The future of the proprietorship business having been assured, customers and clients will be more readily obtained and retained, which in turn tends to stabilize the business on a more permanent and profitable basis. Employees, knowing that the enterprise will not "fold up" on the death of the proprietor, will mold into a far more efficient and stable organization. If credit is necessary in the operation of the proprietorship, it will be more readily extended and probably on better terms because of the knowledge that the death of the proprietor will not bring about the termination of the business and the knowledge that the proprietor's estate will be paid fully in cash for the going value of the business. The purchasing employee, instead of continuously looking for better opportunities elsewhere, will redouble his efforts to help conduct the proprietorship successfully in order to enhance the value of his future business. The interplay of all these favorable factors cannot fail to earn added profits for the present proprietor.

Attractive savings medium provided purchasing employee. Each time the purchasing employee pays a premium for the insurance on the life of the proprietor, he has completed another advance installment payment of the purchase price of the business. To him, therefore, each premium represents a saving—a capital investment immediately put to work for him at compound interest. As a savings plan, it possesses many attractive features. Each amount saved is of a convenient size and is made regularly. Furthermore, the plan contains an element of compulsion, without which most savings plans are soon abandoned. The life insurance has a guaranteed cash value, commencing after a year or two and increasing in amount with each premium payment. And despite the fact that these values are available to the employee at once in the event of an emergency, in most states they receive the highest degree of legal protection against the claims of others. Thus the purchasing employee is furnished with a convenient, regular, efficient, legally protected savings program that is centered directly on the objective most vital to him—assuring his business future by making certain that the funds required to buy the enterprise will be fully saved at precisely the time they are needed.

Proprietor's burden of responsibilities lightened. Simultaneously with the execution of a buy-sell agreement, there will spring up a new interest in the problems and opportunities of the proprietorship on the part of the purchasing employee because, from that day on, he will be vitally concerned with its success. This new interest not only removes the likelihood that the employee may some day leave and set up shop for himself in competition with the proprietor, it also makes the employee anxious to assume more and more of the responsibilities of the business. Thus the proprietor, as he grows older, is, without the necessity of taking in a partner and sharing the profits with him, able to taper off his business activities and find more time for the enjoyment of living. With an associate equally as interested in the future of the enterprise as he is himself, the proprietor's burden of responsibilities is bound to become lighter and his life more pleasurable with the passing years.

Proprietors, like the rest of us, only live once; and this benefit of a buy-sell agreement alone would justify a proprietor in searching out a person whom he could hire and train as a key employee if his organization now lacks such an individual.

Chapter 8

CONTENTS OF THE BUY-SELL
AGREEMENT WITH LIFE INSURANCE

INTRODUCTORY

Agreement must be drawn by a competent attorney. The insured buy-sell plan by which one or more key employees of a proprietor will purchase the business on the death of the owner is comparatively simple. The plan is composed of two elements: (1) a written agreement in which the proprietor binds himself and his estate to sell the enterprise to the employee upon the proprietor's death, and in which the employee binds himself to buy such business upon the owner's death at the stipulated price and agrees to maintain life insurance on the life of the owner in an amount equal to the purchase price; and (2) life insurance policies procured in accordance with the terms of the agreement. Because the proprietor must rely on the agreement for the disposal of his business for its full value in cash upon his death, and because the purchasing employee will be dependent upon it for his future business career, the instrument itself is of such great importance to both parties concerned that only a competent attorney should be entrusted with its drafting.

THE BROAD PATTERN OF THE AGREEMENT

Although no two agreements for the purchase and sale of a proprietorship are exactly alike, all such agreements follow similar patterns. The essential provisions are as follows:

1. A definite agreement as to the assets and liabilities that comprise the proprietorship business.

2. A commitment on the part of the proprietor that he will not dispose of the business during his lifetime without first offering it to the employee at the contract price.

3. A definite commitment on the part of both parties whereby the employee agrees to buy the proprietorship business upon the proprietor's prior death, and whereby the proprietor, binding his estate, agrees to sell and transfer the business to the employee.

4. A definite agreement as to the purchase price to be paid for the business, including underlying provisions for the valuation of the business.

5. A definite commitment to purchase and to maintain, subject to the above agreement, life insurance on the life of the proprietor with which to finance the purchase.

6. A definite stipulation as to the ownership and control of the life insurance policy that is made subject to the agreement, and as to the disposal of the policy should the agreement be terminated during the lifetime of the parties.

7. A definite commitment with respect to the time and manner of paying any balance of the purchase price in excess of the insurance proceeds, including, for the protection of the estate, security provisions covering the unpaid balance; and conversely, provisions with respect to the disposition of any insurance proceeds in excess of the purchase price.

8. A definite commitment that the buyer will assume all business debts and will save the proprietor's estate from harm from them—unless the purchase price is on a "gross" basis, that is, based upon the business assets without the business debts having been deducted.

9. An agreement on the part of the proprietor to grant to the employee the necessary power of attorney to continue the business without interruption. This is advisable if the proprietorship business is of such a nature that a temporary cessation of operations upon the proprietor's death would be injurious, and if a power coupled with an interest can be validly set up in the particular jurisdiction.

10. Provisions with respect to altering, amending, or terminating the agreement.

CONTENTS OF THE AGREEMENT

Since each proprietorship differs in some respects from every other, each insured buy-sell agreement must be individually tailored by the attorney to fit the particular situation. This is accomplished by selecting, from a number of available arrangements, that arrangement most suitable to the situation at hand. A knowledge of the various alternative provisions is therefore necessary, and these will be discussed in the following analysis of the contents of such agreements.

The parties to the agreement. The necessary parties are the proprietor and the purchasing employee or employees. If there is one key employee of the desired calibre, purchase by him alone simplifies matters considerably and is to be recommended. In many instances it is found advisable to have a trustee as an impartial third party both to act as custodian and beneficiary of the life insurance policies during the lifetime of the proprietor and to supervise the carrying out of the purchase and sale upon his death. In community property states, or where the business assets include real property in a state granting dower rights, the wife of the proprietor should also be a party to the agreement.

The purpose of the agreement. Any well-drawn agreement will contain recitals of its purpose as well as essential background information. For example, the agreement should identify the proprietorship, give the status of the purchasing employee, set forth the desire of the parties to sell and purchase the business upon the proprietor's death and to carry life insurance for that purpose, *et cetera.* Such recitals help clarify the intention of the parties and might resolve possible ambiguities in the main provisions of the agreement.

Description of the assets and liabilities of the proprietorship. New York's highest court stated as follows regarding proprietor Noll, in *Matter of Noll:*[1] "... the estate consisted of everything the deceased owned—his business assets, his real estate or any other property.... The debts of the business were his own debts the same as were his living expenses." Since no legal distinction is made between proprietorship assets and liabilities and the other assets and liabilities of the proprietor, in drawing up the agreement it behooves the parties themselves to be particularly careful to describe or define exactly those assets and liabilities that are to constitute the subject matter of the agreement. Any uncertainty in this respect is bound to cause trouble.

The "first-offer" commitment. The agreement should contain a provision stating that if the proprietor should desire to dispose of the proprietorship during his lifetime, he shall first offer in writing to sell it to the employee at the contract price. If the offer is not accepted within a specified time, the proprietor shall be free to dispose of the business to any other person, but shall not sell it without first giving the employee the right to purchase at the price and on the terms offered by such other person. Such provisions not only protect the employee, but also may help govern the Federal estate tax value of the business upon the proprietor's death.

---

[1] 273 N.Y. 219.

The commitment to sell and buy. The agreement should state in precise language that, upon the prior death of the proprietor, his estate will sell, and the other party will buy, the proprietorship business.

The price to be paid, and valuation formula. Discussion of purchase of assets "gross." A choice of several possible provisions is available in designating the purchase price to be paid for the business. Preliminary to the agreement, however, the parties must decide whether the subject matter of the sale is to be the assets and good will of the business, or the assets and good will less the debts of the business. For example, a particular proprietorship may have assets and good will amounting to $35,000 and debts amounting to $10,000. If the employee purchases only the assets and good will, the purchase price should be $35,000, but if he buys the assets and good will less the liabilities, it should be $25,000. Under the first plan, the estate receives a gross amount of cash, including funds with which to pay off the business debts. Under the second plan, the purchasing employee receives a gross amount of property at a net purchase price for the business as a unit and he is required to assume and pay off the business debts. He must pay off promptly; otherwise, the business creditors will retain their right to be paid as estate creditors. (See further discussion of this example on page 107.)

The first plan is most preferable where it can be fully financed with life insurance. Upon the consummation of this plan, the deceased's estate will receive, over and above the net going-concern value of the business in cash, cash with which to discharge immediately the business debts, for which it alone is liable, On his part, the purchasing employee will own the assets and good will of the business, unencumbered with the assumption of the proprietor's business debts. This result, as we shall see later in more detail, eliminates one of the more difficult problems in the purchase and sale arrangement, the problem of assuring the estate of the proprietor that the business debts will be paid. Because of this outstanding advantage, this plan is preferable, even in those situations where life insurance cannot be carried in an amount approximately equal to the value of the assets and good will of the business.

A variation of the first plan may be used, however, to reduce the amount of life insurance needed to cover the purchase price. This variation was used to purchase from the proprietor the business involved in *Harold J. Burke*.[2] Here is the pertinent paragraph from the contract of the parties there:

> 3. It is agreed by and between the parties hereto that vendors are to sell to vendee all of the stock, merchandise, fixtures, customer lists, trade name, formulae, good will, and all personal property, tangible and intangible, now used by vendors in

---

[2] 18 T.C. 77.

> connection with the operation of the business of Killey Cleaners & Furriers whether said items of property are particularly enumerated or not. It is specifically understood that there is not included in this sale any accounts receivable or bank accounts of the said business.

Thus, the buyer did not purchase the accounts receivable or business bank accounts, and did not assume the business liabilities.

There are at least two good reasons why it does not make much sense to purchase the business bank accounts of a deceased proprietor. First, when the purchase price is fully insured, the proceeds that go to purchase the bank account merely buy cash with cash. Second, the problem of determining which bank accounts belong to the business is eliminated. This can be a sticky problem—as we saw earlier in *Shaw v. Shaw*.[3] So far as accounts receivable and accounts payable are concerned, they are owed to, and debts of, the estate; why not leave them that way.

Whichever of the above plans is chosen, the agreement must state clearly the purchase price that is to be paid. Two methods for doing this are available.

The first method is to fix the exact purchase price in advance. The price agreed upon is stated in the agreement at the time it is executed, and there is an accompanying provision to the effect that the parties may revise the stated figure annually or more often by endorsing the revised purchase price upon the contract.

The advantages of this provision are:

1. There can be no misunderstanding as to the amount of the purchase price.
2. The proprietor, knowing exactly what his estate will receive, can plan for the welfare of his dependents with reasonable accuracy.
3. The purchasing employee, knowing in advance the amount he will be required to pay for the business, is enabled to keep the purchase price fully insured.
4. The terms of the agreement and the consummation of the transaction are much simplified.

In spite of these advantages, however, this provision is not well adapted to the average proprietorship. The need for revisions is rather frequent because of changes occurring in the value of the assets engaged in the enterprise or in its net worth. There is always the chance that these revisions may be neglected, and while neglect to keep the purchase price up-to-date would not impair the validity of the agreement, unless the amount stated proved so

---

[3]224 Ark. 833 (1955).

inadequate as to work a transfer in fraud of creditors, still it would result in an unfair bargain. To eliminate this possibility insofar as possible, a further provision is usually included to the effect that the stated price will govern only in the event that the death of the proprietor occurs within one year from the time the last stated figure was agreed upon; in the event of a longer period the purchase price is to be fixed by an alternate method. This is accomplished either by taking the last agreed upon figure as a base and, on the findings of accountants or appraisers, adjusting it for whatever changes in value have taken place in the business from the time its value was last stated until the date of the proprietor's death; or by an entirely different method of valuation, such as the use of one of the formulae which will be discussed later.

A second and more fundamental disadvantage which militates against the use of the stated-value provision is the fact that it calls for a new meeting of the minds of the proprietor and the key employee upon a revised purchase price. With the self-interest of the key employee naturally favoring a low amount and the self-interest of the proprietor naturally favoring a high amount, there is too strong a likelihood that the provision would malfunction by generating future controversies. The natural self-interest of the parties to a proprietorship buy-sell plan with respect to price is quite different from that of two or more partners or stockholders under a "two-way" buy-sell agreement. Under the latter type of agreement, each partner or stockholder has a dual self-interest which tends to be neutralized: each stands to gain from a low price as a buyer if he should survive and to lose as a seller if he dies; and each stands to lose from a high price if he survives as a buyer and to gain as a seller if he dies. Accordingly, there is rarely any difficulty in coming to an agreement on a revised purchase price in the case of partners or stockholders; this provision works well with them. But this is not so in the case of a proprietor and key man; the following method seems better adapted to their "one-way" buy-sell transaction.

The method recommended to proprietorships is the use of a valuation formula set forth in the agreement and to be applied upon the death of the proprietor to ascertain the purchase price. If this method is used, care must be exercised, first, to select a formula that, when applied, will accurately reflect the value of the business, and second, to see that it is stated in the agreement in the clearest possible terms.

The simplest formula fixes the purchase price at the book value shown at the time of the proprietor's death, or as of the date of the last financial statement of the business taken off prior to his death. If the date of death is used, then the provision should specify who is to make the audit and appraisal. Often the provision will instruct the accountant as to the basis on which he is to value each of the various classes of property among the assets—e.g., raw materials are to be valued at whichever is the higher, the cost price or the market value. This formula, however, is inadequate in the case of a well-established business because it fails to include a value for good will. Usually the valuation of good will is provided for in the formula.

There appears to be no fixed rule for good will valuation. Sometimes the agreement stipulates that the value of good will is to be determined by certified public accountants who are experienced in the type of business enterprise involved. Frequently, however, such value is ascertained by the following process: The net earnings of the enterprise over a period of years are averaged; two items—a specified sum representing a reasonable compensation for the personal services of the proprietor, and a reasonable percentage of the book value, representing interest on the proprietor's capital—are subtracted from the averaged net earnings; and the resultant amount is multiplied by a stated figure such as 3, 4, or 5. The size of this last figure will depend largely upon the nature and stability of the business.

To illustrate this formula in action, let us assume that a proprietorship is found to have a book value of $60,000 and average annual net earnings over the last five years of $20,000. Let us assume further that the formula specifies a deduction of $12,000 as representing the proprietor's personal services, that a return of 6 percent is to be credited to interest on book value, and that the net result is to be multiplied by 3. Six percent of the book value is $3,600, which, together with the item of $12,000 representing personal compensation, is subtracted from the $20,000 average annual earnings and the remainder, $4,400, is multiplied by 3. Thus, good will is valued at $13,200; and this figure, added to the $60,000 book value, results in a total valuation of the business at $73,200.

Perhaps a brief explanation should be made of the fact that a sum representing the personal compensation of the proprietor is deducted from the earnings of the business before such earnings are capitalized to arrive at the good will valuation. The reason for this deduction is closely analogous to the reason that justifies the deduction of a reasonable interest return on the book value. The book value represents capital which, if it were not employed in the proprietorship, could be invested elsewhere to produce income. It is therefore proper to pay this invested capital a suitable wage for the work that it does. Or to look at the matter in another light, if the proprietor did not have the capital represented by the book value, he would have to hire that amount and pay it wages in the form of interest to the lender, out of the earnings of the business. So it is also with the proprietor himself. If he were not self-employed, he could be working elsewhere at a salary, in which case he would have to hire another employee and pay him wages to do the work which he himself now performs. Therefore, it is equally proper to credit him with a suitable wage out of the earnings before calculating the good will value of the business. In fact, it would be highly improper not to take this deduction in ascertaining this valuation, for his wage value obviously represents a value that cannot survive his death. Furthermore, the amount to be deducted should be large enough to include any good will value attributable to the proprietor personally, because this value is also lost on his death.

It is suggested that where the parties desire to use a formula to determine the purchase price they consult their accountants, who should be best qualified to recommend the particular formula that will most accurately determine the true value of the business.

Sometimes a provision is made specifying that the value of the business at the proprietor's death is to be ascertained by a panel of three appraisers—often designated "arbitrators" or "arbiters," erroneously so since these words connote an existing dispute or controversy. One such appraiser is to be appointed by the proprietor's personal representative, another by the purchaser, and the third by the two already selected. Serious objections to this method are that delays may result because of the inability of the first two appraisers to agree on a third appointee and that a majority may not agree on a final value.

In each case, the parties should be apprised of the various methods for determining the purchase price and whichever method is, in their opinion, best suited to the situation, should be used.

Financing the purchase with life insurance. The agreement should contain a clause identifying the policies of life insurance made subject to it. It should state that the purpose of such insurance is to provide cash to be applied to the purchase price and that the proceeds when received by either the deceased proprietor's estate or heirs—whether received directly as named beneficiary (not recommended) or indirectly from the purchaser or his trustee—is to be credited to the purchaser as payment on account or in full, as the case may be, of the purchase price for the business. With such statements in the agreement, any danger that the estate or heirs will try to claim not only the insurance proceeds, but the value of the proprietorship as well, is removed.

Provision for adding, substituting, or withdrawing policies. Substantial changes in the value of the proprietorship may take place during the time the buy-sell agreement is in force, in which event the amount of life insurance made subject to the buy-sell agreement should also be changed. Hence the agreement should provide for the addition, substitution, or withdrawal of policies by the joint action of the parties. Any changes in the composition of the insurance should be recorded in an appropriate schedule attached to the agreement and legally made a part of it.

Adjustment when amount of insurance proceeds differs from purchase price. Every agreement, except those few which provide that the amount of insurance proceeds payable shall constitute *ipso facto* the amount of the purchase price, should contain provisions applicable if the insurance proceeds and the purchase price should differ in amount.

If the purchase price proves to be less than the insurance proceeds, it is usually provided that the purchase price will nevertheless be the amount of such proceeds. In other words, the amount of insurance proceeds is made the minimum purchase price. If the purchase price is to be ascertained by formula at time of death, an agreement that the amount of the insurance proceeds is the minimum purchase price has the important advantage of enabling the proprietor to know in advance the minimum amount his estate will receive for the business and of allowing him to plan his estate accordingly.

If the purchase price proves to be more than the insurance proceeds, the payment of the balance may be provided for in one of several ways. If such a balance is relatively small, the purchaser should be required to pay it in cash at the time the assets of the business are transferred to him. If the balance is relatively large, other arrangements must be made. For example, the balance may be provided for by a series of interest-bearing notes, maturing over a period of time and secured by a mortgage on an appropriate part of the business property. In those cases where the balance is not much greater than an amount that the purchaser could raise in cash, this is probably the most feasible arrangement. If it is used, the recommendation is made that the notes be in stated equal amounts and be made payable at stated intervals, thus allowing the number of installments, rather than the amount of the installments, to vary with the size of the total balance owned. The parties usually know approximately the sum that can be paid periodically by the new proprietor without interfering with his successful continuation of the business, and the amount of the periodic payments can, by this provision, be set at a practicable figure. Of course, all such notes should be subject to prepayment at any time.

If it is anticipated that a substantially large balance of the purchase price will be owed by the purchaser, more elaborate provisions may be advisable in order to assure, on the one hand, that the estate of the proprietor will eventually receive the money and, on the other hand, that the purchaser's credit standing will not be impaired beyond the point at which he could be expected to operate successfully.

One of such provisions would call for the formation of a limited partnership between the purchasing employee as general partner and the personal representative of the proprietor, or a person designated by the proprietor in his will, as the limited partner.[4] Under such an arrangement, the unpaid balance of the purchase price constitutes the capital contribution of the limited partner. The partnership exists for a specified term of years or until the contribution of the limited partner is sooner retired. The general partner would be entitled to draw the same amount that he had received in salary as an employee of the proprietor, after which the net profits would be

[4]See page 121 et seq. for brief description of a limited partnership.

shared in proportion to the contributions of each partner. During the term of the partnership, however, the general partner should not be permitted to withdraw any of his share of the profits, and he should be required to pay to the limited partner out of such profits each year at least a pro rata part of the limited partner's original contribution. Thus, if the business continues to prosper, the contribution will be refunded out of the profits, the limited partnership will be terminated and the purchasing employee will become the new proprietor at the end of the specified partnership term or sooner. For the protection of the estate, it can be further provided that, if in any year there are no profits beyond the general partner's amount of drawing in lieu of salary, he must nevertheless pay an amount equivalent to interest on the limited partner's contribution, and that, if the lack of profits persisted for a stated number of years, the limited partner has the right to demand dissolution and termination of the firm.

The foregoing plan is available only in those states that have statutes authorizing the formation of limited partnerships. In other states, the parties may include a provision requiring the formation of a close corporation in which the estate is to receive common or preferred stock—the latter would be logical—representing the amount of the unpaid balance of the purchase price of the business. The details of such an arrangement can be worked out to provide for the gradual retirement of the shares of stock held by the estate or heirs in a manner similar to that outlined for the retirement of the contribution of the limited partner under that plan. It should be noted that under either plan, the estate is not liable for the debts created on the continuance of the business beyond the investment of the estate in the continued business.

Lest the foregoing resume of the various arrangements that can be made to discharge the unpaid balance of the purchase price under an insured buy-sell agreement appear to place undue emphasis on this problem, let us re-examine briefly the basic objectives of such an agreement. The ideal plan is one in which the full purchase price is insured, barring a possible insignificant discrepancy caused by a fluctuation in the value of the business. This is the plan that should be, and is, adopted in most instances. It is only in the exceptional case, therefore, that the parties must resort to one of the more elaborate arrangements sketched above. The parties should adopt the particular plan that will carry out their basic objectives immediately on death of the proprietor: the immediate sale of the business for cash "on the barrel head" paid to the proprietor's estate, and the full ownership of the business by the purchasing employee. Only a fully insured plan will attain these objectives promptly.

The payment of the insurance premiums. Ordinarily it is provided that the purchasing employee is obligated to pay the premiums for the insurance carried on the life of the proprietor, because it is the employee who will benefit from the insurance proceeds in payment for the business. These premium payments may be looked upon as advance installment payments on account for the purchase price of the enterprise which the employee is to buy upon the death of the proprietor. A practical arrangement, and one that assures the proprietor that the insurance will be kept in good standing, is for the proprietor, upon proper authorization from the employee, to deduct the premiums from the employee's salary and himself to make the actual payments to the insurance company.

Occasionally, a situation will exist where an employee, otherwise a logical party to such an agreement, does not receive an income sufficient to enable him to pay the required premiums. In such event, there are several possibilities. In view of the great benefits that the proprietor and his heirs will receive from the buy-sell agreement and in view of the increased value of the purchasing employee to the proprietor because of such an arrangement, the best plan is to increase the salary of the employee at least enough so that he can afford to assume the premium obligation. After all, if his services are not sufficiently valuable to warrant paying him enough so that he can pay these premiums, then the entire plan is probably premature and might better be deferred until a better qualified employee is found.

An alternative to the salary increase is for the proprietor himself to assume part of the premium payments. One way to accomplish this would be through a split-dollar plan, under which the proprietor would pay each year that portion of the premium equal to the policy's increase in cash surrender value. The employee could procure and own the policy, then assign it to the proprietor as collateral security for the latter's premium payments. If the policy is participating and contains the so-called fifth dividend option, the proceeds enuring to the employee may be maintained at a suitable level for many years into the future. Somewhat similar results may be obtained with a special policy the proceeds of which total the face amount plus the amount of cash value upon death within a specified period of years. Under one of these plans, the employee should take advantage of every opportunity to reduce his indebtedness with respect to the policy. By so doing, the employee will build up an equity in the policy which he may use as a down payment for purchase of the business if the proprietor decides to sell it upon reaching retirement age.

Another expedient is the setting up of a partially insured plan, by which the employee carries whatever sum of insurance on the proprietor's life he is able to finance. But here the problem of a large unpaid balance of the purchase price usually must be met, and unless it can be solved satisfactorily, the inauguration of the agreement should be postponed.

Control of the insurance policies. The agreement should specify who is to have the ownership rights in the insurance policies during the lifetime of the proprietor. Logically, the purchasing employee is the owner, unless a trustee is made a party to the agreement and the other parties prefer to have ownership vested in the trustee. If the proprietor is advancing or sharing in the premium payments, then he may be a collateral assignee of the policy. In any event, the agreement should prohibit the exercise of the rights of ownership in derogation of the agreement without prior notice to the proprietor.

The insurance beneficiary arrangements. The trust plan. The agreement should also contain a clause stating who is to be beneficiary of the insurance policy or policies. Here again, there is a choice of several arrangements.

If the proprietor and the purchasing employee decide to have a third party to the agreement as trustee, the trustee (preferably a trust company) is named as insurance beneficiary. In such case, the buy-sell agreement is drawn as a trust indenture, the provisions of which follow the form of the general buy-sell contract, modified and supplemented by the desired trust provisions. These specify that the trustee be made beneficiary of the insurance and custodian of the policies. It is recommended that the ownership rights in the policies also be given to the trustee, with the terms of the agreement outlining the conditions under which he may exercise these rights. However, other agreements provide that ownership be retained by the parties jointly or by the purchasing employee. The trustee is not concerned with the payment of premiums, and therefore the arrangement for their payment is not changed by the adoption of a trust plan. Upon the death of the proprietor, the trustee collects the insurance proceeds and supervises the consummation of the purchase and sale of the business.

This brief sketch of the workings of the trust arrangement illustrates its advantages to the parties.[5] The trustee, a responsible, experienced and disinterested third party, functions smoothly and efficiently to consummate the transaction. The trust arrangement is to be preferred over all others.

The insurance beneficiary arrangements without a trustee. If the parties to the agreement decide against using the trust plan, either because the amount involved is comparatively small or for other reasons, there remain various other beneficiary arrangements they may select.

Among these, the most logical is to designate the purchasing employee as insurance beneficiary. In this arrangement not only is the insurance money paid to the person who has created the fund by the payment of premiums, but also the relationship is equilibrated between the purchasing employee and the deceased proprietor's estate upon the latter's death. The purchasing employee, obligated to buy and pay the purchase price for the proprietorship, holds title to the insurance proceeds. The proprietor's personal representative, obligated to sell and transfer the deceased proprietor's business, holds title to the assets of that business. Each party to the transaction holds something that

---

[5]For further discussion, see page 338.

he is obligated to exchange for something of equal value held by the other. And each is in immediate need of what the other holds; the executor is in need of cash, and certainly the surviving employee is in need of title to the business assets. It is therefore to be expected that the plan will function smoothly.

The agreement can also provide for the designation of the proprietor's estate as insurance beneficiary, although this is not recommended. Such a beneficiary designation creates an imbalance between the purchasing employee and the estate of the proprietor at the time of death for the obvious reason that the estate then holds both the insurance money and the title to the business assets. Although a reasonably balanced situation is not essential because the courts stand ready, if necessary, to enforce the agreement specifically, nevertheless it is wise, as a deterrent to recalcitrance on the part of either side, to arrange for the meeting of the purchasing employee and the proprietor's personal representative on an equal footing to conclude the transaction.

There are at least three other objections to designating the proprietor's estate as beneficiary. First, both the insurance proceeds and the assets of the business are exposed to the claims of creditors of the proprietor's estate. Even though the rights of such creditors are ultimately limited to the insurance proceeds, nevertheless such a one-sided situation might well afford opportunities for interference and might delay the consummation of the purchase and sale. Second, the designation subjects the insurance proceeds to estate taxation. Although the decisions have not permitted taxation both of the value of the business interest being purchased and of the proceeds of insurance constituting purchase-price money for it, yet the placing of the insurance in a taxable status by making it payable to the insured's estate affords the possibility of a controversy on this point.[6] Third, it creates serious doubt whether the insurance proceeds will be included in the purchasing employee's cost basis for income tax purposes of the assets acquired from the deceased proprietor.[7]

Occasionally, a proprietor desires to designate that his personal beneficiaries receive the proceeds, in order to take advantage of the installment settlement options in the policies and to coordinate such insurance proceeds with the proceeds of his personal insurance. Such a designation is possible, but ordinarily it is not recommended. The obstacles in the way of such a designation and the various arrangements that have been devised to get around them are discussed at some length in dealing with insurance made subject to partnership buy-sell agreements. Because the problems and their solutions remain the same in principle whether the subject matter of the

---

[6] See discussion of *Estate of John T. Mitchell v. Commissioner*, page 428.

[7] See discussion of *Legallet v. Commissioner*, and *Mushro v. Commissioner*, page 222.

agreement is a partnership interest or a proprietorship business, and because it is believed that the reader will encounter no difficulty in adapting the partnership material to a proprietorship situation, discussion of this type of beneficiary designation is omitted here to avoid repetition later.

Disposition of insurance if agreement is terminated. Key man insurance also suggested. Normally, the key employee who becomes a party to the agreement is considerably younger than the proprietor, and will survive him to consummate the transaction of purchase and sale as planned. Regardless of the comparative ages of the parties, however, instances occur—and the possibility is always present—in which the key employee dies first. In such event, the agreement is automatically terminated; and it should be provided that the proprietor have an option of perhaps sixty days during which time he may elect to purchase the insurance on his life from the estate of the deceased employee at its then cash value. If the proprietor is at that time uninsurable, or if the policies contain more attractive provisions than those being incorporated in current policies, this will prove to be a very valuable option. Furthermore, with the buy-sell agreement terminated, and assuming that it is not then feasible to set up another such agreement with another employee, the proprietor is well advised to increase his insurance by the amount of shrinkage that he may expect his estate to suffer in liquidating the business upon his death. This he will then be able to do, whether he is insurable or not, if he is given an option to take over the insurance made subject to the agreement.

A far better plan exists, however, by means of which the proprietor, in case the purchase and sale arrangement falls through because of the prior death of the purchasing employee, can hedge against the shrinkage of the business upon its liquidation at his own death. This plan consists of having the proprietor procure, concurrently with the setting up of the buy-sell agreement, a key man insurance policy on the life of the purchasing employee in an amount at least equal to the probable shrinkage that would occur in the value of the business on eventual liquidation if the employee dies first. The proprietor would purchase, own, pay the premiums on, and be beneficiary of such insurance, which could be made subject to the buy-sell agreement to the extent of providing that, on the proprietor's prior death, the policy be maintained by the purchasing employee as collateral for any balance of the purchase price still owed by the employee. Such a policy will prove invaluable to the proprietor if the purchasing employee dies first; it will protect both the proprietor's estate and the purchasing employee if the proprietor dies first and there is a balance of purchase money owed to his estate.

In agreements involving two purchasing employees, it may be provided that, should one of them die during the proprietor's lifetime, the remaining purchasing employee will assume the obligations of the deceased employee and will carry through the agreement. In such event, the surviving purchasing employee obtains additional insurance on the life of the proprietor to cover his added obligations, and the insurance carried on the proprietor by the deceased employee is surrendered by his estate unless, within a specified period, the remaining purchasing employee or the proprietor elects to take over such insurance at its then cash value. The remaining purchasing employee would not be interested in taking over this insurance for value, unless the proprietor were then uninsurable, because he would hold such insurance as a transferee for value, a status that subjects part of the death proceeds to income taxation. Such proceeds, however, are not subject to income tax at his death if the proprietor himself takes over the insurance, and he might well be interested in doing this for the reasons already noted.

Provisions relating to the proprietor's business debts. Alternative of selling assets "gross" recommended. Upon the death of the proprietor, his personal representative is held accountable as a fiduciary for the assets of the estate; first, to collect and conserve such assets and see that they are applied so far as necessary to the payment of all the just debts of the proprietor, whether "business" or "personal," and second, to see that the remaining property of the estate is distributed to those entitled to it. With the above status in mind, let us see what can be done with the outstanding business debts under the buy-sell agreement.

There are two possibilities, and the choice between them is actually made when the parties decide whether the subject matter of the sale is to be the assets and good will of the business, or the assets and good will less the debts of the business. If the assets are sold "gross" to the purchasing employee on the proprietor's death, then no provision need be made in the agreement with reference to the payment of the business debts; they will be paid by the personal representative along with the other debts in the regular course of administration of the estate. If, on the other hand, the business is sold "net," the agreement must contain a provision requiring the purchasing employee to assume and pay off the business debts. Such employee should also be required to give the estate assurances, in the form of suitable releases running to the estate from such business creditors as remain unpaid upon the transfer of the business, or in some other form, to satisfy the personal representative that he will not be called upon to pay such debts. Since the giving of releases to the estate rests with the creditors involved, further provisions should be included to the effect that if the personal representative is not assured to his satisfaction that such business debts will be paid without recourse back to him, he has the right to nullify the sale of the business and to liquidate it.

It is submitted that the plan of selling the business "gross" will in most cases prove more satisfactory to all concerned. To illustrate, we shall reconsider the previous example (page 96) of a proprietorship with total assets and good will of $35,000 and total liabilities of $10,000. If the proprietorship is purchased on a "net" basis, the employee is required to maintain $25,000 of life insurance on the life of the proprietor to pay the purchase price in full upon his death, but he will also have to assume $10,000 in business debts. Moreover, if the estate cannot obtain proper assurances that these debts will be paid without liability on the part of the personal representative, then, to protect himself, the representative will call off the deal. If, on the other hand, the proprietorship assets and good will are purchased for $35,000 and the employee maintains $25,000 of life insurance as before, the purchasing employee will not assume the $10,000 of business debts but instead, he will owe $10,000 balance of purchase price, payable in installments previously agreed upon and in amounts calculated to be reasonably within his financial ability; and the transaction is not subject to nullification on the part of the proprietor's personal representative. Obviously, the purchasing employee will be better suited by this plan. The personal representative, under such an arrangement, will receive immediately $25,000 in cash, out of which he can promptly discharge all business debts and any other obligations owed by the estate, and the estate will receive $10,000 additional in regular installments from the purchasing employee. It appears certain that the estate, too, will be better suited by this plan. Now, if under the gross purchase plan $35,000 of life insurance is maintained, this becomes the better plan. On the death of the proprietor, the purchasing employee will take over business assets worth $35,000, with the full purchase price paid and with no debts assumed. The personal representative will consummate the sale of the business assets and good will for their going-concern value in cash and will be in an excellent position to carry out promptly and efficiently his duties of paying off the debts of the estate and of distributing the residue to the heirs.

We have already referred to a variation of the gross-purchase plan which will usually work out just as satisfactorily and require a lesser amount of life insurance. To illustrate, assume that among the $35,000 of assets is a $5,000 business bank account. By eliminating it from the assets to be purchased, only $30,000 of life insurance will be required to cover the purchase price. If we assume further that the assets also include $5,000 of accounts receivable, and also eliminate them from the assets to be purchased, only $25,000 of life insurance will cover the purchase price. Thus, this variation often requires no more life insurance than purchase of the business on a "net" basis, and under proper circumstances will function more smoothly.

Possible provisions for uninterrupted continuance upon the proprietor's death. If, under the circumstances, a power coupled with an interest can be validly set up in the particular jurisdiction, the agreement should provide that upon the death of the proprietor, the purchasing employee shall immediately take possession of the proprietorship business and continue its operations pending consummation of the transaction of purchase and sale. Where this can be done, an effective way to implement such a provision is for the proprietor to execute, collateral to and simultaneously with the purchase agreement, a broad power of attorney. This power of attorney should be drawn in such fashion that it gives the purchasing employee the power to conduct the business during the proprietor's lifetime if it is supplemented with the proprietor's current consent (this power may be useful on occasion), and the consent would not be revoked upon the occurrence of the proprietor's death but would give the employee the power to continue the business in full operation as a going concern. However, the personal representative of the proprietor should have the right to revoke such power; this he would do upon the consummation of the transaction or upon its failure to go through. With such a power, those doing business with the proprietorship need not hesitate to continue their dealings as usual; without it, they might be unwilling to transact further business until the proprietor's will had been probated, and then only with the personal representative.

Provisions for amending, revoking, or terminating the agreement. The agreement should provide that the individual parties jointly have the right at any time to amend or revoke it. The agreement should further provide that it shall be terminated upon the occurrence of any one of certain specified events—for example: the bankruptcy of either party; the total disability of the purchasing employee, or his termination of employment; the death of the purchasing employee any time prior to the consummation of the transaction; the lapse of the life insurance subject to the agreement; or the sale or liquidation of the business by the proprietor.

Provision binding heirs. The agreement should be made binding specifically upon the heirs of the proprietor. If such a statement is included for all heirs to see, no misunderstanding will develop on this point.

The foregoing discussion has encompassed the principal provisions required in a proprietorship buy-sell agreement. Since the document is of immense importance to all parties concerned, it should be carefully "tailored" to fit the individual case by the attorney of their choice.

Chapter 9

TAX PROBLEMS INVOLVED IN
THE PROPRIETORSHIP INSURED
BUY-SELL AGREEMENT

THE FEDERAL INCOME TAX

The life insurance premiums not deductible expense. The premiums paid for life insurance subject to the buy-sell agreement do not constitute a deductible business expense by the premium payer.

Of course, arrangements are often made whereby the purchasing employee authorizes the proprietor to pay the insurance premiums as they become due and to charge them to the employee's salary account. In these cases the premiums paid by the proprietor are not deductible by him *as premiums* but are deductible by him *as salary* paid out. The employee, the real premium payer, is entitled to no deduction for them.

The life insurance proceeds not taxable income. As a concomitant to the general rule above that life insurance premiums are not deductible, the Internal Revenue Code[1] provides, except in the case of certain policies that have been transferred for value, for the exclusion from taxable income of the face amount received under a life insurance contract paid by reason of the death of the insured.

The sale of the proprietorship by the estate. Section 1014 of the Code provides that the basis for income tax purposes of property acquired by the

---

[1]Section 101.

decedent's estate from the decedent shall be the fair market value of such property at the time of death, or on the optional valuation date if that method of valuation is elected for Federal estate tax purposes. If a buy-sell agreement is in effect, the fair market value of the proprietorship property at death, or on the optional valuation date, if elected, obviously should be the price to be paid under the agreement. Therefore, when the transaction is consummated by the executor or administrator at such price, no gain or loss should result to the estate on the sale of the capital assets.

Uncollected accounts receivable of the proprietor, however, are rights to income in respect of a decedent and do not receive a new basis at the proprietor's death. Therefore, if such accounts are sold by the estate the amount received over unrecovered cost will constitute ordinary income to the estate.[2]

The cost basis of proprietorship assets acquired by the purchasing employee. The cost basis of the assets of the proprietorship taken over by the purchasing employee should be the price he has paid for them. In this respect no material difference results whether the proprietorship assets and good will are bought "gross," without assuming the business debts (see page 96 et seq.), or are bought "net," assuming such debts. If the assets and good will are purchased "gross," the amount paid to the deceased proprietor's estate constitutes the cost basis. If the assets and good will are purchased "net," the amount paid to the deceased proprietor's estate, plus the amount paid in discharge of the debts assumed, constitutes the basis.[3] A moment's reflection shows that in either case the basis is substantially the same total figure. This total is then allocated among the various classes of business assets taken over and forms the basis for determining taxable gain or loss as each asset is disposed of later.

The amount the purchasing employee has paid for the proprietorship will be the purchase price in cases where the employee receives the insurance proceeds as beneficiary and turns the money over to the deceased's personal representative upon consummation of the transaction. The insurance proceeds, together with any remainder of the purchase price paid in installment notes, also constitutes the cost basis of the acquired property if the insurance proceeds are received by a trustee beneficiary and are paid over by it to the personal representative; in so receiving and paying out the insurance money the trustee is acting for the employee. Furthermore, the funds reach the proprietor's estate, not as insurance proceeds, but as purchase-price money in fact.

---

[2] *Dixon, Executor v. U.S.,* 96 Fed. Supp. 986, affirmed 192 Fed. 2d 82.

[3] *Athol Mfg. Co. v. Commissioner,* 54 Fed. 2d 230; *Johnson Motor Co. v. U.S.,* 6 Fed. Supp. 122.

If, however, the insurance proceeds are made payable directly to the proprietor's estate or to his personal beneficiaries, there is grave doubt that such proceeds may be included in the cost basis of the proprietorship assets acquired.[4]

THE FEDERAL ESTATE TAX

Method of applying the tax. Because the Federal estate tax law specifically states the circumstances under which life insurance proceeds are included or excluded from the taxable estate of the insured, the current approach to the application of the estate tax is to ascertain first the tax status of these proceeds. If it is found that the insurance occupies a nontaxable position, then the proprietorship business is generally taxed at the value set forth in the buy-sell agreement. This will be the case if the insurance is purchased, owned and paid for by the purchasing employee and if he or a trustee acting for him is the death beneficiary. If, on the other hand, it is found that the insurance is arranged in such a manner that it comes within the taxable provisions of the law, then the insurance proceeds are included in the taxable estate of the proprietor and the value of the proprietorship is excluded from tax to the extent that such value is represented by the taxable insurance. This will be the case, for example, if the insurance is made payable directly to the proprietor's estate. The net result in the cases where the insurance proceeds occupy a taxable status is that the total measure of taxability involved in the transaction is the total of the insurance proceeds or the total value of the proprietorship, whichever is the greater.

The insured purchase plan should establish value of business for Federal Estate Tax. Numerous decisions have established the rule that when a business is to be sold upon the owner's death pursuant to a binding buy-sell agreement, the value that has been stipulated as the purchase price will govern for estate tax purposes provided that the price, at the time agreed upon, fairly represented the value of the business being sold and the business must be offered at no greater price upon disposal during life.[5]

This rule should be of great benefit to the deceased proprietor's estate. In the absence of an agreement, the ascertainment of the value of a business is an extremely difficult task. The Federal estate tax return calls for statements of earnings and of assets and liabilities for the previous five years and states that "Good will must be accounted for." From this it is readily apparent that much bothersome detail and uncertainty as to the ultimate valuation of the business is encountered if no buy-sell agreement exists, all of which adds to the time and expense of settling of the proprietor's estate.

---

[4]*Legallet v. Commissioner,* 41 B.T.A. 294; cf. *Victor G. Mushro,* 50 T.C. 43 (non-acq.). See discussion of these cases at page 222 et seq.

[5]See cases at pages 382 et seq.

With a buy-sell agreement, entered into fairly, the proprietor gains the definite advantage, in addition to his having the proprietorship disposed of for its full value in cash, of being able to predict his estate taxes in advance. Having this knowledge at hand, he can complete his estate plans with a degree of precision unknown to the proprietor who, without an insured buy-sell agreement, must leave a heritage of liquidation losses, delays and confusion.

PARTNERSHIPS

Part I

FUNDAMENTAL FACTS ABOUT PARTNERSHIPS

Chapter 1

GENERAL INFORMATION
ABOUT PARTNERSHIPS

A knowledge of the fundamental nature of a partnership is prerequisite to an understanding of the problems involved in arriving at the most satisfactory plan for the continuation of the partnership business on the death of a partner. We should know what a partnership is, how it is formed, and the common types of partnerships that are entered into.

WHAT A PARTNERSHIP IS

Partnership defined. The Uniform Partnership Act, of which more will be said later, contains the following concise definition: "A partnership is an association of two or more persons to carry on as co-owners a business for profit." Bates, one of the outstanding authorities on partnership law, says, "A partnership is the contract relation subsisting between persons who have combined their property, labor or skill in an enterprise or business as principals for the purpose of joint profit." Mechem, another outstanding authority in this field, states that "A partnership may be tentatively defined as a legal relation, based upon the express or implied agreement of two or more competent persons whereby they unite their property, labor or skill in carrying on some lawful business as principals for their joint profit."

From these very similar definitions it can be seen that the main characteristics of a partnership are:

1. It is an unincorporated association (as distinguished from a corporation).

2. It is created by the voluntary contract of the parties (as distinguished from a corporation, which is created by law).

3. Its formation requires two or more competent parties.

4. Its capital is constituted by means of contributions from each member of property, labor or skill.

5. Its purpose is to carry on a business for the pecuniary gain of the members (as distinguished from charitable, educational, religious, social or other similar purposes).

6. Its business is transacted by the parties as principals, each of whom is a co-owner.

With these basic distinctions in mind no difficulty should be encountered in recognizing the ordinary partnership relation where it exists. Although difficult questions occasionally arise as to whether or not a partnership relation has been entered into, such situations will be left to those immediately concerned and to their lawyers. Our concern here is for the preservation of businesses conducted by persons who clearly recognize their own partnership relation, and who, therefore, have a continuing solicitude for the future welfare of their enterprises.

HOW PARTNERSHIPS ARE FORMED

A partnership is created only by means of a contract between the persons thereby associated as partners. This contract may be oral or written. When the agreement is in writing, which is always advisable, the instrument is usually known as the "Articles of Partnership." However, a startling number of firms are found to be operating with nothing more than loose oral understandings between their members as the basis of their joint business enterprise. Such oral agreements come within the Statute of Frauds, as a contract to be continued beyond one year, the effect of which is to convert the operating partnership to one at will wherein at any time a partner may bring an action in equity to call his copartner to account.[1] Furthermore, much is left to implication, and it is only because of the close personal relationship of trust and confidence that exists among the partners that misunderstandings about their arrangements are comparatively infrequent. Obviously, it is good legal "housekeeping" and good common sense for a partnership to operate under written articles, and partners should be urged to have their attorneys reduce such agreements to writing if this has not been done.

The Articles of Partnership set forth the agreement of the partners with respect to the formation, conduct and termination of the firm. This contract should cover at least the following essential points: names of the partners;

---

[1] *Sanger v. French*, 157 N.Y. 213, 51 N.E. 979; *Green v. Le Beau*, 281 App. Div. 836, 118 N.Y.S.2d 585 (1953).

partnership name; business to be conducted; place of business and capital; capital contribution of each partner; his share of the profits and losses; his special duties, if any, and any salary or drawing account arrangements; provision for keeping books, and for periodic inventories and accountings; any restrictions of the authority of the partners; provision for settling differences among the partners; the duration of the partnership; and any special provisions operative upon dissolution, unless contained in a collateral agreement.

THE TWO FUNDAMENTAL TYPES OF PARTNERSHIPS

The general partnership. The ordinary type of partnership, in which each partner devotes his entire time to the furtherance of the firm's business, is known as a general partnership. This is the most common form, and is typified by the fact that each partner has full authority to act for the firm within the regular scope of the business and by the fact that each partner is fully liable for the obligations of the partnership. The rights and liabilities of partners in a general partnership are more fully discussed in the two chapters immediately following.

The limited partnership. The second fundamental type of partnership is known as the limited partnership. This type, being unknown to the common law, can be organized only when permitted by special statute. Over three-fourths of the states, however, have enacted, with local variations, the Uniform Limited Partnership Act. This is a model Act prepared some years ago by the Commissioners on Uniform State Laws and recommended to the states for enactment.

This model statute defines a limited partnership as "a partnership formed by two or more persons under the provisions of Section 2, having as members one or more general partners and one or more limited partners. The limited partners as such shall not be bound by the obligations of the partnership." That is its first characteristic. The second characteristic of this form of partnership is that it requires two kinds of partners, general and limited. The general partners conduct the business of the firm, and in so doing they act for themselves as principals and for the other partners as general agents, assuming unlimited liability for the firm's obligations. Thus, their rights and liabilities correspond to those of ordinary partners in a general partnership.

The rights and liabilities of the limited partners, however, must be sharply distinguished from those of the general partners in the limited partnership. A limited partner (often referred to as a special partner), has the right to full information about the affairs of the partnership and to an accounting, but he takes no part in the management of the business. His surname may not appear in the partnership name unless it is also the surname of a general partner or unless it was a part of the partnership name before he became a limited partner. He contributes a specified amount of capital to the enterprise, and unless he exceeds his restricted sphere as a limited partner, his liability for the obligations of the partnership is limited to the amount he has contributed. His contribution cannot be withdrawn, however, until all of the demands against the firm, except those of the partners themselves, have been satisfied. He is entitled to his specified share of the profits, and it is important to note that upon a dissolution, his share of the profits and his contribution have priority over all funds going to the general partners.

The limited partner's interest is personal property and is assignable. If assigned, the assignee may become a substituted limited partner with the consent of the other partners. If the assignee does not become a substituted limited partner, he has neither the right to information about the affairs of the partnership nor access to the books and records. He is entitled merely to his share of the profits, and, upon dissolution, to the assignor's contribution. On the death of a limited partner, his executor or administrator has all the rights of a limited partner for the purpose of settling the estate, including, of course, the power to assign the limited partnership interest of the decedent. *Thus it is of great significance that the death of a limited partner (as contrasted to that of a general partner), does not dissolve the limited partnership.*

Curiously enough, the statute also provides that one person may be both a general partner and a limited partner in the same partnership at the same time. A person occupying this dual role has the status of a general partner, except that in respect of his contribution he has the rights of a limited partner against the other partners. Therefore, as a general partner, his death automatically dissolves the partnership; but as a limited partner, his estate is entitled to the repayment of his contribution ahead of all distributions to the general partners.

The third outstanding characteristic of a limited partnership is the statutory requirement that a sworn certificate be filed for record in a public office setting forth details as to the name and term of the partnership, the character and location of the business, the names and residences of each of the partners and his designation as general or limited partner, the amount of capital contributed by each limited partner, his share of the profits, and other appropriate data of a similar nature. The statute usually requires also that a copy of the certificate or a notice containing its substance be published in local newspapers for a period of weeks.

The subject of limited partnerships has been dealt with at some length here for the reason that it will not again be discussed in detail. Limited partnerships are numerically few as compared with ordinary or general partnerships, and the problems involved on the death of a general partner in a limited partnership are so similar in nature to those involved on the death of a partner in an ordinary partnership that separate treatment would be largely repetitious. Before leaving the subject, however, one point should be emphasized. On the death of a general partner in a limited partnership, the surviving general partners occupy a less favorable position than would be the case had they been partners in an ordinary partnership. In either case, the partnership is automatically dissolved, and unless alternative measures have been set up in advance or can be quickly improvised, the affairs of the enterprise must be wound up promptly and the deceased partner's share of the remaining assets must be paid over to his executor or administrator. When this winding-up process (which is discussed in detail later) has been completed in the ordinary partnership, the surviving partners and the estate of the deceased partner share the remaining assets without precedence. But in a limited partnership the assets remaining after the firm has been liquidated and the creditors of the business satisfied, are first used to pay the limited partners their profits and to return their contributions. Last in line come the general partners and the personal representative of the deceased general partner, who divide what remains. The general partners in a limited partnership, therefore, have an even greater need for a solution of the problems brought about by the death of a general partner than is the case when a death occurs in an ordinary partnership. This should be kept in mind as these problems and their solution with respect to the ordinary partnership are developed in subsequent chapters.

PARTNERSHIPS CLASSIFIED AS COMMERCIAL OR PROFESSIONAL

Historically, all ordinary or general partnerships have been classified legally as trading or non-trading, the latter being partnerships organized to render services rather than to buy or sell commodities. However, general partnerships are more popularly classified as commercial or professional. The legal distinction under either classification relates largely to the implied powers of the partners. Because the general rule is that each partner has the implied powers necessary and proper to conduct the partnership affairs, the scope of his powers varies with the nature of the particular partnership. Thus, a partner of a professional partnership ordinarily will not have the implied power to borrow money or execute negotiable instruments for partnership purposes. For business insurance purposes, however, professional partnerships possess certain distinctive characteristics that justify a separate discussion in a later chapter.

Chapter 2

PROPERTY RIGHTS AND LIABILITIES
IN A PARTNERSHIP

The private ownership of property, one of the fundamental institutions of our free society, forms the basis and constitutes the subject matter of almost all business transactions. The property ownership has assumed many different patterns to suit the varied and ever changing needs of commerce, each form of business organization requiring for its efficient functioning its own particular kinds of property rights. For example, the development of the corporation brought with it the ownership of assets by a distinct legal entity, the corporation itself, and created the special type of ownership evidenced by the stock certificate. Another example, and the one with which we are immediately concerned, is that of the partnership. The evolution of the partnership method of conducting business has been accompanied also by the development of its particular pattern of property rights, including such novel types of ownership as the partnership interest and the tenancy in partnership. A working knowledge of all of these partnership rights is necessary to a clear understanding of the true nature of a partnership.

The principles set forth in this chapter are based on the Uniform Partnership Act. This is a model statute drafted in 1914 by Professor William Draper Lewis under the auspices of the National Conference of Commissioners on Uniform State Laws. Its adoption, with various minor changes to suit local conditions, in more than three-fourths of the states, comprising over 80 percent of the population of the United States, has brought about a gratifying standardization of partnership law in these jurisdictions. In large

124

measure this statute is a codification of the common law, although new rules were made in certain particulars, notably in respect of the real property owned by a partnership.

ASSETS OF THE PARTNERSHIP

The corner grocer is the firm of King & Gay. Who is it that owns that can of beans on the shelf? Probably the wholesaler sold it to the partnership as such. Therefore, title is in the partnership itself, which fact of ownership is both legally possible and customary. Mr. King and Mr. Gay jointly own the beans as "tenants in partnership." As such a co-owner each has an equal right to possession, but only for partnership purposes. Neither can alone assign his individual share of ownership. Only a creditor of the firm can attach his individual ownership rights. If Mr. King dies first, his ownership in the beans and in all other specific property of the partnership automatically goes to Mr. Gay, who then owns all of the assets of the firm as a liquidating trustee. This includes any real property, the title to which was vested in the partnership and which, under the Uniform Partnership Act, is not subject to dower rights. (In those jurisdictions where partnerships are subject to the common law, the rule is that dower, *et cetera,* attaches to the deceased's share of the firm's realty on dissolution, after the firm's creditors are satisfied.)

THE PARTNERSHIP INTEREST OF EACH PARTNER

In addition to, and distinguished from, his property rights in specific partnership assets, each partner owns what is known as his "partnership interest." This consists of his share of the profits and surplus, and is intangible personal property. A short digression for a moment into the field of inheritance taxation will serve to illustrate the nature of this property right.

In the United States Supreme Court case of *Blodgett v. Silberman,*[1] Robert B. Hirsch was a general partner in the firm William Openhym & Sons, organized and doing business in New York under the New York Limited Partnership Act. Among the assets of the firm were land, buildings and other tangible property located in New York and in Connecticut. Hirsch died a resident of Stamford, Connecticut. His will was probated in New York, the Federal and New York estate taxes were paid, and then the will was probated in Connecticut. Blodgett, Connecticut Tax Commissioner, included in the Connecticut inheritance tax computation the value of Hirsch's partnership interest of approximately $1,700,000 on the principle that this interest was intangible personal property and hence, under well established rules of law, had as its situs for taxation the domicile of the owner. Silberman, Hirsch's executor, unsuccessfully challenged this tax in the Connecticut courts, then

---

[1] 277 U.S. 1 (1928).

appealed the case to the United States Supreme Court, which upheld
Connecticut's right to tax. Taxation of other types of property was also
involved in the case, but details have been omitted here as irrelevant to the
nature of a partnership interest. The Supreme Court held that:

> the interest of the decedent in the partnership of Wm. Openhym
> & Sons was simply a right to share in what would remain of the
> partnership assets after its liabilities were satisfied. It was merely
> an interest in the surplus, a chose in action. It is an intangible and
> carries with it a right to an accounting. . . . It thus clearly appears
> that both under the partnership agreement and under the laws of
> the State of New York the interest of the partner was the right to
> receive a sum of money equal to his share of the net value of the
> partnership after a settlement, and this right to his share is a debt
> owing to him, a chose in action, and an intangible. We concur
> with the Supreme Court of Errors that as such it was subject to
> the transfer tax of Connecticut.

Blodgett v. Silberman stands as warning, to those not trained in the law, of
the law's complexity: taxation under the Connecticut inheritance tax was the
basic issue; the New York Partnership Law (following the Uniform Partnership Act and the Uniform Limited Partnership Act) was applied to ascertain
the nature of the partnership interest; and the common law rule of *mobilia
sequuntur personam* (movables follow the person) was the basis for the
holding that the situs of the partnership interest was at the domicile of the
partner in Connecticut.

The foregoing case was followed by New York's highest court in *Re Estate
of Havemeyer.*[2] The court held that the New York estate tax applied to reach
indirectly (by its inclusion in valuing the decedent's partnership interest) the
value of Connecticut realty owned by a New York partnership upon the
death of a partner domiciled in New York, although Connecticut had already
subjected such realty to its inheritance tax.

Under the Uniform Partnership Act a partnership interest is assignable and
an assignment does not of itself dissolve the firm. The assignee does not thereby become a partner; he has neither the right to interfere in the management
of the business nor the right to information about its affairs. But the assignee
is entitled to receive the profits that the assignee would have received and, if
the assignment so provides, the assignor's share of the profits and surplus
upon dissolution, accounting, and winding up of the firm.

Unlike the partner's co-ownership in specific partnership property, his
partnership interest may be reached by an individual judgment creditor of a
partner.[3] On death, the partnership interest goes to an executor or adminis-

---

[2] 17 N.Y.2d 216 (1966).

[3] *Beckley v. Speaks,* 240 N.Y.S.2d 553 (1963).

trator, who is entitled to receive from the surviving partner, for distribution to the heirs, its value in cash as the decedent's share of any profits and surplus remaining after the winding up of the firm's affairs.

THE RIGHT TO PARTICIPATE IN
THE MANAGEMENT

The third property right of each partner is his equal right to participate in the management and conduct of the business. By agreement of the partners, however, restrictions and delegations of authority may be made.

EACH PARTNER A PRINCIPAL AND A
GENERAL AGENT

As a result of the foregoing property rights, each partner in the performance of his business duties acts with respect to himself as a principal having a joint interest in the partnership property, and as a general agent with respect to each other partner. As a general agent, he can bind the firm in any transaction that comes within the ordinary scope of the firm's business. He is restricted, however, from doing certain acts unless authorized by all his associates. For example, he has no authority alone to make an assignment of all of the assets, to sell the good will of the business, to confess a judgment, to submit a partnership claim or liability to an arbitrator or referee, or to do any other act which would make it impossible to carry on the ordinary business of the firm.

PROPERTY RIGHTS IN PARTNERSHIPS UNIQUE

The foregoing highlights dealing with property rights in a partnership show them to be unique. They differ from those encountered elsewhere in the business world. Perhaps the best way to emphasize their uniqueness and to obtain a clearer picture of them is by contrast. Most of us are reasonably familiar with corporations, hence a few comparisons may be fruitful.

CORPORATION AND PARTNERSHIP
PROPERTY COMPARED

If our corner grocer were incorporated, the corporation undoubtedly would have both full title to and ownership of the can of beans, because the corporate business unit is a separate legal entity. In the case of the partnership we had just enough "legal entity" to put title to property in the firm name, but not enough to put ownership there. Consequently our partners held the rights of ownership (but solely for partnership purposes) under the peculiar species of joint ownership known as "tenants in partnership."

To carry our comparison further, if one of the stockholders in the grocery corporation should die, his death would have no immediate effect on the ownership of the beans; they would still be an asset of the corporation itself. In the absence of any special arrangement, the ownership of the deceased's shares of stock passes through his estate to his legatees under his will, or, if no will exists, to his distributees as provided in the intestate laws. The new stockholders have voting powers at stockholders' meetings and the right to receive dividends declared on the stock by the board of directors, but they have no right to demand from the corporation that its assets be liquidated and that the value of their shares of stock be paid to them in cash.

How different the property devolution is when a co-partner dies! His co-ownership in the specific partnership property automatically ceases, the surviving partner or partners becoming vested with the ownership—as liquidating trustees in the absence of a continuation agreement. The deceased's partnership interest goes into his estate. *But the firm is automatically dissolved on the occurrence of the death, and in the absence of a continuation agreement this interest is restricted to the right to the cash value of the deceased partner's share of the assets of the firm upon liquidation, accompanied by the right to demand that the survivor wind up the partnership with all possible dispatch and render a proper account.*

LIABILITIES IN A PARTNERSHIP

A study of all of the legal ramifications of partnership liabilities belongs in the law school. Nevertheless, a knowledge of the broad underlying rules is required by the life underwriter if he is to grasp the full significance of the problems created by the death of a partner. Most readers are familiar with the basic general rule, which may be stated as follows:

> Each partner is fully liable for any contract, wrongful act, or omission, whether the liability is created by himself or by any other partner, while acting in the ordinary course of the firm's business or while acting with the authority of his copartners.

To illustrate, let us look once more at the corner grocer, the partnership of King & Gay. Inquiry brings out the fact that the can of beans was ordered from the wholesaler by Mr. Gay along with a large shipment of other canned goods, costing $800 and billed to King & Gay at 30 days net. Obviously, this was a transaction in the ordinary course of the firm's business; hence partner King is equally liable with partner Gay for the payment of the invoice. But suppose that King dies before payment is made. Gay now owns the stock-in-trade and of course, remains liable for the payment of all of the obligations of the business. What, if anything, happens to King's liability?

The law provides that the individual property of a deceased partner shall be liable for all of the obligations of the partnership incurred *while he was a member, but subject to the prior payment of his separate debts.* King's executor can legally enforce a demand that Mr. Gay, as the surviving partner, apply the partnership property to discharge its liabilities. If this property should prove insufficient, however, the executor will have to contribute out of King's separate estate his share of the deficit, provided there are sufficient funds in the estate to do this after the individual creditors have been satisfied.

If the firm's assets were insufficient and survivor Gay insolvent, then King's executor would be liable for all of the unpaid obligations of the partnership to the extent of King's estate after the payment of separate debts.

On the other hand, if King's estate did not have enough assets after payment of separate creditors to pay in its share of any deficit, Mr. Gay would have to pay all of the deficit out of his own personal savings.

Note that whereas the foregoing illustration covered contract liability, the general rule also covers liability for any wrongful act committed by a partner while acting within the ordinary scope of the firm's business. Under the Uniform Partnership Act, contract liability is joint and liability for wrongful acts is joint and several. This distinction has been abolished in several states. But where it exists the primary effect is that each joint obligor must be made a party defendant to a legal action on the debt; if the liability is joint and several, the obligors may be sued jointly, or separate actions may be brought against one or more of them, as desired.

A judgment generally does not bind partners not named or served. But once a binding judgment has been entered against a partner, whether on a joint or a joint and several partnership obligation, it may be satisfied out of partnership assets or out of the individual assets of the partner. In the latter instance, the partner would have a right of contribution from the other obligors.

Chapter 3

DISSOLUTION OF
A PARTNERSHIP

The outstanding need for a plan which will assure continuation of the partnership business lies in the facts and circumstances surrounding the dissolution, winding up, and termination of a firm. To know accurately these facts and circumstances is to know the urgency of the need for the solution that the life underwriter has to offer. There are thousands of partners throughout the country whose knowledge in this respect is rudimentary at best. Consequently, life underwriters who aspire to sell any substantial volume of partnership insurance must inform themselves thoroughly on the subject in order that they may appreciate properly the need and purpose for their product and thus become qualified to portray the facts to the partners. These facts, to the extent that they relate to our subject, will be set forth in this and the following chapter.

DISSOLUTION, WINDING UP, AND TERMINATION
DISTINGUISHED

Much confused thinking is caused by lack of precision in the use of terms, particularly in the use of the words "dissolution" and "termination." Dissolution is defined by the Uniform Partnership Act as "the change in the relation of the partners caused by any partner ceasing to be associated in the carrying on *as distinguished from the winding up* of the business." "Winding up" needs no special definition. It is the final process in the life history of a partnership, the performing of the acts necessary to the liquidation and closing up of its affairs. "Termination" denotes the end of the firm; it no longer exists. Thus, as stated in *Englestein v. Mackie:*[1]

> The terms "dissolution" and "termination," as employed in the Partnership Act are not synonyms and, as used, have different meanings. Dissolution does not terminate the partnership and does not end completely the authority of the partners. The order of events is: (1) dissolution; (2) winding up; and (3) termination. Termination extinguishes their authority. It is the ultimate result of the winding up and occurs at the conclusion of the wind up.

WHY A DISSOLUTION TAKES PLACE

As stated in 68 Corpus Juris Secundum, §347: "In general a change in the personnel of a partnership works its dissolution. Thus a partnership will be dissolved by the withdrawal of a member from the firm unless the partnership articles provide otherwise . . ." Why is this true? The explanation goes to the core of the partnership relation itself. This is an intimate, confidential, *voluntary*, contractual business relationship in which each partner can act for the others and can subject them to unlimited liability. From the very nature of this important but potentially hazardous business association, it is not surprising to find that a right to choose one's own partner, the *delectus personarum* (choice of the person), has always been a basic tenet. No one can choose a partner for another, nor choose to be the partner of another. It is therefore logical to find a correlative general rule that the disassociation of any partner gives each surviving member a new "choice of the person."

It does not matter why the partner ceases to be associated in the business of the partnership. For example, the cause may be the expiration of the term of the partnership, the agreement of all of the partners to dissolve, or the resignation of a partner at any time, whether it is permitted under their agreement or in contravention of it. As stated by Judge Andrews in *Cahill v. Haff,*[2] regarding a clause in a partnership agreement permitting termination upon sixty days' written notice:

> Notwithstanding this clause, however, either might repudiate it at any time. Then it ended. No agreement can prevent this result. No one can be forced to continue as partner against his will. He may be liable for breach of contract. Nothing more.

Other causes of dissolution stem from such events as the death or bankruptcy of a partner, from any event that would make the business illegal, or from a court decree of dissolution based upon any one of a variety of causes, such as the incapacity or business misconduct of a partner, or the inability of the firm to earn profits, *et cetera.*

---

[1] 182 N.E.2d 351, (Ill. App., 1962).
[2] 248 N.Y. 377, 382.

GENERAL EFFECT OF DISSOLUTION

In the absence of a contrary agreement, dissolution terminates the authority of the remaining partners to act for the partnership except to the limited extent necessary to wind up the firm, including the completion of transactions already begun but not finished. Outstanding contracts are performed, bills receivable are collected, assets are converted into cash for what they will bring, liabilities are paid, and the residue is distributed to the erstwhile partners or their representatives. This winding-up procedure is summed up well as follows in the leading partnership case of *McClennen v. Commissioner,*[3] dealing with Massachusetts law:

> The survivors have the right and duty, with reasonable dispatch, to wind up the partnership affairs, to complete transactions begun but not then finished, to collect the accounts receivable, to pay the firm debts, to convert the remaining firm assets into cash, and to pay in cash to the partners and the legal representative of the deceased partner the net amounts shown by the accounts to be owing to each of them in respect of the capital contributions and in respect of their shares of profits and surplus.

If there is a deficit, each must contribute his share as a minimum, or up to the total amount of the deficit as a maximum, if the others are unable to pay.

---

[3]131 Fed. 2d 165.

Chapter 4

WINDING UP AND TERMINATION
OF PARTNERSHIP ON
DEATH OF A PARTNER

As we have seen, the dissolution of a partnership may be brought about by any cause that results in the severing of a member's association with the firm. The principal cause in which the life underwriter is interested, however, is the death of a partner, for it is following such event that the plan he has to offer can perform seeming miracles in extending the life span of an established business. We have discussed in a broad way what happens to the firm's business on dissolution if the law is allowed to take its course; but there remain several important phases of winding up which need further analysis. Outstanding among these is the status of the surviving, liquidating partner.

SURVIVING PARTNER AS LIQUIDATING TRUSTEE

We have noted that on the death of a partner, the surviving partner (or partners) succeeds to the ownership of the firm's assets as a liquidating trustee. The full significance of his fiduciary status is of great importance to all partners, and, consequently, to all life underwriters soliciting business insurance. A realization of its implications will make it a major motivating factor in the purchase of partnership insurance. It is a formal trust relationship only in a few states where special statutes have so designated it. In practically every jurisdiction, however, the relationship between the surviving partner and the estate is recognized as fiduciary in nature, particularly with respect to remedies available if there has been a breach of this trust. A brief excursion into a few of the leading law cases on the subject bears this out.

Anderson v. Droge.[1] At his death decedent owned a one-third interest in a partnership. Plaintiff, his sole heir, was told by the surviving partners that, although the business had been prosperous in the past, it had suffered a slump in recent years and they doubted if the decedent's estate would realize anything from it. Plaintiff was later referred to the administrator. The administrator had a board of appraisers appointed and they appraised the value of the decedent's interest at $900, in spite of the fact that a financial statement showed capital and surplus of about $37,000 and a bank balance of approximately $26,000. Then the plaintiff received a letter from the administrator stating that the partnership had been sold under court order and bought in by the surviving partners for $950, and enclosing check for $306 net for the one-third interest. Three years later plaintiff filed this suit against the surviving partners for an accounting. The court gave the plaintiff judgment for approximately $8,000, the opinion stating in part:

> Our reason for reaching this conclusion is in accord with that of the District Court, that the surviving partners had a right to continue this business for the purpose of winding it up, and on the death of Thayer they became the trustees of the property and business of the co-partnership for his legal heirs and representatives. The law required of them the utmost good faith in their dealings with those entitled to share in his interest and property left in trust with them. It was their duty as trustees to make a full and fair disclosure of the exact nature and extent of his interest in the partnership and to conceal nothing. They have failed in this duty; they have concealed from the plaintiff the nature and extent of the interest of the deceased in that concern and the value thereof. They have sought by concealment to use the court to defraud the plaintiff out of a valuable right in the concern. In the sale by the administrator only the tangible property was in fact valued, and the interest of the deceased in the other partnership property and as a going concern was not included or sold. They also failed to take into consideration the fact that the business was a going concern and had a good will.

In Re Ducker's Estate.[2] The utmost of good faith and fair dealing will not save a surviving partner who chooses not to obey the mandate of the law to liquidate the firm on the death of a member.

Sol Ducker and one of his sons had conducted a partnership, and on the father's death the son and a friend of the father, as co-executors, decided to carry on the business rather than liquidate it. After operating it about a year

---

[1] 216 Iowa 159, 248 N.W. 344, (1933).

[2] 146 Misc. 899, 263 N.Y.S. 217 (1933).

under the firm name, they formed a corporation, and continued the business for about seven years more. During most of this time profits were plentiful and the business paid to the heirs, a brother and three sisters of the son, in all about $65,000. In addition, the son drew $75 a week as his share. Then came the depression; the corporation could not weather it, and became insolvent. When the account of the executors was rendered, the brother and the three sisters of the surviving partner filed objections to it on the ground that the partnership should have been liquidated on the death of their father and the proceeds invested in legal securities under the provisions of his testamentary trust. The referee appointed by the court held unqualifiedly that the executors had acted throughout in good faith. He also found that the share of the objectants on liquidation of the partnership at death would have been $33,000.

The court held that the executors must reconstitute this entire sum, even though the plaintiffs had already received, in the years since their father's death, earnings from the business five times the amount they would have been paid in interest at 5 percent had the trust fund been originally set up. They had already received about $65,000 and the decree set up $33,000 more for them, a total of $98,000. Had the surviving partner liquidated the partnership on the father's death, as the law prescribed, the objectants would have received principal in trust of $33,000. Interest at 5 percent on this sum for the eight years would approximate $13,000, making a total of $46,000. Furthermore, the court pointed out that if the principal had been set up in trust promptly on the death of the father, it would undoubtedly have been diminished by the universal shrinkage of security values that occurred during the subsequent period. The opinion of the court stated in part as follows:

> Since *Williams v. Whedon,* 109 N.Y. 333, 16 N.E. 365, 4 Am. St. Rep. 460, it has been familiar law that partnership assets as such are not owned by the estate of the deceased partner, and that legal title thereto is completely vested in the surviving partner. The estate had the right only to receive, after liquidation of the firm business, the net value of the share of the deceased partner. . . . The survivor is entitled to the possession and control of the assets and has the right "within the limits of good faith" to dispose of the assets and close the partnership affairs. . . . It is apparent from the record that the accounting son of the deceased with his co-executor, a personal friend of the deceased, unwisely determined to carry on the business of the former co-partnership so as to provide a livelihood for the family of the deceased, four of whom are now attacking the determination. That this decision so to carry on the business exposed the accounting parties to a surcharge has been found by the referee and confirmed by Mr. Surrogate O'Brien. . . . The referee has found . . . that the brother

and sisters of this accounting son ... are in truth invoking the utmost rigor of the law against their brother.

Burden of proof on surviving partner. No one familiar with these and similar cases can doubt the fact that the surviving partner is a liquidating trustee and is "on the spot" whether or not he has acted in good faith. Because of his fiduciary status, he is held responsible to the estate as a trustee of the partnership assets; but this is only part of the story. Because of his superior knowledge of the partnership affairs, he is usually held to the burden of proving that he has not acted in violation of that trust when his conduct is challenged by the personal representative. The rule that the surviving partner has the burden of proof was applied by the Appellate Division of the New York Supreme Court in the case of *Bauchle v. Smylie*.[3] In that case, one of three equal partners had died and his widow was named executrix and residuary legatee in his will. Four months later she sold the decedent's interest to the survivors for $42,500. Not long thereafter, the widow brought an action to have the sale set aside on the ground of fraud. The lower court rendered a decision in favor of the surviving partners, upholding their purchase of the deceased partner's interest on the ground that the widow had not proved that the transaction was unfair to the estate. On appeal, the Appellate Division reversed the decision and sent the case back for a new trial, stating regarding the first trial:

> The action was tried upon an erroneous theory, viz., that the burden was upon the plaintiff to establish the transaction as unfair, whereas the burden was in fact upon the surviving partners to show that it was in all respects fair, and such as a court of equity would sanction and approve.

In short, on the death of a partner we find the surviving partner in the position of trustee of the firm's assets as to the estate of the deceased. In this fiduciary role he must make a fair and complete disclosure of all facts, present or prospective, affecting those assets. He must account for all property values, tangible or intangible. Moreover, if anything goes wrong between him and heirs unfamiliar with the partnership affairs, he will have the burden of proving that his trusteeship was carried out in exact compliance with the high standards of responsibility required of trustees. Lack of good faith and fair dealing will result in disaster; yet good faith and fair dealing will not save him if he departs, as in the *Ducker* case, from the strict mandates of the law governing the winding up of partnerships. Obviously, therefore, the surviving partner stands in great need of a different plan of procedure; he needs a plan that will relieve him of this oppressive fiduciary status.

---

[3]104 App. Div. 513, 93 N.Y.S. 709.

ECONOMIC EFFECTS OF WINDING UP THE PARTNERSHIP

In a typical partnership we see two capable business men combining their diverse talents from day to day in carrying on a modest but successful enterprise. One has the knack of merchandising; the other has the knack of efficient over-all management and supervision. Together, they constitute an effective team, making enough profits to rear their families and enjoy the ordinary comforts and pleasures of life. With the business running smoothly due to their joint efforts, and with orderly plans already developed for the future, they consider themselves "all set." Then without warning, one of them suddenly dies. Gone now is the comparative tranquility of the business day. Gone are the orderly plans for the future of the enterprise. In their stead are the strange and onerous duties of winding up a heretofore thriving business. We are now tolerably familiar with those duties; next let us examine the economic havoc that often follows:

Shrinkage of partnership assets on liquidation. Among the first duties of the surviving partner as liquidator is the collection of accounts receivable. In performing this task he will undoubtedly learn that a substantial part of the total amount cannot be collected. If the firm owned any real estate the surviving partner will be at the mercy of the prevailing market, if any market currently exists. There will be an inventory to dispose of for cash. Bates on Partnerships, S 743, says in part: "the forced conversion of a large stock into money is almost sure to be attended with the most ruinous consequences, not only to the surviving partners, but to the estate of the deceased." Then there will be equipment of various kinds that will have to be converted into cash with reasonable promptness. In this undertaking he may find that these items, which usually must be disposed of through second-hand dealers, are sold only for a fraction of their original value. It is therefore evident that when the surviving partner has completed the liquidation of the tangible property of the firm he will be lucky to have realized fifty cents on the dollar in cash.

But what about the intangible assets, the going-concern value and the good will? In those few fortuitous instances where the business may be sold in bulk, some portion of these values may be salvaged, but in most cases these assets evaporate with the liquidation of the tangible assets. Their loss is total.

Income to the family from the business stops. Up to the day of his death the deceased partner drew out of the partnership a reasonably steady income. The needs and comforts of his family are geared to this income; their standard of living has been erected upon it. Can the family compel the surviving partner to continue these payments or any part of them? No, the survivor is devoid of any authority to make advances to the estate until he has closed out the business. Furthermore, he is accountable only to the executor or administrator of the deceased partner's estate, not to his heirs. This was brought out clearly in *Taylor v. Lint.*[4] There the lower court had directed the surviving partner to pay \$1,200 to each of the guardians of the deceased partner's two minor children, and to pay the fees of such guardians and the attorney who represented them, as a distribution of the partnership assets. Michigan's top court reversed this direction, holding that the surviving partner was accountable solely to the legal representative of the deceased partner's estate.

During the winding-up period the family must rely on the proceeds of the deceased's personal life insurance or on advances that his executor may be able to make from his personal estate. Consequently, immediate hardship will result if the personal sources of income are inadequate. Needless to say, this sudden interruption of the normal family income, followed by a drying up of the source because of drastic liquidation shrinkages brought about by the forced sale of assets, breeds dissatisfaction and suspicion in the minds of the heirs of the deceased partner. Once again we are confronted with the need for a better solution of the partnership problems that arise upon the death of a partner.

Administration of personal estate may be delayed. The executor or administrator of the deceased partner, as the legal representative of his personal estate, has the duty either under the will or under the intestate laws, as the case may be, to wind up the deceased's personal affairs, pay his personal debts, and distribute the remainder to those entitled to it. Under the Uniform Partnership Act he cannot interfere with the liquidation of the partnership unless, or until, there has been misconduct on the part of the surviving partner or there has been an unreasonable delay. If either has occurred, the legal representative can petition the court to have a receiver appointed to take over the winding up.[5] Otherwise, he must wait until liquidation has been completed by the surviving partner. In the meantime, the executor cannot complete his own duties. He cannot fully appraise the estate or complete his estate tax schedules until the partnership has been liquidated and the value of the deceased's share ascertained. Any advances of partnership funds to the widow may be made at his own peril, for there may be an ultimate shortage of assets; and it is in those estates where the assets are meager that executors are hardest pressed to make advances. If it finally develops that there is a cash sum coming to the estate on the termination of the partnership, he is responsible for its delivery to the proper heirs. If there is a deficit, he must contribute the deceased's share out of the assets of the personal estate. If he turns all the personal assets over to the heirs prematurely, he will be surcharged. Thus, if the law of partnership liquidation is allowed to take its course, we find the orderly administration of the

---

[4]338 Mich. 673, 62 N.W.2d 453 (1954).

[5]*State v. The Vanderburgh Probate Court,* 233 Ind. 488, 121 N.E. 2d 723 (1954).

deceased's personal estate delayed, with a frsutrated legal representative and disgruntled heirs as inevitable consequences.

Surviving partner's business career jeopardized. If the surviving partner has carried out his legal mandate, he has brought the business of the partnership to a standstill, liquidated its property for whatever sum it would bring at forced sale, paid its debts, and divided the shrunken residue between the estate of the deceased partner and himself. In the process he has lost a substantial portion of his investment in the business. Nevertheless, the importance of this sacrifice is overshadowed by what may indeed result in disaster. In liquidating the business he has liquidated his job, and with it all his plans for the future. Small wonder it is, then, that so many surviving partners choose to make any deal that opportunity offers at this late date to acquire the deceased partner's interest, even at great risk of subsequent lawsuits and adverse judgements. In the extremity of the situation he will welcome almost any plan that promises to save his business life. Starting his business career all over again is often out of the question. But reliance on the hope of making a satisfactory and conclusive deal with the heirs in the face both of their naturally suspicious attitude and of the strict rules of the law of trusteeship is foolhardy. The surviving partner can least afford, of all the parties concerned, to let the law of partnership liquidation take its course.

Part II

PLANS ATTEMPTED, TO AVOID LIQUIDATION ON DEATH OF A PARTNER

Chapter 5

ALTERNATIVES TO LIQUIDATION
IMPROVISED AFTER A
PARTNER'S DEATH

We have set out in some detail the sacrifices and losses suffered by everyone concerned in the liquidation of a partnership on the death of a partner. The extent of these sacrifices has plainly shown the vital need for a more practical solution than that of allowing the law to take its course, and has caused the parties to improvise various alternative schemes in an attempt to keep the business running and thus by-pass these losses.

MERE CONTINUANCE OF THE BUSINESS

Often a surviving partner will keep on operating, in the hope that he will later be able to come to an agreement with the deceased's heirs, or that they will acquiesce in his conduct. An example of the costliness and futility of this alternative is vividly portrayed in the *Ducker* case, in which the son operated the business with outstanding success for several years after his father's death to the great profit of the deceased partner's family, the son's own brother and three sisters, only to have "the utmost rigor of the law" enforced against him. The results in that case seem harsh, but the court was merely applying the regular rule, that if a dissolution occurs and the business is continued without any settlement of accounts or any contrary agreement being entered into, the legal representative of the deceased is entitled to receive for the heirs the amount of the deceased's interest at date of death, plus his choice either of the interest on it or of the profits attributable to the use of the property after that date.

In *Froess v. Froess*,[1] a case which construed Section 42 of the Uniform Partnership Act where there was no agreement between the surviving partner and the deceased partner's representative to continue the business, the rule was stated as follows:

> The legal rule is fixed on this subject. If the survivors of a partnership carry on the concern, and enter into new transactions with the partnership funds, they do so at their peril, and the representative of the deceased may elect to call on them for the capital, with a share of the profits, or with interest. If no profits are made, or even if a loss is incurred, they must be charged with interest on the funds they use, and the whole loss will be theirs.

Only one high-court case has interpreted the Uniform Partnership Act to call for a different rule. In *Blut v. Katz*,[2] the Supreme Court of New Jersey held that there was a choice between interest and a share of profits only when the partnership business was continued with the consent of the estate, and that where there was a continuance without the consent of the deceased partner's executrix, she had no option to take a share of the profits but was entitled only to the value of the deceased partner's interest at time of his death plus interest thereon to the date of judgment. Two judges, including Chief Justice Vanderbilt, vigorously dissented from this interpretation of the statute, stating that "on the plainest principles of equity and justice the surviving partners should account for the profits ensuing from their unauthorized use of the deceased partner's capital. The principle of unjust enrichment has peculiar application in such circumstances." The result is that except in New Jersey, the general rule appears to be as stated in 68 Corpus Juris Secundum 805:

> The estate of a deceased partner is entitled to a proportionate share of any advantage gained by the surviving partner while continuing the business. If the continuance was unauthorized the representatives may elect between interest on decedent's capital or a proportionate share of the profits.

Lest the impression be left that what the surviving partner loses as a penalty for continuing the business constitutes a gain to the heirs, the case of *Alsworth v. Packard*[3] will be discussed. For a long period of years A.D. Packard and his son carried on a co-partnership. After the father's death, the son continued to operate the business for about six years, when his sister, as

---

[1] 284 Pa. 369, 131 A. 276, 278 (1925).

[2] 13 N.J. 374, 99 Atl. 2d 78 (1953).

[3] 181 Minn. 156, 231 N.W. 916 (1930).

administratrix, brought suit for an accounting on the ground that he should have wound up the partnership affairs promptly. In the lower court a judgment for $66,000 plus a substantial amount of interest was rendered against the son. On appeal, Minnesota's highest court held that although the son was liable, a new trial was necessary to correct certain errors. The following illuminating comment is found in the opinion:

> There must be a new trial. We might say so and stop. We are tempted to go a bit further. A history of the affairs involved, extending over a period of forty years, is possible. The law has the machinery and there is enough time to hunt up early transactions and investigate facts and come to as correct a conclusion as human means can reach on disputed testimony after so long a time. The effort used and the time consumed largely will be wasted effort and time. It is not the fault of the law. It comes because of the shortcomings and delays and faults of the people concerned. The necessary money doubtless can be found to carry on the quarrel. The beneficiaries are well along in years. If the money and property could be had now they would have some enjoyment of it for quite a while. If active in litigation they will probably be able to get their controversy at an end so that one has all, or each has a part, or none of them has anything at all before the end comes.

The general rule that the deceased partner's estate is entitled to receive the value of his interest plus either interest thereon or the profits attributable thereto, if the survivor continues the business, does not obviate the rule that it is the survivor's duty to wind up the partnership where he has no authority to continue. Thus, if the survivor does not proceed promptly with the winding-up process, the legal representative may have the process carried out by a receiver appointed by the court.

The conclusion is inescapable that surviving partners and heirs alike usually suffer heavy losses if the business is improperly continued, and that this irregular procedure offers no alternative solution to the problems of liquidation.

A mere handful of states have enacted special statutes which permit, under certain conditions, the partnership business to be continued with the deceased partner's legal representative as a partner. Thus, in Hawaii, the estate representative may become a limited partner pursuant to a court order and compliance with the Limited Partnership Act, if it appears for the best interests of the estate and the remaining partners approve. In Indiana and Missouri, the legal representative may become a partner pursuant to a court order that defines the extent of the estate's liability, the property subject to the liability, the duration of such partnership, and other appropriate conditions. A few other states have somewhat similar statutes. The plan of continuance with the legal representative as a partner, however, has the fundamental weakness that it will not function unless the surviving partners agree to it. They may refuse because the legal representative is not familiar with the business, because the court has limited his liability, because the plan can at best be only a temporary one—or because they do not like the legal representative's choice of ties. Furthermore, the plan is dependent upon the legal representative's willingness to become a partner. Such a statute may help out where an emergency situation occurs, but is no substitute for a suitable continuation plan made by the partners themselves.

NEW PARTNERSHIP WITH HEIRS

Sometimes, rather than face disastrous liquidation, the surviving partner forms a new partnership with the heirs. This alternative, however, is seldom resorted to because of the well-nigh insurmountable obstacles, both legal and economic, that block its path.

Legal obstacles. The first obstacle is the executor or administrator. Legally, the heirs cannot enter a new partnership with the surviving partner with respect to the partnership property until the administration proceedings have been closed, for the heirs have no right to possession or control of such property until it comes to them by the accounting of the administrator, who is charged with the duty of receiving and accounting for the value of the deceased's interest in the partnership in cash.[4] Therefore, this expedient is eliminated at the outset except in those isolated situations in which the executor or administrator and the sole heir are one and the same person. Even then, the deceased's creditors and the tax authorities must first be satisfied.

A further legal obstacle is the fundamental rule that no one can choose to be the partner of another. If, in spite of all the impediments, the surviving partner wishes to continue the business with the heir, he cannot do so unless the heir also wishes to do likewise rather than to receive the value of the deceased's interest in cash. On the other hand, the desires of the heir to form such a partnership are of no avail if the survivor prefers to liquidate.

Despite the legal obstacles involved, a surviving partner sometimes will continue the business by forming a new partnership with the widow of his deceased partner even though she is not the sole heir. That this can be a costly mistake is well illustrated by a 1951 case.

Spivak v. Bronstein.[5] Jules Bronstein and Jacob Spivak were equal partners conducting a taproom and restaurant business. Spivak died in 1943, survived by his wife and infant son. Spivak left no will and his widow was appointed administratrix. Under the intestate laws of Pennsylvania, the child was entitled to one-half of his father's estate. Without the consent or approval

---

[4]*Taylor v. Lint,* 338 Mich. 673, 62 N.W. 2d 453 (1954).

[5]367 Pa. 70, 79 Atl. 2d 205.

of the probate court, the widow and the surviving partner entered into a new partnership agreement within a month. This agreement recited that the widow executed it on her own behalf and as administratrix, and also as guardian of her minor son (although she could not be the child's guardian under Pennsylvania law). The deceased partner's interest was valued in the agreement at $4,000. Bronstein was required to conduct the business and to pay the widow $40 a week, but he was given an option to purchase the business.

The new partnership continued for three years; then the widow individually and as administratrix sold her interest (recited to be one-half) to Bronstein for $8,500. However, she reserved any right that she might have to an accounting for the profits from the date of death of her husband. A month later she sued for an accounting, alleging that her share of the profits amounted to far more than $40 a week paid her and that she had been fraudulently induced to sell.

The lower court, finding no fraud or mismanagement, decided that the widow as an *individual* was not entitled to an accounting, because of her agreement with the surviving partner. But the survivor must account for the one-half share in the deceased partner's interest which the minor son owned, and must pay the value of that share as of the date of death, together with the profits attributable to the rentention of that share in the business, or 6 percent interest in lieu of profits. As a credit, the survivor was allowed one-half the amounts he had paid to the widow, and on the accounting a judgment for $10,045.81, including interest from date of termination of the partnership with the widow, was entered against the surviving partner. On appeal, the Supreme Court of Pennsylvania affirmed, ordering that the $10,045.81 be paid to the widow as administratrix and that she assign it to the legal guardian of her son.

Thus the surviving partner paid the widow a total salary of about $6,000 during the three years of the partnership; then paid her $8,500 for her interest—and he finally wound up after five ensuing years in the role of a defendant with a judgment against him for an additional $10,000. All this for a partnership interest agreed to be worth $4,000! The courts exact strict justice when legal obstacles are disregarded.

Economic obstacles. From an economic standpoint, a new partnership with the heir is usually sheer folly. Unless the new partner has been active in the management of the business in the past (this is seldom the case, for the heir is usually the deceased partner's widow), the survivor carries almost all of the load for an incommensurate share of the profits. He finds himself in the position of trying to support both his own family and that of the deceased partner. More hopeless still, however, is the clash of basic objectives of the parties. The surviving partner's solicitude is for the future of the business. He wants to plow back for development and expansion any profits beyond a modest current income. The widow as a partner is interested in current income to replace that lost on the death of her husband. She will expect to derive at least as much as he formerly took out of the business, notwithstanding the fact that most of his profits were the result of the personal labor, skill, and experience that he contributed to the firm but that she is not able to contribute. The history of attempts to carry on such partnerships (typified by the *Bronstein* case) shows that the immediate consequences of this divergence of interests are wrangling and dissension, and that the ultimate result is dissolution and the winding up of the new firm. The exceptional case is the one in which the deceased is survived by a son who has been active and competent in the affairs of the business and is sole heir and administrator. In such a case, a new partnership composed of the surviving partner and the son can be arranged if the parties so desire, and should prove successful. Nevertheless, if such favorable circumstances do exist, formation of the new firm is not safely left to improvisation after the death of the father. Adequate provisions for the future partnership should be set up in advance.

From the above it is readily apparent that a partnership with the heirs is almost impossible to arrange after death occurs, is devoid of opportunity for successful operation in the overwhelming majority of cases because of the unequal sharing of the burdens and the conflict of objectives and is, therefore, rarely attempted.

PURCHASE OF SURVIVING PARTNER'S INTEREST BY HEIRS

Once in a while the heirs desire to purchase the interest of the surviving partner. Such a plan is seldom consummated because of its many drawbacks. In the first place, the surviving partner is under a legal duty to liquidate the firm, and can be relieved of that duty only by the consents of the executor and administrator and of all the heirs. Heirs who are minors are unable to give consent; some other heir may be unwilling to. And unless all creditors can be satisfied, the legal representative will not concur. Then too, in carrying through with the plan, the survivor is selling himself out of a job and has to start out in business all over again. The heirs are buying a business strange to them and are required to manage it successfully without the guiding hand of either the deceased partner or the surviving partner.

The unsolvable dilemma. Furthermore, the heirs must withstand the withering competition of the survivor, a man who knows all the details of the business, unless they can obtain a special agreement from him not to establish himself again in the trade or industry in that locality. Unfortunately for the heirs, however, a covenant not to compete is not enforceable unless it contains reasonable restrictions as to time and place such as, for example, a period of five years in the immediate neighborhood. Without such a restrictive agreement, the heirs have no real chance of success.[6] With it, their chances are not much improved. Restricted by such a negative agreement, the survivor is out of a job, and must retire, change his occupation, or start over in a new and strange location. Usually, only a surviving partner who is ready and wants to retire can afford to sign a contract of this nature. Thus, with a negative covenant essential to the heirs but unacceptable to the surviving partner, the use of this plan runs into an unsolvable dilemma. It must be discarded as a solution to the problems of liquidation.

PURCHASE OF DECEDENT'S INTEREST BY SURVIVING PARTNER

The remaining alternative that may be improvised by the parties after the death of a partner to avoid the sacrifices and losses implicit in liquidation of the partnership affairs is the purchase of the deceased partner's interest by the surviving partner. Here again both economic and legal obstacles stand in the way of a satisfactory solution.

The financial barrier. The chief financial barrier is the inability of the survivor to obtain the necessary cash with which to pay for the deceased's interest. If he does not have ample personal wealth, the surviving partner must borrow the purchase price or contract to pay the debt over a period of years. The installment purchase plan will hang a millstone around the neck of the enterprise for years to come. In trying to borrow the cash, the survivor will find that the banks are far more likely to demand a reduction in the line of credit than to grant a new loan. In fact, being cognizant of the fiduciary position occupied by the surviving partner, most financial institutions will avoid becoming involved in any way with the situation. Resort must therefore be made to individual funds. These are not usually available unless the prospects for the future of the business are exceptionally favorable, and then only if the surviving partner takes the money lender into partnership with him or forms a corporation to effect the purchase, giving the lender shares of stock to cover the amount of the loan. Normally then, the raising of the necessary purchase price requires that the survivor go into business and divide the management and profits with an untried, inexperienced, and often incompatible associate.

The legal barriers. The towering obstacles to this plan, however, are legal in nature. First, the deceased's executor or administrator can preemptorily demand that the business be liquidated. Even if willing to sell, he will be unable to do so unless the heirs consent. And, unless it is a cash sale, the creditors may block the transaction if they are not paid off.

Second, an almost insuperable barrier is the surviving partner's task of making a contract that will be able to stand up under any subsequent legal

---

[6]See, for example, *Denawitz v. Milch*, infra at page 161.

attack by dissatisfied heirs. We saw such an attack made in *Bauchle v. Smylie*,[7] and the resultant burden thrust upon the surviving partners to show that the contract was above reproach. His status as a fiduciary lies at the root of this great difficulty. He is a trustee trying to purchase the subject matter of his trust from the beneficiaries. If, perchance, the surviving partner is also the executor of the decedent's estate, he is precluded from making a binding sale to himself in most states unless authorized by special statute, such as the one enacted by the State of Washington. As stated in *Donnelly v. Ritzendollar*,[8] "It is beyond dispute that a fiduciary cannot purchase from himself. [Authorities cited.] Even in the absence of fraud such a sale would be set aside." In many states he cannot make such a contract with another as the legal representative without consent of the beneficiaries of the deceased's estate, no matter how much he offers for the deceased's interest. Michigan's highest court, in *Grigg v. Hanna*,[9] had this to say:

> The surviving partner, as a fiduciary, is in effect the trustee of the assets of the deceased partner ... [citing case]. As such trustee, he may not be interested directly or indirectly as a purchaser in his own behalf of the trust property without consent of the *cestui que trust. 1 Perry on Trusts and Trustees*, 6th Ed. s. 195.

The opinion also quoted the following paragraph from *Kelsey v. Detroit Trust Company*:[10]

> A trustee has no right to act when duty is opposed to interest, fidelity to cupidity, honesty to the desire for personal gain. To act as trustee for a dead man, carries with it the duty to exercise honesty, good faith, and active diligence; the duty to disclose to the beneficiaries and account for the estate, and, stringent as the law is in prohibiting trustees acting in violation of their trust, the rules of law should be more stringent rather than be relaxed.

In a majority of states, however, the surviving partner is allowed to purchase the deceased's interest, provided the terms square with his fiduciary obligations. An excellent summary of the law, in the absence of a special statute, is given in the *Steinmetz* case.[11]

> A surviving partner holds the assets as a quasi trustee for the estate of the deceased partner. . . . Therefore he cannot speculate upon the partnership property for his own advantage and in

---

[7] See page 136.

[8] 14 N.J. 96, 101 A. 2d 1 (1953).

[9] 283 Mich. 443, 278 N.W. 125 (1938).

[10] 265 Mich. 358, 251 N.W. 555, 556.

[11] *Steinmetz v. Steinmetz*, 125 Conn. 663, 7 A. 2d 915, (1935).

disregard of the interests of or under the deceased partner. It is generally held that if he acts with the high degree of good faith which is required by the former partnership relation and his fiduciary relationship to the estate of the deceased partner, he may validly purchase the interest of the latter. . . . A few pertinent cases evince a less favorable attitude toward purchase of the partnership property by the surviving partner at a sale by him or in his behalf. Some hold definitely that a surviving partner cannot validily buy the property of the firm at his own sale, either directly or indirectly, whether the attempt be made by means of public auction or private sale, and regardless of adequacy of the purchase price, his duty as seller and his interest as purchaser being held to be in irreconcilable conflict. . . . The most liberal view entertained is that if the surviving partner attempts to take over the partnership business by selling the partnership property to himself or to someone acting for him the transaction is voidable by or at the instance of the representative of the deceased partner. . . . Therefore the inclusion in the judgment of the provision which impliedly authorizes the defendant to purchase absolutely, although at not less than the fair market value of the property, is unwarranted in law.

Keeping in mind that these cases deal with situations wherein no agreement to purchase had been entered into by the partners prior to death, the opinions show that even in those jurisdictions where the most liberal common-law rule prevails with respect to the purchase of the deceased partner's interest by the surviving partner, his duty of full and fair disclosure of all facts relating to the business is so great and the burden of vindicating the disinterestedness of his action in purchasing such interest for himself so onerous that most survivors left without advance authority to buy might better suffer the losses entailed in liquidation of the firm than assume the risks.

The State of Washington, cognizant of the harsh common-law rules, has enacted a statute under which the surviving partner or partners, upon petition to the court, may be granted a preferred right to purchase the deceased partner's interest at the price, and upon the terms and conditions fixed by the court. The working of this statute may be illustrated by reviewing *In re Glant's Estate.*[12]

Samuel Glant, at the time of his death, owned a 22.54 percent interest in a partnership engaged in the waste materials business for over thirty-eight years. He bequeathed to his widow a 7.51 percent interest, and the surviving partners petitioned the court under the statute to fix the price and determine the terms and conditions of sale of her interest to them. The court, with the

---

[12]50 Wash.2d 309, 356 P.2d 707 (1960).

assistance of appraisers furnished by the parties, fixed the price at $39,130. The widow elected to receive interest rather than profits thereon to date of judgment, bringing the total of $40,369. The terms were $10,369 down and $10,000 in three annual installments with 5 percent interest. The estate was released from liability on a large partnership indebtedness to its bank. The widow, however, appealed the judgment. Her contentions of special interest here were that the price should have included a value for good will, and that the cost of appraisers furnished by her should be paid by the surviving partners. Her expert witness had computed a good-will value of $55,185, and her share as $4,144. The Washington Supreme Court agreed with her on these items, and directed the judgment to be increased by $4,805 to cover the item of good will and the amount she had paid to appraisers. In deciding that good will existed, the court pointed out that the partnership had operated at the same location for over thirty-eight years, that it had retained the same key personnel of exceptional ability from the start, and that it was able to borrow more than $250,000 from its bank on an unsecured loan. It charged the appraisal costs to the surviving partners because they were benefited by the exercise of their preference right to purchase.

Although the widow was unsuccessful in contending that the lower court had erred in certain other respects in fixing the price of her interest, it appears that she, as well as the surviving partners, were well protected in the application of the special statute. It seems a desirable statute to have at hand where the partners themselves have neglected to set up a continuation plan.

The foregoing analysis includes the various plans that have been improvised by the surviving partners and the heirs and legal representatives for the purpose of continuing the business and of thereby avoiding the liquidation losses on the death of a partner. The inevitable conclusion is that, absent a special statute such as Washington has, any scheme formulated after a death occurs eventually creates losses even more disastrous than would have resulted from immediate liquidation. Such alternatives are conceived too late.

Chapter 6

ALTERNATIVES TO LIQUIDATION
SET UP PRIOR TO
A PARTNER'S DEATH

A PLAN SET UP BEFORE A DEATH OCCURS
IS NECESSARY

Examination of the pernicious results that often ensue from arrangements originated and entered into after the death of a partner for the purpose of by-passing the destructive effects of liquidation has demonstrated the necessity of establishing a plan before a death occurs. Various devices have been contrived during the lifetime of the partners; some by one partner acting alone, others by the partners acting in concert. An investigation of these devices and of the attendant results accomplished should lead us to the plan that will solve the problems brought about by the death of a partner.

PLANS MADE BY ONE PARTNER ACTING ALONE

Provision in will for continuance of the business. Sometimes a partner acts alone through provisions inserted in his will in an attempt to forestall liquidation. For example, he may provide in his will that the business be continued after his death, with his share of the capital left in the enterprise as an investment. At first glance this plan may seem advisable, especially if the profits of the enterprise have been large, but actually such a provision damages rather than improves the lot of the heirs. A primary objection is that in legal effect he merely gives the surviving partner an option to continue or

153

to liquidate, no matter how mandatory the terms of the will may be. *Slater v. Slater* [1] is ample authority for this conclusion. In that case, clause "FIFTH" of the will read: "It is my will and desire but I do not so direct that the business now carried on by my brother James and myself as co-partners be continued for the benefit of my Estate so long as it may be practicable and profitable so to do." The opinion, referring to this clause, stated: "The aforesaid paragraph is the only reference in the will to the testator's business, and even had the testator directed his personal representatives to continue the partnership business, they could neither have been compelled to do so by the surviving partner nor could such personal representatives have compelled the surviving partner to admit them as partners." If the survivor elects to liquidate, the provision will be a nullity; the liquidation losses will not be avoided. Ordinarily, the survivor will choose to liquidate, for he will not welcome the prospect of doing all of the work for only a fraction of the profits. On the other hand, if he elects to continue, the testamentary provisions of the deceased partner will take from his heirs the protecting remedies that they would otherwise have. For instance, we saw in the *Ducker* case that where the business was continued without authority, and finally, after several years of attractive profits, became insolvent, the heirs were entitled to keep the profits and were awarded the value of the deceased partner's interest. Had there been no profits, or had there been nothing but losses, the heirs would have been entitled to the value of the decedent's interest, plus interest on it, for the period during which the business was continued. However, if the continuance of the business had been authorized by the will of Sol Ducker, the heirs would have received their share of the profits, but would have lost $33,000, the value of their portion of the partnership interest.

The futility of will plans that authorize the surviving partner to continue the business at the price of supporting two families is further illustrated in *Western Shoe Company v. Neumeister.* [2] There the deceased partner, Neumeister, had bequeathed to his widow all his interest in the partnership of Neumeister & Schultz for the balance of her life, and at her death, to Schultz. Schultz was to control and manage the partnership business at a reasonable salary and was obligated to pay the widow $200 a month, plus one-half the profits. After Neumeister's death the business was continued for eight years, and then the surviving partner went bankrupt. The Western Shoe Company, a creditor of the continuing business, sued the widow on the ground that she had been made a partner. Michigan's highest court held that she was not a partner, and therefore, was not personally liable for the debt. The opinion stated in part:

---

[1] 208 App. Div. 567, aff'd 240 N.Y. 557.
[2] 258 Mich. 662, 242 N.W. 802 (1932).

It was the evident intention of the testator to secure for his wife an income from the partnership business, and to accomplish that purpose he gave possession and control of his interest to Mr. Schultz to be kept and used in the business subject only to certain profits and monthly payment to Mrs. Neumeister. But if he had intended to create a partnership relation between them, it could not be accomplished without their consent and there is no evidence that either of them ever consented.

Thus, to his widow, eight years after his death, the result of this seemingly salutary scheme in the deceased partner's will was the total loss of the value of his partnership interest, accompanied by the legal attempt by the creditors of the continuing business to reach her other property. To the surviving partner, the result of the double burden of work for one-half the profits was bankruptcy.

The net effect of a provision in the will directing the survivor to continue the business is to furnish a dangerous option to the survivor at the expense of the heirs of the will maker. The heirs either receive the liquidated value of the partnership interest or have their funds placed in a highly speculative investment, at the choice of the survivor. The surviving partner has the option of sharing in the liquidation losses or of trying to support two families. Surely, this is not the solution for which we are looking.

Directive in will to form new partnership with executor or heirs. Sometimes a partner directs in his will that his executor or one or more of his heirs be taken into partnership with the survivor, and that the business be continued by the new firm. Here again, we have a provision that may be a nullity, for no one can choose a future partner for another. The survivor may, therefore, disregard the provision and proceed to liquidate, because if he follows the direction of the will he will be embarking on a new partnership venture with an untried associate. If the potential associate is the executor, he cannot be expected to embark on a partnership adventure as a fiduciary for the deceased partner's family unless he can arrange for limited liability. Some courts under statutory provisions may prescribe limited liability, but in such event the survivor is almost sure to choose liquidation of the business. The prospects are no better if the potential associate is an heir of the deceased partner. We have discussed the disadvantages of such an arrangement in a previous chapter.[3] It is rarely attempted, and seldom successful, because of the unequal sharing of burdens and the conflict of objectives between the survivors and the heirs. Whatever the choice of the surviving partner, then, such a provision in the will of the deceased partner will probably fail to produce a desirable solution.

Provision in will for sale to survivor. A partner sometimes provides in his

---

[3]Page 146.

will that his partnership interest may be purchased by the survivor. This provision enables the surviving partner to buy in those states where he could not otherwise do so because of the rule preventing a trustee from purchasing property entrusted to him. In those states that allow a surviving partner to buy the deceased's interest, this provision in a will adds nothing unless it gives further powers. Unless the will stipulates a definite sale price or a specific valuation formula, the transaction is looked upon with suspicion by the courts, and the survivor, as a fiduciary, has the burden of proving that his dealings have been above suspicion. If the will does provide for the sale price, a definite step forward has been made, for then the shackles of the fiduciary relation have been removed from the survivor so long as he proceeds to make the purchase in exact compliance with the offer contained in the will.

In spite of this distinct accomplishment, however, other drawbacks condemn the plan. The survivor cannot rely on it because the provision in the will may be changed at any time prior to death, or the will may be held invalid for other reasons. Furthermore, even though the will remains un-altered and outlives probate, the survivor still has the problem of raising the necessary purchase price. The will maker cannot rely on it because the survivor is not bound in any way to make the purchase, and may exercise his right to liquidate the business.

Attempt by one partner to place his interest in joint tenancy. A partner in an Illinois elevater partnership tried a unique but unsuccessful plan for continuing his interest in the firm beyond his death; he issued a certificate declaring that his one-fourth interest in the partnership belonged to him and his two daughters "jointly or either survivor." The Supreme Court of Illinois held that the certificate was "wholly ineffective under the Uniform Partnership Act" and that the decedent's partnership interest was the property of his estate. The opinion added: "The very nature of a partnership is such that joint tenancy between one of the partners and a stranger to the partnership would be abhorrent to the act."[4]

Thus, we shall have to extend our search for a satisfactory solution beyond the scope of the unilateral contrivances set up by one partner, into the realm of bilateral arrangements made by all the partners.

PLANS MADE BY THE PARTNERS ACTING TOGETHER

A successful plan requires joint action by all partners. It is now clear that the plan which will best solve the problems brought about by the death of a partner must be found among contractual plans entered into prior to death by all of the partners.

Agreement for continuance of the business. Several varieties of such plans

---

[4]*Frey v. Wubbena,* 26 Ill.2d 62, 185 N.E.2d 850 (1962).

have been tried out. One of the simplest was that contained in the partnership articles involved in the New York case of *Steward v. Robinson* and in its related cases. The partners, Colwell and Hepworth, provided in their partnership agreement as follows:

> In the event of the death of either, the business shall be continued by the survivor until the expiration of five years from the first day of February next succeeding such death; the estate of the deceased partner to have the same share and interest in the profits, and to bear the same share of losses of the business, as would have been received and borne by the deceased partner had he lived; provided, however, that if the survivor shall think it necessary to employ an additional clerk in consequence of the death of the deceased partner, in such case the expense shall be charged to and shall be borne by the share in the profits of the deceased partner.

Partner Colwell subsequently died, leaving the value of his partnership interest, $50,000, in the business. Surviving partner Hepworth continued to run the business for a period of approximately five years as provided in the agreement, during which time $35,000 of additional funds were loaned by the executors and trustees of Colwell to the business. At the end of this time, Hepworth was insolvent to the extent of about $500,000, and he then made an assignment for the benefit of creditors.

In the *Stewart v. Robinson* case,[5] certain unsatisfied creditors of the continued business, learning that Colwell's estate had funds, sued his executors and trustees on the ground that the agreement, by providing that the estate would share in the profits and losses, had made the deceased's estate liable for the debts of the continuing business. The opinion pointed out, however, that neither the personal representatives nor the heirs had taken any part in the business with the survivor, that they had not been designated as partners, that an estate as such could not be a partner, and that in fact no new partnership had been formed. The court then held that the estate of the deceased partner was not liable beyond the funds left in the business.

In the *Delamater v. Hepworth* case,[6] other creditors tried to reach the funds in the deceased's estate on the same ground that had been urged by the creditors in *Stewart v. Robinson*. The court decided against the creditors, without opinion, basing its decision on that of *Stewart v. Robinson*.

In the *Butcher v. Hepworth* case,[7] the plaintiffs, who had been appointed receivers of the business, sued the surviving partner and the executors of the

[5] 115 N.Y. 328, 22 N.E. 160.
[6] 115 N.Y. 664.
[7] 115 N.Y. 328.

deceased partner to reach the general assets of the Colwell estate on the specific ground that the business had been conducted by Hepworth and the executors as a new partnership. Here again it was held that no such partnership existed and that the agreement did not involve the general assets of the deceased partner or the personal assets of the executors, but only the funds left in the business.

But the troubles caused by this continuation agreement have not yet been fully explored. In the *Stewart v. Robinson* case the creditors had succeeded in having a receiver appointed for the estate of the deceased partner, pending the outcome of the litigation. After the creditors had lost the decision in the lower court, they were somehow successful in having the receivership continued. In the case of *Colwell v. Garfield National Bank,*[8] the receiver sued the bank to recover a debt owed by that institution to the estate of the deceased partner. The court held that a receiver *pendente lite* had no authority to sue in behalf of the estate he represented after a judgment had been rendered against the party at whose instance he was appointed. These cases reveal that, to add to their misfortunes, the executors of the deceased partner were ousted from their duties for an extended period.

Following the above cases, the surviving partner and the executors of the deceased partner seem to have had a brief interlude of non-litigious quietude. It appears that shortly after Colwell died, the surviving partner had borrowed several thousand dollars from a Mr. Bell and, with the consent of the deceased partner's executors, had given Bell a mortgage on property of the business as security. In *Bell v. Hepworth,*[9] the mortgagee sued to foreclose his mortgage, joining the deceased's executors with Hepworth as defendants. The executors in defense of their suit, apparently somewhat "groggy" from the successive legal blows they had received, contended vainly that the lien of the estate of the deceased partner for the amount he had left in the business was superior to that of the mortgage; that the agreement contained in the partnership articles was invalid because it was testamentary in nature and was not executed with the formalities of a will; and that the agreement to continue the business violated the rule of perpetuities in that it suspended the power of alienation of property for a period of five years. To all these contentions, the court's answers were adverse, and the mortgage was duly foreclosed.

Since each of these five cases was litigated in two lower courts before reaching New York's highest tribunal, the surviving partner and the executors of the deceased partner were called upon to defend themselves legally at least fifteen times as a result of the seemingly innocuous paragraph of the partnership agreement requiring continuation of the business. In the end, the survivor lost everything. The deceased partner's estate lost the $50,000 value

---

[8] 119 N.Y 411.

[9] 134 N.Y. 442.

of the partnership interest left in the business, most if not all of the $35,000 subsequently loaned to the business by the executors, and thousands of dollars in the legal expenses of defending the balance of the estate from the creditors of the continued business. Admitting that this cluster of cases is an extreme example, it is obvious, nevertheless, that any arrangement that can lead to such litigation and financially disastrous results for the surviving partner and estate of the deceased partner must be classed as highly undesirable.

Although the foregoing cluster of cases brought out many weaknesses of a plan whereby a partnership business will be continued by the surviving partner without participation by the deceased partner's estate in the management but only in the profits, they did not bring out clearly a fundamental weakness that exists in this plan. Being a plan that requires the survivor to do all the work, he is entitled to a much greater share of the profits than he received before his partner's death. The estate and heirs, on the other hand, will be dissatisfied with any arrangement that cuts deeply into the share of profits the decedent received. These conflicting viewpoints are such that this plan must be considered a temporary plan of business continuation. This is well illustrated by *Tucker v. Tucker.*[10]

Two brothers, Louis and Joseph Tucker, operated an equal partnership engaged in towing, stevedoring and shipyard business until Louis' death in December 1940. Their partnership agreement contained the following Paragraph Five:

> In the event of the death of either partner all of the property ... of the deceased partner which is in the firm shall remain in the said business for a further period of two years after the deceased partner's death upon the same terms and conditions and operated in the same manner as during his lifetime ... but without any right on the part of ... [his] personal representative to take any part whatever in the conduct, management or direction of the business, the surviving partner having the sole right to continue the conduct and management of the same. At the end of said period of two years the interest of the deceased partner of the firm shall be appraised by a disinterested third person agreeable to the surviving partner and to the Trustees of the deceased partner ... and the surviving partner shall have the right to purchase the interest of the deceased partner in the firm at the appraised value. If the surviving partner will not buy, then the business of the firm shall be liquidated by the surviving partner and the interest of the deceased partner therein shall be paid over to his estate, unless by mutual agreement of the surviving partner and the unanimous consent of all the Trustees

---

[10]370 Pa. 8, 87 A.2d 181 (1952).

of the deceased partner, said interest is allowed to remain in the firm for a longer period upon such terms and for such period as they may agree upon.

Louis named his wife and his son as trustees of his estate, and authorized them to continue his interest in the business as provided in the partnership agreement. The business was continued by the survivor, and in April 1942 he and the trustees agreed that the provisions of Paragraph Five should be extended to December 1946. This extension agreement provided that the survivor was to receive 20 percent of the net profits as compensation, with the balance divided equally between the survivor and the estate. As December 1946 approached, the attorneys for the parties negotiated for another extension agreement, but the trustees were unwilling to grant the salary demanded by the survivor. He nevertheless continued to operate the business, and exercised his right to purchase the estate's interest in the business as of November 30, 1947. The accountant's appraisal showed $38,620 due the estate after allowing the survivor his special compensation of 20 percent of the profits for the year he had operated beyond the extension period. The trustees disputed this allowance, but finally accepted the $38,620 without prejudice and sued the survivor to recover on his allowance and certain other items. Pennsylvania's highest court affirmed a judgment in favor of the survivor on the ground that he had managed the business in good faith during the period of negotiations, was entitled to reasonable compensation for his services, and the amount the parties had agreed upon for the extension period was reasonable.

Thus, while this business continuation plan worked reasonably well for a period of years, it eventually terminated in a purchase plan because the parties, having interests that conflicted, could no longer agree on how the profits should be shared.

Agreement for new partnership between survivor and heirs. A binding agreement may be entered into by the partners and their prospective heirs, providing that on the death of a partner the survivor will form a new partnership to continue the business with specified heirs who are parties to the agreement.[11] Even if all the persons concerned are signatories to such a contract however, the arrangement has one legal weakness that cannot be surmounted: it cannot be specifically enforced by court action. True, if the surviving partner refuses to carry on the business with the designated heir as a new partner, he is liable for damages for breach of contract. And likewise, if the nominated heir refuses to perform, his refusal will subject the deceased partner's estate to damages for breach of contract. But the fact remains that a court will not compel any person to enter or carry on the partnership relation with another. The scheme is therefore tinged with uncertainty and still leaves the possibility of liquidation with its attendant losses as the final outcome.

---

[11]*Estate of Hillowitz* (1968), 22 N.Y.2d 107, 291 N.Y.S.2d 325.

Willingness to go ahead with the new partnership can by no means be assured. Obviously, unless the prospective heirs who are selected to become future partners are active and experienced in the business, the plan will have small chance of success. The surviving partner usually finds himself left with an inexperienced and uninterested prospective partner whose primary objective is to receive current income to replace that lost on the death of the original partner. Such an objective conflicts ruinously with the surviving partner's long range objectives for the future development and expansion of the business, a fact that may well be proved in operating losses if the scheme is carried through.

Even where the surviving partner and the deceased partner's heir are willing to form a successor partnership, it usually breaks up within a few years. This was this history of the successor partnership involved in *Denawetz v. Milch.*[12] There, Joseph Milch and John Denawetz were operating a partnership engaged in the wholesale distribution of brand-name clothing and general merchandise at the time of Denawetz's death in 1954. Their partnership agreement granted to his widow the option of either becoming a partner with Milch or receiving the value of the decedent's interest in cash. She elected to become Milch's partner, and the business continued normally until 1959 with Milch acting as the managing partner and directing operations. Then things ceased to run smoothly. After protracted negotiations to decide who would buy out the other's interest, Milch agreed to sell for $100,000 all his interest in the firm. The agreement did not mention good will or contain a restrictive covenant concerning competition. Milch received his price in cash and notes from the firm's assets, and delivered to the widow a bill of sale wherein he granted her all his interest in the partnership and its assets.

On the following day, Milch opened up his own storeroom and engaged in the same business under the name of the Joseph Milch Company. He was joined by his two sons and a nephew, all of whom had previously worked for the partnership without employment contracts. Shortly thereafter, as a result of direct solicitation, Milch became either the sole or primary distributor in the area of almost every important brand that had been distributed exclusively by the partnership. Also by direct solicitation he acquired the bulk of its customers.

Faced with the loss of most of her business, the widow brought two actions; the first against Milch to enjoin him from competing with her customers and suppliers for a period of two years; the second against his sons and nephews to enjoin their participation. The actions were consolidated and dismissed by the lower court. Pennsylvania's highest court affirmed, stating the following rule:

> ... Unless the partnership articles or the dissolution agreement expressly restricts the right of a former member of a dissolved

---

[12]407 Pa. 115, 178 A.2d 701 (1962).

partnership from competing against the ex-partners by engaging in the same line of business, or by soliciting old customers or suppliers, he may engage in these activities. The courts, however, will not imply such restrictions into agreements.

Of course it is easy to say that the widow should have obtained a restrictive covenant—but we have already emphasized that a surviving partner seldom will agree to one. Certainly this surviving partner would not have done so. His refusal, if he had been asked, would have altered the chain of events, but would not have solved the situation brought about by granting the deceased partner's widow an option to become a partner. In the first instance, the original partners should have chosen a better continuation plan.

The plan of taking in an heir as successor partner is feasible only in the exceptional case in which the heir is already a capable employee of the original partnership and an individual whom the survivor would like to take in as a future partner. For example, the partners might have talented sons employed by the firm. If an agreement to continue the business with a son who has attained his majoirty meets with the favor of all concerned, it should prove satisfactory. Certain precautions, however, must be carefully observed. If a partner's interest constitutes the bulk of his property, his wife should waive any rights that she might otherwise have in the partnership interest. In replacement, such a partner should own sufficient personal life insurance payable to his wife to guarantee her proper maintenance, support and well-being. An alternate plan calls for the purchase by the son of all or part of the father's partnership interest at his death. The purchase should be financed by insurance owned by the son on the father's life, the insurance proceeds to be paid over by the son to the father's estate for distribution to the other members of the family under the terms of the father's will.

It is readily apparent that the existence of the precise circumstances required for the success of a new partnership between the survivor and the heirs is so infrequent that the plan should rarely be set up. Thus it affords a desirable solution only in a few isolated instances.

Agreement for decedent's personal representative to become a partner. This plan is little improved over a provision in a deceased partner's will directing his personal representative to become a partner with the survivor. The will plan has the fundamental weakness that it is binding on no one; whereas, an agreement will bind the signatories to perform or pay damages. Thus, an agreement for a deceased partner's personal representative to become a partner should not only be signed by the partners themselves, but also by their prospective personal representatives if any reliance is to be placed on it. Even then, there is no certainty that the successor partnership will come into being; the surviving partner or the personal representative may prefer to incur liability for breach of his contract to become a member of a new firm. It would be a rare type of personal representative who would agree to become a successor partner unless his liability, and that of the estate, is limited. Therefore, agreements designed to bring in a deceased partner's personal representative usually provide for a limited partnership to be formed, with the personal representative to become the limited partner. Such an agreement may still have its difficulties, however, as illustrated by *Segall v. Altman*.[13]

Martin Saxe and defendant Altman were equal partners in a business dealing in spices. Their articles of partnership provided that the following events would take place upon the death of a partner: Book value would be determined as of the last day of the month following; the surviving partner and the legal representatives of the estate would enter into a limited partnership with the legal representatives as limited partners and contributing the estate's share of the firm's assets; the limited partnership would continue for one year, then from year to year provided there were net profits, but in any event to terminate on the general partner's death; the general partner would receive $100 a week as salary, plus 25 percent of net profits exceeding $25,000, after which the remaining profits would be divided equally; the limited partners would have no right to assign their interests. Each partner made a will containing similar provisions.

Following Saxe's death on May 9, 1945, his widow and daughter were appointed executrices under his will. Altman continued to operate the partnership business in the same manner as before, and filed a partnership income tax return for the period ending December 31, 1945. This return listed Altman as a one-half partner, the widow as a one-third partner, and the daughter as a one-sixth partner. It reported net profits of $22,116 after his $3,500 salary. He drew $14,458 from the business, but paid only $100 to the deceased partner's estate and refused to execute a limited partnership agreement or account to the estate.

The widow first brought a proceeding in the Surrogate's Court to compel the survivor to pay over the estate's $11,058 share of the profits for 1945, but that court held that it had no jurisdiction. (*In re Saxe's Will*, 64 N.Y.S. 2d 123 [1946].) She then brought this action in the proper court. The court, in order to protect the decedent's estate until the issues could be decided, ordered Altman to execute a surety bond for $35,000 to the effect that he would obey all orders of the court in the action, and further ordered that all present and incoming funds of the partnership be placed in bank accounts subject to the joint control of the widow and Altman. If these conditions were not complied with in five days, the widow could have a receiver appointed to take over the partnership affairs.

---

[13]65 N.Y.S.2d 601 (1946).

The public records do not reveal the subsequent events, but it may be assumed that if the carefully planned limited partnership ever materialized it did not endure long. Even if it had started off well, eventually dissatisfaction would arise because it is fundamentally an arrangement whereby the surviving partner is expected to carry the entire burden of running the business while sharing the profits with inactive partners.

Agreement giving survivor option to buy deceased's interest. It is not unusual to find partnership articles which contain a provision allowing the surviving partner an option to buy the deceased partner's interest. That such a plan has an inherent and incurable weakness, which makes it undesirable, is revealed by cases that have dealt with such plans.

A 1968 case in point is *Estate of Frank L. Van Epps*,[14] which involved an equal partnership formed in 1941 by Frank Van Epps and his brother Freeland. Their partnership agreement provided that the surviving partner should have the right at his option to purchase the interest of his deceased partner at a price derived from a formula contained in the agreement.

Frank died in 1965, survived by Freeland. Frank's will specifically bequeathed his interest in the partnership to his three children equally, and requested his brother to defer or forego exercising the option "unless the exercise of such option will be beneficial to the beneficiaries of my will." A codicil to Frank's will named a bank and Freeland as co-executors, and they were so appointed. Shortly thereafter, Freeland gave notice of the exercise of his option at a price approximately $11,000 less than the appraised value of the deceased partner's interest. Objections were filed challenging the sale on the grounds that it was detrimental to the estate beneficiaries and to the personal advantage of Freeland.

The Wisconsin Supreme Court affirmed the trial court's decision that the sale should be set aside. When Freeland accepted the appointment as co-executor he was duty bound as a fiduciary to act in the best interests of the estate beneficiaries. Accordingly, his individual rights became subordinated to his fiduciary duty and prohibited him, in his individual capacity, from exercising the option under the existing facts. The court carefully distinguished this option situation from one involving a mandatory contracual obligation to purchase for a specified or determinable price.

The case reveals several serious weaknesses in the option plan. First, it is not likely to function where, as here, the surviving partner also is a legal representative of the deceased partner's estate. Second, if the option is not exercised, for whatever reason, the surviving partner has the duty to liquidate the firm. For him, this means liquidating himself out of a job; for the heirs, it usually means suffering substantial liquidation losses. Basically, the uncer-

---

[14]40 Wis. 2d 139, 161 N.W. 2d 278.

tainty of not knowing whether the option will be exercised makes this plan undesirable in the vast majority of cases.

AGREEMENT FOR SURVIVOR TO PURCHASE DECEASED PARTNER'S INTEREST

With one outstanding exception, we have now analyzed every scheme, plan, or contrivance that has been used to circumvent liquidation of the affairs of a partnership on the death of a partner. Most of these schemes have culminated in more destructive consequences than would have been the case had liquidation taken place. Each has proved faulty in some vital function. One major plan remains to be analyzed: that calling for a binding contract among the partners whereby the surviving partner or partners agree to purchase the partnership interest of a deceased partner at a price stipulated in the agreement or to be ascertained by the application at time of death of a definite valuation formula contained in it.

A simple agreement of this nature was the bone of contention in *Murphy v. Murphy*.[15] There the partners had agreed that in the event of the death of one, the survivor would pay his widow or legal representative $3,000, and that thereupon the survivor would become the sole owner of the partnership business. The firm, consisting of two brothers, Bartholomew and Patrick Murphy, conducted a liquor business. Upon Patrick's death, Bartholomew tendered the widow and administratrix $3,000 in accordance with the terms of the agreement, but she refused to go through with the transaction. Bartholomew then brought this suit, asking that the widow be compelled to carry out the contract. Massachusetts' highest court held that the agreement was binding and must be specifically performed. The widow as administratrix was required to accept the purchase price of $3,000 that had been stipulated by the partners in the contract and to release the interest of the deceased partner in the partnership to the surviving partner. As this is a leading case, we shall quote freely from the opinion.

> Partnership agreements which provide for the conduct of the business after the death of one or more of the partners, and for the disposition of the interest of partners in the partnership in such event, are frequent. See *Williams v. Brookline*, 194 Mass. 45, 79 N.E. 996. When fairly made, without any illegal purpose and without intent to evade the statute of wills, they are not open to objection.... There are sound reasons why a fair agreement entered into by partners, as to the disposition of partnership property in the event of the death of one or more of the partners, should be sustained. The terms of such an agreement made by those most familiar with the real character and value of the

---

[15]217 Mass. 233, 104 N.E. 466 (1914).

property are quite as likely to be just as an arrangement made after the decease. . . . The contract as bar was executed upon a valid consideration, and having been found expressly not to have been intended as a testamentary disposition, must be upheld.

. . . The plaintiff as the surviving partner, in the absence of any term in the articles of co-partnership covering the matter would take as owner the legal title to firm property. . . . He would take it, however, subject to the duty to pay the firm debts, settle the partnership accounts, and account to the personal representatives of the deceased partner. There is no reason in equity why the defendant should not be required to release this beneficial obligation which, but for the contract, would exist in her favor. . . .

The *Murphy* case finally brings us close to the ideal plan for which we have been searching. In that case there was a binding agreement to buy and sell that, being upheld by the court, eliminated all possibility of liquidation losses. The price was exactly agreed upon in advance, with the result that the survivor never acquired the status of trustee with its attendant burdensome obligations and strict accountability. Furthermore, as the buyer of unique property (the partnership interest of the deceased partner), he was entitled to specific performance of the transaction, rather than to damages, on the refusal of the estate to carry out its part of the contract. The outcome was that the surviving partner owned the entire partnership business and was free to go ahead with whatever future plans he may have had. The estate received in payment for the sale of the deceased partner's interest exactly the amount agreed upon by the partners as the proper price.

BUY-SELL AGREEMENTS BETWEEN PARTNERS GENERALLY UPHELD

The decision in the *Murphy* case, upholding the agreement between the partners providing for the purchase of the partnership interest from the deceased partner by the survivor upon the death of the first to die, probably represents the law in every state. Reference to some of the cases in other jurisdictions will bear this out.

One of the leading cases in the Commonwealth of Pennsylvania is that of *Kaufmann v. Kaufmann,*[16] which involved the large firm of Kaufmann Brothers. The four partners had agreed that on the death of one, the surviving partners would purchase the partnership interest of the deceased partner at a price arrived at by the application of a specified formula that included a valuation of the good will. The court upheld the agreement of the partners, saying in part:

---

[16]222 Pa. 58, 70 Atl. 956 (1908).

Though the most elaborate proof has been submitted by the learned counsel for appellants, the case, after all, is within a narrow compass and absolutely free from doubt and difficulty. The agreements, which are self-interpreting, were made by persons *sui juris*. The one as to the purchase of a deceased partner's interest is not an unusual one, and was fair alike to each of the four partners. If the representatives of Jacob are now disappointed that they cannot get more than the survivors offer them, the law cannot help them, for it was so written by him in his agreement with them.

The court, in *Casey v. Hurley*,[17] had this to say about the agreement of the partners involved there:

While more precise and definite language might have been used to express the intent of the parties, that intent, it seems to us, is unmistakable, and we are unable to perceive any ground upon which it could be held that the contract is not a valid and enforceable one. The agreement between partners that, upon the death of one, the survivors should be entitled to take the interest of the other in the partnership assets at a price named in the agreement, or to be determined thereafter by some method specified therein, rests upon the consideration of the mutual promises of the partners, is enforceable, and relieves the surviving partner of the obligation to account. *Murphy v. Murphy,* 217 Mass. 233, 104 N.E. 466; *Kaufmann v. Kaufmann,* 222 Pa. 58, 70 Atl. 956. . . .

It is now well established that partners may enter into a binding contract for the purchase of the partnership interest of the deceased by the survivor. Furthermore, the courts generally grant specific performance of these contracts in those cases in which their validity is challenged. This means that the partners may set up such agreements with full confidence that their arrangements will be carried out to the letter.

SURVIVORSHIP TYPE OF AGREEMENT
HAS BEEN UPHELD BY MANY STATES

The survivorship type of agreement, providing that the interest of the deceased partner, immediately upon his death, or upon payment therefor, shall vest in and become the property of the surviving partners, must be distinguished from the standard type of agreement calling for the purchase and sale of a partner's interest upon his death. The survivorship agreement has been upheld in such cases as *McKinnon v. McKinnon, Coe v. Winchester,* and others. It has been declared a valid contract in the majority of states, but in a few jurisdictions there may still be some doubt as to its validity. For a period

---

[17]112 Conn. 536, 152 Atl. 892 (1931).

of years, Rhode Island was in that category. The Supreme Court of Rhode Island, in *Ferrara v. Russo,*[18] held ineffective an agreement which provided that in the event of the death of Carmine Ferrara his interest in a certain printing establishment operated by him jointly with Russo would become Russo's property in consideration for a payment of $275 to Ferrara's heirs.

The *Ferrara* case was severely criticized and undoubtedly led to the enactment in 1932 of new legislation which provides that a written partnership agreement, disposing of the assets, firm name, or partnership life insurance policies or proceeds upon the death of a partner, shall not be deemed testamentary in character or for that reason invalid or unenforceable.

The opinion in *McKinnon v. McKinnon,*[19] a Missouri case, stated:

> There are many cases to be found in the books, some of which have been called to our attention and are evidently relied upon in the present case, where an instrument which was intended by the grantor to be a conveyance was held not to be operative as such, because it did not pass any present interest, and to be void as a will, because not executed in conformity with the statute of wills. . . . The distinction between a deed and a will is elementary, and is well understood. The former must pass a present interest, although the right to possession and enjoyment may not accrue until some future time; whereas an instrument which does not pass any interest until after the death of the maker is essentially a will, and must be executed with all due formalities. But we fail to see that these authorities, or the principles which they enunciate, have any proper application to the case at bar. The partnership articles involved in the present controversy were neither intended as a deed or a will. They constitute an executory agreement, which determines the rights of the parties inter se, and provides what disposition shall be made of the partnership property on the happening of a certain event. In the state of Missouri, where these articles were signed, and where both partners at the time resided and carried on business, it is as well settled, as it is in any state of this Union, that an agreement by a person, upon a valuable consideration, to give another the whole or a part of his property at the promissor's death, will be specifically enforced in equity, both as to real and personal property, if the consideration is duly rendered by the promisee . . .

A 1949 case upholding a survivorship type of agreement is *Michaels v. Donato.*[20] The agreement provided that upon the death of a partner the surviving partner should pay the legal representative of the deceased partner

---

[18] 40 R.I. 533, 102 Atl. 86 (1917).

[19] 56 Fed. 409.

[20] 4 N.J. 570, 67 A. 2d 911.

$1,000, "that said sum shall represent the deceased partner's entire interest in the partnership and that upon such payment the surviving partner shall become the sole owner of the partnership business." As in the *McKinnon* case, the decision turned on the distinction between a contract and a will.

Turning to the agreement before the court, the opinion quoted 73 A.L.R. 980 to the effect that "a provision in a partnership agreement that on the death of one of the partners his interest in the partnership shall become the property of the other partners is not invalid as testamentary in nature, and therefore inoperative because of failure to conform to the requirement of the Statute of Wills." The quoted statement was then backed by an imposing array of leading cases and authorities.

A 1953 case, upholding a survivorship type of partnership agreement, is *Silverthorne v. Mayo.*[21] The opinion stated in part:

> It appears to be well settled that a provision in a partnership agreement to the effect that on the death of one of the partners his interest in the partnership shall become the property of the surviving partner or partners is not testamentary in nature, and the fact that the agreement is not executed according to the requirements of the law governing the execution of wills does not render it invalid and unenforceable. Such an agreement is enforceable if supported by fair and adequate consideration.

ADDITIONAL CITATIONS

Among other prominent cases upholding agreements of the partners for the disposal of the interest of a deceased partner to the survivor, or agreements similar in nature, are the following:

In re Orvis' Estate, 223 N.Y. 1, 119 N.E. 88 (1918); *Lockwood's Trustees v. Lockwood,* 250 Ky. 262, 62 S.W. 2d 1053 (1931); *Coe v. Winchester,* 43 Ariz. 500, 33 P. 2d 286 (1934); *Garratt v. Baker,* 5 Cal. 2d 745, 56 P. 2d 225 (1936); *Normand v. Normand,* 90 N.H. 548, 11 A. 2d 816 (1940); *First National Bank of Rome v. Howell,* 195 Ga. 72, 23, S.E. 2d 415 (1942); *Rankin v. Newman,* 114 Cal. 635, 46 Pac. 742 (1896); *Hermes v. Compton,* 260 App. Div. 507, 23 N.Y.S. 2d 126 (1940); *Hirsch v. Bartels,* (Fla.), 49 So.2d 531 (1950), upholding the agreement as creating a joint tenancy of the partnership property; *Lynch v. Ilg,* 348 Ill. App. 545, 109 N.E.2d 362 (1952), leave to appeal denied 413 Ill. 633; *Jones v. Schellenberger,* 225 F.2d 784 (1955), cert. den. 350 U.S. 989 (1956), involving an Illinois partnership; *Van Derlip v. Van Derlip,* 149 Conn. 285, 179 A.2d 619 (1962); *Balafas v. Balafas,* 263 Minn. 267, 117 N.W.2d 20 (1962); *In re Estate of Hillowitz,* 22 N.Y.2d 107, 291 N.Y.S.2d 325 (1968).

A peculiarity of the survivorship agreement in *Jones v. Schellinberger* was

---

[21] 238 N.C. 274, 77 S.E. 2d 678.

a provision that the partners would "participate and own said business and partnership property *as joint tenants* with the right of survivorship, and upon the death of either party hereto, all right, title and interest therein shall vest immediately unto the surviving partner." In upholding the survivorship agreement, the court concluded that since it was evident that the agreement was one in partnership and not in joint tenancy, "the words 'as joint tenants,' are devoid of any legal significance." This case may be distinguished from *Hirsch v. Bartels* on the basis that Illinois operates under the Uniform Partnership Act, which provides specifically that partnership property is held by the partners as tenants in partnership. Surviving tenants under either form succeed to the ownership of the property, but the surviving tenant in partnership succeeds for partnership purposes only and has the duty to account to the deceased partner's estate unless the particular agreement, as in the case of these survivorship agreements, functions to relieve the survivor of such duty. When such agreements are upheld, all that the survivor has to do is perform whatever obligations he has assumed under the agreement.

An Iowa case involved an agreement that would have had the effect of disinheriting a deceased partner's widow, and must be considered on its peculiar facts.[22] The partnership survivorship agreement between four brothers was held in effect a contract to make wills in favor of the survivors and subject to the widow's statutory share in the estate of the deceased. The court pointed out that "there were no creditors except those paid by the surviving partners."

An Arkansas case, which refused to give effect to a survivorship agreement, should be noted here.[23] The surviving partner had obtained the decedent partner's execution of the agreement without informing the latter of her physician's statement that she had a fatal disease and would die soon. Upon learning the facts, the decedent partner bequeathed her partnership interest to her parents and requested that the partnership be liquidated following her death. It was held that the surviving partner had failed to exercise the utmost good faith required of partners in dealing with each other, so as to require the agreement to be set aside, the decedent partner having renounced it by bequeathing her interest to her parents. It would be surprising if any court would uphold an agreement under such circumstances.

A Mississippi case should be mentioned.[24] The survivorship agreement provided that in the event of the death of either partner the farm lands owned by the partners as tenants in common, as well as the personal property

---

[22]*Fleming v. Fleming,* 194 Iowa 71, 174 N.W. 946 (1919), rehearing denied, 194 Iowa 71, 180 N.W. 206 (1920), mod., 194 Iowa 71, 184 N.W. 296 (1921), error dis., 264 U.S. 29 (1924), mod., 211 Iowa 1251, 230 N.W. 359 (1930).

[23]*Alexander v. Sims,* 220 Ark. 643, 249 S.W.2d 832 (1952).

[24]*Conner v. Conner,* 238 Miss. 471, 119 So.2d 240 (1960).

owned by the partnership, should become vested in the survivor. It was held that the instrument was testamentary in character and could not vest title to the property in the survivor. Clearly, the agreement was testamentary as to the property not owned by the partnership, and it may be that Mississippi, which has not adopted the Uniform Partnership Act, would hold any *survivorship* agreement bad. Thus, a regular buy-sell agreement with an adequate purchase price should be used in that state.

FINANCING THE BUY-SELL AGREEMENT

A study of some of the actual cases has shown that if a binding buy-sell agreement has been entered into by the partners, then upon the event of a death, the surviving partner, on tendering the stipulated purchase price of the deceased partner's interest to his executor or administrator, is entitled to a release or conveyance of that interest. If at the time of death, however, the survivor should be financially unable to tender the purchase price, the plan would fall through in spite of any court action that might be brought by the deceased partner's estate. Therefore, the only remaining hazard to such a plan is that the surviving partner may not have the funds with which to carry out the transaction when a death occurs. In some instances a death will not occur for a number of years; in others it will occur in a matter of days. The surviving partner will require a specified amount of cash at an unpredictable time in the future, that is, whenever his partner dies. Obviously therefore, his need for funds will be exactly matched by the obligation of an insurance company to pay funds under a life insurance policy carried on the life of the deceased partner in the amount of the purchase price.

Part III

THE PARTNERSHIP BUY-SELL AGREEMENT FINANCED WITH LIFE INSURANCE

Chapter 7

THE INSURED BUY-SELL
AGREEMENT–
GENERAL CONSIDERATIONS

LIFE INSURANCE ASSURES CARRYING OUT
OF PURCHASE PLAN

Extended examination of the various plans contrived to perpetuate partnership businesses demonstrates that definite assurance of the continuance of the business after a partner's death can be had only by means of a contract in which the survivor, or the partnership, agrees to purchase the interest of the deceased at a stipulated price. From the nature of the transaction, however, such assurance can only be as certain as the ability of the surviving partner, or the firm, to tender the purchase price at time of death.

Life insurance on each partner in the amount of the purchase price is not only necessary to remove the danger that the money to consummate the purchase will not be on hand when needed, but it also offers to the partners the most convenient and attractive method of financing that purchase.

Methods of financing the purchase other than with life insurance. The alternatives to the life insurance plan of financing the purchase are few. If the partners are wealthy, their ability to produce the cash may be conceded, but the survivor will have to put up one hundred cents on the dollar, perhaps at a time highly inconvenient to him. On the other hand, the life insurance contract calls for premiums in installments that seldom total the face amount.

175

If the partners are in ordinary financial circumstances, which includes the vast majority, three choices are possibly open to them: to build up the purchase price in advance through savings; to provide in the agreement for payment of the purchase price in installments; or to borrow the purchase price at time of death.

Attempts to build up the purchase price in advance through ordinary savings plans are impracticable because the money might be required in ten days or in ten years; exactly when, no one can foretell. Certainty that the plan will be completed cannot be attained by this method.

A plan by which all, or substantially all, of the purchase price is to be paid in installments after death is also unworthy of serious consideration because it mortgages the partnership business and the future of the surviving partner, while at the same time it leaves the family of the deceased dependent upon the survivor's success for their money. Moreover, the survivor may find himself in an impossible position to perform.

Assume that two partners each receive $20,000 a year from their partnership. They set a value of $100,000 on each of their interests and agree that in the event of the death of one the survivor will purchase the deceased's interest by paying five annual installments of $20,000, with 5 percent interest. If the partner destined to be the survivor has a wife and a dependent child and ordinary deductions of $2,000, his current Federal income and self-employment taxes, based upon a joint return and 1973 rates, would be $4,161.50, leaving him a net spendable income of $13,938.50. But look at the picture after the death of his associate. The survivor would undoubtedly have to hire a new assistant and pay him at least $7,000 a year. Optimistically assuming that the firm would continue to yield $40,000 annually, an income of about $33,000 would be available for the survivor. After his ordinary deductions of $2,000 as before and the deduction of $5,000 interest on his indebtedness under the agreement, his net income would be $26,000, his Federal income and self-employment taxes would be $6,444, leaving net spendable income of $19,556. If we deduct from this figure his previous spendable income of $13,938.50 as necessary to the maintenance of his established standard of living, only $5,617.50 would remain with which to pay the first installment of $20,000.

Even when income tax rates somewhat lower than the 1973 rates are substituted as those which may prevail at time of a partner's death, it is obvious that the survivor could not carry out his bargain under such ordinary circumstances as those depicted. An agreement spreading the payments over a greater number of years is no answer, for the family of the deceased partner would then be left dependent upon the survivor's success over a dangerously long period.

Since the ability of the surviving partner to borrow the purchase price cannot be assured beforehand, the ultimate completion of this plan is shrouded in uncertainty. This lack of assurance that the plan will function properly overshadows the fact that, even if the survivor is successful in arranging a loan at time of death, he mortgages his future and he will finally have to pay the loan back at one hundred cents on the dollar, probably plus a substantial amount of interest.

The life insurance method of financing the purchase agreement. The life insurance method of financing, on the other hand, guarantees the successful completion of the purchase plan. It is, in effect, an advance installment method of paying the purchase price for the deceased partner's interest. These advance installment payments are in the form of convenient premiums, usually amounting annually to only 3 or 4 percent of the total price with the customary proviso that these premium payments cease at death, no matter how few have been made. Rarely do premiums aggregate the face amount; in fact, the total amount actually paid is often only a fraction of the death proceeds, as some of the following case examples will show, and hence the purchase price is obtained with discounted dollars.

By this plan of financing, the event that causes the obligation to mature and become payable is also made to furnish the money with which to discharge that obligation. By this plan, the survivor owns the entire business, paid for in full; and the deceased partner's estate receives the full amount of the purchase price, in cash, "on the barrel-head." If the life insurance contract had not been devised previously, it surely would have been devised to finance partnership buy-sell agreements, because it so exactly fulfills the requirements.

VALIDITY OF THE BUY-SELL AGREEMENT FINANCED WITH LIFE INSURANCE

The validity of agreements for the purchase and sale of partnership interests, financed with life insurance, rests upon a legal basis no different from that of similar agreements that do not include this financing arrangement. If the agreement is properly drawn to contain the elements of a sound contract, it is binding and enforceable. The cases that involved no insurance which are discussed or cited in Chapter 6 as upholding agreements of this type are also authority for the validity of the complete form of agreement, which includes life insurance financing. Nevertheless, it will be of interest to refer specifically to a few of the cases dealing with agreements that used life insurance.

One of the most interesting of these cases is *Coe v. Winchester.*[1] Ranny V. Winchester and Tasso Coe conducted as partners a merchandise brokerage business in Tucson, Arizona, under the name of Winchester-Coe Company. In the spring of 1926 the partners each purchased $10,000 of life insurance, and

---

[1] 43 Ariz. 500, 33 P. 2d 286 (1934).

entered into an agreement that functioned both as Articles of Partnership and as a Survivor Agreement covering the partnership interest of the first to die. This agreement, which Coe testified in the trial that he had typed while Winchester "more or less" dictated, is unique in more ways than its brevity. Here it is:

> We, Tasso Coe and R.V. Winchester, doing business as Winchester-Coe Company, agree to operate a merchandise brokerage business, dividing the profits equally.
>
> We agree that neither of us shall sign bonds, or endorse any notes unless done jointly.
>
> As a result of a ten-thousand dollar life insurance policy taken out by each of us, Coe's with the Aetna and Winchester's with the Pacific Mutual Life, premiums on which are to be paid by Winchester-Coe Company. In event of Coe's death, his wife or heirs is to receive the face of this policy, and Winchester receives Coe's interest in the business. In the event of Winchester's death his wife or heirs to receive the face of the policy and Coe receives Winchester's interest in the business.
>
> Signed by us this 8th day of May, 1926.
>
> > [signed] Tasso Coe
> > [signed] R.V. Winchester

In the spring of 1930, only four years later, almost to the day, Winchester died. Myrtle Winchester, who was the widow and executrix of the deceased partner, after receiving the $10,000 life insurance proceeds, sued for an accounting. Her principal contention was that, Arizona being a community property state, the agreement covered only her husband's share of the community interest in the partnership, but not her community interest; in other words, that the surviving partner was entitled to only one-half of Winchester's one-half interest by reason of the agreement, and should account to her for the value of her community interest of one-fourth. She also challenged the validity of the agreement, and argued further that it was unfair to her.

Arizona's highest court held the agreement valid, that it entitled the surviving partner to the entire business, and that the arrangement was not only fair to the widow but advantageous to her and "was an admirable one."

The opinion brought out several points worthy of note. In upholding the validity of the contract, *Murphy v. Murphy*,[2] *Matter of Borden's Estate*,[3] and *McKinnon v. McKinnon*[4] were cited. The court had some difficulty in arriving at the decision that the agreement covered the entire community interest of the

----

[2]217 Mass. 233.

[3]159 N.Y.S. 346.

[4]56 Fed. 409.

Winchesters, because of lack of clarity of the wording used. Winchester, however, seems to have been better at writing letters than in dictating agreements, for it was by means of a letter that he had previously written to Coe, which was fortunately admitted in evidence, that the court settled the point as the partners had intended. This letter read in part as follows:

> ... My idea of the proposition is as follows: In case of my death my policy would be paid to my estate, you to receive the entire business. In case you died your policy would be paid to your wife and I would receive the entire business, the two policies to be paid by the firm.
>
> I think this is an excellent proposition and think we should go on with it.

In holding that Winchester had the right to sell the entire community personal property, the court had this to say:

> The partners were married and their contributions to the partnership were from the marital community of each. While the wives of the members of the firm were not actually or nominally partners, therein, because the assets of the firm were community property they had a direct contingent interest in such assets. Under the community law of this state the spouses own their common property and the wife's interest is equal to that of the husband. Such being the rule, the assets of the partnership belonged in equal parts to the partners and their wives. The wife, however, during coverture has no power of disposition of the community personalty. The law, for reasons of convenience and expediency, places that power exclusively in the husband, who may exercise it in any way he chooses, except that he cannot make a testamentary disposition of his wife's interest or dispose of it in fraud of her rights. *La Tourette v. La Tourette,* 15 Ariz. 200, 137 Pac. 426, Ann. Cases, 1915B, 70. These are the only limitations on the husband's control or disposition of the community personalty.
>
> We are satisfied that the agency of Winchester over the community personal property vested him with full and complete power to make a contract in the nature of the one in question. ...

With respect to the advantages of the arrangement, the opinion is also worth quoting:

> The contract was certainly beneficial to the wife of the partner who died first, for the reason that she obtained $10,000 cash instead of her husband's one-half interest in the business worth only $19,819.39, itemized $11,819.39 in personalty and

$8,000 "good will." Without the insurance arrangement the appellee's share would have been a little over $5,000 of the tangible assets and one-half of whatever might have been realized for the partnership "good will" upon a falling market in 1930 and since. It is apparent that the reason which prompted the partners to reduce their contract to writing was not that they feared each other, or that they wanted a written memorial of their agreement, but that their primary purpose in doing so was that the wife of the one who should first die would be provided for as well or better than if she took her deceased husband's one-half interest, and the survivor would have the business without having forced upon him a partner not of his own choosing or some one unfit or incapable of contributing the necessary skill to make the business successful. . . . The arrangement certainly was an admirable one and was made by the two partners to provide for their wives when they could not longer do so. . . .

. . . Nor can it be said that the contract was not most advantageous to appellee. She received $10,000 cash instead of one-half interest in a $19,800 business subject to immediate liquidation. . . . We concur in Winchester's opinion of the arrangement wherein he says: "I think this is an excellent proposition and think we should go on with it."

Considerable space has been devoted to *Coe v. Winchester* because this case illustrates several important phases of our subject. In the first place, it proves the old adage that "when a person acts as his own lawyer, he has a fool for a client." Had the partners engaged the services of a competent attorney to draft their agreement, the case probably would never have gone to court. Unambiguous language would have made it clear that Coe was to get the entire business, and having the wives also sign a properly drawn agreement (which is advisable in community property states even though held not necessary in this particular case in which only personal property was involved), would have left Mrs. Winchester with no plausible ground on which to bring suit. In the second place, the facts show that not more than five years' premiums could have been paid on the life insurance. Therefore, the purchase was financed by Coe through insurance premiums at only a small fraction of the price actually paid over to Mrs. Winchester. In the third place, the case shows that enlightened court opinion not only upholds such agreements, but applauds their use.

Lockwood's Trustee v. Lockwood.[5] The facts of this case show that John W. Lockwood and his son, William, conducted the partnership of J.W. Lockwood & Son. On October 30, 1931, when the father was age 67, they entered into a partnership buy-sell agreement, financed by $10,000 of

---

[5]250 Ky. 262, 62 S.W. 2d 1053 (1933).

insurance on each life. On November 9, 1931, only ten days later, the son died. The case came to court because the agreement was poorly worded, two of the clauses being in conflict on the amount that was to be paid to the estate. The court upheld the particular clause that awarded the full amount of insurance in payment of the partnership interest.

The case had three interesting facets that merit our attention. First, the validity of the agreement as such was not questioned. Second, there would have been no dispute had the agreement been properly drawn, a fact which emphasizes that this is a task for a competent and experienced lawyer. Third, the case illustrates again the superiority of the life insurance method of financing such agreements. In the normal course of events, the father would have died first, yet it was the son who died just ten days after the buy-sell agreement had been executed. Only a small amount could have been paid out in premiums; nevertheless, the estate of the deceased received the full purchase price of $10,000. The all-important reason for using the life insurance method of financing is that it guarantees the completion of the plan by making certain that the purchase price is in the hands of the purchaser when it is needed.

It is impossible to avoid the conclusion that life insurance is the most efficient method of financing when it is considered purely from a dollars and cents standpoint. The risk of having to pay the purchase price in a few days or in a few years because of the premature death of a partner is ever present and should be transferred to a life insurance company whose prime economic function is to neutralize such risks by the application of the law of averages to large numbers. John Lockwood and his son acted wisely in doing this.

We now turn to Michigan and to the case of *Ireland v. Lester.*[6] Clyde Ireland and Cleveland J. Lester were partners in the sand and gravel business. In April, 1936, they entered into a buy-sell agreement. The purchase price in the agreement was set at $50,000 and was never changed. It was partially covered by life insurance that was to constitute the initial payment upon death; the remainder was payable at the rate of $1,000 per year. The agreement was prepared by an out-of-town attorney whom "the partners never saw, the data being furnished by the insurance agent." As originally drawn, it was provided that the deceased's estate should receive the money. However, before its execution the partners erased the word "estate" and inserted the word "wife" with respect to the initial payment, but by oversight they did not do so with respect to the subsequent payments. The agreement was signed by the partners and their wives.

Ireland died in December, 1939, without leaving a will, and was survived by his widow and two children by a former marriage. The surviving partner was ready to perform, but the question arose: Who should receive the

_____

[6]298 Mich. 154, 298 N.W. 488 (1941).

money? The widow brought suit to have the instrument reformed to accord with the terms intended by the parties and for an order directing the money to be paid to her. The two children intervened, contending that the contract was invalid as testamentary in character and that the estate was entitled to the value of the partnership interest, in which case they would receive their intestate shares as heirs at law.

Michigan's highest court affirmed the decision in favor of the wife, holding that the contract was not a testamentary in character, but that it was "a bilateral contract consisting of mutual promises to sell or buy, to be determined in the future by an event sure to occur." It was held "a valid and binding agreement, not testamentary in effect," the court declaring that the lower court had jurisdiction to reform it, regardless of whether the money was payable to the estate or the widow, and that there was no reason why the administrator could not carry out the terms of the agreement. The court also pointed out that the widow was a third party beneficiary under the agreement, and that by reason of a special Michigan statute her rights under it had vested at the time it was signed.

In summary, the cases involving partnership buy-sell agreements financed with life insurance have universally upheld these agreements, based upon the earlier authorities, outstanding among which are the *Murphy* and *McKinnon* cases. We have found no case that has held such a contract void by nature. On the contrary, we have seen that the courts are upholding these agreements in spite of inept draftsmanship, which demonstrates their conviction of the inherent legal soundness of the underlying transaction.

COURTS REQUIRE PARTNERSHIP BUY-SELL AGREEMENTS TO BE SPECIFICALLY PERFORMED

From time to time, reference has been made in the text to the fact that the courts grant specific performance of agreements for the purchase and sale of a partnership interest. This was done by the courts, for example, in the leading cases of *Murphy v. Murphy* and *McKinnon v. McKinnon.* Before the matter is discussed further, however, the significance of a decree of specific performance should be made clear. Perhaps this may best be done by contrasting it with the judgment rendered in the ordinary contract action at law.

In the case of the breach of an ordinary contract, the person aggrieved will sue for, and if successful receive, a judgment entitling him to money damages. Because the other party failed to perform his part of the contract, the plaintiff is awarded a sum of money in the amount of the pecuniary loss caused by this lack of performance; and he then must recontract with someone else if he wants to have the contract terms carried out.

In the case of the breach of certain special types of contracts, however, money damages are obviously not an adequate remedy, and in such cases courts of equity will require the parties to carry out what they have agreed to do. In other words, a decree of specific performance is granted. Among these special types of contracts, as we have seen, is the agreement for the purchase and sale of a partnership interest. Money damages would not be just to the surviving partner. He has contracted to buy the deceased partner's interest, and if the particular transaction is not carried through, he must liquidate the business, and with it, his job. Justice can be done him only by requiring the estate of the deceased partner to transfer the deceased's interest in the partnership to the survivor on receipt of the purchase price.

This was the decree in the *Murphy* case, and it was also the decree in the *Lockwood* case and in many others that we have reviewed. But what of the deceased partner's estate? Can the executor or administrator of the deceased partner require the survivor, by court decree if necessary, to carry through his obligation to buy so that the estate may be sure to avoid liquidation losses? The following case shows that the surviving partner may also be made specifically to perform his part of the contract.

Kavanaugh v. Johnson.[7] Thomas J. Kavanaugh and George W. Johnson conducted The Graphic Press, as partners. They entered into an insured buy-sell agreement in which the survivor was obligated to purchase the deceased partner's interest at a valuation based upon an inventory to be made at time of death by three appraisers, but the minimum valuation was further stipulated to be the amount of life insurance on the deceased subject to the agreement. The facts show that insurance was purchased by the partners from time to time. Insurance was last taken out on Kavanaugh in 1931, at which time Johnson was found to be uninsurable and an "income bond" was issued to him. In 1933, no doubt because of adverse business conditions, $9,000 of insurance on each life, all subject to the agreement, was allowed to lapse. Then on January 12, 1934, the insurable partner, Kavanaugh, died. There was $13,266.67 of business insurance in force on his life, $6,008.51 of it being subject to the buy-sell agreement. All of this insurance was made payable to the surviving partner. When an appraisal revealed that the physical assets of the partnership at the time of Kavanaugh's death were $5,273.92 less than the liabilities, the survivor refused to pay over the insurance proceeds on the ground that one-half the net liabilities, or $2,636.96, should be subtracted. The executrix of the deceased partner brought this suit in equity to reach the insurance proceeds.

The court decreed specific performance, ordering the surviving partner to pay $6,008.51, the full amount of life insurance proceeds made subject to the agreement, with interest from the date the inventory had been taken, and ordering the executrix thereupon to release her rights in the partnership.

---

[7] 290 Mass. 587, 195 N.E. 797 (1935).

Thus we see that the estate, as well as the surviving partner, is entitled to have these agreements carried out to the letter. The court followed the general rule that, if the property is such that the court would have given specific performance to the buyer if he had sued for it, the seller may have specific performance. The rule has ample justification in these cases because there is no open market for a deceased partner's interest.

Before leaving *Kavanaugh v. Johnson,* it will be worthwhile to emphasize a few of its interesting aspects. First, it was the insurable partner, Kavanaugh, who died. Furthermore, his death occurred only three years after he was last insured, and less than a year after $9,000 of insurance on his life had been allowed to lapse. The insurance obviously showed considerable profit, but it was unfortunate that some insurance had to be dropped only a few months before Kavanaugh's death. Second, in view of the settled state of the law in Massachusetts, few words were written by the court regarding the validity of the agreement. The opinion merely stated on this point:

> It is apparent that one of the main objectives of the agreement was to provide a method for the disposition of the interest of a deceased partner without disrupting the business as a going concern. Such an agreement when not made with intent to evade the statute of will is valid.

Third, the agreement should have stated that the survivor was to assume the partnership debts upon the purchase. This omission in all probability brought the case to court. On this point the opinion reads:

> In the light of all the facts the plaintiff should receive under clause 4 the full amount obtained by the defendant on the policies covered by the agreement, without deduction for debts. The principle that in the absence of agreement partners share losses equally, *Lavoine v. Casey,* 251 Mass. 124, 127, 146 N.E. 241, is overcome by the principle that where one partner takes all the assets and continues the business only slight evidence is necessary to warrant the inference that the partner also assumed the debts of the firm, *Shaw v. McGregory,* 105 Mass. 96, 102. This construction is supported by the uncontradicted evidence that the policies and "income bond" of 1929 and 1931, which were not within the terms of the agreement, were taken out for the purpose of providing the surviving partner with cash to pay the debts and carry on the business, because in all probability there would be a good many debts and the partners felt that "whoever survived would need the cash to pay those debts and go on with the business as survivor."

Fourth—and we repeat for emphasis—the decision shows that the courts will grant specific performance to the deceased partner's estate if there is the ability to perform on the part of the survivor, in other words, if he is able to pay. It is a rule in equity never to make a futile decree, but it is submitted that if there are life insurance proceeds in the amount of the purchase price in the hands of the surviving partner, or better still, in the hands of a trustee, with which to carry out a buy-sell agreement, such agreement when brought to court will be ordered performed to the letter. In short, a properly executed agreement for the purchase and sale of a partnership interest, financed with life insurance, definitely assures the continuance of the partnership business.

Before leaving the subject of specific performance, we should emphasize that resort to litigation is rarely required where the agreement is carefully set up. Of the cases reviewed here, two involved agreements that were open invitations to court actions. In *Coe v. Winchester,* the partners not only used the more frequently challenged survivorship type of agreement, but acted as their own lawyers as well. In *Ireland v. Lester,* the partners attempted to revise their agreement at the last moment and in only half doing so, compelled a suit for reformation. The remaining cases, *Lockwood's Trustee v. Lockwood* and *Kavanaugh v. Johnson,* were taken into court mainly because controversies arose over the meaning of the respective valuation clauses, undoubtedly the most important part of such an agreement and demanding the greatest skill in draftsmanship. The *Kavanaugh* case also demonstrates the likelihood of a court contest when there is a gross difference between the value of a deceased partner's interest and the purchase price to be paid for it. In that case, the purchase price strongly favored the widow.

In *More v. Carnes,*[8] the converse was true. That case involved an insured survivorship agreement under which on a partner's death the survivor would automatically become the owner of the business and the insurance on the deceased partner's life would be paid to his wife as beneficiary. Because the appraised value of the deceased partner's interest was more than double the value of the insurance proceeds, the widow challenged the validity of the agreement. The court expressed regret over the resulting inequity, but held the agreement valid and enforceable. These comprise most of the available top court cases of this type, and the ultimate decision in each instance enforced the agreement in the manner the parties had intended when it was made.

---

[8] 309 Ky. 41, 214 S.W.2d 984 (1948).

Chapter 8

SPECIFIC BENEFITS OF THE
BUY-SELL AGREEMENT
WITH LIFE INSURANCE

Interspersed throughout the text have been discussions and examples that have revealed the advantages to be derived from an insurance-financed agreement between partners for the purchase by the survivors of the deceased partner's interest. For convenient reference, we shall devote this chapter to a recital of these advantages.

BENEFITS TO THE SURVIVING PARTNERS

Survivors' business future assured. The insured buy-sell agreement, by replacing the ordinary course of the law on the death of a partner, which would require prompt liquidation of the partnership affairs, assures the continuation of the partnership business without interruption or loss of momentum, because the continuation plan includes provisions that will effect the purchase of the deceased partner's interest immediately, with the greatest smoothness and dispatch. The agreement to buy and sell has been set up previously, the price has been agreed upon in advance, and the purchase money with which to consummate the transaction is at hand. Nothing has been left over which to bargain or dicker. Consequently, the survivors take over the business as a running machine, with equipment, employee organization, customers and good will all intact; and they may go forward with their daily routine and future plans as entire owners of the business, free and clear of any debt to the deceased partner's estate. Their future business careers have been assured.

Survivors avoid liquidating losses. The liquidation of a going business invariably results in substantial pecuniary losses, outstanding among which is usually total loss of good will. The insured buy-sell agreement, providing for the uninterrupted and undisturbed continuation of the business by the surviving partners, completely by-passes these losses in business equities that often have been built up by years of hard work.

Survivors avoid becoming liquidating trustees. Without a buy-sell arrangement, the surviving partners, on the death of an associate, become liquidating trustees of the partnership property and affairs. As such, they are held to the highest standards of conduct, and to the strictest accountability for every asset of the partnership in closing out the business. That this fiduciary status is burdensome and often costly has been amply demonstrated again and again by the cases examined. With a binding buy-sell agreement all this is avoided; a fiduciary relationship between the surviving partners and the deceased's estate is never established.

If further proof is needed that such an agreement prevents this onerous fiduciary relationship between the survivors and the deceased's estate or heirs from arising, it may be found in *Hermes v. Compton*,[1] from which opinion the following self-explanatory quotation is taken:

> That there was a complete severance of the relationship of trust and confidence that existed prior to the death of Hermes is also clear, because the agreement further provides that nothing contained therein "shall be so construed as to constitute as a partner the estate of any deceased partner." In other words, Hermes' death effected not only a termination of the relationship of confidence and trust which theretofore existed, but also a sale to the surviving partners of his interest in the partnership assets. While after Hermes' death his estate was interested in the profits because the consideration of the sale was to be determined by the net income, it had no proprietary interest in the business or the profits. Hence, plaintiff has an adequate remedy at law and is not entitled to an accounting.

Thus, instead of being trustees, the surviving partners with a buy-sell agreement occupy the status of purchasers bound by a contract previously entered into, dealing with sellers also previously bound by the contract with respect to all the terms of the transaction. If the contract is properly drawn, no difficulty whatever should be encountered. No one can examine the host of court cases dealing with the fiduciary relationship—many of them are contests arising years after the death of a partner and all placing the burden

---

[1] 260 App. Div. 507, 1027 (New York, 1940).

of proof of good faith and irreproachable conduct on the surviving partners—without being convinced that the survivors under a modern insured buy-sell agreement are indeed in a fortunate position.

Courts will enforce carrying out of purchase contract, if necessary. Because the future business careers of the surviving partners are tied up with the buy-sell arrangement, it is vitally important to them that the plan be carried through on the death of a partner. They cannot afford, therefore, to rely on any plan for the continuance of the firm's business that the courts will not specifically enforce if necessary. As we have seen, the insured buy-sell agreement will be specifically enforced by the courts according to its terms.

BENEFITS TO THE DECEASED PARTNER'S ESTATE AND HEIRS

Estate receives payment in full, in cash, at once. The functioning of the *fully insured* buy-sell agreement places in the hands of the executor or administrator of the deceased partner the full amount of the sale price of the decedent's interest in the firm, in cash, at once. There is no basis for acrimonious bickering and bargaining between the personal representative, usually the widow, and the surviving partners. Furthermore, by provision to that effect in the agreement, the amount of the proceeds may be set as a minimum price, thereby guaranteeing such striking contrast with the certainty that losses will be suffered through forced liquidation and the uncertainty of the amount that will finally be received in the absence of a purchase agreement.

Deceased's estate can be settled promptly and efficiently. If there is no purchase agreement effective after the death of a partner, the survivors are required to wind up the partnership with reasonable dispatch; but the process necessarily consumes considerable time—more than it will usually take the personal representative of the decedent to administer the decedent's personal estate. But the personal representative, among other important duties, cannot complete this estate and inheritance tax schedules until he knows the liquidated value of the decedent's share in the firm, nor is it usually possible for him to ascertain the respective amounts that are to go to various legatees. Therefore, in the normal course of settling the affairs of a deceased partner, the executor or administrator will find it necessary to hold open the estate until the partnership has been closed out and the share of the deceased partner has been received from the surviving liquidating partners, which delays the accounting and settling of the entire estate. This delay is eliminated by the insured buy-sell arrangement, by means of which the executor or administrator promptly receives the value of the decedent's business interest in cash.

The executor has need for a substantial amount of cash with which to pay final expenses, outstanding bills, taxes, fees, and other probate costs.

Furthermore, ready cash frequently enables him to take advantage of discounts offered for prompt payment of bills and taxes. To obtain the required cash, the forced sale of valuable estate assets at a sacrifice is often necessary. An insured purchase agreement eliminates any such loss, and since cash is immediately available, discounts may be saved.

In the ordinary course of liquidating a partnership on the death of a partner, a formal accounting procedure is called for between the surviving partners and the personal representative of the deceased. An insured buy-sell agreement eliminates this time-consuming, costly, and often irritating procedure.

Where the agreement is properly set up—as discussed later—the purchase price will establish the value of the deceased partner's interest for Federal estate tax purposes. Because in the absence of such an agreement small businesses tend to be overvalued for such purposes, this benefit alone may save thousands of dollars in taxes.

In short, with ample cash immediately available from the buy-sell agreement and with delays, uncertainties and costly procedures eliminated, the personal representative can carry out a prompt, efficient and economical administration of the deceased's estate.

The widow is relieved of business worries. Many different plans not making use of insurance financing and under which the welfare of the widow has been made dependent upon the future success of the surviving partners over a period of years, have been set up as an alternative to liquidation. *Hermes v. Compton* is typical of such arrangements. The agreement in that case fixed the purchase price as a percentage of profits in excess of a stated sum to be earned by the surviving partners for the five years subsequent to death. Profits of the survivors were large the first year following Herme's death, and his widow received a substantial payment; then the senior surviving partner retired, profits fell below the stated sum, and payments were discontinued. The widow brought suit for an accounting, which suit was defeated in equity because of the agreement. The widow continued the litigation as an action at law, but here too, lost the decision. An insured buy-sell agreement would have furnished the purchase price "on the barrel head," and the widow would have been relieved of the worries and losses consequent upon the provisions made in that case.

Under an insured buy-sell agreement, the widow is entirely free from any future responsibilities in connection with the partnership. The estate receives payment in cash, which may be invested in the highest type of securities for her benefit. This is as it should be; for a widow to keep her money in a small business, no matter how successful its past record may be, is hazardous.

BENEFITS DURING THE LIFETIME OF
THE PARTNERS

The partnership business if profitably stabilized. With an insured buy-sell agreement, the future of the partnership business is assured. This fact has several important and valuable consequences of immediate benefit to the partners. The partners and their customers or clients, knowing that the business of the firm will continue in spite of the death of one of the members, are at liberty to enter into more permanent and farsighted dealings that will tend to stabilize the business on a more profitable basis. Employees, knowing that the continuance of the business has been assured, and with it, their jobs, are welded into a more stable and efficient organization. The firm's bankers—knowing that the business will not be interrupted on the death of a partner; that the purchase price of a deceased partner's interest will be forthcoming automatically at the needed time from an outside source, the insurance company, without draining one cent from the business treasury; that the partners each year are building larger cash values in their business insurance policies; and that the firm's business and organization has been stabilized by the arrangement—will extend a more favorable line of credit over the years. All of these beneficial business factors, taken together, spell out more profits for the firm during the lifetime of all the partners.

An attractive saving medium is provided. The insured buy-sell arrangement is in effect an advance installment method of purchasing the interest of a deceased partner. Each premium paid on the insurance under such an arrangement represents a current saving for future benefit. As a savings plan, it has many attractive features. Obviously most important is the fact that the accumulation program is automatically completed for the full amount needed on the death of the insured, no matter how little has been put in by way of premium payments. Among other desirable characteristics, the amount to be saved each year is convenient in size, is made regularly and has an element of compulsion, without which few savings projects are ever carried through to completion. After a few years, the policies contain guaranteed cash values, which receive the highest degree of legal protection in most states, and which are available at once should a real financial emergency arise. In other words, it is a convenient, effective savings program focused directly on an objective vitally important to all the partners, assuring them that the money required to buy out the business interest of a deceased partner will be fully saved when needed.

The future of the partners is made predictable. An insured buy-sell agreement enables each partner to predict what will take place in the event of the death of any partner. If fate decrees that he become the surviving partner, he knows that he will be the owner of the business, paid for in full. On the other hand, he knows that if he should die first, his estate will at once receive the full value of the share of the business in cash. Each partner, therefore, can freely give his best efforts to the promotion of the partnership affairs, secure in the knowledge that if he lives his career will be kept open and his property ownership enhanced; and that, if he does not survive his associates, the value of his estate will be enhanced by his hard work. Each partner, also, knowing that if he dies first his estate will have the cash benefit of a specified amount, is thereby enabled to plan his estate in an orderly manner for the support and welfare of his family. Contrast this picture with that of partners without a purchase plan, faced with the prospect of sudden termination of the business, trustee responsibilities, unknown liquidation losses, loss of careers, unknown estate values for the support of dependents, bickering and dissension between widow and survivors; and the conclusion is obvious that the partners, while all are yet living, derive substantial benefits from an insured buy-sell arrangement.

Chapter 9

SELECTING TYPE
OF AGREEMENT

The two basic types of agreements. A partnership buy-sell agreement with life insurance may take either of two available forms: a cross-purchase agreement, or a so-called entity agreement.

A cross-purchase agreement is most commonly used in small commercial partnerships. It is an agreement whereby the partners individually agree to purchase the interest in the firm of a deceased partner. Customarily, each partner owns insurance on the life of the other partners in an amount approximating his share of the purchase price should one of the other partners predecease him. The partnership is not a party to such an agreement.

In the case of a partnership composed of several partners, who desire to continue the partnership regardless of deaths occurring among their number, the use of an entity type of agreement has become increasingly popular. The partnership itself is a party to such an agreement, along with the partners. The agreement provides for the uninterrupted continuation of the partnership upon the death of a partner and the purchase or liquidation of his interest for the account of the survivors from the partnership funds, furnished in whole or in part for this purpose by insurance on the lives of all partners. The policies are owned by, paid for by, and payable to, the partnership.

FACTORS DETERMINING CHOICE OF AGREEMENT

Equity of results. In the case of a cross-purchase agreement, the insurance usually is arranged on the cross-purchase plan. Each partner agrees that upon

192

the death of a co-partner he will purchase a proportionate part of the deceased partner's interest at a price based upon its agreed value pursuant to the agreement, and each partner purchases and maintains insurance on the lives of the others in the approximate amount of purchase price he will be called upon to pay when a co-partner dies. Under this plan, the insurance is owned personally and does not enter into the purchase price. Assuming that the price set represents true value, the cross-purchase agreement functions with complete equity among the partners—regardless of the variations in their ages or in their respective interests in the firm.

In the case of an entity purchase agreement, the payment of the premiums by the partnership is the same mathematically as if each partner had paid that portion of the premiums which is proportionate to his fractional interest in the firm. As contrasted with the arrangement under a cross-purchase agreement, however, none of the insurance is owned by a deceased partner's estate as recompense for his portion of the premiums that have been paid by the partnership. Thus an entity agreement will not function equitably among the partners unless the purchase price paid to a deceased partner's estate takes into consideration the life insurance owned by the partnership to the extent of his fractional interest in the firm. Partial equity is obtained if the purchase price takes into consideration his share of the value of all the policies immediately before a death occurs. Substantially complete equity results if his share of the proceeds of the insurance on his own life is also taken into consideration. If the entity plan is to achieve this result and at the same time have the purchase price fully insured, however, additional amounts of insurance will be required.

Number of partners. In the case of partnerships composed of only two partners, cross-purchase agreements are used most frequently. The arrangement is free from estate tax complications. By reason of the fact that each partner pays the correct cost of his benefits under the agreement, complete equity is attained.

In the case of partnerships composed of more than two partners, however, the plan whereby each partner maintains insurance on the life of each other partner becomes less convenient as the number of partners increases. With three partners, the arrangement under a cross-purchase agreement whereby each owns and maintains policies on the lives of the others—a total of six policies in all—is only slightly less convenient than is the case with the partnership owning and maintaining three policies under an entity type of agreement. But where there are nine partners, for example, there would be seventy-two policies under the usual cross-purchase agreement, compared with only nine policies under an entity type of agreement. In such a case the cross-purchase agreement could be insured with only nine policies: one on the life of each partner, with the other eight partners joint premium payers and joint and survivor owners. But the difficulties that might be encountered in the form of future adjustments and complications where there are so many joint owners and premium payers makes such a plan impracticable. Hence one must conclude that where there are a substantial number of partners, the entity plan, under which the partnership pays the premiums and owns a small number of policies, is simpler in operation than a cross-purchase plan, under which each of several partners owns and maintains a cluster of policies.

Ages and fractional interests of the partners. Where a partnership is composed of only a few partners who do not differ greatly in age or in respective fractional interests owned in the firm, these factors are neutral so far as choice of plan is concerned. Under either type of agreement, the financial load of premium payments is distributed in approximately the same proportion although in a different manner. But where there are large differences in the respective ages of the partners or in their respective fractional interests in the firm, these factors may favor an entity agreement. In such a firm, the younger partners customarily own the smaller interests, with the result that they may be unwilling or unable to pay the premiums required to maintain the insurance on the older partners with the larger interests in the firm. The indirect premium load under an entity type of agreement, on the other hand, rests largely upon the partners who are older and who own the larger interests. Thus the premium load is distributed according to ability to carry it. As previously noted, the plan will work out equitably provided the purchase price under the entity agreement takes into consideration the deceased partner's share of the insurance values when a death occurs.

Status of insurance in relation to partnership. Under a cross-purchase agreement, the insurance is owned personally by each respective partner. Under an entity type agreement, the policies and proceeds are partnership assets. The increasing cash values continuously contribute to the building up of the financial worth of the partnership—whereas the insurance policies personally owned under a cross-purchase agreement build up the personal assets of the individual policy owners. The value of the policies owned by the partnership under an entity agreement will strengthen the financial statement of the firm, a result which the partners may desire. But such policies are at all times subject to the claims of the partnership creditors. Hence difficulties may be encountered in carrying out the entity agreement when a death occurs, unless the firm has ample funds, aside from the insurance proceeds collected at that time, to satisfy its creditors. In this connection, however, it is well to recall the fact that general partners have unlimited liability for partnership obligations.

Ratio of partnership interests desired among surviving partners. When a partnership liquidates a deceased partner's interest under an entity agreement, the surviving partners will share the ownership of the firm in the same ratio that their respective interests bore to one another prior to the death. If this ratio is not satisfactory, they will have to realign their interests by means of a supplementary purchase and sale transaction among themselves. The provisions of a cross-purchase agreement, on the other hand, may specify that each survivor will buy whatever proportion of a deceased partner's interest is set forth therein—regardless of their current proportionate interests.

Federal estate tax factor. Where the insurance acquired to finance a cross-purchase agreement is arranged so that an insured will not possess any incidents of ownership in the policies on his own life, the value of the proceeds will not be subject to Federal estate tax. Subject to the tax, however, will be the value of the policies the deceased partner owned on the lives of the survivors and the value of the deceased's partnership interest. If the agreement is drawn and set up properly, the value of that interest will be its purchase price in the agreement—as is brought out later in Chapter 14.

Where the insurance is owned by the partnership to finance an entity agreement, it appears that the value of the insurance on the life of a deceased partner will not be includible *as insurance* in his gross estate. In valuing the deceased partner's interest the proceeds of the insurance on his life and his proportionate share of the value of the policies on the lives of the surviving partners, being partnership assets, will be taken into consideration. The only exception would be where the purchase price has not taken into consideration the insurance values and the purchase price is held to establish the value of the deceased's partnership interest for Federal estate tax purposes. The discussion in Chapter 14, will show that there is no case or ruling directly on these facts.

Income tax status of payments. The sale of an interest in a partnership under a cross-purchase agreement is treated as the sale of a capital asset, except as to payments received from the surviving partners for the seller's interest in the firm attributable (on the basis of relative fair market values) to unrealized receivables and to inventory items that have appreciated substantially in value. Unrealized receivables are uncommon in the case of a commercial partnership reporting its income on an accrual basis. They are typical of a personal service partnership reporting on a cash basis, such as a law firm.[1] Where substantially appreciated inventory items exist, they are usually possessed by a commercial partnership. Such items are defined broadly and are considered to have appreciated substantially in value if their fair market value exceeds 120 percent of their adjusted basis to the partnership and exceeds 10 percent of the fair market value of all partnership property except money. Payments received that are attributable to unrealized receivables and to substantially appreciated inventory items are deemed

---

[1]See discussion of professional partnerships in Chapter 13 *infra*.

amounts realized from the sale of property other than capital asset, with the result that any consequent gain or loss is ordinary income or loss.[2]

In the case of a cross-purchase agreement, this ordinary income or loss is computed first. In determining the amount, "a portion of such partner's adjusted basis for his interest in the partnership must be allocated, under regulations, to his share of unrealized receivables or substantially appreciated inventory items. The amount of basis to be so allocated shall ordinarily be his pro rata share of the partnership basis for such property with appropriate adjustments for any transferee basis with respect to him under section 743(b). This amount shall be subtracted from the basis of such partner's interest before computing his capital gain or loss on the sale of his interest under section 741."[3]

To delineate further the income tax consequences to a deceased partner's estate under a cross-purchase agreement, something must be said about the basis of a deceased partner's interest. In general, such interest is considered a capital asset. It takes a new basis at the partner's death consisting of its fair market value for Federal estate tax purposes, increased by the estate's share of partnership liabilities and reduced by the value of its share of items constituting income in respect of a decedent.[4] The *Quick* and *Woodhall* cases upheld such reduction in basis of the deceased partner's interest, holding that payments for his share of the firm's unrealized receivables constituted income in respect of a decedent. This result was held to follow even though the partnership had elected under Code Sections 743 and 754 to adjust the basis of its assets upon the partner's death. Thus, the income tax result to a deceased partner's estate under a cross-purchase agreement, where the firm possesses unrealized receivables, usually will be little or no capital gain or loss, but ordinary income to the extent payment are received for the decedent's interest in unrealized receivables. Where the partnership does not possess unrealized receivables, the purchase price paid for the decedent's interest under a cross-purchase agreement should result in little or no capital gain or loss, and no ordinary income.

Payments made by a partnership under an entity agreement receive somewhat different tax treatment. First, payments are allocated, on the basis of relative fair market value, between payments in exchange for the deceased's partnership interest and other payments. Payments in exchange for the partnership interest do not include amounts paid for the deceased's proportionate share of unrealized receivables, and do not include amounts paid for good will except to the extent the agreement provides *specifically* for

---

[2]I.R.C., Secs. 741, 751.

[3]83d Cong., 2d Sess., S. Rep. No. 1622, p. 401.

[4]I.R.C., Secs. 742, 1014(c); Reg. Sec. 1.742-1; *Quick's Trust v. Commissioner,* 444 F.2d 90; *Woodhall v. Commissioner,* 454 F. 2d 226 (1972).

reasonable payments with respect to good will. Payments in exchange for the partnership interest do include payments attributable to inventory items that have appreciated substantially in value, but are considered amounts paid for property other than a capital asset. First, an amount of the basis of the partnership interest being liquidated equal to the partner's share of the partnership basis for its substantially appreciated inventory items, with appropriate adjustments for any transferee basis with respect to him under section 743(b), is allocated to his share of such items, and ordinary income results to the extent that his share of the fair market value of such items exceeds this allocated basis.[5] The remainder of the basis of the partnership interest is measured against the value of the liquidated partner's portion of the capital assets of the firm, including good will if payments for it are specified in the agreement, to ascertain the capital gain or loss on the liquidation of such interest.[6] Any other payments received, including amounts received for unrealized receivables and unspecified good will, are usually ordinary income to the estate and are classed as income in respect of a decedent. However, if any of these payments are determined with regard to the income of the partnership they are treated as a distributive share of the partnership income and retain their character as ordinary income or capital gain, as the case may be.

It should be emphasized that under an entity agreement there is tax flexibility with respect to any payments for good will. If the agreement specifies that a reasonable amount is to be paid for the deceased partner's share of existing good will of the firm, such payments constitute part of the payments for the deceased partner's interest. As such, they get capital gains treatment in the hands of the recipient (usually resulting in no gain or loss) and are not deductible by the partnership. If the agreement does not specify payments for good will, any payments actually made for it are not considered paid on account of his partnership interest but are classed as other payments made which are deductible by the partnership and income to the recipient.[7]

Closing of taxable year. When a partner dies, the partnership taxable year closes with respect to him at the end of the normal partnership taxable year, or at the time when such partner's interest is sold or completely liquidated, whichever is earlier. The last return of the deceased partner includes his share of partnership taxable income for the partnership taxable year or years ending within or with the last taxable year of such partner. For example, assume that the partners report on the calendar year basis and the partnership has a taxable year ending June 30. One of the partners dies on October 31,

---

[5] 83d Cong., 2d Sess., Conf. Rep. No. 2543, pp. 62, 65.

[6] I.R.C., Secs. 736(b), 751(b)(1)(B); 83d Cong., 2d Sess., S. Rep. 1622, p. 404.

[7] *Smith v. Commissioner* 313 F.2d 16 (1962).

and under a cross-purchase agreement his interest is purchased as of that date. The taxable year of the partnership beginning the previous July 1 closes with respect to the deceased partner and his final return will include his distributive share of taxable income of the partnership for its taxable year ending the previous June 30, plus his share of the partnership taxable income for the period July 1 to October 31.

Where both the partnership and the partners report on the calendar year basis, the final return of a partner dying on October 31, and whose partnership interest was purchased as of that date, would include his distributive share for the period of ten months in the year of death. On the other hand, if such partner's interest was sold after the date of death, or was liquidated with payments from the partnership after such date, none of his distributive share for the year of death would be included in his final return even though he might have withdrawn the funds. Not only would the estate have to pay the tax on such income without having received the funds, it would not have the advantage of deductions that might have been taken in the decedent's final return. This points up one disadvantage of an entity agreement under present tax provisions, as compared with a cross-purchase agreement effective at date of death, where the partners and the partnership use the same taxable year. Conversely, the advantage is the other way and prevents bunching of income in the decedent's final return, where different taxable years are used.

Income tax bases of the surviving partners. Upon the purchase of a deceased partner's interest under a cross-purchase agreement, the basis of the partnership interest of each surviving partner is increased by the amount he has paid to purchase a portion of the deceased partner's interest. In such amount is included an amount representing the proceeds of the insurance he has collected on the life of the deceased partner.

The effect of the workings of an entity agreement upon the bases of the interests of the partners is somewhat complex. The policies are owned by the partnership and payable to it. Ordinarily, the partnership will pay the premiums out of partnership income, charge off as expense that portion of the premiums not reflected in an increase in cash values, and carry the cash values as an asset. The portion of premiums thus charged off is a nondeductible expense, and as such does not reduce the distributive income of the partnership nor the taxable incomes of the partners. Nevertheless, such expense paid by the partnership reduces the bases of the partners' interests to the extent allocated to each. The net result is that the payment of premiums by the partnership, as contrasted with the withdrawal of a like amount of distributive income by the partners, increases the respective basis of each partner's interest by his share of the increase in cash values each year.

The insurance proceeds received by the partnership upon the death of a partner are excluded from its gross income. But it appears that the excess of the death proceeds over the cash value of the policy as carried on the partnership books increases the bases of the partnership interests of the partners.[8]

To sum up the effect under an entity agreement, the interest of the deceased partner (as always) gets a new basis at his death. But the basis of the partnership interest of each surviving partner should reflect his attributable portion of the cash values of all the policies owned by the partnership, plus his attributable portion of the nontaxable income of the partnership represented by the insurance proceeds collected on the life of the deceased partner. It may be that a provision allocating all of such nontaxable income to the capital accounts of the surviving partners will hold for basis purposes. Lacking that, however, a portion will represent the deceased partner's share. Therefore, amounts with respect to the insurance on the life of the deceased partner totalling less than the insurance proceeds will go to increase the bases of the surviving partners' interests.

Cost basis of partnership assets acquired from deceased partner. The cost basis of the deceased partner's share in the property of the partnership acquired by the surviving partners under a cross-purchase agreement should be the purchase price the survivors have paid for it, provided they have elected under Code Section 754 to adjust basis. This will undoubtedly be the case if the surviving partners have been designated beneficiaries of the insurance proceeds used to finance the agreement. The insurance proceeds, together with any remainder of the purchase price paid, should also constitute the cost basis of the acquired property if the insurance proceeds are received by a trustee and paid over by it to the deceased partner's legal representative in return for a transfer of the deceased's interest in the firm, provided the election under Section 754 to adjust basis is made.

On the other hand, if the insurance proceeds are made payable directly to the insured partner's estate or to his personal beneficiaries, there is grave doubt that such proceeds may be included in the cost basis of the property acquired from the deceased partner.[9] The arrangements that appear to raise no doubt that the insurance proceeds will be reflected in the cost basis of the partnership property of the surviving partners, provided election under Section 754 is made, are those under which the survivors paid the premiums and under which they, or a trustee acting for them, have been the policyowners and beneficiaries of the deceased partner's insurance and have made the payments to the estate.

The proper functioning of an entity agreement under the tax law requires that the payments in liquidation of the deceased partner's interest be made

---

[8] I.R.C., Section 705(a)(1)(B).

[9] *Paul Legallet,* 41 B.T.A. 294; *cf. Victor G. Mushro,* 50 T.C. 43 (1968), nonacquiescence (1970). See discussion of these cases in Chapter 11.

by the partnership itself.[10] These payments will have no effect on the basis of the partnership assets, however, unless the election to adjust bases of such assets is made under Section 754.

Thus, partners have a substantial number of important factors to be considered in making their choice between an individual cross-purchase agreement and a partnership entity agreement.

---

[10]*Karan v. Commissioner*, 319 F.2d 303.

Chapter 10

CONTENTS OF THE
BUY-SELL AGREEMENT
WITH LIFE INSURANCE

Introductory. Agreement must be drawn by a competent attorney. A written buy-sell agreement that includes provisions for life insurance financing is the basic legal medium used to assure uninterrupted continuation of the business of a partnership by the survivors, following the death of an associate. The agreement can be incorporated in the Articles of Partnership, but rather than add to the cumbersomeness of the Articles, the established practice is to execute a separate contract. The contract may take either of two forms: a cross-purchase agreement in which the individual partners are the parties, or a so-called entity agreement in which the partnership itself is also a party.

With the surviving partners depending upon their agreement for acquisition of full ownership of the enterprise instead of having to liquidate their business and jobs, and with the deceased's estate and heirs relying upon it for prompt payment in cash of the full value of the deceased's interest in the firm instead of the shrunken, forced-sale value of his share, this document is obviously one of the most important contracts the partners will ever execute. Because of this, a competent attorney should be engaged to draft the instrument.

BROAD PATTERN OF THE AGREEMENT

The growing realization that the insured business continuation plan is the only method by which the partners can make certain that their objectives will be carried out has brought about the adoption of this arrangement by literally thousands of firms. And this, in turn, has brought about a modicum of standardization in the forms of agreements used. Furthermore, every agreement of this type, because it deals with like subject matter, must of necessity follow a similar broad pattern with which life underwriters must be familiar if they are to render intelligent and profitable service to partners. This broad pattern consists of the essentials that the insured buy-sell agreement must accomplish. They may be itemized as follows:

1. A definite commitment on the part of each partner that he will not dispose of his interest in the partnership during his lifetime without first offering it for sale to the other partners at the contract price.

2. A definite commitment, not merely an option, on the part of all the partners in which they agree, binding their estates, that the surviving partners (or the partnership, in case of an entity agreement) will buy, and that the deceased partner's estate will sell and transfer to the survivors (or the partnership), the partnership interest of a deceased partner.

3. A definite commitment as to the purchase price to be paid by the surviving partners (or partnership) for the deceased partner's interest.

4. A definite commitment by the partners (or partnership) to purchase and maintain under the agreement life insurance policies in an agreed amount with which to finance the purchase, the proceeds of which policies are to constitute purchase-price money for the partnership interest when it is received by the deceased partner's estate.

5. A definite commitment as to the ownership and control of the life insurance policies made subject to the agreement and as to the disposal of policies on the lives of surviving partners.

6. A definite commitment with respect to the time and manner of paying any balance of the purchase price in excess of the insurance proceeds, and conversely, with respect to the disposition of any insurance proceeds in excess of the purchase price.

7. A definite commitment that the surviving partners will assume all obligations of the partnership and will save harmless and indemnify the deceased partner's estate therefrom.

CONTENTS OF THE AGREEMENT

Introductory. Since no two partnerships are exactly alike, no two insured buy-sell agreements can be identical in form and content. The provisions of each such contract must be individually "fitted" by the attorney to the circumstances of each particular case. This "fitting" is made possible because various alternative methods are available to provide for such matters as, for example, establishing the purchase price, designating the life insurance beneficiaries, and allocating premium payments. Nevertheless, since all agreements must deal with the same subject matter, that is, the buying and selling of a deceased partner's interest and the use of life insurance to supply the purchase money, the general structure and contents of such agreements are sufficiently delimited to make a somewhat detailed analysis practicable. Life underwriters should be reasonably familiar with the general provisions usually contained in them, and should be cognizant of the various alternative arrangements available. Accordingly, an inexhaustive topical analysis will be made of the principal provisions that are usually contained in a standard agreement, without, however, considering the technical legal wording to be used in setting out these provisions in the finished document, since that is the peculiar province of the drafting attorney.

The parties to the agreement. Preferably, all the partners, together with a trustee selected by them, are the parties to a cross-purchase agreement. The partners, being the buyers and sellers, are necessary parties. The trustee is not a necessary party, but is recommended as an impartial "third party," to act as custodian and beneficiary of the life insurance policies during the lifetime of the partners, and, when a death occurs, to supervise the consummation of the transaction. In the case of an entity type of agreement, the partnership itself is a party along with the partners. A trustee is seldom a party, but may be desirable as an additional party in some instances.

In community property states, it is advisable, although held not necessary in Arizona under the facts present in *Coe v. Winchester*,[1] to include the wives of the partners as parties.

The purpose of the agreement. The preamble of a well-drawn agreement contains a recital of the purpose of the agreement. It should state that the partners desire to create a ready market for the interest of a deceased partner, and that the survivors desire to acquire such interest in order to be able to continue the business without the necessity for liquidation and an accounting. This preamble serves the purpose of clarifying the intention of the parties and might play an important role should ambiguities creep in elsewhere in the agreement.

The "first offer" commitment. In those instances in which any of the partners owns sufficient property to call for the payment of estate taxes upon his death, the agreement should contain a clause requiring any partner who retires to offer his interest in the firm for sale to the partnership or the other partners at the same price that governs a purchase in the event of a partner's death, before he can make any other disposition of it. Such a provision seems to be required if the price is to be binding on death as to valuation of the partnership interest in a deceased's estate under the Federal estate tax law.[2]

The commitment to sell and to buy. A cross-purchase agreement should set out in unequivocal language that each partner, binding his heirs, personal

[1]See page 177 et seq.
[2]See the *Hoffman* case, discussed at page 387 et seq.

representatives and assigns, agrees to sell to the surviving partners, and that the surviving partners agree to purchase all right, title and interest which the deceased partner may have in the partnership at the time of his death. Where the agreement is of the entity type, the partners commit their estates to sell their interests to the partnership, and the partnership agrees to buy a deceased partner's interest for the accounts of the survivors.

The agreement should also show the present share of ownership each partner's interest represents, and if more than two partners are involved in a cross-purchase agreement it should clearly designate the portion of a deceased's interest that each survivor is to acquire.

The price to be paid, and valuation formula, if used. The purchase price to be paid for a deceased partner's interest must either be stated in the agreement in dollars and cents, or the agreement must set out a crystal clear valuation formula or procedure to be used at time of death to determine the price. A cross-purchase agreement should further state that the proceeds of any life insurance made subject to it are not to be included in setting the value of a deceased's interest. An entity agreement, on the other hand, should directly or indirectly take into consideration the insurance values if it is to arrive at an equitable price.

If the purchase price is a stated amount, the agreement hould also provide that the parties may revise the stated figure annually or more often by endorsing the revised purchase price upon the contract. This method has several distinct advantages. First, it cannot be misunderstood. Second, each partner knows at all times the exact amount his estate will receive for the sale of his business interest in the event of his death, and can plan his estate and for the welfare of his dependents with an accuracy not otherwise possible. Third, knowing in advance the amount to be paid, the partners, by maintaining a like amount of insurance directly or through the partnership, may keep the purchase price fully insured, and in this way eliminate any necessity for supplementary payments. In short, a stated purchase price simplifies and makes definite the whole arrangement.

Against the advantages of a fixed-dollar price stand some disadvantages. One of these is that the partners may neglect to keep the figure current. If the partners are satisfied with the stated price, however, the efficacy of the agreement will not be impaired unless the amount is so inadequate at death as to work a fraud on creditors of the estate. Thus, we saw an agreement with a stated but inadequate price specifically enforced in *More v. Carnes*.[3] And a partner's refusal to negotiate in good faith the revision of a stated price, in accordance with the terms of the buy-sell agreement, would justify a court in abrogating the entire agreement[4] because the partners are obligated to deal

[3] 309 Ky. 41, 214 S.W.2d 984 (1948).

[4] *Helms v. Duckworth* 249 F.2d 482; *Duckworth v. Helms,* 268 F.2d 584.

with each other in utmost good faith and fairness. A critical disadvantage, however, is that a fixed-dollar price fails to reflect the fluctuations in the partners' capital and income accounts resulting from withdrawals and contributions. This disadvantage may be largely overcome by providing that the stated price be adjusted for changes in the deceased partner's capital and income accounts that have taken place since the date was last agreed upon.

Many agreements use as the purchase price the actual book value of the deceased's interest at time of death. While this method looks satisfactory at first glance, it has serious defects. First, the courts do not always agree on what is book value. Usually, they hold it to be "the value as shown by the books of the business, and no other value," as in *Succession of Jurisich*.[5] Another case [6] added that it presupposes the existence of a proper set of books, and held that book value included the proceeds of a policy on the deceased partner's life payable to the partnership and the cash surrender value of the policy it owned on the survivor's life, even though neither item appeared on the firm's general ledger. In a third case, New York's highest court in *Aron v. Gillman* [7] held 4 to 3 that book value as determined by audit included inventory at its actual value and not as posted on the books. The remedy is to describe in the agreement exactly what is meant by book value, if the term is used. The agreement should also identify the person who is to determine such value.

Another serious defect is that book value alone never approximates actual value and is not intended to, as any accountant well knows. For example, the depreciation charged off reflects the provisions of the income tax law rather than actual depreciation of the firm's assets. Moreover, the *Jurisich* and other cases hold that book value does not include good will not carried on the books, hence does not reflect the going-concern value of the partnership. Thus, if the partners insist on using book value despite it defects, at least it should be supplemented in the purchase price with an amount for good will if it exists.

How important it may be to include good will is well illustrated by *Succession of Conway*.[8] There, "capital and effects" were held to include good will, and the deceased partner's interest in the firm's good will was held to be $10,000 while his interest in other assets was only $6,655.77. Sometimes a stated amount is agreed upon as the good will value. Quite frequently, good will is valued by including a provision by which the average annual earnings in excess of a stipulated percentage of the book value will be

---

[5] 224 La. 325, 69 So.2d 361 (1953).

[6] *Rubel v. Rubel,* 224 La. 325, 69 So.2d 361 (1953).

[7] 309 N.Y. 157, 128 N.E.2d 284 (1955).

[8] 215 La. 819, 41 So.2d 729 (1949).

capitalized. For example, such a formula might stipulate that the net earnings, averaged over the five years previous to death—after deducting a specified amount as equivalent to compensation for the personal services of the partners, and after deducting 6 percent of the book value as earnings on invested capital—will be multiplied by five to ascertain the good will value to be added to the net ledger assets in arriving at the total value.

Where an entity agreement is used, the partners should keep in mind in considering good will that if the agreement specifies a reasonable amount to be paid for good will, the payment will be treated as part of the purchase price for a deceased partner's interest. As such, it will not be deductible by the partnership and under ordinary circumstances will not create tax liability for the recipient. On the other hand, any payments made for unspecified good will are deductible by the partnership and taxed as ordinary income to the recipient [I.R.C., Section 736(b)]. Any substantial payments to be made of the latter type should be spread over several taxable years of the recipient, in order to minimize the amount of income taxes involved.

Another method requires that the value of the deceased's interest be fixed by a board of appraisers. For instance, a three-man board might be required, one to be appointed by the surviving partners, one by the deceased's personal representative, and the third to be selected by the other two.[9]

It is most important that, whatever method is adopted to ascertain the purchase price, its details be incorporated in the agreement in the clearest possible words so that no controversy will arise over the amount due the deceased's estate. If the provisions are susceptible to more than one interpretation, then they should be rephrased by the attorney. The accountant for the partnership is the person usually best qualified to select the method that will most accurately reflect the true value of the partnership interest, and the attorney is, of course, the proper person to draft the wording of the provision in the agreement. However, this provision is so vital that neither the accountant nor the life underwriter should hesitate to criticize the nomenclature used if its meaning is not entirely clear to them.

The financing of the purchase with life insurance. A recital should appear in the agreement definitely stating that the life insurance made subject to it is for the purpose of providing the necessary cash to consummate the purchase of a deceased partner's interest. The agreement should also definitely state that the proceeds of such insurance when received by the deceased partner's estate or heirs, whether received directly as insurance beneficiary or indirectly from the trustee or the survivors, shall be credited to the surviving partners as payment on account or in full, as the case may be, of the deceased partner's interest in the partnership.

---

[9]For other discussions of book value and good will value, see pages 328–331, *supra*, and pages 98–99 *infra*.

By making these statements in the contract in so many words, any danger is removed that the estate or heirs will contend they are supposed to receive both the insurance proceeds and the value of the deceased's business interest.

Schedule of the life insurance policies. In the body of the agreement or in a schedule attached to and made a part of the instrument, there should appear a description of each life insurance policy made subject to it. Ample identification is provided if the agreement sets forth the name of the insured, the policy number, the insurance company, and the face amount of each policy. In addition, a schedule should be provided in which to record any future changes made in the insurance coverage by the adding, substituting, or withdrawing of policies, if the agreement permits such changes to be made.

Careful scheduling, so that the identity of all policies subject to the agreement is clear at all times, is important. It is not uncommon for the surviving partners, rather than a trustee, to be designated as beneficiaries of the insurance made subject to a cross-purchase agreement. Frequently, too, partners carry business insurance payable to the survivors in addition to the purchase-money insurance coverage. In such a situation it is imperative that an accurate schedule of policies be maintained. Careful scheduling of policies is also advisable under an entity agreement.

Provisions for adding, substituting, or withdrawing policies. A partnership buy-sell agreement will normally remain in effect over a period of years, during which time substantial changes are likely to occur in the value of the business. Therefore, the agreement should provide for the addition, substitution, and withdrawal of life insurance policies by the joint action of the partners.

Again, the precaution must be carefully observed to record in an attached schedule the details of any future changes made in the composition of the insurance policies subject to the agreement.

Adjustment to be made when the amount of insurance proceeds differs from the purchase price. When the death of a partner occurs, the amount of life insurance proceeds payable subject to the agreement may be exactly equal to the purchase price to be paid for the deceased partner's interest, or it may exceed or fall short of that figure. It cannot be expected that these amounts will coincide if a valuation formula is used to ascertain the purchase price. And even if the purchase price is a stated amount, a death may occur when, for one reason or another, the full amount of insurance is not carried. Hence, every agreement should contain provisions specifying the adjustments that are to be made when the insurance proceeds and the purchase price differ in amount.

When the insurance proceeds exceed the purchase price, it is usually provided in a cross-purchase agreement that an amount equal to the full amount of such proceeds shall nevertheless be paid over as being the minimum purchase price. Although any other disposition of the excess proceeds that the partners desire can be provided for, the establishment of the insurance money as the minimum has the important advantage that it enables each partner to know the minimum amount his estate and heirs will receive. This is particularly valuable information if the purchase price is to be derived from the application of a formula after death. Where an entity agreement is used, it is customary to provide that any excess of insurance proceeds over the purchase price collected by the partnership on the deceased partner's life shall be retained as general partnership funds.

When the purchase price exceeds the insurance proceeds, it is customary to provide that the balance will be paid by the delivery of a series of interest-bearing notes made by the surviving partners or the partnership, depending upon the type of agreement, and payable to the estate of the deceased partner. This series of notes may be specified to run for a few months or for a period of years, depending upon the circumstances of the particular case and the wishes of the partners. Some agreements leave the details of paying any balance entirely in the hands of the surviving partners and the personal representative of the deceased, to be agreed upon by them at the time of death. There are, however, two objections to this. First, it may lead to bickering and controversy and it may result in arrangements too harsh for the survivors, or, on the other hand, it may be too liberal for the best interest of the deceased's estate. Second, one of the basic requirements of a valid contract is that its terms be definite; and it is possible that some court might construe such a loose provision as too indefinite. Whether or not this danger is remote, it can easily be avoided; and at the same time the provisions can be made sufficiently flexible. For example, it may be provided that any balance of the purchase price is to be paid in installments of a specified amount at specified intervals, thus allowing the number of installments to vary with the size of the total balance. The partners usually know approximately how much a survivor or the firm, as the case may be, will be able to pay periodically without financial embarrassment. Therefore, this arrangement seems to afford the most satisfactory solution, supplying as it does, both definiteness and flexibility. Under any installment arrangement, there should always be the privilege of accelerating payments.

Before leaving this topic, it should be emphasized again that maximum benefit can be obtained from an insured purchase and sale arrangement only when the partners keep the purchase price as fully insured as possible. Most partners realize this, with the result that in the great majority of cases the balances payable over and above the insurance proceeds are either non-existent or represent an insignificant part of the total purchase price.

The payment of premiums. The agreement should designate who is obligated to pay the premiums on each policy included under it. In the case of an entity agreement, the premiums are paid by the partnership. A cross-purchase agreement usually provides that the premiums for each policy will be paid by the partners other than the insured in the same ratio that the interest of the insured will be acquired and shared between them upon the insured's death. However, because there are several other arrangements available for allocating premium payments among the partners, each requiring considerable explanation, discussion of the entire subject of premium payments is deferred until a later chapter.

Ownership of the insurance policies and restrictions on use for other purposes. The agreement should state who will own the right to exercise the benefits, privileges, and advantages contained in each policy during the insured's lifetime. This will be the partnership, in the case of an entity agreement. The logical partners to own these rights in the case of each policy under a cross-purchase agreement are the particular premium payers. However, an exception to this may well be made in a trustee beneficiary case, referred to under the following heading.

The agreement should further state that the rights in the policies shall be exercised by the respective owners only for the purpose of carrying out the terms of the agreement.

The insurance beneficiary arrangements. The agreement should definitely state who are to be designated beneficiaries of the life insurance policies made subject to it. This is another provision, however, that offers the partners and their attorneys considerable choice.

The agreement may stipulate that a specified individual or trust company, preferably the latter, be designated as beneficiary. However, a necessary antecedent to this is the selection by the partners of the trustee plan of administering the terms of the agreement and the preparation and execution of the instrument as a trust indenture.[10]

Instead of setting up an agreement under which a trustee is designated beneficiary of the life insurance, the partners may select any one of several other arrangements, each of which has its advantages. The space required for an adequate discussion of these other arrangements, however, makes it advisable to devote a separate chapter to them.

Disposition of insurance on the lives of surviving partners. The question of the disposition of the insurance policies on the lives of the surviving partners does not come up in the case of an entity type of agreement that continues in force irrespective of the death of one or more partners. Also, this question does not arise on the death of a partner in a two-man partnership under such an agreement because the deceased partner's estate will be paid the value of his interest from the partnership funds, which include the proceeds of the insurance on the deceased partner's life, and the remaining business assets, including the policy on the life of the survivor, will belong absolutely to the

---

[10]See discussion of the trustee plan, as used with corporate stock, beginning at page 338, *infra.*

survivor. Where there are more than two survivors, the policies on their lives continue to be operative under the entity agreement.

An individual cross-purchase agreement should contain provisions relating to the disposition of the insurance subject to it on the lives of the survivors. The nature of these provisions depends upon whether the agreement is to continue beyond the first death, or is to terminate upon the purchase of the interest of the partner first to die. If the agreement is to terminate, as in the case of a death in a partnership composed of two partners, the agreement should contain provisions disposing of the policies on the life of the surviving partner and allowing him the option to take over the contracts if he so desires. Such an option is valuable to him for several reasons. Foremost is the possibility that he might not be insurable at the time of his partner's death. And even if he is insurable, new insurance would require a higher premium outlay to maintain. Furthermore, the policies that have been maintained on his life under the agreement have usually been in force a sufficient time to make them incontestable, and they often contain other privileges and benefits on a more favorable basis than is the case with new policies. Because of these advantages to the survivor, and further, because the contracts usually have substantial cash values that have been created in whole or in part out of premiums paid by the deceased partner, the surviving partner should be required to pay the deceased's estate a reasonable sum for their acquisition.

Most cross-purchase agreements provide that the estate will be reimbursed to the extent of the cash values created under the plan by premiums that have been paid by the deceased partner. For example, if there were only two partners and each had paid the premiums for the insurance on the life of the other, the premiums that have been so paid by the deceased partner have created the entire cash value in the survivor's policies; the agreement would provide that the survivor may acquire this insurance upon paying the deceased's estate the cash value of it—plus any unearned amount of premium paid.

It should be noted that, under this arrangement, the surviving partner can easily finance the taking over of these contracts, because he can always borrow from the insurance company the amount he must pay over. If two partners have contributed equally to the premiums, then the agreement would require the surviving partner to pay the deceased's estate one-half of the joint cash values of all the policies as of the day before the death occurred. It should be noted here, however, that, except in the case of equal ages, the cash values of the insurance taken over on this basis will be greater or less than the amount the surviving partner is required to pay over for the policies. It is apparent that either of these methods is also applicable if there have been three or more partners. Ordinarily the surviving partner is given at least thirty days from date of the personal representative's appointment in which to act, after which period the deceased's personal representative may surrender the insurance for the account of the estate.

A popular modification of the cash-value-reimbursement method is to require the surviving partner to reimburse the deceased's estate for the premiums paid, in the event that a claim occurs before the policies on the life of the survivor have been in force a sufficient period of time to contain cash values. This seems just, for in such a case the insurance gain of the survivor would be large, and he can well afford to refund to the estate the premiums that the deceased partner has paid.

As already indicated in the case of a two-man partnership, where a cross-purchase agreement does not run beyond the first death, the agreement should grant the respective insureds an option to purchase the policies on their own lives owned by the deceased partner's estate. Where there are more than two partners and the agreement is to continue beyond the first death, the surviving partners other than the insured in each instance are granted an option to purchase the insured's policy. Thus if Jones and Smith are the surviving partners, Jones will have an option to purchase from the deceased partner's estate its policy on the life of Smith; and vice versa. In this manner, all of the insurance on surviving partners subject to the agreement can remain subject to it on a cross-insurance plan, as long as the partnership operates. Such purchases will not subject the death proceeds of the policies to income tax as having been transferred for value, because policies may be transferred for value to a partner of the insured (or to a partnership in which the insured is a partner) under an exception to the transfer-for-value rule.[11]

Provision that the deceased's estate be held harmless from claims of creditors of business. In agreeing upon the value of their partnership, the partners will have in mind, not its gross assets, but its net worth: its assets, less its outstanding obligations. Therefore, when the deceased partner's interest is purchased at the agreed valuation, his estate receives payment based upon the net worth of his share in the firm. In other words, the deceased's share of the outstanding liabilities having been subtracted in arriving at the purchase price of his interest, his estate receives no money with which to pay these obligations. The deceased has in effect paid his share of the debts of the firm by accepting the valuation of his interest on a net-worth basis. It clearly follows, then, that the buy-sell agreement should contain a provision that the surviving partners should assume all the obligations of the partnership, and that the deceased's estate should be held harmless from the claims of the creditors of the firm.

Provisions for amending, revoking, or terminating the agreement. It is customary to include in the buy-sell agreement a statement that it may be amended or revoked by a writing signed by all the partners. If a trustee is a

---

[11] I.R.C., Section 101(a)(2)(B).

party to the agreement, it is usually necessary to provide that no amendment may be made that will increase the obligations or reduce the rights of the trustee without its written consent.

It is customary, also, to include in the agreement a clause stating that the agreement will automatically terminate upon the happening of such events as, for example, the lapse of insurance subject to the agreement, or the dissolution, other than by death, of the partnership. This clause should provide that upon termination of the agreement, each partner is entitled to acquire the policies on his own life after completing whatever financial adjustment is stipulated. For instance, if there were two partners, each of whom had paid premiums on the other's policies, then it could be stipulated that each partner could acquire the policy on his own life by paying the other the cash value of it.

The foregoing analysis has touched upon the principal provisions that should be contained in a partnership buy-sell agreement. Sample forms of agreement have been omitted purposely. The inclusion of one or two would tend to narrow the discussions; the inclusion of an adequate number would be impracticable. They are readily obtained from the form books, from the legal departments of trust companies and insurance companies, and from the specialized business insurance services and trust services. However, lest the impression be left with those who are not familiar with such agreements that they are bulky and many-paged documents, it should be said that well-drawn agreements of this type are on the average only about eight or nine pages in length, if trustee arrangements are used, and are otherwise only about half that long. It is a reasonably concise instrument, but the mission it performs for the partners is so important that there must be no carelessness in its preparation. Such a possibility is remote if the partners engaged an experienced attorney for the task.

Chapter 11

LIFE INSURANCE PREMIUM
AND BENEFICIARY ARRANGEMENTS

WHO SHOULD PAY THE LIFE INSURANCE PREMIUMS

There are a variety of ways in which payment of premiums for the life insurance made subject to a buy-sell agreement may be allocated. Premiums may be paid by partners other than the insured under each policy, they may be pooled and paid pro rata by the partners, they may be paid by the insured partner in each case, or the partnership itself may pay them. In order than an intelligent choice may be made from among these methods, each arrangement will be discussed in this chapter.

Premiums paid by partners other than the insured. Where a cross-purchase agreement is used, this is the logical arrangement. Keeping in mind that the true nature of the insurance method of supplying the purchase price is an advance-installment accumulation plan under which the insurance premiums constitute the installments, then it follows logically that the premium payer in the case of each policy under the plan should be the partner or partners to whose account the insurance proceeds payable on death will be credited as purchase money. Applying this basic principle, the premiums for each policy should therefore be paid by the partners other than the one insured under it, and such premium payments should be contributed by these other partners in the same ratio in which the interest of the insured will be purchased and shared between them upon the insured's death. Perhaps this allocation of premiums appears more complicated than it really is; a few examples may prove helpful.

213

If there are only two partners, each should pay the premiums on the insurance covering the other's life, for it is the survivor who will be given purchase-money credit for the insurance proceeds paid, and the survivor will take over all of the deceased's interest in the business.

If there are three equal partners, each should pay one-half of the premiums for the insurance on the lives of the other two; for in the event one of the others should die, each will receive purchase-money credit for one-half of the insurance proceeds, and each will acquire one-half of the deceased's interest in the firm. Exactly the same principle can be followed with a larger number of partners.

Again, this is the correct principle to apply if the partnership interests in the partnership are not equally divided, or if, the interests being equal, the partners deisre unequal interests between the survivors in event of a death.

For instance, Jack, Jim and Joe are equal partners. If Jack should die, Jim and Joe desire to own the business equally between them; hence they will each contribute one-half the premiums for the insurance on Jack's life. If Jim or Joe should die first, however, Jack does not want to increase his one-third interest in the business; hence Jim will pay the entire premiums for the insurance on Joe's life, and vice versa, and in the event of the death of either, the other will own a two-thirds interest.

To illustrate further, Ben might have a one-half interest in a three-member partnership, with Bill and Bob each owning a one-fourth interest. They desire a continuation plan that in the event of a death will allow the interests of the survivors, after they acquire the interest of the deceased, to bear the same ratio to each other as before. In other words, the ratio of Ben's interest with each of the others is one-half to one-fourth, or two to one. To maintain this fixed relation he will have to acquire two-thirds of the interest of either Bill or Bob; hence he should pay two-thirds of the premiums for the insurance carried on each of them. However, the ratio between Bill and Bob is one to one, or equal; hence each would pay one-half the premiums for insurance on Ben's life.

The following exhibits in tabular form (in fractions of the total premiums for each coverage) the premium allocation for Ben, Bill and Bob, based on the above facts:

	by Ben	by Bill	by Bob
Insurance on Ben's life	–	1/2	1/2
Insurance on Bill's life	2/3	–	1/3
Insurance on Bob's life	2/3	1/3	–

In cases in which there are three or more partners it is a simple matter to prepare and include in the agreement a schedule of premium allocations, worked out on whatever basis is decided upon by the partners. It is a simple matter, also, to arrange for the partnership to draw the premium checks, charging them to the accounts of the individual partners in accordance with the allocation schedule agreed upon.

Suggestions are outlined in Chapter 12 as to adjustments that may be made in the event a partner holding a smaller interest is unable to pay all the premiums allocated to him.

Pooling of premiums. Although the foregoing method of allocating premium payments in the case of a cross-purchase agreement is correct in principle, and is ordinarily used, other methods are also used. One such other method is to "pool" the entire premiums and require each partner to pay a part. If the partnership interests are equal and the partners' ages are close, rough equity is achieved among the partners by requiring equal contributions from them to the pool. If the ages vary considerably, however, the plan unduly favors the younger partners at the expense of the older ones. If the interests are unequal, then the pooling of the premiums merely "scrambles" the equities, regardless of the basis upon which the partners contribute to the pool. If there are substantial differences, both in the ages and in the interests of the partners, then by a pooling of premiums the equities of the individual partners in the financing arrangement might be said to have been beaten into an "omelet."

The pooling arrangement results in an equal sharing of the premium payments; but on principle they should not be equally shared except in the rare situation where both ages and interests are equal. Moreover, if premiums are shared equally, then it logically follows that the resulting benefit in the event of a death should likewise be shared equally. In other words, it follows logically that the deceased partner's estate should be entitled to his aliquot share of any insurance profits made: insurance death proceeds received in excess of premiums paid. Of course, no such sharing of profits is provided for the practical reason that the balance of proceeds left to be credited against the purchase price would fall short of the amount required. The principle of the sharing of benefits, however, is usually applied partially, by giving the deceased partner credit for his pro rata share of the cash values of all policies as of the date of death. Sometimes he is also credited with his pro rata share of any death proceeds that may be in excess of the purchase price, but the fact remains that the pooling arrangement is a "share and share alike" method on the debit side only.

Premiums paid by respective insureds. Employing another method, a cross-purchase agreement could specify that each partner pay the premiums for the insurance on his own life. It should not be necessary to point out that this is totally wrong in principle, for in effect each partner is maintaining the fund with which to purchase property that he already owns, his own partnership interest.

Premiums paid by the partnership itself. Under an entity type of agreement, the premiums should of course be paid by the partnership. The firm will own the policies and the cash values will appear on the partnership books as assets. Mathematically, the payment of the premiums by the firm is the same as if each partner had contributed that part of the total premiums which is proportionate to his distributive share of the partnership income. Therefore, the purchase price set under this type of agreement should at least take into consideration the cash values of all the policies immediately before the death of a partner. Ideally, the purchase price should also take into consideration the excess of the death proceeds over the cash value of the policy on the deceased partner's life—as such proceeds collected by the partnership constitute partnership assets for which the deceased partner indirectly has contributed his proper share.

THE LIFE INSURANCE BENEFICIARY ARRANGEMENTS

In chapter 10, it was pointed out that the partners and their attorneys are offered a considerable choice in the matter of the beneficiaries that may be designated to receive the life insurance proceeds payable under the insured partnership buy-sell agreement. In that chapter it was also pointed out that an arrangement by which a trustee is made a party to the agreement to carry out its provisions as an impartial third party and is accordingly designated as the life insurance beneficiary, was to be preferred. However, cases frequently occur in which the partners, either because the amounts involved are comparatively small, or for other reasons, do not desire a trust plan. It is important, therefore, to know what other beneficiary arrangements are available to the partners and the relative merits of each arrangement.

Designation of the surviving partners as beneficiaries. If the trustee plan is not selected, then the designation of the surviving partners as insurance beneficiaries is the most logical alternative choice in the case of a cross-purchase agreement. By the terms of the continuation agreement, the survivors have usually paid the premiums for the insurance on the deceased's life, and have owned it, subject to the necessary restrictions against its use for other purposes; therefore, to pay the death proceeds to those who have created and owned the fund makes sense. Furthermore, this designation logically puts the purchase money in the hands of the individuals who owe it.

This arrangement also tends to set up an equilibrium between the deceased's estate and the surviving partners after the insurance proceeds are paid to the beneficiaries. The surviving partners who are obligated to buy and to pay the purchase price for the deceased's interest hold these insurance proceeds. The executor or administrator, who is obligated to sell and to transfer the deceased partner's interest, holds the title to that interest. (The surviving partners also hold the specific partnership property, but no change in the title or possession of that property is required by the plan.) Hence this beneficiary designation results in a reasonably balanced situation, with each side of the transaction holding something that it is obliged to deliver over to the other side simultaneously upon receipt of something that the other side possesses. Accordingly, the consummation of the purchase and sale should go through smoothly, upon the survivors paying over the purchase price and receiving back a transfer of the deceased's interest in the firm. The possibility that a serious difficulty will develop is remote if all the parties concerned realize that, should one side balk at going through with the plan, the other side may demand and obtain, by court enforcement if necessary, specific performance of the transaction.

The trustee plan is superior in that, among other things, it segregates the insurance proceeds by having them paid to a disinterested third party as stakeholder; but there is no basic reason why a properly set up cross-purchase plan that pays these proceeds into the hands of the surviving partners should not function satisfactorily.

The surviving partners should not be the beneficiaries of the insurance where an entity type of agreement is used.

Designation of the deceased partner's estate as beneficiary. The designation of the deceased partner's estate as beneficiary of the insurance policies place under the buy-sell agreement is another (but usually unsatisfactory) choice available to the partners and their attorneys.

If this designation is made, it is imperative that the agreement contain a clear and positive statement that the insurance proceeds thus received by the estate direct from the insurance company are to be credited as payment on account or in full, as the case may be, of the purchase price for the deceased partner's interest. This is obviously necessary in order to preclude any possibility that the estate or heirs will contend they are entitled both to the insurance proceeds and to the value of the deceased's interest.

From the above comments, it is apparent that the designation of the insured partner's estate as the beneficiary does not result in a balanced situation after a death occurs, for the reason that the executor or administrator holds both the insurance money and the title to the partnership interest of the deceased partner. Consequently, delivery of everything, or almost everything (in case the purchase price had not been fully insured), that the personal representative is entitled to receive under the agreement has already been made before the parties are brought together, and there does not remain an equal exchange of values to be made between them. In other words, the parties do not meet on an equal footing to conclude the transaction. This arrangement creates an obstacle to the smooth functioning of the plan.

The designation of the insured's estate as beneficiary creates the possibility that the principle of the *Legallet* case will be applied so that the insurance proceeds will not be included in the income tax bases of the partnership interests of the surviving partners.

Proceeds paid to a deceased partner's estate as beneficiary are includible as such in his gross estate for Federal estate tax purposes. Therefore, with such a beneficiary there is the possibility that the Government will attempt also to include the value of the deceased partner's interest. Such an attempt at double estate taxation was made in the *Mitchell* case, involving close corporation stock. Although such attempts have consistently failed,[1] insurance arrangements that make such attempts possible are to be avoided.

It should be pointed out that the designation of the deceased partner's estate as beneficiary is not suitable unless the agreement specifies that the insurance proceeds shall constitute the minimum price in the event the stipulated method of valuation produces a lesser amount. If the insured's estate is the beneficiary, the insurance proceeds become part of the taxable estate of the deceased partner, against which the personal representative is allowed to credit the value of the deceased's interest to the extent that the amounts overlap. Hence, if the insurance proceeds should be in excess of the value of the deceased's interest and if the agreement should call for a sharing of that excess with the surviving partners, the personal representative must persuade the Treasury Department that it is entitled to deduct the amount of excess paid back to the survivors. He thus creates another possible source of controversy over the amount of estate taxes due.

Designation of personal beneficiaries of the insured partners. Considerable demand has developed, particularly in connection with smaller partnerships, for an insured buy-sell plan that will allow each partner to designate his personal beneficiaries to receive the proceeds of the policies on his own life in order to take advantage of the installment settlement options contained in the policies. Pressure for such a plan has been and is being exerted by life underwriters as well as by partners because of a laudable desire to reap double benefits from the insurance. The objective is to have the insurance proceeds function, first, as business insurance, to supply the purchase money for the deceased partner's interest, and second, as personal insurance, to have the purchase money remain in the form of insurance proceeds payable to the deceased's family in installments under the policy options, which enables the partners to use it as part of their personal insurance programs.

Although there are double benefits to be derived from the successful working of such a plan, there remain a number of very serious obstacles in it that must be overcome. The partnership interest of the deceased partner is an asset of his estate, and the insurance proceeds are the purchase money for it. Therefore, if the surviving partner is to have the undisturbed right to all of the assets of the partnership, it follows that these insurance proceeds must be made available for the payment of claims of creditors of the estate unless other funds are available to satisfy such claims. *Silverthorne v. Mayo.*[2]

---

[1] See *Estate of Ray E. Tompkins,* 13 T.C. 1054 (1949), involving a partnership interest.

[2] 238 N.C. 274, 77 S.E.2d 678 (1953).

A second obstacle is the possibility that heirs of the deceased partner will be able to interfere with the buy-sell plan where the partners have designated personal beneficiaries to receive the insurance proceeds.

A third obstacle is raised by the case of *Legallet v. Commissioner,*[3] in which it was held that partnership purchase insurance proceeds paid direct to a deceased partner's widow as beneficiary could not be included in the cost basis of the assets of the business in the hands of the surviving partner. This case is discussed later.

A fourth obstacle inherent in the designation of personal beneficiaries is the danger that such beneficiaries will claim both the insurance proceeds and their share of the value of the partnership interest on the ground that the insurance was personal.[4] This obstacle, however, may be disposed of at once by stating that whenever a personal beneficiary arrangement is set up, the wording of the agreement must leave no doubt whatever that these insurance proceeds are in payment of the insured's interest in the firm.

The problem involved in the first obstacle will arise if the transfer of the deceased partner's interest to the survivor, with the purchase money for that interest going directly to the deceased partner's personal beneficiary, will leave his executor or administrator with insufficient estate funds to pay debts, administration expenses, and taxes. If in such a situation the purchase plan does not make it possible for the personal representative to obtain a portion of the insurance proceeds sufficient to pay the claims against the deceased's estate, the personal representative has ample power under the Fraudulent Conveyance laws to prevent the transfer of the deceased partner's interest to the survivor to the extent necessary to satisfy the estate creditors.

The foregoing is affirmed by *Silverthorne v. Mayo.*[5] In that case the partnership agreement specified that the purchase price for the deceased partner's interest was to be paid directly to his widow. In holding that the widow had received the right to the purchase price as the designee of the payments in a valid third-party beneficiary contract, thereby eliminating any problem with the deceased partner's heirs, the court noted that the arrangement did not eliminate the claims of any unsatisfied creditors of the deceased partner. Here is a quotation from the court's opinion:

> Ordinarily, a surviving partner, in the absence of a partnership agreement providing otherwise, is charged with the duty to pay the firm debts, collect the partnership accounts, and account to the personal representatives of the deceased partner. It naturally follows that a partnership agreement is not binding on the firm's

---

[3]41 B.T.A. 294.

[4]There are many such cases; see, for example, the successful claim in *Strumberg v. Mercantile Trust Company,* Mo., 367 S.W.2d 535 (1963).

[5]Cited in note 2 *supra.*

creditors unless they assent. 68 C.J.S. Partnership, §401(d), page 921. Furthermore, an interest in a partnership may be subjected to the payment of the individual debts of the partner. Therefore, the disposition of the property by contract, enforceable at death, does not exempt such property from liability for the debts of the decedent any more effectually than if the property had been disposed of by will.

At this point we shall discuss the obstacle that may be presented by the deceased partner's heirs if personal beneficiaries are designated for the life insurance.

By means of a properly prepared will, the possibility of interference from heirs other than those who are given a right to renounce the benefits of the will and to take under statutory provisions, can be eliminated. But a problem may be presented by the fact that the laws of most states give certain heirs, ordinarily the widow and usually any children born after the making of the will and not mentioned in it or not otherwise provided for, an election to take against the will up to the amount they would have been entitled to receive in the absence of a will. The widow, at least, usually has an indefeasible right to a share of a decedent's estate, will or no will, and she cannot be denied this right except by her own voluntary waiver in a formal manner commonly prescribed by statute. In this connection, it should be noted that insurance proceeds in any amount payable to her as a direct beneficiary do not defeat or reduce a widow's statutory rights in most, if not all, jurisdictions, because her rights are in the property passing through the decedent's probate estate. Therefore, should she or any other heirs simply be designated as personal beneficiary of the partnership purchase insurance, will or no will, there is a possibility that the widow will attempt to upset the plan, unless a valid waiver has been obtained from her in advance.

An example of this is shown in *Buehrle v. Buehrle*.[6] Two brothers, a few years after having inherited a wholesale liquor business from their father, insured themselves for $5,000 under a joint-life fifteen-year endowment policy, payable to the widow of the first to die, and they entered into an agreement stating that each would make a will leaving his partnership interest to the other. They also agreed that on the death of one the entire business "shall belong to the survivor of said parties, provided said insurance policy above mentioned is kept in full force and valid and payable to the widow of such deceased party." On the same day the agreement was signed, the brothers also executed wills in conformity with the agreement and conditioned upon the policy being in full force and effect at the first death. Premiums on the policy were paid by the partnership.

---

[6] 291 Ill. 589, 126 N.E. 539 (1920).

Upon the death of one brother seven years later, his widow collected the $5,000 proceeds. However, an audit of the partnership books made the day after the death showed the assets to be worth $69,905.10. As soon as the widow learned of the contents of the will and the contract she renounced her rights under the will, elected to take her statutory share, and charged herself with the insurance proceeds. The surviving brother contended that the partnership interest passed to him under the terms of the agreement itself, but Illinois' highest court held that it was an agreement for the making of mutual wills rather than a survivorship contract and that the wife was entitled to her statutory rights in her husband's estate upon her renunciation and her election to take under the law. The court further held that, since the insurance premiums had been paid by the partnership, the proceeds would be considered as partnership assets. The case shows clearly the absolute necessity for proper waivers from pretermitted heirs if the plan adopted calls for the partnership interest to pass *by will* to the surviving partner.

We now come to the problem presented by the *Legallet* case,[7] as it relates to the modified personal beneficiary arrangement. In that case the partners originally executed a regular insured cross-purchase agreement with $20,000 of life insurance on each partner, payable to the other as beneficiary. A few months later they each purchased $5,000 additional insurance. Three years later they substituted a new agreement for their standard agreement and made all of the life insurance payable directly to their wives as personal beneficiaries under the installment income options. The new agreement included the wives as parties, each of whom agreed to accept the $25,000 insurance proceeds as first payment on the deceased partner's interest (valued in the agreement for the current year at approximately $55,936 each) with the balance payable in a series of fifty monthly notes of equal amount. Several months later partner O'Neill died, and the purchase and sale transaction was consummated as agreed upon. Afterwards in the same year the surviving partner Legallet sold some accounts receivable and merchandise that had belonged to the former partnership of Legallet & O'Neill. In reporting the profit on the sale in his income tax return for that year Legallet used the full purchase price of $55,936 as the cost basis of the assets acquired by him from the deceased partner. However, the government assessed him an additional income tax of $4,680.04 on the sale, on the ground that the cost basis of the assets acquired did not include the life insurance proceeds of $25,000 and was, therefore, only $30,936, the amount of notes paid. Legallet then petitioned the Board of Tax Appeals to set aside the assessment, but was unsuccessful. The court stated:

> The $25,000 was not in fact received by him, but by O'Neill's
> wife, and was not in fact paid by petitioner to her. Is the effect,

---

[7] *Paul Legallet v. Commissioner*, 41 B.T.A. 294 (1940).

for the present purpose, as if he had so received and paid the
$25,000 as purchase price of the partnership interest acquired?
... Petitioner, in effect, contends that looking through form to
substance, the insurance should be considered as received by
petitioner as provided by earlier agreements between the partners,
though not by the last agreement, that they were constructively
received by him, and that the insurance proceeds when received
by O'Neill's wife was impressed with a trust and subject to use as
part payment of the purchase price of the partnership interest
acquired by petitioner, in accord with the use in the contract of
the expression "part payment."

Legallet's argument that the insurance proceeds should be considered
constructively received by him and paid over as part of his cost was answered,
and the case decided upon the authority of the *Mitchell* case,[8] as follows:

Petitioner's argument that we should look to substance
through form and find that the parties intended that petitioner be
the beneficiary, as in previous transactions, is nullified by the
mere fact that the parties, for reasons duly considered, deserted
the older form of agreement and method of insuring with the
other as beneficiary and adopted a different one. They wished a
change of substance as well as form, for they wished a certain
kind of distribution, and in order to obtain it, found it necessary
to deviate from the old payment in a lump sum to the survivor.
We cannot reasonably now say that the change was unintentional
or ineffectual. Likewise the idea that the insurance proceeds was
a trust fund for payments to the petitioner is, we think, not
accurate. It was, as in the three cases above discussed, subject to a
contract, but not by way of such trust as to dictate constructive
receipt of the amount by petitioner. A mere contract entailing
the elements here involved does not constitute constructive
receipt.

Upon the authority of the *Dobrzensky* and *Mitchell* cases,
supra, above discussed, we conclude and hold that petitioner's
cost basis does not include the $25,000 insurance proceeds
received by the wife of his deceased partner.

The issue in the *Legallet* case has been in court only once since that
decision. It came before the Tax Court in the 1968 case of *Victor G.
Mushro.*[9] Fortunately for the surviving partners, the court distinguished the
Legallet case. The Internal Revenue Service, however, published a nonacquies-
ence in the *Mushro* decision in 1970.

Victor, Louis and Lawrence Mushro, who operated a motel partnership,

---

[8]*Estate of John T. H. Mitchell,* 37 B.T.A. 1.
[9]50 T.C. 43.

engaged a lawyer to draft a regular partnership buy-sell agreement. Lawrence refused to sign it because the partnership was to be the insurance beneficiary. He insisted that his wife be named beneficiary of his policy because of animosity then existing between his brothers and his wife. He was afraid that if the partnership was the beneficiary, his brothers would make it difficult for his estate to get the money. Consequently, a new agreement was drafted and signed which provided that the insurance policies were to be owned by the partnership but made payable to the beneficiaries designated by the partners. The proceeds were to constitute payment "in behalf of the surviving partners for so much of the partnership interest of the decedent as could be purchased with said insurance proceeds." Premiums were paid by the partnership and a part proportionate to his interest charged to each partner's account.

When Lawrence died in 1960, $100,000 of insurance proceeds became payable to his wife Pauline as beneficiary. At that time an agreement was executed between the widow and the surviving partners which provided that the proceeds belonged to her and "shall be applied in like manner as if said funds were paid by said first parties [surviving parties] to [Pauline] in full payment of all right, title and interest of LAWRENCE MUSHRO (now deceased) in his share and interest in the partnership and the assets and good will thereof."

Subsequently, the surviving partners formed a new partnership, elected to increase basis under I.R.C. Section 754, then dissolved the new firm and distributed all of its assets to Victor and Louis. Neither reported a gain from the distribution, each having increased the basis of his interest by one-half the value of Lawrence's partnership interest at his death.

The Tax Court held that the deceased partner's policy had named his wife as beneficiary solely as a security device and that in reality the surviving partners had received the proceeds and then paid them to Pauline in exchange for the deceased partner's interest. It followed that each survivor had an increased cost basis pursuant to I.R.C. Section 1012 for half the value of the deceased partner's interest. The court's opinion distinguished the *Legallet* case as follows:

> When the partners in *Legallet* named their wives beneficiaries of the life insurance policies, they were carrying out their basic intent—to provide an annuity to the wife of the first partner to die. It follows that in *Legallet* the partners did not intend, in their buy-sell agreement, for anyone other than their wives to receive the proceeds of the insurance policies. In the case at bar, however, the partners' real intent was to have either the surviving partners or the partnership [the court decided the former] receive the insurance proceeds. When the partners named their wives beneficiaries of the policies, they were not carrying out

their real intent; they were only creating a security device to satisfy Lawrence.

One judge, in concurring, took the view that the decision in effect overruled *Legallet* rather than distinguished it. As previously noted, however, in 1970 the Internal Revenue Service published a nonacquiescence in the *Mushro* decision. That means, of course, that the Service will continue to follow the *Legallet* case. And as long as *Legallet* is followed, it obviously adds another primary difficulty to any plan that includes the naming of personal beneficiaries under buy-sell insurance policies.

From the foregoing analysis it is apparent that the matter of designating personal beneficiaries in business insurance policies involved special problems. However, a workable plan can be set up under which personal beneficiaries may be designated in the modified form. One such modified personal beneficiary arrangement permitted by some insurance companies involves a cross-purchase plan without a trustee. The surviving partner, owner of the policy on the other partner's life, will be the primary beneficiary under the interest option with full withdrawal rights during a limited period. The insured's wife will be named secondary beneficiary. Upon the insured's death, his executor will proceed with the estate administration, and in due course will be ready to transfer the decedent's interest in the firm to the survivor. The survivor will supply the purchase price to the extent of the proceeds either by withdrawing them and paying them over to the executor or by releasing his interest in the proceeds in favor of the secondary beneficiary. If the latter, the secondary beneficiary may then elect a settlement option if desired. Under this arrangement the insurance proceeds are made available to the executor if and to the extent needed to administer the estate, thus to pay any otherwise unsatisfied creditors as well as heirs, if any, who have unsatisfied and indefeasible rights in the estate. Furthermore, the surviving partner's right of withdrawal appears clearly to give him constructive receipt of the proceeds so as to eliminate the basis problem encountered in the *Legallet* case.

In some instances the partners desire to have the insurance proceeds under the control of a disinterested third party during the interest period. Thus, some insurance companies are willing to permit the designation of a trustee as primary beneficiary. The trustee is given the right to withdraw and pay over cash to the estate if and to the extent required in its administration and to otherwise follow the procedure set up under a plan that does not use a trustee.

Choice among the various plans depends upon the state of the law in the particular jurisdiction, the circumstances of the individual case, the wishes of the parties involved, and the beneficiary rules of the particular insurance company whose policies are concerned. It is also apparent, however, that such a plan will probably have to accept some disadvantages. Furthermore, the proper execution of such an arrangement will require the skillful selection and coordination of provisions best suited to the circumstances of the individual partnership. The conclusion seems evident, therefore, that the standard agreement with a trustee or the surviving partners as insurance beneficiaries (or the partnership in the case of an entity agreement) will prove the most satisfactory in the great majority of partnerships, and that a plan using personal beneficiaries should be adopted only in the exceptional case in which a qualified local attorney has approved it after a careful study of all the advantages and disadvantages of the plan in the particular situation.

Designation of the partnership itself as beneficiary. The partnership itself should be designated beneficiary of the insurance only in the case of an entity type of agreement. Under such an agreement the policies are partnership property and are properly payable to the firm. Under a cross-purchase agreement, the policies are owned by the individual partners, and needless confusion would result from naming the firm as beneficiary.

On the other hand, needless confusion and litigation may result if the proceeds of insurance under an entity agreement are not payable to the partnership, or to a trustee acting for it. In the first place, an income tax issue may be raised as to whether the proceeds are to be considered payments from the partnership under Code Section 736. In the second place, there is the danger that both the proceeds and the value of the deceased partner's interest may be claimed by the representative of the deceased partner's estate. This happened, for example, in *Jones v. Morrison.*[10] That case involved a limited partnership comprising two general partners and one limited partner. The partnership was to continue for one year or until the death of any partner. The partnership insured each partner for $50,000 for the specific purpose of repaying the limited partner's $50,000 contribution to the firm should it be dissolved by death, and all of the policies were assigned to the limited partner or his executors to be applied for such purpose. Upon repayment of the limited partner's contribution during his lifetime, he had the option of acquiring the policies on his own life by paying the firm their cash surrender value, if any. The partnership purchased term insurance, but it later converted a $22,000 policy on the limited partner to straight life on his agreement to pay the difference in premium. Following the firm's dissolution after the limited partner's death, his estate claimed the proceeds of the $22,000 policy as well as his $50,000 contribution. The Appellate Division agreed, but New York's highest court held that such proceeds must be applied in repayment of the insured's contribution. In this particular instance a trustee beneficiary was indicated, and probably would have kept the parties out of court.

---

[10] 263 N.Y. 447, 189 N.E. 545 (1934).

Chapter 12

UNUSUAL CONTINUATION
PROBLEMS DISCUSSED

The discussion of the insured partnership business continuation plan has been based in general upon the circumstances found in the typical firm: namely, a partnership composed of two or more members, all of whom are insurable, and whose respective interests in the partnership are somewhere near equal. It is recognized, of course, that these typical circumstances do not always obtain and that unusual circumstances may call for appropriate modifications of the standard purchase and sale arrangement. Accordingly, a few of these abnormal situations will be pointed out and a few ways by which they may be met will be suggested.

PARTNERS WITH GREATLY DISPROPORTIONATE INTERESTS

Occasionally a partnership is encountered in which the respective shares of the members are greatly disproportionate to each other. A simple example would be our old firm of King & Gay, if we assume that King holds a three-fourths interest and Gay a one-fourth interest. The standard procedure would require Gay to purchase insurance on the life of King in the amount of his three-fourths interest and pay the premiums on it. If this can be done it should be done, for these premiums are the scientifically correct amounts that Gay should be called upon to pay for the acquisition of King's three-fourths interest upon the latter's death. But very often the problem of premium paying of the partner with the smaller interest is aggravated by the fact that the other partner is considerably older. We shall assume this to be the case with King, with the result that it is financially impossible for Gay to pay the entire premiums for the insurance on King's life.

A satisfactory solution to Gay's premium-paying problem could be worked out as follows: Gay will pay as great a portion of the premiums for the insurance on King's life as he is able. King will pay the remainder of the premiums for the insurance on his own life as a loan to Gay. A special schedule should be appended to the agreement on which to record and initial these loans as they are made, and the agreement should provide that these loans be repaid out of the first insurance moneys collected upon King's death. Of course, unless the amount of insurance carried on King's life is in excess of the purchase price of his interest, this provision will cause the proceeds to fall short, but the discrepancy will be absorbed by the usual note arrangement covering any balance of purchase price remaining after crediting the insurance proceeds received. Over the life of an agreement it very often happens that the partners will adjust their interests to a more nearly equal basis, in which event loans of this nature may be paid back before a death occurs.

Another solution, not so satisfactory, is for Gay to purchase insurance on King's life in the amount Gay is able to maintain, leaving the remainder of the purchase price to be absorbed by the usual installment note arrangement.

A third solution would be to set up a partnership entity type of agreement, under which the insurance premiums are paid by the partnership and the firm is the owner and beneficiary of the policies. Such an agreement is particularly suitable to a partnership consisting of several partners, but it can be used in the case of two partners. Under this form of agreement, a partner with a large interest indirectly pays a proportionately large share of the premiums, but the plan works out equitably where all insurance values are taken into consideration when the interest of a deceased partner is acquired.

THE UNINSURABLE PARTNER

When we realize that, on the average, approximately one person in every twenty who applies to the insurance companies for life insurance is unable to obtain a policy, we may expect that partners who desire to set up an insured buy-sell plan will occasionally find that one of their associates is uninsurable. The problem is solved immediately if the uninsurable partner has sufficient personal insurance that he is willing to sell and assign to the partnership or the other partners to finance the purchase price of his interest. Where this cannot be done, the first reaction of the partners usually is to abandon their plan to execute a continuation agreement. But they need not and should not desert their purpose. We have gone to considerable lengths to demonstrate what happens to a partnership business when the law of partnership liquidation is allowed to take its course. The losses resulting are serious to everyone concerned, and they can be avoided even though a partner cannot be insured. In fact, if there were no such thing as life insurance it would still be advisable for partners to set up continuation agreements under which the surviving partners would finance the purchase of a deceased partner's interest with down payments accumulated in ordinary sinking funds and with a series of notes to cover the remainder of the purchase price. The "dog" is the buy-sell agreement; the "tail" is the method by which the agreement is financed. With every partner insured for the value of his interest, we have a "wagging tail" to denote that everything is as it should be. But the tail should not be allowed to wag the dog. If it is impossible to set up the ideal insurance method of financing with respect to the interest of every partner, then it should be used for the insurable partners, and the sinking fund method should be used to finance the purchase of the uninsurable partner's interest.

The buy-sell agreement is modified to provide that the partners other than the uninsurable member, instead of maintaining insurance on his life, will deposit annually into a segregated reserve fund an amount at least equal to the premiums that would have been paid by them had the partner been insurable. With the preferred trust plan, this sinking fund may be built up in the trust, thus affording a perfect segregation; otherwise it may be placed in a separate bank account, or invested in government bonds. Another feasible method under certain circumstances is to build up the fund by means of discounted premiums paid in advance on the policies of those insured, provision being made for the reversion of the fund to the contributors upon the insured's death or upon the death of the uninsurable partner.

As a concomitant to the provision for a sinking fund, the agreement must allow the remainder of the purchase price to be paid in installments spread over a period of time sufficient to avoid financial embarrassment to the survivors. This is taken care of automatically if the note arrangement suggested earlier in the text is employed, namely, that notes of a specified amount become payable at specified intervals; thus, the number of installments will vary automatically with the size of the total remainder of the purchase price to be paid.

Where an entity agreement is used, a sinking fund may be built up in the form of discounted premiums or in a special reserve account. The partnership also may find it feasible to own key-man insurance on the insurable partners, in order to augment the sinking fund should any of the insurable partners predecease the uninsurable partner. It should not be assumed that because one of the partners is uninsurable, he will die first; in the case of *Kavanaugh v. Johnson,* for example, it was the uninsurable partner who survived. If the uninsurable partner dies first, however, the additional cash value created by the key-man insurance will be available to make partial payment for the decedent's partnership interest.

THE PROBLEM OF LARGE PARTNERSHIP
LIABILITIES

The death of a partner does not free his estate from liability for the debts of the partnership. In the ordinary situation, however, if the firm's debts are largely composed of current liabilities, the regular provision in the buy-sell agreement requiring the surviving partner to assume these debts and to hold the estate of the deceased partner harmless therefrom has proved satisfactory. Nevertheless, situations will be encountered in which a partnership has outstanding comparatively large liabilities not immediately due and in which the ordinary provision in the agreement will not be sufficient protection to the deceased's estate. Such a situation is not within the province of the life underwriter to work out, but he should recognize that it does exist in certain cases, and he should know something about one or two of the remedies that might be used.

One possible remedy in a proper situation that life underwriters would naturally think of is a special joint policy of life insurance covering the partners in the amount of the deferred obligations. If there are only one or two large creditors such a policy can be made payable to them as their interests may appear, with any balance payable to the firm. If a trusteed partnership purchase plan is used, such a policy can be made payable to the trustee with instructions to apply the proceeds to the debts of the firm in whatever manner desired.

The proceeds of any life insurance arranged to pay off obligations of the partnership should be included in valuing the partnership interests under a purchase and sale agreement, for such proceeds increase the net worth of the business to the extent thereof.

Another possible remedy, if the partners are unable to maintain the amount of insurance required to retire the deferred obligations in full, is for them to purchase an amount of insurance sufficient to obtain releases from these creditors of the estate's liability.

A third possible remedy is the purchase of a surety bond by the surviving partner that would require the surety company to indemnify the deceased's estate for any loss resulting from the failure of the survivor to discharge the outstanding debts of the firm. The difficulty with this solution, however, is that it cannot be known in advance whether the survivor will be able to obtain the issuance of such a bond.

It should be evident from this discussion that because of the large amount of their deferred liabilities, some partnerships should postpone any continuation plans until they have achieved a more suitable ratio of liabilities to net worth. In other words, an insured purchase and sale plan cannot logically be set up in every situation. In a great majority of partnerships it will be of immense service to the partners and their families, but in a few firms the partners might better solve the outstanding liabilities problem first.

Chapter 13

PROFESSIONAL PARTNERSHIPS

Because of the fact that a professional or personal-service partnership, typified by a law firm or a firm of accountants, differs in some material respects from the ordinary commercial partnership, there is need for a separate discussion of its continuation problems and their solutions.

DISTINCTIVE CHARACTERISTICS

In the ordinary business or commercial firm, capital, in the form of such tangible property as real estate, fixtures, machinery, equipment, materials and supplies, and merchandise, is an important factor and represents a substantial portion of the purchase price to be paid on acquisition of a deceased partner's interest. In such a firm, going-concern and good-will value also account for a sizable part of the total value. In contrast, the usual professional or personal-service partnership interest represents only a small amount of capital in the form of tangible property and, in legal contemplation, little or no good will attributable to a partner that survives his death.

Professional partnerships may be further distinguished from commercial partnerships by the fact that the former generally use the cash method of accounting in keeping their books and in reporting income. One important result is that such firms usually have substantial amounts of unrealized receivables outstanding, including unbilled work in process, representing potential income not yet accounted for. As emphasized later, these items pose a particularly difficult fiduciary problem to the surviving partners following the death of a partner, in the absence of a suitable buy-sell agreement.

231

Another characteristic of most professional partnerships is the fact that a retiring or deceased partner's interest therein must be disposed of only to a licensed member of the particular profession, or must be liquidated.

SPECIAL NEED FOR A CONTINUATION AGREEMENT

Because of the peculiar characteristics of professional partnerships, they stand in greater need of a suitable continuation agreement following the death of a partner than do commercial partnerships. One, just mentioned, is the necessity of liquidating a deceased partner's interest or of selling it to another licensed member of the same profession.

Another need is to relieve the surviving partners from what otherwise would be unusually burdensome fiduciary duties owed the decedent's personal representative and heirs. We have previously emphasized the unenvious fiduciary position occupied by the surviving partners in a commercial firm in accounting to the deceased partner's estate, and the litigation that often results. Where a professional partnership is concerned, the situation is even more acute. Since the tangible assets do not amount to much, the decedent's share is likely to be of insignificant value. The partners in such firms, however, usually enjoy substantial incomes from the personal services rendered, and on the death of a partner the firm may be expected to have uncompleted work in process of considerable value to which the decedent has contributed. Without an agreement to the contrary the surviving partners must account for the decedent's interest in the work in process, no matter how difficult is the task of evaluating it. With little to be derived from the decedent's interest in the firm's tangible assets, his estate and heirs probably will expect much from his interest in the uncompleted work and will litigate the matter if the amount falls below expectations. There have been many such cases; perhaps *McNutt v. Hannon* is typical.[1]

McNutt's death dissolved a law partnership that had been in existence for about fifteen years. His executor and the surviving partner could not agree upon the amount the estate was entitled to receive for the decedent's interest in uncompleted work. The executor sued for an accounting, and the trial court proceeded with the difficult problem of ascertaining the value of the deceased partner's interest in the complex legal cases in process at his death. That court's evaluation satisfied no one, and both parties appealed. Eight years after McNutt's death, the matter became settled when California's highest court affirmed the trial court's decree.

Finally, most professional partners feel the need and have the desire to treat a deceased partner's estate and heirs as fairly as is reasonably possible under the circumstances. Among other things, this involves the matter of good will. Even though the firm possesses little or no good will from a legal

---

[1] 183 Cal. 537, 191 Pac. 1108.

standpoint, from a practical standpoint a capable and well-established professional partnership actually possesses a considerable quantum of good will that will inure to the financial benefit of the surviving partners. A realization of this fact has been one of significant reasons why such firms have set up continuation agreements. Whether or not such agreements specify payments for any good-will value, the total amount payable on behalf of a deceased partner usually will take such value into consideration. Then there is the matter of a deceased partner's interest in work in process, previously mentioned. The partners desire an agreement with payments that will avoid a complicated and protracted accounting with respect to a deceased partner's share therein and at the same time that will cushion the shock to his family caused by the sudden loss of the decedent's income from the firm.

SELECTING THE TYPE OF AGREEMENT

Chapter 9 contains a detailed discussion of this subject with reference to partnerships in general. Most of that discussion also applies to professional partnerships and need not be repeated here. But because most professional partnerships use the cash method of accounting and possess substantial amounts of unrealized receivables, the previous discussion of such items in relation to the type of agreement to be selected by a professional partnership is of special significance and calls for further emphasis here. Also, the treatment of good will in relation to the type of agreement to be selected is of great significance and needs further discussion here. We shall discuss these matters further in separately discussing entity and cross-purchase types of agreements for professional partnerships.

Entity agreements. In order to solve the various problems, professional and personal-service partnerships customarily have set up a species of continuation plan resembling an entity type of agreement except that all or the greater part of the payments to be made by the partnership consist of an agreed percentage of the continuing firm's income, payable to the deceased partner's estate or heirs for a fixed period of years.

Following considerable confusion in the courts as to the income tax incidence of payments made under such agreements, the Internal Revenue Code of 1954 set our fairly definite rules by separating the payments received from the partnership into two groups. The first group consists of nondeductible payments in acquisition of the deceased partner's interest in the partnership property. This group includes payments for good will only to the extent that the agreement *specifically* provides for such payments in a reasonable amount. Because the partnership interest of a deceased partner receives a new income tax basis at death, which is its value at that time or on the optional valuation date for Federal estate tax purposes, the recipient of these payments should have little or no income tax thereon. Normally, these payments will constitute the purchase price received upon the sale of a capital asset under circumstances in which the price and income tax basis are the same.

Payments in the second group consist of those in excess of the value of the deceased partner's interest in partnership property at time of death. They include any payments made for the deceased partner's share of any unrealized receivables of the partnership. If these payments are based upon partnership income, they are treated as a distributive share, thus reducing the distributive shares of the surviving partners. If these payments are not based on partnership income, they are deductible by the partnership as a business expense. In either event, the payments in this group are treated by the recipient as ordinary income in respect of a decedent. The value of these payments (as well as of those in the first group) are includible in the deceased partner's gross estate for Federal estate tax purposes,[2] but the recipient is entitled to an income tax deduction for any estate tax paid attributable to such payments.[3]

Because payments in the second group are income in respect of a decedent, their value at the deceased partner's death must be deducted from the value of his partnership interest. Thus, as pointed out in Chapter 9, the value of such interest takes a new basis at the partner's death consisting of its fair market value for Federal estate tax purposes, increased by the estate's share of the firm's liabilities and reduced by the value of its share of items constituting income in respect of a decedent.[4]

The *Quick* case is particularly in point here. It concerned an equal partnership between Quick and another, which provided architectural and engineering services and used the cash method of accounting. Following Quick's death in 1960, his estate, and later his *inter vivos* trust, succeeded as partner. In its 1960 tax return, the partnership elected under Sections 743(b) and 754 to adjust the basis of its assets. At that time, the firm had a large amount of outstanding unrealized receivables with a zero basis. It proceeded with their collection. The Quick Trust, claiming a new basis for its one-half share of the collected receivables because of the new basis for the decedent's interest at his death and the firm's election to adjust the basis of its assets, did not include the collections in its taxable income. The Tax Court (54 T.C. 1336), affirmed by the Court of Appeals for the 8th Circuit, held that the collections were income in respect of a decedent, that Section 1014(c) applied to reduce the death basis of the decedent's partnership interest by the fair market value of his share of the unrealized receivables, and that therefore the optional basis adjustment of the firm's assets under Section 743(b) did

---

[2] *Reigelman's Estate v. Commissioner*, 253 F.2d 315.

[3] I.R.C., Section 691(c).

[4] I.R.C. Secs. 742, 1014(c); Reg. §1.742-1; *Quick's Trust v. Commissioner*, 444 F.2d 90 (1971); *Woodhall v. Commissioner*, 454 F.2d 226 (1972).

not give a new basis to such receivables. Consequently, collection of them constituted ordinary income, and the Quick Trust's share was reportable as income in respect of a decedent. This case was cited and followed by the 9th Circuit in *Woodhall,* which concerned a buy-sell agreement between two partners individually.

Note that where a partnership possesses good-will value, the firm by inserting or omitting a provision in its entity agreement to provide for the purchase of a deceased partner's interest in good will, can determine whether the survivors or the recipient of the payments will bear the income tax on payments actually representing the decedent's interest in good will.[5]

The fact that the payments in the second group constitute ordinary income to the recipient makes it desirable that by the terms of the agreement these payments be spread over a period of years and not bunched into too few taxable years of the estate or other recipient.

Life insurance is an exceedingly valuable adjunct to an income continuation plan. In essence, the survivors under the plan are committed to the payment through the firm of a substantial amount of money each year for several years after a partner's death. Except insofar as these payments represent fees for work done by the decedent prior to death in connection with unfinished business, the payments consist of money earned by the survivors which they cannot keep. Even though the arrangement is such that they are relieved from the additional burden of paying taxes on this money, the steady drain on the funds of the continuing members is bound to retard their progress over the years the payments are required. How much better it would be for them if, at the time of the death, the partnership was able to collect insurance proceeds on the deceased's life, free from taxes, in the amount of the estimated payments to be made to his estate or widow. They can readily put themselves in a position to do this if each partner is insured by the partnership in the amount of the estimated post-mortem payments to be made on his account.

Before concluding this discussion of entity agreements for personal-service partnerships, something should be said about the advantages to the estate or heirs of making payments falling in the second group of a definite agreed amount, as against a sharing of an agreed percentage of future income. We need only to revert to the case of *Hermes v. Compton,* 260 App. Div. 507, quoted on page 169 for illustration. The continuation agreement involved in that case, in addition to certain capital sums that were paid in lump sum, called for the payment to Hermes' estate for a period of five years of a sum equal to a specified percentage of the annual net income derived by the surviving partners over and above $75,000. The estate received a substantial amount covering the first year after Hermes' death, for in that year the senior

---

[5]I.R.C., Section 736(b).

surviving partner alone (two partners survived) earned in excess of $100,000. The following year, however, the senior partner retired, except as a consultant, with the result that earnings fell below $75,000 and payments under the continuation agreement stopped. The same result, of course, would have been brought about had the senior partner died that year instead of retiring, which shows clearly the weakness implicit in any plan of sharing the income of survivors.

Payments in a definite agreed amount for an agreed period also have distinct advantages for the surviving partners. Such payments eliminate any checking into the future partnership income by the deceased partner's executor or heirs. Furthermore, with a known total amount to be paid in the event of a partner's death, the other partners or the partnership may cover such payments with the correct amount of insurance.

Cross-purchase agreements. A small professional partnership comprising only two or three partners may prefer to set up an insured cross-purchase agreement under which each partner will purchase, own and maintain a policy on the life of each of the other partners. Upon the death of a partner, the survivors will buy the deceased partner's interest, using the insurance proceeds for this purpose.

We should recall at this point that the sale of an interest in a partnership is treated as the sale of a capital asset except as to payments received for the seller's interest attributable to unrealized receivables and substantially appreciated inventory. Payments received that are so attributable are considered amounts realized from the sale of property other than a capital asset, and the consequent gain or loss is ordinary income or loss. Because most professional partnerships will possess substantial amounts of unrealized receivables, the estate will receive ordinary income gain in the form of income in respect of a decedent to the extent payments are received for the decedent's interest in such receivables when it sells the deceased partner's interest to the surviving partners.[6]

The *Woodhall* case is directly in point. It concerned an equal partnership between brothers Lyle and Eldon Woodhall, engaged in the plastering contractor business. Because it was located in Washington, a community property state, Lyle's wife Chrissie owned a one-half share of his partnership interest. The brothers entered into a buy-sell agreement providing that upon the death of either partner the partnership would terminate and the survivor would purchase the decedent's interest at a price to be determined by formula. The purchase price was payable over five years, with $5,000 payable within 30 days of death. The agreement apparently was uninsured. When Lyle died, in 1964, Chrissie was appointed executrix and received the first

---

[6]Rev. Rul. 66-325, 1966-2 C.B. 249; *Woodhall v. Commissioner,* 38 T.C.M. 1438, affirmed 9 Cir. 1972, 454 F.2d 226.

payment of $5,000 from the survivor. The tax status of this payment was the immediate issue, brought on by the fact that at Lyle's death the firm possessed unrealized receivables representing 83.3 percent of the firm's value. Chrissie, as executrix and as surviving spouse, claimed that the basis of the decedent's partnership interest at death was its then fair market value, which was the amount to be received under the buy-sell agreement; therefore, no gain or loss was realized. She also purported to elect an increased basis adjustment under Code Section 732(d).

The Tax Court, affirmed by the 9th Circuit, held that 83.3 percent of the $5,000 and subsequent payments to be received by both Chrissie and the estate were taxable as ordinary income and income in respect of a decedent. In reaching this decision the court first computed the basis of the deceased partner's interest by taking its fair market value at death, adding one-half the firm's liabilities, and deducting one-half the unrealized receivables. This basis was then split equally between Chrissie individually and the estate, she having received a new basis for her community share on her husband's death. Next, the court arrived at the gross sales price by adding to the amount to be paid one-half the liabilities to be assumed by the survivor, then splitting the total equally between Chrissie and the estate. From these latter amounts the court subtracted the bases of the deceased partner's interests to Chrissie and the estate, leaving gain to each of an amount exactly equal to their shares of the unrealized receivables. And since ordinary gain was to be computed first under a cross-purchase agreement, the entire gain here, being attributable to unrealized receivables, was held taxable as ordinary income and income in respect of a decedent. A concomitant result was that, because of the reduction in the deceased partner's basis on account of the unrealized receivables, there was no capital loss as an offset to the ordinary income gain. Section 732(d) was held inapplicable in the absence of a property distribution by the partnership. In affirming the Tax Court's decision, the 9th Circuit cited the *Quick Trust* case, previoulsy summarized, which concerned an entity type of liquidation arrangement, as calling for a similar result.

From these cases the conclusion is obvious that any cross-purchase (or entity) agreement set up by a partnership that has a substantial amount of unrealized receivables should anticipate that they will generate ordinary income to the estate on the sale of a deceased partner's interest and should spread the payments for such receivables over a period of at least two or three years.

Payments made by the surviving partners under a cross-purchase agreement do not reduce their incomes. But, if an election to adjust basis of assets under Section 754 is made, such payments do increase the basis of assets, including unrealized receivables. The effect of this is that when the partnership collects the unrealized receivables the surviving partners will not be taxed on the portion purchased from the estate if the amount collected therefor is the same as the price paid.

Summarized comparison of the two types of plans. From the foregoing discussion and those in Chapter 9, we can present a brief comparison of the two types of continuation plans. Where there are several partners and the partnership is expected to continue despite deaths of members, the entity plan has distinct advantages. The handling of the insurance policies is greatly simplified, and their cash values are readily available to the firm in an emergency. Also, where income payments are to be made on behalf of a deceased partner, handling such payments by the partnership not only results in clear-cut income tax deductions by the partnership, but also is considered the most reliable arrangement from the standpoint of the estate and heirs. Further, the entity plan permits a tax choice regarding payments for good will. And as discussed in some detail in Chapter 9, the entity plan prevents the closing of the firm's taxable year and the bunching of income, where different taxable years are used.

On the other hand, a cross-purchase plan effective at the date of death closes the partnership's taxable year with respect to the deceased partner, an advantage where the same taxable years are used. The cross-purchase plan is also simpler in operation where the partnership has only two or three members. Furthermore, as discussed in Chapter 9, an insured cross-purchase plan results in a higher increase in the bases of the surviving partners' interests than does an insured entity plan.

In choosing their plan, the members of professional partnerships should consider carefully these and all other characteristics of the two types of plans and select the one that best suits their particular circumstances. Whichever plan is selected, the partners will find it to their advantage to make sure that it is fully insured.

WHAT THE PLAN SHOULD ACCOMPLISH

The plan adopted by the members of a professional partnership should accomplish several important objectives. First, it should transfer to the continuing partnership, or to its surviving members, the deceased partner's interest in the fixed assets. This may be accomplished by a provision for paying the exact amount of his capital account, or for paying an annually agreed—upon stated amount. Second, it should provide payment to the decedent's estate of his share of undistributed partnership profits realized before his death. Third, it should provide for income payments over a stated period of a few years, representing the decedent's interest in uncollected accounts and work in process. This may be accomplished by a provision to pay a stated percentage of future partnership profits, or to pay a fixed amount of payments annually or more often, for a stated period of years. The latter provision is again stressed as the most advantageous because it assures the deceased partner's family of a fixed income, rather than one that fluctuates with the firm's profits, for the agreed period; it assures the continuing partnership against interference from the decedent's executor because he will have no right to an accounting of the firm's profits; and it assures funding of the amount in advance with life insurance because it calls for a known fixed amount. Thus, the objectives that a suitable continuation plan may accomplish should make such a plan most attractive to a professional partnership.

PROFESSIONAL PARTNERSHIP PLANS
SPECIFICALLY ENFORCEABLE

As in the case of continuation plans of commercial partnerships, professional partnerships' continuation agreements are specifically enforced by the courts. A recent case on the subject, involving the continuation agreement of a medical partnership, is *Adams v. Jarvis.*[7]

---

[7] 23 Wis.2d 453, 127 N.W.2d 400 (1964).

Chapter 14

TAX PROBLEMS INVOLVED IN THE INSURED BUY-SELL PLAN

THE FEDERAL INCOME TAX

The partnership return and scheme of taxing partners. Partnerships, as such, are not taxpayers under the Federal income tax law. Each partnership, however, must file a return. In this return the ordinary net income of the firm is calculated by totaling the gross profits and other income of the partnership and subtracting from this gross income the regular business deductions such as salaries and wages of employees (including any salaries paid to partners), rent, repairs, interest, taxes, depreciation, *et cetera*. (This calculation closely follows the schedule in the individual tax return that the life underwriter is accustomed to fill out in order to show his gross income, business expenses, and net income from conducting his insurance business.) The share of the net income of the partnership to which each partner is entitled is then shown on an appropriate schedule in the partnership return.

Another schedule itemizes gains and losses from sales or exchanges of capital assets of the partnership, and the share of each partner in the short term capital gains and losses and in the long term capital gains and losses is separately shown. The return also reports each partner's share in the charitable contributions made by the partnership, and includes may other schedules for the purpose of itemizing details that are of no interest to us here.

This partnership return having been made, each partner then includes in his individual income tax return his salary, if any, and his share of the ordinary income of the firm, whether or not it has been distributed to him. Each partner also includes with his personal capital gains and losses his share of the capital gains and losses of the partnership. There are other important items, such as the deduction of the partner's share of charitable contributions made by the firm, but our principal concern at this point is merely to outline the broad scheme of taxation as it relates to the partnership and to the individual partners.

The life insurance premiums not deductible. The premiums paid for life insurance made subject to a buy-sell agreement are not deductible as business expenses. This holds true whether the premiums are paid by the insured partner, by the other partners, or by the firm itself.[1] If paid by the firm, the result taxwise or otherwise is the same as it would have been had each partner paid premiums in proportion as he shares in the earnings of the partnership.

The rule that premiums are not deductible business expense also holds true regardless of the beneficiary designations contained in the policies.[2]

The life insurance proceeds generally not taxable income. Life insurance proceeds paid by reason of the death of a partner insured under a buy-sell agreement are not subject to income tax, as a general rule.[3] Formerly, there was an exception in the case of a policy that has been transferred for value to a partner or to his firm. The Internal Revenue Code of 1954, however, provides that a policy may be transferred for value to a partner of the insured, or to a partnership in which the insured is a partner, without subjecting the proceeds at death to income tax as the proceeds of a policy transferred for value.[4] Thus, an uninsurable partner with a surplus of personal insurance can sell some of it to the partnership or to the other partners for the purpose of purchasing his interest in the firm at his death. Likewise, under a cross-purchase agreement the surviving partners may purchase from a deceased partner's estate the policies the deceased owned on the lives of the survivors and continue such insurance under the agreement.

The sale or liquidation of a deceased partner's interest. In discussing Chapters 9 and 13 the various factors to be considered in making a choice between a cross-purchase and an entity agreement, the income tax implications of each type of agreement have been discussed in adequate detail. Therefore, reference should be made to those discussions; no useful purpose would be served in repeating them here.

---

[1]I.R.C., Secs. 262 and 264(a)(1); *Clarence W. McKay,* 10 B.T.A. 949; *Ernest J. Keefe,* 15 T.C. 952.

[2]*Clarence W. McKay, supra; Ernest J. Keefe, supra; Joseph Nussbaum,* 19 B.T.A. 868.

[3]I.R.C., Sec. 101(a)(1).

[4]I.R.C., Sec. 101(a)(2)(B).

THE FEDERAL ESTATE TAX

No double taxation. In general, it may be said that the existence of an insured partnership buy-sell plan does not materially affect the amount of estate taxes a deceased partner's personal representative will be called upon to pay. This is because the courts have repeatedly prohibited inclusion in the taxable estate of both the value of the deceased partner's interest and the insurance proceeds received by the estate in payment for the sale of that interest.[5]

The decisions of the courts, however, have not been consistent in determining which of the two types of property, to the extent that the partnership interest and the purchase price for it represents the same value to the estate, should be included in the taxable estate. For example, the Board of Tax Appeals in *Boston Safe Deposit and Trust Co. (Estate of Scovell)*,[6] held that the full value of the partnership interest, $129,247.19, was to be included in the decedent's taxable estate, and that the insurance proceeds, $100,000, applied on the purchase price were to be excluded. Then, in the subsequent case of *M.W. Dobrzensky, Executor,*[7] the Board reversed its reasoning by holding that the insurance proceeds were taxable, and that the value of the deceased partner's interest represented by the insurance was to be excluded. The current trend is to look at the tax status of the insurance first, taxing it if the policies are so arranged as to come within the taxable provisions of the statute, and exempting from the taxable estate an equivalent amount representing the partnership interest. With reference to an entity agreement, it is interesting to note that a partner has been held not to possess any incidents of ownership in a policy on his life owned by and payable to his partnership.[8]

Another interesting case is *Infante's Estate.*[9] That case concerned an insured cross-purchase agreement. Each partner was the owner and beneficiary of the policies on his co-partner's life, pursuant to the agreement, but it also provided that ". . . so long as this agreement remains in force and prior to the death of either of the partners, neither partner will borrow against or surrender the policy or policies which he owns for the purpose of this agreement, or change the beneficiary or make settlement thereof without the consent of the other partner thereto." Upon Infante's death, the agreement valued his partnership interest at $55,000, which also was the price the

---

[5] *Estate of Ray E. Tompkins,* 13 T.C. 1054.

[6] 30 B.T.A. 679.

[7] 34 B.T.A. 305.

[8] *Estate of Frank H. Knipp,* 24 T.C. 153 (1955).

[9] 29 T.C.M. 903 (1970).

survivor paid for it. The survivor, however, collected $125,500 of insurance proceeds (partially accidental death benefits) on the policies he owned on the decedent's life under the agreement. The decedent's estate tax return included $55,000 as the value of his partnership interest, plus the cash value of the insurance he had owned on the survivor's life. The Revenue Service, contending that the veto power given the decedent under the agreement was an incident of ownership, included the $125,000 insurance proceeds in the decedent's estate instead of the $55,000 value of his partnership interest. The Tax Court disagreed, holding that the decedent's veto power in the agreement was not an incident of ownership in the policies on his life; its purpose was to obligate each in a manner that would give assurance that the proceeds would be available for the purpose intended. The opinion added:

> ... By so obligating themselves, each gave up the right to any of the economic benefits of the policy except those provided for in the partnership agreement. Each also gave up any right to control the flow of economic benefits for any purpose other than the one specified in the agreement. If either partner had acted to violate the agreement, the other would have a valid cause of action against him on the contract. On this basis, restrictions of the type utilized in this case, which are included in the partnership agreement to insure that funds are available for the purchase of a deceased partner's interest, should not form a basis for the inclusion of the policy in the estate of the decedent where the decedent does not otherwise possess any "incidents of ownership" under the terms of the policy itself.

We add that this must be considered a liberal decision until it has been supported by the higher Federal courts. A provision that requires adequate notice to the insured before the policy owner can exercise his ownership rights in a cross-purchase policy is safe taxwise and may be just as satisfactory to the partners.

The insured purchase plan establishes Federal estate tax value. The insured buy-sell plan performs an important function in connection with Federal estate taxation. The value agreed upon as the purchase price of the deceased partner's interest is held to govern for estate tax purposes, even though the actual value is higher at time of death, if (1) it fairly represents the value of the interest at the time the purchase price is stipulated in an arm's length transaction, and (2) the partner has been prohibited from disposing of his interest from the time of the execution of the buy-sell contract until his death without first offering it to the other partners at the contract price.[10]

This fact may be of great benefit to the deceased's estate. Without a

---

[10]*Estate of Lionel Weil,* 22 T.C. 1267 (1954); *Angela Fiorito,* 33 T.C. 440 (1959); *Brodrick v. Gore,* 224 F.2d 892 (1955).

subsisting agreement, a difficult appraisal must be made at the time of the death, not only of the value of the tangible assets of the partnership, but also of the value of good will. At best, the values to be established in such an appraisal are to a considerable degree matters of opinion about which honest men may disagree. Therefore, it is not unusual for the Government and the deceased's estate to be far apart in their respective opinions as to the value of a deceased partner's interest, a divergency that often leads to dispute, prolonged negotiations, and sometimes to litigation, in order to determine the value. The result to the estate is a delayed and costly settlement of the deceased partner's affairs, all of which is avoided by a properly set up insured purchase agreement.

The fact that the purchase price in a properly set up buy-sell agreement controls for Federal estate tax purposes appears sound in principle because the partnership interest cannot be worth any more to the estate than the estate is bound to accept in an obligatory sale. The proviso that the purchase price must be adequate when it is established is, of course, necessary to prevent undervaluations made to avoid estate taxes.

STATE DEATH TAXES

Two divergent rules have developed in the states as to the effect of a buy-sell agreement on the valuation of a business interest for death tax purposes. A few of the states follow the Federal rule under which the purchase price in a properly arranged agreement governs for valuation purposes. Among these states are Maryland, Mississippi, New York and Pennsylvania (by statute), as well as the District of Columbia.

Several other states follow the so-called inheritance tax rule, to the effect that the agreement does not govern value but will be considered with other evidence of value. States having an inheritance tax justify the rule on the ground that this tax, as distinguished from an estate tax, falls upon the value of property *received* by the estate beneficiaries, rather than upon the value of property as it passes from the decedent. These states tax any excess value over the purchase price as a transfer for an inadequate consideration intended to take effect at death. Among the states applying the rule are Kentucky, Massachusetts, New Jersey, Ohio, Tennessee, Texas, Washington and Wisconsin. Many states have not decided the issue, but the trend in states levying inheritance taxes is to adopt that rule.

CORPORATIONS

Part I

FUNDAMENTAL FACTS
ABOUT CORPORATIONS

Chapter 1

GENERAL INFORMATION
ABOUT CORPORATIONS

Knowledge of the fundamental nature of a corporation is necessary to understand and appreciate both the problems brought about by the death of a close corporation stockholder and the most satisfactory arrangements for the continuation of the corporate business, in the best interests of the deceased's family as well as the surviving stockholders.

WHAT A CORPORATION IS

Corporation defined. One of the early definitions of a corporation was recorded in the year 1613 when Lord Coke, in the case of *Sutton's Hospital*,[1] said: "A corporation aggregate of many is invisible, immortal, and rests only in intendment and consideration of the law." In the year 1819, Chief Justice Marshall of the United States Supreme Court, in the case of *Dartmouth College v. Woodward*,[2] nearly repeated the words of Lord Coke by stating: "A corporation is an artificial being, invisible, intangible, and existing only in contemplation of law." These and similar definitions, however, have been severely criticized as overemphasizing the nature of a corporation as an artificial legal entity and failing to give proper emphasis to the association of natural persons that comprise its membership. A modern and realistic

---

[1] 10 Coke's Rep. 1, 32.
[2] 4 Wheat. (U.S.) 518.

249

definition by the late Professor Wormser is as follows: "In the last analysis, it would seem correct to state that a corporation is a group of one or more human beings acting as a unit and vested with personality by the policy of the law."[3]

HOW CORPORATIONS ARE FORMED

A corporation may be created only by virtue of sovereign authority. So far as we are concerned here, such authority rests with each state and with the Federal government. Ordinary business corporations, the type in which we are interested, are chartered by the Federal government if they are set up in the District of Columbia, otherwise, by the various state governments.

Originally, each corporation charter was granted by a special legislative act. But the tremendous development of the corporate form of conducting business proved this method too cumbersome, and general incorporation laws, under which corporations can be organized with greater speed and better supervision, were enacted.

Under the most modern of these laws, the procedure to be followed in creating a corporation is concise and well-defined. The organizers prepare a certificate of incorporation that includes such facts as the name of the corporation, the location of its principal office, its purpose in detail, data regarding its capital stock, its duration, the number of its directors, the names and addresses of the incorporators and the number of shares of stock each has agreed to take, and any other information required by the particular state statute. (Usually, the law lays down specifications as to minimum number of incorporators and directors, and as to a minimum number of them who must be citizens of the United States and residents of the state of incorporation.) The completed certificate is then sent to the proper state official, often the Secretary of State, together with the necessary incorporation tax and fees. If it is found to be in proper form and otherwise in compliance with the law, copies will be filed in the required locations, and the new corporation is born. It will become fully organized when the organization meetings of the incorporators and of the directors have been held, at which time by-laws will be adopted for the government of the corporation, its officers will be elected, and any other business will be transacted that the incorporators then wish to complete. At this point, the corporation is ready for business.

Thus a corporation comes into being by the incorporators complying with the stipulated requirements of the state. The state, by enacting the corporation law, has made a general offer to prospective incorporators to form a corporation. The incorporators, by their compliance with the terms of the offer set out in the statute, have accepted the offer. The resulting relation-

---

[3]I. Maurice Wormser, *Frankenstein, Incorporated.* New York: McGraw-Hill Book Company, Inc., 1931, p. 62.

ship, therefore, between the incorporators and the state is contractual in nature.

TYPES OF CORPORATIONS

Corporations may be classified in many different ways, but an exhaustive classification will not be attempted here. For our purposes, we may start by making a division between public and private corporations. The public corporation is a governmental body, as, for example, a state or political subdivision of a state. Private corporations may be subdivided into stock corporations and non-stock corporations.

Non-stock corporations are usually subdivided into various types of membership, including religious and eleemosynary corporations.

A stock corporation is one that has a capital stock divided into shares and that is empowered by law to distribute dividends or shares of surplus profits to its stockholders. Such corporations may be further classified as moneyed or financial corporations (such as banks and insurance companies), public service corporations, and business corporations.

A business corporation may be defined as one organized to carry on manufacturing, trading, or other ordinary commercial pursuits. These corporations, for our purposes, may be subdivided into publicly-held corporations and close corporations. The former is typified by those corporations owned by a substantial number of stockholders, most of whom take no part in the active management of the enterprise.

Close corporations. A close corporation may be defined as a corporation whose franchise is owned by a small group of stockholders, all of whom usually are actively engaged in its mangement. Frequently, all of this group comprises the board of directors and officers, as well as the only shareholders. It is a business organization that, in its unity of ownership and management in the hands of a small, closely knit coterie of persons, strongly resembles a partnership. Because of this resemblance, the close corporation owners are exposed to business continuation problems somewhat similar to those of partners and stand in need of an equally satisfactory solution. Consequently, this text will be concerned primarily with the close corporation.

Special forms of close corporations. Principally to obtain certain Federal income tax benefits, two special forms of close corporations have developed in recent years. One of these, although in other respects a regular close corporation, is commonly called a Subchapter S corporation because it has elected to qualify and be subject to Federal income tax under Subchapter S of the Internal Revenue Code, enacted in 1958. Among the qualifications for this election are that the corporation have only one class of stock and have ten or fewer stockholders, all of whom are individuals or estates. The tax results are that the corporation is not subject to the accumulated earnings tax and avoids the corporate income tax; its profits are taxed directly to its stockholders. Such corporations are discussed in more detail later.

The other special form of close corporation is the professional corporation. Such corporations are creatures of special enabling statutes enacted in recent years by all of the states to overcome the prohibition in pre-existing statutes and court decisions against the practice of a profession through the corporate form. Tax results are that the corporation is subject to the Federal income tax on corporations (or, if qualified, it may elect Subchapter S taxation), and it may take advantage of tax-favored corporate employee benefit plans. These corporations also are discussed in more detail later.

Chapter 2

THE POWERS AND MANAGEMENT
OF A CORPORATION

POWERS IN GENERAL

A corporation has only such powers as are expressly granted to it by the state and as are found in the formal corporate charter and applicable statutes, together with such implied powers as are incidental to, or consequent upon, or reasonably necessary to the carrying out of those powers specifically conferred upon it.

It has power to conduct the type or types of business authorized by its charter and no other. Therefore, it is customary to make the expressed powers in the charter as broad as possible in order to avoid any question of *ultra vires* acts, acts that are beyond the powers of the corporation. A corporation may ordinarily be formed for any lawful purpose. Special statutes and requirements govern the organization and conduct of corporations to carry on banking, insurance, transportation, and other businesses closely related to the public interest.

The practice of law, however, occupies a special status in that the inherent power to control it in most states lies in the state's highest court rather than in its legislature.[1] Thus, although the Committee on Professional Ethics of the American Bar Association has stated that the practice of law by a professional corporation may not violate the Canon of Ethics (Opinion No.

---

[1] *In re Opinion of the Justices,* 289 Mass. 607, 194 N.E. 313.

303, 1-11-61), and although a state has enacted an enabling statute, final authority for such practice must come from the state's top court.[2]

Among the incidental powers of a corporation is the power of continued existence during the period designated in its charter, subject to any reserved right of the state to dissolve it sooner. It has the right to use its corporate name and it has the power to change such name, subject to applicable laws relating to this. It has the right to have and use a corporate seal, although in most states its use is not required except for such formal documents as deeds, bonds, mortgages and the like in cases in which the seal of an individual would be required under similar circumstances. It has the power to enter into all contracts necessary to carry on its business. It has the power to employ officers and other employees and agents to conduct its affairs. It has the power to acquire, hold, and otherwise deal with property for purposes consistent with the powers granted to it. It has the power to borrow money and to contract indebtedness, to furnish security for any debt and to loan money if necessary. It has power to sue and be sued in its corporate name. It has power to make by-laws for the government of its affairs consistent with its formal charter and the applicable statutes. It has power to enter into joint ventures, but not to become a partner unless specifically authorized by charter. Generally, unless authorized by statute or charter, it has no power to purchase the stock of another corporation, but this rule is modified in cases in which it is necessary to acquire such stock to protect some right in which event the stock of another corporation may be acquired. A typical example of this is the acquisition of such stock in liquidation of a debt that might be worthless otherwise.

POWER OF A CORPORATION TO ACQUIRE ITS OWN STOCK

In England the courts have held that a corporation, unless expressly authorized, has no right to purchase its own shares of stock. At common law in America, a small coterie of states have followed the English doctrine that such a purchase was *ultra vires,* but the majority of our courts have held that a corporation has an implied power to acquire its own shares, provided it does so in good faith and without injury to its creditors or stockholders. To prevent such injury, it is held almost universally that such purchase must be made out of surplus. Massachusetts, however, appears to require only that the purchase be made in good faith and that it does not result in loss to its creditors or stockholders. In *Barrett v. W.A. Webster Lumber Co.,*[3] it is said: "The contention of the plaintiff that a corporation cannot purchase its own stock except out of surplus profits cannot be sustained."

---

[2]*In re Forida Bar,* (Fla.), 133 So. 2d 554 (1961).

[3]275 Mass. 302, 175 N.E. 765 (1931).

In recent years, many states have legislated on this matter, and nearly all of the states that formerly followed the English rule have enacted statutes permitting such purchases under proper circumstances. Because of the frequency with which changes occur by reason of new statutes and court decisions, no attempt will be made here to present the current status of such a transaction in each state. The most suitable media for such an exhibit are the loose-leaf business insurance services, to which the reader is referred for up-to-the-minute information with respect to any state in which he is particularly interested. Furthermore, a local attorney should be consulted if the matter is not entirely clear.

Distinction should be made between the power of a corporation to make a present purchase of its own shares and its ability to enter into a valid contract in which the corporation agrees to make such a purchase at some future time. If, for example, the particular state law allows a purchase only out of corporate surplus, such a contract obviously cannot be consummated by the corporation when the time for performance comes if at that time the corporate surplus is insufficient to pay for the stock. This fact introduces a contingency, a possible circumstance under which the corporation will be unable to perform, which in turn raises the vital question as to whether such a contract is binding at all. It would seem that the promise of the corporation to make the purchase can be construed as a promise to do so unless at the time for performance it had no surplus with which to make the purchase, and as so construed, the corporation's promise can be deemed to be more than illusory and therefore to constitute sufficient consideration for the agreement. However, one New York case held to the contrary.[4]

In that case, a close corporation sold 114 shares of stock to an employee and entered into an agreement with him in which the corporation was to repurchase the stock at its book value upon termination of the employment of the employee. Bearing on the case was Section 664 of the New York Penal Law which provides that it is a misdemeanor for a director of a corporation to vote "to apply any portion of the funds of such corporation, except surplus profits, directly or indirectly, to the purchase of shares of its own stock." Upon termination of employment, the employee refused to sell the stock on the ground that the agreement was not binding. The corporation brought suit for specific performance, but New York's highest court sustained the employee's position. The reasoning of the court appears to have been that because it would have been impossible for the corporation to perform the contract if no surplus existed when the employee left, the contract was one not mutually binding on the parties and therefore lacking in consideration. It is very important to note, however, that the court also pointed out that, if the corporation had given as consideration something other than its bare

---

[4]*Topkin, Loring & Schwartz v. Schwartz,* 249 N.Y. 206 (1928).

promise to buy the stock, e.g., had given employment to the employee *in consideration* for his agreement to sell the stock at the end of his employment, then the contract would have been enforceable unless, as a matter of defense by the corporation, no surplus existed with which to make the purchase. Up to the effective date of the New York Business Corporation Law, September 1, 1963, this latter point had an important bearing on our main subject, which will be developed later.

THE MANAGEMENT OF A CORPORATION

The stockholders. As we have seen, the nature and extent of the powers of a corporation are those specifically granted to it and contained in its charter and in the applicable statutes, together with those incidentally implied therefrom. To set these powers in motion, the stockholders will elect a board of directors and will adopt by-laws (or will delegate this task to the board) that define the duties and regulate the conduct of the members and officers.

The stockholders, as such, have no authority to participate in the conduct of the ordinary business of the corporation, since these activities are managed by the board. In addition to the election of directors, however, there is usually reserved to the stockholders, by law, decisions on various important matters pertaining to the existence, powers, and capital structure of the corporation. Among these matters are the approval of the disposal of the aggregate corporate assets; approval of a mortgage on the corporate property; amendment of the corporate charter; increase, reduction or other change in the capital stock; and approval of the dissolution of the corporation or its merger or consolidation with another corporation.

In some of these matters, the stockholders decide by majority vote; in others, for example, the mortgaging of the corporation's realty, a two-thirds or greater vote is usually required by statute. In addition, the laws of a few states now require the vote of the stockholders before a corporation may purchase its own stock and they specify the affirmative percentage necessary to secure approval.

The board of directors. Following their election, the board of directors chosen by the stockholders meet and take up the management of the ordinary affairs of the corporation, since such management is placed in their hands by the laws of most states. It should be noted, however, that a board member as such has no individual authority to act for the corporation; he acts only as a *board* with his fellow members when they are assembled at a duly held meeting of the directors. Corporate officers are elected and their salaries fixed by the directors. These officers proceed through their own efforts and the efforts of hired agents and employees, to carry into execution the daily routine of the corporation's business.

The board of directors, however, can delegate to officers and agents only ministerial power to administer the affairs of the corporation. As manager of the corporation and the primary possessor of all the power conferred by the corporate charter, the board cannot delegate the exercise of the discretionary powers vested in it, such as, for example, the election of officers or the declaration of corporate dividends.

In their possession and use of the property of the corporation and in their management of its business, the directors, although not strictly trustees, occupy a fiduciary relation to the corporation and its stockholders, and are obligated to exercise the same degree of care and prudence in conducting its affairs as would be exercised by the ordinary prudent man in conducting his own affairs, to the end that the corporate assets will not be wrongfully wasted, dissipated or misapplied. Accordingly, a director may not exercise his official position for his own benefit; he must act only for the benefit of the corporation. Furthermore, by the weight of authority, any contract between a director and his corporation is voidable by the corporation.

Ordinary routine contracts of a corporation are usually entered into on its behalf by its officers. The board of directors, however, may make any ordinary contract that the corporation is empowered to make. But as previously stated, an individual director has no such power to act for the corporation; he functions solely through the collective action of the board in its duly constituted meetings.

In sizable corporations, it is common practice for the board of directors to set up subcommittees from among their members and to delegate to these committees various advisory and ministerial duties. The board may, for example, form an executive committee or a finance committee reporting to, and responsible to, the board of directors.

Officers and agents of the corporation. Since the board of directors acts only in an official meeting and since such meetings cannot be held continuously, it delegates the performance of ministerial duties on behalf of the corporation to officers and agents. The officers are elected by the board of directors, which board also regulates their salaries. The official positions to be filled and the duties of each office are customarily specified in the by-laws and usually consist, as a minimum, of a president, one or more vice-presidents, a secretary and a treasurer.

Upon these officers falls the task of carrying on the business of the corporation, including the hiring and supervision of the agents and ordinary employees of the organization.

Chapter 3

PROPERTY RIGHTS AND LIABILITIES
IN A CORPORATION

The corporation, of all types of business organization, presents the most interesting and unique pattern of property rights and liabilities, both in respect of the corporation itself and of the stockholders. Some of the details of this pattern will be discussed.

THE ASSETS OF THE CORPORATION

The corner grocery is a close corporation, King & Gay, Inc., with Mr. King and Mr. Gay the only stockholders. Now, who owns the can of beans on the shelf? The title is vested in the corporation as a separate legal entity and the can of beans can be sold to a customer only by the corporation, acting through its authorized representatives. Neither Mr. King nor Mr. Gay has any legal ownership in the beans. If someone takes unlawful possession of them, the beans can be recovered only in the name of the corporation. In other words, the assets of a corporation are owned by the corporation and not by the stockholders, and this is true even though there is only a single stockholder. If Mr. King, for example, wants to own the beans, he may purchase them from the corporation; or he may receive title to them if a dividend, payable in property, is declared by the corporation out of surplus profits; or he may receive title to the beans as part of his share upon a dissolution of the corporation, liquidation of its affairs, and distribution of the remaining assets to the stockholders.

THE INTEREST OF EACH STOCKHOLDER

What property, then, do Mr. King and Mr. Gay own in connection with the corporation? Do they own the capital stock that they contributed to it when they dissolved their partnership and formed the corporation? No, the capital stock of a corporation is the money or property put into the corporate fund by the subscribers, which fund becomes the property of the corporation. What they do own are certain valuable but intangible rights.

First, they collectively own the franchise of the corporation *to be* a corporation. This primary franchise of its being a corporation is a special privilege conferred by the state and vests in the group of individuals who compose the corporation. Second, they own the bundle of rights accruing to one who holds a share in a stock corporation. As expressed in the case of *Burrall v. The Bushwick R.R. Co.,*[1] "A share of the capital stock, is the right to partake, according to the amount put into the fund [the capital stock], the surplus profits of the corporation; and ultimately on the dissolution of it, of so much of the fund thus created, as remains unimpaired, and is not liable for debts of the corporation."

In addition to the two basic rights that, according to the quoted definition, go to make up a share of stock, namely, the right to receive an aliquot share of surplus profits in the form of dividends when they are declared and the right to receive a like share of the residuum upon the dissolution of the corporation, a stockholder has other important rights, some of which are exercisable by him alone. His remaining rights are exercisable only when he acts with the other stockholders as a body.

Among these additional rights are: The right to receive a certificate as evidence of his share of the stock; the right to transfer his stock interest and to have the transfer made on the corporate books; the right to inspect the books and records of the corporation; the right to attend stockholders' meetings and to vote for directors; the right to adopt by-laws; the right to require that the property of the corporation be employed for proper corporate purposes; the right to subscribe for any new shares of stock; and usually, the right to vote on such fundamental matters as change of corporate name, increase or decrease in (or other alteration of) the capital structure of the corporation, or any material change in the scope of the corporate business. Some of these rights have an important bearing on our subject and will be discussed further.

The right to dividends. A stockholder's "right to partake, according to the amount put into the fund, of the surplus profits of the corporation" is his right to share in dividends as and when they are declared by the board of

---

[1] 75 N.Y. 211.

directors of the corporation. Dividends are corporate funds derived from the earnings and profits of the corporation and appropriated by a corporate act to the use of, and to be divided among, the stockholders.

It should be reiterated that dividends of a corporation are declared, not by the stockholders, but by the board of directors of the corporation. Even though a majority of the stockholders want such action, the directors may honestly refuse to vote for dividends. Probably in most jurisdictions, a dividend could be declared by the unanimous vote of all the stockholders but such action, for obvious reasons, is a rare exception. Normally, the only recourse of the stockholders is to vote for a change of directors at the next election of the board.

But if the stockholders can prove to a court of equity that the directors, in refusing to declare dividends, are acting not in good faith in the interest of the corporation, but rather to serve their own personal ends, the court will grant relief. Nevertheless, successful prosecution of such a suit is exceedingly difficult, for the stockholders "must establish as matter of law that the action of the directors on this record was inimical to the welfare of the corporation and all its stockholders."[2]

The cited case was an action brought to compel the payment of dividends. It was proved that earnings and assets were ample to do this. It was also proved that the president and director of the corporation had shown personal animosity toward the widow and child who owned the beneficial interest in the block of stock held in trust by the plaintiff bank. But the court, in refusing to interfere with the policy of the directors in not declaring dividends, had this to say in part: "That such personal animosity is visible may not be denied, but it does not follow that the impelling motive of the action of the board was such ill feeling. On the contrary, the old policy has been continued, not as a freeze-out policy, but to pay debts and provide against emergencies. . . ."

One of the few successful cases of this nature, and well worth reading, is that of *Dodge v. Ford Motor Co.*[3]

On July 31, 1916, the Ford Company, a gigantic close corporation, had capital stock of $2,000,000 and surplus of about $112,000,000. Notwithstanding the fact that it was selling cars for $440 (reduced to $360 on August 1st, 1916) its profits during the last fiscal year had been over $60,000,000 and it had on hand approximately $54,000,000 of bonds and cash. The company was paying a regular quarterly dividend equal to 5 percent monthly on the capital stock and since 1910 had paid the stockholders $41,000,000 in special dividends. No special dividends had been voted after October, 1915,

---

[2]*City Bank Farmers Trust Co. v. Hewitt Realty Co.*, 257 N.Y. 62, 177 N.E. 309 (1931).

[3]204 Mich. 459, 170 N.W. 668, 3 A.L.R. 413 (1919).

however, and the Dodge brothers, owners of one-tenth of the stock, brought this action to compel an additional dividend payment. Although the corporation declared a special dividend of $2,000,000 in November, 1916, before filing an answer in the action, the court decreed the payment of 'an additional dividend of over $19,000,000. While justifying the decree on the facts, the court nevertheless quoted the applicable rule as phrased by various authorities, including Cook on *Corporations* (7th ed.) section 545, which reads in part:

> It requires a very strong case to induce a court of equity to order the directors to declare a dividend, inasmuch as equity has no jurisdiction, unless fraud or a breach of trust is involved.

If there exists only one class of stock, namely, common stock, each share is entitled to its pro rata amount of the total dividends declared. In many instances, however, one or more classes of preferred stock are also issued. Preferred stock is a class of stock entitling the owner to whatever preferences are agreed to in the stock certificate and in the charter. The rights of the holder are contractual and are confined to these provisions. Usually there is a preference as to dividends and often there is included, also, a preference in the distribution of the remaining assets of the corporation in the event of its dissolution. These shares may be given a priority in the appropriation of dividends up to an agreed percentage, such as 6 percent, which may be made the maximum dividend rate on such stock. Or, it may be provided that dividends beyond the stated preferential figure shall be shared equally with the common stock, in which case the preferred stock is usually called "participating." The priority granted the preferred stock may be cumulative or non-cumulative. If it is non-cumulative, the preferred shareholders are entitled to receive the specified dividends in any one year before any dividends may be declared on common stock during that particular year, but each year is taken by itself. If the stock is cumulative, the shareholders are entitled to receive the specified dividends accumulated from the time the preferred stock was issued before any dividends may be declared on the common stock.

The general rule is that ordinary dividends on any class of stock, common or preferred, may not be paid except out of surplus, and every shareholder must be treated in the same manner as every other shareholder of the same class.

The right to inspect the corporate books and records. At common law, and by statute in most states, a stockholder has a right to inspect the books and records of the corporation at reasonable times and places and for proper purposes. In fact, most state statutes grant this right, regardless of the motive or purpose behind the inspection. Generally, this right may be exercised in person or by the stockholder's authorized agent or attorney, and copies and memoranda may be made for reference. In most instances, this right will be enforced in a court proceeding if such inspection has been wrongfully denied by the corporation. It is a valuable privilege, especially in the case of a minority stockholder.

The right to attend stockholders' meetings and vote. Incident to the ownership of a common share in a private corporation is the right of the shareholder to attend meetings of the stockholders and to vote upon the corporate matters acted upon at such times as, for example, the election of members of the board of directors. In large corporations the right to vote by proxy—conferred by statute, charter or by-law—is frequently exercised. In close corporations, all the stockholders are usually present to vote in person. In a stockholders' meeting, a shareholder represents himself and his own interests and has a right to vote as he desires. Ordinarily, his motives are irrelevant, although there is an implication that the corporate affairs will be conducted in the interest of all of the stockholders.

As a general rule, the majority of outstanding stock must be represented at a meeting to constitute a quorum for transacting business, and a majority vote of the stock represented at such a meeting will carry the matters voted on, except as to certain extraordinary matters that, by statute or by-law, may require the affirmative vote of the holders of perhaps as much as two-thirds of the outstanding stock.

One vote is generally allowed by statute for each share of voting stock. In corporations having more than one class of stock outstanding, such as common and preferred, it is often provided that the preferred shall be non-voting stock, or shall not have voting power unless dividends on the preferred have been in arrears for a stipulated period.

In many states, statutes authorize cumulative voting by stockholders when two or more vacancies are to be filled on the board of directors. Under such statutes, a stockholder may cast as many votes as there are offices to be filled, multiplied by the number of his shares of stock, all of which votes may be cast for one candidate or distributed among the candidates as the stockholder sees fit. A stockholder with 50 shares, for example, could cast 50 votes each for three candidates to fill three vacancies on the board; he could "cumulate" all the votes he is entitled to cast for all three vacancies and divide them among the candidates in whatever proportion he desires; or he could cast the total 150 votes in favor of one particular candidate. By means of this cumulative voting device, minority stockholders are often able to obtain representation on the board when they otherwise could be outvoted on every office to be filled. It should be kept in mind, however, that the decisions of the board of directors in conducting the affairs of the corporation are usually made by majority vote and therefore that mere representation on the board still will leave the minority stockholders with little "say" in the actual management of the corporation.

The right to transfer stock. As an incident of his ownership of stock, a shareholder has a general property right to transfer his shares at will. This inherent right of alienation, however, may be reasonably restricted by the corporate charter or by contract between the stockholders, although "an absolute prohibition unlimited in point of time against transfer of stock would be invalid as against public policy."[4] Accordingly, it is generally held that a restriction against the sale of shares of stock unless other stockholders or the corporation have first been given the opportunity to buy, contained in the corporate charter (and not merely in the buy-laws), or in a stockholders' agreement, with the stock certificates adequately inscribed, is valid.[5] The law on the subject is well summed up by Judge Untermeyer in *Penthouse Properties, Inc. v. 1158 Fifth Ave., Inc.,*[6] as follows:

> The general rule that the ownership of property cannot exist in one person and the right of alienation in another . . . has in this State been frequently applied to shares of corporate stock . . . and cognizance has been taken of the principle that "the right of transfer is a right of property, and if another has the arbitrary power to forbid a transfer of property by the owner, that amounts to annihilation of property". . . . The same rule has been applied in other States. . . . But restrictions against the sale of shares of stock, unless other stockholders or the corporation have first been accorded an opportunity to buy, are not repugnant to that principle. . . . The weight of authority elsewhere is to the same effect. See annotations on *Validity of Restrictions,* 65 A.L.R., pp. 1168-1171. . . .

It may be said in general, however, that the courts look more leniently upon restrictions against the transfer of close corporation stock than upon restrictions involving the shares of large corporations. Furthermore, restrictions imposed as a provision of a private contract between particular stockholders may be considered valid, although similar restrictions appearing only in the corporate by-laws might be held invalid.

It is readily apparent from the foregoing that the scheme of property rights in a corporation is entirely different from that subsisting in a partnership. Because of this, it may be expected that the death of a stockholder has a quite different effect than the death of a partner. A later chapter will show this to be the case.

GENERAL COMMENT ABOUT LIABILITIES

A thorough study of all the phases of liability involved in the corporate

---

[4]*Bloomingdale v. Bloomingdale,* 107 Misc. 646, 177 N.Y.S. 873 (1919).

[5]*Weissman v. Lincoln Corporation,* Fla. 76 So. 2d 478 (1954).

[6]11 N.Y.S. 2d 417, 422 (1939).

form of conducting business is beyond the scope of this text. Some understanding of the subject is necessary, however, and an attempt will be made to review the general rules of liability that concern the corporation itself, its officers and agents, its directors and its stockholders.

LIABILITY OF THE CORPORATION

A corporation is held liable for all acts of its officers, agents and ordinary employees performed within the general powers of the corporation and with the express or implied authority of the corporation. Furthermore, if the representative, although unauthorized, acts within the powers of the corporation, which subsequently ratifies the act or accepts its benefits, the corporation will be held liable.

If an authorized corporation representative enters into a contract which is beyond the powers of the corporation, an *ultra vires* contract, such a contract cannot be enforced against the corporation, unless the other party has already performed and the corporation has received the full benefit of such performance. If such a contract has been fully performed by both parties, the court will usually leave the parties as it finds them. Some courts, however, declare all *ultra vires* contracts void, whether executory, partially executed, or fully executed. Contracts that not only go beyond the express powers of a corporation but are also in themselves illegal, or that go against public policy, are held void in all jurisdictions. But this latter doctrine is not peculiar to corporations; all such contracts are held void, regardless of the identity of the parties involved.

The liability of the corporation for the acts of its representatives when acting within the general scope of their authority goes beyond the field of contracts into the field of torts and sometimes into the field of crimes. Moreover, in these fields the fact that the wrong was committed in the course of a transaction that was *ultra vires* does not relieve the corporation of liability.

LIABILITY OF THE OFFICERS, AGENTS
AND EMPLOYEES

In a contractual matter, a representative acting for a corporation assumes no personal liability if his act, whether within the powers of a corporation or merely *ultra vires,* either is within his authority or is later ratified by the corporation. Without proper express or implied authority or ratification, however, the representative would ordinarily be liable to the corporation for any damages caused it and liable to the party dealt with for breach of implied warranty of authority, but since he did not purport to act for anyone but the corporation, he would not be liable under the contract terms, except in the case of a negotiable instrument.

If a representative of the corporation commits a tort, as, for example, a trespass or a negligent or willful injury to another, while acting within the general scope of his authority, such representative, as well as the corporation, will be liable for the damage or injury caused. The same result would probably follow in the case of a crime, although this would depend upon the scope of the particular criminal statute involved.

LIABILITY OF THE DIRECTORS

Directors are obligated to exercise the same degree of care in their management of the corporation that they would use in the prudent handling of their own affairs. They must be honest, diligent, and loyal in performing for the corporation the duties they have undertaken. This rule is applied against each director individually as to his own acts or neglect, unless two or more directors have joined in a wrongful act. In applying the rule, however, directors are not held liable for mere mistakes or errors in judgment, but they may be held liable for damage or injury to the corporation resulting from their neglect to act, their failure to act with reasonable prudence, or their negligent or willful acts inimicable to the welfare of the corporation.

In some states, specific laws impose statutory liability upon directors and officers for breach or neglect of certain duties, as, for example, the failure to make a required report or the making of a false report on behalf of the corporation.

In general, directors assume no contractual liability, because all contracts made by them are the corporation's contracts. In some jurisdictions, however, directors are held personally liable on *ultra vires* contracts made by the corporation.

Any tort or criminal liability of a director is determined by application of the general rules previously outlined.

LIABILITY OF THE STOCKHOLDERS

For the reason that stockholders as such are not concerned with the active management of the corporation, the imposition of any tort liability against them in such capacity would be rare indeed. The same may also be said of contractual liability, since any special contracts that the stockholders might enter into would be executed for and in the name of the corporation as the contracting party.

This brings us to a general rule, and one of the distinguishing characteristics of a corporation, namely, that the stockholders are not liable for the debts of their corporation. In the absence of special statutes or special individual agreements, therefore, the stockholders, in the event of the corporation's becoming insolvent, stand to lose only their capital invested in it plus any unpaid balances that they might owe the corporation on their stock.

By the laws of some states, however, stockholders of certain types of corporations have what is known as statutory liability. These statutes usually provide that such stockholders shall be personally liable for a sum equal to the par value of their shares in the event that the assets of the corporation prove insufficient to meet its liabilities. Such statutory liability is sometimes imposed against stockholders of banks and trust companies. A few states impose statutory liability against shareholders in manufacturing corporations. But the trend is toward abolishing such statutes.

Of course, a stockholder is liable to creditors of the corporation for the amount distributed to him in dividends or capital stock in a case in which such a distribution was made while the corporation was insolvent, for this is a clear case of a transfer in fraud of creditors.

Chapter 4

CHARACTERISTICS OF
A CORPORATION SUMMARIZED

IN GENERAL

We are now in a position to summarize the unique characteristics of the corporation as a form of organization for the conduct of a business enterprise.

The primary characteristic of a corporation is its own recognized legal entity, separate from the group of individuals who compose its stockholders. From this it follows that the death of a stockholder or the disposal of his stock does not affect the identity of the corporation. As stated by Blackstone, it is "a person that never dies; in like manner as the River Thames is still the same river, though the parts which compose it are changing every instant."[1] It remains the same corporation, irrespective of changes in the ownership of its stock. Its span of life is limited only by its charter and applicable laws, and may be perpetual. By way of contrast, a partnership dissolution takes place upon the death of a partner or upon the disposal of his partnership interest.

Another characteristic is that a corporation is the creature of the state. A franchise from a state or the Federal government is necessary to create it. In contrast, a partnership is formed by the written or oral agreement of the parties themselves.

A third characteristic of a corporation is the limitation of its powers to

---

[1] 1 Bl. Com. 468.

those expressly granted to it by its charter and those incidental to it or consequent upon such enumerated powers. A partnership, on the other hand, may delve into any lawful business at the whim of the partners, subject, of course, to laws applicable to certain businesses and professions that may require proper licenses or appropriate evidence of the individual qualifications of the partners, as in the case of a firm of lawyers, doctors, or dentists.

A fourth characteristic of a corporation is the so-called limitation of liability of the stockholders. They are not liable for the debts of the corporation. In the absence of special statutory liability, a stockholder stands to lose only what he has put into the corporation by way of capital stock. This feature, together with the fact that an investor can buy as much or as little stock as he sees fit and need not participate in the management of the enterprise, has made possible the gigantic corporations of today, of which the American Telephone & Telegraph Company is an example. Without such corporations, the national government would remain the only instrumentality capable of carrying on the "big business" of the country, and socialism would be forced upon us. Again, in contrast, partners are fully liable for the debts of their partnership. This fact, together with the intimate business association required of them, sets a relatively low limit on the capital that a partnership can assemble, and this, in turn, restricts the scope of ordinary partnerships to comparatively small business operations.

A fifth characteristic of a corporation is that its management, although elected by the stockholder-owners, is not in their hands but in the hands of its directors. A stockholder cannot bind his corporation by individual action unless, of course, he is acting as its authorized agent, in which event he is acting not in his capacity as a shareholder but as a servant of the corporation. In the general partnership, each partner is *ipso facto* an agent of the partnership and binds all of the partners by his acts within the ordinary scope of the business carried on by the firm.

PECULIAR CHARACTERISTICS OF THE CLOSE CORPORATION

The general characteristics of corporations extend to close corporations as well as to the huge enterprises with hundreds of thousands of stockholders. The fact remains, however, that the method of operation of the usual close corporation requires that some important distinctions be made.

We have defined a close corporation as one whose franchise is owned by a small group of stockholders, all of whom usually are actively engaged in its management. In other words, in the composition of its ownership and management, it closely resembles the usual partnership. From this resemblance flow some special characteristics important to our subject.

First, there is the same intimate association of a few men pooling their talents and industry in the conduct of a business enterprise that is found in the case of a partnership. Each of the close corporation stockholders is usually a director and an officer as well and, furthermore, is making the business of the corporation his life work. It is his full-time career as well as his investment. The natural result is that in the event of the death of one stockholder, the survivor or survivors are just as anxious for the enterprise to be continued as in the case of a partnership, and it is just as vital for him or them that this be done.

Second, a stockholder's limitation of liability often assume minor importance in a close corporation because large creditors frequently require the joint and several personal obligations of the stockholders before dealing with them. The extent of any such outstanding obligations is of great consequence to all concerned in the event of the death of a close corporation stockholder.

Third, stockholders of a close corporation are accustomed to taking the profits of their enterprise mostly in the form of salaries rather than in the form of dividends. This is natural and proper, for in many cases the overwhelming share of such profits is attributable to the personal services performed by the stockholders as against the earnings on their invested capital. The full significance of this practice, however, is not realized until the death of a stockholder and the consequent discontinuance of his salary.

Fourth, because the stockholders in a close corporation conduct themselves and their business affairs largely as if they were partners, often referring to each other as such, the courts are lenient in applying the rules of corporate law, especially with respect to stockholders' agreements relating to the management of such corporations and to restrictions on the transfer of shares to outsiders. In fact, such an outstanding jurist as Chief Judge Cullen has referred to close corporations as "little more than (though not the same as) chartered partnerships,"[2] and described the two-man corporation there involved as "what has frequently been called in this court an 'incorporated partnership.' "

Fifth, and again because they look upon themselves as partners, the stockholders of a close corporation pay little attention to majority and minority stockholdings. Their business sessions resemble conferences of partners much more than the formal meetings of stockholders or directors. They are accustomed to a unanimous meeting of the minds on every important decision before going ahead. And once a decision is made, all pitch in to work for its success. The various legal rights of controlling and minority stockholders are foreign to them. Foreign to them, also, are stockholders who want a voice in the management of the corporation but not in its work. "Drone" stockholders have no suitable place in such a corporation. Yet the

---

[2]*Ripin v. U.S. Woven Label Co.*, 205 N.Y. 442 at page 447. And Justice Shearn, at page 639 of his dissenting opinion in *Cuppy v. Ward*, 187 App. Div. 625.

death of a close corporation stockholder will bring them in, unless careful plans are made in advance to keep them out.

Sixth, because the stock in a close corporation is owned by only a few individuals, all of whom are usually active in its management, the shares have no ready market. Consequently, the only persons ordinarily interested in purchasing a deceased associate's shares are the surviving stockholders. This characteristic, alone, makes such stock an unsuitable investment for the family of a deceased close corporation shareholder.

There is another type of close corporation, often called a family corporation, which differs from the "chartered partnership" type in that its stock is owned by one family and it is usually dominated by the family head. It has continuation problems peculiar to itself which will be discussed separately later, and will be alluded to from time to time.

Chapter 5

THE EFFECT OF DEATH OF
A CLOSE CORPORATION
STOCKHOLDER

The death of a stockholder in a close corporation usually has important and far-reaching consequences in spite of the fact that such event has no automatic legal effect on the life-span of the corporation. As the incidence of these consequences depends upon whether the deceased was a sole stockholder, a majority stockholder, a minority stockholder, or owned exactly one-half of the shares of stock in the enterprise, an analysis will be made of the effect of the death of a stockholder occupying each such status.

DEATH OF A SOLE STOCKHOLDER

We have seen that one of the prime characteristics of a corporation is its continued succession for the period specified by its formal charter or by statute, unless it is sooner dissolved by affirmative action, and that its legal existence is not disturbed by any changes in the ownership of its shares of stock. The death of a stockholder, even though he owned all of the shares of stock in a corporation, does not *ipso facto* affect the life of the corporation. Its stock merely passes on to new owners: first, to the executor or administrator of the deceased stockholder's estate, and later, unless the corporation is liquidated by the estate, to the heirs, or purchasers from the estate, as transferees of the executor or administrator.

Status of the stock in the hands of the executor or administrator. The

271

rights and duties of the personal representative are significant to us with respect to the shares of stock. These are succinctly set out in the case of *In re Steinberg's Estate*,[1] a case in which the testator had been the sole stockholder:

> The executor in the case at bar received certain property rights as a result of his qualification. For present purposes, these consist primarily of three things, namely: First, the right to receive dividends which may be declared on the shares of the company; second, the right to vote upon such shares; and third, the right to receive all of the net assets of the company on its dissolution after the payment of its obligations to third parties. His possession of these rights, however, is not beneficial but purely fiduciary, and he is answerable to his beneficiaries who are primarily the creditors and secondarily the distributees of the estate, for the manner of his conduct in the holding of, and transactions or omissions in respect to, every item of the property thus held in trust.

But what about the personal representative's right, if any, to continue the corporate business? He has only such rights of continuance as are given to him under the decedent's will.[2] In other words, if a decedent owned all or substantially all of the shares of stock of a corporation, his personal representative is subject to substantially the same business continuation rules that govern in the case of a proprietorship business and he must deal with the corporation in the same manner that he would be required to if it were an unincorporated business. This is clearly brought out in the case of *In re Stulman's Will*,[3] in which Surrogate Wingate stated:

> The question in the case at bar is really broader, however, than that of mere continuance of investment by the fiduciaries, and in essence concerns the continuance by them of the testator's business, since he was virtually its possessor by reason of almost complete stock ownership. [The testator had owned 925 shares and his son 75 shares.] Under such circumstances the rule of law has been inflexible for the last half century, at least, that, to permit a testamentary fiduciary so to continue, a power to that effect "must be found in the direct, explicit and unequivocal language of the will or else will not be deemed to have been conferred." *Willis v. Sharp*, 113 N.Y. 586, 21 N.E. 705. . . . The equitable powers of a Surrogate's Court permit it to penetrate to the inner verities of the situation. Thus, where the business in

---

[1] 150 Misc. 339, 274 N.Y.S. 914 (1934).

[2] *In re Estate of Muller*, 24 N.Y.2d 336, 300 N.Y.S.2d 341 (1969).

[3] 263 N.Y.S. 197, 146 Misc. 861 (1933).

question is actually within the sole control of the testator, his testamentary fiduciaries will be held to a strict accountability in this regard, whether or not the formality of incorporation has taken place. In the absence of unequivocal authority for continuance contained in the will, "an executor or administrator has no authority virtute officii to continue it, except for the temporary purpose of converting the assets employed * * * into money." *Willis v. Sharp,* 113 N.Y. 586, 589. . . .

The conclusion seems evident from the above quotations that the problems and hazards brought about by the death of a sole stockholder are similar to those faced upon the death of a sole proprietor.

DEATH OF A MAJORITY STOCKHOLDER

At this point it is important to recall to mind the outstanding characteristic of a close corporation of the "incorporated partnership" type, namely, that there is the same intimate association of a few men, combining their full time, talent and industry in the conduct of a business enterprise as was found to exist in a partnership. Therefore, although the death of a majority stockholder in a close corporation does not automatically dissolve the business association *legally,* as would be the case in a partnership, it nevertheless shatters the well-balanced combination of diverse human talent that has been working together as a successful business team.

The position of the surviving minority stockholders. In many instances, on the death of the majority stockholder, the surviving minority stockholders are left occupying a worse position than would have been the case had the organization been a partnership. In either situation, there is the loss of the chief member of the "team." But if the enterprise had been a partnership, they, as surviving partners, could wind up the old concern and would then be free to seek out a new associate, if one could be found, who could bring like talent and congeniality to the new firm. Because the enterprise is a corporation, however, the controlling interest of the deceased stockholder passes into the hands of a new majority stockholder, first to the executor or administrator and ultimately to a legatee or a purchaser from the estate. The choice of the new associate is entirely out of the hands of the survivors; and the chance is slim indeed that his personality and special abilities will harmonize agreeably and successfully with those of the survivors. In fact, it is probable that the stock will pass into the hands of an heir, such as the deceased's widow, who is incapable or unwilling to contribute to the work of the corporation and is interested only in substantial future dividends.

But whoever the heir is, whatever his temperament and qualifications, whether he is an active or a "drone" stockholder, as the new owner of the deceased's shares he will have the deciding voice in future meetings. Since the directors of the corporation are elected by vote of the stockholders, the new interests can dominate the board. The board of directors, in turn, not only appoints the officers and fixes their salaries, but dictates the dividend policy of the corporation as well.

Picture, in this new setting, the unenviable position of the surviving minority stockholders. Left to carry the burden of the work of the corporation, they nonetheless can be outvoted at all meetings, and their very jobs and salaries as officers are placed in jeopardy. Of course, they can resign, and perhaps start a new organization of their own, but first, they will probably need to sell their stock in order to raise capital, and there is little or no market for minority holdings in a close corporation. Then too, they have been identified with a corporation whose name and location is familiar to the trade, and they will be handicapped by a strange name at a strange location. Had there been a partnership, then as surviving minority partners they would at least have had the right to wind up the affairs of the old firm and to have thus eliminated it and its name as a competitor before they started a new enterprise. In such a case, they would obviously have had a better opportunity to acquire the customers that had been "orphaned" by the dissolution of the partnership. The minority stockholders in a close corporation stand in dire need of a plan that will give them control of the organization in the event of the death of a majority stockholder.

The position of the estate and heirs of the majority stockholder. The first destination of the shares of stock of the deceased majority stockholder is with the executor or administrator, who, as we have seen, holds the stock during the administration of the estate primarily for the creditors of the estate and secondarily for the heirs or legatees.

If the deceased stockholder has left no will, it is the duty of the administrator of his estate to dispose of the personal property of the estate for cash, to pay the creditors of the decedent and the taxes and administration costs, and to turn over the residue to those heirs or distributees entitled to it under the intestate laws of the state. (If the personal property is insufficient to pay the debts and charges, the real property may be resorted to.) If other property is sufficient to pay the debts, taxes and expenses of administration, and if the consent of all the heirs, provided they are all adult, is obtained, the administrator can conserve the deceased's close corporation stock and ultimately deliver it to those agreed upon to receive it under any agreement of consent. Without such a fortuitous post-mortem arrangement, the administrator has no right to hold the stock beyond the time necessary for the prudent liquidation of it.

Because the estate has a controlling interest to dispose of, it would seem at first glance that this should bring the estate a fair price, but the result is usually disappointing. In the first place, the stock is sold under a forced sale, for the administrator must carry through the administration of the estate with reasonable promptness, a fact well known to all prospective buyers. In the second place, the administration of the estate may take place during a general business depression or during a depression in the particular trade or industry involved. Hence, such a sale ordinarily results in a bargain for the buyer and a substantial loss to the stockholder's estate and heirs.

If the deceased stockholder has left a valid will, which is the least he should do in view of the above, the situation with respect to his close corporation stock is unchanged unless he has dealt specifically in the will with such shares of stock. If they have been specifically bequeathed or placed in trust, the stock will not be liquidated to pay creditors' and other claims except as a last resort. But if such shares represent almost all of the deceased's assets, some portion will have to be sold in order to raise money for the discharge of the debts of the decedent and the post-mortem obligations, including estate and inheritance taxes, of the estate. Should such a sale become necessary, it may involve disposing of sufficient shares to alter the balance of control, in which event the shares sold will no doubt command an attractive price from the surviving stockholders if they are able to finance the purchase, but the remaining shares in the estate will be of little value.

If, on the other hand, it is possible to pass on the majority shares intact to the legatees, the recipients will then inherit control of the corporation. But unless the recipients are capable of taking an active and successful part in the management of the business of the corporation, trouble, disappointments, and losses lie ahead. Control of any vehicle without the requisite ability and experience to operate it safely, be it a highly powered car or an erstwhile smoothly running business organization, usually means that the vehicle and all aboard are headed toward disaster. If the surviving experienced minority stockholders decide not to risk remaining with the corporation, calamity is sure to follow.

Perhaps the legatees will be content to remain inactive and to allow the surviving minority stockholders to run the business. Such a course is much less hazardous at the start, but it cannot subsist for long because of the conflict of interests engendered. The surviving stockholders, called upon to conduct the business alone, will feel that the profits should go to them in the form of salary increases, if they are not "plowed back" into the enterprise for future development. The inactive stockholders, not being on the payroll, can derive benefit from the business only from dividends on their stock. Accordingly, they will insist on a dividend income if there are any profits, and because of their voting control, they will be in a position to command dividend distributions in lieu of salary increases to the active minority stockholders. Thus, the latter, left to do all the work, are expected to share a substantial portion of the fruits of their labor. Such an arrangement obviously will not long endure.

The conclusion is evident that unless the majority stock passes into the hands of an experienced legatee such as a capable son or other relative of the deceased majority stockholder who is already active in the affairs of the corporation, who has proved to be a congenial associate, and who will be ready and willing to shoulder his share of the burden, the heirs will be far better served with the prompt receipt of the cash value of the stock.

DEATH OF A MINORITY STOCKHOLDER

From the standpoint of the business "team," the death of a minority stockholder may be just as serious as the loss of a majority stockholder. In fact, there are many close corporations in which the minority stockholder contributes the major part of the work while the other associate contributes the major part of the capital. In any event, the death of the minority shareholder disrupts the intimate group of well-balanced business talent and leaves the survivors with the problem of reorganizing the management of the corporation.

The position of the surviving majority stockholders. Faced with the necessity of reorganizing their management staff, the surviving majority stockholders are in a position to readjust this particular matter promptly. By means of their controlling number of votes as stockholders, they can reconstitute the personnel of the board of directors. The board, in turn, can search out and appoint, at a suitable salary, a new officer to take over the duties of the deceased stockholder.

Provided always that the surviving majority stockholders, in their capacity as controlling directors, act in good faith for the best interests of the corporation, the new minority stockholder will be unable to interfere successfully with the future dividend policy that the survivors adopt.

In the matter of their own future salaries, however, the majority stockholders may find themselves vulnerable. The underlying difficulty here is that the vote of a director in the matter of his own salary is a nullity and should not even be cast. While all of the original stockholders were alive, this point was of no moment, for they were accustomed to act unanimously and there was no one to complain. But the death of one of their number may bring a vital change in this respect. Now, there is a new minority stockholder who is likely to complain if any salary increases are attempted. The vulnerability of the surviving stockholders on this point is demonstrated in the following quotation from the opinion in *Fitchett v. Murphy*,[4] referring to the lower court opinion:

> The learned court, in its opinion, correctly held that "Directors of a corporation have no right to vote salaries to one another as mere incidents of their office as was done here. They are not debarred from becoming employees of the incorporation and they are entitled to a reasonable compensation for their services

---

[4] 46 App. Div. 181 (N.Y.).

as such. But as in fixing their compensation they are in the position as trustees dealing with themselves in respect of their trust, their action is subject to question by the stockholders or to review by the court of equity at the suit of a stockholder. In the case of a large board of directors the fixing of a salary of one of their number for prescribed services might be deemed conclusive, where the influence of one employed was not a factor therein. This case is quite different."

The fact that the by-laws of the corporation provide for the salaries to be established by the board of directors does not surmount the difficulty. This is shown by the following quotation from the opinion in *McConnell v. Combination M. & M. Co.,*[5] in which the court said at page 568:

The directors had power to adopt a code of by-laws (Comp. Statutes, 1887, Div. 5, Sec. 454), but they could not, even under a by-law, vote a salary to one of their number when the vote of such director was necessary to make up a quorum.

Under such circumstances, it is not established whether the salary resolution is void or merely voidable. Some jurisdictions hold it void. At least one jurisdiction holds the resolution voidable, and that it can be validated in a stockholders' meeting by a majority vote. Probably most jurisdictions hold that the salary resolution is voidable at the instance of a dissenting stockholder. Regardless of the jurisdiction, however, it is not to be expected that the future acts and decisions of the surviving majority stockholders will go unchallenged. On the contrary, unless the minority stockholders are treated more liberally than good business judgment usually dictates, their plight will be such that they will take advantage of every opportunity to harass the majority. The survivors will be fortunate indeed if they succeed in avoiding not only unpleasantness and bickering in every stockholders' meeting but ultimately, a hostile, expensive and time-consuming shareholders' suit.

The position of the estate and heirs of the minority stockholder. The shares of the deceased minority stockholder pass first into the hands of his executor or administrator, but their ultimate destination is dependent upon the status of the estate and the provisions of the deceased's will, if any.

If there is no will, the administrator is called upon to dispose of the stock for cash unless all of the heirs, provided they are all adult and thus capable of consent, agree to accept the shares themselves and unless there is also sufficient other property in the estate for the payment of all the debts and obligations of the deceased and his estate.

---

[5]31 Mont. 563.

If the deceased stockholder leaves a will without specific provisions with respect to his stock, the situation is the same. The executor is required to sell the stock in the absence of a valid post-mortem agreement among the legatees to accept the stock certificates in lieu of cash, again keeping in mind that such an agreement cannot be effectuated unless there is sufficient other property in the estate available to the executor for the discharge of all estate obligations.

In either of the foregoing situations, the position of the executor or administrator appears at first glance to be identical with that which prevails in the case of the death of a majority stockholder, but in reality there is a vast difference. Because he has a controlling interest in a close corporation to dispose of, the personal representative of a deceased majority stockholder usually possesses a marketable estate asset. This is not true of the personal representative of a deceased minority stockholder. In most instances, his only available market consists of the surviving majority stockholders who, already having control of the corporation, can well afford to play a waiting game. Fortunate is the personal representative who, in this situation, is able to dispose of the minority interest at a price acceptable to the probate court and pleasing to the legatees, if, indeed, he is able to dispose of it at all during the limited probate period of the estate.

If there is a valid will specifically bequeathing the shares of the minority stockholder to one or more legatees, or an effective post-mortem agreement on the part of the heirs to accept such shares, and there are funds available for the payments of estate obligations, the minority stock ownership will pass ultimately into the hands of one or more members of the deceased's family. If the ultimate owner is a son or other relative ready, willing, capable, and acceptable to the surviving majority stockholders as an intimate business associate, no difficulties should ensue. But if, as is usually the case, the new owner proves to be an inactive stockholder, then the trouble starts.

Often the new owner is the widow of the deceased. Before his death, the minority stockholder derived a good livelihood from the corporation and it will be difficult, if not impossible, to persuade his widow that her deceased husband's income resulted almost entirely from his personal activity as a working associate rather than from the fact that he happened to own some shares of stock in the enterprise. In all probability, she will never cease to expect more income in the form of dividends on the stock than the board of directors is willing to declare. In fact, the payment of substantial dividends on the common stock of close corporations is the exception and not the rule. Any residue of corporate earnings left after the payment of commensurate salaries to the active stockholders is usually needed for the further development and expansion of the corporate business.

It is in this setting that the new minority stockholder will attend stockholders' meetings, there to participate in the discussions and to vote, however impotently, upon all the matters brought up. These discussions may well become bitter as time goes on and as the true situation of the inactive stockholder unfolds. If the cumulative system of voting for directors is used, the minority stockholder will be able to gain representation on the board and thus to carry such bitterness into the deliberations and actions of the board on the vital matters of salaries paid and dividends declared.

Eventually, the minority stockholder will either give up the unequal struggle and sell the stock at a bargain price or, bitterness turning to rancor, will bring the majority stockholders into court on charges of mismanagement in an attempt to compel the payment of smaller salaries and greater dividends.

Such suits are common (see following chapter), but few of them are successful in procuring larger dividends because the underlying situation usually justifies the conduct of the majority stockholders. Such a lawsuit causes the controlling stockholders considerable expense and embarrassment and sometimes loss of newly voted salaries. But instead of forcing payment of larger dividends, it usually only demonstrates to the inactive minority stockholder that the income-producing power of his shares of stock in the close corporation is relatively small.

Clearly, it is the duty of every minority stockholder in a close corporation to make sure that his stock interest does not pass into the hands of an inactive member of his family. This he can readily prevent by becoming a party to a plan by means of which his shares will be purchased at his death for a fair price by the surviving majority stockholders, or redeemed by the corporation.

DEATH OF AN EQUAL STOCKHOLDER

Scattered throughout the country there are a host of "two-man" corporations. In each of these corporations, the enterprise is carried on by two men, each owning one-half of the shares of stock. Many of these concerns originally started out as co-partnerships and were incorporated later to obtain the advantage of limited liability. They are typical "incorporated partnerships," in which the work and the profits are shared equally in an atmosphere of harmony and unanimity on all important decisions. Informality is the rule, and voting power is never thought of as such. In fact, the stockholders consider themselves, and customarily refer to themselves as, "partners," to the dismay and confusion of their more legally minded friends.

A detailed analysis is hardly necessary to depict the situation brought about by the death of one of these equal stockholders. The equal sharing of the work of the corporation is terminated, and the survivor, for some time at least, must carry the burden alone. Gone, also, is the spirit of harmony that prevailed in the management of the enterprise. First, the personal representative, in a new and strange atmosphere of formality, will occupy the place of the deceased associate at stockholders' and directors' meetings. Representing primarily the creditors of the deceased stockholder and secondarily his heirs and legatees, the viewpoint and objectives of the executor or administrator will be foreign to that of the surviving stockholder. Ultimately, the deceased's place will be occupied either by a purchaser of the deceased's stock, if the personal representative is required to sell, or by a member of the deceased stock-representative is required to sell, or by a member of the deceased stock-holder's family. In either event, there is little possibility that the new stockholder will prove to be an acceptable "partner" to the surviving stockholder. The probability verges into certainty that the resultant differences in experience, burdens or objectives, in combination with equal ownership and voting power, will rapidly develop into a stalemate that can be resolved only by the liquidation of the corporation.

Surely, equal stockholders stand in need of a plan that will eliminate any such unfortunate result.

Part II

PLANS ATTEMPTED, TO AVOID DELETERIOUS EFFECTS OF CLOSE CORPORATION STOCKHOLDER'S DEATH

Chapter 6

PLANS IMPROVISED AFTER
A STOCKHOLDER'S DEATH

In the previous chapter, we have seen that the death of a close corporation stockholder has important and often deleterious consequences to all concerned, even though such a death does not of itself affect the life span of the corporation. As the adverse effects of such a death become apparent, it is only natural that the parties concerned will attempt to remedy the situation in which they find themselves. We shall review some of these attempted remedies in order to demonstrate the sterility of all such post-mortem improvisations.

DEATH OF A SOLE STOCKHOLDER

The death of a stockholder who owns all or nearly all of the stock of a corporation leaves his estate and heirs in much the same position as if the business were not incorporated. The personal representative has no authority to continue the corporation business but must proceed promptly to dispose of it or to dissolve it, unless the will states otherwise in language that is direct, explicit and unequivocal. If, therefore, the sole stockholder has neglected to act prior to his death with respect to the future of his corporation, it devolves upon his personal representative to sell or to liquidate the enterprise. This is not easy to do, however, if the corporation has been a profitable one that provided the livelihood of the deceased stockholder and his family, and occasionally the personal representative or the heirs will attempt to keep the business operating despite the lack of proper authority to do so. This was the situation in the following case, which again illustrates the folly of dealing with estate assets without proper authority.

The case of *In re Kinreich's Estate* [1] was a proceeding in the Surrogate's Court in which the widow, as executrix, and Turkus, as co-executor, were called upon for an accounting of the estate assets of Leo Kinreich. At his death, Kinreich owned all of the stock of the Sterling Wax Paper Manufacturing Company. His will contained certain legacies to two employees and named his wife residuary legatee, but it did not give her the authority to continue the corporate business. Approximately ten days after Kinreich's death the personal representatives and their attorney held a conference to plan for the continuance of the corporation at which the widow was elected its president, at a salary of $300 a week. Thereafter, she actively conducted the business for two years and four months until it became bankrupt in January, 1929. During this period, the co-executor refrained from taking any active part in the affairs of the corporation, although the widow sent him periodic reports.

Following the failure of the business, the legatees under the will brought this proceeding in an effort to hold the personal representatives accountable for the loss. The court held both executors liable and surcharged them with the book value of the business at the date of the sole stockholder's death. With reference to the liability of the widow, the opinion stated, in language reminiscent of that used in cases dealing with sole proprietorships and already familiar to us in that connection:

> As to the liability of testator's widow, who qualified as executrix and actively managed the business, it clearly appears that, in the absence of any authority in the will, she must be held strictly accountable for the loss sustained in continuing the business. . . .

With respect to her salary of $300 per week, the opinion stated:

> The payment of this excessive amount furnished a strong motive on the part of the widow to continue the business in disregard of her legal duty.

In holding co-executor Turkus also liable, the court said:

> From the entire record it appears that the executor, Turkus, was properly held responsible with the executrix for the loss to the beneficiaries of the estate. His duty, as the developments show, was to insist that the business be sold or liquidated as soon as reasonably possible after testator's death. [Several cases cited as authority, also Harvard Law Review, March, 1921, p. 483.]

With reference to the corporation, the opinion commented as follows:

---

[1] 137 Misc. 735, 244 N.Y.S. 357 (1930).

That the estate held only shares of stock in the business corporation does not affect the question of the executors' liability. This question has been decided by the Court of Appeals in *Matter of Auditore's Will*, 249 N.Y. 335, 345, 164 N.E. 242, 244, the Court saying: "The surrogate is not dealing with the corporation, but with the value of its stock at specified times."

Root v. Blackwood[2] involved the basic rules where the decedent widower, owning 290 of the 300 shares of his corporation, bequeathed them to his minor children. Two executors were appointed, one being the decedent's brother-in-law, a nonresident who also was appointed guardian of the children. The executors called a stockholders' meeting at which they and another were elected directors, and without obtaining a court order they continued to operate the corporation for a period of over four years. The stock, worth $29,000 at the decedent's death, was worth little or nothing at the end of this period, and the executors obtained a court order for the appointment of a trustee to liquidate the corporation. When the resident executor and the trustee filed their reports fourteen years later, three of the children sought to charge the executor with the value of the stock on the date he was appointed, and the trustee with the value of the corporation's assets when he took over. The trial court relieved the executor of responsibility, on the ground that responsibility for the stock rested on the guardian for the children. The appellate court reversed and ordered a new trial, stating in part:

It is not within the general scope of his powers or authority for an administrator or executor to carry on the business of his decedent, and if he does so without the order of some proper court, or the authority of a will, he does so at his own risk and will be personally liable for all losses sustained, while he will be required to account to the estate for all profits he may make.

... The executor was bound to know that he had no right to turn the administration of the estate over the guardian or to the Root Manufacturing Company without order of court and without complying with the law. No statute or court order authorized any such delegation of authority and responsibility.

When Executor Arnt assumed control of the corporate stock of the Root Manufacturing Company, he could have either sold said stock for its value at that time, or distributed it under order of the court.

He chose instead, without any authority from either the court or will, to continue operation of the business through others, for a period of over four years and until said stock is now probably of no value.

The personal representative is liable for the actual loss to the

---

[2] 120 Ind. App. 545, 94 N.E.2d 489 (1950).

estate resulting from negligent failure to sell securities. 33 C.J.S., Executors and Administrators, §248, p. 1259.

Since it is patent that the sole stockholder of a corporation is confronted with substantially the same business continuation problems as the sole proprietor, it should be equally patent that those problems are susceptible to like solutions. Furthermore, since the solutions of the problems encountered by the proprietor in perpetuating his enterprise and in assuring its full going value to his heirs have been fully discussed in the section on Proprietorships, our discussion here of the sole stockholder will be concluded by referring the reader to the appropriate material in that section and by calling attention to the fact that in working out a satisfactory solution, the sole stockholder has the distinct advantage of dealing with more readily identifiable and more easily divisible property, for he is dealing with shares of corporate stock instead of the divers items of real and personal property used in the conduct of a proprietorship business.

DEATH OF A MAJORITY STOCKHOLDER

There are in existence many close corporations made up of two stockholders, one of whom owns a few more shares of stock than the other. While both stockholders are alive, this difference in holdings is disregarded, and they conduct the business as if they were equal partners in the enterprise. Upon the death of the majority stockholder, however, this difference will sooner or later assert itself, and the new owners of the majority stock will take the control away from the surviving minority stockholder. Such a development is illustrated by the following cases.

Gaines Bros. Co. v. Gaines and *Gaines v. Gaines Bros. Co.* Frank Gaines and his brother, James Henry Gaines, had organized a partnership in 1893 for the purpose of farming, stock raising, and the conduct of a general trading business.

In June, 1907, the two brother formed the corporation of Gaines Bros. Co. with capital stock of $40,000, divided into 1600 shares of $25 each. The incorporation papers showed James the owner of 820 shares and Frank the owner of 776 shares, four shares being assigned to one Walter Gaines in order to have the necessary three incorporators.

The handling of the affairs of both the former partnership and the new corporation was entirely informal. During their days as partners, the two brothers had kept a joint bank account, against which they drew such checks as they desired for the operation of the partnership and for their own individual needs. After the formation of the corporation, the finances were continued in the same manner, no detailed records being kept.

This harmonious relationship continued until the death of James in 1914, at which time the first formal meeting of the corporation took place in order to elect one of the deceased's two sons a director, the majority interest having passed to James' widow and sons.

The business of the corporation was then carried on as before for a period of nearly sixteen years. Eventually, however, the heirs of the deceased brother constituted themselves a majority of the board of directors and in about the year 1930 they began to assert their authority. Friction developed immediately, and soon afterward the majority put through a dividend declaration of $260,000.

Frank then brought these two actions, *Gaines Bros. Co. v. Gaines*[3] and *Gaines v. Gaines Bros. Co.*,[4] with various objects in mind but with the primary purpose of establishing his right to equal ownership of the shares of stock in the corporation, based upon an alleged oral agreement to that effect made with his deceased brother at the time of its incorporation. This object, if established, would of course give Frank the equal say in the management of the corporation that he had always exercised in operating the partnership and the corporation with his brother. The court, however, refused to go beyond the written and verified articles and agreement of incorporation and decided against him. And not only did Frank lose his major contention, he also, since he had not alleged any wrongdoing on the part of the heirs, failed to obtain the other forms of relief requested, including an injunction against further dividends and for an accounting. On the subject of majority control, the court said as follows:

> In the absence of any allegations in the petition of negligence, misfeasance, fraud, oppression, or mismanagement on the part of the officers and directors of the corporation, the plaintiff has no standing in a court of equity to enforce an accounting or for dissolution of the corporation. The majority interest in a corporation have a right to dictate the business policy of the company so long as it is done in an honest, reasonable, competent, and efficient manner. The law has always recognized the right of majority stockholders of a corporation to control its business and affairs, and a court of equity will never interfere with such control except for the very best of reasons.

It is clear from this case that the death of a majority stockholder leaves the surviving minority stockholder in a precarious position, barring affirmative wrongdoing on the part of the heirs, and it takes little imagination to foresee what the next step will be in most instances. Because of the acrimony developed in the advanced stages of litigation, in all probability the stockholders are never again able to work together harmoniously. Therefore, unless the services of the surviving minority stockholder are absolutely indispensable

---

[3] 176 Okla. 576, 56 P. 2d 869.

[4] 176 Okla. 583, 56 P. 2d 863 (1963).

to the corporation, the "final act" will find the controlling majority stockholders dispensing with his services.

What can the surviving minority stockholder, acting alone, do to protect his position in the corporation? He can buy out the heirs of the deceased majority stockholder, *if* they are willing to sell, *if* an agreement can be reached as to the purchase price, and *if* the survivor can raise the necessary purchase money. Provided that the corporation is prosperous, there is little likelihood that the new majority stockholders will consider selling their stock, let alone do so at a price that the survivor can pay. Second, the survivor can sell his stock interest, *if* he can find a buyer. Outsiders are usually not interested in purchasing a minority interest in a close corporation, and therefore, probably the only prospective buyers are the new majority stockholders. But since they already have control of the corporate affairs, they have no particular incentive to purchase the additional shares and will offer little for them. Moreover, this alternative sells the survivor out of a job instead of protecting his position in the corporation. Third, the survivor can submit to the control of the new majority stockholders and hope for the best.

The mere recital of these alternatives makes it obvious that a minority stockholder cannot afford to trust his future to the chance that, after the majority stockholder's death, he will somehow be able to conclude a satisfactory arrangement with the heirs. To protect his position in the corporation, he must enter into an arrangement with his majority associate; he must act before death occurs.

DEATH OF A MINORITY STOCKHOLDER

By far the greater number of associates in close corporations own a minority stock interest. The situation most frequently involved, therefore, is that brought about by the death of a minority stockholder. In the previous chapter, this situation was discussed in general terms. Now, let us observe what actually happens in some of these cases in the absence of any special arrangements between the original stockholders to take care of such a contingency.

Situations frequently occur in which it becomes the duty of the executor or administrator of a deceased stockholder to sell his shares of stock in the process of administering his estate. In the case of the death of a minority stockholder who has made no specific provision with respect to his stock, this duty often presents an embarrassing dilemma to the personal representative. If he holds the stock, he may be surcharged for any losses to the estate resulting from the retention of a non-legal investment. On the other hand, because the market for a minority interest in a close corporation is extremely limited, if any market exists at all, he may be surcharged for selling the stock at what is ruled to be an inadequate price. Such a dilemma was barely avoided by the personal representative in the following case.

Matter of Middleditch. Livingston Middleditch died possessing a minority interest in a close corporation, and it was the duty of his personal representative to dispose of this stock, if possible. When the time came for an accounting of the affairs of the estate however, the personal representative, unable to find a buyer, still held the stock among the estate assets. The heirs then entered objections to an approval of the account and urged that a surcharge should be made. The rest of the story appears in the following quotation:[5]

> ... The burden rested upon the objectors to demonstrate that the actions of the executors in retaining the stock of the company have resulted in loss to the estate (*Matter of Pollock,* 134 Misc., 212, 214.) In this they have failed. It may be conceded that it would have been the duty of the executors to sell the stock if a reasonable market could have been found. This consideration is, however, pointless on the record since no suggestion has been made that any such market has ever existed. This is not surprising since the purchase of a minority interest in a close corporation is a transaction which would appeal to few persons. There is no more reason for criticising the accountants for failure personally to buy the stock than for the like failure of the objectants. The difficulties encountered by the executors in liquidation were inherent in the nature of the property in the hands of the testator and the situation was not altered by his death. ...

The real lesson from this case, however, is not the final avoidance of personal liability by the executors of Middleditch, but the plight of his legatees. The failure of minority stockholder Middleditch to make specific plans for the satisfactory disposal of his stock resulted in an unsuccessful litigation that was costly to the heirs. Moreover, they took possession of the stock because no buyer could be found. In fact, it is difficult to foresee how it could ever be sold for more than a fraction of its true value, and further loss to the heirs seems inevitable. How much better it would have been, both for his executors and for his family and probably for the surviving majority stockholders, as the next case will show, had Middleditch arranged to sell his minority holdings to the surviving stockholders for an adequate cash price.

The typical case involving the heirs of a minority stockholder is not one brought against the decedent's executor or administrator for failing to dispose of his shares, as in *Middleditch,* but one brought against the surviving stockholders through the corporation to recover for the corporation increased salaries paid and/or to force the declaration of adequate dividends. One of these actions was *Godley v. Crandell & Godley Co.*[6] It was brought by the

---

[5]N.Y., Kings County Surrogate, *N.Y. Law Journal,* Feb. 18, 1935.

[6]212 N.Y. 121, 105 N.E. 818 (1915).

widow of a stockholder who had bequeathed his large minority interest' to her. She succeeded in recovering over $145,000 in additional and increased salaries, and another $103,000 in connection with the liquidation of the corporation into a new corporation without consideration for the former's substantial good will value.

That an action of this type frequently follows upon the death of a minority stockholder in a close corporation is born out in the intermediate court opinion in this same case, in which, at pages 706, 707 of 153 App. Div., the following vivid portrayal of the underlying situation is given:

> The basic reason of the corporate disputes which have produced the crop of representative actions, similar to the case at bar, is this: the original members of a joint enterprise or partnership engaged in trade, business or manufacturing, seeing certain real advantages in incorporation—the two most important being (1) a limitation of personal liability for the debts of the business to the amount invested therein, and (2) freedom from dissolution by reason of the death of a partner—transform the trading partnership into a business corporation, the partners receiving stock in proportion to their interests. So long as they all live, and agree, they treat it as a partnership, and, whether they distribute the surplus profits among themselves as dividends or by way of salaries, the financial result is precisely the same and there is no one to complain. But when a partner (that is, such a stockholder) dies, or by reason of disagreement with the majority is ousted from the management, the majority refuse to regard the stock of that deceased or ousted partner as entitled to the treatment that he was when alive or in agreement. They think that as they do the work and have the responsibility, they are entitled to keep to themselves and divide among themselves all, or the substantial part, of the profits or gains of the business, thus losing sight of the fact that the very form of the enterprise which they have created, to wit, a corporation, which has conferred upon them the benefits of a limitation of liability and a survival notwithstanding the death of a member, couples with those advantages the equality of all the stock, irrespective of ownership, whether original or recent, and irrespective of the participation in the affairs of the company or of the work or labor for it. All the stock is on the same basis of partnership *inter sese* and the right of the majority, or the surviving original partners, to still treat the enterprise as their own and as they will, has ceased. That is the penalty or payment which they have to make for the original advantage which they have received by incorporating. It is for this reason that, chafing under the legal necessity of treating all the stock alike and of dividing the profits *pro rata* to the holders thereof, they became ingenious in devising methods to evade and

avoid their corporate responsibilities. The only safeguard lies in strict adherence to the equitable principle that the directors are fiduciaries, and may not, therefore, deal with themselves. The court is still the refuge and the support of the minority. Whenever a minority stockholder can show that the directors, his fiduciaries, have deviated from the path of square and honorable dealing for their own benefits, the court will exercise its power to right the wrong.

The outstanding specific import of the *Godley* case to close corporation stockholders is that surviving majority stockholders are held accountable to the heirs of a deceased minority stockholder for salaries voted themselves against the wishes of the heirs who take over the deceased's stock. In the previous chapter two cases were quoted to the same effect, but the rule is of such supreme importance and is so frequently overlooked that further authorities will be quoted.

An excerpt from the case of *Raynolds v. Diamond Mills Paper Co.*, is in point:[7]

> Now, in this case the salaries have been fixed by the directors themselves—these three salaried agents, who collect $29,000 per annum for their services and control the board of directors. . . . The rule is well settled that the burden is upon the directors and managers in such a case as this to satisfy the court that the salaries which they have paid themselves have been earned. The situation is absolutely different from that which I described in dealing with the claim of the stockholders to have a dividend declared. Here the court cannot avoid or evade the discharge of a duty, however difficult it may be. I must confess that it is a difficult task for this court, upon such proofs as have been taken here and upon such proofs as might have been taken, if every piece of evidence possible had been adduced to fix the just compensation which these men are entitled to receive for their services. But they cannot fix it themselves. They cannot pay themselves. They cannot be the judges of their own case. They are acting very differently in awarding themselves salaries from what they are doing when determining whether dividends shall be declared or not, although, of course, they have an interest in the declaration of the dividends as stockholders.

Here are some excerpts from *Bates Street Shirt Co. v. Waite*[8] that contrast in bold relief, first, the situation as to the stockholders voting themselves salaries prior to 1923 when all them were alive, all were actively engaged in the corporate business and all were on the board of directors; and second, the

---

[7] 69 N.J. Eq. 299, 60 Atl. 941 at page 946.

[8] 130 Me. 352, 156 Atl. 293 (1931).

changed status in this respect in 1923 after the death of a minority stockholder, Fosdick, who had owned one-fifth of the common stock of the corporation:

> In the years prior to 1923, salaries were fixed by vote or by agreement of boards of directors consisting in whole or in majority part of the officers to whom the salaries were to be paid, all participating in fixing each individual salary, in violation of the general rule which is well settled.
>
> "Directors cannot vote salaries to themselves. Nor can they vote a salary to one of their number as president or secretary or treasurer, at a meeting where his presence is necessary to a quorum. And such votes, if passed, are voidable by the corporation, and if money has been paid it may be recovered back." *Camden Land Co. v. Lewis,* 101 Me. 78; *Pride v. Pride Lumber Co.,* 109 Me 452.
>
> The reason and justice of the rule is apparent. Directors have no authority to act for the corporation in matters in which they are personally interested. They owe their whole duty to the corporation and they are not to be permitted to act when duty conflicts with interest. They cannot serve themselves and the corporation at the same time. . . .
>
> But the peculiar circumstances of this case take it out of the general rule. Here the directors were the only bona fide common stockholders. It is not illegal for a corporation to distribute its profits in salaries provided that all of the stockholders assent. 2 Cook on Corporations, 6th Ed., Sec. 657.
>
> . . . The year 1923 stands by itself. Mr. Fosdick died in 1922. The stock which he had owned was held by his estate until it was purchased by the corporation in September, 1924. Salaries for 1923 were voted at a directors' meeting in which defendants appear to have participated in fixing the amounts which they were to receive. Their action in this respect was not ratified by the stockholders, nor was it acquiesced in by the executrix of the Fosdick estate. On the contrary, she vigorously protested against it. In so doing, she was quite within her rights as a representative of minority stockholders. No dividends were being paid on the stock. Prior to Mr. Fosdick's death, it was immaterial whether the profits of the business were distributed in salaries or in dividends, but when his salary ceased, a different situation obtained. The objections of his executrix were finally silenced by the sale of the stock, but until that was arranged she was entitled to register pertinent protest against the action of the directors.

Incidentally, the "pertinent protest" of Fosdick's widow and executrix was registered in the form of two lawsuits. The comment that concerns these lawsuits that appear in this opinion should be of particular interest to surviving majority stockholders:

> ... Although the first bill was dismissed and the second never came to a hearing, the allegations contained in both were widely published, as a result of which both these defendants and the corporation were subjected to unpleasant criticism; applications for loans were more closely scrutinized than had been ordinarily the case; and those connected with the company believed with good reason that the pendency of the litigation was injurious to its business.

The economic reason that Fosdick's widow registered "pertinent protest," followed by two lawsuits, is also set forth in the opinion of this case as follows:

> ... His family was left with an investment which was necessarily unproductive, unless the method of distributing profits which the corporation had followed for many years was abandoned, and even then, it was not such an investment as would recommend itself to any but an active business man valuing it as a means of securing profitable employment.

The legal troubles of the surviving majority stockholders, Parker R. Waite and his wife, culminated in the principal action, *Bates Street Shirt Co. v. Waite,* from which we have been quoting. In addition to the common stock of the corporation, all of which was owned by the Waites except that which was sold by them to Fosdick and later purchased by the corporation from his estate, there was still outstanding $300,000 of preferred stock under a covenant providing that in the event of failure to pay preferred dividends for six months, the voting power of the common stock would pass to the preferred stockholders.

This did happen in 1928, and the preferred stockholders took over the entire control of the corporation. Subsequently, this action was brought against the Waites, alleging various charges of fraudulent conduct in their handling of the corporate affairs, among which was the matter of salaries they had received and the purchase of the Fosdick stock by the corporation. The court held that the preferred stockholders were "in quite a different position than" the Fosdick estate in challenging the salaries paid; they could not question the salaries voted during the period that the Waites were in control, for during that period the preferred stockholders had received all they were entitled to, that is, full dividends on their stock. The court also held that the purchase of the Fosdick stock was justified, and dismissed the action.

In examining the facts of the *Bates* case, one is led to a conjecture of what might have happened under different circumstances. If a plan for the purchase of Fosdick's minority stock had been set up before his death, the lawsuits brought by his estate, with their damaging publicity and injurious effect on the business, could have been avoided. And the avoidance of these injurious actions, in turn, well might have enabled the company to continue the payment of preferred dividends and the Waites to remain in control of the business they had founded. The troubles of the surviving majority stockholders and of the widow of the deceased minority stockholder could easily have been avoided if a stock purchase plan had been arranged.

Lest the impression be left that a deceased minority stockholder's widow will complain only when she has received unfair treatment from the surviving majority stockholders, two important cases involving the same parties will be presented.[9]

Originally, all of the stock of the Pennsylvania corporation involved had been owned by one Mrs. Scheer. She had placed L.H. Maguire in charge of the corporate business, and in recognition of his services she had given him 12 of the 40 outstanding shares. When Maguire died in 1946 he was practically the only corporate employee, the business dwindled to such an extent the company was verging on insolvency. His shares were appraised at $450. His widow was appointed administratrix of his estate, and she later became a member of the corporation's board of directors.

Following Maguire's death Mrs. Scheer called in Arthur Osborne, her nephew, and he called in Charles A. and Joseph C. Hofmann, Jr., to participate in the corporation's management under a corporate agreement whereby the Hofmanns received, in addition to salaries, one-half of the net profits before taxes. Following Mrs. Scheer's death, Osborne became president and majority stockholder of the corporation.

The corporation began in 1947 to make money, and there followed an amazing financial success evolved out of a practically defunct corporation through the ability, industry and faithful service of the Hofmanns. In 1951 and 1952 the corporation paid dividends of $4,000, of which the widow as administratrix received $1,200—nearly three times the value of the 12 shares of stock at Maguire's death. Nevertheless, the administratrix brought an action to compel the Hofmanns to return to the corporation certain moneys they had received under their profit-sharing agreement with the corporation on the ground that the aggregate amount was excessive and unconscionable. Pennsylvania's highest court, however, sustained the agreement.

Because of the phenomenal success of the corporation, funds were needed for expansion and improvement. With only $2,000 of authorized capital, the corporation was under-capitalized and could borrow money only if the officers would assume personal liability. To solve the problem, the stockholders in a 1954 meeting amended the corporate articles to increase the

---

[9]*Maguire v. Osborne,* 384 Pa. 430, 121 A.2d 147 (1956); *Maguire v. Osborne,* 388 Pa. 121, 130 A.2d 157 (1957).

authorized capital to $100,000 (2000 shares of $50 par value). The following year the board of directors passed a resolution for the issuance of 200 additional shares at par value of $50 each, and voted to grant preemptive rights (though not required by the articles) under which the administratrix was given the right to buy 60 shares. She, however, had voted against the increase of authorized capital at both the stockholders' and the directors' meetings. Her position was that she was financially unable to purchase the additional shares. She then brought the second action, one to enjoin issuance of the additional stock on the ground that the price was grossly inadequate. Pennsylvania's highest court affirmed the lower court's decree dismissing the complaint, and adopted as its opinion excerpts from that of the lower court. Among those excerpts were the following:

> ... The fixing of the value of the new stock at par with the offer of preemptive rights gave to all of the stockholders, including the plaintiff, the right to purchase the newly issued stock at the same price as that of the original issue. The fact that plaintiff is financially unable to purchase the newly issued stock is unfortunate but it is to be observed that the fixing of the value of the newly issued shares at a higher price would be no solution to her predicament. ... Moreover, the directors were not obliged to consider plaintiff's necessitous circumstances, nor is there a shred of testimony to indicate that in the policy they pursued the directors were influenced by selfish motives or that they were scheming against plaintiff's interests. *Jones v. Costlow,* 349 Pa. 136, 142, (36 A. 2d 460).
>
> It is hornbook law that officers and directors owe a duty to stockholders to act in the utmost good faith and that they must act for the common interest of all the stockholders. The offer to plaintiff of preemptive rights is evidence of good faith. Plaintiff is a minority stockholder and the directors of the corporation owe her a duty to take no action for the purpose of injuring her minority holdings. A careful review of the record does not disclose that the defendant directors acted in bad faith or with improper motives. In fact plaintiff's expert witness concedes that the corporation was undercapitalized. The growth of this corporation required increased capitalization. The action taken by the directors is a proper one. They fixed a value which is fair in the light of all the circumstances and should not be subject to the peril of having a court or expert witness merely differ as to its value.

*   *   *   *   *

Defendant directors acted in good faith and did not scheme to deprive plaintiff as a stockholder of a substantial part of her interest in the surplus of defendant corporation.

Here again we see that a decedent's minority interest, in the hands of an inactive stockholder, can cause the active majoirty stockholders no end of trouble despite what appears to have been very fair treatment. A stock purchase agreement, effective at Maguire's death, would, among other troubles, have saved the majority stockholders two costly trips up to the Pennsylvania Supreme Court.

DEATH OF AN EQUAL STOCKHOLDER

The remaining situation is that brought about by the death of a close corporation stockholder owning or controlling (some stock is often put in the name of the wife) one-half of the outstanding stock. The forerunner of the corporations involved in these cases, as was pointed out in the previous chapter, is usually a co-partnership between two men who have subsequently incorporated the business to obtain the advantage of limited liability, or for tax reasons. Upon the death of one of these two men, dissension and eventual deadlock may well develop from this new situation, in which the surviving active stockholder is called upon to carry perhaps the full burden of the work of the corporation at the same time that the control of the corporation's management and its earnings are to be shared equally. Let us look at an actual case of this type.

Matter of Brown.[10] About the year 1908, Brown and Ferraro formed a co-partnership to carry on the cooperage business. The enterprise prospered, and in 1918 the two men formed a corporation to continue the business, one-half of the stock being issued to Brown and his wife and one-half being issued to Ferraro and his wife. The opinion in the case stated: "The business, by its nature, required the personal attention, skill, knowledge and labor of both the former partners. Since its inception the business has afforded both families a comfortable living."

The former co-partnership enterprise was carried on harmoniously and profitably under the corporate form for eighteen years, until the death of Brown in December, 1936. Less than three months later, Brown's widow brought the surviving equal stockholder into court in this proceeding to prevent him among other things from raising his salary. Mr. Justice Lockwood tells the story in his opinion as it had developed during this short interval after the death:

> After the death of petitioner's husband in December, 1936, dissension arose and there appears to be little likelihood that petitioner and respondent, each owning or controlling one-half of the corporation's stock, will be able to agree and carry on the business.
>
> The grounds for the dispute are set forth at length in the petition and affidavits, each party, of course, furnishing his or her version of the circumstances.

---

[10]N.Y. Supreme Court, *N.Y. Law Journal,* March 26, 1937.

Petitioner seeks an order enjoining the respondent Anthony Ferraro from issuing checks on the corporate account and upon his sole signature, and from drawing salaries to himself in excess of $35 per week, and to enjoin the respondents from holding a meeting of the directors. No action has been brought and no proceeding is pending other than this application.

The court has conferred with the parties and their attorneys in an unsuccessful endeavor to effectuate an amicable settlement satisfactory to both parties. Nothing remains but for the parties to secure a judicial determination of their rights by appropriate action.

Another deadlocked corporation was involved in the case of *Krall v. Krall.*[11] Prior to its incorporation in 1929, the business of the Krall Coal Company, Inc. was operated as an equal partnership between Moses and William Krall. Upon incorporation, one share of stock went to Moses, 49 shares went to his wife, and 50 shares were issued to William. Moses died in 1943. With the stock equally divided, vacancies in the offices of director and president were never filled. However, William took charge of the corporate affairs, withdrawing $125 a week in salary and operating the business "as though he personally owned all the outstanding stock."

As might be expected, dissension soon arose between the widow and William. In 1947 she brought this action against him, in which she charged various acts of fraud and mismanagement and asked for the appointment of a receiver and the dissolution of the corporation. The trial court concluded that there had been no fraud or mismanagement, but that William's actions in assuming complete and exclusive control of the business were improper and illegal, and that there was a total deadlock between the two stockholders. Accordingly, the court ordered the appointment of a permanent receiver for the corporation. This order was upheld unanimously when appealed to Connecticut's highest court. While it was felt that the appointment of a receiver for a going, solvent corporation was strong medicine, such appointment was justified here because a "complete deadlock has persisted for more than a decade."

The trouble, in the cases of equal stockholders, lies in the fact that a business enterprise founded and conducted by two men is what might be called a "business marriage" in which the parties work together for financial success in a spirit of harmony, implicit trust and confidence, and in whole-hearted co-operation.

The natural form of business organization for such business enterprises is the partnership, the rules of law concerning which have been derived from just such intimate business associations. In such cases, it is a fiduciary relationship, in law and in fact. To the original founders, however, it does not

[11]141 Conn. 325, 106 Atl. 2d 165 (1954).

matter whether the organization is a partnership or a corporation, for their dealings with each other will in either event be on the same intimate, informal, and harmonious basis.

But the form of organization becomes immensely important and significant once the original association is broken up by the death of one of the associates. In the case of a partnership, the form of organization is automatically dissolved. Not so with the corporation. When an equal stockholder dies, the surviving equal stockholder is faced with a situation entirely foreign to the original intimate business association and, as we saw in the *Brown* and *Krall* cases, trouble is inevitable. Moreover, as we also saw in those cases, the difficulties are usually insolvable because of a deadlock brought about by the equality of control. Often the only recourse is the dissolution of the corporation itself.

A sure way to prevent a deadlock from developing, following an equal stockholder's death, is for one of the parties to buy the other's stock. In fact, this is the ideal solution where it is properly planned and contracted for before a death occurs. If a plan is improvised after a stockholder's death, however, it may lead to serious difficulties. This is what happened in *Matter of Prenske.*[12]

At the time of Prenske's death in 1945, he and another were equal stockholders in a New York corporation. He was survived by his wife and three minor children, and the widow was appointed administratrix. His stock was valued at $30,000, and also among the estate assets was some $17,000 in demand notes and unpaid salary owed decedent by the corporation. The surviving stockholder refused to continue operations, stating to the administratrix that he would sue for dissolution of the corporation unless one would buy the other out. He then contracted with the widow to give her a five-day option to buy his shares for $42,700, in default of the exercise of which he agreed to buy the estate's shares at the same price. The widow exercised her option and operated the business until it was petitioned into bankruptcy in 1949. When she presented her account as administratrix, the probate court held her liable for the entire loss: some $17,000 of indebtedness she had failed to collect from the corporation, plus the $30,000 value of the stock at the decedent's death. The court's reasoning is shown by the following quotation from its opinion:

> There was no excuse for the administratrix to conduct this business for almost four years at the risk of the estate when her primary duty was one of liquidation (*Willis v. Sharp,* 113 N.Y., 586, 589 . . .). It is not a question of hindsight being better than foresight. This fiduciary, without the authority of any will or the leave of any court, deliberately embarked on a risky venture with

---

[12]115 N.Y.S.2d 184 (1952).

estate assets. She had no intention to liquidate. She was not even seriously looking for a buyer. Indeed, she not only spurned the generous offer of the surviving stockholder, reduced to a binding obligation within two months of decedent's death, but she instituted legal action to compel him to sell to her so that she might continue the business for the supposed benefit of herself and her children. Her action was a deliberate violation of her trust. The result is that she must be surcharged for the entire loss. . . .

The court only applied settled rules to surcharge the widow. Although she was probably trying to do what was right, as she saw it, she received harsh criticism from the court. The real criticism, however, deserved to fall upon her deceased husband, who had failed to make a will or to set up any plan with respect to his stock.

Summary. The cases reviewed in this chapter illustrate how, in the absence of specific plans set up in advance to take care of the situation, the death of a close corporation stockholder, regardless of the extent of his stockholdings, brings about an unwanted and economically unsound relationship between the surviving stockholders and the heirs of the deceased. The cases also demonstrate that attempts of the parties involved to "cure" the situation in which they find themselves after a stockholder's death usually result only in multiplying their difficulties. What is needed is the proverbial "ounce of prevention" in the form of a plan set up by the original stockholders before a death occurs that will prevent "unnatural" stockholder relationships from coming into being upon the occurrence of a death among their number.

Chapter 7

PLANS SET UP BY STOCKHOLDERS PRIOR TO A DEATH

It now seems clear that stockholders of partnership-type close corporations stand in need of some workable plan by which, in the event of the death of one of their number, the survivors will be able to continue the enterprise without outside interference or control, while at the same time the heirs of the deceased will be justly provided for. It also seems apparent that these two essential objectives can be accomplished only by a plan that will result in the acquisition of the shares of stock of a deceased stockholder by the surviving stockholders or the corporation, and the prompt receipt of the full value of such stock by the deceased's estate. The certainty and efficiency with which any plan will attain these essential objectives, therefore, constitute the proper basis for testing the relative merits of the various plans available to the stockholders.

"FIRST OFFER" ARRANGEMENTS

It is not uncommon to find, either in the certificate of incorporation of a corporation or in a separate agreement entered into by all of its stockholders, a clause providing that no stock of the corporation shall be transferred to a person not already a stockholder unless the stock shall have been first offered for sale to the other stockholders at an agreed price.

Such a restrictive agreement is essential to govern transfers of stock that may be made during a stockholder's lifetime, in order to give the remaining stockholders a fair opportunity to prevent any shares of stock from passing into the hands of outsiders. More than this opportunity cannot be granted in most jurisdictions for protection against this particular contingency because a total restriction against the alienation of shares of stock is invalid in a majority of the states.

Little discussion is required, however, to show that a "first offer" arrangement will not solve the problems brought about by a stockholder's death, for it merely provides that *if* the estate or heirs decide to sell, they must give the corporation or surviving stockholders the first opportunity to buy. They are left free to retain the stock if they wish. This they may very well wish to do if they have inherited a majority stock interest, thus leaving the surviving stockholders in a difficult situation. If, on the other hand, a minority interest is involved, the estate and heirs will probably desire to sell; but neither the corporation nor the survivors are under any compulsion to buy and they can sometimes take advantage of the situation by waiting. This appears to have been the result in *Estate of Blanche Potter.*[1]

In the Potter case there was a "first offer" restriction in the by-laws and in the stock certificates of O.B. Potter Properties, Inc., to the effect that the shares could not be sold until an offer to sell them to the corporation at the same price had been made and refused. Blanche Potter had owned a one-fourth interest of 2,500 shares of $100 par value. By her will, she specifically bequeathed 360 shares and the corporation voluntarily offered to buy the remaining 2,140 shares from her executor at $33 per share. This proposal was rejected, and her executor then made a formal offer of the stock to the corporation at $100 a share. The corporation, in turn, rejected this offer. At this point, restrictions against an outside sale were removed but the efforts of the executor to sell the stock to outsiders were unsuccessful. Ultimately, the stock was put up for sale at public auction, at which the corporation purchased the shares on a bid of $60 per share. Then, to increase the difficulties of the estate of the minority stockholders even further, it was held that the executor must pay New York estate taxes on the stock based upon a valuation of $97.84 per share, which figure was computed by taking the appraised value of a share, $115.11, and deducting 15 percent from it because the stock comprised a minority interest in the corporation.

Obviously, a "first offer" provision cannot prevent the development of the undesirable after-death situations that we have examined. Consequently, its use should be confined to its proper function of protecting suitably against *inter vivos* transfers to outsiders. We must search further for a plan adequate to provide for the situation created upon a stockholder's death.

OPTION ARRANGEMENTS

The stockholders of a close corporation often enter into an agreement

---

[1]*N.Y. Law Journal,* Nov. 19, 1946, p. 1379.

which provides that upon the death of one of their number, the survivors shall have an option during a limited specified period of time to purchase the deceased's shares at a stipulated price.

A brief analysis of a few of the situations that may obtain upon the death of a stockholder with this type of agreement outstanding will show that the option arrangement functions in some instances but not in others. If the facts are such, for example, that the surviving stockholders desire to buy the deceased's stock at the agreed price and are also in a position to pay this price, the survivors will thus be able promptly to regain the full ownership and control of the corporate enterprise, and at the same time the heirs will be well served if an adequate price has been set. Furthermore, the survivors will be able to obtain specific performance of their option to purchase the stock when the option is properly exercised, as evidenced by the following quotation from *Johnson v. Johnson*[2] which case involved an option given to the surviving stockholder that permitted him to purchase 100 shares:

> The corporation is a close corporation. The stock has no fixed or market value and is not quoted in the commercial reports or sold upon the stock boards. The 100 shares in question are essential to the control of the corporation. In such circumstances an action for damages would not afford adequate relief; hence a suit for specific performance will lie.

On the other hand, if the survivors are unable to purchase because of lack of funds, or if they prefer to play a waiting game rather than exercise their option, nothing is accomplished by the arrangement.

Because of the very definite possibility that the surviving stockholders, particularly in those instances in which they already own the majority of the stock, will prefer to let their option rights go by default, coercive "teeth" are sometimes worked into option agreements in an effort to assure their exercise. This was evidently the purpose of the provisions involved in the case of *In re Block's Will.*[3]

Four brothers, Wolfe, Tony, Herman, and Maurice Block, had conducted a partnership engaged in the business of importing bristles. In 1939, they incorporated as Block Bros., Inc., with Wolfe and Tony each owning forty shares, and Herman and Maurice each owning ten shares. They then entered into an option agreement that provided:

> In the event of the death of any of the parties, the survivors shall have the right ... to purchase the stock of the deceased. If the surviving parties do not elect to purchase ... then the executor or personal representative of the deceased may sell the said shares to any other person. If the said executor or personal

---

[2] 87 Colo. 207, 286 P. 109 (1930).

[3] 60 N.Y.S. 2d 639 (1946).

representative . . . shall be unable to sell the said stock, then at the option of the executor or personal representative . . . , the parties hereto agree that the corporation shall forthwith be dissolved and liquidated and distribution of assets promptly made.

This agreement was destined for heavy duty, for Wolfe died in 1942, Tony died in 1943 and Herman died in 1945.

At Wolfe's death, his will left all of his property to his widow, Bessie F. Block. She was nominated as executrix but renounced the appointment. She subsequently requested Maurice to purchase the 40 shares owned by her as a result of Wolfe's death, Tony and Herman having died in the interim.

Upon Tony's death, his will left his shares in trust to pay his widow, Minnie, $25 a week for life, with the widow, his brother Maurice, and one Scheer as trustees. The will also provided that upon the dissolution of the corporation within five years after Tony's death, seven-twelfths of the amount received on his shares by the trustees upon the dissolution and distribution of the corporate assets should go to Maurice and the balance be held in further trust for the widow. The trust was set up in accordance with these provisions.

Upon the death of Herman, who was the third of the four brothers to die within a span of three years and one month, the survivor, Maurice, found himself in no financial position to purchase either the shares formerly owned by Wolfe or those formerly owned by Herman. Herman's widow, Dora, then joined with Wolfe's widow, Bessie, in demanding the dissolution of the corporation, apparently without either of them having made any effort to sell the stock to outsiders. Herman left no will, and Dora was appointed administratrix of his estate. Pursuant to the demand, a call was issued for a special meeting of the stockholders to consider, among other things, the matter of dissolution of the corporation.

The widow of Tony brought this suit to remove Maurice and Scheer as trustees under Tony's will, on the ground that they were about to vote for a dissolution and that Maurice was personally interested in seeing the corporation dissolved because in such an event he would receive seven-twelfths of the value of the stock held in the trust. Maurice's removal was also requested on the ground that he was receiving a salary from the corporation while he was acting as trustee. It was contended that the demand made by Wolfe's widow could have no legal effect because she had renounced her appointment as personal representative, and that the demand made for dissolution by Herman's widow should be disregarded by Maurice because the widow had made no prior effort to sell the stock to outsiders.

By the time the case reached a hearing, the meeting of the stockholders had been held and a dissolution of the corporation directed, Maurice and

Scheer voting in its favor. The practical question, therefore, was whether they had violated their duties as trustees.

The court dismissed the petition, holding that the fact Maurice would receive a portion of the trust property on dissolution of the corporation did not disqualify him as trustee. It was also pointed out that his salary from the corporation was proper since he had always been a salaried officer of the corporation and, under another provision of the agreement, had promised to devote all his time and attention to the business of the corporation. On this point the court said further:

> It is apparent that without Maurice, the last survivor of the firm of Block Bros., Inc., there would be *no business,* since it is evident that it depends upon his knowledge and experience. The salaries which he has received have not been unreasonable. No misconduct or overreaching has been shown.

The court took the position that the widow of Herman could validly demand the dissolution of the corporation under the agreement, saying:

> Under the agreement, the demand made by her was sufficient for the purpose of obtaining a dissolution without considering the legal effect of the demand made by Bessie . . . who did not represent the estate of Wolfe . . . as a fiduciary. It was not obligatory upon her to make efforts to sell the shares to any other person upon Maurice Block's refusal to purchase. The agreement provided that the executor or personal representative "may" sell the shares to any other person. Furthermore, in view of the nature of the shares themselves, being those of a closely held corporation, having no general market and not saleable to the general public in the usual manner, it would be extremely difficult if not impossible to obtain a ready buyer for the shares. The agreement plainly provides an estate fiduciary with a method of liquidating these shares where the fiduciary deems it necessary to do so.

Thus, the "teeth" put into this option arrangement proved to have a powerful "bite," but the ultimate result was the reverse of that intended. Instead of remedying the inherent weakness of the option arrangement, that is, freedom of choice on the part of the optionee, it resulted in dissolving the corporation.

Occasionally, the corporation rather than the surviving stockholders possesses an option to acquire a deceased stockholder's shares. Such an arrangement must in the first instance come within the province of the applicable state laws regarding a corporation's power to redeem its own shares, and regarding the persons who must act on its behalf in exercising the option. How important the latter can be is typified by a recent case where the decedent's estate held the majority stock interest and voted against the corporation's resolution to exercise its option. Since, held the court, the corporation had declined to exercise its option, the estate was free to sell its majority interest to outsiders—a result hardly contemplated when the option arrangement was set up. This case teaches us that where the corporation is given an option (or first offer), it should be accompanied by a similar option (or first offer) given to the other stockholders if the corporation is unable or unwilling to purchase the shares.

No doubt there are rare and unusual circumstances in which an option arrangement is justified as the best solution obtainable. The uncertainty of its exercise and its one-sidedness in favor of the surviving stockholders, however, classify it as a distinctly second-rate arrangement, incapable of furnishing a certain solution to the problems faced upon the death of a close corporation stockholder.

PURCHASE AND SALE ARRANGEMENTS

The most common arrangement to solve the situation brought about by the death of a stockholder in a close corporation is an agreement among all the stockholders, providing that upon the death of one of their number, the survivors agree to purchase the deceased's stock at a specified price.

Such an arrangement eliminates the defects encountered in the use of "first offer" and option plans. "First offers" need not be made at all, and if they are made, they need not be accepted, as we saw in the *Potter* case. Options compel an offer to be made, as held in the *Johnson* case, but again the offer need not be accepted, as is illustrated by the *Block* case. Under the purchase and sale arrangement, on the other hand, the estate of the deceased stockholder is bound to sell and the surviving stockholder or stockholders (or corporation) are bound to buy the deceased's shares of stock in the corporation at a figure that all have agreed upon in advance.

The purchase and sale arrangement, therefore, is the only workable plan by which, upon the death of a close corporation stockholder, the survivors may be certain that they will acquire full ownership and control of the enterprise and by which the family of the deceased may be certain that they will receive the full value of his stock. A proper agreement to that effect among the stockholders while they are all alive binds the transaction. The only remaining hazard is the possibility that the survivors (or corporation) will not have the funds at hand, when death occurs, to pay for the deceased's stock interest. The elimination of this hazard is a simple matter, however, provided that the stockholders are insurable. In such a case, all that remains to be done is to include in the purchase and sale arrangement an insurance policy on the life of each stockholder in the amount of his interest. The purchase price is then assured.

Part III

THE STOCK BUY-SELL AGREEMENT FINANCED WITH LIFE INSURANCE

Chapter 8

THE INSURED BUY-SELL
AGREEMENT--
GENERAL CONSIDERATIONS

LIFE INSURANCE ASSURES CARRYING OUT
OF PURCHASE PLAN

Detailed examination of the situation confronting the surviving stock-holders and the estate and heirs upon the death of a close corporation associate has demonstrated the urgent need for a plan, effective at death, that will place the entire ownership and control of the enterprise in the hands of the survivors and that will promptly reimburse the deceased's estate in full for the value of his stock interest. Careful scrutiny of the alternate plans available to the stockholders has shown that only one arrangement, a binding buy-sell agreement financed with life insurance, guarantees the attainment of these essential objectives.

The life insurance method of financing the purchase of the deceased's stock at death not only removes the hazard that the survivors will not be in a position to buy, but also provides them with the most convenient and attractive method of obtaining the purchase money when it is needed. In discussing partnership buy-sell plans, we compared the advantages of the life insurance method of financing the buy-sell agreement with other methods. Because that discussion is equally applicable to corporation buy-sell plans, no need exists to repeat it here.[1]

---

[1]See pages 175-177.

Types of stock buy-sell agreements. As in the case of partners, the stockholders of a close corporation have a choice between two types of buy-sell agreements: a cross-purchase agreement or a stock redemption agreement. Under a cross-purchase agreement, the stockholders agree that the survivors will purchase, and the deceased stockholder's estate will sell, the deceased stockholder's shares in the corporation, and each stockholder acquires insurance on the lives of the others to fund his obligations under the agreement. Under a stock redemption agreement, the corporation and the stockholders agree that the corporation will buy (redeem), and the deceased stockholder's estate will sell, his shares in the corporation, and the corporation acquires insurance on the lives of the stockholders to fund its obligations under the agreement.

FACTORS DETERMINING CHOICE OF AGREEMENT

In choosing between an individual cross-purchase agreement and a stock redemption agreement, several factors must be considered. Some of these will be discussed fully here; others will be mentioned here but discussed in detail in a later chapter devoted to stock redemption agreements.

Legality and enforceability of the agreement. The legality of a cross-purchase agreement is discussed later in this chapter. The legality of a stock redemption agreement is discussed in a subsequent chapter devoted to such agreements. Also discussed later is the enforceability of these respective agreements.

Convenience and practicality. A corporation may fund its stock redemption agreement with only one policy on the life of each stockholder. A cross-purchase agreement among several stockholders, on the other hand, calls for a multiplicity of policies. Furthermore, a stock redemption agreement often may be more practicable if the other stockholders own relatively more stock, because the younger stockholders may be unable or unwilling to pay the consequent larger premiums required of them under a cross-purchase agreement. Split-dollar insurance plans with the younger stockholders may, however, solve this problem.

Equity of results. Under a cross-purchase agreement, with cross-ownership of the life insurance policies, the plan functions with substantially complete equity among the stockholders where the purchase price is adequate. It seems proper to disregard the likelihood that the surviving stockholders, whoever fate decrees them to be, may have an insurance gain over the premiums they have paid, because they have owned and maintained the policies on the decedent's life. His estate will, of course, own the cash values of the policies he has owned and maintained on the lives of the survivors.

Under a stock redemption agreement, the corporation's payment of premiums is mathematically as if each stockholder had contributed to the premiums in the same proportion as his stockholdings. As contrasted with a cross-purchase plan, however, a deceased stockholder's estate does not own any policies on the lives of the survivors as recompense for his indirect proportion of the premiums paid by the corporation. Therefore, the purchase price under a stock redemption agreement should at least take into consideration the cash value of all policies immediately prior to a stockholder's death, if it does not take into consideration the entire proceeds of insurance on the deceased stockholder's life.

Availability of policy values. Under a stock redemption agreement the policy cash values are corporate assets, hence available for business purposes if needed. Under a cross-purchase agreement, the policies are owned individually and are not directly available for business purposes. By the same token, however, they are not automatically exposed to corporate creditors. Here, we have advantages and disadvantages that should be weighed carefully.

Ratio of stockholdings among survivors. A stock redemption agreement functions so as not to disturb the ratio stockholdings among the survivors but may, for example, convert a minority interest into a majority interest. Under a cross-purchase agreement, the stockholders may achieve whatever ratio of stockholdings among the survivors they mutually desire.

General income tax considerations. If the deductible salaries of the individual stockholders enable them to pay the necessary premiums to maintain insurance under a cross-purchase agreement, the income tax advantage here between the types of agreement will depend upon a comparison of individual tax rates with the corporation's tax rate. If, on the other hand, the stockholders would have to pay individual premiums from corporate dividends, the advantage here favors a stock redemption agreement.

Where the corporation has more than two stockholders and they desire that their agreement extend beyond the first death, some of the insurance will run afoul of the transfer-for-value rule if the surviving stockholders take over on a cross-ownership basis the policies owned on their lives by the decedent. The life insurance under a stock redemption agreement does not encounter this problem since the policies at all times are owned by the corporation.

When a cross-purchase agreement functions at the death of a stockholder, the purchase price paid by the surviving stockholders becomes the income tax basis of the shares acquired. When a stock redemption agreement functions, however, the redemption price paid does not increase the basis of the stock owned by the survivors. This difference is discussed in a later chapter and is important only if a surviving stockholder sells some of his shares rather than holding them until death, when they would obtain a new basis.

Federal estate tax considerations. This factor presents little choice between plans. As we shall see in a later chapter, the purchase price set in a properly arranged agreement of either type will establish the Federal estate tax value of the decedent's stock. Under a stock redemption agreement, the price should reflect the decedent's indirect interest in the insurance values owned by the corporation. The purchase price in a cross-purchase agreement will not reflect such values, but the value of the policies owned by the decedent on the lives of the survivors will be includible in his gross estate along with the value of his stock.[2]

Special tax problems under a stock redemption agreement. These problems involve consideration of the penalty accumulated earnings tax that may be assessed against corporations, consideration of the question whether the corporation's premium payments may be taxed to the stockholders as dividends, and consideration of the question whether the corporation's payments in redemption of a deceased stockholder's shares may be considered a dividend, either to the surviving stockholders or to the estate. The problems are discussed later in the chapter devoted to stock redemption agreements.

The foregoing considerations should be studied carefully by close corporation stockholders and their advisors in choosing the type of agreement most suitable for them.

LEGALITY OF THE INSURED
CROSS-PURCHASE AGREEMENT

It is undoubtedly true to say that today practically every jurisdiction will uphold the legality of a mutual agreement executed by the stockholders of a close corporation which provides that, upon the death of one of their number, the surviving parties will buy, and the deceased's estate will sell to the survivors at a specified price and terms, his shares of stock in the corporation.

As in the case of partnership agreements of a similar nature however, the fact that such a contract calls for performance at time of the death of a party has caused it to be challenged from time to time on the ground that it is testamentary in character and therefore must qualify under the law of wills if it is to be valid. This challenge is not surprising in view of the fact that agreements of all types that call for performance at or after a certain death occurs have had to meet this same challenge because of a failure to distinguish the fundamental nature of such a contract from that of a last will and testament.

It is in order to consider a case involving a specific agreement of stock purchase upon the death of a stockholder. The case is that of *Fawcett v. Fawcett.*[3] George Fawcett and his brother owned the stock of a bank, George

---

[2]*Estate of Richard C. du Pont,* 18 T.C. 1134.

[3]191 N.C. 679, 132 S.E. 796 (1926).

being its president and his brother the cashier. In 1908, they entered into the
following rather unorthodox agreement:

> Whereas, upon the death of either party of this contract, it is
> the desire and will of each and both that any and all shares of
> stock in the First National Bank of Mt. Airy, N.C., owned by
> either of the parties of this contract, at the time of death, shall
> become the property of the survivors, upon a par basis, and this
> instrument is a contract made by each and both parties hereto, to
> sell the survivor said stock at par, and to give the survivor five
> years during which to make payment for said stock, to be divided
> into five equal annual payments. And this contract shall be
> binding upon the administrators, executors or assigns of either
> party. This contract may be canceled by either party upon a
> change of mind, circumstances or sentiment with proper notice to
> the other party hereto in writing.

When George died intestate in 1920 he possessed bank stock amounting to
$29,250 and was survived by a widow and three minor children. The surviving
brother then took over the deceased's bank stock, had it retired or canceled,
and caused a new stock certificate to be issued to himself in lieu of it.
George's widow, as administratrix of the estate and as guardian of the
children, sued to recover the stock on the ground that the agreement was
against public policy, was testamentary and was without consideration.

The court upheld the agreement as a valid and binding contract.

On the question of public policy the opinion stated:

> Nor do we find in the contract anything inconsistent with the
> doctrine of public policy. . . . A contract, for example, whereby
> A agrees to make a will in favor of B, or to refrain from making a
> will, is not of itself void on any ground of public policy; and a
> contract which is to be performed at the death of one of the
> parties is not for this reason illegal.

In making the point that the agreement was not void as testamentary, the
court said:

> The agreement in question is not open to the objection that it
> is a testamentary disposition of property. . . . [Citing cases] It has
> only one witness, and purports to be, not a will, but an executory
> agreement. Six times it is specifically designated a "contract";
> evidently it is "a present contract presently executed," the
> performance of which is deferred until the death of one of the
> parties. . . . In *McKinnon v. McKinnon*, 56 F. 409, 5 C.C.A. 530,
> the court said that such a contract is an executory agreement,
> which determines the rights of the parties *inter se* and provides
> what disposition shall be made of the property on the happening
> of a certain event—a contract which at the promisor's death will

be specifically enforced in equity or become the foundation for an action at law. It is upon this principle that a negotiable instrument may be made payable after death or a contract enforced which provides that compensation shall be made after death for services rendered in the lifetime of the promisor. [Cases and texts cited]

The agreement nearly failed however, by reason of the insertion of its last sentence with reference to cancellation. The widow claimed that the birth of three children since the date of the agreement had wrought a change in the deceased stockholder's circumstances that was equivalent to a written notice and that made the agreement void. Some of the court's comments on this point are quoted here.

A contract may be discharged by performance; by a breach of such a material nature as to justify the innocent party in treating it as rescinded; by fraud, mistake, or duress; by release; by renunciation, merger, or impossibility of performance. 3 Williston on Contracts, §1793 et seq.; Page on Contracts, §2447 et seq. None of these conditions is pleaded or established by the evidence; and mere change in the circumstances of the parties is not sufficient to work a cancellation. The parties to a bilateral contract may agree to rescind it in a particular way, for, as there must be mutual assent to form a contract, there may be mutual assent as to the method by which it may be rescinded; that is, as the parties are bound by their agreement, so by their agreement they may be loosed from their mutual tie. Clark on Contracts, 606. Here the method of revocation was agreed on; by the express terms of the contract there must have been, not only a change of mind, or circumstances, or sentiment, but "proper notice to the other party hereto in writing." Such notice was not given, and presumptively there was no change that made notice necessary or desirable.

Now we come to one of the very few cases that have reached the courts challenging the validity of an insured stock purchase agreement entered into by the individual stockholders; and the facts of the case make it readily apparent why this agreement was destined to be challenged in court. The case is *In re Estate of Soper; Cochran v. Whitby.*[4]

Ira Soper, a native of Kentucky, in 1911 married the plaintiff, Adeline Westphal, who was a widow with three children. After living together until August, 1921, Soper disappeared under circumstances strongly suggesting suicide. In fact, however, he went to Canada and from there to Minneapolis, where he lived the remainder of his life under the name of John W. Young. In

---

[4]196 Minn. 60, 264 N.W. 427 (1935).

1922, he married another widow and they lived together until her death in 1925. In 1927 he married the defendant Gertrude Whitby, also a widow.

Under the name of Young, he and one Karstens organized the Young Fuel Company with $10,000 capital, each family owning one-half the stock. Subsequently, Young and Karstens each procured $5,000 of insurance payable to a Minneapolis trust company, and the insurance policies and certificates of stock were delivered to the trust company under an agreement that provided:

> Upon the decease of either John W. Young or Ferdinand J. Karstens, the Trust Company shall proceed to collect the proceeds of the Insurance Policies upon the life of such deceased Depositor, and shall handle and dispose of such proceeds as follows:
>
> The Trust Company shall deliver the stock certificate of the deceased Depositor to the surviving Depositor and it shall deliver the proceeds of the insurance on the life of the deceased Depositor to the wife of the deceased Depositor if living, and if not living, then to the representatives of his estate, and the stock certificates that were deposited by the Depositor who is then the surviving Depositor, together with the policies of insurance upon his life shall be delivered to such surviving Depositor.
>
> All of the stock deposited hereunder and all of the policies deposited hereunder or any part thereof may be withdrawn by said two Depositors on the joint receipt of both of them.

Soper (Young) actually did commit suicide in 1932, at which time the trust company collected proceeds of the insurance policy on his life and paid the money over to Gertrude Whitby as his surviving wife, and at the same time delivered to Karstens the policy on his life, together with the decedent's shares of stock.

Several months after these matters had been closed out, Mrs. Soper, the true wife of Young, made her appearance; Cochran was appointed administrator of the estate, and he and Mrs. Soper brought this suit against Gertrude Whitby and the trust company to recover the insurance money.

The court held the agreement valid against the contention that it was a testamentary disposition, and held that Gertrude Whitby was the person under the agreement intended as the recipient of the insurance proceeds. The opinion of the court on the first point is quoted at some length because it ties in most of the important cases on partnership agreements. This case shows clearly that the principle involved in the contract is the decisive factor, not the subject matter of the contract. Because this particular agreement was in the form of an "escrow agreement" or revocable insurance trust, the first part of the opinion upholds the validity of such an agreement as follows:

> ... Nor do we think the escrow agreement can be considered a

testamentary disposition of the insurance money or of any other property included in that instrument. It was not so intended, and nothing therein contained can be so construed. Rather, so it seems to us, it takes the form of and functions as an insurance trust. The legal right to demand and receive the insurance money was by the agreement vested in the trust company. It was the payee in both policies. The legal title to the stock certificates vested in it. Immediately upon the death of the insured the rights of the settlors and beneficiaries were finally established. The duty of the trustee to act as in the agreement stipulated became operative. What had theretofore been a passive or inactive matter became at once upon Young's death an obligation requiring action. The trustee performed thereunder. It could do no more, and duty required it to do no less. . . .

An insurance trust having been created, the cases seem to hold with practical unanimity that such trusts are nontestamentary. The mere fact that the settlor reserves the right to revoke the trust does not destroy its efficacy as an insurance trust if the event upon which the trust depends takes place before revocation is made effective. A late and very important case bearing on this subject is *Gurnett v. Mutual Life Ins. Co.*, 356 Ill. 612, 191 N.E. 250.

The opinion then goes on to discuss the validity of the arrangement on the assumption that the "escrow receipt" might not constitute an insurance trust, and it brings in a discussion of the contract law on this subject:

Even if it be conceded that this was not an insurance trust, the authorities generally seem to hold that such arrangements, even if not involving the trust aspect, are valid as inter vivos transactions because they are contractual in nature. Thus in *Coe v. Winchester* (Ariz.) 33 P. (2d) 286, it appears that two partners entered into a written agreement whereby each agreed that he would effect a policy of life insurance payable to his wife. On the death of either, the wife of the deceased was to get the insurance and the surviving partner was to take the deceased's interest in the partnership. Under Arizona law each partner's interest in the business is community property belonging equally to the partner and his wife. But as to such property the husband has complete right to disposal of the entire interest by any deal inter vivos, but cannot make a testamentary disposition of his wife's interest. One of the partners died. His wife claimed a one-fourth interest in the business on the theory that the attempted disposition of the property was testamentary and therefore could not affect her community interest. The court came to the conclusion that the contract was not a testamentary disposition of property and that as such the entire one-half interest of the deceased partner had been validly transferred. Other cases upon this phase are *Murphy v. Murphy*, 217 Mass. 233, 104 N.E. 466 . . . *Thompson v. J.D. Thompson Carnation Co.*, 279 Ill. 54, 116 N.E. 648. In the last cited case the court held an agreement between a stockholder and a corporation, of similar nature, import, and purpose to those of partnership cases hereinbefore cited, to be mutually binding upon each and all the parties thereto from the date of its execution. It was held that there was no testamentary disposition of the property.

The decisions arrived at in the foregoing cases, based upon a proper and fundamental distinction between a valid executory contract and a last will, leave no doubt that stockholders in a close corporation may enter into a contract, financed with life insurance, by which, upon the death of one of their number the surviving stockholder or stockholders are legally bound to purchase, and the estate of the deceased stockholder is legally bound to sell, the deceased's stockholdings in the enterprise.

COURTS WILL SPECIFICALLY ENFORCE CLOSE CORPORATION STOCK CROSS-PURCHASE AGREEMENTS

Ordinarily, upon the failure of a party to carry out his obligations under a contract, a court will award money damages to the aggrieved party. In the case of a contract for the purchase and sale of close corporation stock by its active stockholders however, it is readily apparent that an award of money damages constitutes an inadequate remedy for the refusal of the seller to carry out his part of the transaction. In such a case, there is no open market in which the buyer may procure like shares of stock; indeed, the stock is otherwise non-procurable. And from the standpoint of the seller, there is little or no other market. For this reason, the courts usually grant the buyer specific performance of such agreements.

The best evidence that the courts will specifically enforce a close corporation stock cross-purchase agreement financed with life insurance is such a case as *Bohnsack v. Detroit Trust Co.*[5]

In 1926, Bohnsack, Fouts, Pomfret, and two others organized the Mich-I-Penn Oil and Grease Company. In 1931, they entered into a written agreement providing that if any stockholder wished to dispose of his shares during his lifetime he would sell them to his fellow stockholders, and providing also for mandatory sale to the survivors upon death. Each stockholder was to take out life insurance in the amount of $20,000, payable to the Union Guardian Trust Company as trustee. On his death, the value of the deceased's stock was to be ascertained by a stipulated method, the shares

---

[5]292 Mich. 167, 290 N.W. 367 (1940).

of stock were to be turned over to the surviving stockholders, and the avails from the insurance were to be applied in payment. Life insurance was purchased as agreed upon and deposited with the trust company for the purposes of the agreement.

In 1934, the other two stockholders sold their shares to Bohnsack, Fouts and Pomfret, and were released from the agreement; however, the remaining stockholders agreed in writing that the original agreement would remain in full force and effect as to them.

Then occurred an incident that ultimately brought the agreement into court. One policy for $10,000, taken out by Pomfret, lapsed and he took out another for the same amount, but instead of his making it payable to the Union Guardian Trust Company under the stock purchase trust agreement he designated his wife and relatives as beneficiaries and deposited it with another trust company. Shortly afterward Pomfret died and the defendant, the Detroit Trust Company, was appointed executor of his estate.

Upon the refusal of the executor to carry through the purchase and sale transaction, Bohnsack filed this bill for specific performance of the agreement, asking that he and Fouts be decreed the owners in equal shares of the stock that was held by Pomfret and that was now in the hands of his estate.

The court granted the surviving stockholders specific performance of the agreement, the opinion stating:

> The agreement was valid and under it the plaintiff is entitled to have specific performance.
>
> An action at law to recover damages for breach of the contract would not afford adequate remedy but, in effect, destroy the very purpose of the agreement by opening the way for holding of the stock by third persons.

Manifestly, the failure of Pomfret to substitute the new insurance in the place and stead of the lapsed policy under the purchase agreement created a situation that was bound to be litigated. With respect to this the court said:

> When Mr. Pomfret took out the mentioned policy, with his wife and relatives named beneficiaries, it was a breach of the contract but valid as to the beneficiaries and may not be disturbed as to them in this proceeding inasmuch as the beneficiaries are not parties, but that does not release the estate from performing the contract and giving creditor for the amount of that policy in payment for the shares of stock.

Once an agreement goes to court, it is the duty of the opposing attorneys to attack it assiduously from every possible angle. It was to be expected, therefore, that the validity of this agreement would be challenged. The opinion, in addition to citing the *Lindsay* cases, 205 Pa. 79 and 210 Pa. 224

(enforcing an option agreement), and *Coe v. Winchester*, quoting from the headnotes, had the following to say:

> It was the legitimate desire of the organizers and sole stockholders to have and maintain a close corporation, with consequent benefit, and to that end entered into the contract. The contract was of mutual benefit, upon sufficient consideration and legitimate, unless it can be said that the insurance feature rendered such part thereof invalid.
>
> Mr. Pomfret had an insurable interest in his own life, with right to designate a trustee beneficiary and direct such beneficiary to carry out his contract.
>
> The validity of the insurance is unquestioned. The contest is over the contract application of the insurance.
>
> The contract carried out the purpose of a close corporation and the insurance feature was in furtherance of that end, and was not a speculation in human life but a protection, by mutual desire, of business relations and interests.

In a 1955 case,[6] New York's top court held that the deceased stockholder's administrator must specifically perform an agreement between the corporation's two stockholders whereby on the death of one the stockholdings of the deceased should be sold to, and purchased by, the survivor "at the book value thereof." The agreement further provided that book value "shall be determined by the most recent audit of the books of the corporation provided such audit has been made not more than sixty days before the death of such individual. The payment therefor is to be made in eighteen (18) equal monthly installments."

The principal stockholder, owning two-thirds of the stock, died in 1953. The last previous audit had taken place within sixty days, but it reflected an estimated inventory that was much too low and contained no adjustment but merely a notation regarding accrued income taxes. Claiming that the surviving stockholder had breached the agreement, the administrator of the estate refused to perform. The survivor then brought this suit for specific performance. The New York Court of Appeals upheld the lower court's decree of specific performance, holding also that book value not only should reflect the actual value of the inventory, as the lower court had held, but also the corporation's estimated liability for income taxes. The latter adjustment lowered the purchase price of the deceased's stock by approximately $54,000.

Another case holding that the surviving stockholder was entitled to specific performance of a cross-purchase agreement is *Bailey v. Smith*.[7] The

---

[6]*Aron v. Gillman*, 309 N.Y. 157, 128 N.E.2d 284.

[7]268 Ala. 456, 107 So.2d 868 (1959).

agreement, however, cannot be recommended since it left the deceased stockholder's widow in an unenviable position. The agreement ran between the two principal stockholders of a corporation, each owning 334 of the 691 voting shares outstanding. Their agreement provided in part:

> Upon the death of either of said Stockholders, the surviving Stockholder shall purchase and the estate of decedent shall sell that number of shares of the stock of the Company which, when added to shares owned by the surviving Stockholder, will give the surviving Stockholder voting control of the Company. The purchase price of each share shall be double its book value at the end of the month in which the death of the Stockholder occurs. In determining book value any insurance on the life of the deceased Stockholder owned by and payable to the Company and which is reasonably certain to be collected shall be taken into consideration.

The purchase price was to be paid within thirty days after the personal representative of the deceased's estate qualified. The agreement also gave the survivor an option to purchase all of the deceased stockholder's shares, and contained a first-offer obligation in event one stockholder desired to sell during life.

Following Bailey's death, Smith offered to purchase from the estate twelve shares, which would give him voting control, but the deceased's widow as executrix refused to accept the purchase price and deliver the shares. Alabama's highest court held that Smith was entitled to the relief of specific performance. It held further that any insurance on the deceased stockholder's life payable to the corporation was to be taken into account as a corporate asset in arriving at book value, "whether the proceeds of the insurance have or have not been collected, provided the insurance is reasonably certain to be collected."

This agreement obviated the possibility of a deadlocked corporation, but did so at the expense of the widow, who was left a life estate in all the deceased's property.

We now come to the question of whether the courts will decree specific performance of a cross-purchase agreement at the behest of a deceased stockholder's personal representative or heirs. The general rule is that a court of equity will not decree specific performance of an agreement if it appears that the plaintiff has an adequate remedy at law. And it is said: "The remedy of specific performance has been refused to the vendor when the only purpose of the suit was to recover the purchase price, for which the remedy at law was adequate."[8] Some courts hold, however, that when one party may specifically enforce, the other party may do likewise. But that rule is being

---

[8] 49 Am. Jur., Sec. 130, page 154.

eroded as more and more courts adhere to the rule in Restatement of Contracts, Section 372(a): "The fact that the remedy of specific performance is available to one party to a contract is not in itself a sufficient reason for making the remedy available to the other; but it is of weight when it accompanies other reasons, and it may be decisive when the adequacy of damages is difficult to determine and there is no other reason for refusing specific enforcement." Now let us look at two cases on the subject.

Cardos v. Cristadoro[9] involved a cross-purchase agreement whereby the five incorporators of a company agreed that upon the death of any one of them, the survivors were obligated to purchase, and the decedent's estate was obligated to sell the decedent's stock "at its book value as determined by the last fiscal audit of the company, or last quarterly statement if one has been prepared." The agreement also contained the following paragraph:

> (2) The remaining parties are bound among themselves to purchase the stock of the decedent party in the proportion of their then ownership of stock in the company, but should any of said parties refuse or fail to purchase his proportion upon demand, the remaining parties shall be entitled but not bound to purchase the stock in proportion to their ownership of stock, provided, however, that nothing contained in this paragraph shall prevent the decedent's estate from enforcing performance of their obligation to purchase against any or all the surviving parties.

Cardos was one of the incorporators. At the time of his death in 1950, he and Cristadoro were the only remaining parties affected by the agreement, the latter having bought out the other three. Following Cristadoro's refusal to purchase the decedent's shares, on the ground that the agreement had been abrogated, the heirs of Cardos sued for specific performance. Louisiana's highest court upheld the lower court's judgment ordering Cristadoro to specifically perform the agreement and purchase the decedent's stock at its book value, and further decreeing that if he failed to so perform within fifteen days then there be judgment in favor of the heirs in the sum of the book value plus interest. The court noted that there was mutuality of obligations under the contract, "expressly intended to keep the ownership of these shares of stock within the original incorporators." It did not discuss, however, the right of heirs to a decree of specific performance; perhaps it concluded that the terms of paragraph (2) gave them that right. In any event, the heirs obtained, either through the decree that the survivor specifically perform or through the alternative money judgment, the purchase price of the decedent's stock.

Gingerich v. Protein Blenders, Inc.[10] involved a contract for the present

---

[9]228 La. 975, 84 So. 2d 606 (1955).

[10]250 Ia. 654, 95 N.W.2d 522 (1959).

sale, rather than sale at a stockholder's death, of a block of a corporation's stock. It illustrates, however, the trend of judicial decisions on the question of whether the seller of close corporation stock may have specific performance of his agreement against a recalcitrant buyer. Under the contract, the defendant corporation agreed to purchase from Gingerich 4,505 shares of preferred stock of another corporation at a stated price of $236,512.50. Such shares were tendered by the seller but refused by the defendant corporation, whereupon the seller brought this suit for specific performance. The lower court held that the seller had an adequate remedy at law because the amount of his recovery was definite and fixed, and did not depend upon whether the stock had a known of ascertainable value. We quote from the court's opinion to show the evolution of new rules in this area.

> It is true that we have in the past laid down the rule that "Equity will not interfere to compel specific performance of a contract by one party where similar relief would not or could not be granted against the other party upon his refusal to perform." [Authorities cited.] The converse of this rule, if followed, must necessarily be that when one party may specifically enforce, the other may likewise do so. But the rule is not sound, has been much criticized, and so many exceptions have been engrafted upon it that it is no longer recognized as controlling. Plaintiff's counsel recognize this, and with commendable candor cite Restatement of Contracts, Sec. 372(2). . . . A thorough discussion of the question, with citation of many authorities, will be found in *Vanzandt v. Heilman,* 54 N.M. 97, 214 P.2d 864, 22 A.L.R. 2d 497; and see *Peterson v. Johnson Nut Co.,* 204 Minn. 300, 283 N.W. 561; . . . ("mutuality of remedy is not always essential to a decree of specific performance"); and 81 C.J.S. Specific Performance §11, pp. 427, 428. So far as the Iowa cases cited above in this division hold that mutuality of remedy is essential to an action for specific performance or, by inference and conversely, that if one party is entitled to the remedy the other must likewise be, they are overruled.
>
> * * * * *
>
> . . . We hold that the plaintiff's petition states a case for recovery of the agreed sale price of the stock at law, which forum affords adequate relief; and accordingly no ground for equitable remedies exists.

Thus, while the courts disagree on whether a deceased stockholder's estate may pursue the remedy of specific performance, they all agree that the estate may recover the purchase price to which it is entitled.

Before leaving the subject of the enforceability of stock buy-sell agreements, we call attention to the statutory provisions that require any restrictions on the transfer of shares to be stated on the stock certificates if such restrictions are to be valid. Section 15 of the Uniform Stock Transfer Act, in effect in practically all states that have not adopted the Uniform Commercial Code, provides that "... there shall be no restrictions upon the transfer of shares so representated [by certificate] by virtue of any by-laws of such corporation, or otherwise, unless the ... restriction is stated upon the certificate." Section 8-204 of the Uniform Commercial Code provides: "Unless noted specifically on the security a restriction on transfer imposed by the issuer, even though otherwise lawful, is ineffective except against a person with actual knowledge of it." The law as to the reach of these provisions is still developing and is beyond the scope of this text. Suffice it to say that it is advisable in all instances of stock buy-sell agreements to inscribe on the certificates involved the restrictions being imposed upon their transfer.

Summary. A buy-sell agreement financed with life insurance furnishes close corporation stockholders with the most certain and most economical method of providing for the situation brought about by the death of an associate. It is the safest plan available because it sets up in advance, through the medium of a valid contract, usually enforceable specifically, a binding obligation to buy and sell at time of death. It is the most economical plan because it takes advantage of compound interest and the insurance principle to provide the purchase money, often with a great discount of dollars. For an excellent example of this, consider the *Bohnsack* case, in which a binding obligation was specifically enforced and in which the death of Pomfret occurred during the third policy year of the insurance originally purchased to finance the plan.

Chapter 9

CONTENTS OF THE INSURED STOCK BUY-SELL AGREEMENT

Introductory. Agreement must be drawn by a competent attorney. A carefully written buy-sell agreement, including in it provisions for life insurance financing, constitutes the legal basis for assuring that upon the death of an associate in a close corporation the surviving stockholders will succeed to its full ownership and control and that the estate of the deceased stockholder will receive in cash the full value of his stock interest.

The agreement, in most states, may take either of two forms: a cross-purchase agreement in which the individual stockholders are the parties and the surviving stockholders the purchasers of the shares of a deceased stockholder; or a so-called stock redemption agreement, in which the corporation is a party and is the purchaser of the shares of a deceased stockholder. Since the stock redemption plan has many distinct characteristics, that plan is discussed separately in Chapter 11. Until that chapter is reached, the text will be concerned largely with plans of individual purchase of stock under cross-purchase agreements. Such an agreement stipulates that, upon the death of a stockholder, the surviving stockholders will buy the deceased's stock in the corporation at an agreed price; that insurance will be carried on the life of each stockholder to supply the purchase money; and that simultaneously with the payment of the purchase price, the executor or administrator of his estate will transfer the deceased's shares of stock to the surviving stockholders. Because the surviving stockholders rely upon this contract for the ultimate acquisition of full ownership and control of the

323

enterprise, and because the deceased's family relies upon it for prompt cash payment of the full value of the deceased's stock, the document assumes a role of such obvious importance to all concerned that the parties are reckless indeed if they fail to entrust its preparation to a competent attorney.

THE BROAD PATTERN OF THE AGREEMENT

Insured stock buy-sell agreements have been in common use for a substantial number of years; thousands of them have been drafted, each "tailored" to fit the particular circumstances involved. Since all of these agreements have dealt with similar problems and like subject matter, however, their contents have followed a broad general pattern consisting of the essential commitments that such agreements should include. They may be itemized as follows:

1. A definite commitment on the part of each of the stockholders not to sell or otherwise to dispose of his stock during his lifetime without first offering it for sale to the other stockholders (or to the corporation, in case of a stock redemption agreement) at a stipulated price.

2. A definite commitment, not merely an option, on the part of all the stockholders in which they agree, binding their estates, that the surviving stockholders will buy, and the deceased stockholder's estate will sell and transfer to the survivors, the shares of stock of a deceased stockholder. In the case of a stock redemption agreement, the corporation commits itself to purchase (redeem) the shares.

3. A definite commitment as to the purchase price to be paid for the deceased stockholder's shares.

4. A definite commitment by the stockholders to purchase and maintain under the agreement life insurance policies in an agreed amount with which to finance the purchase, the proceeds of these policies to constitute purchase-price money for the shares of stock when it is received by the deceased stockholder's estate. In the case of a stock redemption agreement, the policies are purchased and maintained by the corporation.

5. A definite commitment as to the ownership and control of the life insurance policies made subject to the agreement, and as to the disposal of the policies on the lives of surviving stockholders.

6. A definite commitment with respect to the time and manner of paying any balance of the purchase price in excess of the insurance proceeds, and, conversely, with respect to the disposition of any insurance proceeds in excess of the purchase price.

CONTENTS OF THE AGREEMENT

Introductory. Because each close corporation differs in some respects at least from every other corporation, no two insured stock buy-sell agreements can be identical. Nevertheless, since they all serve to accomplish the same basic objectives, that is, the buying and selling of a deceased stockholder's shares and the payment for them from the proceeds of business insurance carried on his life, the general structure of such agreements is sufficiently circumscribed to permit an analysis and discussion of the principal provisions usually contained in them. This will now be attempted from a functional standpoint without our considering the important matter of the appropriate technical legal wording of such provisions, since this last is the special province of the drafting attorney.

The parties to the agreement. Ordinarily, all the stockholders, together with a trustee selected by them, constitute the parties to a cross-purchase agreement. Obviously then, all the stockholders must become parties if the arrangement is going to make certain that upon the death of any stockholder the survivors will succeed to full stock ownership in the enterprise. A trustee is not a necessary party to the agreement, but he is desirable as an impartial "third party" to act as a depositary for the shares of stock and the insurance policies during the lifetime of the stockholders and, when a death takes place, to supervise the consummation of the transaction. More will be said later of the functioning of the trust plan, in discussing insurance beneficiary arrangements.

In the case of a corporation stock redemption agreement, the corporation itself will acquire the shares of a deceased stockholder, and is made a party to the agreement for that purpose.

In community property states, it is recommended that the agreement include the wives of the stockholders as signatories unless the attorney for the stockholders in the particular case, who is familiar with the requirements of the local community property law, decides that this is unnecessary.

The purpose of the agreement. The preamble of a well-drafted buy-sell agreement contains a recital setting out in brief the purpose and intent of the parties in entering into the agreement. These recitals state, for example, that the parties all are active in, and together own the stock of, the close corporation involved; that in the event of the death of one of their number, the transfer of his stock to any person other than the surviving stockholders (or the corporation) would tend to disrupt the harmonious and successful management and control of the corporation to which the parties concerned have devoted years of time, attention, and personal energy; that it is the desire of the parties to avoid any such unfortunate contingency and to assure that the estate of a deceased party will receive the full going-value of his stock interest by making provision for the purchase of a deceased's shares at time of death by the surviving parties (or the corporation) and for the use of life insurance to aid in funding such purchase. Recitals of this nature serve to clarify the intentions of the parties and have proved of real significance in cases in which ambiguities have inadvertently crept into the agreement elsewhere.

The "first offer" commitment. The preservation of the enterprise as a close corporation among the original associates who remain active obviously calls for a provision in the agreement that requires that any stockholder who retires or desires to dispose of his stock for other reasons shall first offer his shares for sale to the other stockholders (or to the corporation) before he shall have the right to make any other disposition of them. The usual provision of this type allows a period of at least thirty days during which to accept such an offer and may provide that upon refusal and subsequent failure of the offering stockholder to dispose of his stock elsewhere within a specified period, such as six months, a new "first offer" must be made of the stock to the other stockholders (or the corporation). Furthermore, the other stockholders (or corporation) should be given the right to purchase such stock at the same contract price that governs on purchase in the event of a stockholder's death, if such a price is to be binding on death as to the valuation of the stock in the deceased's estate under the Federal estate tax law. There are other important phases in the matter of estate tax valuation, however, and more will be said on this point later in a chapter devoted entirely to tax problems.

The commitment to sell and buy. A cross-purchase agreement should stipulate in unequivocal terms that each stockholder, binding his heirs, distributees, personal representatives, and assigns, agrees to sell to the surviving stockholders and the surviving stockholders agree to purchase, all of the stock that the deceased stockholder may own in the corporation at the time of his death. In the case of a stock redemption agreement, the stockholders commit their estates to sell their stock to the corporation, and the corporation agrees to buy (redeem) a deceased stockholder's shares.

(For purposes of identification and clarity, it is advisable to state, either in the recitals or in an appended schedule, the certificate number and the number of shares owned by each stockholder. An appended schedule is preferable, since provision may be made to register in it any subsequent changes in stockholdings among the parties.)

The provision for stamping stock certificates. As stressed in a previous chapter, each stock certificate should be stamped or inscribed with a legend to the effect that the certificate is subject to a stock buy-sell agreement of specified date between its owner and the other stockholders and is transferable only in accordance with the agreement.

The price to be paid, and valuation formula, if used. The purchase price to be paid per share for the stock of a deceased stockholder may be fixed by the use of any one of a variety of available methods. The stockholders should choose whatever method is most satisfactory to them and see that it is clearly set out in the agreement.

One method often used is to fix the exact purchase price in advance. At the time of entering into the agreement the price per share will be agreed upon and stated, with the further proviso that the parties may revise the stated figure at any time by indorsing the revised figure upon the contract, the last price stated prior to death to control. If it is expected that there will be need for frequent revisions, it is usually provided that a price must be indorsed upon the contract in each fiscal year; and in case of failure to do so, the purchase price will be fixed by taking the last stated figure as a base and adjusting it for subsequent changes in book value to date of death as determined by the accountants of the corporation. Or if the parties prefer, they may provide for the substitution of an entirely different method of valuation in case no stated price has been filed within a year prior to death. Either one of these provisions should develop a satisfactory purchase price in event the stockholders neglect to keep their stated price current.

The method of using a stated purchase price has the following advantages: First, there can be no misunderstanding as to the amount itself; second, each of the stockholders, knowing exactly what his stock will bring, can plan his estate with precision; third, the stockholders, knowing the exact purchase price that will be required, are afforded an opportunity to keep the price fully insured; fourth, it simplifies the terms of the agreement and the consummation of the transaction.

The courts ordinarily show no hesitancy in specifically enforcing stock cross-purchase agreements containing a stated purchase price for a decedent's stock, as was done in *Krebs v. McDonald's Ex'x.*[1] The agreement called for fixing the price at a special stockholders' meeting to be held annually on the first Monday in February, and the stockholders had not neglected annual review. As sometimes happens, however, they were satisfied to keep the price low. The agreement functioned without a hitch on four separate occasions following the death of a stockholder, but following the fifth death, that of McDonald, his widow as executrix refused to perform. In holding the agreement specifically enforceable, the Court of Appeals of Kentucky stated in part:

> ... As heretobefore stated, the valuations under the agreement never sensitively reflected changes in actual value through the prior twenty years of its operation, and Mr. McDonald was one of the architects of this method. His widow, as executrix and sole successor in interest, cannot now be heard to complain about this method of valuation.

A cross-purchase agreement containing a stated price, with provision for revision from time to time upon agreement of the stockholders, implies that

---

[1] 266 S.W.2d 87 (1953).

each stockholder intends in good faith to cooperate in carrying out the provision. Where such intent is lacking, a court may abrogate the agreement, as was done in *Helms v. Duckworth*[2] and *Duckworth v. Helms*.[3] There, the agreement between the two stockholders contained a provision for review of the stated price each January, but no change was ever requested or made. Following the death of one stockholder, his administratrix brought suit to have the agreement cancelled unless the surviving stockholder agreed to pay the true value of the stock. The surviving stockholder stated in an affidavit that "it was never his intention at any time to consent to any change in this provision. . . ." The court, stating that "holders of closely held stock in a corporation such as shown here bear a fiduciary duty to deal fairly, honestly and openly with their fellow stockholders and to make disclosure of all essential information," held that the survivor's failure to disclose "to his corporate business 'partner' his fixed intent never to alter the original price constituted a flagrant breach of a fiduciary duty" which warranted cancellation of the agreement.

Sometimes the agreement will provide that the purchase price of a deceased's shares will be their book value at time of death, this to be determined by taking the value from the last company statement drawn off prior to death and by subtracting any dividends paid in the interim. A variation of this method is to take the book value as found by the corporation's accountants as of the date of death. Whatever plan is used to obtain book value, however, the fact remains that this method is deficient in that it does not set the purchase price of the deceased's stock at a figure that reflects the going value of the business; it usually fails to include any value for good will, and consequently it is not to be recommended under normal circumstances.

How unreliable book value is as an indicator of market value is shown by a study published in February 1956 by the New York Stock Exchange. That study compared the market value with the book value of the 1055 listed common stocks. It revealed that 660 stocks were selling above book value and 395 below book value. Moreover, 202 stocks were selling at double book value or more, and 72 stocks were selling at one-half of book value or less.

As we pointed out in discussing book value in relation to partnership agreements, the courts do not always agree on what constitutes book value. In *Piedmont Publishing Co. v. Rogers*,[4] for example, occurs this statement: "When we come to the question whether or not good will must be included in book value, we find the decisions in conflict." That case held good will includible where the agreement used the words "total book value." And in

---

[2]249 F.2d 482 (1957).

[3]268 F.2d 584 (1959).

[4]14 Cal. Rptr. 133 (1961).

Aron v. Gillman,[5] we see this statement: "There appears to be no agreement among the decisions or textbook writers on a complete and authoritative definition of the term 'book value.'" There, the agreement called for book value as determined by the most recent audit. The court held that book value included inventory at its actual value and not the estimated value shown on the books, and excluded estimated income taxes for the year although not deducted on the books. The lesson from these and many other cases is that if book value is to be used as an element in determining the purchase price of a decedent's stock, the agreement should define the term with great precision and identify the person or firm designated to apply it. This is vital since, as we have seen, "book value" is not an exact term of art. Because it is not, the Committee on Terminology of the American Institute of Accountants a few years ago recommended discontinuance of the term in buy-sell agreements.

Many stock buy-sell agreements provide that the purchase price shall be determined by the application of a stated formula. The purpose of this method is to place suitable emphasis on net profits as an important measure of value, and also to reflect as accurately as possible the value of good will in setting the price, but unfortunately there is no consensus that any one formula among those in use will do this best. A few of these formulas will be discussed.

One formula calls for the "straight capitalization" of the average net profits of the corporation at a definite rate, for example, 10 percent, the result being taken as the total value of all the stock, including good will. This is then divided by the number of shares to arrive at the price per share. It should be explained that capitalization of net earnings is simply the capital figure that, at the rate of capitalization used, would yield those net earnings. To illustrate, such a formula might require that the net profits be averaged for the last five complete fiscal years prior to death and then capitalized at 10 percent to obtain the total value. Assume, then, that the average net profits for the last five years have been $20,000. Dividing this figure by 10 percent gives a total figure that, at 10 percent, will yield $20,000 per year; namely, $200,000. Dividing this total value by the number of shares gives the value per share; and multiplying that value by the number of shares owned by a deceased stockholder determines the total purchase price for his shares.

This plan is flexible in that a capitalization percentage may be selected by the stockholders to approximate most closely what they believe to be the value of their stock. It is often an impractical plan in the case of a small close corporation because the corporate books rarely portray the true profits of the enterprise; most of the earnings are absorbed in the form of salaries. Then too, abnormally profitable and unprofitable years should not be used in striking an average of past net profits; and it would be a difficult matter to

---

[5] 309 N.Y. 157, 128 N.E.2d 284 (1955).

provide properly for doing this in a purchase agreement. And lastly, the past profits have been earned by *all* the stockholders and may very well overvalue the stock in the light of the fact that one of the two, three, or more associates will be gone when the valuation is made.

Sometimes a formula is used that combines book value and the value derived from the straight capitalization method, and takes the average of the two as the purchase price. Often a weighted average is used. An illustration of this method is found in *Felder v. Anderson, Clayton & Co.,*[6] except that appraised net asset value was used instead of book value. Net asset value was found to be $700.05 per share, and capitalized earnings value found to be $365.23. The latter amount resulted from averaging the net profits of the most recent five years and multiplying by 8.4. This multiplier was obtained by averaging the earnings-price ratios of representative stocks for the same five years and discounting by 10 percent for lack of marketability. The court then gave a weight of 80 percent to capitalized earnings and 20 percent to net asset value, and held the stock worth $432.09 per share as follows:

Earnings Value .... $365.23 X 8 = $2,921.84
Net Asset Value .... $700.05 X 2 = $1,400.10

Per share Value   10) $4,321.94

$ 432.19

Had the court not assigned weights, the result would have been $532.64 per share. A formula along these lines, specifying weights appropriate to the particular corporation, has much to recommend it.

Another formula is that known as the "years' purchase method." Under this method, a return of 6 percent is usually allowed on the average book value (averaged over a stated period of years) and this amount is deducted from the average earnings (also averaged over a stated period of years). The remaining profits are then multiplied by the stated number of years' purchase, such as three, four, or five, to compute the value of good will. The value of good will so determined is thereupon added to the book value to arrive at the total value under the formula. The following illustration should make this method clear:

Average book value (capital stock and surplus) $120,000
Average annual net profits $12,000
6 percent return on average book value 7,200

Excess of profits over 6 percent of book value .... $ 4,800
$4,800 multiplied by 5 years' purchase, shows a goodwill
valuation of . . . . $ 24,000

Total value of the corporation $144,000

[6]39 Del Ch. 76, 159 A.2nd 278 (1960).

It will be noted that the years' purchase method is also flexible in that the number of years taken may be varied with the circumstances of the particular corporation. Like the straight capitalization method, however, it must rely upon average net profits, which may or may not reflect the true profits earned by the enterprise. To correct this, it would probably be necessary to provide in the formula that salaries beyond a specified amount be considered part of the profits. Again, provision should be made for the elimination of abnormal years when applying the formula. And to all of these difficulties must be added the drawback inherent in every formula; the purchase price established by it cannot be ascertained finally until a death occurs.

Thus it is apparent that the use of any method of valuation except that of taking book value alone, which is patently deficient, calls for some arbitrary decision on the part of the stockholders. In the case of a stated purchase price, the stockholders must set the actual figure. If the straight capitalization method is employed, they must decide upon the rate to be used. And if the years' purchase method or a similar method is decided upon, they must stipulate in the formula the number of years to be used. In addition, there is the problem of defining and eliminating the abnormal years before applying any formula that uses average net profits, not to mention the problem of isolating only normal salaries in place of the actual salaries drawn by the stockholders. It is submitted that in most agreements the parties might as well go "whole hog" in the first place by stipulating the exact purchase price, with provision for its future revision from time to time as circumstances dictate. After all, the value of shares of stock in a close corporation cannot be ascertained with exactitude, and there is good reason to believe that a stated purchase price determined and agreed to by the stockholders among themselves while they are all alive not only will be as accurate as any other obtainable, but will be the most practical figure to use.

The financing of the purchase with life insurance. The life insurance policies made subject to the agreement should be recorded in the body of the agreement or, preferably, in an appropriate schedule appended to it. The agreement should state that the purpose of the insurance is to provide cash to be applied against the purchase price of a deceased insured's shares of stock and that the proceeds of the insurance when received by the deceased's estate or heirs, whether the estate receives it directly as named beneficiary or indirectly from the surviving stockholders or from their trustee, shall be credited to the survivors as payment on account or in full, as the case may be, of the purchase price for the deceased's stock. Careful scheduling of all policies made subject to the agreement is essential in order to eliminate any possible confusion with the personal insurance owned by the stockholders or with any business insurance that may be carried for the purpose of indemnifying the enterprise for the loss of services of a valuable associate, or for credit purposes.

Provisions for adding, substituting, or withdrawing policies. A stock purchase agreement is likely to remain in effect for a number of years, during which time substantial changes may occur in the value of the stock of the corporation. If the value of the stock increases substantially, a common development, the stockholders will want to cover the commitment to buy with additional insurance. On the other hand, if the value decreases, they may desire to release some of the insurance from the obligations of the agreement. And even though no appreciable changes take place in the value of the stock, it is possible that a stockholder (or the corporation, in case of a stock redemption agreement) might prefer at a later date to substitute a different policy of like amount. Hence the agreement should provide for the addition, substitution, or withdrawal of policies on notice to, or written consent of, all the parties. It is essential, of course, to record in the agreement any changes made in the composition of the insurance made subject to the agreement.

Adjustment when amount of insurance proceeds differs from purchase price. Every agreement should contain provisions specifying the adjustments that are to take place if the insurance proceeds and the purchase price of a deceased's stock differ in amount.

When the insurance proceeds exceed the purchase price, it is usually provided in a cross-purchase agreement that the full amount of such proceeds will nevertheless be paid over as the minimum purchase price. In other words, it is provided that the purchase price will be the amount called for under the regular price-fixing clause of the agreement or the amount of the insurance proceeds, whichever amount is greater. Although any other disposition of excess insurance proceeds may be made that the parties desire, a provision establishing the insurance proceeds as the minimum amount of money that a deceased stockholder's estate will receive has the distinct advantage of enabling the parties to plan their estates with a precision otherwise unobtainable, particularly if a valuation formula is to be applied at time of death. Where a stock redemption agreement is used, it is customary to provide that any excess of insurance proceeds over the purchase price collected by the corporation shall be retained as general corporate funds. Thus, such excess functions as key-man insurance proceeds.

When the purchase price exceeds the insurance proceeds, it is customary to provide that the balance, if not paid in cash, will be paid by the delivery of a series of interest-bearing notes made by the surviving stockholders or by the corporation, depending upon the type of agreement, and payable to the estate of the deceased stockholder. This series of notes may mature over a period of months or over a period of years, depending upon the circumstances of the particular case and the wishes of the stockholders. Better than merely providing for the period over which the notes are to run, however, is a provision to the effect that any balance of the purchase price be paid in stated equal amounts at specified intervals, thus permitting the number of installments, rather than their amount, to vary with the size of the total balance owed.

The advantages of this arrangement are obvious. The stockholders usually know approximately what amount can be paid periodically by a survivor (or by the corporation under a stock redemption agreement) without financial embarrassment. Often the amount of these installments can be set at a figure to approximate the amount of salary payments being made to the deceased stockholder at time of death. This arrangement affords both definiteness and flexibility. Under it, a small balance will be quickly retired. On the other hand, a large balance will not impose too heavy a financial burden upon the survivors. Any installment arrangement should include the privilege of prepaying any outstanding notes at any time. Provision may also be made, if desired, for the immediate maturing of all the notes outstanding in the event of default in making any payment.

Securing any unpaid balance. Collateral security for any unpaid balance of the purchase price may be provided for by stipulating in the agreement that the personal representative of the deceased stockholder shall retain stock to perhaps 150 percent of the amount of, and allocable to, each unpaid note; the personal representative is to transfer the stock held as collateral for this amount as each note is subsequently paid. Collateral assignment of the insurance policies on the lives of the survivors subject to the agreement may also be specified.

At this point it should be emphasized again that the maximum benefit cannot be obtained from an insured buy-sell agreement unless the stockholders keep the purchase price as fully insured as possible, in the light of the valuation method used by them. Most stockholders realize the great value to them of doing this, with the result that in the vast majority of cases the balance payable, over and above the insurance proceeds, is either nonexistent or insignificant in amount.

The payment of premiums. The agreement should state clearly who is obligated to pay the premiums on each life insurance policy made subject to it. In the case of a stock redemption agreement, the premiums are paid by the corporation. Most cross-purchase agreements provide that each stockholder will procure, own and pay the premiums on policies on the lives of the other stockholders. The proceeds of each policy will represent the portion of the insured's shares that the premium payer is obligated to purchase on the prior death of the insured. Where there are three stockholders, for example, A and B each will own and pay the premiums on a policy on C's life; A and C each will own and pay the premiums on a policy on B's life, and B and C each will own and pay the premiums on a policy on A's life. This plan is in keeping with the true nature of the insurance method of supplying the purchase price: and advance installment accumulation method under which the insurance premiums constitute the installments.

The corporation should not be designated the premium-payer unless the stock redemption plan discussed in a later chapter is used. In any case, however, the corporation may be authorized to make the actual payments to the insurance company and to charge such payments to the salary accounts of the individual stockholders in accordance with the method of premium allocation adopted by them. In fact, this procedure is highly recommended, for it gives assurance to all the stockholders that all the premiums payable under the agreement will be paid when they fall due and that none will be overlooked. Any method of premium allocation is readily implemented by this procedure.

Premiums may be pooled and shared pro rata by the stockholders if their stockholdings are equal. This method, however, introduces other complications. If there is a substantial difference in the ages of the stockholders, it has the effect of requiring the older stockholders to pay more than their just portion, which complicates the adjustments that must be made when a death occurs. If each stockholder has shared equally in the premium burden, he is entitled to share equally in the cash values of the policies at the time of a claim. The difficulty created in this situation is that the cash value credits do not correspond with the cash values in the policies on their own lives that the survivors will take over upon the adjustment.

On the other hand, had each paid the premiums on the policy on the other's life, the proceeds of the policy on the deceased's life would have discharged completely the purchase price for the deceased's stock, and the surviving stockholder could be given the privilege of taking over the policy on his own life by paying the deceased's estate the exact amount of the cash value of that policy. If necessary, the money with which to do this can be made available by a policy loan. If he does not desire to take over the policy, the deceased's estate is fully paid off upon surrender of the policy to the insurance company.

A plan requiring each stockholder to pay the premiums for the insurance on his own life is totally wrong in principle, for in effect each stockholder is then maintaining the fund with which to purchase his own property, that is, his own shares of stock.

Ownership of the insurance policies and restrictions on use for other purposes. The agreement should specify who is to own the right to exercise the benefits and privileges contained in each policy during the insured's lifetime. If a trustee is made a party to the agreement, the ownership may be vested in the trustee if desired. If this is not done, then the logical owners of each policy are the particular premium payers. This will be the corporation, in the case of a stock redemption agreement. The agreement should provide restrictions upon the exercise of ownership rights in derogation of the objectives of the agreement.

Disposition of policies on the lives of survivors. The matter of the disposition of the insurance policies on the lives of the surviving stockholders does not come up in the case of a stock redemption agreement that continues in force irrespective of the death of one or more stockholders. On the other hand, an individual cross-purchase agreement should contain provisions disposing of the insurance policies on the lives of the stockholders after a death occurs.

The usual arrangement is to grant each insured an option, exercisable within a specified period, such as thirty or sixty days after the appointment of the executor or administrator, to take over the insurance in force on his own life under the agreement after he has made a suitable financial adjustment for differences in cash values. This plan is readily accomplished by crediting each stockholder, including the deceased, with the cash values that have been created in the survivors' policies by the premiums each has paid, charging each surviving stockholder with the cash value of the insurance he is acquiring on his own life, and settling the balances with those entitled to them. In the event any policy is not taken over during the option period, its owner is empowered to surrender it to the insurance company for cash.

It should be noted that by the above process, the deceased's estate will receive credit for the premiums the deceased has paid to the extent of the cash values created, in addition, of course, to receiving the full purchase price for his shares of stock in the enterprise.

It should also be observed that, if each stockholder has contributed to the premiums on the insurance other than that in force on his own life, the amount that any survivor must put up in order to take over the policy on his own life will never exceed the cash value of that policy, and therefore under such circumstances the exchange may be financed in full, if need be, by a policy loan. In fact, the only situation in which he would owe the full cash value of his insurance on the adjustment, if each has paid the other's premium, is in the case of the death of one of only two stockholders, in which event the survivor would have the option to take over his policy from the deceased's estate upon paying to the estate the cash value of it. If more than two stockholders are involved, the adjustment calls for the surviving stockholders in taking over their policies to pay considerably less than the cash values of the policies being acquired on their own lives, since each receives credit for part of the cash values of the policies on the other survivor or survivors.

Assume, for example, that the stockholders are Able, Baker and Cain, and that each is insured for $20,000 on the cross-purchase plan. Baker dies ten years later, and the survivors use the proceeds of the insurance on his life to buy his shares from his estate. The survivors desire to take over the policies on their respective lives. Each of the policies on Able's life, one owned by Cain and the other owned by Baker's estate, has a cash value of $1,800. Each of the policies on Cain's life, one owned by Able and the other by Baker's estate, has a cash value of $2,400. Therefore, Able must pay the estate $1,800 for one policy on his life, and will owe Cain $1,800 for the other policy. Cain must pay the estate $2,400 for one policy on his life, and will owe Able $2,400 for the other policy. Thus, on the adjustment Cain will pay Able the difference of $600, and will pay $2,400 to the estate. His payments of $3,000 are considerably less than the $4,800 total cash value of the policies he takes over. Able will pay the estate $1,800 and will collect $600 from Cain on their adjustment. Able's net payment of $1,200 is far below the $2,400 total cash value of the policies he takes over. As the tax law stands when this is written, neither surviving stockholder can acquire from a deceased stockholder's estate the policy on the other surviving stockholder's life without running afoul of the transfer-for-value rule—although a surviving partner is protected from application of the rule in a similar situation. Each survivor could, of course, continue the policy he owns on the other's life for purposes of a cross-purchase agreement between them.

If the premiums have been "pooled" and paid pro rata by the stockholders, then the cash values of all the policies as of the day before a death occurs should be totaled and divided pro rata to ascertain the credit to be given each party. On taking over his policy, each survivor, as before, will be charged with its cash value. Thus, in addition to its other shortcomings the plan of pooling premiums produces an imbalance in the adjustment after death. This is not a serious problem, however, except in the case of the death of the older one of two stockholders. In this event, the survivor must pay to the deceased's estate an amount greater than the amount of the cash value of the policy being acquired.

If the insurance carried under the plan has been substantially less than the purchase price, which leaves a sizable balance for the survivors to pay in installments, then it may be provided in the agreement that upon taking over the insurance on their own lives the survivors will make collateral assignments of their policies to the deceased stockholder's estate as security. Obviously, this procedure furnishes valuable protection to the survivors as well as to those interested in the estate of the deceased.

Provisions for amending, revoking, or terminating the agreement. The agreement should reserve to the stockholders jointly the right at any time to amend or revoke it by a writing signed by all of them. Of course, if a trustee is also a party, it will be necessary to provide that the stockholders shall not make any change in the terms of the agreement that will increase the obligations or reduce the rights of the trustee without its consent.

The agreement should also contain provisions for its automatic termination upon the happening of any one of certain specified events as, for example, the dissolution or bankruptcy of the corporation, or, in the case of two stockholders, the death of both prior to the consummation of the purchase and sale of the stock of the stockholder first to die.

The agreement may also provide that any stockholder except the offending stockholder (or a majority of the stockholders, if preferred) has the right to call for a revocation of the agreement if the insurance of any other stockholder, who is obligated to maintain insurance subject to the agreement, is allowed to lapse without value or is withdrawn.

Supplemental to the provisions for revocation and termination, there should be included provisions giving each stockholder the right, upon suitable adjustment, to take over the insurance in force upon his own life, and any other provisions relating to the shares of stock or insurance appropriate to the circumstances.

The foregoing comprise the principal provisions that should be contained in an insured stock buy-sell agreement entered into by the individual stockholders. Again, sample forms and clauses have been left out of the text purposely. Their inclusion, if only a few were set out, would tend to cramp the discussion; and the inclusion of a number sufficient to illustrate all the available variations in arrangements would be impracticable. Furthermore, many such forms are accessible in the legal form books and in the specialized business insurance and trust services, and still others may be obtained by attorneys from the law departments of insurance and trust companies. Lawyers will find these forms of assistance in drafting the tailor-made finished document that each situation requires.

Chapter 10

INSURANCE BENEFICIARY
ARRANGEMENTS

The buy-sell agreement should state to whom the life insurance policies are to be made payable upon death. In this matter, one may choose from among a number of different arrangements.

The corporation as beneficiary. If a plan is adopted in which the corporation will be the purchaser of a deceased's shares of stock, then preferably the corporation should be designated to receive the insurance proceeds.

A trustee as beneficiary. If the stockholders desire to have a cross-purchase plan administered by a trustee as an impartial "third party," then the trustee, preferably the corporation's bank, if it has trust powers, should be designated beneficiary of the life insurance made subject to the agreement. This plan is highly recommended.

Under the plan, the trustee becomes a party to the agreement along with the stockholders. The contract is in the form of a business insurance trust agreement, the provisions of which follow the general cross-purchase contract form, modified and supplemented by the necessary trust provisions. It will be provided that the life insurance policies be made payable to the trustee and deposited with it. Ownership rights under the policies may be given to the trustee or may be retained by the stockholders who pay the respective premiums on them. Funds with which to pay the insurance premiums also may be deposited with the trustee, but ordinarily the stockholders themselves, or the corporation as their agent, will pay the premiums directly to the insurance company. The stockholders will indorse their stock certificates in blank and deposit them with the trustee for the purposes of the agreement, reserving to themselves, however, the right to receive all dividends payable on the stock and the right to vote their respective shares.

The foregoing arrangements place the trustee in an ideal position to carry through the consummation of the purchase and sale in the event of a stockholder's death. The proceeds of the insurance on the deceased stockholder's life are collected by the trustee. Then, if the agreement provides for the application of a valuation formula to ascertain the purchase price of the deceased's shares, the trustee applies the formula or supervises its application, whichever procedure is called for by the agreement. Upon ascertainment of the purchase price, either from a clause in the agreement stipulating a predetermined figure or from the application of a specified formula, the trustee, after reserving its commissions, delivers to the deceased's executor or administrator as much of the insurance proceeds as is required to pay the purchase price of the deceased stockholder's shares, and disposes of any excess of insurance proceeds as directed in the agreement. The shares of stock owned by the survivors and the shares purchased by them from the deceased's estate are then indorsed over to them and the insurance policies on the lives of the survivors are made over to the respective owners, who will offer to transfer them to the insureds in accordance with the terms of the agreement covering such an exchange.

If the insurance proceeds, however, are less than the purchase price, then the trustee procures from the surviving stockholders a series of notes as called for by the agreement, payable to the deceased's estate and aggregating the balance of the price owed by the survivors. These notes, together with the insurance proceeds and any specified collateral in the form of a portion of the deceased's stock, or collateral assignments of the insurance on the lives of the survivors, or both, are delivered to the executor or administrator. Any shares of stock and any insurance policies not required as collateral are delivered to the proper owners by the trustee; and the stock and insurance held as collateral by the deceased's personal representative are made over by him to the surviving stockholders as the notes are subsequently paid. Upon the discharge of the trustee's duties, the trust is terminated.

This brief outline of the trustee plan shows that when an experienced corporate trustee is made a party, the consummation of the purchase and sale of a deceased's stock will be carried through smoothly in an impartial and responsible manner; thus the stockholders are relieved of most of the details and bother, while at the same time they are assured that the interests of all concerned will be supervised by a capable, unbiased third party. All things considered, there is no better plan.

The surviving stockholders as beneficiaries. If the trustee plan is not chosen, the designation of the surviving stockholders as beneficiaries of the insurance is a logical choice under a cross-purchase agreement. It places the purchase money in the hands of those who are to be the purchasers and who are obligated to use the insurance proceeds in payment for the deceased's stock. It places the purchase money in the hands of those who have created it and own it if, as is usually the case, the survivors have paid all the premiums on the deceased's insurance and have possessed the incidents of ownership during his lifetime.

Furthermore, this arrangement tends to balance the situation at death between the surviving stockholders and the deceased's estate. The survivors, obligated to buy and to pay the agreed purchase price for the deceased's stock, hold the insurance proceeds pending consummation of the transaction. The personal representative, obligated to sell and transfer the deceased's stock in the corporation, holds the shares. Thus, each side of the transaction holds something that is obliged to deliver over to the other side upon the receipt of that which the other side possesses. Given this balanced status, together with the realization that the survivors may, if necessary, obtain specific performance of the agreement by court decree, and that the estate may obtain a decree or judgment for the purchase price, the purchase and sale should function smoothly.

Under this arrangement, as under the trustee plan, if the survivors have been the premium payers and policy owners of the deceased's insurance, the proceeds are not subject to estate taxation, and will be included in figuring the cost basis of the shares of stock acquired by the survivors, to give them the most favorable income tax position possible should the survivors later sell any of these shares.

Attention should be called, however, to the fact that the proceeds and avails of insurance made payable to the surviving stockholders are not protected against the claims of their creditors. But in this connection, it should be kept in mind that the creditors of the corporation are not creditors of the individual stockholders. It should be remembered also that aside from the secured creditor, such as a mortgagee, who holds by contract a contingent right of disposal of a specific item of the debtor's property, the relationship between the debtor and his creditor is personal; the creditor, as such, has no property interest in his debtor's assets. Upon default in payment of a debt that has become due, the creditor has the right to sue, and the debtor has the right to defend the action on the merits. It may be said in general that unless a debtor, after the maturity of a claim against him, conceals himself or his property or removes himself or his property from the state, or is about to do this, with intent to defraud his creditor; or has made a transfer in fraud of his creditors; or until a creditor obtains a judgment against him, the creditor has no right to touch or interfere with any of the debtor's property.

That any conduct or transactions in fraud of creditors will occur is improbable. If, however, the financial status of any of the stockholders should deteriorate to the extent that he may have unsatisfied judgment creditors, they can levy not only on the insurance that he owns under the plan payable to himself, but also on his shares of stock in the corporation and on his other available property as well. The result would be that, until the judgment was satisfied, the agreement, unaltered, would be impracticable and the parties would no doubt take advantage of their reserved right to amend or revoke it, as dictated by the changed circumstances.

Moreover, the creditors of a stockholder-beneficiary not only must be in a legal position to attach his property, but must act before the insurance death proceeds are paid over by him in payment of a deceased's stock. Assuming the purchase price to have been set at a fair figure, the transfer of the proceeds, since it is in good faith and for a fair consideration, cannot be set aside as a transfer in fraud of creditors. Therefore the transaction, if consummated, will hold, even though creditors of a surviving stockholder under certain circumstances might be able to attach or levy on his shares of stock, including such stock as he might have acquired from the deceased's estate.

It is believed that substantially the same creditor status as outlined above would ultimately prevail if the trust plan is used, although in most jurisdictions the courts would then be called upon to resolve the conflict between statutes protecting insurance payable to "third person" beneficiaries and the rule of law or its statutory counterpart which holds that a transfer in trust for the transferor's benefit may be reached by his present and future creditors. There seems to be a paucity of cases on the subject, and this fact alone indicates that in the great majority of cases there will be no need for protection of the insurance from claims of creditors.

The insured's estate as beneficiary. Among the other arrangements that may be chosen is that of designating the respective estates of the insured stockholders as beneficiaries. Although this is a plan that is sometimes used, there are several objections to it.

A deceased stockholder's death finds his executor or administrator holding the title to both the subject matter of the sale and the purchase money for it. This creates an imbalance in the situation in favor of the estate and against the surviving stockholders. Although this alone is not serious, nevertheless if the agreement does not contain a clear and positive statement that the insurance proceeds thus received by the estate directly from the insurance company are to be credited to the surviving stockholders as purchase money for the deceased's shares of stock, the personal representative or heirs may contend that they are entitled not only to the insurance proceeds but to the full purchase price as well. Furthermore, if this plan called for all or any part of an insured's premiums to be paid by himself, a contention that all or part of the insurance proceeds constituted personal insurance might prove formidable.

Another objection is that both the deceased's shares of stock and the insurance proceeds are exposed to claims of the creditors of his estate. Here, we have a quite different debtor-creditor relationship than subsisted during the deceased stockholder's lifetime. After death, his estate constitutes a fund impounded in the hands of his personal representative for the benefit, first, of his creditors, and second, of his distributees. True, the personal representative is charged with the duty of carrying out the executory contracts of the deceased stockholder, except those calling for the deceased's personal services and those expressly terminable upon death, and is therefore bound to carry through the stock purchase and sale agreement. But in case the deceased's assets prove inadequate, the surviving stockholders well might be forced to resort to litigation in order to assert their rights. Estate creditors, including the tax collectors, are naturally militant in the situation, for they are afforded their last opportunity to collect their debts, and because of this, the personal representative may actually desire litigation for his own protection in the premises. Again we are dealing with a situation best avoided by the trust plan, in which the title to the stock and the insurance proceeds are vested in the trustee, the former to be made over to the survivors and the latter to be made over to the deceased's personal representative upon the consummation of the agreement.

A further objection to designating the respective estates of the insured stockholders as beneficiaries is the possibility of controversies over the amount of estate taxes. It seems to be well settled by the court decisions that if there is an insured buy-sell agreement effective at death, an estate tax is not imposed on both the purchase price and the value of the business interest being sold under the agreement, but the taxing authorities nevertheless from time to time continue their efforts to impose "double" taxation. They are given the opportunity to attempt this under every arrangement by which the insurance proceeds are estate taxable, that is, if the insured has any of the incidents of ownership in the policy on his own life, or if, as is here under discussion, the proceeds are payable to his estate.

If the estate of the insured is named as insurance beneficiary, there is also some danger that the rule of the *Legallet* case[1] will be applied on a subsequent sale of the stock. If applied, the insurance proceeds paid directly to the estate will not be included in the cost basis of the stock acquired from a deceased associate when the survivor computes his gain or loss on a subsequent sale. (See discussion of these cases at page 221 et seq. of the section on Partnerships).

Lastly, the estate beneficiary arrangement is not suitable, for obvious reasons, unless the agreement stipulates that the insurance proceeds shall constitute the minimum purchase price.

---

[1] 41 B.T.A. 294; cf., *Victor G. Mushro,* 50 T.C. 43.

Designation of personal beneficiaries of the stockholders. At this point it is apropos to re-emphasize that the purpose of a stock cross-purchase agreement is to enable the surviving stockholders to purchase the shares of a deceased stockholder in the corporation and in this way to continue in full ownership and control of the enterprise, and at the same time guarantee that the estate of the deceased will receive full value for his interest in the business promptly, in cash. The function of life insurance in connection with such an agreement is to guarantee that the surviving stockholders will have the cash available with which to pay over the full purchase money promptly at the time of a stockholder's death, whenever it may occur. However, other arrangements are designed to go still further; that is, instead of providing that the deceased's estate receive the purchase price in cash, the insurance proceeds are paid directly to the personal beneficiaries of a deceased party. In other words, the objective in some instances is that the insurance proceeds function, first, as business insurance to supply the purchase money to pay for the stock of a deceased stockholder; and second, as personal insurance, the purchase money remaining in the form of insurance proceeds held by the insurance company and payable in installments to the deceased stockholder's family under the settlement options of the policy.

The possibility and feasibility of making such insurance arrangements have been discussed at some length in the section on Partnerships, to which the reader is referred, since the discussion there is equally applicable to close corporation stock purchase agreements.

To sum up the matter of designating personal beneficiaries: the designation of personal beneficiaries and the use of settlement options are foreign to the basic purposes to be accomplished by a business buy-sell agreement. Such a designation probably will give rise to an income tax problem as presented in the *Legallet* case, unless the special settlement arrangement previously discussed is utilized. It raises the problem of satisfying estate creditors and heirs with statutory rights in the estate, where they are not otherwise satisfied. In the great majority of cases there is need in a deceased stockholder's estate for all or nearly all of the cash supplied by the purchase price for his stock. Consequently, most stockholders are well advised to eschew the advantages of settlement options under the insurance used to fund a buy-sell agreement, and to adhere to a plan which provides for a lump sum payment of insurance proceeds used to fund the plan.

Chapter 11

THE CORPORATION AS PURCHASER

IN GENERAL

In some cases, close corporation stockholders will find that the cross-purchase plan providing for the purchase of a deceased stockholder's shares by the survivors is the best one suited to their situation. Many instances will occur, however, when the stockholders will desire a plan in which the corporation agrees to purchase (redeem) a deceased's stock and retire it into the corporate treasury. In one or two states, this latter plan may not be available because of restrictions against the purchase of its own stock by a corporation, but where the transaction is not prohibited, the stockholders are offered a choice between these two basic plans. Because the corporation purchase plan, often called the stock redemption plan, has many distinct characteristics, a separate discussion of it has been reserved for this chapter.

When stock redemption plan is considered useful. Under certain circumstances, as already noted in Chapter 8, the stock redemption plan appears to offer close corporation stockholders the most suitable means of preserving ownership of the enterprise for the survivors. For example, if there are more than two or three active stockholders this plan offers a simpler method of continuing the purchase arrangement in operation beyond the first death. Again, if a corporation has an ample surplus after paying full salaries and commensurate dividends on its stock, it may well be in a better economic position, because of an income tax differential existing in its favor, and in a better financial position, to purchase a deceased's stock. Situations of this

344

latter type were frequent during World War II, with high corporate earnings on the one hand and salary freezing on the other.

Situations such as those described, however, by no means account for all of the corporation purchase plans adopted. Many are set up in place of an individual purchase plan for no other reason than the stockholders' fallacious rationalizing that if the corporation agrees to purchase the stock and if it pays the premiums on the insurance with which to finance the purchase, such premiums do not in effect come out of their pockets.

General characteristics of the usual corporation plan. Under the usual stock redemption plan, the corporation becomes a party to the agreement along with the stockholders. The agreement stipulates that upon the death of a stockholder, his estate will sell, and the corporation will buy (redeem), his shares of stock in the enterprise. To make as certain as possible that the corporation will have surplus funds on hand at the death of a stockholder with which to carry out its end of the bargain, the corporation agrees to purchase and maintain a specified amount of life insurance on each stockholder.

It is readily apparent that this arrangement differs in many respects from the individual purchase plan. The life insurance is bought and owned by the corporation. The policies constitute a corporate asset; the creditors of the corporation must therefore be considered. The premiums are paid by the corporation; hence each stockholder, including in each instance the stockholder whose stock will be sold on consummation of the plan, contributes indirectly to the purchase plan in proportion to his stockholdings.

Characteristics of other stock redemption plans. Unfortunately, some diversity of opinion exists among respectable authorities as to what a corporation can properly obligate itself to do toward the purchase of its own stock and as to the possible tax consequences that may result. Assuming a jurisdiction in which a corporation can legally buy its own shares, some authorities nevertheless feel that a direct contract by the corporation to do so and to carry life insurance for the purpose of financing the purchase may run some risk of not being considered for a corporate purpose, and that, consequently, the arrangement may encounter difficulty from Section 531 of the Internal Revenue Code. This section imposes a penalty accumulated earnings tax on the income of a corporation that, instead of being distributed, are accumulated for the purpose of avoiding income tax upon its stockholders. These authorities, therefore, believe that the life insurance must be divorced from any agreement to purchase stock, and that it must be purchased, owned and justified by the corporation as insurance to compensate it for the loss of the services of valuable men. This viewpoint, however, has been refuted by certain recent cases, discussed later. Then too, various methods are used to implement the purchase of a deceased's stock. Some recommend a definite agreement between the corporation and the stockholders to this effect, and others recommend an agreement among the individual stockholders committing the survivors, when a death occurs, to vote their stock in favor of having the corporation purchase the deceased's stock.

Obviously, indirect stock purchase arrangements such as these differ radically from the individual purchase plan, as well as from the direct or formal corporation purchase plan.

LEGALITY, VALIDITY, AND ENFORCEABILITY OF STOCK REDEMPTION PLANS

Legality. The first inquiry in any case is whether the law of the state of incorporation permits a corporation to purchase its own shares of stock. In England, the courts have held such a purchase to be illegal, unless the particular corporation is expressly authorized to do so. (See the leading case in that country, *Trevor v. Whitworth.*[1]) In the United States, the courts of a few states followed the English rule in the absence of an enabling statute. But the nearly unanimous court authority in this country today upholds the right of a corporation to buy its own stock if the purchase is made in good faith and does not impair its capital.

However, nearly all of the states today have statutes on the subject, some of them enacted to grant corporations the right to purchase their stock when previous local court decisions had held to the contrary. These statutes differ somewhat in each jurisdiction as to their conditions and limitations; some of the statutes are very broad and others confine the right to purchase within very narrow bounds. The situation, therefore, requires reference to the applicable law in each instance. No attempt is made here to set out the present status of the law in the various states. Up-to-date digests of the prevailing law, state by state, may be found in any of the various periodic supplement loose-leaf business insurance services, to which the reader is referred.

Validity of executory contract by corporation to purchase its own stock. Assuming that the laws of the particular jurisdiction permit a corporation to purchase its own stock, if it is done in good faith and out of surplus so that the rights of creditors are not endangered, the next inquiry in any case is whether the proposed contractual arrangement actually imposes upon the corporation a legally binding obligation to buy. The general rule is stated in 5 Thompson, Corporations, s. 4086 (4080), as follows: "In jurisdictions where corporations have the power to purchase their own shares of stock, within the foregoing rules [as to good faith, rights of creditors, *et cetera*], there is nothing to prevent the corporation from entering into a valid contract to

---

[1]L.R., 12 App. Cas. 409.

repurchase shares sold by it." The pertinent inquiry, therefore, is what constitutes "entering into a valid contract" on the part of the corporation.

Probably in most jurisdictions where such purchase is authorized, a simple agreement in which at death the stockholders agree for their estates to sell, and the corporation agrees to buy, their shares of stock at the stipulated price or terms is valid and binding, except only, that it could not be enforced against the corporation if at time of performance the purchase would impair its capital. In such jurisdictions, the purchase agreement may be set up independent of the life insurance, if such an arrangement is considered desirable.

Effective Sept. 1, 1963, New York has been listed among such jurisdictions. Before a new statute went into effect on that date, however, there was some doubt whether a stock redemption agreement which made no reference to life insurance was specifically enforceable against the corporation. That doubt was caused by the *Topken* case.[2] Schwartz had bought and paid $15,200 for 152 shares of the corporation's stock under an agreement whereby on termination of his employment the corporation was to repurchase the shares at book value, exclusive of good will. Upon his termination of employment five years later, when the stock had no book value, the corporation claimed his stock—for free. On his refusal to deliver, the corporation sued in equity for specific performance, asking that it be decreed the owner of the shares. New York's highest court held that specific performance would not be decreed. The decision was based on the reasoning that the purported consideration for the contract was the mutual promises of the parties, that the Penal Code made it impossible for the corporation to buy its stock at any time it failed to have a surplus; therefore, "One of the promises may or may not be good, the same as if a discretion were left to one of the parties to perform or not to perform. Under such circumstances there is no consideration and the contract cannot be enforced." But the opinion went on to state:

> If in the case before us the defendant had been given employment and the employment had furnished the price or the consideration for his agreement to return the stock at the end of his employment, we would then have a contract resting not on a mutuality of promises, but upon a consideration given and paid in part by the corporation. . . . The contract then would be good unless it appeared that the stock would be purchased out of capital. This would be a matter of defense.

Everyone agreed that equity was done by the court in not allowing the corporation to get back for nothing the shares for which Schwartz had paid the corporation $15,000 only a few years previously. But the court's

---

[2]*Topken, Loring & Schwartz v. Schwartz,* 249 N.Y. 206, 163 N.E. 735, 66 A.L.R. 1179 (1928).

reasoning received wide criticism, on the ground that a conditional promise is illusory only where the condition is within the arbitrary control of the promiser.

Instead of employing the criticized reasoning, the court might have declined to decree specific performance under this rule: "A bill in equity for specific performance is an appeal to the conscience of the court, and generally, in such a proceeding, the inquiry must be whether, in equity and good conscience, the court should specifically enforce the contract.... If plaintiff's case is lacking in equity, relief will be denied."[3] However, the same court has refused to follow the *Topken* decision in subsequent cases involving similar contracts.[4]

Even if the Topken case had been followed, however, cases in New York involving insured stock redemption agreements made it clear that such agreements were valid as coming within the exception stated in the *Topken* case where the corporation agreed to maintain the insurance policies.[5] The effect the *Topken* case had was extinguished on the date when New York's new Business Corporation Law went into effect. Section 514, relating to agreements for the purchase by a corporation of its own shares, provides as follows:

> (a) An agreement for the purchase by a corporation of its own shares shall be enforceable by the shareholder and the corporation to the extent such purchase is permitted at the time of purchase by section 513 (purchase or redemption by a corporation of its own shares).
>
> (b) The possibility that a corporation may not be able to purchase its shares under section 513 shall not be a ground for denying either party specific performance of an agreement for the purchase by a corporation of its own shares, if at the time for performance, the corporation can purchase all or part of such shares under section 513.

Section 513(a) reads as follows:

> (a) A corporation, subject to any restrictions contained in its certificate of incorporation, may purchase its own shares, or redeem its redeemable shares, out of surplus except when currently the corporation is insolvent or would thereby be made insolvent.

---

[3] 81 C.J.S. Specific Performance §3, p. 411.

[4] *Cross v. Beguelin*, 252 N.Y. 262, 169 N.E. 378; *Matter of Estate of San Giacomo*, 14 N.Y. 2d 615, 198 N.E. 2d 268 (1964).

[5] *Greater New York Carpet House, Inc. v. Herschmann*, 258 App. Div. 649, 17 N.Y.S.2d 483 (1940); *Ionic Shop, Inc. v. Rothfield*, 64 N.Y.S.2d 101 (1946); *Murphy v. George Murphy, Inc.*, 7 Misc. 2d 647, 166 N.Y.S.2d 290; *In re Farah's Estate*, 215 N.Y.S.2d 908 (1961).

Subsection (b) permits redemption out of stated capital for certain enumerated purposes. Thus was laid the ghost of a hard case that made bad law.

Enforceability. Assuming a jurisdiction in which a corporation is permitted to purchase its own stock and a valid contract running between the corporation and the stockholders to make such purchase upon the death of a stockholder, there remains the question of the enforceability of the contract upon the occurrence of a death.[6] This question has been answered for New York by quoting its new statute. This statute, patterned after the Model Act, reflects the law generally. It is the law of practically all jurisdictions, however, that even though a valid stock redemption contract has been set up, it will not be enforced to the prejudice of the creditors of the corporation. The best way, therefore, to assure the enforceability of such a contract is to make sure that the corporation maintains at all times life insurance on each stockholder to the full amount of the purchase price for his stock. With a valid contract, and with adequate surplus funds at hand with which to make the purchase, in most states either party, if necessary, can have specific performance decreed.

There is a further precaution, however, that the stockholders in most states should observe in order to make sure that their agreement will be enforced by specific performance, if necessary. Most states now have statutes that require any restrictions on the transfer of shares to be stated on the stock certificates if such restrictions are to be valid. Practically all of these statutes constitute either Section 15 of the Uniform Stock Transfer Act or Section 8-204 of the Uniform Commercial Code. Because such sections were quoted previously in Chapter 8, they will not be repeated here. We add, however, that they are particularly applicable to the restrictions which usually surround stock redemption agreements. Accordingly, all stock certificates made subject to such agreements should have subscribed thereon the restrictions imposed upon their transfer.

We have mentioned that a stock redemption agreement will not be enforced to the prejudice of the corporations creditors, and that a fully insured agreement is the best way to assure enforceability. If the corporation, however, has agreed with any creditor not to redeem any shares without the creditor's consent while its debt is outstanding, obviously something more should be done. The typical example is a bank loan agreement with a corporation to that effect. Where such an agreement exists, additional life insurance on the appropriate key men in the corporation should be bought to discharge the loan.

Enforceability as against preferred stockholders. The ordinary close corporation has only common stock outstanding. Occasionally, however, a

---

[6]A recent case is *Brigham v. M & J Corporation,* 352 Mass. 674, 227 N.E.2d 915 (1967).

close corporation will also issue nonvoting preferred stock, usually to obtain additional capital from outsiders. The rights of preferred stockholders are contractual and differ from one issue to another. In such cases, therefore, care must be exercised to make sure that any plan by which the corporation is to purchase the common shares of an active stockholder upon his death will not conflict with the preferential contract rights of the preferred stockholders. The latter cannot interfere with the plan so long as their rights are properly observed. It is readily apparent, however, that they can interfere with a purchase of common stock at a time when preferred dividends are in arrears; hence, in any case in which this is a possibility, a different purchase plan should be adopted.

INSURANCE ARRANGEMENTS

Under the usual stock redemption plan the corporation will procure, pay the premiums on, and be the beneficiary of, the life insurance carried to supply the purchase money for a deceased's stock. During the life of the agreement, therefore, the cash values of the policies constitute assets of the corporation and are subject to the claims of creditors of the corporation. But because "A solvent corporation, of course, holds its property as an individual holds his,"[7] the matter of corporate creditors becomes important only in the event of the corporation's insolvency.

Some authorities seem to feel that an arrangement by which the insurance policies and the certificates of stock are placed in escrow with a third party trustee is improper, so far as the corporation is concerned. The authors fail to share their view. Granted that the corporation has the right to purchase its shares of stock, we see no reason why it cannot employ a trustee to act as its agent in consummating the transaction and to act as custodian for it of the insurance policies meanwhile. Under the trust arrangement, it seems to be an open question whether, in the event of the corporation's insolvency during the executory period, the policy cash values are subject to the corporation's creditors. Most states have statutes protecting insurance payable to a third person beneficiary, but under this arrangement the trustee beneficiary is to act as the corporation's agent in collecting the proceeds. Furthermore, at common law, and by statute in most states, property placed in trust for the use of the grantor remains subject to the grantor's present and future creditors. But regardless of how this question might ultimately be resolved in any particular jurisdiction, the fact remains that employing the services of an impartial trustee, whose only interest in the transaction is to perform faithfully its prescribed duties in the premises, has many advantages.

The naming of personal insurance beneficiaries under a corporation purchase plan, raises the question whether the premiums paid by the

---

[7]*In re Fechheimer Fishel Co.*, 212 Fed. 357.

corporation might not be considered taxable income to the respective insureds. This income tax question came to the fore in two celebrated cases.

Prunier v. Commissioner.[8] Two brothers owned almost all of the stock of a Massachusetts corporation. They and the corporation set up an insured stock redemption plan under which the insurance policies did not name the corporation as owner, assignee or beneficiary. Each policy indicated that it belonged to the insured and the co-stockholder jointly, with the latter as beneficiary. However, a signed agreement between them in the corporation's minute book obliged the stockholders to turn any death proceeds over to the corporation, which would use the funds to purchase the decedent's stock. The corporation paid all premiums, but did not take a deduction for them. The Tax Court, concluding that the corporation was neither equitable owner nor beneficiary of the policies, held the premiums taxable income to the respective insureds. The Court of Appeals for the First Circuit reversed. It found, under applicable state law, that a court of equity would have enforced the corporation's claim to any death proceeds. Thus, the corporation was held the equitable owner and beneficiary of the policies, and the corporation-paid premiums were not taxable income to the stockholders. Here, confused records and poor coordination between plan and policy arrangements invited the tax challenge.

If the corporation retains the incidents of ownership in the policies, including the right to change the beneficiaries, and if the insurance is "tied in" clearly with the agreement to buy and sell, there seems to be no sound basis upon which the premiums can properly be taxed to the stockholders. In substance, the premiums represent neither compensation nor dividends. This was substantially the arrangement in the second case.

Sanders v. Fox.[9] This case involved an insured stock redemption agreement entered into by a corporation and its four stockholders. The corporation owned the insurance policies and paid the premiums, but each insured stockholder had the right under the agreement to name his own beneficiary. Upon the death of a stockholder, the corporation agreed to deliver the policy to the named beneficiary for collection. Thereupon, the corporation would transfer to itself as much of the decedent's stock as the proceeds would purchase at the stated dollar price, the shares having been endorsed in blank and delivered to the corporation. The insurance proceeds were to be the minimum purchase price. A Federal district court held the premiums paid by the corporation to be dividends constructively received by the stockholders. The Court of Appeals for the Tenth Circuit reversed. Since the proceeds must be applied to the purchase price of the stock, the result was held to be the

---

[8]248 F.2d 818 (1957).

[9]253 F.2d 855 (1958).

same as if the corporation had been named beneficiary of the policies and it
had separately agreed to buy the decedent's stock at a price equal to the
insurance proceeds. The court summed up its opinion as follows:

> The immediate present benefits to the stockholder arising
> from the execution of the agreement, such as the assurance of a
> market at a guaranteed minimum return on his stock, the
> appreciation of the value of his stock, and the retention of
> corporate officers acceptable to his limited group, are not taxable
> incidents. Whatever taxable benefits he may receive from this
> agreement and policy are contingent upon future happenings and
> incapable of present determination. The immediate benefits of
> this investment rebound to the corporation. Under such
> circumstances it is not proper to impress premiums presently
> being paid with the label of constructive dividends. . . .

The Revenue Service has accepted this decision.[10] Notwithstanding, this
arrangement should not be used unless each stockholder has made ample
provision for supplying his estate with cash from other sources. As was said in
Silverthorne v. Mayo, ". . . the disposition of property by contract, enforceable at death, does not exempt such property from liability for the debts of
the decedent any more effectually than if the property had been disposed of
by will." In contrast, the problem of estate creditors is solved automatically
under a conventional stock redemption agreement. The policy proceeds will
be collected by the corporation as beneficiary, and it will pay the purchase
price of the decedent's stock to his estate in cash. Any cash not needed to
discharge estate obligations may form part of the principal of a testamentary
trust and be administered in whatever manner desired. With such a trust, and
with personal insurance payable under the policy options, if desired, the
peculiar advantages of each method of furnishing income for dependents are
gained.

**Special financial adjustment required at death or retirement of a
stockholder.** Under the corporation purchase plan, the payment of the life
insurance premiums by the corporation is generally the same mathematically
as if each stockholder had contributed directly to the premiums in proportion
to his stockholdings. This is so because premiums for insurance for the
purpose of purchasing the corporation's own stock must be paid out of
surplus funds that would otherwise be shared ultimately by the stockholders
on the basis of the number of shares owned by each. It is obvious that a stock
redemption plan will not function equitably unless the purchase price paid
for a deceased stockholder's shares takes into consideration the life insurance
owned by the corporation to the extent of his proportionate number of the
total shares outstanding. Partial equity is achieved if the purchase price takes

---

[10]Revenue Ruling 59-184, 1959-1 C.B. 65.

into consideration his proportionate share of the value of all policies immediately before a death occurs. Substantially complete equity is achieved if his proportionate share of the insurance on his own life is also taken into consideration.

The agreement, of course, should contain provisions giving the corporation a limited option to buy the stock of any stockholder who desires to sell during his lifetime. The same plan of adjustment as outlined above can be used in setting the final purchase price for his stock. Following such an adjustment, a retiring stockholder can be permitted to purchase the insurance in force on his own life at its then cash value, or the adjustment and purchase can be handled on a net basis.

SPECIAL TAX CONSIDERATIONS INVOLVED

The Accumulated Earnings Tax. The Internal Revenue Code of 1954 authorizes the assessment in particular instances of a special accumulated earnings tax on the earnings of a corporation that, instead of being distributed, are accumulated for the purpose of avoiding the income tax with respect to its stockholders. The fact that earnings and profits are permitted to accumulate beyond the reasonable needs of the business is proof of the purpose to avoid income tax upon shareholders, unless the corporation proves to the contrary. Under certain circumstances, however, the details of which are beyond the scope of this text, the burden of proof will be on the Government.

Where the accumulated earnings tax is assessed, it falls only upon the earnings that have been accumulated beyond the reasonable needs of the corporation during the year assessed. In this respect, reasonable needs include reasonably anticipated needs. In order to tax unreasonably accumulated earnings only, a credit is allowed consisting of that part of the earnings and profits of the corporation which is retained for its reasonable needs. The minimum credit is not less than the amount by which $~~100,000~~ exceeds the $150,000 (1976) accumulated earnings and profits at the close of the preceding taxable year after deducting any dividends paid within two and one-half months thereafter.

For example, a corporation had accumulated earnings and profits of $15,000 at the end of its previous taxable year. For the current taxable year it has earnings and profits of $105,000 after deducting $10,000 in dividends paid. The accumulated earnings credit, based upon the reasonable needs of the business, is determined to be only $20,000. But the minimum allowable credit will be $85,000, the amount by which $100,000 exceeds $15,000, the accumulated earnings and profits at the close of the preceding year. Thus the tax, if assessed, would fall on $20,000 ($105,000 less $85,000 credit), assuming at least that amount of accumulated taxable income. Such income is derived from the corporation's taxable income, with certain adjustments that include deduction of income tax and dividends paid and the credit for reasonable needs, as illustrated, but that do not include tax-exempt income such as is represented by life insurance proceeds. The tax rates imposed are 27½ percent on the first $100,000 of accumulated taxable income and 38½ percent on the excess over $100,000.

The earnings of a corporation used to pay premiums for insurance on the lives of stockholders under a stock redemption agreement represent undistributed earnings and profits. This raises the question as to whether the financing of a stock redemption plan fulfills a reasonable need of a corporation. An important case dealing with a former excess profits tax held that premiums paid to finance a stock redemption agreement implemented a proper corporate purpose in that the plan provided for continuity of harmonious management. That case was *The Emeloid Co., Inc. v. Commissioner.* [11]

In the *Emeloid* case, the corporation in 1942 purchased $100,000 of single premium insurance on the life of each of its two equal stockholders. Most of the premiums were borrowed from a bank, presumably because at that time the law permitted the deduction of interest paid on money borrowed for such a purpose. In 1946, a trusteed stock redemption agreement was set up, financed by the $200,000 of single premium insurance and $200,000 of new annual premium insurance on the stockholders. In the meantime, the corporation in its excess profits tax return for 1944 had taken a borrowed-capital credit based on the loan. This credit was disallowed by the Tax Court, on the ground that the loan merely served the purposes of the individual stockholders. On appeal, the United States Court of Appeals for the Third Circuit reversed and held that the corporation was entitled to the credit as being based upon a loan which served a proper corporate purpose. The court held that whether the insurance be viewed as key-man insurance—as was concluded on the facts—or as stock redemption insurance, the policies implemented a proper corporate objective. Referring to the corporate function of key-man insurance, the opinion stated:

> What corporate purpose could be considered more essential than key man insurance? The business that insures its buildings and machinery and automobiles from every possible hazard can hardly be expected to exercise less care in protecting itself against the loss of two of its most vital assets—managerial skill and experience.

The opinion went on to justify the corporate purpose of stock redemption insurance, both from the standpoint of its direct and immediate functioning as such, and its indirect and ultimate functioning as key-man insurance. As to the latter, the opinion stated:

----

[11] 189 Fed. 2d 230, (1951).

Petitioner, in the situation provided for by the trust agreement, would also indirectly have the benefit of key man insurance. . . . The shares purchased by petitioner would become treasury shares and could be resold in the same manner as other corporate assets. *Borg v. International Silver Co., supra.* The trust agreement provides petitioner with a method of subjecting all potential purchasers to a screening test, thus permitting the corporation to choose its new shareholders in a highly selective manner. Funds derived from the resale would then be available to the petitioner and provide it with needed working capital.

What the opinion had to say of the insurance as stock redemption insurance was this:

We need not, however, rest this decision on the state of the record in the absence of the trust agreement, as it is not in the least inconsistent with the purpose originally underlying the purchase of the insurance. The trust was designed to implement that original purpose, and, at the same time, add a further business objective, viz., to provide for continuity of harmonious management. Harmony is the essential catalyst for achieving good management; and good management is the *sine qua non* of long-term business success. Petitioner, deeming its management sound and harmonious, conceived of the trust to insure its continuation. Petitioner apparently anticipated that, should one of its key stockholder-officers die, those beneficially interested in his estate might enter into active participation in corporate affairs and possibly introduce an element of friction. Or his estate, not being bound by contract to sell the stock to petitioner, might sell it to adverse interests. The fragile bark of a small business can be wrecked on just such uncharted shoals.

Although the *Emeloid* case was concerned with the excess profits tax, it must be conceded from its reasoning that the payment of premiums by a corporation for a proper type and amount of life insurance for the purpose of implementing a plan "to provide for continuity of harmonious management" does not result in an accumulation of the earnings and profits of the corporation beyond the reasonable needs of the business and is not a plan designed for the purpose of preventing the imposition of income tax upon its shareholders through the medium of permitting earnings or profits to accumulate instead of being paid out in dividends. Thus, even though this tax may be assessed against other funds of a corporation that have been unreasonably accumulated, the tax should not reach the funds that have been used to pay premiums for stock redemption insurance.

This conclusion is strengthened by another case, *Mountain State Steel*

Foundries v. Commissioner.[12] The corporation involved succeeded an equal partnership. When partner Ben Miller died, his one-half interest passed to his widow and two daughters, and when the business was incorporated shortly thereafter they received one-half the stock. Being inactive stockholders of a corporation with fluctuating profits and uncertain dividends, the Millers demanded that the business be sold or liquidated. Following unsuccessful efforts to find a suitable purchaser, the corporation agreed to redeem the stock of the Millers with payments over a number of years. The corporation continued to meet its payments, but the Commissioner assessed 1939 Code section 102 penalty tax (predecessor to the present tax). His theory was that, since the active stockholders might have bought the stock and declared additional dividends with which to pay for it, the corporate redemption was entered into for the purpose of avoiding personal taxes by corporate accumulation. The Tax Court agreed, on the ground that the redemption served no corporate business purpose. The Court of Appeals for the Fourth Circuit reversed, stating in part:

> We disagree with the premise of the Tax Court that these disbursements served no corporate purpose.
>
> The problems which confronted the widow and daughters of Ben Miller and the Strattons [the active stockholders] is one that frequently arises upon the death of one co-venturer in a relatively small business enterprise. Many of those enterprises are worth substantially more to those who are able and anxious to manage them, deriving livelihoods from salaries, than to passive investors who must look only to prospective dividends for a return upon their investment. The Miller stock clearly was worth much less as a continuing investment to Mrs. Miller than it would have been worth to Ben Miller had he survived and remained active in the management of the business. It was natural that she should demand that the business be sold or liquidated, and it would have been essentially unfair to have left her and her daughters indefinitely in a position in which they could expect relatively small and uncertain income from what everyone regarded, with reason, as a valuable property.
>
> This sort of situation leads to demands for dividends out of consideration of the stockholders' personal financial need, perhaps without appropriate regard for the need of the corporation to make capital expenditures in order to maintain a competitive position. On the other hand, those stockholders active in the management of the business deriving salaries from it may be able to afford indulgence of an ambition to enlarge future earnings through still larger current capital expenditures, an indulgence which other stockholders may ill afford.

---

[12]284 F.2d 737 (1960).

When the stockholders have such conflicting interests, the corporation and its future are necessarily affected. When the situation results in demands that the business be sold or liquidated, as it did here, the impact of the conflict upon the corporation is direct and immediate. . . . The resolution of such a conflict, so that the need of the corporation may govern managerial decision, is plainly a corporate purpose.

Many businessmen now anticipate such problems and provide solutions through agreements, and implementing devices, to take out the estate of a co-venturer, who dies, on a basis designed to be fair to the estate, to the enterprise and to the surviving co-venturers. It has been held that corporate disbursements to pay insurance premiums to provide a fund with which to purchase stock from the estate of the person whose life is insured do serve a corporate, business purpose. [A footnote cited the *Emeloid, Prunier* and *Sanders* cases.] If disbursements to create a fund with which to purchase stock serve a corporate purpose, surely the disbursement of the created fund in purchasing the stock serves the same purpose.

Thus, in the light of the *Emeloid* and *Mountain State Steel* cases, an insured stock redemption should not attract the accumulated earnings tax.

Unfortunately, a subsequent case involving premiums for key man insurance did not follow the precepts set forth in the foregoing cases—perhaps because of its particular facts. This was *Novelart Mfg. Co. v. Commissioner.*[13] The corporation had only one stockholder, and over a sixty-year period had built up over $5 million in accumulated earnings and profits. It increased such accumulations by $359,000 during the fiscal years 1961, 1962 and 1963, and the Commissioner assessed the accumulated earnings tax on such increases. During these three years, the corporation paid total premiums of $68,600 on $955,000 of key man insurance, of which $875,000 was on the sole stockholder's life. In each of the three years, the corporation paid dividends of $15,400 and salary of $42,000 to its sole stockholder. At the beginning of the three-year period, the corporation had over $3 million in cash and liquid securities. The Tax Court held that the reasonable needs of the business, including anticipated needs, during the three-year period, amounted to only $782,000, most of which was expended for additional plant space. And since the corporation had sufficient available earnings accumulated from prior years to more than provide for the necessary funds, the court upheld the Commissioner's assessment of the penalty tax on the earnings accumulated during the three years.

The corporation had argued unsuccessfully that its accumulated taxable income should have been reduced by the premiums paid on the key man

---

[13]434 F.2d 1011 (1970), affirming 52 T.C. 794 (1969).

insurance. The Tax Court concluded that since Congress had specifically provided in Section 535(b) for the deductions to be taken into account in computing accumulated taxable income, and since the insurance premiums did not fall within any of the prescribed deductions, they could not be deducted. The court noted, however, that the corporation had not contended that the premiums should be included in the calculation of the accumulated earnings credit in Section 535(c), as being accumulations for the reasonable needs of the business. The corporation made the same argument before the Court of Appeals for the 6th Circuit, and received the same negative answer.

Here, the comparatively large and liquid accumulation of earnings and profits in years prior to those assessed, and the fact that it had a sole stockholder who could benefit taxwise if it did not increase its dividends, militated against the corporation's chances of avoiding imposition of this penalty tax. And the fact that over 90 percent of the key man insurance coverage was on the sole stockholder's life didn't help. Nevertheless, it must be added that the corporation's argument regarding the insurance premiums was based upon the wrong subsection; it should have been based upon subsection (c) of Section 535, which allows a credit against accumulated taxable income for all amounts accumulated in the assessed taxable years for the reasonable needs of the business.

Finally with respect to the premiums paid for stock redemption insurance, it should be said that they represent a comparatively small accumulation in any one taxable year and therefore should not, by themselves, be significant enough to encourage assessment of this penalty tax in the first instance. And where such small amounts are included along with other accumulations made in any assessed taxable year, such premiums should be eliminated from the tax as being reasonable accumulations under the doctrine of the *Emeloid* and *Mountain State Steel* cases.

The last-quoted sentence from the *Mountain State Steel* opinion bears on the question whether a corporation's collection and disbursement of the death proceeds of life insurance under a regular stock redemption agreement should be considered in levying the accumulated earnings tax. As this is written, only one case has answered the question. The decision was to eliminate the insurance proceeds as committed to a valid business purpose: redemption of a deceased minority stockholder's shares. The case was *Oman Construction Co., Inc.*[14]

In the *Oman* case, the corporation's plan was to build up its net worth so that it could obtain and perform an increasing volume of heavy construction work. Accordingly, its retention of earnings during the 1957-1960 period increased from $436,000 to $3,379,000. The corporation paid a small amount of dividends in 1959 and 1960.

---

[14]24 T.C.M. 1799 (1965).

The corporation's stock was owned by three stockholders. John Oman owned a minority stock interest and was its president. Pursuant to an understanding among them that on John's death the corporation would redeem his stock so as to enable it to avoid changing to a conservative business policy for the protection of his family, the corporation insured his life for $1,500,000.

Upon John's death in 1960, the corporation collected the insurance proceeds. Shortly thereafter, but in the corporation's 1961 fiscal year, it redeemed John's shares for $2,250,293, using the insurance proceeds plus other assets for the purpose.

Following the Commissioner's assessment of the accumulated earnings tax for the years 1958-1960, the Tax Court held that the tax didn't lie. Here is that part of the court's opinion that dealt particularly with the life insurance proceeds:

> ... During the year [1960] petitioner was contracting for a work program of $50 million and carrying out $27 million of work and with a net worth of $832,000 at the start of the year. It invested $1,200,000 in additional construction equipment. It began to distribute dividends for the first time in December 1959 and March 1960. ... Just after the dividend was distributed in March and just before the end of the fiscal year, John was killed. This was hardly the occasion for the distribution of more and larger dividends. The effect on the petitioner's business of the loss of a principal officer could not be predicted. The proceeds of the life insurance, while increasing the amount of the assets, were committed by previous agreement to the redemption of John's stock. Redemption of the stock of a minority stockholder is a valid business purpose, and funds retained for such a purpose are retained for the reasonable needs of a corporation's business.[15] Although the petitioner had an increased amount of cash on hand at the end of the fiscal year, much of this was withdrawn from uncompleted joint vetures and was subject to future income taxes and renegotiation, or possibly to repayment if the venture turned out badly.... Although the surplus per books was increased to $2,414,000, this amount should be reduced by the life insurance in appraising the actual surplus available for needs of the business and possible dividends, leaving about $1 million in net worth.... Retention of those earnings for fiscal 1960 was for the reasonable needs of the business.

In the *Oman* case, the life insurance proceeds were received by the corporation in fiscal 1960 and retained for the stock redemption made in

---

[15] Citing *Dill Manufacturing Co.*, 39 B.T.A. 1023 (1939); *Gazette Pub. Co. v. Self,* 103 F. Supp. 779 (E.D.Ark., 1952).

1961. In 1960, the corporation had a large amount of accumulated taxable income upon which the penalty tax could fall even though the insurance proceeds, being tax-exempt, did not increase such income. But, as pointed out later in this chapter, such proceeds did increase the corporation's earnings and profits for 1960. Consequently, it was important to the corporation that its retention of the earnings and profits represented by the insurance proceeds be held for the reasonable needs of the business. It is gratifying that not only the insurance proceeds, but also the additional dollars of the purchase price paid for the decedent's shares, were held to be retained for the reasonable needs of the business.

Special considerations are involved where there is an insured partial stock redemption plan under the protection of Code Section 303. See further discussion of this penalty tax in Chapter 16, infra.

Distributions in redemption of stock. The functioning of a regular stock redemption agreement results in the purchase of all the shares of stock of a deceased stockholder. As a result, the funds received from the corporation in payment of the stock should be treated as purchase price paid and not as a distribution of a taxable dividend. The funds will be so treated under the provisions of Sections 302(b)(1) and 331 of the Code, "if the redemption is not essentially equivalent to a dividend." As this is a general provision which depends upon the facts of each case, it cannot be relied on. Section 302(b)(3) usually can be relied on, however, as it provides that a distribution by a corporation in complete redemption of all the stock owned by a shareholder will be considered as the purchase price paid for his stock. Nevertheless, exceptions occur in the case of certain family corporations, because under some circumstances the rules of constructive ownership of stock attribute the ownership of stock to the deceased's estate where it is owned by certain other individuals or organizations.

The basic rule of constructive ownership applicable here is that an estate is considered as owning the stock that is owned directly or indirectly by or for a beneficiary of the estate. Therefore, a redemption of all the shares actually owned by a deceased stockholder's estate is not protected by Section 302(b)(3) if the estate is considered as constructively owning any shares in the corporation.

Thus, if a father and son each owned one-half of the outstanding shares of stock of a corporation, then upon the father's death his estate is considered as owning all the shares if the son is a beneficiary of the estate. Under such circumstances, the redemption of the father's previously owned shares would not come within the protection of Section 302(b)(3).

The regulations deems a person an estate beneficiary only if he inherits a present interest in probate property.[16] They also state that a person is no longer considered an estate beneficiary after he has received all the property

---

[16]Reg. § 1.318-3(a)

to which he is entitled and there is only a remote possibility that he will be required to return property or make a contribution to the estate to satisfy its claims and expenses. A residuary beneficiary, however, remains an estate beneficiary until it is finally closed.

That this regulation can be a trap is illustrated by the case of *Webber's Estate v. U.S.*[17] There, all of the corporation's stock had been owned by the decedent and his son, and the son had received all the property to which he was entitled from the decedent's estate before the latter's stock was redeemed from his estate. Nevertheless, the son was held still to be an estate beneficiary because at the time of the redemption he remained subject to a claim by the estate for his share of Federal and state death taxes. Thus, his stock was attributed to the estate and the distribution to it in redemption of his father's stock was held a taxable dividend. This unfortunate result would have been avoided had the decedent provided in his will that all death taxes be payable out of his residuary estate without apportionment to any estate beneficiary.

Other stock attribution rules must be considered along with the estate attribution rule when stock is redeemed from an estate, because there can be a chain of stock attribution except that stock is not attributed twice under the family attribution rule. Under that rule, a stockholder will be treated as owning the stock owned directly or indirectly by his spouse, children, grandchildren and parents. There is, however, an important exception to the family attribution rule in certain instances of complete redemptions. This exception, known as the "ten-year rule," applies if the stockholder whose shares are redeemed (1) is left with no interest in the corporation as a stockholder, officer, director or employee; (2) does not acquire any such interest (except by bequest or inheritance) within ten years following the redemption, and files timely agreement with the Revenue Service to notify it of any violation; and (3) has not engaged in any stock transfer to or from his spouse, children, grandchildren or parents or, if so, the transfer was not made to avoid income taxes. This exception might be used, for example, under a special arrangement involving a corporation the stock of which is owned by a father and son. The father would bequeath his stock to his wife subject to a stock redemption agreement that obligates her to sell such stock to the corporation.

The other rules attribute stock to or from a partnership, corporation or trust under circumstances beyond the scope of this text. We add, however, that once stock is attributed from an individual to an entity (partnership, estate, trust or corporation), it will not then be attributed sidewise from the entity to another partner, beneficiary or stockholder whose shares are redeemed. Nevertheless, the illustration of chain attribution that was the subject of Revenue Ruling 59-233, 2959-2 C.B. 106, should serve as a

---

[17]403 F.2d 411 (1968), affirming 263 F. Supp. 703.

warning to check each situation with great care. There, a testamentary trust for the decedent's children owned the stock to be redeemed, and the decedent's husband owned the remaining stock. The father's stock was attributed to the children under the family attribution rule, and then to the trust under the rule that stock owned directly or indirectly by a trust beneficiary is attributed to the trust. Thus, it was ruled that the redemption of the stock actually owned by the trust would not be considered a complete redemption under Section 302(b)(3).

This ruling would have been the same had the redemption been from the wife's estate, provided the children were estate beneficiaries at the time. And had the husband been an estate beneficiary, his stock would have been attributed directly to the estate. Hence the ruling, if upheld, points up the danger involved in a stock redemption agreement where members of a stockholder's family also own some shares.

One important case, however, refused to uphold the provision in the ruling stating that the waiver agreement called for under the ten-year rule described before is not available to suspend family attribution if the redemption is from an estate or trust.[18] In that case, one-third of the stock of two family corporations was owned as community property by Walter and Lillian Crawford. The remaining stock of each corporation was owned equally by their two sons. Stock redemption agreements were executed by all the stockholders in 1962. Walter died in 1965, leaving Lillian as the sole beneficiary of his estate. Both Lillian and the estate filed Section 302(c)(3) waiver agreements and, pursuant to the stock redemption agreements, the two corporations redeemed the stock held by Lillian and Walter's estate. Thereafter, they ceased to have any interest in the corporations other than as creditor. The Tax Court, disagreeing with the provision in Revenue Ruling 59-233 that an estate or trust was not eligible to use the waiver agreement in Section 302(c)(3), held that the estate's waiver agreement was effective to prevent attribution to it of the stock owned by the two sons; therefore, the distributions in redemption should be treated as in exchange for the redeemed stock under Section 302(b)(3). If this case holds up, it should be a boon to family corporations planning stock redemptions.

An estate redemption plan will function safely if the redemption of the decedent's shares qualifies as a disproportionate redemption under the formula in Section 302(b)(2). This formula requires that after the redemption the estate must own, directly or through attribution, (a) less than 50 percent of the voting power, and (b) its ratio each of voting and non-voting common stock must be less than 80 percent of the ratio that it owned before redemption. Note that this provision is of little use where there is a redemption at a stockholder's death, because it would leave the decedent's

---

[18]*Lillian M. Crawford,* 59 T.C. #81, 3-19-73.

heirs in the undesirable position of minority stockholders. An estate redemption will function safely also if the link of attribution from the beneficiary to the estate is broken before the redemption takes place. But in most instances where the corporation's stock is spread among various members of the family, the only safe plan is an individual cross-purchase agreement, or a partial redemption to the extent protected from dividend treatment by Section 303.

Note that the estate attribution rule may apply even though the stockholders are unrelated. For example, a decedent's estate owns 50 shares of stock of a corporation. The decedent bequeathed his golf clubs to an unrelated co-stockholder who owns 20 shares. Th estate will be considered to own 70 shares, and the redemption of the decedent's 50 shares under a stock redemption agreement will not be protected by Section 302(b)(3). There is much more likelihood, however, that a redemption will be considered as not essentially equivalent to a taxable dividend, and thus protected under Section 302(b)(1), where the stockholders are unrelated.

The preceding examples show that the provision covering redemption of all of the shares of a deceased stockholder may not furnish protection to a stock redemption agreement of a family corporation, under certain circumstances. This provision, nevertheless, protects the stock redemption agreements of most other corporations by eliminating the danger that the purchase price for a deceased stockholder's shares will be treated as a dividend to the recipient.

The possible application of the rules of constructive ownership should not be overlooked in any stock redemption plan.

Effect of stock redemption on corporate earnings and profits. Although the redemption of the shares of a deceased stockholder is not usually treated as a dividend distribution, it has the effect of increasing the earnings and profits of the corporation. Under the provisions of Section 101(a) of the Code, the death proceeds of the stock redemption insurance are excluded from the corporation's gross income. Nevertheless, the excess of such proceeds over the aggregate sums of the premiums paid will constitute earnings and profits available for later distribution.[19] Under Section 316, distributions out of earnings and profits are taxable dividends; but Section 312(e) provides that a distribution treated under Section 302 as the purchase price paid for stock is not treated as a distribution of earnings and profits to the extent properly chargeable to capital account. Therefore, this payment would only partially offset the increase in earnings and profits created upon receipt of the death proceeds of the insurance by the corporation. This result may be important to the surviving stockholders, for it may make a subsequent distribution to them taxable as a dividend that otherwise would not be taxable since not made from earnings and profits.

---

[19]Rev. Rul. 54-230, 1954-1 C.B. 114; and see *J. Paul McDaniel,* 25 T.C. 276.

Establishing value of stock for Federal estate tax. As is more fully discussed in a later chapter, it has been held in a long line of decisions that if the purchase price of a deceased shareholder's stock fairly represented its value at the time agreed upon, and if prior to his death he has been prohibited from disposing of his shares during the period from the execution of the purchase and sale contract until his death without first offering them to the corporation or to the other stockholders at the contract price, that price will control for estate tax purposes. This rule should hold whether the purchase and sale agreement runs between the stockholders themselves or between the corporation and the stockholders, with one possible exception as to the corporation purchase plan. If one of the stockholders owns a majority of the shares, it may be argued that under the corporation plan this dominant stockholder possesses sufficient power to force its amendment or abandonment at any time and that he is not in reality bound by such a contract; consequently the purchase price cannot be held to represent the estate tax value of his stock. If the purchase price is fairly set, however, and the agreement is properly drafted so that the mutual agreement of *all* the parties to it is required to effect any changes, it would seem that this argument should not prevail. A corporation is no less bound by its proper contracts than is an individual. The real question should be whether the agreement was entered into "at arm's length," which would appear to be answered satisfactorily if there were several stockholders and if the price set was a fair one.

Effect of corporation stock purchase on value of survivors' shares. Normally, stock purchased by the corporation under a stock redemption plan is retained in the corporate treasury. As long as it comprises treasury stock, it will remain dormant, bereft of voting or dividend or distribution rights. The further effect of this is to increase the book value of the outstanding shares held by the survivors without increasing the cost basis of such shares. Should the survivors subsequently sell any of their stock, therefore, presumably this enhancement in book value would be reflected in the sale price, in which event an additional and sizable capital-gains tax would be incurred.

Assume, for example, a corporation with $60,000 of capital stock consisting of 600 shares of $100 par value each, contributed equally by three stockholders. If the corporation has $30,000 of surplus, each share will have a book value of $150 as compared with the income tax basis of $100 per share. Assume further, that upon the death of a stockholder the corporation collects $30,000 of life insurance proceeds under a policy with no cash value, and pays out the same amount of money to acquire the deceased's one-third stock interest. The capital stock account of the corporation will now show $60,000 issued stock, less $20,000 treasury stock, leaving an amount outstanding of $40,000. The surplus account will show $30,000, plus $30,000 life insurance proceeds and less the $10,000 amount over par paid for the deceased's shares, or a net amount of surplus of $50,000. The total book value of the 400 shares of stock held by the survivors, therefore, will be $90,000 and the value per share will be $225, as compared with the unchanged income tax basis of $100 per share.

Had these stockholders arranged an individual purchase plan, the book value of $150 per share would have remained unchanged; and each surviving stockholder would have owned 300 shares, the original 200 of which would have had an income tax basis of $100; and the 100 shares acquired from the deceased stockholder would have had a basis of $150.

To return to our discussion of the assumed corporation plan, the corporation, of course, can sell the treasury stock. If it sold the shares to a new stockholder at $150 per share, it would have no gain or loss on the transaction.[20] The capital account would then be restored to $60,000 of outstanding stock and the surplus account would stand at $60,000, making the book value $200 per share. The corporation has increased its surplus by $10,000, but there appears to be no normal way this increased amount can reach the stockholders except through the channel of taxable dividends.

The corporation, instead of selling the treasury stock, can transfer it to the surviving stockholders by declaring a stock dividend. Because of a special exception made in I.R.C., Section 305 for constitutional reasons, such a stock dividend no doubt is non-taxable, but by the provisions of I.R.C., Section 307, the basis of the old stock held must be allocated between the old and the new stock received. The basis of the old stock of $40,000 would therefore be allocated between the 400 original shares held by the survivors and the 200 shares comprising the stock dividend, with a resulting basis per share of only $66.67. This procedure again restores the capital stock account to $60,000 of outstanding stock; and with the surplus account remaining at $50,000, the book value per share becomes $183.33. The declaration of a stock dividend, therefore, will not solve the problem of the spread between the income tax basis of the survivors' shares and their value.

> Note: In the foregoing illustrations showing the effect of the purchase and sale of treasury stock on the balance sheet, the accounting method that seems to be in most general use has been followed, namely, the deduction of the par value of the treasury shares from the stated capital and the deduction from surplus of that portion of the purchase price paid in excess of par, with a reversal of the entries upon sale. From a legal standpoint, treasury shares should be shown on the balance sheet simply as a deduction from the number of shares issued and outstanding, without deduction from the stated capital, and the surplus should be reduced by the purchase price paid. On subsequent sale, the money received should be credited to surplus. For our

[20]I.R.C., Section 1032(a).

purposes here, however, it is immaterial which of these two accounting methods is used, for both arrive at the same book value of the remaining outstanding shares.

It is apparent that the corporation stock redemption plan puts the surviving stockholders in an unavoidable position to incur considerable additional capital gains tax liability upon a subsequent sale of their shares during life, as contrasted with the plan of individual purchase. The importance of this disadvantage depends, in each particular case, upon the entire picture. The purchase of the deceased's stock by the corporation normally will transfer corporate surplus to the deceased's heirs tax free, since the basis of the stock in their hands will be its value at death, which is the price to be received. The survivors may not sell their shares during their lifetimes, thereby avoiding any capital gains tax. But even if a sale is made, the maximum effective rate of tax will be comparatively low, assuming that the shares will be held for a period sufficient to result in a long-term gain. These possibilities must be weighed in the light of all the other considerations in choosing the most desirable type of stock purchase plan.

The foregoing discussion of its various phases shows that special considerations are involved in the corporation stock purchase plan that are not present in the individual stock purchase plan. In nearly all the states a choice between these plans is offered the stockholders.

COMBINATION PURCHASE PLANS

On rare occasions a combination of the two plans may be found best to serve the purposes of the stockholders. One of these occasions might exist, for example, if all the circumstances pointed to the advisability of a corporation purchase plan except that the surviving stockholders desire a different ratio of stockholdings between themselves after a death occurs. An individual purchase plan for some of the stock can be set up to ensure the proportionate holdings desired, with the remainder of the stock made subject to a corporation purchase arrangement. Another occasion for the use of a combined plan may arise if there are two stockholders, one of whom owns only a small minority interest and whose income is not sufficient to purchase all of the majority stock. An individual purchase plan could be set up to the extent that the minority stockholder could finance it, with the balance of stock to be purchased by the corporation. Combination plans, however, call for carefully worked out adjustments to be made upon death and the arranging of them necessitates double the ordinary amount of "machinery." Their use should be restricted to those situations in which no other solution is satisfactory and, in view of the provisions in Section 302 of the Internal Revenue Code, the individual purchase should function ahead of the corporate purchase.

Chapter 12

PLANS OF SUBCHAPTER S CORPORATIONS

Several thousand small business corporations have elected taxation under Subchapter S, comprising sections 1371 through 1377 of the Internal Revenue Code. As a result of such election, a corporation avoids the corporation income tax and is not exposed to the penalty accumulated earnings tax. Instead, the tax on corporate earnings falls on its stockholders.

QUALIFICATION REQUIREMENTS

A small business corporation must meet a number of rigid requirements before it can elect to be taxed under Subchapter S. First, it must be a domestic corporation, one created in the United States. Furthermore, it must not derive more than 80 percent of its gross receipts from foreign sources, nor more than 20 percent from passive investment income. The latter requirement, however, is suspended during the first two years of operation if such passive income does not exceed $3,000. Second, it must not belong to an affiliated group, except that it can own the stock of a completely inactive subsidiary. Third, it can have only one class of stock—which necessarily is voting common stock. Fourth, it must have ten or fewer stockholders. Fifth, all of its stockholders must be individuals or estates, and no stockholder can be a nonresident alien.

In determining the number of stockholders, each co-tenant is counted separately unless they are husband and wife. Spouses owning stock as co-tenants or as community property are counted as one unless both also own stock as separate property. Even then, or where spouses in certain community

367

property states (Idaho, Louisiana and Texas) only own stock as separate property the dividends on which belong to the community, they count as one stockholder. Where a guardian or custodian holds stock for more than one child, count each child as a stockholder. On the death of a stockholder, count his estate as a new stockholder even though title to the stock may go direct to the legatees under state law.

MAKING THE ELECTION

The election by the stockholders of a qualifed corporation to be taxed under Subchapter S must be unanimous, and spouses who are co-tenants must both consent. The stockholders must make the election either in the months preceding the taxable year for which it is to be effective, or in the first month of such year.

A new stockholder must file his consent to a subsisting stockholders' election within thirty days after his stock acquisition, unless he has obtained an extension from the Revenue Service. An estate becomes a new stockholder when the personal representative has qualified. His consent for the estate is required even though he is already an individual consenting stockholder.[1] He has thirty days thereafter to file his consent, except that he must act within thirty days after the close of the corporation's taxable year unless he obtains an extension.

DURATION OF THE ELECTION

Once the election to be taxed under Subchapter S is made, it continues until terminated. And once terminated, it cannot be made again for five years without the consent of the Internal Revenue Service. It may be terminated affirmatively by the unanimous vote of the stockholders. If such vote is made in the first month of the corporation's taxable year, it will terminate the election for that year; otherwise, it will take effect the following taxable year. Of great importance, however, is that the happening of certain events will automatically terminate the election effect the following taxable year retroactively to the beginning of the taxable year. These are: (1) failure of a new stockholder to file timely consent; (2) an eleventh person, a nonresident alien, or a trust, partnership or corporation becomes a stockholder; (3) the corporation issues a second class of stock; or (4) the corporation exceeds the percentage limitations on either gross receipts from foreign sources or on passive income.

TAX CONSEQUENCES

A Subchapter S corporation computes its taxable income in the regular manner except that it cannot take the deductions for net operating loss, for

---

[1]*Lewis Building & Supplies, Inc.,* 25 T.C.M. 844 (1966).

partially tax-exempt interest and for dividends received. Any net operating losses pass through to the stockholders, and long-term capital gains retain their character when distributed. This is not the case, however, with tax-exempt income such as life insurance proceeds. While such proceeds do not enter into the corporation's taxable income, they are taxable to the stockholders if paid out in dividends. The corporation's taxable income is exempt from the corporate income tax. It pays dividends generally from either current taxable income or "undistributed taxable income." The latter for any year equals its taxable income less any cash dividends paid during the year. Cash dividends paid within two and one-half months after the end of the corporation's taxable year are treated as distributions of undistributed taxable income for the year just ended. Any remaining undistributed taxable income for a given year becomes previously taxed income, which is "locked in" to the extent that distributions of it can occur only in a year when the cash dividends exceed current earnings and profits.

Each stockholder of a Subchapter S corporation includes in his income his share of the corporation's current taxable income, whether or not distributed to him. He reports actual dividends when he receives them. He is deemed to receive his portion of undistributed taxable income on the last day of the corporation's taxable year; only shareholders of record on that day realize such income. The basis of his stock is increased by any undistributed earnings of the corporation taxed to him, and is reduced upon distribution of such earnings to him as a stockholder. Since he is taxed currently on his share of undistributed taxable income, he is not taxed on its subsequent distribution to him. His right to receive such later distribution tax-free, however, is entirely personal to him; in the event he dies or sells his stock, the exemption is lost and does not pass to his successor.

The foregoing sketches merely some of the more important highlights of taxation under Subchapter S, but it should be sufficient to demonstrate that an electing corporation has a special need for a stock purchase agreement. Without such an agreement, the corporation's election will terminate abruptly if a deceased stockholder leaves many heirs or bequeaths his stock in trust.

CHOICE OF PLAN

The stockholders of a Subchapter S corporation may choose either a stock redemption or a cross-purchase plan. Under a stock redemption plan, the stock attribution rules apply. In addition, there are other differences between the two plans that should be noted here.

Under both plans, the premium burden falls on the stockholders since the premiums are not deductible. Under a stock redemption plan, they bear the premium burden directly in proportion to their stockholdings. Under a cross-purchase plan, age differences and differences in stockholdings inversely affect the distribution of the premium burden.

Under a stock redemption agreement, each stockholder's share of the nondeductible premiums increases the basis of his stock. The amounts become previously taxed income and are "locked in" to the extent previously noted. Under a cross-purchase agreement, the premiums paid by the stockholders have no effect on the basis of their stock, but the proceeds of insurance they receive and pay out for a decedent's stock become the basis of the shares purchased.

The consummation of an insured stock redemption agreement usually increases the corporation's earnings and profits in some degree, as discussed earlier, although the insurance proceeds are received tax-free by the corporation. This increase does not occur under a cross-purchase plan. This and other differences in results follow the pattern of differences pointed out previously in discussing the factors to be considered in choosing between the two types of agreements. Thus, all of those factors should be considered by the stockholders of a Subchapter S corporation.

There are some special factors unrelated to the choice of plan that such stockholders should consider in relation to a stock purchase agreement. As we have noted, the shareholders of record on the last day of the corporation's taxable year are taxed ratably on its undistributed taxable income for the year. Therefore, to prevent the tax on this income from falling entirely on the survivors, they should provide either for distribution of such income before the decedent's shares are purchased from his estate, or provide that the purchase be made on the first day of the taxable year following the decedent's death. Also, since the tax exemption of undistributed income previously taxed to the decedent will be lost on his death, it behooves all Subchapter S corporations to have as little of such income on hand as conveniently possible.

Chapter 13

PLANS OF PROFESSIONAL CORPORATIONS

Although presently there are several thousand in existence, they are of recent origin for traditionally, a corporation could not practice a profession. The canons of ethics of the various professions, as well as some state laws, prohibited such practice on the basis that no legal entity could properly intervene between a professional man and his clients or patients. Eventually, however, the tax-favored benefits available to corporate employees under the Internal Revenue Code proved to be the catalytic agent that precipitated changes in the canons of ethics and the enactment of new enabling laws that permit the organization of professional corporations.

BRIEF HISTORY

Over the years, the professional canons of ethics and a large body of case law prohibited corporate practice of such representative professions as law, medicine, dentistry and optometry. Then came the gradual inclusion in the Internal Revenue Code of various tax-favored benefits for corporate employees. These included qualified employee pension and profit-sharing plans, the $5,000 death benefit exclusion, group life insurance plans, employee health insurance plans, deferred compension plans and split-dollar plans. This development led certain enterprising medical groups to form noncorporate associations through which they could ethically practice medicine but which, under the Code, were taxable as corporations provided they had a majority of the corporate characteristics of continuity of life,

371

centralization of management, limited liability, and free transferability of interests. Several of these professional associations immediately installed employee retirement plans that included the doctors as employees, and a landmark case held that such an association was taxable as a corporation and could have a qualified retirement plan that included its member-doctors.[1]

The *Kintner* and other cases led to a 1960 change in the Federal regulations covering the taxation of associations whereby state law was to be determinative of whether an organization had a majority of corporate characteristics. This change encouraged most of the states to enact special statutes designed to meet the requirements of the regulations, either by means of a professional association or a professional corporation. The details of these special statutes are beyond the scope of this text. In general, they permit only persons licensed to practice the particular profession in the state to own interests in the association or corporation. Thus, for example, if a doctor-stockholder of a medical corporation dies, his estate must sell his interest promptly to a licensed doctor or to the corporation.

Although a number of these special statutes include lawyers, many cases have held that inherent power to control the practice of law lies in the highest court of the state. Following decisions in Florida and Colorado that lawyers could incorporate, the American Bar Association issued opinions stating that the corporate practice of law may not violate the canons of ethics under certain circumstances, but limited the type of profit-sharing plans that would be proper.

The rapid development of statutory law was not to the liking of the Internal Revenue Service and led to amended regulations in 1965 which stated that the Code, rather that state law, would determine whether a professional organization had a majority of the corporate characteristics.

Not surprisingly, the Federal courts confronted with the issue brought on by the 1965 regulations refused to ignore the many state statutes that had been enacted in reliance on the previous regulations and held the new regulations invalid as discriminatory. Faced with the array of decisions against it, the Revenue Service in 1969 announced in Technical Information Release 1019 that properly conducted organizations created under the state professional corporation and association acts would generally be treated as corporations for tax purposes.

NONTAX ADVANTAGES OF INCORPORATION

We have already pointed out that a professional corporation must have a majority of the corporate characteristics of continuity of life, centralization of management, limited liability, and free transferability of interests if it is to

---

[1] *U.S. v. Kintner*, 216 F.2d 418 (1954).

be taxed as a corporation. Actually, to the extent these characteristics are achieved, they are nontax advantages.

Continuity of life. This corporate characteristic is achieved, provided the professional corporation keeps within the requirements of the special law under which it was organized. Unlike a partnership, the corporation is not dissolved by the death or withdrawal of a member.

Centralization of management. This characteristic requires that the professional stockholders organize and manage their corporation by means of by-laws, a board of directors and officers, as they would if it were a commercial corporation. The result of adherence to established corporate practice usually is a more efficient organization than many professional partnerships.

Limited liability. This characteristic can be achieved only partially, and is an advantage to that extent. The personal liability that runs between a lawyer and his client, or a doctor and his patient, is not altered by incorporation. In contrast with partners, however, professional stockholders are not liable for the acts of their fellow stockholders. Furthermore, corporate creditors cannot reach the personal assets of the stockholders, as partnership creditors can do.

Free transferability of interests. This characteristic is achieved only partially. The stock of a professional corporation, although transferable, may be transferred by a stockholder or his estate only to the corporation or to another licensed member of the same profession.

THE QUESTION OF ELECTING SUBCHAPTER S STATUS

Some professional corporations will not be eligible to elect to be taxed under Subchapter S, usually because the stockholders exceed the number permitted. Most such corporations, however, have a choice and should study carefully the advantages and disadvantages before making it. Their study may reveal that they need not be concerned with exemption from the accumulated earnings tax because in most personal service organizations capital is not an important income-producing factor; therefore, they do not plan to accumulate in the corporation a large amount of its profits. Furthermore, the stockholders may desire to establish a pension or profit-sharing plan under the regular rules applicable to corporate plans, rather than under the restricted rules applicable to stockholder-employees of Subchapter S corporations. For example, such stockholders owning more than 5 percent of the stock must include in his income any amount contributed on his behalf that exceeds the lesser of $2,500 or 10 percent of his salary. And under a profit-sharing plan, he cannot share in any forfeitures. Obviously, these and the many other factors of choice should be considered carefully.

THE NEED FOR A BUY-SELL PLAN

A professional corporation's need for a buy-sell plan under which a deceased stockholder's shares will be sold at his death to his fellow stockholders, or redeemed by the corporation, is inherent in the nature of the corporation and the state law under which it was created. As we have noted, these laws provide that only members of the same profession may be stockholders. In fact, the statutes of some states require sale or redemption of a deceased stockholder's shares within a stated time limit. Hence, upon the death of a stockholder, there is no recourse but to sell his stock promptly to another licensed member of the same profession or have the corporation redeem it. In most instances of a sale, the stockholders will want to be the purchasers rather than an outside professional.

CHOICE OF PLAN

The factors to be considered by the stockholders of a professional corporation in making a choice between entering into an insured cross-purchase agreement to acquir the shares of a deceased stockholder, or having the corporation enter into an insured stock redemption agreement, are basically the same factors previously discussed and need not be repeated here. If the corporation has elected to be taxed as a Subchapter S corporation, however, a stock redemption plan will not be feasible unless it is kept fully insured. This is because such a corporation in most instances will adhere to the practice of paying out substantially all of its income each year or within two and one-half months thereafter and, consequently, cannot expect to build up sufficient surplus with which to redeem a decedent's shares. Thus, it must expect to have on hand adequate surplus for redemption purposes only by means of insurance on a decedent's life. Because of this factor, and the other special factors discussed in the chapter on such corporations, probably most such corporations will be well advised to choose an insured cross-purchase plan under which to acquire the shares of a deceased stockholder.

SETTING THE PRICE

Some of the state statutes require, in the absence of a buy-sell agreement or provision, that a deceased stockholders shares be redeemed by the corporation at their book value. Such a statutory requirement furnishes another reason why the stockholders of a professional corporation should set up their own buy-sell agreement, for book value is an inadequate price to pay for a decedent's shares for three basic reasons. First, since capital is not an important income-producing factor in such corporations, their tangible assets are of little value as contrasted with those of a commercial corporation. Second, since professional corporations almost invariably use the cash method of accounting, their balance sheets will not include accounts receivable—a substantial asset in such corporations. Third, their balance sheets will not recognize any value for good will, although most professional corporations in operation for at least a few years will engender good-will value among its patients and clients.

Thus, an adequate price for a decedent's stock should encompass a suitable value for the tangible assets, including accounts receivable less accounts payable, and an amount representing the decedent's share of good-will value. A preferred way to arrive at the latter amount is to capitalize the corporation's averaged earnings before professional salaries. This may be done by using a multiple of one to five years, the number depending upon the financial history and progress of the particular corporation. The decedent's share is allocated from this final amount. Frequently this is accomplished by reducing the overall value to a price per share and stating such price in the buy-sell agreement, subject to a revaluation and restatement annually or oftener.

Chapter 14

TAX PROBLEMS INVOLVED
IN THE INSURED
STOCK BUY-SELL PLAN

THE FEDERAL INCOME TAX

Where a corporation stock redemption is set up, special income tax considerations are involved. These were discussed previously in Chapter 11. Special tax considerations are involved also in connection with plans of Subchapter S corporations, discussed in Chapter 12, and in connection with plans of professional corporations, discussed in Chapter 13. Here, we discuss income tax considerations that involve plans generally.

The life insurance premiums not deductible expense. The general rule is that premiums paid for life insurance made subject to a stock buy-sell agreement are not deductible as business expense. This is so whether the premiums are paid by the individual stockholders under an individual cross-purchase plan or by the corporation itself under a corporation stock redemption plan.[1]

In this connection, mention should be made of one common situation that furnishes an apparent, but not an actual, exception: when a cross-purchase plan is set up under which the stockholders authorize the corporation to pay the insurance premiums and charge them to the respective salary accounts of the stockholders. Premiums thus paid by the corporation are of course deductible; not as premiums, however, but as salary. This is not only a convenient method of paying premiums, but also has the advantage of

---

[1] I.R.C., Sections 264(a) and 265; Rev. Rul. 70-117, I.R.B. 1970, 11.

assuring all the stockholders that the payments will be made when due. The stockholders merely appoint the corporation to act as their agent for this purpose; they will report their full salaries for income tax purposes, including the premium payments charged to them.

In some instances, stockholders have financed their cross-purchase agreements with so-called jumbo group term life insurance coverage, with the thought that the regular income tax rules would apply to allow the corporation a tax deduction for the premiums while such premiums would not be taxed to them. In a ruling letter to one of such corporations, however, the Internal Revenue Service ruled that the premiums paid for the excessive coverage on the stockholders were not deductible.[2] The New York Insurance Department has ruled that such group coverage violates Section 204 of the New York Insurance Law and has warned the insurance companies against its issuance. Congress, however, in new Section 79, enacted by the 1964 Revenue Act, settled the matter of premium taxation of "jumbo" group term life insurance in another manner. This section provides that an insured employee is taxable on employer-paid premiums for such coverage in excess of $50,000. An exception applies to a terminated employee who either has reached normal retirement age or has become disabled. Other exceptions apply when the beneficiary is a charitable organization, or is the employer. In the latter event, the employer (corporation) would not be allowed to deduct the premiums.

Other tax and practical questions are raised in connection with the use of group term life insurance to fund a stock buy-sell agreement. The question of a transfer for value is a serious one since the income tax regulations provide that "... the creation, for value, of an enforceable contractual right to receive all or a part of the proceeds of a policy may constitute a transfer for a valuable consideration of the policy or an interest therein." [Reg. §1.101-1(b)(4).] Perhaps this result might be avoided by naming the insured stockholder's wife as beneficiary, but the purchasing stockholder's basis for the stock acquired under the agreement in such case would not include the insurance proceeds.[3] For these and other cogent reasons, such as the steadily increasing premiums with each advance in age and the entire lack of cash surrender values, stockholders should not attempt to finance buy-sell agreements with group life insurance coverage.

The life insurance death proceeds generally not taxable income. Life insurance proceeds paid upon the death of a stockholder insured under an insured buy-sell agreement are not, as a general rule, subject to income tax.[4] But the income tax applies if a policy was transferred for value during the

---

[2]Ruling letter to Century Planning Corporation, New York, dated 6-28-62.

[3]*Paul Legallet,* 41 B.T.A. 294; *cf. Victor G. Mushro,* 50 T.C. 43.

[4]I.R.C., Section 101(a)(1).

insured's lifetime unless the transfer was in a transaction that did not change the basis of the policy, or unless the transferee was one of the following: the insured, a partner of the insured, a partnership in which the insured was a partner, or a corporation in which the insured was a shareholder or officer. Where the income tax applies, the amount of proceeds received at death of the insured in excess of the sum of the consideration paid for the transfer plus any subsequent premiums paid by the transferee is taxed to him as ordinary income. [I.R.C., Section 101(a)(2).]

This obviously militates against the use of old insurance for financing a new cross-purchase agreement among stockholders. Sometimes stockholders overlook the statute, however, as was done in *Monroe v. Patterson*, 197 F. Supp. 146 (1961). There, two old policies that had been payable to the corporation as key-man insurance on one of the stockholders was transferred to two other stockholders in trust to apply the proceeds to the purchase price under their cross-purchase agreement. The transferee stockholders paid nothing for the transfer, but did pay part of the subsequently due premiums. Upon the insured's death, the court held that the policies had been transferred for value and that the transferee stockholders must include in gross income the amount of proceeds received in excess of the premiums they had paid. This case points up the danger involved in using old life insurance policies bought and arranged for a different purpose, to fund a cross-purchase agreement, so long as the exceptions to the transfer-for-value rule fail to shelter transfers for value to co-stockholders. It also points up the danger of concluding that no transfer for value has occurred merely because the transferee has not specifically bought the policy from the transferor for a stated price.

On the other hand, old insurance may be transferred for value to the corporation and used to finance a stock redemption agreement. This might be done, for instance, where a stockholder is presently uninsurable, but has an ample amount of other personal insurance.

The problem of a transfer may be encountered also if a corporation is owned by three or more stockholders and it is desired to continue a plan after the first death has occurred. Probably the most desirable solution is to transfer the insurance on the surviving stockholders to the corporation and set up a stock redemption plan.

From the foregoing, it seems obvious that the problem of a transfer for value of the insurance is best solved in the case of three or more stockholders by starting out with a stock redemption agreement.

The sale of the deceased's stock by his estate. Before a death occurs under an insured stock buy-sell agreement there is only a contract to sell, binding the personal representative of a deceased stockholder actually to sell and transfer his stock upon receipt of the agreed purchase price. Consequently, the cost basis of the deceased's stock to his estate will be its value at death, or on the optional valuation date used for Federal estate tax purposes, the statutory basis generally for property passing at death.[5] The value of the stock to the deceased's estate cannot be other than the price at which he has obligated his estate to sell it; therefore, the estate, in consummating the sale at that agreed value, has no gain or loss in the transaction.

The cost basis of stock acquired from deceased stockholder. The cost basis to the surviving stockholders of the shares of stock they acquire from the deceased's estate under their cross-purchase agreement should be the purchase price they have paid for it. There seems to be little doubt of this result if the surviving stockholders have been designated beneficiaries of the insurance proceeds used to finance the transaction, regardless of the method of premium allocation. The insurance proceeds, together with any balance of the purchase price paid in installments or cash, should also constitute the cost basis of the acquired stock if the insurance proceeds are received by a trustee and paid over by it to the deceased stockholder's personal representative in return for a transfer of the deceased's stock, when the surviving stockholders have paid the premiums and they or their trustee owned the policy.

One case held that the purchase price paid was the basis of the stock purchased under a cross-purchase agreement even though it provided that upon payment of such price the policy which the decedent had owned and paid for on the survivor's life was to become the insured's property "without charge of any kind."[6] The lower court had held that the purchase price for basis purposes must be allocated between the stock and the value of the policy, the latter having a cash surrender value of over $29,000. If the issue again confronts the courts, some of them may well agree with the lower court. In any event, the case illustrates a poor provision, one that favored the surviving stockholder at the expense of the deceased stockholder's estate and heirs.

If the deceased stockholder has owned and paid the premiums on the insurance covering his life, especially if there has been no accompanying provision for reimbursement of premiums paid by the deceased, the surviving stockholders may anticipate that the Treasury Department will challenge the inclusion of the insurance proceeds in the cost basis of the shares acquired. If the insurance proceeds under a stock buy-sell agreement are made payable directly to the deceased's estate or to his personal beneficiaries, there is slight reason to believe that such proceeds may be included in the cost basis of the shares acquired from the deceased stockholder, if the deceased has owned and participated in paying the premiums on his own insurance.[7] (See discussion

---

[5]I.R.C., Section 1014.

[6]*Storey v. United States,* 305 F. 2d 733 (6 Cir. 1962), reversing 193 F. Supp. 769.

[7]*Paul Legallet,* 41 B.T.A. 294.

of this in Chapter 11 on Partnerships.) In respect of the holding in the *Legallet* case, a distinction based upon the difference in subject matter of the agreement, i.e., shares of stock rather than a partnership interest, would seem to have no probative force. It would seem that the premiums, at least, should be includible in the cost basis if the premiums have been paid by the stockholders other than the insured and if the other stockholders have also owned the policies on the life of the deceased, but we know of no holding to that effect.

To sum up, the arrangements that appear to raise no doubt that the insurance proceeds will be included in the cost basis of the surviving stockholders are those under which the survivors have been the premium payers and they, or a trustee in their stead, have been the policyowners and beneficiaries of the deceased partner's insurance.

THE FEDERAL ESTATE TAX

No double taxation. The existence of an insured stock purchase agreement does not "double up" on the amount of estate taxes a deceased stockholder's personal representative will be called on to pay.[8] In fact, there is no such possibility if the life insurance is arranged so as to be excluded from his taxable estate. This is the case if, for example, the deceased has held no incidents of ownership in the insurance in force on his life under the plan and if his estate has not been designated as beneficiary. In such cases nothing could be taxed except the value of his transferred shares. Even if the life insurance is arranged subject to estate taxation, the value of the stock for purposes of this tax is held decreased by the amount of insurance taxed and applied to its purchase price.[9]

The *Mitchell* case is the leading adjudication with respect to the application of the preceding estate tax rule to close corporation stock. In 1924, Mitchell and Philip W. Lennen organized the advertising corporation of Lennen & Mitchell, Inc., each subscribing to one-half of the 1,800 shares of stock, which each held up to Mitchell's death in 1930. In April, 1929, they executed an individual stock cross-purchase agreement financed in part by $200,000 of insurance on each, payable to the respective insured's estates, "the said sum of $200,000 . . . to be received on account of the purchase price as if the surviving party had paid the sum." In addition, Lennen owned $400,000 of insurance on Mitchell, not subject to the agreement. The following year Mitchell died and proceeds of the policy subject to the agreement, amounting to $202,666.67, were paid to his estate. It was then agreed between Lennen and the administratrix and the next of kin that Mitchell's shares at death had a value of $313,771.93 in accordance with the

---

[8] *Estate of Ealy*, 10 T.C.M. 431 (1951).

[9] *Estate of John T.H. Mitchell*, 37 B.T.A. 1 (1938).

purchase and sale agreement, and Lennen paid the balance of $111,105.26 in cash to the administratrix.

In the estate tax return the administratrix reported the shares as having a value of $111,105.26 and reported the $202,666.67 as proceeds of insurance payable to the estate. The Commissioner increased the value of the stock to $313,771.93, made no change with respect to the insurance proceeds and assessed an estate tax deficiency of $35,769.14. Thus we have a clear case of an attempt to "double tax" the amount represented by the insurance proceeds.

The administratrix petitioned the Board of Tax Appeals to set aside the deficiency, and was successful. Some of the reasoning of the Board is as follows:

> In our opinion there can be no doubt that the insurance proceeds in the amount of $202,666.67 must be included in determining the value of the decedent's gross estate, as proceeds of insurance, within the meaning of section 302 (g) *supra* [1926 Revenue Act] . . . .
>
> However, such insurance proceeds were received by decedent's estate subject to the terms of a valid and binding contract that they be applied to reduce the purchase price to be paid by Lennen for the decedent's 900 shares of Lennen & Mitchell, Inc. stock which by the same contract Lennen was obligated to buy. These shares, being so burdened, were not subject to the unfettered ownership of the decedent's estate. The effect of the contract was to reduce the value of the estate's interest in such stock by an amount equal to the amount of the proceeds of the insurance policy, and the value of the stock as so reduced must be deemed as its value for estate tax purposes. . . . As so reduced that amount was $111,105.26 for which amount the decedent's estate was obligated to and did transfer the said shares to Lennen. . . .

Aside from the tax feature, it should be noted that not more than two premiums could have been paid on this insurance, again demonstrating the unique value of the life insurance method of financing.

Estate tax cannot be by-passed. It was formerly urged in some quarters that an insured buy-sell agreement could be designed so that the proceeds of the life insurance credited to the payment of the purchase price would not be subject to the Federal estate tax and at the same time the business interest being purchased would be valued for estate tax purposes at the agreed value *less* these insurance proceeds. The case of *Estate of Herbert G. Riecker,* [10] however, held to the contrary. The court held that, if the insurance was not subject to estate tax, the business interest was taxable at its full value.

---

[10] 3 T.C.M. 1293 (1944).

The net result of the cases appears to be that, if the insurance is arranged in such manner as to require its inclusion in the taxable estate of the insured, then it will be taxed and will be considered to have lowered *pro tanto* the value of the stock purchased with it for estate tax purposes; but if the insurance proceeds are not includible in the taxable estate, then the stock will be included at its full value, undiminished by any insurance proceeds credited against the purchase price. This result seems to be fair and equitable to all concerned.

The insured purchase plan establishes share value for Federal estate tax. As pointed out in Chapter 10, many cases uphold the rule that if the purchase price of a deceased stockholder's shares fairly represents their value at the time agreed upon and if prior to his death the stockholder has been prohibited from disposing of his shares from the time of the buy-sell contract until his death without first offering them to the c her stockholders or to the corporation at the contract price, then this price will control for estate tax purposes, even though the actual value of the stock would be much higher at time of death if freed from the agreement. A brief resume of a few of these cases shows this to be the rule.

Wilson v. Bowers.[11] In 1909, A.R. Wilson, the decedent, contracted with his nephew and one Betts not to sell or assign his 3000 shares of stock in Earl & Wilson Company without first offering them to this nephew at $6.667 per share. If the nephew did not accept the offer, a similar offer was to be made to Betts. It was further provided that upon Wilson's death, the nephew should have the right for four months after the qualification of the personal representative to purchase the stock at the agreed purchase price, and in the event of his failure to exercise the option, a similar right of purchase was given to Betts. When Wilson died many years afterward, his will bequeathed his 3000 shares to his nephew. On the estate tax return, Wilson's executors reported the value of the shares at $20,000, the option price. The Commissioner increased the valuation to $23.55 per share and assessed an additional estate tax of $3,039. The Court of Appeals affirmed the lower court in holding that the option price of $20,000 governed for estate tax purposes, the opinion stating in part:

> Since the contract was specifically enforceable, it seems obvious that the sale value of the stock during the testator's life could have been no more than the low price at which he was obliged to offer it, first, to Franklin Wilson, and then to Betts; nor could his executors have sold it for more, unless both the option holders had allowed their options to lapse. Even if each were penniless, money could readily have been borrowed on the stock when it was worth nearly four times the option price. We

---

[11]57 Fed. 2d 682 (1932).

are to deal with actualities; and the suggestion that the shares may have had a greater market value because of the possibility that the options would not be exercised seems too extravagant to require further refutation . . .

Finally, the appellant argues that the option was never exercised, and that Franklin Wilson took under the will thereby relinquishing his option and leaving the interest which passed by will the full value of the shares. Logically, subsequent events should not be considered in determining value at the time of death. It is true that this court held the contrary with respect to the relinquishment of dower in *Schuette v. Bowers* (C.C.A.) 40 Fed. (2d) 208, 213. But the ruling there made was put squarely on the precedent and was recognized as illogical. We shall not extend it where authority does not compel.

In 1936, two important decisions on this subject were handed down, both also involving option agreements. These were *Helvering v. Salvage*[12] and *Lomb v. Sugden*.[13] The latter case concerned the value for tax purposes of 1,500 shares of Bausch & Lomb Optical Company stock in the estate of Mrs. Carrie B. Lomb. About a year before her death, Mrs. Lomb had entered an agreement with all the other stockholders of the company, under which none of them could sell their stock without first offering the shares to the others at a price that, when computed at the time of her death, amounted to $69.445 per share. The stock, however, could be donated to the other stockholders or could be bequeathed under certain restrictions. On her death, Mrs. Lomb had bequeathed her holdings as part of her residuary estate to her husband. The Commissioner assessed the shares at $100; the executor paid the additional estate tax required and brought suit to recover the alleged overpayment. The Court of Appeals reversed the lower court's decision and held that the option price of $69.445 governed. The opinion stated as follows:

> . . . As Holmes, J., said in *Edwards v. Slocum,* 264 U.S. 61, 63, quoting from *Knowlton v. Moore,* 178 U.S. 41, the tax is on "not the interest to which some person succeeds on a death, but the interest which ceased by reason of the death." Mrs. Lomb at the time of her death was restricted to a price of only $69.445 because she was obliged either to donate her stock to the other stockholders or to offer it to them at that low price. In either event that price was the most that she could obtain for her stock in the natural course of events. . . .

The decision of the Supreme Court on January 13, 1936, in *Helvering v. Salvage,* 56 S. Ct. 375, 377, 80 L. Ed.–, recognizes an option agreement as restricting the market value of stock in

---

[12]297 U.S. 106.

[13]82 Fed. 2d 166.

the hands of the owner to the option price. There Justice
McReynolds said: "Considering the option to repurchase at par,
outstanding in 1922, there could be no proper finding of fair
market value at that time in excess of $100 per share." Because
of the agreement, the decedent could not have secured a price
greater than $69.445 at the time of her death. It is as of that time
that the value of the stock must be determined. Then she could
only give it or sell it to the other stockholders at the price fixed.
Its value to the estate can be no greater than that with which the
decedent parted. *Edwards v. Slocum,* 264 U.S. 61, 63.

We think that *Helvering v. Salvage,* supra, and *Wilson v.
Bowers,* (C.C.A.) 57 Fed. (2d) 682, govern, and that the judgment should be reversed.

Another important case went through the courts during the following two
years: the *Bensel* case.[14] This case was brought to set aside an estate tax
deficiency of $297,101.11 assessed against the estate of F.L. Driver, Sr., based
upon the value of 50,830 shares of Driver-Harris Co. common stock that the
decedent had transferred to a trustee pursuant to an agreement made with his
son. The facts show that the father and son had not been on friendly terms
prior to and during the period involved in their stock negotiations. In fact, the
father had originally opposed his son's employment by the company.

As time went on, however, the son's unusual business ability was
recognized, and in 1924, when the son demanded some guarantee as to his
future with the company, an agreement regarding the father's stock was
entered into. By this agreement, the father transferred all his common stock
in the company to a trustee, reserving the income during his life, with the
provision that upon his death the son could purchase the shares from the
trustee at $65 per share, although current sales of the stock were being made
in 1924 at a much lower figure. The son had endeavored to have the price
fixed at less than $65, and in 1925 persuaded his father to reduce it to
$34.428 per share. In 1926, during which year sales of the stock had been
made ranging from $25 to $65 a share, the father insisted that the price be
restored to $65, and it was finally changed to $59.02, or a total of $300,000,
with a certain discount allowed if paid in lump sum. In 1929 the share price
became $5.902 when the par value of the stock was reduced from $100 to
$10 per share.

Upon the father's death in 1930, the son paid the full purchase price at
once, which, after a disagreement over the amount of discount had been
settled, came to a net payment of $232,500. The father's executors reported
this figure as the value of the stock in his gross estate.

The Board of Tax Appeals held, and the Court of Appeals affirmed, that

---

[14]*Edith M. Bensel et al., Executors,* 36 B.T.A. 246 (1937), aff'd as *Commissioner v.
Bensel,* 100 F.2d 639 (1938).

the value of the stock for estate tax purposes was the contract price at which the son had bought it, namely, $232,500, although the parties had stipulated that the stock's value exceeded $3 million at the decedent's death.

The Court of Appeals affirmed the Board in a very brief opinion, part of which follows:

> It will thus be seen that instead of the ordinary creation of a trust by an individual by a unilateral indenture, we have here settlement of a business problem by the contract of two parties hostile to each other and dealing at arm's length, the object of which was the purchase of the father's stock at a price which was lower than full value.
>
> Under the proofs, the Board had warrant for holding that the price at which the son was to acquire the father's stock was a proper figure. Such being the case, the appeal of the Commissioner is dismissed and the order of the Board affirmed.

A very important principle may be inferred from the *Bensel* case, namely, that if the relationship of the contracting parties to an agreement is such that the prospective buyer would be a natural object of the prospective seller's bounty, the agreed purchase price certainly will not hold for estate tax valuation unless the parties, "dealing at arm's length," set up a fair figure (for confirmation, see the quotation from the *Hoffman* case on page 387.) Presumably this would be done if, in such a case the parties at the time of making the agreement called in an accredited and independent public accountant or professional appraisal firm to appraise and report in writing the value of the stock, and the parties then incorporated the reported value in their agreement as the purchase price. Of course, any subsequent change in the purchase price should be based entirely upon a similar independent appraisal currently made. Any such procedure would have been superfluous in the *Bensel* case for, as stated in the opinion of the Court of Appeals, "Father and son were hostile to each other; both employed counsel to represent them, and the agreements were only reached after protracted contentions and negotiations."

In 1943 we find two more important case decisions on this subject handed down, both of which drew lines of distinction between the types of agreement that will establish share value for estate tax purposes and the types that will fail to do this.

One of these cases was *Worcester County Trust Company v. Commissioner*,[15] involving the estate tax value of 12,760 shares of stock of the Southwell Wool Combining Company in the estate of James Smith. This company had been organized by the members of a few families, and in order to keep the stock in the hands of these families the articles of incorporation

---

[15] 134 Fed. 2d 578.

were amended in 1935 to provide that before any stockholder could transfer his stock by way of gift or otherwise, he must first offer it for sale to the corporation at its book value as of the end of the previous month. The directors were given thirty days to accept any such offer, and if not accepted the stockholder was at liberty to sell at any price. It was further provided, however, that the board of directors could in specific instances vote to waive compliance by a seller, and also that the restriction did not apply to any transfer by the executor or administrator of a deceased stockholder to his legatees or next of kin.

Smith died in 1937, leaving his stock to his son. His executors reported the value of the shares in the estate tax return at $15.46 per share, the book value as prescribed in the articles of incorporation. The Commissioner determined the value to be $35 per share, a figure exactly ten times the average net earnings of the company over the previous five years, and assessed a deficiency accordingly. The executors petitioned the Board of Tax Appeals for a redetermination. The Board[16] upheld the Commissioner's valuation on the ground that the restrictions imposed on the sale of the stock did not affect its value and that the executors had not shown some other value to be correct. The Board's opinion, however, stated that cases which hold that restrictions obligating the owner to sell at a fixed price do provide a ceiling for valuation and are distinguishable, citing *Helvering v. Salvage, Commissioner v. Bensel, Wilson v. Bowers* and *Lomb v. Sugden.* The executors then appealed the case to the Court of Appeals, First Circuit.

The Court of Appeals reversed the decision and sent the case back to the Board for further proceedings to establish the correct value of the stock. It held that the Board's determination of value, based upon the formula used by the Commissioner, was "without rational foundation and excecessive" and should not have been taken even though the executors had failed to prove some other value to be correct. It stated that "the question of fair market value is ever one of fact and not of formula." It held further that the restrictions in the articles necessarily depressed the value of the stock and were among the relevant factors to be considered, although not restrictive to a degree that would establish value.

Thus we see that a "first offer" or "first refusal" restriction or agreement depresses the value of the shares affected but does not establish their value in the owner's estate. To accomplish the latter, the agreement must as a minimum grant to others on the critical date (at the owner's death) an enforceable option to purchase the stock at the agreed value. An insured stock purchase agreement goes even further; it requires the actual sale of the stock as of the critical date at the agreed value. It is significant, indeed, that the cases bearing on the option and the purchase agreements were clearly

---

[16]46 B.T.A. 337.

distinguished in the Board's opinion and were not even mentioned by the Court of Appeals.

The second important case in 1943 was that of *Claire Giannini Hoffman*.[17] There, the decedent during his lifetime had given his brother the option to acquire, upon his death, whatever interest he might then have in a securities business operated as a partnership, and in certain notes of the nominal partners, upon the payment of the balance then due on a promissory note of the decedent and the payment to his estate of a sum equal to 20 percent of the value of the assets of the partnership. The court held that because the restriction imposed by the option agreement did not become effective until the decedent's death, the fair market value of the property and not the option price was the measure of value for estate tax. The opinion briefly reviewed the *Wilson, Lomb, Bensel, Mitchell* and *Salvage* cases and distinguished the agreements involved in those cases from the option here, as follows:

> In view of some of petitioner's arguments it will not be amiss to refer briefly to the effect of what he refers to as the "option" given by Virgil to Lawrence. In the cases cited by him the optionee had been given an unqualified right to purchase at a designated price and the optioner could not dispose of the property during the continuance of the option. Such an option restricts the market value of the property in the hands of the owner. *Helvering v. Salvage, supra;* c.f. *Edwards v. Slocum,* 264 U.S. 61. Virgil, however, could have disposed of his interest in Walston & Co. and the note of Hoffman upon any terms or conditions he saw fit to impose and at any time he saw fit to do so. No argument is required to show that such an option did not restrict or limit the value of the property in his hands.

There were other important angles to this case, namely the fact that the optionee was the natural object of the bounty of the optiner and the fact that there was some question as to the enforceability of the "option" involved. The court commented on this as follows:

> The opinion of the Board in the *Bensel* case suggests the reason for, though we do not intend to imply that it completely delimits the extent of, the rule relied upon by petitioner. Thus the fact that the option is given to one who is the natural object of the bounty of the optioner requires substantial proof to show that it rested upon full and adequate consideration. Whether a unilateral agreement made by an unmarried man to his brother constitutes an enforceable contract is at least a debatable question. There is no showing that Virgil was indebted to his brother in any amount, nor was the brother required to do more than

[17] 2 T.C. 1160.

elect whether he would take the property upon the terms specified. If the agreement were fair and reasonable when originally entered into, would it be upheld by the court—no reciprocity being shown—when the actual investment of the donor or optioner had been more than quadrupled? In the event of litigation between the other heirs at law of the optioner and the optionee, would the court have upheld the agreement? Was the so-called option a valid substitute for testamentary disposition of property? While none of these questions need be answered, they suggest that there must be some limit to the passage of substantial property rights under a unilateral agreement granting to the natural object of the bounty of a deceased an option to purchase at a grossly inadequate price. In other words, we are of the opinion that while a bona fide contract, based upon adequate consideration, to sell property for less than its value may fix the value of the property for the purposes of the estate tax, a mere gratuitous promise to permit some favored individual, particularly the natural object of the bounty of the promissor, to purchase it at a grossly inadequate price can have no such effect.

This comment would seem to bear out very clearly the rule inferred from the *Bensel* case.

The *Hoffman* case as a whole shows that an agreement calling for purchase and sale at death, standing alone, is not sufficient to establish estate tax value; the agreement must also contain restrictions on the disposal of the stock prior to death. The opinion, as previously noted, distinguished the main line of cases in this respect. For instance, it said: "In the Lomb case an agreement had been made by the stockholders whereby none could sell his stock without first offering it to the others who were to have the right to purchase in proportion to their common stockholdings at approximately $69 per share." A fair inference from this comment, and from the facts in the other cases, is that a "first offer" restriction during life is sufficient, when coupled with an obligatory purchase and sale (or binding option) effective at death.

In 1944, the Tax Court held in the much more clear-cut case of *Estate of James H. Matthews,*[18] that restrictions must be imposed on the parties during life if their option agreement or their agreement to purchase at a stipulated price at death is to establish estate tax value. In this case, shares of stock were the subject matter of the agreement and there were questions neither with respect to close relationship nor as to the enforceability of the contract. Matthews, president and a large stockholder in the James H. Matthews Company, had entered into an agreement with William Jenkins, another officer and stockholder, in which reciprocal options were given for the survivor within three months after the death of the other to purchase from

[18]3 T.C. 525.

the estate of the deceased all the shares of stock of the company that might be owned by the deceased at the time of his death. The corporation carried life insurance on each party independent of the agreement, except that if a dividend were paid by the corporation within the option period from the proceeds of the policy on the life of the decedent the option price per share was to be $75; otherwise it was to be $90. Matthews confirmed the agreement in his will.

Matthews died in 1938 owning 785 shares. No dividend was paid by the corporation from the insurance proceeds of the policy on his life and Jenkins purchased his shares from the executor for $90 per share, paying $70,650. The executor reported this figure as their value on the estate tax return, but the Commissioner determined their value to be $120 per share or a total of $94,200 and assessed a deficiency accordingly. The executor petitioned the Tax Court for a redetermination.

The Tax Court held that the fair market value of the stock, rather than the option price, governed, because the agreement did not impose restrictions during the decedent's lifetime. The court's opinion related this case closely to the *Hoffman* case, first, by "briefing" the basic facts the opinion handed down in that case, and then continuing:

> ... The restrictions there imposed upon the property by the option agreement did not become effective until the decedent's death and did not affect its value until after his death. That was the situation in the present case. The option agreement was to apply only to the stock which might be owned by the decedent at the time of his death and decedent was under no obligation to retain ownership of any of the shares until his death. He was free up to the very moment of his death to sell or otherwise dispose of the shares for the best price obtainable. That right terminated with and by reason of his death. Likewise the right of the optionee to purchase the shares came into existence at the time of and by reason of decdent's death.

The opinion went on to distinguish the main line of cases as follows:

> The instant case, like the *Hoffman* case, is distinguishable from the cases relied upon by the petitioner, such as *Wilson v. Bowers,* 57 Fed. (2d) 682; *Lomb v. Sugden,* 82 Fed. (2d) 166, and *Edith M. Bensel et al., Executors,* 36 B.T.A. 246, affd. 100 Fed. (2d) 639. In all of those cases the option agreement, or other restriction on the sale of the property, became effective during the lifetime of the decedent and the value of the property was not affected by his death. In *Lomb v. Sugden,* supra, for instance, the court said:
>
> "... Because of the agreement, the decedent could not have secured a price greater than $69.445 at the time of her death. It is

as of that time that the value of the stock must be determined. Then she could only give it or sell it to the other stockholders at the price fixed. Its value to the estate could be no greater than that with which the decedent parted. *Edwards v. Slocum,* 264 U.S. 61, 63."

In 1951, the value of the stock owned by a deceased stockholder and sold to the corporation under a stock redemption option agreement was held in the *Salt* case to be the option price in the agreement.[19] The decedent, a retired president of Graybar Electric Company, Inc., held a voting trust certificate representing 4,000 shares of the company stock. He had acquired the shares in an exchange upon consolidation at par value of $20 a share, subject to a restrictive agreement whereby he was required to offer the shares to the corporation if he desired to sell them during life, and whereby at his death his estate was required to offer them to the corporation at $20 a share. All of the common stock of the corporation was subject to this restrictive agreement, and the corporation followed its practice of exercising its option by doing so at the death of Salt. The Commissioner determined that the value of the stock for Federal estate tax purposes was $60 a share, but the Tax Court held such value to be the $20 a share option price paid under the agreement. In so holding, the opinion stated in part:

> Not only was the estate required to offer the stock to Graybar after decedent's death for $20 per share but also, if during decedent's lifetime he had desired to dispose of the stock, he was required to offer it to Graybar at $20 per share. The stock being subject to this restrictive agreement and which in practice had always been adhered to by Graybar we conclude that the value of the stock for estate tax purposes was $20 per share. . . .

The case of *May v. McGowan,*[20] cited in the opinion in the *Salt* case, was affirmed by the United States Court of Appeals for the Second Circuit in 1952. Prior to taking his son into partnership, May had borrowed extensively from his bank for business purposes. This indebtedness was assumed by the partnership, but as between father and son the father agreed to pay it. A corporation was organized subsequently, to which was transferred all of the assets of the partnership in consideration of the assumption by the corporation of the bank indebtedness up to $161,500 and of the issuance of 500 shares of stock to each partner. Thereupon the stockholders entered into an agreement providing that neither would dispose of his shares without first offering them to the other at $100 a share. But because the son had personally agreed to guarantee to the bank its loans to the corporation, the

---

[19]*Estate of Albert Salt,* 17 T.C. 92.

[20]97 F. Supp. 326, aff'd 194 F.2d 396.

price per share as to him was to be reduced by 1/500 of the indebtedness due the bank at the date of exercise of his option. The agreement further provided that upon the death of either, the survivor would have an irrevocable option to purchase on the above terms.

When the father died, the indebtedness to the bank exceeded $50,000 with the result that under the agreement the son was entitled to his father's stock for nothing. The executors reported the value of the stock at zero in the estate return, but the Commissioner determined its value to be $50,000. The lower court upheld the executors. The Commissioner appealed the case to the United States Court of Appeals for the Second Circuit in the hope that this court, which had decided the leading cases of *Wilson v. Bowers* and *Lomb v. Sugden* many years previously, would change its position. The court saw no reason to question its prior decisions and affirmed the lower court. The following quotation from the court's opinion is of particular interest:

> It seems clear that with the option outstanding no one would purchase the stock of the decedent at its value unrestricted by the option when it was subject to call by Harry A. May at zero. This was the rationale of our decisions in *Wilson v. Bowers,* 2d Cir., 57 Fed. 2d 682, and *Lomb v. Sugden,* 2d Cir. 82 Fed. 2d 166. In *Lomb v. Sugden supra* (at p. 168), we said that this view was supported by the Supreme Court's decision in *Helvering v. Salvage,* 297 U.S. 106, to the effect that an outstanding option to purchase restricts the market value of stock in the hands of the owner to the option price. We see no reason for questioning the foregoing decisions. If they leave a loophole for tax evasion in some cases, here the district court found that there was no purpose to evade taxes. Such a loophole, if important, should be closed by legislative action rather than by disregarding the cases we have cited.

In 1958, the Tax Court again held that the purchase price set in a stock redemption agreement controlled the Federal estate tax value of the decedent's shares.[21] The decedent was suffering from an incurable disease when he and his two brothers, the three stockholders in a publishing corporation, entered into the agreement. In the event of any stockholder's death, his shares were to be purchased for $200,000. The decedent died one year later. The opinion stated the rule as follows:

> Where for the purposes of keeping control of a business in its present management, the owners set up in an arm's length agreement, which we consider this to be, the price at which the interest of a part owner is to be disposed of by his estate to the

---

[21]*Estate of Orville Littick,* 31 T.C. 181.

other owners, that price controls for estate tax purposes, regardless of the market value of the interest to be disposed of.

The Tax Court briefed the facts in the partnership case of *Broderick v. Gore*,[22] which is considered somewhat similar, and concluded its opinion with the following paragraph:

> We recognize that here it was likely that Orville would die before his brothers, but that was not a foregone conclusion and it is not such fact as should destroy the validity of his agreement with his brothers. Had either brother predeceased him we think the agreement to purchase the stock at the $200,000 figure would clearly have been enforceable. We think the principles followed in the *Gore* case are applicable here and hold for petitioner.

The foregoing completes the examination of the important cases that have litigated the question of the binding force of agreements in establishing the value of close corporation stock at the time of the owner's death. In addition to these cases, however, and directly related to the subject here, are some of the cases involving insured stock buy-sell agreements previously examined under other headings. In the *Mitchell* case, for example, the contract price was accepted by the Commissioner as a base figure of stock valuation without question, the litigation there having to do with whether the stock should be taxed either in full at the base figure or as reduced by taxable insurance received by the estate as part of the purchase price for the sale of the stock under the terms of the agreement.

All of these cases, taken as a whole, confirm the rule that an insured stock buy-sell agreement, entered into at arm's length, establishes share value for Federal estate tax purposes as well as for the purposes of the agreement if the price fairly represented the value of the shares at the time agreed upon and if prior to death each stockholder has been prohibited from disposing of his shares from the time of the agreement until his death without first offering them to the other stockholders or to the corporation at the same contract price. The rule is sound in principle, because the stock cannot be worth any more to the estate than the decedent or his estate is bound to accept for it. It is beneficial alike to Government and to stockholders, for it saves both the trouble and expense of ascertaining the value of close corporation stock as "a fact," in the light of the company's net worth, earning power, dividend paying capacity, and all other relevant factors, including consideration of values of listed stock of other corporations engaged in a similar line of business—a difficult and discouraging task usually ending in disagreement.

Effect of insured buy-sell agreements on valuation for state death taxes.

---

[22] 224 F.2d 892.

Most of the states levy inheritance taxes, as distinguished from estate taxes. Partially because of the difference in nature of these two types of death taxes, two divergent rules have developed as to the effect of a buy-sell agreement on the valuation of a business interest for purposes of state death taxation. Several of the states follow the Federal rule, just discussed. A number of other states, mostly those levying inheritance taxes, follow the so-called inheritance tax rule. This rule is that such an agreement does not control value for death tax purposes but will be considered along with other evidence of value. States applying this rule appraise the business interest, and if found to be worth more than the contract price, tax the excess value to the purchasers as a transfer for an inadequate consideration intended to take effect at or after death. A third group comprises many states that have not decided the issue. Since the matter is in a developing stage, the loose-leaf tax services should be consulted with respect to its status in any particular state.

Chapter 15

SPECIFIC BENEFITS OF THE
INSURED STOCK BUY-SELL PLAN

BENEFITS TO THE SURVIVING STOCKHOLDERS

Survivors protected from control or interference by outsiders. We have seen that in the absence of an agreement, the surviving stockholders stand unprotected against the intrusion into the corporate affairs of unacceptable or hostile outsiders. We have noted that surviving minority stockholders, unable as a last resort to liquidate the business, are placed in a worse position than they would have occupied as surviving minority partners. We have observed cases in which surviving equal stockholders have become deadlocked in attempting to continue a corporate business with the stockholding heirs. And we have followed the litigation that has resulted in holding surviving majority stockholders accountable to the heirs of a deceased minority stockholder in such vital matters as the salaries and expenses of those remaining in control. The trouble that develops in these different situations springs from a common generating cause, the separation of the ownership of a block of the stock from the active management. When any shares in a close corporation go out of the hands of the active managers, the spirit of harmony and efficient cooperation that formerly exited cannot help but be impaired. As was stated in the *Emeloid* case: "The fragile bark of a small business can be wrecked on just such uncharted shoals." Active management and owner-ship in a small corporation are like "Siamese twins"; they must be kept together for it to live and thrive.

The insured stock purchase agreement keeps active management and ownership together in the hands of the surviving stockholders. By acquiring ownership of all of the shares through the functioning of the plan, they have every opportunity to continue the thriving business enterprise free from the control or interference of outsiders.

Survivors or corporation guaranteed the opportunity and ability to purchase deceased's stock. In the absence of an agreement, the surviving stockholders have no assurance that they or the corporation will be able to acquire the shares of stock owned by the deceased. If he has bequeathed them to specific legatees, the shares may be unprocurable. Even if the executor or administrator is obliged to sell them, the survivors or the corporation must outbid all competitive offers. With a buy-sell agreement, the survivors are enabled to acquire complete ownership of their corporation; the transaction will be specifically enforced against the estate, if such step becomes necessary. The agreement has made the transfer of ownership certain, and has made the purchase price definite. And when insurance of the purchase price is added to the agreement to buy and sell, the purchase money will be at hand at the precise time for payment.

Survivors acquire full stock ownership by most convenient and economical plan. The life insurance plan of financing not only eliminates the hazard that the surviving stockholders or the corporation will not have the purchase price for the deceased's stock ready when death occurs, it represents the most convenient and economical method of acquiring the necessary funds. It constitutes an advance installment purchase plan. Since these installment payments are only about half the legal rate of interest and are self-completing upon death for the full amount, they are convenient to make and rarely indeed do the total payments made aggregate the purchase-price money made available. The insurance plan, therefore, provides the purchase money for the deceased's shares with discounted dollars.

BENEFITS TO THE DECEASED STOCKHOLDER'S ESTATE AND HEIRS

The deceased's estate receives payment in full, in cash, at once. Prompt consummation of the fully insured buy-sell agreement puts into the hands of the executor or administrator of the deceased stockholder the full amount of the sale price of the decedent's shares. Nothing remains over which to bicker and bargain in a setting in which the survivors would have all the advantages. The money is forthcoming immediately and, if the agreement so provides, the insurance proceeds will constitute the minimum amount the estate will receive as the purchase price.

Speculative business interest converted into a cash certainty for deceased's family. While all the primary stockholders are alive, the efficient and harmonious blending of their combined talents and industry equips them well to cope successfully with the inherently speculative nature of a small business enterprise. Indeed, they relish the hazards, knowing that success will usually bring profits commensurate with the risks taken and that failure can be followed with another attempt. Far different, however, is the situation of the family of a deceased stockholder. Risky stocks in an inherently hazardous undertaking have no proper place, let alone a predominating place, among the investments of a widow and children. No stockholder in a small corporation can possibly foresee what the future destiny of the organization will be after his death. And as for the widow, any failure will be permanent. The insured stock purchase plan recognizes these fundamental truths by providing for the prompt disposal of the deceased's close corporation stock for its full value in cash in the interests of his family welfare.

Deceased's family protected against "freezing-out" process. If, in the absence of a stock purchase plan, the surviving stockholders are able to continue the business successfully, they will not long submit to the task of doing all the work and dividing the profits with the deceased's family. Then the customary pattern is an attempt to "freeze out" the widow by raising salaries and lowering or eliminating dividend payments on the stock. Perhaps the widow will be able to uphold her rights in a court of equity. She has only an outside chance of interfering with the dividend policy of the survivors— and costs of litigation are high. Consequently, assuming the continued success of the enterprise, the deceased's stock nevertheless fails to prove a suitable investment for his widow. With the prompt sale of this stock under an insured purchase plan, the widow is saved from the possibility of being subjected to the "freezing-out" process, with its attendant costs, anxieties, disappointments, and the personal animosities certain to be engendered. Far superior is a plan that recognizes the undeniable fact that the profits of an enterprise belong to those who earn them and that saves the widow from a situation in which her livelihood would be dependent upon her ability to sustain an unnatural financial arrangement.

The insured buy-sell agreement establishes share value for Federal estate tax. As brought out in previous chapters, the purchase price payable in a properly drafted cross-purchase or redemption agreement will constitute the Federal estate tax value of the decedent's shares. Having this value thus established probably will save the estate some estate tax dollars, for the records show that the Revenue Service tends to overvalue the shares of a small close corporation where no buy-sell agreement exists. Furthermore, with the value of the shares readily established, the settlement of the stockholder's estate will be expedited.

Deceased's estate can be administered promptly and economically. The executor or administrator has need for a substantial amount of cash to discharge the ante-mortem and post-mortem obligations of the deceased stockholder. Among his ante-mortem obligations will be the cost of last illness, current bills, unpaid property and income taxes, and outstanding special debts such as bank loans or mortgages. His post-mortem obligations will include funeral and burial expenses, estate and inheritance taxes, and the fees and costs attendant upon the probate and administration of his estate. In the aggregate, these items loom large, totaling 20 to 30 percent of the average moderate estate.

Ready cash with which to pay these obligations saves the shrinkage and loss inevitably suffered if it is necessary to liquidate a substantial portion of the general estate property or the close corporation stock quickly. Furthermore, the possession of ready cash enables the executor to take advantage of any discounts allowed for prompt payment of bills and taxes and to avoid any penalties for delinquent payment. Indiana, for example, allows 5 percent discount for inheritance taxes paid within one year from date of death. Conversely, under the Indiana law, interest is charged against any inheritance taxes remaining unpaid after eighteen months. Under the Federal law, interest is charged after one year against unpaid Federal estate taxes, assuming that proper extensions are procured.

An insured buy-sell agreement gives the executor ample cash to pay all obligations of the deceased stockholder, which eliminates any possibility of a disastrous liquidation of assets in a depressed market or the incurring of any penalties. Instead, discounts are saved, liquidation is avoided, and a prompt, efficient, and economical administration of the deceased stockholder's estate is assured.

BENEFITS DURING THE LIFETIME OF THE STOCKHOLDERS

This subject has been discussed beginning at page 190 in relation to partnership buy-sell agreements. There, we discussed the benefits of having the business profitably stabilized, having an attractive saving medium provided through the insurance policies, and having the future of the partners made predictable. Since these lifetime benefits of a buy-sell agreement are substantially the same whether the business owners are partners or close corporation stockholders, the reader is referred to the previous discussion.

Chapter 16

RETENTION OF CLOSE CORPORATION STOCK FOR THE FAMILY

FACTORS INDICATING RETENTION OF CLOSE CORPORATION STOCK

The discussion of close corporations that has preceded this chapter has dealt largely with the type of small close corporation aptly described as an "incorporated partnership." With very few exceptions, the stockholders of such corporations are well advised to enter into insured buy-sell agreements under which a deceased stockholder's shares will be purchased by the survivors or redeemed by the corporations. Here, we are concerned primarily with close corporations that are controlled by one family, and usually by the head of that family. In many instances, the stockholders of these corporations also would be well advised to enter into insured buy-sell agreements. In many other instances, however, particularly where the head of the family owns the controlling stock, factors are present which indicate that his stock might better be retained after his death for the benefit of his family. Thus, where a family corporation is encountered, a careful study should be made to determine whether such factors are present or could reasonably be brought into existence.

It should be stock of a commercial corporation. Most personal-service businesses, particularly those involving professional practice, are operated as proprietorships or partnerships. But some are operated in corporate form, including some organized under the recently enacted professional corporation statutes. The stock of such a corporation, however, is not suitable for retention since, as noted in a previous chapter on this subject, the statutes require that a decedent's shares either be redeemed by the corporation or acquired by a locally licensed member of the same profession. To be suitable, the stock should be that of a corporation engaged in a commercial enterprise.

Generally, it should be a controlling stock interest. The stock to be retained usually should represent a controlling interest in the corporation. An exception occurs with respect to the stock interests of members of the controlling stockholder's family. We have already said enough about the possibility of a deadlocked corporation to warn against retention of stock in a corporation equally owned by two families. And in this regard, the stock equally owned by two married brothers should be put in that category. Even though the corporation is operated smoothly while both brothers are alive, the possibilities of dissension developing after the death of one, if his shares are passed along to his heirs rather than being sold to his brother or redeemed should be canvassed thoroughly before a decision is made on the manner of disposition of the stock at death.

Where retention of a controlling interest seems indicated, the plan should be accompanied by agreements to purchase the interest of any stockholder outside the family circle upon his death. In *Bates Street Shirt Co. v. Waite,*[1] we saw the trouble that may ensue in the absence of such an agreement. Many other cases could be cited on this point, but it is too obvious to be labored further.

It should be a stock interest the owner wants to perpetuate. Typical of one type of corporation being discussed here is a company founded by the present controlling stockholder. He has succeeded in building up a substantial enterprise that often bears his name, as a result of his business acumen and some luck, and he wants to perpetuate it in the family as a monument to himself. This is fine, provided there is another member of the family, such as a son, who is interested in the corporation as a business career and who possesses the requisite business ability—and provided the other factors are present that indicate successful retention of the stock within the family.

The corporation must have capable successor management. Here, we come to the factor that is the *sine qua non* of successful retention of a controlling stock interest. Unless this factor is present at the stockholder's death, his interest should be sold or liquidated at that time; it would be foolhardy to retain a business interest within the family if there is no successor management able to continue it on a profitable basis. Not only must capable successor management be present, but any necessary steps should be taken now to assure that such management will remain with the corporation after the stockholder's death. Some inducements to interest and hold such management will be discussed later. We add here that there should be no indication

---

[1] 130 Me. 352.

that after the controlling stockholder's death those who could succeed to the management of the corporation would quarrel among themselves or with the successors to the controlling stock interest. This is no problem, normally, where a capable and experienced son will succeed both to the management of the corporation and to its controlling stock.

The corporation should have the likelihood of continuing satisfactory profits. The corporaton should not only be one with a record of satisfactory profits to date, but one which shows strong likelihood that such a record can be continued after the controlling stockholder's death. Furthermore, the present and anticipated profits should be at a level higher than might reasonably be expected from investing the same amount of capital in prime investments. Otherwise, there is no sense in passing along to the family the risks inherent in a small corporate enterprise.

Satisfactory profits cannot be anticipated after the stockholder's death if they are dependent upon his services, or upon the services of any other individual such as an inventor or other specialist. Nor should the profits be dependent upon patents about to expire, upon a franchise that will be lost on the stockholder's death, or upon a fad the demand for which may quickly disappear. If satisfactory profits are to be anticipated, the corporation should be in a good competitive position, and have good business momentum, in a line of business that is at least holding its own in a fast-changing world. The demand for buggy whips, for example, is not what it once was.

The corporation should have adequate capital. The corporation should have adequate working capital. It should also have adequate capital, when the time comes, to stabilize the business during the transition period following the controlling stockholder's death. It should have adequate bank credit facilities that are not being used to excess and are not dependent upon the controlling stockholder alone. It should have little or no long-term debt owed to outsiders that would drain substantial earnings away from the family. If inactive members of the family are expected to derive future income from the corporation, it must have a reasonable policy for dividing profits between that portion to be retained for growth, and that portion to be paid out to the stockholders.

Cash must be available for estate settlement without disrupting stock retention plan. Planning for the retention of a stockholder's shares is a futile exercise unless effective plans are made also to supply his executor with cash for estate settlement adequate to keep the retention plan intact. Assuming that we are concerned with a stock interest of substantial value, which should be the case if it is to be retained, a sizable Federal estate tax may be anticipated. Furthermore, without a buy-sell agreement effective to establish the value of the stockholder's shares in his estate and to pour cash into the estate as purchase money special plans for providing cash should be made. Some of these plans will be discussed later. The point here is that the estate owner's plan for stock retention may never come to fruition if supplying his estate with cash for estate settlement is left to chance. This was what happened, for example, in *Re Setrakian's Estate*.[2] The residue of the decedent's estate which was to include a 50 percent interest in one corporation worth over $2 million, was directed into a trust under his will for the benefit of his four daughters. The stock never reached the testamentary trust. Six years after the decedent's death, the court ordered the executors to sell all of the stock owned by the estate, based upon the following finding:

> No. 12. That the decedent's estate has now been in the course of probate administration for over 6 years, and the reason said estate has not been heretofore expeditiously closed and distributed is that said estate has had no funds wherewith to pay the aforesaid debts, expenses of administration and legacy, which while not determinable with entire accuracy at this time, will approximate $170,000.00; that the decedent's estate has no workable or practicable way or method of raising the cash funds necessary to be raised in order to close and distribute the decedent's estate except by a sale or sales of capital assets of said estate, which said capital assets consist almost wholly of the shares of [the two corporations].

The other 50 percent stock interest in the $2 million corporation was owned by the decedent's brother. Had they set up an insured buy-sell agreement for that stock, the estate no doubt could have been settled within a period closer to six months than six years, and at far less cost.

The stockholder should have other assets that will supply family income. No close corporation stockholder should leave his family entirely dependent upon whatever income they may receive from the corporation. Aside from his corporate stock, he should create reasonably adequate sources of income for his family's support and welfare during and after the transition period following his death. Several methods of providing such outside sources of income will be discussed later. They are necessary because no close corporation, no matter how sound or how ably managed, can be expected, month by month and year by year, to furnish a steady flow of income. At best, recessions will come and go, profits will advance and recede, and the need to plow profits back into the business will fluctuate from time to time. At worst, continuation of the business may prove a failure; no family of a decedent should be asked to rely solely on it for needed funds.

The stockholder's estate must be capable of suitable division among family members. This is a factor that assumes prime importance where the controlling stockholder has a capable son associated with the corporation to whom he desires to leave the control. He can accomplish this by bequeathing his

---

[2]140 Cal. App. 2d 926, 295 P.2d 924.

stock to the son, provided he has other property that he can bequeath to other members of the family so that each will be treated equitably. If he lacks such other property, he may accomplish and equitable division, at least of the fruits of the stcok ownership, by various methods later to be discussed.

All of the foregoing factors should be present at the stockholder's death, to assure profitable retention of his stock. Some of these factors will be present currently; some never will be present, indicating that the stock should not be retained; some, not currently existing, may be supplied by proper lifetime planning. Plans for remedying the deficiencies that are remediable will be discussed.

ARRANGEMENTS TO SAFEGUARD A STOCK INTEREST TO BE RETAINED

Assuring capable management. If the corporation lacks capable management, aside from the controlling stockholder, steps should be taken immediately to remedy this deficiency. If the business is too small to support second-line mangement, it is too small to consider retaining for family support and welfare. Assuming that is not the case, and that there are no sons to be groomed to take over, it will be necessary to bring new managerial talent into the organization unless such talent can be found among present personnel. In any event, it must be located and groomed.

In order to attract the right man from the outside, it may be necessary to offer him a stock interest. If so, it usually is desirable to arrange a buy-sell agreement with him under which his stock will be repurchased or retired upon severance of employment, by death or otherwise.

Given capable second-line management, special arrangements may be necessary to assure that it will remain with the corporation and ultimately become successor management. The controlling stockholder cannot be sure, of course, that his understudy will survive him. But the corporation can insure the new executive's life so that, should he predecease the controlling stockholder, it will have funds at hand to offset the loss of his skill and experience, and to finance his replacement. In order to protect against the possibility that the new executive will leave the corporation, it may enter into a deferred compensation agreement with him, backed by an appropriate amount of key-man insurance on his life. Because of rapidly accelerating income tax brackets, deferred compensation contracts are becoming one of the most effective techniques for attracting and holding key executives. Life insurance on such an executive will protect the corporation in event he dies prematurely, and will function to offset the deferred payments if he lives to receive them. Furthermore, it will function to finance any payments, either contractual or voluntary, to be made to the executive's widow. Payments to her, however, might better be provided through a so-called split-dollar insurance arrangement with the executive since the insurance proceeds payable under such an arrangement are generally free of income tax.

In order to assure that successor management will stay with the corporation after the controlling stockholder's death, the latter may provide special inducements in his will. We saw an interesting application of this techniques in *Matter of Noll.*[3] The decedent, a sole proprietor, directed in his will that the business be incorporated, and that the employee who had managed it for him be retained at an adequate salary and given 25 percent of the stock. Another interesting and effective arrangement is portrayed in *Kress v. Stanton,*[4] the details of which will be given later in discussing arrangement to assure the continuation of satisfactory profits.

Assuring a capable employee organization. A controlling stockholder will fall short of his objective of successful stock retention for his family if, having provided for capable successor management, he fails to provide also for a capable employee organization. He has at hand several business insurance arrangements that will help build up and hold such an organization, arrangments that are attractive also to his management personnel.

Assuming that the corporation has a sufficient number of employees— which it should have if its stock is to be retained—it may purchase for a low, tax-deductible premium, a group life insurance policy that will provide every permanent employee with a substantial amount of life insurance. It also may protect the employees and make their jobs more attractive by purchasing for them and their dependents group disability, hospitalization and major medical insurance coverage. Again, the corporation may deduct its premiums as a business expense.

The corporation may purchase a group annuity plan, or establish a qualified pension trust funded with life insurance and annuity contracts. These plans are tax-favored as to the corporation, the trust or insurance company, and the employees. From the employee's current standpoint, it is as if he received a tax-free increase in pay and put it toward his retirement in a tax-free fund.

The corporation may establish a deferred profit-sharing plan, which may include a substantial amount of life insurance on each participant. Such a plan not only attracts and hold high-calibre employees, but also gives them a powerful incentive to contribute more effectively to the corporation's profit-making ability. Such a plan, being dependent upon the corporation's profits, should include life insurance on the key profit-producing people in the organization.

That such plans as the foregoing will aid materially in building up and holding a capable employee organization is evidenced by *Lincoln Electric*

---

[3] 273 N.Y. 219.

[4] 98 F. Supp. 470, aff'd 196 F.2d 499.

Co.[5] The Tax Court, in approving the corporation's rights to deduct large contributions to a group annuity contract and to a profit-sharing trust, stated:

> The record clearly establishes that petitioner's incentive system materially contributed to increased productivity, enhanced earnings, reduced selling prices, avoided labor strife and work stoppages, and developed and retained a cooperative, loyal, efficient and satisfied force of employees.

Assuring continuation of satisfactory profits. Given capable successor management and employee organization, the corporation and its controlling stockholder still have additional arrangements that may be made to help assure the continuation of satisfactory profits after his death. A few of these will be discussed.

The corporation whose stock is to be retained must have a good record of profits to date,, but close scrutiny may reveal that the profits are coming from a dangerously narrow range of products or items. The obvious need here is to broaden the range, to diversify. A corporation that generates all of its profits from only one or two sources should start immediately on a search for other sources that can profitably be fitted into its type of operation. The same principle of diversification applies where a corporation is manufacturing products for only one or two large customers. The stock of such corporations as these, as presently operated, involves too great a business hazard to qualify for family retention; the controlling stockholder should move rapidly to correct the lack of spread, even though some current profits must be sacrificed in the process.

If the controlling stockholder is actively managing his corporation, as is usually the case, the corporation should own adequate key man insurance on his life to help assure continuation of profits after his death. An example of the importance of such insurance is found in *Helen Irene Rhodes,*[6] and *Fred F. Fischer.*[7] Both cases involved the stock of the Fischer Meat Company. When the founder, Otto Fischer, died, the corporate surplus was $45,000; key man insurance on his life increased this figure to $110,000. Obviously, this increase in the corporation's surplus supplied it with additional working capital and funds to stabilize its operations during the transition period following the founder's death.

In discussing the factors that indicate retention of stock, we pointed out that the corporation should have little or no long-term debt owed to outsiders since the effect would be to drain substantial earnings away from the family.

---

[5] 17 T.C. 1600.

[6] 3 T.C.M. 963.

[7] 6 T.C.M. 520.

Key man insurance on the controlling stockholder's life also will function in the event of his death to retire such debt. A classic example was reflected in *Newell v. Commissioner.*[8] In that case the Ingalls Stone Company, through its president, had negotiated a $300,000 issue of bonds, secured by a like amount of insurance on the president's life. The corporation paid off portions of the bond issue from time to time, and retired the remaining bonds from the insurance proceeds following the president's death some years later.

Under certain circumstances, a controlling stockholder will be interested in having his stock retained for his family's benefit only for a limited period, after which he prefers that the stock be replaced with conventional investments. An ingenious arrangement for implementing such a plan, an arrangement that assured capable successor management and satisfactory profits during the period, is revealed in *Kress v. Stanton.*[9] In that case the controlling stockholder, Frederick J. Kress, owned approximately three-quarters of the stock of Kress Box Company after having placed about one-sixth of his shares in a living trust. His wife owned a few shares, Vice President Le Clere owned a few, and a few were spread among other employees. Kress left his shares in a testamentary trust which directed that Le Clere have an option, in any of the next ten years in which the corporation earned at least 6 percent on the par value of its stock and the trustees decided that he had contributed to such profits, to purchase from the trust at book value up to 25 percent of the outstanding stock. Then at the end of the ten years, if Le Clere had purchased 25 percent of the stock, he was given a two-year option to purchase the trust's remaining shares but no number less. The options were to terminate if Le Clere left the company, or if the trustees accepted an advantageous sale of the shares. Following Kress' death, Le Clere was elected president of the corporation. Profits exceeded 6 percent, and Le Clere exercised his option to purchase 25 percent of the outstanding stock within two years after the controlling stockholder's death. Thus was a successful stock retention accomplished, to the benefit of all concerned.

PROVIDING CASH FOR ESTATE SETTLEMENT

As we saw in *Re Setrakian's Estate,*[10] a stockholder's plan for retention of his stock will be defeated if his executor is forced to sell the stock in order to pay the debts, death taxes, and other costs of settling his estate. Perhaps the example depicted by *Moran v. Sutter,*[11] is in order at this point. The decedent owned 53½ percent of the outstanding stock of The Reardon Company, of which he was president. He left 50 percent of his stock outright

---

[8] 66 F.2d 103; (see facts on this at 25 B.T.A. 773).

[9] 98 F. Supp. 470, aff'd 196 F.2d 499.

[10] 140 Cal. App. 2d 926, 295 P.2d 924.

[11] 360 Mo. 304, 228 S.W. 2d 682 (1950).

to his widow, 10 percent to his brother and sisters, and 40 percent in trust for his minor daughter. His estate was worth over $900,000, of which all but about $15,000 represented the corporation's stock. With estate debts, death taxes, widow's allowances and administration expenses totaling about $400,000, the probate court ordered the sale of 90 percent of the decedent's stock. Fortunately for the surviving stockholders, because it shifted control to them, the corporation was in a position to buy the stock for some $942.000.

Although the decedents in the *Setrakian* and *Moran* cases neglected to make plans for supplying their estates with cash, the requirement that the estate have the necessary cash is a factor that the stockholder may bring under control. The first thing he should do, of course, is to ascertain with reasonable accuracy the amount of cash his executor will need. Since the amount can be only an intelligent estimate, it should be a liberal one. Then, he should consider the various arrangements available to supply the projected amount and implement one or more of them for the purposes of his estate.

SECTION 303 REDEMPTION TO PROVIDE CASH

Fortunately, this section of the Internal Revenue Code was enacted for the specific purpose of making available to many close corporation stockholders a prime method of supplying their estates with most of the cash that will be needed. The statute lays down certain requirements and limitations, and provides that if these are met the redemption payments will be treated as purchase price for the stock and not the distribution of a dividend.

What stock qualifies. Where the value of the decedent's stock of a corporation (including a Subchapter S corporation) is included in his gross estate, and comprises either more than 35 percent of the gross estate or more than 50 percent of the taxable estate, it qualifies for partial redemption under Section 303. Where the decedent owned more than 75 percent of the stock of two or more corporations, they may be treated as one corporation in applying these percentage requirements. If the stock of the corporations is community property, the community stock interest of the decedent's wife is treated as having been included in his gross estate to meet the 75 percent test but not the 35 or 50 percent requirement. If qualifying stock is exchanged for new stock in a tax-free reorganization, or new stock is issued as a tax-free dividend on the qualified stock, the new stock qualifies for the redemption. Thus, where the decedent's stock represents bare voting control, control may be retained by the redemption of new, nonvoting stock.

It should be noted that where the stockholder is survived by his wife and full advantage is taken of the estate tax marital deduction, the 50 percent requirement is more liberal than the 35 percent requirement. If, for example, the gross estate is $400,000, the value of the decedent's stock of the corporation included therein must exceed $140,000 under the 35 percent test.

If we assume that administration expenses are $20,000 (leaving an adjusted gross estate of $380,000), and that the marital deduction is $190,000, then after also deducting the $60,000 specific exemption the taxable estate is $130,000. Thus, under the alternative 50 percent requirement, the value of the decedent's stock in his gross estate must exceed $65,000 only.

If the stockholder anticipates that the value of his stock will be uncomfortably close to the more-than 35 or 50 percent borderline for qualification, he may increase the applicable percentage by making *inter vivos* gifts of property other than the stock. Or, he may increase the value of his stock by having the corporation purchase additional key man insurance on his life. Sale to the corporation of some personal insurance, and its replacement with new insurance owned by his wife, will have a double-barreled effect; it will increase the stock's value and decrease the value of other property includible in his gross estate.

Who may have stock redeemed. Normally, the stock redeemed under Section 303 will be part of the shares in the executor's hands, for it is the estate that has need for cash with which to settle the estate (although the section does not require its application to such purpose). However, the redemption may be made from a person who acquired the stock as an heir, a beneficiary under the decedent's will or trust, surviving spouse, surviving joint owner, appointee, or donee, so long as the stock was included in the decedent's gross estate. But a shareholder who acquired his stock in satisfaction of a specific monetary bequest, or by gift or purchase from any person to whom the stock had passed from the decedent cannot have his stock redeemed under the protection of Section 303.

Maximum redemption distribution protected. Section 303 protects from possible dividend treatment the amount distributed in the redemption of qualified stock to the extent it does not exceed the aggregate amount of allowable funeral and administration expenses, and death taxes plus any interest thereon. To the extent the amount distributed does exceed the protected amount, such excess will be subject to the rules of Section 302 in determining whether it represents a sale or exchange, or a taxable dividend.

Limited period allowed for Section 303 redemption. The distribution in redemption of stock under the protection of Section 303 must be made within three years and ninety days after the Federal estate tax return is filed. But if a bona fide petition for a redetermination of Federal estate tax has been timely filed with the Tax Court, the distribution is protected if it is made within the period ending sixty days after the court's decision becomes final.

Use of life insurance with Section 303 redemptions. The state law and the corporation's charter must, of course, permit the corporation to redeem its stock. Nearly all states permit redemption if the corporate surplus is sufficient for the purpose. As a practical matter, the corporation needs not only the requisite surplus, but also cash at hand with which to make redemption payments without crippling its working capital. The corporation may supply itself with the necessary cash and increase its surplus with the proceeds of key man insurance on the controlling stockholder's life. Where his stock qualifies, such insurance gives the stockholder assurance that the redemption will be made and that the redemption payments will pour needed cash into his estate. Thus, the insurance so arranged might be said to furnish double-duty dollars: dollars which first ensure that the corporation has surplus out of which to make the redemption and cash in hand with which to make it and second, ensure that the executor has cash for estate settlement purposes. The descriptive phrase "double-duty dollars," however, has been appropriated to describe another plan for making a redemption under Section 303.

The so-called plan of using double-duty dollars in making a redemption under Section 303 assumes that a corporation has ample surplus for redemption purposes, although it might be short of cash for the purpose. Since the corporation does not need to bolster the amount of its surplus with the proceeds of key man insurance, the insurance under this plan is arranged differently to play a part in accomplishing a different objective: draining off corporate surplus or future earnings for family support after the stockholder's death. This is accomplished by a series of steps. The insurance on the stockholder's life is purchased, owned by, and payable to one or more members of his family. Following the stockholder's death, the insurance beneficiaries lend the proceeds to the corporation in exchange for its interest-bearing notes or bonds. The corporation then uses the borrowed cash to redeem stock from the executor under Section 303. Family support comes from the corporation's tax-deductible interest payments on the notes or bonds, and from its ultimate repayment of principal. Principal payments, from the standpoint of the beneficiaries, are simply a return of their own funds. Thus, the insurance dollars are said to perform a double duty: first, dollars with which to redeem the stock; second, dollars with which to support the family. Given a corporation with ample surplus, of substantial size, and assured earning power regardless of the stockholder's death, plus family members who may be relied on to lend the insurance proceeds to it, the plan should function suitably.

A comparison of the two Section 303 redemption plans is interesting. The personal insurance plan patently involves far more risk: risk that the corporation will not have the required surplus for redemption purposes; risk that the insurance beneficiaries will refuse to lend a large amount of money in hand; risk that the corporation may run into financial difficulties before it is able to pay back the insurance proceeds borrowed. It saddles onto the corporation a substantial fixed obligation at just the time when it must readjust for the loss of its key stockholder. These risks are foreign to the key man insurance plan.

The personal insurance plan has the advantage of draining off some of the corporation's future earnings in the form of tax-deductible interest payments, and probably of draining off some of the corporation's surplus in principal repayments. These advantages obviously are dependent upon a strong corporation whose profit-making ability will not suffer from the death of the controlling stockholder. From the standpoint of the family, it is imperative that other assets be available to supply dependents with basic income.

The personal insurance plan appears to have an estate tax advantage over the key man insurance plan, since the latter should enhance the value of the decedent's stock in his gross estate. In fact, it is relied on to do so where otherwise such value might not qualify for a Section 303 redemption. But that is only part of the tax picture; the income tax picture should be viewed also.

Under the key man insurance plan, the corporation will pay the insurance premiums—let us say a total of $100,000 in a given case. If the personal insurance plan is used instead, this $100,000 either will be accumulated by the corporation to increase the value of the decedent's stock—thus tending to equalize the estate tax results—or will be paid to the stockholders as dividends and be pared down substantially by personal income taxes. What is left would have to be supplemented by other personal income—after tax—to make the premium payments. Consequently, the personal insurance plan appears to have an income tax disadvantage, coupled with the disadvantage of reducing substantially the spendable income of the premium payers.

In summary, each plan has its own collateral objectives, and its peculiar advantages and disadvantages. The stockholder should study both in the light of his own situation and objectives, and then choose the most suitable plan for his corporation, estate and family.

For many stockholders the value of stock will not exceed 35 percent of the gross estate, but will exceed 50 percent of the taxable estate if the wife survives so as to preserve the marital deduction. Given these circumstances, the stockholder should protect against his wife dying first. One effective plan is to insure her life and place the policy in an irrevocable funded trust for the benefit of the children or other heirs. The trustee should be authorized to purchase assets from the estate of either spouse. If the wife predeceases the stockholder, the insurance proceeds will help offset the loss of the marital deduction in his estate and the chance to make a Section 303 redemption, and at the same time give his executor a possible source of estate cash. If she survives him, her estate will have substantial cash needs and her executor will have a source of cash through the trustee.

Section 303 redemption and accumulated earnings tax. This penalty tax on earnings accumulated beyond the reasonable needs of the business, in relation to a complete redemption of a deceased stockholder's shares under a regular stock redemption agreement, was discussed in Chapter 11. Here, its special relationship to Section 303 partial redemptions is discussed.

Prior to the 1969 amendments to Section 537, a series of cases had held that accumulations of earnings for purposes of a Section 303 redemption were not for the reasonable needs of the business but primarily for the personal needs of the stockholder and his estate. Thus, in several instances, such accumulations were subjected to the penalty tax.[12]

The 1969 amendments provide that accumulations made in the year of death or a later year, required for a Section 303 redemption, are for the reasonable needs of the business. They also direct that if funds are used for such a redemption, no inference is to be drawn that accumulations in the years prior to death represent unreasonable accumulations but a determination is to be made without regard to the redemption.

Thus, the amendments afford some protection from the penalty tax, but not very much. To the extent that they do not protect against the tax, it appears that the safest procedure is to fund a Section 303 redemption with annual-premium life insurance. Such premiums represent a comparatively small accumulation in any one taxable year and rarely should be significant enough in amount to draw assessment of this tax. As noted previously, the death proceeds are not subject to this tax since they are tax-exempt income and therefore are not part of the accumulated taxable income upon which the tax falls. But even if this were not so, the 1969 amendments would eliminate the death proceeds from this tax.

Insurance on stockholder's life. Where a Section 303 redemption is entirely out of the picture, estate cash can best be supplied by some plan that will call for insurance on the stockholder's life sufficient for the purpose. If he has a son active in the business who is to succeed him, for example, a purchase agreement may be entered into whereby the son will buy enough stock at his father's death to supply the cash needed by his estate. The agreement will be financed with insurance on the father's life owned by, and payable to, the son. In fact, such a plan is required in many situations for the purpose of dividing the stockholder's estate equitably among the members of his family. Failing such a plan, one of the regular insurance plans for supplying the estate with cash should be set up; in the final analysis, such cash must be provided if the stock retention plan is to be feasible.

Installment payment of estate tax under Section 6166. On the matter of providing cash for the estate, we add only that the provision in section 6166 of the Internal Revenue Code for payment of the Federal estate tax

---

[12]*Youngs Rubber Corp. v. Commissioner*, 331 F.2d 12; *Dickman Lumber Co. v. U.S.*, 355 F.2d 670; *The Kirlin Co. v. Commissioner*, 361 F.2d 818.

attributable to the corporation's stock into two ten annual installments with interest is too costly as well as too impractical, even though it might be available. The statute contains so many qualifications, limitations and tax traps that it "should be avoided like the plague," as one prominent authority put it.

BUILDING OTHER ASSETS FOR FAMILY INCOME

As we have stated, a stockholder who desires to retain his stock interest should create other reasonably adequate sources of income for his family's support and welfare; he should not leave them entirely dependent upon whatever they may receive from the corporation after his death. He has several methods available for providing such income.

Personal life insurance. The stockholder should set up a program of personal life insurance that will at least provide for the minimum income needs of his family. Optional settlements will provide guaranteed income, and will enable his wife to benefit from the $1,000 annual income tax exclusion of the interest element therein.

Tax-free death benefit. The stockholder should schedule a $5,000 tax-free death benefit from his corporation under Section 101(b) of the Internal Revenue Code. Although the amount is not too impressive in the case of a controlling stockholder, this is an income tax exemption that should not be overlooked.

Pension and profit-sharing plans. The stockholder has an excellent opportunity to build up substantial funds by establishing qualified pension and profit-sharing plans through his corporation and becoming a participant therein. Substantial amounts of life insurance may be purchased under these plans, if desired. Funds contributed to these plans grow free of income tax. The stockholder can select joint and survivor payments under these plans, thereby guaranteeing his wife a lifetime survivorship income. Or, he can create a living trust and designate it as the beneficiary of any lump-sum distribution payable at this death. The lump-sum distribution will qualify for capital gains treatment to the extent it represents employer contributions made before 1970, employee contributions, and earnings on all contributions. That portion of a lump sum distribution representing employer contributions made in 1970 and thereafter will be taxed as ordinary income—in some cases under a seven-year averaging rule. The trust qualifies as a named beneficiary to eliminate Federal estate tax on the amount attributable to the corporation's contributions. Furthermore, the trust may be arranged so as to save Federal estate tax on the income beneficiary's death. The estate tax would apply, however, if the distribution is payable to the stockholder's estate; for this reason, such distribtuions are not desirable sources of estate cash unless payable to a named beneficiary under a special arrangement, such as might be made with a trust, authorizing it to purchase assets from the stockholder's estate. Furthermore, a participant may not provide that his retirement benefits be accumulated and held until his death.

The foregoing and other methods are available to the stockholder for providing income for his family from sources outside the corporation. Such income is important for two solid reasons. It protects his family in the event the corporation gets into financial difficulties. It enables his successor to operate the corporation as a businessman should operate it: conserving some of the earnings, rather than paying out every cent in current dividends.

TESTAMENTARY AND OTHER ARRANGEMENTS
FOR STOCK RETENTION

A controlling stockholder has two basic arrangements for disposition of his stock under his will: one or more outright bequests of the stock, with or without conditions attached, or bequest of the stock to a testamentary trust. In any event, he has the problem of providing for retention of the stock in such a manner that suitable provision will be made for each member of his family without jeopardizing the continued success of the corporation. Sometimes a simple plan will do; sometimes a complex plan is required.

Specific bequest of the stock. A condition precedent to such a disposition is a prospective heir willing and capable of stepping into the controlling stockholder's business shoes. Thus, if he has a son with the ability and experience to continue the corporate operations successfully, bequest of the stock to him should be all that is required, if there is no problem of equitable division of the estate. If two such sons are in the business, the stock could be divided between them.

If the stockholder has other property sufficient to treat the other members of the family equitably, he plans his will accordingly. Where that is not the case, he will have to work out another solution. Spreading the stock by outright bequests among the various members of the family, associated with the corporation or not, would not be a solution; more likely, it would sow the seeds of family bickering and discord. One obvious solution, already mentioned, called for an agreement whereby the son will purchase an amount of his father's stock sufficient to accomplish an equitable division of the latter's estate.

Assume for example, that the stockholder has a wife, a son associated with him in the corporation, and a daughter. His stock is worth $100,000, and his total net estate is estimated at $240,000. His son is to receive the stock, but he wants his wife to receive one-half of his net estate, and each child to receive one-fourth. This logical division will be accomplished if the son purchases at his father's death $40,000 of the stock with a like amount of insurance on the father's life, the proceeds of which the son will pay into the estate. The stock bequeathed to the son will be worth $60,000. The remaining estate property comprises $140,000 plus the $40,000 insurance proceeds, of which $120,000 will go to the wife and $60,000 to the daughter. Similar solutions can be worked out to fit any reasonably similar family and estate situations. While exact figures cannot be known in advance, sufficiently close estimates usually can be made to make the method practicable.

Another method of equitably dividing the stockholder's estate calls for recapitalizing the corporation before his death. For example, non-voting preferred stock may be issued and bequeathed to his wife, with voting common bequeathed to the son active in the business. Much could be written about the possibilities of recapitalization, but it would take us beyond the scope of this book. Its ramifications, however, should be probed by the stockholder who plans to retain his stock for the benefit of the family.

Sometimes a stockholder will create what amounts to a division of his estate by attaching a condition to the bequest of his stock. This is what the stockholder did in *Meyerson v. Malinow.*[13] The decedent and his two sons by a former marriage each owned one-third of the stock of an iron and metal company. His will bequeathed his stock to his sons subject to a charge upon the stock that the sons pay to his widow $50 a week "as long, during her life or widowhood, as she shall reside in Spartanburg County." The sons paid the weekly charge for five years and then stopped. The court held them liable for the weekly amount up to the date of the widow's death, which occurred while the action was pending. Because of the family relationship of the survivors, the decedent might better have sold the stock to his sons at his death and provided for his widow out of the purchase price.

Another will provision for equitable division was involved in *Garner v. Beskin.*[14] There the decedent and her son each owned one-half the stock of a department store. She was survived by the son and a daughter. She bequeathed her stock to the son with the proviso that if the bequest amounted to more than one-half of her estate the son was directed to pay the difference in money to her daughter "so that each of my said two children will receive an equal amount from my estate." This proviso accomplished its purpose, but the decedent had cut the estate division so fine that it took Virginia's top court to settle a dispute over valuation.

When taking up the subject of suitable division of the controlling stockholder's estate, we stated that spreading the stock among the various members of his family was no solution, but was an invitation to family dissension following his death. Many cases show this to be true. A typical example is *Black v. Parker Manufacturing Co.*[15] The decedent left his controlling stock interest to his son, but left small minority interest to each of three daughters. One daughter sued her brother and the corporation,

---

[13] 231 S.C. 14, 97 S.E.2d 88 (1957).

[14] 198 Va. 653, 96 S.E.2d 117 (1957).

[15] 329 Mass. 105, 106 N.E.2d 544 (1952).

claiming that he was receiving an excessive salary from the corporation; further, that he had started other businesses in order to siphon off profits for himself alone. The daughter's suit was unsuccessful, but the case shows the folly of spreading small amounts of stock around among family members. The controlling stockholder and his son should have had an agreement whereby the son would have purchased from the father's estate the stock he unwisely bequeathed to his daughters.

Another example of family dissension caused by spreading stock around is reflected in two cases referred to previously in this chapter: *Helen Irene Rhodes*[16] and *Fred F. Fischer.*[17] On the decedent's death, his son inherited stock control of the Fischer Meat Company and became its president and manager. But the decedent's widow and two daughters held minority interests, acquired by gifts and bequests from the decedent. One daughter was dissatisfied with her legacy, and became dissatisfied with her brother's management of the corporation and its failure to pay dividends. She threatened court proceedings to have her father's will declared invalid, and to have a receiver appointed for the corporation. The upshot was a redemption of her stock at a price nearly double its book value. Her Tax Court case held that she had realized ordinary income on the redemption of some of her shares. Her brother's case held that the redemption of his sister's stock did not result in a dividend to the remaining stockholders. Here again, an estate division plan was needed. It could have been accomplished by an agreement whereby the son would have purchased at his father's death the shares that, without such an agreement, sowed the seeds of dissension.

Testamentary trust of the stock. A bequest of close corporation stock in trust for the controlling stockholder's family is a desirable arrangement in many situations. The trust accomplishes an equitable division of the stockholder's estate without dissemination of stock ownership among the various members of the family, and at the same time achieves centralized supervision and voting control. It allows whatever division of the corporation's dividend income the circumstances of the family members warrant, and such division can result in substantial income tax savings. It can be arranged so as to save the second estate tax on the stock, if that objective is desired. Or, it can span the period until the son becomes qualified to take over.

If the stockholder plans to bequeath his shares to a trust under his will, the corporation should possess all of the factors favoring retention previously discussed. Of special importance here are ample capital, capable successor management and arrangements that will assure the payment of dividends. In most instances, the corporation whose stock is to be retained should be of substantial size, larger than might be required were the stock to be

---

[16] 3 T.C.M. 963.

[17] 6 T.C.M. 520.

bequeathed outright to a son who is active in the business. Where the corporation is quite small, the trustee will have little chance of success if business conditions take a bad turn. This is what happened in *Blauvelt v. Citizens Trust Co.*[18]

In that case, the decedent owned most of the stock of a small laundry company, each of his two sons and an employee owning the few other shares. He and his sons had operated the business successfully for a number of years, and following his death in 1927 his stock went into a testamentary trust along with his mill property on which it was located. The trust was to pay from its income $150 monthly to his widow, with any excess income to be accumulated for the sons. It was to continue during the lifetime of the widow and sons. The decedent's shares were worth less than $40,000 at his death, and the mill property was worth about $20,000, subject to a $10,000 mortgage. The depression struck in 1929, and the monthly payments to the widow were discontinued in March 1932 for lack of trust income. She died in 1935. The trustee sold the mill property in 1944; and it sold the laundry business in 1947 "for a sum sufficient to satisfy all of its creditors but leaving nothing for distribution to the stockholders." Under the circumstances, the court refused to hold the trustee liable for the losses incurred. The case, however, teaches some lessons. Basic is the fact that the corporation was too small to place in trust for the duration of three lives. It was certainly too small to be relied on for support of the stockholder's widow, with or without a business depression.

The stockholder should possess stock that will give the trustee voting control, and should make sure that his executor has ample cash with which to settle the estate so that the controlling stock will reach the trustee. This was the flaw that defeated testamentary trust plans with respect to close corporation stock, you will recollect, in the *Setrakian* and *Moran* cases. In this connection, the stockholder should have estate tax estimates made from time to time since the value of his stock will not be established as in the case of a buy-sell agreement. He must consider, of course, whether the contemplated trust will qualify the stock for the estate tax marital deduction.

Usually the stockholder should select as trustee a willing trust company, experienced in supervising businesses. Where it appears advantageous, he may designate as co-trustee an individual familiar with the business. He will be well advised, however, to select a co-trustee who will not have a conflict of interest with the trust beneficiaries. Other members of the family who own stock of the corporation and are active in its management are not desirable as trustees. Their primary interest lies in salaries and in conserving profits for growth, thus conflicting with the interest of the trust beneficiaries in corporate dividends. Nevertheless, many stockholders refuse to follow this

---

[18] 3 N.J. 545, 71 A.2d 184 (1950).

advice; and most of the lawsuits against trustees of close corporation stock stem from such refusal. Let us look at just one of them.

In re Keyston's Estate.[19] The decedent owned 1,450 shares and his brother 500 shares of a saddle manufacturing company. The decedent died in 1945. His will provided a testamentary trust of his shares, with his brother as trustee and his widow and minor sons as beneficiaries. The trustee sold 200 shares to his father for cash to pay death taxes, leaving 1,250 shares in trust valued at about $81,000. The corporation was authorized to issue 700 additional shares in 1946; these were purchased by the brother to bring his shares to 1,200. Thus, the shares he held in the testamentary trust were diluted to a minority interest. A fair amount of dividends were paid to the trust beneficiaries in 1946 and 1947, advances of funds were made to them in 1948 and 1949, but nothing was paid to them the following two years. The widow petitioned for removal of the decedent's brother as trustee on the ground that he was using the corporation for his own purposes. His corporate salary was $1,000 per month, but he voluntarily reduced it to $750 monthly ten months before trial. He was not removed, but ordered to render an accurate accounting. The case was remanded to see whether some trusteed stock should be sold to pay expenses and advances made.

In that case we see a trustee with interests that conflicted with the beneficiaries'. But that was not all that was wrong. There was no cash with which to pay estate settlement costs, a fact that started the events leading to the change in the trust holdings from a controlling to a minority interest. Basically, the company was too small to assure reasonably steady dividends; it was a two-man corporation the stock of which should have been subject to a buy-sell agreement rather than a testamentary trust.

The stockholder should discuss his contemplated trust plan with the trustee he intends to designate, and ascertain whether the trusteeship will be accepted. Then he should discuss the details and eliminate any contemplated provisions which the trustee does not consider workable or feasible. He should give the trustee adequate express powers and authority, since the statutes will fall short of doing so. He should include provisions to protect the stock from dilution by giving the trustee the authority to acquire a proportionate part of any additional stock, whether a new issue or resold treasury stock. Thus, the trust corpus should contain assets other than the corporate stock.

The stockholder should limit the trust duration to a reasonable period, such as the remaining lifetime of his widow or until his son (or sons) has reached maturity and has demonstrated his ability to operate the business successfully. In the *Blauvelt* case, for example, we saw a trust term far too

---

[19]102 Cal. App.2d 223, 227 Pac.2d 1 7 (1951).

long; with two sons in the laundry company, that trust should have provided for termination at the widow's death.

The stockholder also should discuss his contemplated testamentary trust with his wife, and include provisions therein or elsewhere which should assure that she will not upset his plan by electing against his will. Without such assurance, an *inter vivos* trust of the stock would be indicated.

CONCLUSION

A fitting way to close this discussion of stock retention is to return to the case of *Kress v. Stanton*,[20] because it reflects well the factors necessary for successful retention of close corporation stock. There, the decedent was the controlling stockholder of a profitable commercial corporation worth over $2 million at his death. It had capable successor management: Le Clere. There must have been cash available for estate settlement, since the decedent's stock was trusteed as planned. Living and testamentary trusts of the stock were created, with a corporate trustee; there was no trustee with interests conflicting with the interests of the trust beneficiaries. There was an optional limited period of stock trusteeship. The trust arrangement provided an incentive plan to hold the key executive and to assure satisfactory profits during the trust term. When such factors as these are present, the stockholder has the factors at hand to assure successful retention of his stock.

---

[20] 98 F. Supp. 470, aff'd 196 F.2d 494.

OTHER USES OF LIFE AND HEALTH INSURANCE TO BENEFIT THE BUSINESS ORGANIZATION

Chapter 1

DISABILITY BUY-SELL AGREEMENTS
AND SALARY CONTINUATION PLANS

Up to this point considerable time has been spent on documenting the need for a business owner during his lifetime to plan for the disposition of his business interest in the event of his death. He must determine whether it will be in the best interests of his family to allow one or more of them to succeed to his business interest. If not, he must arrange for its sale with the purchase money invested in some form that will provide adequate income for the family without unduly jeopardizing the security of the principal. If a sale of the business interest is determined to be the best course of action, a buy-sell agreement funded with life insurance that provides for the interest of a business owner to be sold at his death to either the business itself or to his co-owners is generally the recommended procedure.

A creative plan for the disposition of a business interest at death before retirement that does not provide for the contingency of an active business owner becoming totally disabled is statistically doing less than half the job. Statistics show that the probability of an active business owner becoming totally disabled before retirement is much greater than the probability that he will die before retirement. Nevertheless, many plans for the disposition of a business interest at death are silent with respect to its disposition in the event of a total disability. The finality of death when compared with the uncertainties surrounding a disability make it easier to plan for the former. However, the fact that on the average one out of every three persons now age thirty-five will suffer a long term disability of at least three months duration

421

before reaching age sixty-five and that the average length of such disability will be over five years, makes it imperative to plan ahead.[1]

OVERCOMING PROBLEMS ASSOCIATED WITH LONG TERM DISABILITY OF AN OWNER-EMPLOYEE IN A CLOSELY HELD BUSINESS

Just as with death, the long term disability of a business owner will create problems for the healthy active owners of the business and the disabled inactive owner and his family. Where there is no prior planning and a disability occurs, the bargaining positions of the parties involved will no longer be equal. Prior to the disability all of the owners shared a unity of purpose and all actively contributed to the success of the business. Now, one of their number has been transformed from an asset into a liability. Not knowing how long this unproductive status will last, it is difficult to determine what steps should be taken. The problems become more apparent with each passing day. In the view of the disabled owner his past activity with the firm and his continuing proprietary interest, to say nothing of his need for income, entitle him to continue to receive his full salary until he "gets back on the job." In the view of the healthy owners, they are now doing all or a portion of the work of their disabled co-owner. Or perhaps a new man has been hired at substantial expense to fill the gap that has been created. In addition, profits may be suffering because as yet no one has learned to perform the functions of the disabled owner as well as he did. In hopes of a quick recovery all may agree to continue the full salary of the disabled owner. However, as the chances for recovery diminish, the financial drain on the business, together with the ebbing moral responsibility of the healthy owners, will often lead to a crisis situation.

Disabled minority owner. If the disabled individual owns a minority interest in an incorporated business he has no control over the continuation of his salary or the dividend-paying policies of the corporation. The eventual outcome usually will be a sale of his interest to the healthy co-owners at a price which reflects his weak bargaining position. If the business is a partnership, a minority owner technically may be in a stronger position since he can force a dissolution of the partnership. Nevertheless, if the partnership is liquidated the disabled partner will generally receive far less than the value of his partnership interest in the business as a going concern. In addition, the healthy partners are free to reorganize without him.

Disabled majority owner. If the disabled individual owns a majority interest in an incorporated business, he may control the continuation of salary payments to himself as well as the dividend-paying policy of the corporation. However, he must now rely more heavily than ever on the

---

[1]*C.L.U. Journal,* Vol. VIII, No. 1, p. 52.

minority stockholder-employees to successfully run the business. If the business cannot be run at a profit without him, his control becomes meaningless. If the minority stockholder-employees can run the business successfully, the majority stockholder-employee's dependence upon them will make their bargaining position much stronger than their stock ownership would normally allow. Unless they are well compensated for their extra efforts they may move on and leave the disabled majority stockholder with a failing business.

TWIN ISSUES ASSOCIATED WITH DISABILITY

The possible long term disability of a closely held business owner gives rise to two major problems. The first involves the continuation of the disabled owner's salary during the period of his disability. The second involves the disposition of the disabled owner's business interest when it becomes apparent that he is not likely to recover sufficiently to resume his duties with the firm. These issues can be dealt with most satisfactorily through the establishment of express plans prior to the occurrence of a disability. The plans should stipulate how long salary payments of a disabled owner are to be continued, either in whole or in part; and, set out the circumstances that will trigger a buy-out of the business interest of the disabled owner by the firm itself or by his co-owners. Advance knowledge concerning the continuation of his income and the disposition of his business interest if he should become disabled allows each business owner to plan for the eventuality of a disability. He can compare his income needs as he sees them in the event he becomes disabled with the sources of income that would be available at that time. If it appears there would be an income deficiency he can take the steps necessary to eliminate it, such as the purchase of additional personal disability income insurance.

WHAT CONSTITUTES A SALARY CONTINUATION PLAN

A "salary continuation plan" may exist as a separate document, or where it covers only owner-employees it may be incorporated into the disability buy-sell agreement. Generally, salary continuation payments will be made for at least the period of time from the inception of a disability until a buy-out of the disabled owner's business interest takes place. Under the Federal income tax laws a "salary (wage) continuation plan" (the terms "salary" and "wage" are used here interchangeably) is entitled to favorable tax treatment. Therefore, it is important to understand what constitutes a "salary continuation plan."

A salary continuation plan is a form of accident or health plan under which salary, or payments in lieu of salary, are paid to an employee for a period during which he is absent from work on account of a personal injury or sickness. A plan may cover one or more employees, and there may be different plans for different employees or classes of employees. There is no one model plan for all purposes. Specimen plans are available from such sources as life insurance companies and banks. They may be either insured or non-insured, and it is not necessary that the plan be in writing. The employee's rights to benefits under the plan need not be enforceable. However, if the employee's rights are not enforceable, an amount will be deemed to be received under a plan only if: (1) on the date the employee became sick or injured, the employee was covered by a plan (or program, policy, or custom having the effect of a plan) providing for the payment of amounts to the employee in the event of personal injuries or sickness, and (2) notice or knowledge of such plan was reasonably available to the employee. It is immaterial who makes payment of the benefits provided by the plan. For example, payments may be made by the employer, an association of employers or employees, or by an insurance company.[2] Some of the elements that comprise a "salary continuation plan" are deserving of closer scrutiny.

Payment of benefits must be to an "employee." To qualify for favorable tax treatment benefits under a "salary continuation plan" must be paid to an employee. Thus, although a partnership or sole proprietorship may establish a salary continuation plan, any benefits paid under the plan to a partner or to the sole proprietor will not qualify for favorable tax treatment. This is because a partner or sole proprietor is treated as a self-employed individual and not as an employee for this purpose.[3] On the other hand, an employee of a corporation who is also a stockholder of that corporation is treated as an employee. The employee-employer relationship must exist not only at the inception of a disability but as long as salary continuation payments are being made. Therefore, only salary continuation payments attributable to periods during which the employee would be at work were it not for a personal injury or sickness are considered as received under a salary continuation plan. Any payments received by an employee who would not be expected to be at work because he has reached retirement age would no longer qualify as payments made under a salary continuation plan.[4] Payments received by a disabled stockholder-employee after his interest in the business is sold may lose their favorable income tax treatment. This will be so unless it can be shown that such payments are not received in return for his business interest and he is still an employee of the business who would be expected to come to work if he were not disabled, even though he is no longer a stockholder.

---

[2]Regs. Secs. 1.105-4(a)(2)(i) and 1.105-5(a).

[3]Reg. Sec. 1.105-5(b).

[4]Reg. Sec. 1.105-4(a)(3)(i)(a)—however, a Federal court of appeals has held that if the employee was eligible for early retirement based on his years of service at the time he was forced to retire because of his disability, any payments he receives prior to reaching the firm's mandatory retirement age will still be treated as amounts received under a salary continuation plan. *Brooks v. U.S. Ct. of Apps.*, 6th Cir., No. 72-1457, (2/8/73); contra, *Walsh v. U.S.*, 322 F. Supp. 613.

A plan designed to benefit "employees." The Treasury Regulations state that "a plan may cover one or more employees, and there may be different plans for different employees or classes of employees."[5] Based on this statement it generally is assumed that a salary continuation plan can discriminate with respect to the employees that are covered and benefits provided covered employees. Despite this apparent license to discriminate, the Internal Revenue Service has attempted to deny "plan" status in certain cases where the only employees covered were stockholder-employees. The Service seems to be promoting the view that where a plan covers only stockholder-employees this fact of discrimination should be taken into account in determining whether a salary continuation plan has been established for the benefit of employees in their capacity as stockholders rather than as employees. This view was upheld by the Tax Court in the *Larkin* case.[6] In that case a corporation established an alleged plan providing medical reimbursement. No insurance was involved and benefits were paid subject to the discretion of the two stockholder-employees. In fact, with only one exception, benefit payments were made only to the stockholder-employees and their dependents. Based on the facts, the Tax Court held that no "plan" for tax purposes existed because the purpose of the alleged plan was not to benefit employees but to benefit stockholders and their relatives and only incidentally to benefit employees. Factors that influenced the court in reaching its decision included its findings that benefits were not related to the performance of services and there was no limitation on the amount of benefits.

Subsequently, in the *Bogene* case,[7] on somewhat different facts, the Service was rebuffed by the Tax Court when it argued that there was not a "plan for employees" because plan coverage was limited to stockholder-employees. Here the corporation adopted a plan by board resolution providing that all medical expenses of its two stockholder-employees and their dependents would be paid by the corporation. The corporation employed fifty people. Although the plan was not in writing, its existence was recorded in the corporate minutes. In addition, the plan was specific as to the employees who were covered and the benefits that would be payable. Furthermore, the stockholder-employees who were covered knew of the existence of the alleged plan. Based on these facts the court found that the purpose of the plan was to benefit a class of employees and not merely to benefit stockholders. The result in the *Bogene* case seems to indicate that discrimination in coverage under a "salary continuation plan" that takes the form of limiting coverage to stockholder-employees will not *per se* require the

---

[5]Reg. Sec. 1.105-5(a).

[6]Alan B. Larkin, 48 T.C. 629, Affirmed 394 F. 2d 494 First Circuit, 1968.

[7]Bogene Inc. T.C. Memo 1968-147.

conclusion that a plan for the benefit of employees which qualifies for favorable tax treatment does not exist.

It appears from these cases that a salary continuation plan that benefits only stockholder-employees could, under proper circumstances, withstand an attack by the Internal Revenue Service. The issue could probably be avoided entirely if the class of covered participants is worded so that it could include nonstockholder-employees, if they meet the class requirements. This would especially be true if the plan expressly states who the covered employees are and the extent of the benefits to be provided. Although the Treasury Regulations do not require that the plan be in writing, an employer would be well advised to draft a written document as evidence of the existence of a plan.

A salary continuation plan may be insured or noninsured. The loss of a key man through disability can put more financial strain on a business than the death of a key man. In both cases profits may suffer, credit may be tightened and the costs of hiring a replacement may be incurred. However, where the key man is lost through disability the business may incur the additional expense of having to pay all or a portion of his salary in accordance with its salary continuation plan.

For the benefits payable under a salary continuation plan to receive favorable tax treatment it is not necessary to fund the plan with disability income insurance. The employer is free to self-insure any obligations he may have under the plan. Nevertheless, it is evident that this is an inopportune time to add another financial burden to the firm. It is generally preferable to provide benefits through the use of disability income insurance that will be paid for in installments over the period of time when the disabled key man was an active, healthy contributor to the business.

Another reason to use disability income insurance is to provide a workable definition of disability and an independent third party (the insurance company) to decide for the firm whether an individual's disability entitles him to benefits under the salary continuation plan.

The definition of disability varies in different disability income contracts. Therefore, the firm should be sure that the policies it selects contain the definition which best meets its needs. For example, some policies base disability on the ability of the individual to work in any occupation for which his education and background reasonably fits him. This definition is often found in disability income riders attached to life insurance policies. Where the purpose of the salary continuation plan is to benefit a key employee when he is not able to perform his regular duties with the business, such a definition would be inappropriate. A policy containing a more liberal definition of disability should be sought. An example would be one that paid disability benefits when the individual is unable to work at his own occupation or profession. A popular definition of disability found in many policies combines these two approaches. It provides that benefits will be payable for the first two years (some policies use up to five years) if the individual is unable to work at his own occupation or profession and thereafter if he is unable to work at any reasonably gainful occupation for which he is or may become fitted by education, training, or experience, having due regard for the nature of his previous occupation and for his prior average earnings.

Although one of these definitions of disability could be written into a salary continuation plan that is self-insured, the business owners would still have the problem of determining when that definition was met. To avoid having to make that determination themselves, a self-insured plan may provide that the decision will be made by a specified physician or the concurrence of two or more physicians. This solution still requires the business owners to decide which physicians to use. It also necessitates the payment of fees for their services.

THE TAX TREATMENT OF SALARY CONTINUATION PAYMENTS

Numerous references have been made to the tax favored treatment accorded a salary continuation plan. In order to appreciate the significance of qualifying for "plan" status, it is necessary to compare the tax treatment of salary continuation payments made when there is no plan with those made pursuant to a plan.

INCOME TAX TREATMENT OF SALARY CONTINUATION PAYMENTS MADE BY A CORPORATION

Salary continuation plan without disability income insurance. Salary continuation payments made by a corporation under a salary continuation plan without disability income insurance will be deductible if they are reasonable in amount when taken together with all other forms of compensation provided the employee.[8] Some difficulty may be encountered in meeting the reasonableness test where the disabled employee is a stockholder of the corporation. In such case the benefits may be construed as a constructive dividend and not deductible to the corporation.

Salary continuation payments made pursuant to a plan will be received by the disabled employee as "sick pay." Under the sick pay rules, after the first thirty days of continuous absence from work due to a disability the employee may exclude from taxable income up to a maximum of $100 per week. Any salary continuation payments in excess of $100 per week will be taxable to the employee as ordinary income. During the first thirty days of absence from work if the salary continuation payments exceed 75 percent of the employee's regular pay for a comparable period, the employee must include

---

[8]I.R.C. Sec. 162(a)(1).

in his taxable income the entire amount of the salary continuation payments received for the first thirty days of disability. On the other hand, if the salary continuation payments during the first thirty days do not exceed 75 percent of the disabled employee's regular pay for a comparable period, he may exclude from taxable income up to a maximum of $75 per week for the first thirty days. However, no salary continuation payments for the first seven days of the initial thirty-day period may be excluded from taxable income unless the employee is hospitalized for at least one day at some time during his absence from work.[9]

Without a salary continuation plan and without disability income insurance. Even though no plan exists and there is no disability income insurance, salary continuation payments made by a corporation should be deductible by the corporation if they are reasonable in amount when taken together with other compensation received by the disabled employee. However, salary continuation payments made to an employee of a corporation qualify for the sick pay exclusion from taxable income only if they are received under a salary continuation plan.[10] Where there is no plan, the entire amount of such benefits will be includible in the taxable income of the employee.

Salary continuation plan with disability income insurance. Where a corporation has established a salary continuation plan funded with disability income insurance, the tax treatment will depend upon whether the right to receive disability income benefits from the insurance company belongs to the insured-employee or to the corporation. If benefits are payable by the insurance company directly to the employee, premium payments made by the corporation will be income tax deductible to it provided they are reasonable in amount when taken together with the insured-employee's other compensation.[11] Furthermore, the insured-employee will not have to include any part of the premium payments in his taxable income.[12] Disability income benefits received by the insured-employee directly from the insurance company under a salary continuation plan will qualify for sick pay tax treatment. Thus, subject to the rules previously discussed for the first thirty-day period of disability, the disabled employee will receive up to $100 per week tax free with any excess subject to ordinary income tax treatment.

Where disability income insurance benefits are payable directly to the corporation pursuant to a salary continuation plan, the benefits will be received tax free by the corporation,[13] but the corporation will not be

---

[9]I.R.C. Sec. 105(d).

[10]I.R.C. Sec. 105(a); Regs. Secs. 1.105-4(a)(1) and 1.105-4(a)(2)(i).

[11]I.R.C. Sec. 162(a); Reg. Sec. 1.162-10(a).

[12]I.R.C. Sec. 106.

[13]I.R.C. Sec. 104(a)(3); Rev. Rul. 66-262, 1966-2 CB 105.

permitted to deduct its premium payments.[14] Any salary continuation payments made by the corporation to the insured-employee will be income tax deductible to it and taxable to the disabled employee as sick pay.

Without a salary continuation plan but with disability income insurance. Although the existence of disability income insurance is strong evidence that a salary continuation plan exists, it does not guarantee "plan" treatment. Where there is no plan and disability income insurance benefits are payable directly to the employee, any premium payments made by the corporation should be deductible if they meet the reasonableness requirement. Regardless of whether the corporation will be entitled to a deduction, such premium payments will be treated as taxable compensation to the employee used to purchase personally owned disability income insurance. Premiums for individually purchased, personally owned, disability income insurance are not deductible by the insured as a medical expense or otherwise. However, any disability income benefits from such insurance will be received tax free without limit by the insured employee.[15]

Where disability income insurance benefits are payable directly to the corporation without a salary continuation plan, such benefits will be receivable free of income tax by the corporation.[16] Since the disability income benefits are receivable tax free, premiums paid by the corporation are expenses incurred in the acquisition of tax free income. As such, they are not tax deductible.[17] Where the right to receive disability benefits from the insurance company belongs to the corporation, the insured-employee having no interest in the disability income policy, premium payment will not be taxable income to the employee. Subsequent payments of salary continuation to the insured employee by the corporation will be deductible to the corporation subject to the usual caveat that they must be reasonable in amount. Since no plan exists, salary continuation payments received by the employee do not qualify as sick pay. They are therefore fully taxable as ordinary income to the employee.

INCOME TAX TREATMENT OF SALARY CONTINUATION PAYMENTS MADE BY A SOLE PROPRIETORSHIP OR PARTNERSHIP

For non-owner employees. Salary continuation benefits provided by a sole proprietorship or partnership for an employee who has no ownership interest in the business are treated for tax purposes in the same manner as salary continuation benefits provided by a corporation for its employees. For further details see the previous discussions under the general heading "Income

---

[14]I.R.C. Sec. 265(1).

[15]I.R.C. Sec. 104(a)(3).

[16]Supra footnote 13.

[17]Supra footnote 14.

Tax Treatment of Salary Continuation Payments Made By a Corporation."

For owner-employees. A sole proprietor or partner is not considered an employee for salary continuation plan purposes. Therefore, the fact that the firm has a salary continuation plan does not affect the tax treatment of an owner-employee. Where there is no disability income insurance a sole proprietor merely continues to include in his taxable income the net profits of the proprietorship. In a partnership, if a partner receives guaranteed salary continuation payments during a period of disability, they are regarded as the disabled partner's distributive share of taxable ordinary income of the partnership. Such payments are not treated as sick pay made to an employee under a salary continuation plan.

The purchase of disability income insurance by a sole proprietor for himself or by a partnership for a partner does not alter the rule that sole proprietors and partners are self-employed individuals and not employees for the purpose of participating on a tax favored basis in a salary continuation plan. Where disability income benefits are payable by the insurance company directly to a sole proprietor or to a partner, the rules applicable to personally owned disability income insurance apply. Thus, premiums paid on disability income insurance for a sole proprietor or a partner, even though paid from business funds, cannot be deducted as a business expense or otherwise. However, benefits will be receivable free of income tax without limit. In a partnership it is also possible to have disability income insurance benefits for a partner paid directly to the partnership as beneficiary. Where this is done any benefits should be received tax free by the partnership. However, if the partnership then makes salary continuation payments to the disabled partner, they may be taxable to him as guaranteed income.[18] This may be true at least to the extent such payments exceed his proportionate share of the tax-free disability income benefits received by the partnership. Premiums paid by a partnership for disability income insurance on a partner are not deductible regardless of whether the insurance benefits are payable directly to the partner or to the partnership. Therefore, it is obviously preferable from a tax standpoint to have such benefits payable directly to the partner so that they may be received by him free of income tax.

ADDITIONAL TAX CONSEQUENCES OF A
SALARY CONTINUATION PLAN

Disability income payments received by an employee under a salary continuation plan are not subject to social security taxes.[19] In addition, no withholding tax is required with respect to disability income payments made to an employee under this plan to the extent that such payments are

---

[18]Reg. Sec. 1.707-1(c).

[19]I.R.C. Secs. 3101(a) and 3121(a)(2).

excludable from the gross income of the employee under the rules applicable to sick pay.[20]

SPLIT-PREMIUM DISABILITY INCOME PLAN

Where an employee has substantial income from sources other than his salary he may prefer to receive any disability income benefits income tax free even if it means he cannot exclude all the disability income insurance premiums from his taxable income. In such case, maximum tax benefits can be provided by having the employer and the employee each pay a portion of the premium for the disability income insurance with all of the benefits payable directly to the employee. Specifically, the employer pays that portion of the premium which will be sufficient to purchase a weekly disability income of $100. The premium for any additional disability income coverage desired by the employee will be paid for by the employee. If the disability income benefits paid for by the employer are payable under a salary continuation plan, the entire amount of the disability income benefits will be received income tax free by the employee. In addition, he will not have to include in his taxable income the portion of the premium paid by the employer. The first $100 per week of benefits will be excludable from the employee's taxable income as sick pay. Any excess benefits over $100 per week will be excludable from the employee's taxable income as disability income benefits received under a personally paid for disability income policy. The portion of the premium paid for by the employer is excludable from the employee's taxable income as premiums paid under a salary continuation plan. The premium paid by the employee, however, is not tax deductible. If the employee would rather not pay his share of the premium out of his current income and he has enough control over the employment situation, the employee can request the employer to pay the entire premium and charge the portion that should have been paid by the employee as additional compensation to him. In this case the employee's only out-of-pocket cost will be the additional income tax he must pay on the inclusion in his taxable income of an amount equal to his share of the premium.

PROVISIONS OF A DISABILITY BUY-SELL AGREEMENT

A disability buy-sell agreement may be prepared as a separate document or the necessary provisions may be included in the buy-sell agreement applicable to the death of a business owner. Where a separate document is used many of its provisions will be identical to those that will be found in a buy-sell agreement covering the contingency of death. However, there will be certain provisions which would not be included in the latter agreement. Since the buy-sell agreement covering the contingency of death has already been

---

[20]Reg. Sec. 31.3401(a)-1(b)(8)(ii).

treated in great detail in previous chapters, only those provisions specifically applicable to a buy-out upon disability will now be discussed.

Definition of disability. Where a salary continuation plan is included as part of a disability buy-sell agreement, the same definition of disability that is used to activate the salary continuation provision will normally be used to activate the buy-out provision. What is important is that the parties select a definition of disability that is in keeping with their objective. This may be stated to be the purchase of the interest of a disabled owner-employee who is not likely to be able to perform his regular business duties for a period of time that will seriously impair his ability once again to perform his regular duties even if he could eventually return to work. Almost as important as the definition of disability itself is the establishment of a mechanism by which it will be determined whether an individual has met the definition selected. The most effective way of removing the onus for making that decision from the owners of the business is to fund the agreement with disability income insurance and utilize the definition of disability contained in the policy. Care should be taken, however, that the definition in the policy is in keeping with the objectives of the parties. Furthermore, the agreement should clearly state that this definition will be applicable even if the disability income insurance policy is not in effect at the time a disability occurs. In the latter event, the agreement may provide for a designated physician or concensus of physicians to make the determination of whether the individual has met the definition of disability as stated in the lapsed policy.

Salary continuation payments. Until the time a buy-out of the disabled owner-employee's interest is required, some provision should be made for continuing all or a portion of his salary. Where the salary continuation plan is contained in the buy-sell agreement, it will normally provide for the continuation of all or a portion of the disabled owner-employee's salary from the date of his disability until the time when the buy-out takes place. A salary continuation plan covering owner-employees may exist separate and apart from the disability buy-sell agreement. In such case it may be appropriate for the plan to provide for disability income benefits to continue beyond the time when the buy-out goes into effect. If a stockholder-employee maintains his "employee" status even though he is no longer a stockholder, the receipt of such disability income benefits should qualify as sick pay if made pursuant to a salary continuation plan.

Where a disability buy-sell agreement requires the healthy stockholders to purchase the disabled stockholder's stock (a cross-purchase plan), disability income insurance used to fund the purchase should be paid for and owned by the stockholders on the lives of each other. Despite this arrangement, if the salary continuation payments made to a disabled stockholder-employee prior to the buy-out are to be eligible for tax favored plan treatment they should come from the corporation and not from the healthy co-stockholders. Disability income insurance used to fund the salary continuation plan should be paid for by the corporation and owned either by the corporation or the respective insureds regardless of whether the buy-out is arranged as a cross-purchase or stock redemption.

Time when the buy-out becomes effective. When planning in advance for a disability buy-out, the most difficult decision to reach is an objective determination of the point in time when the buy-out will become mandatory. One way of hedging the making of this decision is to provide that at the end of a stipulated period of time following a disability either the healthy owner-employees have an option to purchase or the disabled owner-employee has an option to sell the business interest in question. However, the use of an optional buy-out provision distorts the benefits of the agreement in favor of the holder of the option. If the healthy owner-employees hold the option they could refuse to exercise it and vote to discontinue salary payments to the disabled owner-employee if doing so would be to their advantage. In that event, the disability optional purchase agreement would be no protection whatsoever for the disabled owner-employee. The situation may be reversed if it is the disabled owner-employee who has the option to sell his interest. This would be the case especially where he owns a controlling interest in the business. He might be content with continuing to receive his salary or forcing the declaration of dividends while not performing his normal business duties. In such case it is the healthy owner-employees who would receive no protection from the disability optional sale agreement.

To avoid the situation where one individual is put in a more or less favorable position than the others in the event of a disability, it is best to provide for a mandatory buy-out after the expiration of some specified period of time following a disability. Where this decision is made before a disability occurs it stands the best chance of being an objective one.

The actual period of time selected will vary among businesses. Useful criteria for reaching a decision are the importance to the business of personal services performed by the owner-employees, the skill involved in carrying out their functions in the business, the difficulty of finding a replacement, the ages of the individuals involved and their interpersonal relationships. The most popular period of time before a buy-out becomes mandatory appears to be two years. It is for this reason that some of the key man disability income policies specially designed for funding a disability buy-sell agreement are geared to a two-year waiting period. However, whatever period of time the parties deem appropriate should be the most important consideration in determining when a buy-out should take place.

Who should be the purchaser, the business or co-owner? In a previous chapter dealing with a buy-out at the death of a business owner, considerable time was spent on the pros and cons of having either the business or the surviving owners be the purchaser. All of the factors raised such as who would have to be the premium payor for any insurance used to fund the agreement, how many insurance policies would have to be purchased, the effects of the attribution rules and the possibility of dividend treatment, the stepped-up income tax basis for the purchaser and the availability to creditors of the monies used to fund the agreement are all also applicable to a determination of who should be the purchaser in the event of a disability buy-out.

When the purchaser under the disability buy-sell agreement is the owner, premium payor and beneficiary of a disability income policy insuring the seller in order to fund the buy-out, the tax consequences associated with the policy will be the same regardless of whether the purchaser is the business or the healthy co-business owner. In both cases premium payments will not be deductible and disability income benefits will be received tax free by the purchaser.[21] When these disability benefits are turned over to the disabled owner-employee they are received by him as payments in exchange for his business interest and are taxed accordingly. If the business is in corporate form, and assuming no constructive dividend treatment, the exchange will be treated as a capital transaction. That portion of the purchase price in excess of the disabled stockholder's cost basis will be taxed as a capital gain in the year of sale unless the transaction qualifies as an "installment sale" based on rules soon to be discussed.

Where the business interest is unincorporated, a portion of the purchase money is considered to be received in exchange for a capital asset and a portion is considered to be received in exchange for ordinary income items such as accounts receivable, substantially appreciated inventory, and good will if the purchaser is the partnership. This ordinary income tax treatment of good will can be avoided even where the purchaser is the partnership by specifically providing in the agreement that a reasonable portion of the purchase price is in exchange for good will. If this is done such portion will be treated as payment received in exchange for a capital asset.[22]

Whether the purchase of a disabled business owner's interest is arranged under a cross-purchase plan or stock redemption (corporation) or entity (partnership) plan will usually depend on what conclusion the parties reach concerning the method of purchase for a buy-out at death.

Valuation of the business interest to be purchased. There are two decisions which must be reached in determining the purchase price for a business interest in the event of a disability. First, the method for arriving at the purchase price; second, the date upon which the valuation will be made. The methods of valuation are the same as those applicable to a buy-out at death.

---

[21] Rev. Rul. 66-262, 1966-2 C.B. 105.

[22] I.R.C. Sec. 741.

A stated purchase price may be used with a provision for resetting the stated amount at periodic intervals usually no greater than one or two years. Another common approach is to select a formula for valuation that automatically adjusts itself with changes in the value of the business.

The date upon which the valuation should be made is a more difficult decision to reach. The obvious choices are either the date upon which the owner-employee first becomes disabled so as to entitle him to salary continuation payments or the date upon which the buy-out of his interest becomes mandatory. Arguments in favor of the earlier date include the fact that once the disabled employee is no longer associated with the business as an active participant he should not be responsible for diminutions in value nor should he benefit from future increases in value. In addition, if the later date is used in combination with a stated purchase price that calls for a re-evaluation between the date that the disability first occurs and the date when the buy-out will become mandatory, a clear conflict of interests will arise. When attempting to revalue the business the parties would know who the likely purchaser will be and who the likely seller will be. When this approach is used with a buy-out at death the parties are always renegotiating the price at a time when no one can be sure who will be the purchaser and who will be the seller so that it will be relatively easy to reach unanimity on a fair price. Such will not be the case if a new price must be arrived at after disability occurs. This is a strong argument for using the date the disability occurs as the valuation date when the stated purchase price method of valuation combined with a periodic re-evaluation is utilized.

Arguments in favor of using the date upon which the buy-out becomes mandatory as the valuation date include the fact that it is not until that date that the disabled owner-employee becomes obligated to sell and his co-owners become obligated to buy. If the value of the business has fluctuated considerably, either up or down, from the date of disability to the date the buy-out becomes mandatory and the earlier date is used, the business interest will exchange hands at a price which may be much lower or much higher than the interest is actually worth on the date of the transfer. This is particularly true where a formula for valuation that automatically adjusts itself is used.

Once the parties decide whether or not they want a disabled owner-employee to share in any increase or decrease in value of the business between the time of his disability and the time a buy-out becomes mandatory, they can then pick the method of valuation that will work best with the valuation date they have selected. This would appear to be the stated purchase price method if the date upon which the disability occurs is selected as the valuation date and the formula method if the date upon which the disability becomes mandatory is selected as the valuation date.

SOURCE OF FUNDS TO FINANCE A DISABILITY BUY-OUT

Sources other than insurance. It is possible to fund a disability buy-out without the use of disability income insurance. However, the various alternatives all have shortcomings which can be overcome in whole or in part through the use of disability income insurance. The simplest arrangement would be to pay for the disabled business owner's interest out of future income. However, this requires the disabled owner to rely solely on the future success of the business as the primary source of funds with which to pay for his interest starting at a time when the business may not yet have found an adequate replacement for him. Another alternative would be for the business to establish a sinking fund prior to the time a disability occurs to accumulate sufficient funds to purchase the interest of a disabled owner. The obvious problem with this solution is that there is no guarantee when a disability will occur. If there is sufficient time to accumulate an adequate amount, this may be a good solution. However, if a disability occurs soon after the plan is put into effect, the sinking fund will amount to no more than a down-payment and the remaining installments will have to come from future profits. A third possibility is to borrow the money necessary to finance the buy-out. The ability of the business or the healthy owners to make such a loan at a point in time when a key man in the business will no longer be playing an active role is problematical. Even if a loan can be secured, it may require the payment of a substantial rate of interest.

Funding with disability income insurance. There has been one consistent criticism leveled against the use of disability income insurance to fund a disability buy-sell agreement. It is that the amounts of disability income insurance one can purchase within the underwriting limits of the various life insurance companies are too low to adequately fund the typical disability buy-out. Even if the disability insurance benefits would be sufficient, they are typically payable in installments, which requires the buy-out to be made over a number of years.

The reason for the traditionally low limits on the amount of disability income insurance that a company will write is based on the fact that the primary function of a disability income policy is to replace a portion of the disabled insured's income during the period of time when his disability does not permit him to work. Thus, if the net benefits from a disability income policy after taxes were at or near the after-tax value of the insured's lost earnings, there would be little or no financial incentive to "get well." To avoid the potential for malingering, most insurance companies limit the amount of disability income insurance they will sell an individual to 50 or 60 percent of his gross earned income. In addition, most companies also limit the dollar amount they will issue to monthly amounts between $500 and $1,000, although it is now possible to buy non-cancellable disability income policies

paying up to $2,500 per month with benefits to age sixty-five or beyond.[23]
Some insurance companies now recognize that these underwriting requirements are not applicable where disability income insurance is used to fund
the purchase of the business interest of a disabled owner, rather than to
replace his lost earnings. These companies now make available a disability
benefits policy with underwriting limits geared to the value of the insured's
business interest rather than his earnings. For example, one company will
issue an additional $3,000 per month disability insurance with a maximum
benefit period of one year ($36,000 total benefit) where the benefits are to
be used to fund a disability buy-sell agreement. This policy will only be issued
to a business as owner. Furthermore, the beneficiary must be a trustee who is
authorized to use the benefits of the policy only for the purpose of
implementing the buy-sell agreement. The disability must last for one year
before benefits will be payable under this policy. Another company now
makes available a lump sum disability benefit with underwriting limits based
on the value of the insured's business interest. In this case "total disability,"
which is defined as "inability to engage in the insured's own occupation or
employment or any other reasonable occupation or employment available in
the business organization specified in the application for the policy," must
last for two years before the lump sum benefit will be payable. Under this
policy there appears to be no limitations on who the loss payee may be. With
these types of disability benefit policies in addition to the traditional
disability income policies, enough insurance should be available to fully fund
a disability buy-sell agreement for most closely held business interests either
in a lump sum or over a relatively short period of time.

Other sources of funds. Additional dollars can be freed to fund a disability
buy-sell agreement if the waiver of premium benefit is included with the
disability income policy, and any life insurance policy that is purchased to
fund a buy-out at death. Where a disability activates the waiver of premium
benefit, dollars that were previously being spent to pay premiums on
insurance can be used to help meet the payments required under the terms of
the buy-out. Other sources of funds are the guaranteed cash value and any
dividends from the life insurance policy on the life of the now disabled
owner. Where the life insurance policy is being paid for by the insurance
company under the waiver of premium benefit, the guaranteed cash value
which continues to grow during the period of disability can be made available
through a policy loan.

Thanks to more liberal disability income underwriting requirements, the
development of specially designed disability income policies to fund buy-sell
agreements, and the sources mentioned above, it is now possible to ade-

---

[23]Huebner & Black, Jr., Life Insurance 8th Ed. Appleton-Century-Croft, 1969, p.
272.

quately fund through insurance the buy-out of the average-sized closely held business interest in the event of a disability.

LUMP SUM BUY-OUT VS. INSTALLMENT SALE

It may not always be desirable to arrange for a *lump sum* buy-out in the event of a disability. When a buy-out takes place at death, for income tax purposes the estate receives a stepped-up cost basis for the business interest equal to its estate tax value. Where the purchase price in a buy-sell agreement establishes the value of the business interest for estate tax purposes, there will be no taxable gain on a sale at death. However, where a disability buy-out takes place the disabled seller will not receive a step-up in his cost basis for purposes of computing any taxable gain on the sale. Any excess of the purchase price over his cost basis will be taxable all in one year. Where the value of the business has undergone substantial appreciation since the disabled owner first acquired his interest there may be a heavy income tax liability.

It is possible to decrease the tax liability if the transaction qualifies as an "installment sale."[24] In order to qualify as an installment sale, the total amount of purchase money received in the first year may not exceed 30 percent of the selling price. If the transaction does not require the payment of at least 4 percent simple interest on the declining balance, that portion of the selling price that would bring interest payments up to 5 percent compounded semi-annually will be treated as "unstated interest" for tax purposes.[25] Any portion of the selling price which is considered to be unstated interest is not taken into account when determining whether more than 30 percent of the selling price was paid in the first year. For example, if the terms of the sale are $15,000 in the first year and $5,000 each year thereafter for seven years (total selling price $50,000) without interest, the arrangement will not qualify as an installment sale because approximately $6,000 of the $50,000 purchase price will be treated as unstated interest. In order to qualify as an installment sale in this case the maximum amount that should have been paid in the first year is 30 percent of only $44,000 or $13,200.[26]

Where a transaction qualifies as an installment sale any capital gain is prorated over the installment payment period and the seller need include in his taxable income each year only that portion of the year's installment that is considered to be capital gain.[27] This is especially significant for a disability

---

[24] I.R.C. Sec. 453.

[25] Regs. Secs. 1.483-1(c)(1) and (2), and 1.483-1(d)(1) and (2).

[26] Reg. Sec. 1.453-1(b)(2).

[27] Reg. Sec. 1.453-1(b)(1).

buy-out because the disabled seller is likely to be in a sharply reduced income tax bracket for a number of years following his disability.

Where a disability buy-out has qualified for income tax treatment as an installment sale and the seller dies before all of the installments have been paid, any unpaid payments will be treated as "income in respect of a decedent" to the extent of any gain that would have been taxable to the decedent had he received such payments while he was alive.[28] The recipient of these payments will be taxed in the same manner that the deceased would have been taxed if he had received them himself. However, the recipient will be allowed to deduct an amount equal to the increase in estate taxes caused by the inclusion of the "income in respect of a decedent" in the decedent's gross estate from the amount that would otherwise be taxable.

The portion of the unpaid installments that are considered a return of the decedent's cost basis and thus not treated as "income in respect of a decedent" are nevertheless includible at their discounted (present) value in the gross estate of the decedent for Federal estate tax purposes.

DEATH OF DISABLED OWNER BEFORE
FULL PAYMENT FOR HIS INTEREST

The buy-sell agreement should provide for the contingency of the disabled owner dying prior to the receipt of full payment for his interest. Where the agreement is also funded with life insurance it may be appropriate to provide that the unpaid balance of the purchase price will be payable in a single sum from the death proceeds. Any excess death proceeds over the unpaid balance could be used to reimburse the buyer for any prior payments he made. Where there is no life insurance it may be appropriate to provide that any unpaid installments due after the death of the disabled owner will be reduced in amount with the balance paid out over a longer period of time. The reason is the buyer may no longer receive disability income benefits to fund his obligation after the disabled seller dies.

PROVISION IN EVENT OF RECOVERY OF THE DISABLED OWNER
AFTER THE BUY-OUT HAS STARTED

It was stated earlier that the period of time before a buy-out becomes mandatory should be based, at least in part, on when the disabled owner would no longer be able to effectively carry out his functions as an employee even if he should subsequently recover. If this factor was taken into account in establishing the waiting period before a buy-out becomes mandatory, it may be appropriate to provide that the disabled owner cannot come back into the business once the buy-out has started even if he does recover. Of course, if all the parties agree that the recovered owner should be allowed

---

[28]I.R.C. Sec. 691(a)(4).

back into the business, they are free to alter the terms of the buy-sell agreement. Where the buy-out will continue despite a recovery, the agreement might provide for the remaining buy-out period to be extended with the dollar amount of each payment reduced to reflect the fact that the buyer is no longer receiving disability income benefits with which to fund his obligation.

DISPOSITION OF LIFE INSURANCE ON THE DISABLED OWNER AFTER THE BUY-OUT IS COMPLETED

Once the disability buy-out is completed, any life insurance that was purchased to fund a death buy-out will no longer be needed. At this point the life insurance policy on the disabled ex-owner will probably be worth even more than its cash value because of the probable reduction in life expectancy of the disabled insured. Despite this fact an equitable approach might be to allow the disabled insured to purchase the life insurance policy on his life for an amount equal to its interpolated terminal reserve plus any dividends on deposit plus the portion of any premium paid but not yet earned less any loans outstanding.

CONCLUSION

When a business owner has answered in the affirmative concerning a plan for the sale of his business interest at death, he also should be queried as to its disposition in the event of a permanent disability. The coordination in a buy-sell agreement of a plan providing for both contingencies, entered into before the fact, and adequately funded with life insurance and disability income insurance, will make the business and personal future of all those involved more secure.

Chapter 2

KEY MAN INSURANCE

The term "business insurance" encompasses more than insurance used to fund the purchase of a business interest. It may be used to identify any life and health insurance policies that are owned by and payable to a business. Examples include insurance used to fund a salary continuation plan, a nonqualified deferred compensation plan, a disability income plan and insurance purchased to idemnify a business or business owner for an economic loss that will be suffered in the event of the death or permanent disability of the insured. Insurance purchased for this latter purpose is traditionally referred to as key man insurance. The term "key man insurance" is sometimes applied to the other forms of business insurance. However, this chapter will be limited to exploring the characteristics and uses of key man insurance in the traditional sense only.

CHARACTERISTICS OF A KEY MAN

A key man in a business may generally be defined as one whose death, prior to retirement, will have an adverse economic effect on the business, evidenced by a loss of profits or credit standing and the extra expense of hiring a capable replacement.

The characteristics to look for in order to seek out the individuals who meet the definition of key men in a business are many and varied. An objective test is the size of a man's salary. Although taken by itself a high salary is not conclusive of key man status, in most businesses it is an indication that management believes this person to be a valuable asset.

Another important factor is the decision-making powers of the individual.

If his position allows him either to make important managerial decisions himself or exert substantial influence over the management decision making body, he may be thought of as instrumental to the success of the business and thus a key man.

In addition to the "planners," the "doers" can also be key men. That is, those employees who bear direct responsibility for carrying out management directives in the areas of production, sales or otherwise, will often fit the definition of key men. An individual who interacts directly with customers or clients of the business and who, through his personal efforts, has built a "following" is usually a key man. His death may result in loss to the firm of a substantial portion of his "following."

An individual whose presence in the business represents a source of capital, either on a direct basis or through his prestige with banks and other lending institutions, may be a key man. Where banks consistently request a particular individual to co-sign for loans to the business, the death of that individual will surely have an adverse effect on the sources of capital available to the firm.

An individual may be classified as a key man because he possesses a unique talent. Depending on the type of business, he may be an artist, writer, inventor, designer, or quarterback with an uncanny knack of "threading the needle." The common factor in all these examples is the possession of a unique talent which at best would be difficult and costly to replace.

RECOGNIZING THE BUSINESS THAT NEEDS KEY MAN INSURANCE

Key men may be found in all types of businesses, large and small, incorporated and unincorporated, capital oriented and personal service oriented, new and old. However, the need for key man insurance is not the same for all businesses that have key men.

The need for key man insurance to indemnify the business for the loss of a key man will usually be minimal when the business:

1. spreads its management responsibilities among a number of individuals,
2. has a well thought out management training program.
3. has sufficient liquid surplus to meet emergencies, and
4. can borrow money on its own name without the personal guarantee of any of its owners.

The need for key man insurance to indemnify the business for the loss of a key man may be very great indeed when:

1. management of the firm rests in the hands of a chosen few who are dominating factors, either from the standpoint of ownership, management, or both,
2. there is no highly refined management training program to provide back-up management support,

3. a few individuals are doing the work of many,

4. liquid surplus to meet emergencies in virtually nonexistent, and

5. business loans cannot be negotiated without the personal guarantee of one or more of the business owners.

Although most businesses will not possess all of the characteristics of either of the preceding groupings, they will nevertheless tend to fit into one mold or the other. In general, businesses that are likely to have characteristics that allow them to benefit most from the lifetime and death benefits of key man insurance are closely held enterprises in which one or more of the owners are actively engaged in management. On the other hand, with certain exceptions, large publicly held companies will generally possess those characteristics mentioned before that minimize the need for the benefits provided by key man insurance.

ADVERSE CONSEQUENCES ASSOCIATED WITH THE LOSS OF A KEY MAN IN A CLOSELY HELD BUSINESS

When two or more individuals agree to form a business it is usually because they each recognize that by combining their separate resources of money, connections and talents more total profit can be produced than would be the case if each attempted to "go it alone." The death or permanent disability of any one of the active business owners can destroy this synergism that has been created. The reasons for the concomitant loss of profits will depend upon the attributes which the now missing key man brought to the business. Where management skills are lost, the efficiency of the entire business suffers. Results include increased expenses and smaller profit margins, without any offsetting increase in production or sales. Where production skills are lost, the result will be smaller profits because of an increase in unit costs and a decrease in the ability to fill orders. Where sales skills are lost, profits will be less because the unit sales cost will increase. Key man life insurance and disability income insurance purchased by a business can provide the dollars that will offset a decrease in profits caused by the loss of a key man with management, production, or sales skills.

Effect on credit standing. The credit standing of a business may suffer because of the potential, as well as the actual, death of a key man. Suppliers of goods and services may be less likely to provide a business with liberal credit terms where, because of a thin management team, the sudden loss of a key man might disrupt the profitable running of a business. After the death of a key man, trade credit is likely to be tightened even more. The lifetime benefits, as well as the death proceeds, of a key man life insurance policy can help to improve the credit terms available to a business, both during the lifetime of the key man and after his death. Trade creditors can rely on the fact that if the key man should die while amounts are owed to them, cash from the life insurance policy will either be available directly to pay any loans or may be used to maintain the business on an even keel after the death of the key man, so that amounts due creditors can be paid from business earnings.

When a bank is considering making a loan to a business, it looks to such items as the firm's cash position, its management depth and ability, its credit standing, and its potential for profits. Where a business fails to meet bank standards in these categories, if a loan is granted at all, it will be at a relatively high interest rate. In addition, the bank may require the personal guarantee of one or more of the business owners. The maintenance of a permanent key man life insurance policy will improve the cash position and the credit standing of the business during the key man's lifetime. The cash value during lifetime, as well as the potential death proceeds, may be used as collateral for securing a bank loan. In addition, the existence of key man insurance helps to establish that the financial managers of the business are concerned with safety of capital and the long range success of the business. These assurances can lead to less stringent loan terms. For example, the business may be able to secure a loan without the personal guarantee of one or more of the owners; or the bank may be willing to lend money at a better rate where key man insurance has been purchased. Another loan provision that may be avoided by the existence of key man life insurance is the requirement that the balance of any loan outstanding becomes due and payable upon the death of a particular key man. The knowledge that cash will flow into the business upon such death may be sufficient to convince a bank that this provision need not be included in the loan agreement. Where a bank insists upon an owner personally guaranteeing a business loan, and especially where the loan automatically becomes due upon the death of that business owner, the existence of a key man life insurance policy on his life will serve to benefit him personally, as well as to benefit the business. The personal guarantee of the business owner will carry over to his estate. As a contingent debtor of the bank, the estate may have to remain open until the debt is paid. The use of the death proceeds from the key man policy to pay the loan removes this contingent liability from the estate and allows the estate to be settled promptly.

A permanent key man life insurance policy is itself a source of credit. In general, an amount up to the cash value of the policy may be borrowed from the life insurance company at a guaranteed rate of interest. For many years the guaranteed rate of interest was 5 percent. Some life insurance policies issued in the 1970s now contain a 6 percent guaranteed interest rate. In either case, the interest required compares very favorably with the going rate of interest for business loans. In addition, the fact that a policy loan is obtainable upon request and is non-callable, makes it an attractive source of funds.

COST OF REPLACING A KEY MAN

The extraordinary expenses incurred by a business in locating, hiring, and training a replacement for a lost key man can substantially reduce its profits. During the period of time when a replacement is being located, the work of the missing key man may have to be performed by persons ill-equipped to do the job. The hiring of a capable replacement may require the payment of greater compensation than the amount that was being paid to the key man. This is especially true where the key man was an owner-employee willing to accept less than his true worth at present because of the opportunity, as an owner of the business, to make a handsome profit in the future. In any case, the hiring of a new man may require the payment of thousands of dollars in employment agency fees and reimbursement for moving expenses. Even after the replacement is hired it will take him some time before he is able to perform at or near the level of efficiency reached, perhaps over many years, by the key man. The death proceeds of a key man life insurance policy can help to meet these expenses of hiring a new man, as well as offset the loss of profits that may result during the period of time the replacement is acquiring the necessary experience to become a key man himself.

INSURABLE INTEREST IN LIFE OF KEY MAN

If a life insurance policy is purchased by a business or an individual on the life of another person in whom the purchaser does not have an insurable interest, the death proceeds may be treated as taxable income arising from a wagering contract rather than as death proceeds of a life insurance policy that are receivable free of income tax.[1] The question of whether an insurable interest exists in a particular case is a matter of state law. Although the case law and statutes of the various states are not all the same, it is generally held that the purchaser of a life insurance policy has an insurable interest when he has a reasonable expectation of deriving economic benefit from the continuation of the insured's life, or of suffering economic detriment by reason of the insured's death.

The business as purchaser. A business that purchases a key man policy on the life of an individual who is active in the business and whose continued activities are reasonably expected to increase the future profits of the business has an insurable interest because of the economic benefit the business will derive from the continued life of the insured. If the business purchases a key man life insurance policy on the life of an individual whose activities on behalf of the business are instrumental in securing capital or credit for the business or upon whose death an outstanding loan of the business will become callable upon demand, the business can be said to

---

[1] *Atlantic Oil Co. v. Patterson,* 331 F. 2nd 516 (CA-5, 1964).

possess an insurable interest because it will suffer an economic detriment in the event of the death of the insured. This fact is proven by a long line of court decisions.[2] In addition, by statute, a number of states expressly permit a corporation to purchase insurance on the life of an officer or stockholder.

A business owner as purchaser. Where a corporation or partnership has an insurable interest in a key man, each stockholder or partner may also have an insurable interest in that key man in proportion to his ownership interest in the business. This is so regardless of whether the business owner is an individual, a trust or an estate. For example, if a business interest has been transferred in trust for the benefit of the grantor's family, the trust agreement may empower the trustee, in carrying out his duties of protecting trust assets, to purchase insurance on the life of a key executive in the business. A profit-sharing trust is a distinct legal entity and as such can and does have an insurable interest in those key men in the business whose efforts are responsible for the production of profits and whose loss would result in a decrease in profits.

Where a partner is the key man to be insured, his co-partner(s) (rather than the partnership) may want to be owner and beneficiary under the policy. The reason may be to avoid having the deceased partner's estate share in the proceeds in proportion to its partnership interest. Such would be the case if the proceeds were paid to the partnership, unless there existed a buy-sell agreement which called for the sale of the insured-partner's interest at a fixed price stated in the agreement.

The first few years after the formation of a new business in corporate form are often critical to the determination of whether the business will be successful. During this period of time, it is not unusual for a business to operate at a loss. Under these circumstances, any key man insurance that is purchased may be personally owned by and payable to the stockholder-employees (rather than the corporation) so that if the business fails because of the death of a key man, they may recoup their investments without subjecting the death proceeds to the claims of corporation creditors.

After business relationship is terminated. It is held in virtually all states that the requirement of an insurable interest exists only at the time when a life insurance policy is purchased. Thus, where a key man terminates his relationship with a business, the business may continue to pay the premiums for the policy and upon the insured's subsequent death receive the life insurance proceeds income tax free.

Mere existence of a business relationship. Keep in mind that it is the expectance of an economic gain by the continued life, or an economic loss by the death of the insured, which gives rise to an insurable interest, rather than

---

[2]*U.S. v. Supplee-Biddle Hardware Co.*, 265 U.S. 189 (1924); *Wellhouse v. United Paper*, 29 F. 2nd 886 (1929); *McMullen v. St. Lucie Bank* 175 So. 721 (1937).

the mere existence of an employer-employee or other business relationship. This fact is borne out in the *Lakin* case[3] where the court held that an insurable interest does not necessarily arise by virtue of the fact that the owner of the policy and the insured were partners. In that case, the insured had made no financial or capital contribution to the partnership; had no technical knowledge, skill, or ability as a worker or manager to add to the partnership; did not have any experience in the type of work he was to do or in the business of the partnership; and could not be expected to bring any business to the partnership, nor favorably affect the partnership good will. Based on these facts, the courts concluded that no insurable interest existed. This was obviously an extreme case. In most business situations the facts will support the conclusion that an insurable interest does exist.

INCOME TAX CONSEQUENCES OF KEY MAN INSURANCE

Premiums. A business entity will usually be the owner, beneficiary, and premium payor for a key man life insurance policy. Under this arrangement, if the insured is an officer or employee, or a person financially interested in any trade or business carried on by the business entity, no income tax deduction will be allowed for the premium payments.[4]

Even if the business is entitled to receive only a portion of the proceeds, the entire premium will be nondeductible. This is also true where the business is only indirectly a beneficiary under the policy. For example, where a policy is purchased by a corporation as security for a loan to it, with the lender named as beneficiary, no deduction is allowed for premium payments made by the corporation since it indirectly benefits from the policy by having its loan obligation reduced when the proceeds are paid to the lender. This rule has been extended to deny a deduction for premiums if the business has any beneficial interest in the policy, including the right to change the beneficiary, to surrender the policy for cash, or to make policy loans.[5]

In some instances a partner or stockholder may be the owner, premium payor, and beneficiary of a key man policy on the life of a person who, although he is an employee of the partnership or the corporation, is not an employee of the partner or stockholder (the taxpayer) and is not financially interested in the taxpayer's business. Nevertheless, such premium payments would not be deductible because they would not qualify as ordinary and necessary business expenses incurred in a trade or business.[6] Instead, they will be treated as either personal expenses, or expenses attributable to the

[3]*Lakin v. Postal Life & Casualty Co.,* 316 S.W. (2nd) 542 (Mo., 1958).

[4]I.R.C. Sec. 264(a)(1).

[5]Rev. Rul. 66-203, 1966-2 CB 104; Rev. Rul. 70-148, 1970 1 CB 60.

[6]I.R.C. Sec. 162.

acquisition of tax exempt income represented by the death proceeds. In either case, the premiums will not be deductible.[7]

The nondeductible income tax treatment accorded key man life insurance premiums is counterbalanced by the fact that the premiums are not treated as taxable income to the insured. This is the case even when the insured is controlling stockholder of a corporation that is owner, beneficiary, and premium payor of the policy.[8]

Proceeds. The same rules applicable to the income taxation of the proceeds of a personal life insurance policy also apply to the proceeds of a key man policy. Thus, in most cases, any life insurance death proceeds will be free of income taxation, regardless of whether the beneficiary is an individual or a business entity.[9] Where the proceeds of a life insurance policy are paid to a corporation as beneficiary, the proceeds lose their identity as life insurance after such payment. Therefore, the income tax exemption accorded the death proceeds of life insurance when received by a corporation is not applicable where the proceeds are subsequently distributed to stockholders.[10] Instead, such a secondary distribution is taxed to the stockholders as a dividend to the extent of the earnings and profits available for the payment of dividends. The result is ordinary income taxation to the stockholders with no deduction allowed the corporation. Even if the corporation has selected to be taxed as a Subchapter S corporation, the life insurance death proceeds it receives do not retain their tax free character when distributed to the stockholders. Instead, any distribution of such proceeds to the stockholders will be taxed as a dividend. Note that although the receipt of life insurance death proceeds in excess of premiums paid increases the current earnings and profits of a corporation, it does not increase its taxable income. Thus, regardless of whether the corporation has elected Subchapter S tax treatment, the stockholders will not be taxed on the death proceeds unless and until they are distributed from the corporation to the stockholders.

Unlike a corporation, a partnership acts merely as a conduit for income tax purposes with any taxable income of the partnership taxable directly to the partners, regardless of whether such income is distributed or not. Although this tax treatment is similar to that accorded a Subchapter S corporation, unlike the latter, life insurance death proceeds received by a partnership do retain their tax exempt status when passed on by the partnership to the individual partners.

Transfer for value. In most instances a key man policy will be purchased by a business directly from an insurance company. In some cases, however, an

---

[7]I.R.C. Secs. 262, 265(1).

[8]*Casale v. Comm.,* 247 F. 2d 440 (1957); Rev. Rul. 59-184, 1959-1 CB 65.

[9]I.R.C. Sec. 101(a).

[10]Rev. Rul. 71-79, IRB No. 1971-7 (2/16/71).

existing policy may be acquired from an individual or another business in exchange for valuable consideration. Under these circumstances, the death proceeds will be subject to income taxation to the extent that they exceed the sum of the original consideration paid upon the transfer plus the net premiums paid subsequent to the transfer, unless the transfer meets the requirements of one of the express exceptions to this rule.[11]

One set of exceptions to the "transfer for value" rule is based on the relationship which the insured bears to the transferee. If a life insurance policy is transferred for value to the insured, to a partner of the insured, to a partnership in which the insured is a partner, or to a corporation in which the insured is a shareholder or officer, despite the fact that the policy was transferred for value, the death proceeds will be receivable by the transferee entirely free of income tax.[12] Conspicuous by its absence from this list of safe transfers is a transfer for value to a co-shareholder of the insured. Although the omission of an exception for a transfer to a co-shareholder of the insured is aimed at public corporations, it is equally applicable to co-shareholders in a closely held corporation.

This set of exceptions to the transfer for value rule permits the transfer of an in-force policy to a partnership or to a corporation for use as a key man policy, if the insured is either a partner of the partnership or a shareholder or officer of the corporation. However, if the insured is merely an employee of either business entity, no exception will be applicable and the proceeds in excess of the sum of the consideration paid for the policy at the time of the transfer plus any additional net premiums paid will be subject to ordinary income taxation.

Note that where there is more than one transfer, the applicability of one of the "relationship to the insured" exceptions to the transfer for value rule is controlled by the final transfer. For example, if a shareholder transfers for value a policy of insurance on his life to a co-shareholder, such transfer would not come within one of the exceptions to the transfer for value rule. If the insured died while the co-shareholder owned the policy, a portion of the proceeds would be subject to ordinary income taxation. However, if prior to the death of the insured, the co-shareholder transfers the policy to a corporation of which the insured is a shareholder and the insured then dies, the final transfer would come within one of the exceptions to the transfer for value rule. Therefore, the corporation would receive the proceeds entirely free of income taxation.[13]

An example of an in-force policy that might be transferred to a partnership or corporation to serve as key man insurance is one that was originally

---

[11] I.R.C. Sec. 101(a)(2).

[12] I.R.C. Sec. 101(a)(2)(B).

[13] Reg. Sec. 1.101-1(b)(3)(ii).

purchased to fund a cross-purchase buy-sell agreement. After the death of the first to die of the business owners, his estate will still own the life insurance purchased on the life of the surviving business owner. If the surviving business owner does not want to purchase this policy for personal use, it may be good planning to have the business purchase the policy to serve as key man insurance.

Another exception to the transfer for value rule permits the death proceeds to be free of income taxation if the policy has a basis for determining gain or loss for income tax purposes in the hands of the business (transferee) that is determined in whole or in part by reference to the basis, for income tax purposes, of such policy in the hands of the transferor.[14] This exception to the transfer for value rule may be applicable to a partnership that owns a key man policy and decides to incorporate. If the assets of the partnership, including the life insurance policy, are transferred to the new corporation by the partners who, immediately after the transfer, own at least 80 percent of the voting power of voting stock and at least 80 percent of the total shares of other classes of stock, the transfer will qualify as a tax free exchange and the basis for the life insurance policy in the hands of the corporation will be the same as it was in the hands of the partnership.[15] The same result regarding the application of the transfer for value rule would be reached where an existing corporation transfers a key man life insurance policy, along with its other assets, to another corporation in return for stock or securities in such other corporation as part of a tax free reorganization.[16]

Note, however, that even though the final transfer for value meets the "carry over basis" exception, if there was a previous transfer for value which does not meet any of the exceptions to the rule, the amount of death proceeds which will be excludable from the taxable income of the final transferee will be limited to the sum of the amount which would have been excludable by the previous transferee if the final transfer had not taken place plus any net premiums paid by the final transferee.[17] For example, assume that a corporation purchases an existing policy on the life of a key employee who is neither a shareholder or officer of the corporation. Subsequently, the policy is transferred to another corporation as part of a tax free reorganization. Despite the fact that this last transfer falls within the "carry over basis" exception to the transfer for value rule, if the insured then dies, the proceeds in excess of the sum of what the first corporation originally paid for the policy plus the premiums paid by both corporations will be taxable income.

---

[14] I.R.C. Sec. 101(a)(2)(A).

[15] I.R.C. Sec. 351(a).

[16] I.R.C. Sec. 354(a)(1).

[17] Reg. Sec. 1.101(b)(3)(iii).

ACCUMULATED EARNINGS TAX

The accumulated earnings tax, which was discussed in some detail earlier (see pages 353 to 360), is a penalty tax levied upon current taxable income of a corporation that is accumulated beyond its reasonable needs rather than being paid out as dividends.[18] However, even without demonstrating a reasonable business need, accumulations of current taxable income will not be subject to the accumulated earnings tax to the extent that, when taken together with earnings and profits accumulated in prior years, the sum does not exceed $100,000. To the extent that there is accumulated taxable income as defined in Internal Revenue Code Section 535, after taking into account the $100,000 credit, it will be subject to the accumulated earnings tax unless it can be shown that such accumulation is required for the reasonable needs of the business.

Effect on key man insurance. Since premiums paid by a corporation on key man life insurance are not deductible for income tax purposes, the dollar amount of each year's premium must be taken into account in arriving at a determination of the corporation's accumulated taxable income for a given year. Where the accumulated earnings and profits of the corporation exceed the minimum credit of $~~100,000~~ *150,000*, the key man life insurance premium paid in the tax year in question will be subject to the accumulated earnings tax, if levied, unless it can be shown that the life insurance purchase was for the reasonable needs of the business.

The death proceeds of a key man life insurance policy are receivable by a corporation free of income tax. As such, the proceeds are not a part of the corporation's accumulated taxable income and hence will in no event be subject to the accumulated earnings tax. However, earnings and profits of the corporation will be increased by the excess of such life insurance proceeds over the net premiums paid.[19] If accumulated, they will be taken into account in determining whether the earnings and profits of the corporation exceed the $100,000 minimum credit allowable.

In general, where a corporation accumulates taxable income in the form of premium payments on a key man life insurance policy purchased to indemnify the corporation for the loss of services of the insured in the event of his death, such purchase will be considered to meet a reasonable business need so that the earnings used to pay premiums will not be subject to the accumulated earnings tax.[20] For a discussion of the *Emeloid* case, frequently cited to support this conclusion, see pages 354 to 355.

---

[18] I.R.C. Sec. 531.

[19] Rev. Rul. 54-230, 1954-1 CB 114.

[20] *Harry A. Koch Co. v. Vinal,* 228 F. Supp. 783 (1964); *Bradford Robinson Printing Co.,* 1 AFTR 2d 1278 (1957); *Emeloid Co. v. Comm.,* 189 F.2d 230 (1951).

To meet the reasonable business needs test, insurance purchased to indemnify a corporation for the loss of the services of a key man should not exceed an amount which represents the reasonably anticipated needs of the corporation that will arise as a result of the death of the key man. To some extent the life insurance company will prevent a corporation from purchasing more key man insurance than it needs by refusing to underwrite the risk for coverage that exceeds the value of the corporation's insurable interest in the key man.

The type of life insurance purchased should also reflect the needs of the corporation. Where the purpose of the insurance is to indemnify the corporation at the death of the insured, rather than to accumulate a cash fund, the coverage should probably not be in the form of an endowment policy or other high cash value policy. Instead, the insurance should be one of the types such as whole life insurance or term insurance, in which the bulk of the premiums go towards providing a death benefit rather than the accumulation of cash values.

SURRENDER OR SALE OF KEY MAN LIFE INSURANCE

Where an insured key man terminates his relationship with the corporation (or other business entity), the firm has several alternatives when it comes to the disposition of the life insurance policy. Despite the fact that the insured is no longer associated with the firm, it could continue to pay premiums and at the death of the insured receive the life insurance proceeds free of income tax. Instead, it may be determined that the best course of action is to surrender the policy to the insurance company for its cash surrender value. Where the insured is in need of additional personal life insurance protection, it may be best to have the firm sell the policy to him.

Income tax consequences. Where the policy is either surrendered or sold, the question of the income tax treatment of the firm arises. If the amount received by the firm upon surrender or sale of the policy exceeds its net premium cost, such excess will be taxable to the firm as ordinary income in that year.[21] Where there is a *gain* on the transaction, it is permissible to include the portion of each premium payment that went towards providing current life insurance protection when computing the net premium cost.[22] One might assume that if a key man life insurance policy is surrendered or sold at a loss, such loss would be deductible for income tax purposes as one incurred in connection with the taxpayer's trade or business.[23] However, in most cases there will be no deductible loss even where the cash surrender value is less than aggregate net premiums paid. This is because the portion of

---

[21] I.R.C. Sec. 72(e).

[22] I.R.C. Sec. 72(e)(1)(B).

[23] I.R.C. Sec. 165.

aggregate premiums paid that is attributable to the cost of life insurance protection may not be taken into account in determining net premium cost where a *loss* will result. The cases that have dealt with this issue hold that this portion of the aggregate premiums is not a recoverable investment, but a nondeductible expense.[24]

ESTATE TAX CONSEQUENCES

Under the Federal estate tax law the death proceeds of a life insurance policy will be includable in the gross estate of the insured if: (1) the proceeds are payable to or for the benefit of the insured's estate, or (2) the insured, at the time of his death, possessed any incidents of ownership in the policy, regardless of the beneficiary.[25] The term "incidents of ownership" as used here is not limited in its meaning to ownership of the policy in the technical legal sense. Generally speaking, the term has reference to the right of the insured or his estate to the economic benefits of the policy. Thus, it includes among other powers the power to change the beneficiary, to surrender or cancel the policy, to assign the policy, to revoke an assignment, to pledge the policy for a loan, or to obtain from the insurer a loan against the surrender value of the policy.[26]

Where a key man policy is properly arranged, a business or, in some instances, a business owner, will be owner and beneficiary of the policy with the insured possessing no incidents of ownership therein. Under these circumstances, no portion of the proceeds should be includible in the insured's gross estate for Federal estate tax purposes.

Stockholder-employee as key man. Where the insured, under a key man life insurance policy, also is a stockholder in the corporation which owns the policy, the additional issue arises as to whether the insured may be deemed to possess incidents of ownership in the policy by virtue of his stock ownership. Until October of 1971, the Internal Revenue Service took the position, in its regulations, that only where the insured was the sole stockholder of a corporation which had the power to change the beneficiary on a policy of insurance on his life, would the insured be considered to possess an incident of ownership in the policy so that its proceeds would be includable in his gross estate for Federal estate tax purposes.[27] In October of 1971, the Internal Revenue Service issued Revenue Ruling 71-463, which extended the "sole ownership" rule to a majority stockholder-insured who had the power, through his stock ownership, to exercise the incidents of ownership in the

---

[24]*London Shoe Co., Inc. v. Comm.*, 80 F 2d 230, Cert denied 298 U.S. 663; *Keystone Consolidated Publishing Co.*, 26 BTA 1210.

[25]I.R.C. Sec. 2042.

[26]Reg. Sec. 20.2042-1(a)(2).

[27]Reg. Sec. 20. 2042-1(c)(2).

policy on his life that are possessed by the corporation.[28] However, the Service soon had second thoughts on the matter. The response was the issuance of another revenue ruling in which the Service announced its withdrawal of Revenue Ruling 71-463 and stated that it would also reconsider its position on a sole stockholder-insured as well.[29] In August of 1972, the Internal Revenue Service expressed its latest thinking on this matter when it issued new *proposed* regulations dealing with the treatment of corporate owned life insurance where the insured is a stockholder.

In place of the present language in the regulations which attribute incidents of ownership to a sole stockholder, the proposed regulation, if adopted, would provide that where the economic benefits of a life insurance policy on the insured's life are reserved to a corporation, of which the insured is the sole or controlling stockholder, the corporation's incidents of ownership will not be attributed to the insured through his stock ownership to the extent the proceeds of the policy are payable to the corporation. Any proceeds payable to a third party for a valid business purpose, such as in satisfaction of a business debt of the corporation, so that the net worth of the corporation is increased by the amount of such proceeds, will be deemed to be payable to the corporation. If any part of the proceeds of the policy are not payable to or for the benefit of the corporation, and, thus, are not taken into account in valuing the insured's stockholdings in the corporation, any incidents of ownership held by the corporation as to that part of the proceeds will be attributed to the insured through his stock ownership where the insured is the sole or controlling stockholder. The insured will not be deemed to be the controlling stockholder unless he is the majority stockholder of the corporation. The insured will be considered to be a majority stockholder if he has *actual* legal or equitable ownership of stock possessing more than 50 percent of the total combined voting power of the corporation.

Thus, it appears that under the proposed regulation, if a corporation owns a life insurance policy on the life of a majority stockholder and the proceeds are payable to the insured's wife, the incidents of ownership held by the corporation will be attributed to the insured through his stock ownership and the proceeds will be includible in the insured's gross estate for Federal estate tax purposes. However, where the policy proceeds are payable in part to the insured's wife and in part to the corporation, only the portion of the proceeds payable to his wife would be includible in the insured's gross estate.[30]

As part of its new approach to this matter, the Service also issued a proposed regulation dealing with the valuing of unlisted stock for estate tax

---

[28] Rev. Rul. 71-463, IRB No. 1971-42 (10/18/71).

[29] Rev. Rul. 72-167, IRB No. 1972-15 (4/10/72).

[30] Proposed Reg. Sec. 20.2042-1(c)(2).

purposes. In spelling out the relevant factors to be considered when determining the value of unlisted stock for Federal estate tax purposes, the proposed regulation specifically provides for consideration to be given to nonoperating assets, including life insurance policies owned by or payable to the corporation.[31] Although the value of life insurance policies owned by a corporation have been taken into account before in valuing its stock, the regulations did not expressly provide for such consideration.

If the proposed regulations are adopted, even a sole stockholder may be insured under a key man policy owned by and payable to the corporation, without the proceeds being directly includible in his gross estate. However, where a decedent owned stock in a corporation that owned a key man life insurance policy on his life, the proceeds of the policy will be taken into account in valuing his stock for estate tax purposes. Note, however, that the value of the key man policy will not have an effect on the value of the deceased insured's stock where such stock is sold under the terms of a properly drawn buy-sell agreement that pegs the value of the stock at the purchase price in the agreement for Federal estate tax purposes.

It may also be possible to negate the increase in value of a key man's stock due to the receipt of key man life insurance proceeds by demonstrating that the value of the corporation has been reduced by a like amount due to the death of the key man. However, the loss sustained by a corporation as a result of the death of a key man is not assumed, but must be proved.[32] Although self-serving declarations will not be determinative of the issue, they may be helpful in establishing that the loss of the insured's services have resulted in economic loss to the corporation. Thus, at the time of the purchase of key man life insurance, a resolution should be adopted by the board of directors authorizing the purchase and stating that the purpose for acquiring the insurance is to offset an anticipated economic loss to the corporation at the death of the insured.

Partner as key man. There are no regulations or revenue rulings dealing specifically with the estate tax treatment of a key man life insurance policy on the life of a partner that is owned by and payable to the partnership. However, where this issue has come before the courts it has been held that a partnership is a separate legal entity distinguishable from the individual partners, so that incidents of ownership in a life insurance policy possessed by a partnership should not be attributable to the partners.[33] Thus, where a life insurance policy on the life of a partner is owned by and payable to the partnership and all premium payments are paid out of partnership funds, the

---

[31] Proposed Reg. Sec. 20.231-2(f).

[32] *Newell v. Comm.* 66 F. 2d 102; Rev. Rul. 59-60 1959-1, CB 237.

[33] *Estate of Frank H. Knipp*, 25 TC 153 (1955), Acq. 1959-1 CB 4.

death proceeds should not be includible as such in the insured's gross estate. However, the proceeds received by the partnership will be included as a partnership asset when valuing the insured partner's interest in the partnership for Federal estate tax purposes, unless there is a properly drawn buy-sell agreement in effect which pegs the value of the insured partner's interest at the purchase price for Federal estate tax purposes.

PLACING A DOLLAR VALUE ON A KEY MAN

Once the decision to purchase key man life insurance has been reached, the question becomes how much insurance should be purchased on the key man's life. Since the primary purpose of key man life insurance is to indemnify the business for the economic loss it will suffer as a result of the death of the key man, it is the value of this loss which should determine the dollar amount of insurance purchased. Note that what must be measured is not the intrinsic worth of the key man, that is, what his services are worth in the job market, but the value of the key man in its totality to the business in question. How this will be done may range from a "gut" reaction by the firm's decision-making body, to the utilization of a highly sophisticated formula in an attempt to arrive at an objective decision for what is basically a subjective problem.

Depending on what services the key man renders to the business, it may be possible to identify certain criteria that will provide a fair estimate of the share of the annual earnings of the business that are attributable to the efforts of the key man. For example, if a person is designated a key man because he is heading up a special project whose success is dependent upon his services, the potential investment which may be lost if the project has to be abandoned will be an important factor in determining his value. If the key man is a salesman, the net value of the business which he produces would be a good indication of his value to the firm. If the personal contacts of the key man are responsible for attracting customers to the firm, the net value of the business attributable to these customers would be an important valuation factor. In most cases, however, the key man will be a member of top management and it will not be possible to single out any particular portion of the earnings of the business which can be attributable directly to his services.

Use of a formula. When the key man is a member of top management, whose decisions cut across all areas of the business so that he may be thought of as responsible in part for all the earnings of the business, his worth may be determined by first placing a value on the entire top management's contributions to earnings and then determining what portion of this figure should be attributed to the key man. This method works best when dealing with a closely held business in which the key man is an owner-manager of the business. Following is a description of a formula that employs this technique. Begin with the average annual net earnings of the business over the past five years. For this purpose, "average annual net earnings" is defined as total salaries paid to all owner-managers plus any amount added to earned surplus plus any amount paid in dividends. From this figure two items are subtracted. The first is the total estimated replacement salaries that would be required to hire individuals to perform the routine duties of all the owner-managers. The second is the annual income which would be produced if the net worth of the business were invested at a given interest rate, such as 6 percent. After subtracting "replacement salaries" and "interest on net worth" from "annual net earnings," the amount remaining may be thought of as the annual net earnings attributable to the expertise of the top management team. The next step is to determine what fraction of this amount should be attributable to the owner-manager who is to be insured. This is a decision which will have to be made by the management team itself. The final step is to determine the number of years it will take for an inexperienced replacement to contribute to annual net earnings in the same amount as the key man. A typical number of years that may be used might range anywhere from two to seven. The value of the key man is arrived at by multiplying the number of years selected by the fractional share of annual net earnings attributable to management expertise that is apportioned to the key man. Here is an example of how this formula works:

1. Average annual net earnings of the business over the last five years (total salaries paid to all owner-managers + amount added to earned surplus + amount of dividends paid) $220,000

Less: 2. Estimated replacement salaries to perform routine duties (for all owner-managers) $130,000

3. Earnings on net worth of $200,000 at 6%. 12,000

4. Annual net earnings attributable to management Expertise [(1) - (2 + 3)] 78,000

5. Fraction of annual net earnings due to management expertise attributable to key man who is to be insured (assume 1/3). 26,000

6. Dollar amount of (5) above x number of years before replacement can contribute to annual net earnings to the same degree as key man to be insured (assume 5 years) = value of key man . . . . 130,000[34]

Valuations arrived at through the use of formulas such as the preceding one are almost always dependent upon certain subjective assumptions. In this case, replacement salaries, earnings on net worth, and the number of years required to completely replace the key man all must be assumed. However, the firm's decision makers are usually in a position that permits them to make fairly

---

[34]To arrive at an even more accurate valuation it may be appropriate to reduce this figure by an amount assumed to be the contribution to annual net earnings of the replacement during the portion of the five year period he is on the job.

accurate estimates in these areas. At the very least, such formulas serve as a useful guide for arriving at a sound figure for the value of a key man.

One simple method for arriving at the worth of a key man is merely to pick some multiple of his current salary as his value to the firm. The most often mentioned multiple is five times the key man's annual salary. The "five times" rule of thumb is apparently derived from the fact that this is the typical underwriting limit used by life insurance companies when determining the maximum amount of life insurance coverage they will issue on the life of a key man where the proceeds are to be used to indemnify the business. However, where special circumstances exist and it can be shown that a particular key man has a greater value to the business, most insurance companies will increase this limit. This is particularly true where the key man happens to be an owner-manager of the business.

DISABILITY OF THE KEY MAN

The loss of a key man through permanent disability has the same adverse economic affects on the business as the death of a key man. Key man disability income insurance owned by and payable to the business can indemnify it, at least in part, for any financial loss that results. Premium payments for such coverage will not be income tax deductible. However, any benefits received by the firm will be income tax free.

One drawback to the use of key man disability income insurance is that it may reduce the amount of coverage that the key man can purchase for his own income protection. This will be the case when it is taken into account by the insurance company in determining how much total disability income insurance it will underwrite. One reason for doing this is that the firm is free to pass on any benefits to the insured key man even though the policy is purportedly purchased to benefit the firm. A solution would be to design a disability income policy for funding a key man plan with underwriting limits geared to the value of the insured key man to the business, rather than to his income.

Waiver of premium benefit. In addition to the possible purchase of key man disability income insurance, a business that purchases key man life insurance can protect its investment in the event of disability by adding the disability waiver of premium benefit to the life insurance. Under this provision the business would be excused from the payment of premiums during a period of total and presumably permanent disability from either accident or sickness. Even though no premium payments are being made, the life insurance policy will remain in full force, with the cash values continuing to increase in the same manner as when premiums were actually being paid. In addition, the dollars which were previously being spent in the form of nondeductible premium payments can now be diverted to the payment of deductible disability income benefits which the business may be obligated to pay to the disabled key man. The switch from a nondeductible expense to a deductible one enables a "50 percent income tax bracket" firm that was paying a $2,500 annual premium on a nondeductible basis to pay a $5,000 annual disability income benefit on a deductible basis without increasing its after tax cost.

RETIREMENT OF KEY MAN

In many cases, an insured key man will live to his normal retirement age and the need for key man insurance to indemnify the business will no longer exist. There are several options available to the business concerning the disposition of a key man policy in this event. The business could ignore the fact that the key man has retired, continue to pay the premiums, and upon his death receive the proceeds income tax free. Another alternative would be to offer the policy to the key man for its then present value. This would be an especially attractive offer to the key man if he is in need of additional personal life insurance protection and is presently uninsurable. If the key man does not want to purchase the policy, the firm could surrender it to the life insurance company for its cash surrender value. Another possibility would be to use the cash values of the policy to fund a nonqualified deferred compensation plan which would provide benefits to the key man only in the event he lived to retirement. It would not be appropriate to use a true key man policy to fund a deferred compensation plan which also provided a death benefit to the personal beneficiary of the key man in the event he dies prior to retirement, because, in that event, the proceeds are earmarked to be used to indemnify the business for the economic loss it will suffer at the death of the key man.

THE MECHANICS OF A KEY MAN PLAN

There is no requirement that a written agreement be entered into in order to establish a key man life insurance plan. Where a corporation wants to establish a key man plan, all that is needed is a simple resolution of the board of directors spelling out the value of the key man to the company and the economic loss that will be suffered at his death, with authorization to the appropriate company officer to purchase an insurance policy on the life of the key man. If an officer of the corporation is to be the insured key man, a different company officer should sign the life insurance application on behalf of the corporation. The key man will, of course, sign the application as the proposed insured.

If a partnership or sole proprietorship wants to institute a key man plan, there is not even the requirement of a resolution. However, if one of the partners is to be the insured key man, another partner, other than the insured, should sign the life insurance application on behalf of the partnership.

The ease with which a key man plan can be set up, taken together with the multiplicity of benefits that can be provided by such a plan, make it one of the most popular uses of life insurance by a business.

Chapter 3

DESIGN AND TAX ASPECTS OF NONQUALIFIED DEFERRED COMPENSATION

In this chapter nonqualified deferred compensation plans will be explored in depth, with emphasis put on the uses of life insurance to aid an employer in meeting its obligations under such plans.

DISTINGUISHING BETWEEN QUALIFIED AND NONQUALIFIED DEFERRED COMPENSATION

The term "deferred compensation" may be defined to include all agreements by the terms of which compensation for services rendered is postponed until some time after the services in question have been performed. A "nonqualifed" deferred compensation plan is simply one which does not meet the requirements set out in the Internal Revenue Code for a "qualified" deferred compensation plan. The Code requirements for qualification of a deferred compensation plan include nondiscriminatory participation of employees under a classification established by the employer that meets either a fixed percentage coverage requirement, or is found by the Service, as a matter of fact, not to discriminate in favor of employees who are officers, shareholders, supervisors, or highly compensated employees.[1] In addition, contributions to the plan, or benefits provided under the plan, must not

---

[1] I.R.C. Sec. 401(a)(3).

discriminate in favor of the so-called prohibited group of employees previously enumerated.[2]

For meeting these requirements along with a host of others, a qualified plan enjoys certain tax benefits. These include an immediate income tax deduction to the employer for its contributions to the plan,[3] deferral of a participating employee's taxation until he begins to receive benefits under the plan,[4] and tax exemption of earnings on plan contributions until they are distributed from the plan.[5] Despite these tax advantages, a company may be willing to provide only limited benefits under a qualified plan because of the cost implications of covering employees on a nondiscriminatory basis.

The single most distinctive feature of a nonqualified deferred compensation plan is the opportunity it gives the employer to discriminate in its selection of the employees to be covered under the plan. Thus, the employer may choose to cover only those employees who contribute most to the success of the business. In addition, the employer is free to discriminate among employees covered under a nonqualified plan in terms of the benefits to be provided. If the plan is properly arranged, a participating employee will not be taxed as a result of the plan until he begins to receive his benefits. However, the employer will not receive a current income tax deduction for its contributions to the plan, and any earnings derived from its contributions will not be tax exempt. The income tax consequences of a nonqualified plan will be covered in greater detail shortly. Throughout the remainder of this chapter the term "deferred compensation" will refer to a nonqualified deferred compensation plan unless specifically stated otherwise.

MOTIVATION BEHIND A NONQUALIFIED
DEFERRED COMPENSATION PLAN

A deferred compensation plan may be established to meet the needs of either the employee or employer.

"Savings" deferred compensation. Where a deferred compensation plan is instituted at the request of the employee, generally he will voluntarily take a reduction in current compensation or defer an offered increase in compensation. In lieu of the amount deferred by the employee, the employer agrees to pay a stipulated amount beginning at termination of employment or at the employee's prior death.

The primary purpose of this voluntary savings deferred compensation plan is to maximize the amount of each dollar that will be available for personal use by minimizing the amount of each dollar that will have to be paid in

---

[2]I.R.C. Sec. 401(a)(4).

[3]I.R.C. Sec. 404(a).

[4]I.R.C. Sec. 402(a).

[5]I.R.C. Sec. 501(a).

taxes. For example, an employee now in a top income tax bracket of 50 percent (taxable income of at least $44,000 on a joint return) has become an equal partner in himself; that is, he will have to split every additional dollar he earns equally with the government. After retirement, if his top income tax bracket is only 28 percent (maximum taxable income of $20,000 on a joint return), by the simple expedient of postponing the receipt of income and thus its taxation until retirement, the employee is able to turn 50 cent dollars into 72 cent dollars. That is, he will have available for personal use 22 cents more out of every dollar that was deferred rather than received as compensation currently.

The possible spread between an individual's top income tax bracket during his working years and after retirement has been somewhat reduced by a provision of the Tax Reform Act of 1969 which establishes a 50 percent maximum tax rate on earned income.[6] The maximum tax rate for all other ordinary income is 70 percent. Prior to the passage of this law, earned income, which includes wages, salaries, professional fees, and other amounts received as compensation for personal services actually rendered[7] was also taxed at a maximum rate of 70 percent.

Deferred compensation payments received by an individual do not qualify as earned income and, therefore, are not eligible for the 50 percent maximum tax rate. However, it would be a rare situation for a person who has begun to receive deferred compensation payments also to be receiving a sufficient amount of earned income in any one year to benefit from the 50 percent maximum tax rate limit.

Certain factors must be present before it will benefit an employee to seek deferral of a portion of his current compensation. The employee must be in a strong financial position with current income substantially in excess of current expenses. In addition, the employee's current top income tax bracket must be high with prospects of remaining high only until retirement. Where the deferred compensation payments will be equal to the amount of income deferred, the savings produced by having the payments taxed at the lower bracket should exceed the after tax income that could have been earned by the employee if he had received this compensation currently, paid the tax on it, and invested the remainder. Finally, the employer should be in sound financial condition with the likelihood of remaining so throughout the period when the deferred compensation payments will be made. This is particularly important in most deferred compensation plans where the employee is usually relying on the mere promise of the employer, unsecured in any way, to pay benefits in the future.

"**Inducement to stay**" **deferred compensation.** The second path to a

---

[6]I.R.C. Sec. 1348.

[7]I.R.C. Sec. 1348(b) and 911(b).

nonqualified deferred compensation plan is one that may be taken by an employer who must actively compete in the fringe benefit arena to attract and retain valuable employees. The firm already may be providing group life and health insurance and qualified retirement plan benefits to all its employees. Now it seeks to benefit only its key employees to tie them closer to the firm and to discourage them from seeking employment elsewhere. The firm may accomplish its objective through a deferred compensation plan. Here the key employee will not be given the choice of receiving additional present compensation or deferred compensation. The employer will choose the deferred compensation plan for him. This may then be referred to as an involuntary "inducement to stay" deferred compensation plan.

It is the employer who will initiate an inducement to stay deferred compensation plan. The employee's consent to the arrangement is not required. The important distinction is that the employee is not given the choice of receiving additional current compensation in lieu of the deferred compensation plan. Some of the characteristics which might suggest the need for an inducement to stay deferred compensation plan include: an industry in which competition for key men is keen; a firm whose profits are dependent upon the activities of a few highly talented individuals; and an employer in sound financial shape who is willing to "sweeten the pot" for key employees in order to provide a further inducement to stay with the firm.

UNFUNDED AND FUNDED DEFERRED COMPENSATION PLANS

To understand the tax treatment that will be accorded a deferred compensation plan, it is necessary to distinguish between an unfunded and a funded plan.

Unfunded plan. A deferred compensation plan is unfunded when the employee must rely on the mere unsecured promise of the employer to make the deferred compensation payments. No assets are set aside by the employer in which the employee has a current beneficial interest. In the event the employer defaults on its promise, the employee will be in the position of a general creditor. The plan will continue to be treated as unfunded for tax purposes even though the employer establishes a reserve to meet future obligations under the plan by creating a fund through the purchase of life insurance, annuities, mutual funds, or other securities, as long as the fund remains the unrestricted asset of the employer. The employer's intention to ultimately use these funds to discharge its contractual obligations to the employee will not make this a *funded* deferred compensation plan if the employee has no present interest in the funds.[8]

Funded plan. A deferred compensation agreement will be considered

---

[8]Rev. Rul. 68-99, C.B. 1968-1, 193; Rev. Rul. 72-25, I.R.B. No. 1972-4, 8.

funded for tax purposes when the employer promises to make payments to the employee at some future date and to meet its promise contributes specific assets to a fund in which the employee has a current beneficial interest. Amounts so set aside by the employer will be placed beyond its control and will not be available to the general creditors of the employer. Examples of funding would be contributions made by the employer to a nonqualified trust or escrow account for the benefit of the employee; or the purchase by the employer of a life insurance policy or nonqualified annuity owned by the *employee.*

ROADBLOCKS TO DEFERRING
TAXATION OF COMPENSATION

Under the Federal income tax law, income, in whatever form it takes, is taxable in the year it is either actually or constructively received by the taxpayer.

Constructive receipt. Under the doctrine of constructive receipt, income is taxable in the year it is constructively received. Income is constructively received by a cash basis taxpayer in the taxable year during which it is credited to his account, set apart for him, or otherwise made available so that he may draw upon it at any time. However, income is not constructively received if the taxpayer's control of its receipt is subject to substantial limitations or restrictions.[9] Thus, where an employer tenders a year-end bonus to an employee and the employee requests that the employer retain the bonus until the employee asks for it, the bonus will be taxable to the employee in the year tendered. On the other hand, where the employer merely credits the employee with a bonus, but the money is not available to the employee until some future date, the mere crediting on the books of the employer does not constitute constructive receipt until the future date when the bonus does become available to the employee.[10]

Economic benefit. Under the economic benefit doctrine, a cash basis taxpayer may be taxed if property has been dealt with in such a manner as to provide him with compensation in the form of an economic or financial benefit in the current taxable year that can be valued in terms of money. This is true regardless of whether there are substantial limitations or restrictions on the ability of the cash basis taxpayer to make full use of the property in question by reducing it to his own possession. This doctrine is exemplified in *E.T. Sproull v. Commissioner.*[11] In that case, an employer in 1945 set up a nonqualified trust for the benefit of an employee in the amount of $10,500. The trustee was directed to pay out of principal to the employee the sum of

---

[9] Reg. Sec. 1.451-2(a).

[10] Reg. Sec. 1.451-2(b).

[11] 16 T.C. 244, affirmed, 194 Fed. 2d 541.

$5,250 in 1946 and the balance, including income, during 1947. In the event of the employee's prior death the amounts were to be paid to his estate. On appeal, the court stated:

> It is undoubtedly true that the amount which the Commissioner has included in petitioner's income for 1945 was used in that year for his benefit . . . in setting up the trust of which petitioner, or, in the event of his death then his estate, was the sole beneficiary. . . .
>
> The question then becomes. . . was 'any economic or financial benefit conferred on the employee as compensation' in the taxable year. If so, it was taxable to him in that year. This question we must answer in the affirmative. The employer's part of the transaction terminated in 1945. It was then that the amount of the compensation was fixed at $10,500 and irrevocably paid out for the petitioner's sole benefit. . . .

In the *Sproull* case, an amount was set aside for the employee; however, the employee was not able to draw upon it at any time during 1945. Thus, the employee did not have constructive receipt of the cash itself in that year because there existed a substantial limitation on his control of it. What he did have was *actual* receipt of the economic or financial benefit conferred upon him in 1945 when the employer set up an irrevocable trust for his benefit in which the employee's rights were nonforfeitable. Hence, to successfully defer compensation under a nonqualified plan, not only must there be a substantial limitation or restriction on the employee's control over receipt of the compensation to avoid the constructive receipt doctrine, but also the plan must be so designed that it does not confer an economic or financial benefit on the employee in the current year to avoid the economic benefit doctrine.

WHAT MUST BE DONE TO EFFECTIVELY DEFER TAXATION OF COMPENSATION

Unfunded plan. Revenue Ruling 60-31[12] sheds considerable light on the question of when an unfunded nonqualified deferred compensation plan would effectively defer an employee's (or independent contractor's) taxable income. This ruling analyzed several situations to arrive at some basic conclusions concerning the requirements for successful deferral of income. The most important conclusion reached is that an employer's mere promise to pay compensation in the future, not represented by notes or secured in any way (an unfunded plan), is not regarded as the receipt of income by a cash basis taxpayer. Thus, under a plan of deferred compensation where an employer merely promises to make payments in the future, even if the employee's (independent contractor's) rights under the plan are nonforfeit-

---

[12]1960-1 C.B. 174.

able, the plan will not confer an economic or financial benefit on the employee in the current year. The ruling indicates this does not mean that a taxpayer may deliberately turn his back upon income he has already earned and that his employer is willing and able to pay him and thereby select the year that he will report it. However, where compensation has not yet been earned, an agreement may be entered into that provides for unearned compensation to be paid upon some specified date in the future, or upon the happening of a specified event rather than at the time services are rendered. The specified event that starts the payments is usually termination of employment for any reason agreed to by the parties, such as retirement, death, disability, dismissal, and resignation. The employee's control over the receipt of the income payments will then be considered subject to a substantial limitation (the passage of time) or restriction (need to terminate employment). Hence, there will be no constructive receipt of income and taxation will be deferred until the payments are actually made.

Funded plan. If current taxation under the economic benefit doctrine is to be avoided when property such as life insurance, annuities, or securities is transferred from an employer directly to an employee, or into an escrow account or nonqualified trust for the benefit of an employee in connection with the performance of services, the rights of the employee in such property must be either subject to a substantial risk of forfeiture *or* be nontransferable.[13] Although the requirements for exclusion from current taxation are stated as alternatives, the Internal Revenue Code expressly provides that property rights will be nontransferable only if the rights of a transferee in such property will be subject to a substantial risk of forfeiture.[14]

The Internal Revenue Code states that the rights of a person in property are subject to a substantial risk of forfeiture if such person's rights to full enjoyment of the property are conditioned upon the future performance of *substantial* services by an individual.[15] The proposed regulations under Internal Revenue Code Section 83(c) indicate that whether such services are *substantial* depends upon the particular facts and circumstances. The regularity of the performance of services and the time spent in performing such services will tend to indicate whether they are substantial.

In addition, the proposed regulations expand the definition of a substantial risk of forfeiture to include a situation where a person's rights to full enjoyment of such property are conditioned upon refraining from the performance of substantial services by an individual. Factors that may be taken into account in determining whether a covenant not to compete constitutes a substantial risk of forfeiture include:

---

[13]I.R.C. Sec. 83(a).

[14]I.R.C. Sec. 83(c).

[15]I.R.C. Sec. 83(c).

1. age of the employee,
2. availability of alternative employment opportunities,
3. likelihood of the employee's obtaining such other employment,
4. degree of skill possessed by the employee,
5. employee's health, and
6. practice (if any) of the employer to enforce such a covenant.

Rights in property transferred to a retiring employee subject to the sole requirement that it must be returned unless he renders consulting services upon the request of his former employer will not be considered subject to a substantial risk of forfeiture unless he is in fact expected to perform substantial services.

The requirement that there exist a substantial risk of forfeiture, not only prior to retirement but after retirement as well, to defer taxation under a funded deferred compensation plan substantially limits the occasions when a funded plan will be a viable solution. In most cases, the difficulty will be in maintaining a substantial risk of forfeiture after retirement. As can be seen from the previous discussion, the use of a forfeiture provision that will be triggered by the failure to render consulting services or the violation of a covenant not to compete will be considered to give rise to a *substantial* risk of forfeiture only where clearly indicated by the particular facts and circumstances. Where there is no longer a substantial risk of forfeiture after retirement, the entire value of the fund set aside for the employee will be taxable as ordinary income in that year. Since deferred compensation payments do not qualify as earned income for purposes of the 50 percent maximum tax rate on earned income, the inclusion of the entire fund in taxable income in one year could drive the employee's top tax bracket up to the maximum of 70 percent. This could result in the compensation that was deferred being taxed at a higher rate than if it were received during employment.

THE EMPLOYER'S TAX PICTURE

Now that we have analyzed the employee's tax treatment under both unfunded and funded deferred compensation plans, consideration must be given to the employer's tax picture.

Unfunded plan. Where an employer gives an employee nothing more than his unsecured promise to make deferred compensation payments in the future, regardless of whether the employee's rights are forfeitable or nonforfeitable, the employer will not be entitled to an income tax deduction until benefits are actually received by the employee and are includible in his gross income.[16] This will be the result even where the employer has purchased life

---

[16] I.R.C. Sec. 404(a)(5).

insurance, an annuity, or other property over which the employer retains full control to meet its future obligations to the employee.

If the employee dies, any salary continuation payments made to his beneficiary under an unfunded deferred compensation plan will be deductible by the employer in the year they are taxable to the beneficiary. The fact that the beneficiary may be allowed to exclude from taxation the first $5,000 of such payments as a tax free employee's death benefit under Internal Revenue Code Section 101(b) will not reduce the amount the employer is entitled to deduct.[17]

Funded plan. Where an employer makes contributions to a funded deferred compensation plan, its deduction will be postponed until the year in which an amount attributable to such contribution is includible as compensation in the gross income of the employee or his beneficiary. Here also, if the employee dies and payments made to his beneficiary qualify for the $5,000 tax free death benefit, the employer's deduction will nevertheless not be reduced.[18]

Thus, it can be seen that under the present state of the law there is no way to establish a nonqualified deferred compensation plan under which the employer receives a current income tax deduction for contributions to the plan while at the same time the incidence of income taxation to the employee, for whose benefit the contributions are made, is deferred.

Reasonableness of compensation. The availability of a deduction to the employer in the year in which deferred compensation benefits are includible in the taxable income of the employee is contingent upon the assumption that the payment of such benefits qualifies as an ordinary and necessary business expense during that taxable year, and is compensation for personal services actually rendered. In no case will a deduction be allowed to an employer for a deferred compensation benefit to an employee which, when taken together with other compensation for such employee's services, constitutes unreasonable compensation for the services actually rendered. What constitutes reasonable compensation depends upon the facts of the particular case. Among the elements to be considered are the personal services actually rendered in prior years, as well as the current year, and all compensation and contributions paid to or for such employee in prior years, as well as in the current year. Thus, it is possible for a deduction to be allowed even though a deferred compensation benefit taken together with other compensation for the current year is in excess of reasonable compensation for services performed in the *current* year. This may be the case when total compensation and contributions paid to or for the employee represents

---

[17]Proposed Reg. Sec. 1.404(a)-12. The $5,000 tax free death benefit is covered in greater detail beginning on page 473.

[18]I.R.C. Sec. 404(a)(5); Proposed Reg. Sec. 1.404(a)-12.

reasonable compensation for all services rendered by the employee up to the end of the current year.[19]

The issue of reasonableness of compensation will usually be raised by the Internal Revenue Service only in the case of a stockholder-employee. Payments to a stockholder-employee deemed to be in excess of reasonable compensation for services will be taxable as a dividend. The result will be ordinary income tax treatment to the stockholder-employee and no deduction to the corporation.[20]

An employer must file Treasury Forms 4848 and 4849 each year to substantiate his deductions for annual contributions to a funded deferred compensation plan regardless of whether it is qualified or not. On Form 4848 the employer must record information necessary to justify his income tax deductions. On Form 4849 the employer must provide a financial statement for the fund that has been established as a part of the plan.

Overcoming the effect of the postponement of the employer's deduction. Where an "inducement to stay" deferred compensation plan is being recommended to an employer as the means of retaining a key man, the loss of a current income tax deduction by the employer may be raised as an objection to the plan. For example, the employer, a corporation, might state that it would be willing to increase the employee's salary by $5,000 per year if it could get a current income tax deduction, which in its 48 percent income tax bracket would mean an after-tax cost of only $2,600.

However, if the corporation were merely to set aside $5,000 per year, perhaps in the form of insurance premiums on a policy on the key man's life which would be owned by and payable to the corporation, as a means of *informally* funding the plan, there would be no current income tax deduction and the corporation's after tax cost would be $5,000. This objection may be overcome by suggesting to the corporation that it purchase an insurance policy with an annual premium of only $2,600 (the after tax cost of a deductible increase in salary of $5,000). Following is an example of how this might work in a specific case: Assume the key employee is male and presently age forty-five with the plan calling for deferred compensation benefits to begin at age sixty-five. Assume that a $61,000 participating life paid-up at sixty-five contract could be purchased with an annual premium of $2,600. At age sixty-five this contract will have an estimated cash value of $63,069 (a guaranteed cash value of $45,140 plus an estimated cash value from paid-up additions of $17,929). If the corporation elects to receive the total cash value under a life income option with a guarantee of payments for ten years, the annual payments from the life insurance company will be $4,657. Of this

---

[19]Reg. Sec. 1.404(a)-1(b).

[20]*Willmark Service System, Inc.* T.C. memo 1965-294, affirmed 368 F. 2d 359 (C.A.-2 1966).

amount, applying the annuity tax rules, only $1,709 or 36.7 percent will be subject to income taxation when received by the corporation. Assuming that the corporation is in a 48 percent tax bracket, the total amount of each annual payment remaining after taxes will be $3,837. Since the amounts paid to the employee as deferred compensation normally will be fully deductible, the corporation can pay the employee $7,378 per year at an after tax cost of only $3,837—exactly the amount available to the corporation each year, after taxes, from the life insurance company.[21] Obviously the figures will vary depending upon the age of the employee at the time the plan is entered into. However, at an age of forty-five, it can be seen that by setting aside an amount equal to the after tax cost of a present increase in salary, a life income can be provided for the employee in an amount substantially greater than the assumed annual increase in salary that is deferred without any additional expense to the employer.

DEATH BENEFITS

It is not unusual for a deferred compensation agreement to provide for the payment of a death benefit in the event the employee dies either before or after the deferred compensation payments begin, as long as all of the payments due him have not been made. The payment of such a death benefit may have both income and estate tax consequences.

Estate tax. If, at the time of his death, an employee was receiving deferred compensation payments or he possessed the right to receive such payments in

---

[21]To test result assume that exclusive of deferred compensation plan the corporation has $100,000 of taxable income and that it is taxed at a flat rate of 48% (actually, first $25,000 of taxable income taxed at 22% and excess at 48%):

No Deferred Compensation Plan		Deferred Compensation Benefits Payable	
Taxable income	$100,000	Taxable income without considering deferred compensation plan	$100,000
Less income tax	48,000	Plus: taxable portion of annuity paymts.	1,709
Net income after taxes (Net funds Available)	$ 52,000		101,709
		Less: deferred compensation benefit paid to employee	7,378
			94,331
		Less: income tax	45,279
		Net income after tax	49,052
		Plus: tax free portion of annuity paymt.	2,948
		Net funds available	$ 52,000

the future, the present value of any survivor benefits payable under the agreement will be includible in his gross estate.[22]

An employee will be considered to possess the right to receive payments at some time in the future, even though his right was subject to a substantial risk of forfeiture, if he complied with his obligations under the agreement until the time of his death. In determining whether the death benefit should be includible in an employee's gross estate, all rights and benefits accruing to the employee and to others by reason of his employment, with the exception of those under qualified retirement plans, will be considered together as if they were all provided under one contract or agreement.[23] An example should help to clarify these concepts. Assume that an employer and employee enter into a deferred compensation agreement which contains the following provisions:

1. If the employee continues to work for the employer until his retirement at age sixty-five, then starting at that time, the employer will pay him $5,000 per year for life.

2. The employee must be available for consulting services after age sixty-five upon request of the employer.

3. The employee forfeits his right to any benefits if he does not meet his obligations before and after retirement.

4. In the event the employee should die prior to having attained age sixty-five, the employer will pay $5,000 per year for ten years to his designated beneficiary.

5. In the event the employee dies after reaching age sixty-five, but before having received ten annual payments of $5,000 each, the employer will continue to make such payments to the designated beneficiary of the employee until a total of ten payments have been made.

Under this agreement, if the employee dies after having reached age sixty-five but before having received ten annual payments, the present value of any unpaid payments at the time of his death will be includable in his gross estate since the employee was in fact receiving payments at the time of his death. This is the result even though the employee's right to continue to receive payments was forfeitable up to the time of his death.

If the employee dies before having reached age sixty-five, his designated beneficiary will receive $5,000 per year for ten years. The present value of such payments as of the employee's death will be includable in his gross estate for Federal estate tax purposes. This is so since, immediately before his death, the employee had an enforceable right to receive the deferred compensation payment commencing at age sixty-five. The fact that the employee's rights

---

[22]I.R.C. Sec. 2039(a).

[23]Reg. Sec. 20.2039-1(b).

were entirely forfeitable in the event his employment was terminated prior to his reaching age sixty-five will not alter this result as long as he was an employee at the time of his death.

The outcome would be the same even if the employer and employee had established two separate nonqualified plans: one to provide the employee with benefits during his lifetime, and the other to provide his designated beneficiary with a death benefit. In such case all rights and benefits accruing to the employee and to his beneficiary by reason of his employment will be considered together in determining whether the death benefit will be includable in the employee's gross estate.

If an agreement between an employer and employee provides for only the payment of a death benefit to a named beneficiary and, except for benefits payable under a qualified retirement plan, the employee is entitled to no other post employment benefits, the value of the death benefit should not be includable in the employee's gross estate as a survivorship benefit.[24] However, if the death benefit is payable in return for services rendered by the employee, it may be includable in his gross estate as a lifetime transfer where certain powers over the transferred property rights are retained by the employee. Retention of the power to change the beneficiary at any time or to change the beneficiary in the event that the designated beneficiary predeceases him might require inclusion of the death benefit in his gross estate.[25] However, the fact that the employer and employee could agree to negotiate a new death benefit plan, or that the employee could force a termination of the plan by quitting his job, should not be considered as the type of power that would result in inclusion of the death benefit in the employee's gross estate.[26]

Where an employer *voluntarily* pays a death benefit to the family of an employee, it normally will not be includable in the gross estate of the employee. However, if the employer has consistently paid a voluntary death benefit to the family of each employee with whom he had entered into a formal deferred compensation plan that provides by its terms living benefits only, the death benefit may be considered as having been made under a "contract or agreement." Taken together with the formal plan of the employer, this will result in inclusion of the death benefit in the employee's gross estate.[27]

Income tax. Deferred compensation benefits received by an employee will be taxable as ordinary income since they are consideration for the rendering

---

[24]Estate of Fusz 46 T.C. 214, acq. 1967-2 CB 2.

[25]I.R.C. Sec. 2036 through Sec. 2038.

[26]*Kramer v. U.S.* 186 Ct. Cl. 684, 406 F. 2d 1363 (1969); *Estate of Whitworth*, T.C. Memo 1963-41.

[27]Reg. Sec. 20.2039-1(b) example (4).

of past services. After the death of the employee, any deferred compensation benefits paid to his estate or to a named beneficiary will be treated in the same way for income tax purposes in the hands of the recipient as they would have been if received by the employee.[28] Thus, such death benefits are taxable as ordinary income. There is a limited exception to this rule. The Internal Revenue Code specifically provides that the first $5,000 of any death benefit payable by an employer on account of the death of an employee will be excludable from the taxable income of the beneficiary.[29] However, for this exclusion to be applicable, the employee must *not* have possessed, immediately before his death, a nonforfeitable right to receive the benefits himself while living. For this purpose, it appears that an employee will not be considered to possess, immediately before his death, a nonforfeitable right to receive benefits while living, as long as his rights were forfeitable up to the time of his death. The exclusion will still apply even where the act that would give rise to the forfeiture was entirely within the control of the employee provided that up to the time of his death, the employee had not committed any such act. For example, the $5,000 exclusion will apply where the agreement provides that the employee will forfeit all benefits either if he terminates his employment without the employer's consent, or if he enters into competition with the employer after the termination of his employment.[30]

Where the present value of death benefits under a deferred compensation agreement is includable in the gross estate of the employee for Federal estate tax purposes, and the right to receive such benefits was created prior to the employee's death, they qualify as "income in respect of a decedent." As such, the person who receives the benefits will be entitled to an income tax deduction equal to the increase in the employee's estate tax attributable to the inclusion of the present value of the right to receive these benefits in the employee's gross estate. To compute the amount of the deduction, first compute the estate tax due with the income in respect of a decedent included in the gross estate and then recompute the estate tax due without its inclusion in the gross estate. The difference between the two results is the amount of the income tax deduction.

Note that where an income in respect of a decedent item qualifies for the estate tax marital deduction, it may result in reducing the income tax deduction. This will occur whenever there are not enough other assets that qualify to entitle the estate to the maximum marital deduction when

---

[28] I.R.C. Sec. 691(a).

[29] I.R.C. Sec. 101(b).

[30] Reg. Sec. 1.101-2(e)(2) example (6). This requirement that the employee not have had a nonforfeitable right to receive the benefits while living does not apply to a lump sum death benefit received under a qualified retirement plan. Reg. Sec. 1.101-2(d).

recomputing the estate tax that would be due without inclusion of the income in respect of a decedent item in the gross estate.[31] Nevertheless, the employee often will want his wife to receive the death benefits under a deferred compensation plan in a manner that they will qualify for the marital deduction. This can be done without reducing the income tax deduction for income in respect of a decedent and without unnecessarily overqualifying the estate for the marital deduction. To do so the employee should utilize a formula marital deduction clause in his will that automatically gives his wife a sufficient portion of the estate to qualify for the maximum marital deduction regardless of the size of the estate or the assets comprising the estate.

DESIGNING THE DEFERRED COMPENSATION PLAN

The ultimate design of a deferred compensation plan is limited only by the requirements that must be present to obtain the desired tax consequences. Within these limitations the plan will be shaped primarily by the relative bargaining positions and needs of the employer and the employee. Where the employee voluntarily takes a reduction in current compensation or defers an increase in compensation that he could receive currently, the provisions of the plan will tend to be controlled more by the employee and his needs. Where the employer initiates a deferred compensation plan as an additional benefit to attract and retain a key employee, the plan provisions will tend to be controlled more by the employer and his needs.

Forfeiture provisions. Except for a funded deferred compensation plan, it is not necessary to have forfeiture provisions to defer the employee's income. Thus, in an unfunded plan, regardless of whether or not the employer informally funds its obligation by setting aside certain property which remains the unencumbered assets of the employer, the assurance of income tax deferral for the employee need not be a consideration in determining the extent to which forfeiture provisions should be used.

Forfeiture for termination of employment prior to normal retirement age. Where a deferred compensation plan is instituted by the employer as an added inducement to keep a key employee with the firm, the employer is likely to require that the employee forfeit all rights under the plan in the event that he terminates his employment prior to normal retirement age without the consent of the employer. To make the plan more attractive to the employee, the employer may agree to a vesting schedule which provides that the portion of the employee's benefits subject to forfeiture decreases as the employee's term of employment increases. For example, the plan may provide that if the employee terminates before having worked five years under the agreement, he loses all benefits; if he terminates after five years but

---

[31]Reg. Sec. 1.691(c)-1(a)(2)

before ten years, he loses 75 percent of his benefits; if he terminates after ten years but before fifteen years, he loses 50 percent of his benefits and so on. In addition, the employer usually is agreeable to the payment of some benefits if the employee dies or becomes permanently disabled prior to his normal retirement age.

Where the deferred compensation plan is instituted at the request of the employee who is going to accept a voluntary deferral of current compensation, he is not likely to agree to the arrangement unless all of his benefits are nonforfeitable in the event of early termination of employment regardless of the reason.

Covenant not to compete. Where the employer initiates the plan he may require the inclusion of a provision providing for the forfeiture of any unpaid benefits in the event the employee enters into competition with the employer, either directly or by going to work for a competitor. In a voluntary savings deferred compensation plan the employee may sometimes utilize this forfeiture provision when he has no intention of competing in order to qualify any death benefit payable under the plan for the $5,000 exclusion from income taxation. For a covenant not to compete to be enforceable in a court of law, it should be reasonable in terms of the geographical area over which it is applicable. That is, the prohibited area should not extend beyond the locality in which the employer carries on its business. Also, the period of time over which the restriction will remain in force should be reasonable to avoid violating the public policy against restraints on a person's right to work.

Consulting services. Where the deferred compensation agreement is instituted by the employer as an additional benefit, he may require the employee to render consulting services after his retirement or else forfeit any benefits under the plan. The terms of the provision requiring consulting services may give the employer the right to exercise direction and control over the retired employee. To the extent that the employee must render such services on substantially a full-time basis if called upon to do so by the employer, the deferred compensation payments may be classified as "wages" received by an employee in the current year. As such, they may be taken into account when determining whether the otherwise retired employee must forfeit any social security benefits. Under the 1972 Amendments to the Social Security law, in any month in which the supposed retired employee actually performs consulting services and receives an amount classified as wages earned in the current year he will lose one dollar of social security benefits for each two dollars of such monthly wages in excess of $175.

It is possible to have a consulting services provision in an unfunded deferred compensation agreement without causing this adverse social security consequence. To do so the provision should provide the following:

1. The retired employee is required to remain available to render

consulting services (he is not given a formal schedule of duties on a regular basis);

2. The employer cannot require compliance with detailed orders nor exercise supervision over how he carries out his duties;
3. There is no established work schedule and the retired employee could stay home from work without securing the permission of the employer.

If this approach is taken the employer should not be found to have retained the right to exercise the direct control required to establish the relationship of employer and employee. Under these circumstances, assuming the rendering of occasional consulting services does not amount to performing substantial services as a self-employed individual, the deferred compensation payments should not be considered as wages or self-employment income earned in the *current* year for the purpose of reducing the retired employee's social security benefits.[32] Note that even if the deferred compensation payments are treated as wages earned in *prior* years, they will be subject to employer and employee social security taxes. However, the deferred compensation payments may then be the basis for a later recomputation and increase in social security retirement benefits.[33]

Where the deferred compensation agreement provides that the retiring employee may have to render consulting services, this can also affect the tax treatment applicable to a lump sum distribution from a *qualified* retirement plan, if one exists. If the consultation services provision gives rise to the conclusion that the alleged retired employee is still an employee so that there has been no separation from service, the entire lump sum distribution from a qualified plan will be taxable as ordinary income. If it can be established that the consulting services requirement is such that the employer does not exercise or retain the right to exercise direction and control over the performance of the advisory services, the employee should be considered to have separated from the service of the employer. This results in a lump sum distribution from a qualified retirement plan being taxed as a long term capital gain except for that portion of the distribution which represents the employer's contributions made in 1970 and thereafter, which will be taxed as ordinary income, in most cases, under a favorable seven-year averaging rule.[34]

Thus, from the employee's standpoint a consulting services provision should be avoided if possible. Where the employer insists upon such a provision care should be taken when wording the clause to avoid the conclusion that the employer will continue to exercise direction and control over the services to be performed by the retired employee.

[32]Rev. Rul. 69-647, I.R.B. 1969-52, 12.

[33]Social Security Ruling 73-30, July '73.

[34]*Supra* footnote 32.

PAYMENT OF BENEFITS

When drafting a nonqualified deferred compensation agreement, consideration must be given to the circumstances under which benefits will be payable and the amount of such benefits. The events that generally give rise to a right to receive benefits include retirement, termination, disability, and death. Within each of these categories further specification is necessary concerning the variations in benefits payable, if any, dependent upon the circumstances surrounding the happening of the event. For instance, retirement may occur at the normal retirement age, or it may occur later or earlier than the normal retirement age. In addition, early termination may be at the request of the employer or at the election of the employee. Disability may be temporary or permanent. Death may occur prior to separation from service or after separation from service. Each of these contingencies may be dealt with differently in different plans depending upon the purposes behind the institution of the plan and the relative bargaining strengths of the employer and the employee.

Inducement to stay plan. Where a deferred compensation plan is instituted by an employer as an added inducement to keep a key employee with the firm, it will usually be in the form of a definite benefit plan. That is, the plan will state that a specified dollar amount will be payable, generally for a specified period of time, upon the happening of any of those events that the employer deems appropriate for the payment of benefits. For example, the agreement might provide that if the employee has been continuously employed by the employer from the date of the agreement until his sixty-fifth birthday, then beginning at that time, the employee will receive $500 per month for 120 consecutive months (normal retirement benefit). In the event the employee dies after normal retirement but before having received 120 monthly payments, any unpaid payments at the time of his death may be paid to a designated beneficiary (post retirement death benefit). The employer may decide that if the employee terminates his employment prior to age sixty-five, without the consent of the employer, that no benefits will be payable under the deferred compensation agreement. In the event of early termination with the consent of the employer, benefits may be payable in a reduced amount from what the benefit would have been if the employee had stayed until age sixty-five (early retirement benefit). This may be accomplished through the use of a schedule contained in the agreement which gears the size of the monthly benefit to the number of years that the employee has served since the agreement went into effect. In lieu of the schedule approach, a formula clause could be used. For example, an employee who is age forty-five when an agreement is entered into that provides a benefit of $500 per month commencing at age sixty-five could be credited with a monthly benefit of one-twentieth of $500 for each year of employment from the date of the agreement to the date of his termination of employment.

Where the main purpose of the plan is to induce an employee to stay with the firm, an employer may nevertheless be willing to pay a benefit in the event of early termination. However, the employer may insist that any early termination benefits be payable to the employee only after he attains age sixty-five. Where the employer agrees to pay a preretirement death benefit, the amount of the benefit may be the same as that which would have been payable at normal retirement or upon early retirement at the date of his death. Where the employer agrees to pay a preretirement death benefit it will generally want to purchase insurance on the employee's life to help meet its obligation.

The agreement may provide that in lieu of the stated monthly benefit, the actuarial equivalent may be paid beginning at such time, in such amounts and for such periods as are agreed upon by the employer and employee or his beneficiary. This will provide additional flexibility in the method of paying benefits. When an actuarial equivalent of the standard method of payment can be elected, it should be available only with the consent of the employer to avoid the possibility of constructive receipt of benefits. The method to be utilized in determining actuarial equivalents should also be stated specifically in the agreement.

Voluntary savings plan. When a voluntary savings deferred compensation plan is instituted at the request of an employee in order to postpone the payment of income tax on the deferred portion, the agreement will often take on the attributes of a defined contribution plan. That is, no attempt is made in the plan to designate the specific benefits payable under the plan. Instead, the benefits payable are based upon the amount of compensation that has been deferred each year until the time payments become due. Here, benefits are generally payable upon termination of employment for any reason whatsoever, including early termination elected by the employee without the consent of the employer. To avoid the tax problems associated with a funded deferred compensation plan, the amount of compensation deferred by the employee each year should remain the unencumbered assets of the employer. However, the employer may set up a bookkeeping account to determine the value of the amount credited to the employee. The employer may also use the deferred compensation to purchase insurance on the employee's life that is owned by and payable to the employer without the plan being considered "funded" in the sense that will cause current taxation for the employee if his rights under the plan are not subject to a substantial risk of forfeiture.

The amount credited to the employee's account should be at least equal to the dollar amount of compensation deferred each year. Sometimes the plan provides for a specific rate of interest to be credited to the employee's account. Another alternative is to credit the employee's account with the actual gain or loss attributable to the investment of an amount of money equal to the compensation deferred by the employee. Such investments may be specified by the terms of the agreement itself. Where this is done, the size of the benefits payable should be related to what the value of the investments stipulated in the agreement would be at the time the benefits become payable, regardless of whether the employer has actually made the investments called for by the agreement.

SAMPLE APPROACH TO THE BENEFIT PROVISIONS
UNDER A DEFERRED COMPENSATION AGREEMENT

At the time a voluntary savings deferred compensation agreement is entered into, the employer may purchase insurance on the employee's life with a gross premium equal to the annual compensation deferred by the employee. This life insurance policy may then be identified by number, insured, face amount, and life insurance company in the agreement.

Normal retirement. The agreement can then provide that, at age sixty-five, the employee will begin to receive monthly installments over a ten-year period (or some other method of payout) in an amount equal to what the cash surrender value of the policy including the value of any accumulated dividends would provide at age sixty-five, if the policy had been kept in full force until that time.

Early termination. The same approach may be taken for early termination. That is, equate total benefits to the value that the policy would have had if kept in full force until the date upon which the employee terminates his employment. If, in the event of early termination, benefits are deferred until the employee reaches age sixty-five, the agreement can provide that total benefits will be equal to the value the policy would have produced if the nonforfeiture option elected was reduced paid-up insurance and the policy values remained with the insurance company unitl the employee attained age sixty-five.

Death benefit. Where the employee dies while employed, the death benefit can be the amount that would have been payable under the policy if it had been kept in full force up to the time of his death. Where plan benefits for a terminating employee are to be deferred until age sixty-five, and the employee dies after terminating his employment but prior to having attained age sixty-five, the death benefit payable under the deferred compensation plan can be measured by the amount payable under the policy if the reduced paid-up insurance nonforfeiture option had been elected on the date the employee terminated his employment.

Earnings after benefits begin. In the preceding approach, total benefits payable to the employee or his beneficiary are equated to the size of the insurance fund as of the date payments are to begin. After that date, any earnings on the fund do not increase the employee's benefits but help the employer to meet its obligations. To further benefit the employee the agreement could provide that earnings after payments under the plan have begun also will be credited to the employee. For example, where the plan is informally funded through life insurance, the total amount of benefits will be equal to what would be payable if the employer elected to receive the insurance proceeds under the terms of the appropriate settlement option. Thus, where the payout is to be over ten years, the monthly benefit would be the same as would be payable by the insurance company where the employer elects to receive settlement in monthly payments over a specified period of ten years. In this way, interest earned on the fund would increase the benefits receivable by the employer from the life insurance company and in turn would increase the benefits receivable by the employee or his beneficiary. This can be an especially attractive device as an offset to inflation during the payout period when a variable annuity is the designated method of settlement.

Where a hedge against inflation is important to the employee during the accumulation period as well as during the payout period, the deferred compensation agreement can provide that the amount deferred annually be assumed to be invested partially in life insurance and partially in mutual funds or a variable annuity. Benefits can then be geared to the values that would have been built up in the life insurance policy if it had been kept in full force and the values that would have been built up in the mutual fund or variable annuity if it had been purchased with the specified portion of compensation deferred each year.

Disability benefits. Where the employee is deferring a portion of his current compensation and benefits are geared to the values of a given life insurance policy, the employee should benefit if because of his disability the waiver of premium provision under the policy goes into effect. This can be accomplished by having the employer pay disability income benefits to the employee equal in amount to the premium that has been waived. This could be in addition to the other benefits called for by the terms of the deferred compensation agreement in the event of permanent disability.

To ensure tax deferment. Where life insurance or some other asset is purchased by the employer, regardless of whether the benefits payable under the terms of the deferred compensation agreement are geared to the value of such assets or the employer merely elects to purchase such assets to help meet its future obligations under the agreement, the rights of the employee and his beneficiary under the deferred compensation agreement should be those of an unsecured creditor of the employer. Any assets acquired by the employer in connection with the deferred compensation agreement should not be held under any trust for the benefit of the employee or his beneficiary or as security for the performance of the obligation of the employer. Instead, such assets should remain the unencumbered assets of the employer. If this is done, the value of such assets should not be currently taxable to the employee even if the employee is a majority stockholder of the employer and his rights under the deferred compensation plan are nonforfeitable.[35]

It does not appear that a prohibition against assignment of the employee's rights under a deferred compensation agreement is required to defer taxation where the employer makes an unsecured promise to pay benefits in the future. However, it may be advisable to include a provision barring assignment or transfer by the employee or his beneficiary. This will avoid the economic benefit issue, and also shield the benefits payable under the plan from creditors of the employee or his beneficiary.

A deferred compensation agreement generally does not contain a prohibition against the employer assigning its liabilities under the plan. Therefore, the agreement should expressly state that the employer will not merge with another business or be sold to another firm without provision being made for its successor to assume the obligations of the employer under the deferred compensation agreement.

LIFE INSURANCE IN DEFERRED COMPENSATION PLANS

We have already cited some example of how life insurance may be used by an employer to establish a reserve against his future liabilities under a deferred compensation plan. Informal funding through life insurance is especially attractive where the plan provides for the payment of death benefits. When a reserve is established through investment in assets other than life insurance, and the employee dies shortly after the plan is entered into, the size of the fund may be inadequate to meet the employer's obligation. Where life insurance is used as an informal funding device, the premature death of the employee will not only give rise to the employer's obligation to pay death benefits, but also will create the funds with which to meet that obligation.

Another factor which enhances the attractiveness of life insurance as an informal funding device is the income tax free status of the cash value build-up in the policy during the accumulation period. Earnings on most other forms of assets that might be used to accumulate a reserve will be currently taxable to the employer.

An additional advantage of life insurance funding is the option it gives to the employer at the time the employee reaches retirement age. The employer

---

[35] See *Casale v. Comm.*, 247 F. 2d 440 (C.A.-2, 1957); acq. Rev. Rul. 59-184, C.B. 1959-1, 65. In *Casale*, a 98% stockholder-employee was held not to be currently taxed on premiums paid by his corporation where it was policyowner and beneficiary and the policy was an unrestricted corporate asset.

may either use the cash values of the policy to meet its obligation to pay retirement benefits or, if other assets are available for that purpose, keep the policy in force and at the death of the employee collect the death proceeds. Where the latter is done, and the deferred compensation plan calls for the payment of a definite benefit determined as of the date the plan is entered into, the employer will often receive more from the insurance company as death proceeds than it will pay out to the employee and his beneficiary as benefits under the plan.

Life insurance funding also makes available the waiver of premium benefit. This will relieve the employer's obligation to pay premiums in the event the insured-employee becomes permanently and totally disabled. Even though premiums are waived, the insurance policy will remain in full force and cash values will continue to grow. The dollars that are no longer needed to pay premiums can be used to either provide disability income to the employee or reduce the employer's costs under the plan.

Where life insurance is used in an informally funded deferred compensation plan, the employer will normally be the policy owner, premium payor and beneficiary of the policy on the employee's life. Premium payments by the employer will not be deductible since the employer has a beneficial interest in the policy.[36] However, the guaranteed cash value and policy dividends will accumulate income tax free. Note, however, that if dividends are left on deposit at interest with the insurance company, any interest earned by such individuals will be taxable each year. Any death proceeds received by the employer will not be subject to income taxation.[37] Where the policy matures or is surrendered during the lifetime of the insured, only the excess of any maturity proceeds or cash surrender value over the total net premiums paid will be taxable as ordinary income to the employer.[38]

The availability of settlement options, especially where the deferred compensation plan requires the employer to pay a life income to the employee, is another reason for informal funding through life insurance. By electing a life income option, the employer can pass on to the insurance company the risk of the employee living beyond his normal life expectancy. Where a settlement option is used, care should be taken not to designate the employee or his beneficiary as the direct beneficiary under the terms of the life insurance policy. This is to avoid the conclusion that the policy has, in effect, been distributed to the employee or his beneficiary so that the full value of the policy would be taxable to the recipient all in one year. To avoid this result, the employer should designate itself as beneficiary under the terms of the settlement option. The employer will then receive the installment

---

[36]I.R.C. Sec. 264(a)(1).

[37]I.R.C. Sec. 101(a)(1)

[38]I.R.C. Sec. 72(e).

payments from the insurance company and in turn pay the employee out of its funds. Where the employer elects to receive payment in installments from the insurance company, the installments will be taxed under the rules applicable to the taxation of an annuity.[39] That is, the portion of each payment that is considered to be a return of the employer's basis will be receivable income tax free, while the balance of each payment will be taxable as ordinary income to the employer.

COLLATERALIZED DEFERRED COMPENSATION

Where an employee is considering the deferral of a portion of his current compensation in return for his employer's promise to make payments to him after retirement, a key consideration is the probable ability of the employer to make the payments to him when due in the future. Since the employee is postponing the receipt of a portion of his current income he will probably want his right to receive benefits in the future to be nonforfeitable. This eliminates the possibility of using a funded trust or escrow arrangement, since the employee would be taxable currently where his rights are not subject to a substantial risk of forfeiture. Another suggestion is to have the employer collaterally assign to the employee, as security for its promise, the assets which comprise the fund the employer is accumulating to meet its future obligations under the deferred compensation plan. The asset, for example, a life insurance policy, remains in the possession of the employer and there is no transfer of ownership from the employer to the employee. Rather, the employee is given a priority ahead of other creditors of the employer to collect his benefits from the proceeds of the life insurance policy only in the event of a default by the employer under the terms of the deferred compensation agreement. The requirement of a default by the employer before the employee can get at the asset in question should represent a substantial limitation on the employee's control over the asset. Therefore, he should not be held to be in constructive receipt of its value prior to a default.

Although the constructive receipt doctrine would not seem to apply, there may be a tax problem for the employee under the economic benefit doctrine. The addition of security could be held to permit a value to be placed on the employer's promise resulting in receipt by the employee of a present economic benefit where his rights under the plan are not subject to a substantial risk of forfeiture. To reach the conclusion that the employee would be granted tax deferral, the pronouncement in Revenue Ruling 60-31 that the employer's "mere promise to pay, not represented by notes or secured in any way, is not regarded as a receipt of income...," would have to be construed *not* to imply that where the employer's promise *is* secured in any way, it necessarily follows that the employee will be currently taxed.

---

[39]I.R.C. Sec. 72.

Assuming current taxation can be avoided, if at the time the employer defaults on his promise the employee forecloses on the assigned asset, he will be in receipt of its full value and that amount should then be currently taxable to him. However, paying tax on a lump sum all in one year is obviously preferable to receiving little or no benefits as purely a general creditor of the employer. Since the employee's income tax treatment under collateralized deferrred compensation is still in the gray area, it is probably wise to avoid such arrangements unless deemed absolutely necessary by the employee.

NONQUALIFIED DEFERRED COMPENSATION: THE "DISCRIMINATING" RETIREMENT PLAN

The most distinctive characteristic of a nonqualified deferred compensation plan is the fact that it allows the employer to discriminate freely in favor of highly paid key employees, including stockholder-employees when choosing those persons to be benefited. Such a plan may stand alone or be used in conjunction with a qualified retirement plan that must be provided by the employer on a nondiscriminatory basis.

The soundness of having the employer create a fund to meet its future obligations under a deferred compensation plan is well established. The advantages of using life insurance as a vehicle for accomplishing this objective, either alone or in conjunction with a mutual fund or variable annuity, are also well recognized.

Chapter 4

THE FINE POINTS OF
SPLIT-DOLLAR INSURANCE PLANS

A split-dollar insurance plan is an arrangement designed to allow a person who needs insurance protection, for whatever reason, to secure it at a cost to him that is less than if he simply purchased the insurance on his own. This is accomplished by having the individual who is in need of insurance *split* the premium cost with another individual or entity.[1] The other person or entity who contributes toward the premium cost will share in the proceeds of the insurance to the extent of his premium contribution. The balance of the proceeds will be payable to or for the benefit of the individual who is in need of the insurance protection.

Thus, a prerequisite to a split-dollar insurance plan is the existence of another person or entity willing to contribute toward the cost of insurance protection needed by someone else. In some cases, the individual who has an insurance need controls an entity which can assist in the payment of the premiums. For example, a controlling stockholder-employee can elect to have his corporation participate in the premium cost; or the grantor of a trust can direct the trustee to participate in the purchase of insurance for the benefit of someone other than the trust.

Uses of split-dollar plans. The uses to which the split-dollar method of purchasing insurance can be put are many and varied. A split-dollar plan may

---

[1]In some cases, the other person or entity will contribute the entire premium cost, with the person who needs the insurance contributing nothing. This so-called noncontributory split-dollar plan is discussed beginning on page 503 of this text.

be established by an employer as a fringe benefit for a key employee. It may be established by a stockholder-employee and his corporation to provide personal protection for his family at a cost to him that will be less than if he merely purchases the insurance himself. Split-dollar may be utilized by a sole proprietor and a key employee to enable the employee to secure the funds with which to purchase the proprietorship at the death of its owner. Split-dollar may be used to help fund a cross-purchase buy-sell agreement where that method of purchase is deemed preferable to a stock redemption plan and the stockholders nevertheless want the corporation to assist in the purchase of the insurance needed to fund the plan. Split-dollar may be used to provide a salary continuation benefit to the widow of a key employee. It may be the means by which an individual will provide a contribution to charity and at the same time provide himself with personal insurance protection. A split-dollar plan may be used by a father who wants to protect his daughter by contributing toward the purchase of insurance on her husband's life. In order to emphasize the business uses of insurance, this chapter will deal primarily with split-dollar plans that involve an employer and employee.

THE BASIC SPLIT-DOLLAR PLAN

Although there are many variations of split-dollar plans, it will be helpful to an understanding of the concept to explain its operation by reference to what is generally referred to as the basic split-dollar plan. This is the arrangement that is dealt with by the Internal Revenue Service in its Revenue Rulings on split-dollar plans between an employer and an employee.

In the basic split-dollar arrangement, the employer and employee join in the purchase of an insurance contract on the life of the employee in which there is a substantial investment element. The employer provides the funds to pay that part of each annual premium equal to the annual increase in the cash surrender value. The employee pays the balance of each annual premium. The employer is entitled to receive from the proceeds of the policy an amount equal to the cash surrender value, or at least a sufficient part thereof to equal its total premium payments. The employee has the right to name the beneficiary for the balance of any proceeds payable by reason of his death.

Although the employee's share of each annual premium may be substantial in the early years, it will decrease each year as the annual increases in cash value grow progressively larger. In some cases the employee's share may even reach zero after a relatively short time. As the employer takes over more of the obligation to pay premiums its share of the death proceeds will increase. Nevertheless, with relatively little cost to the employee he is able to obtain valuable insurance protection that remains substantial for a long period of time, although it decreases each year.

SPLIT-DOLLAR SYSTEMS

There are two major systems that have been developed for the establishment of a split-dollar life insurance plan. One method is generally referred to as the endorsement system and the other as the collateral assignment system.

Endorsement system. Where a split-dollar plan is established under the endorsement system, insurance on the life of an employee is applied for and owned by the employer. Since the employer owns the policy, it is primarily responsible for the payment of the premiums. However, in a basic split-dollar arrangement, the employee agrees to reimburse the employer for the portion of each premium payment that exceeds the annual increase in the cash surrender value of the policy The employer is named the beneficiary for that portion of the proceeds equal to the cash surrender value as of the end of the year in which the employee dies. The employee will then designate a personal beneficiary to receive the remainder of the proceeds. The employee's rights are protected by an *endorsement* on the policy which modifies the employer's rights as policy owner. This endorsement provides that the designation of the employee's personal beneficiary to receive the proceeds in excess of the cash surrender value cannot be changed without the consent of the insured employee. This protects the employee by eliminating the employer's power, as owner of the policy, to change the beneficiary designation so as to benefit only itself.

Some life insurance companies have adopted a slightly different approach to the endorsement system of split-dollar plan. These companies permit the designation of the insured employee as owner of that portion of the death proceeds in excess of the cash surrender value, and the designation of the employer as owner of all the other rights and benefits under the policy.

Under the endorsement system the employer will recover an amount equal to its premium payments at the death of the insured employee as a beneficiary under the policy. If the split-dollar plan is terminated prior to the death of the insured employee, the employer will be able to recover its premium outlay directly from the cash surrender value which it controls as owner of the policy. This may be accomplished by surrendering the policy or giving the insured employee the option to purchase it for an amount equal to its cash surrender value.

Collateral assignment system. When a basic split-dollar insurance plan is established under the collateral assignment system, the insured employee applies for and owns the policy on his life. He then designates his own personal beneficiary to receive the proceeds in the event of his death. As owner of the policy, the insured employee is primarily liable for the payment of premiums. However, in a separate agreement, the employer obligates itself to "lend" the employee an amount of money each year equal to the annual increase in the cash surrender value. Generally, this loan will be made to the employee interest free. Thus, the employee's out-of-pocket cost will be limited to that portion of each annual premium that exceeds the annual increase in cash surrender value. To protect the employer, the employee will collaterally assign the policy to the employer as security for the amount of the loan. At the insured employee's death, the employer will recover the amount of its loan from the death proceeds, not as a beneficiary of the policy, but as a collateral assignee. The employer and employee may prepare their own collateral assignment form or utilize a standard form, such as the American Bankers' Association Form No. 10—Assignment of Life Insurance as Collateral. Under the ABA form, the insured employee assigns to the employer the right to collect the death proceeds of the policy. In addition, the employer agrees to pay any balance of the death proceeds remaining after satisfaction of its loan to the beneficiary designated in the policy. To protect the employer in the event the split-dollar arrangement is terminated prior to the death of the insured employee, the right to surrender the policy or make policy loans is also assigned to the employer. However, the employer agrees that, except for obtaining a policy loan to pay a portion of the premium, it will not surrender the policy or obtain a policy loan until there has been a default by the insured employee on his obligation to repay the employer's loan. Since the life insurance company involved is not a party to the collateral assignment, it will not be bound by it unless put on notice of its existence. Therefore, a copy of the collateral assignment should be sent to the insurance company that issues the policy.

Where a collateral assignment split-dollar plan involves a corporation and one of its officers, shareholders, or directors, the applicable state law and the by-laws of the corporation should be checked to determine if there are any restrictions on the capacity of a corporation to make loans to these individuals. Some states specifically prohibit the making of such loans, subject to criminal sanctions. Another group of states merely hold the corporate directors who approve such loans personally liable for any loss that occurs as a result of nonpayment. However, the chance that a director will have to reimburse the corporation for a loss under a collateral assignment split-dollar plan is unlikely since the loan will generally be fully secured by the cash value of the policy. There is a possibility that these state statutes do not apply to a collateral assignment split-dollar plan based on the position of the Internal Revenue Service that such a plan involves a loan in form only and not in substance. In substance it is considered to be taxable compensation to the insured employee. However, the application of these state statutes is not governed by Federal tax law and, therefore, such payments may nevertheless be treated as loans for this purpose.

FACTORS BEARING ON CHOICE OF
SPLIT-DOLLAR SYSTEMS

There are several factors that help determine which split-dollar system should be used. Although the Federal income tax treatment will not vary with the system used, the Federal estate tax treatment may. Where avoidance of estate taxes is desired and the insured is a majority stockholder-employee, the collateral assignment system should be used. The reasons are discussed in greater detail under the heading "Estate Tax Treatment of Split-Dollar Plans," beginning on page 496.

Another factor to consider is whether the employer wants the cash value available for use in its business during the term of the split-dollar plan. If it does, the endorsement system is preferable. Under the collateral assignment system, the policy cash value will generally not be available to the employer unless and until the insured employee is in default on his obligation. However, the employer usually will be permitted to make policy loans to pay premiums even if the insured employee is not in default. Under the endorsement system, the employer, as owner of the policy, is free to borrow from the policy at any time and for any reason. Where the parties intend to use the policy to fund a nonqualified deferred compensation arrangement in the event the insured employee lives to retirement, the endorsement method should be used. This is especially true when the insured employee is *not* a shareholder or officer of the corporation. Under the endorsement method, the employer owns the policy and the cash value. At the retirement of the insured employee, the employer can elect to receive the cash value under a settlement option or continue to pay the premiums on the policy until the death of the employee. In the latter case, the death proceeds could be used to offset the benefits paid under the deferred compensation agreement. If the collateral assignment system is used the insured employee is owner of the policy. If the policy is to be used to fund a deferred compensation plan it will have to be transferred to the corporation. This would involve a transfer for value that would not come under the exceptions to the transfer for value rule unless the insured employee was a shareholder or officer of the corporation. The result would be ordinary income tax treatment of the death proceeds less the amount the employer paid toward the purchase of the policy where no exception applies.

If a policy already in force and personally owned by the insured employee is to be used to establish a split-dollar plan, it will be simpler to adopt the collateral assignment system. However, if the policy already in force is a key man policy owned by the employer, the simpler approach would be to utilize the endorsement system.

A SEPARATE SPLIT-DOLLAR AGREEMENT

Parties to a split-dollar plan may be well advised to execute a separate agreement setting out their rights and obligations. However, the existence of such an agreement is not an absolute necessity.

A separate agreement may be more important when the collateral assignment system is used than when the endorsement system is used. Under the endorsement system, the employer already owns the policy and controls the cash value to which it will be entitled. Each party's share of the death proceeds is specifically spelled out in the beneficiary designation. This is not the case under the collateral assignment system where only the personal beneficiary of the insured employee is named in the policy. The employer generally will receive the entire death proceeds as collateral assignee. It then is obligated to pay any excess proceeds over the amount of the loan to the insured employee's personal beneficiary. Without a specific agreement, the amount of the employer's interest as collateral assignee will not be spelled out in a written document. A separate agreement can eliminate this shortcoming by a provision covering the distribution of proceeds between the employer and the insured employee's beneficiary. In addition, the agreement can spell out the premium payment obligations of the parties, the application of any policy dividends, the conditions under which the plan will be terminated, the rights of the parties to the policy cash values prior to termination, and the various methods of disposing of the policy after termination of the plan. Other provisions may be desirable depending upon the specific situation involved. Regardless of whether a written split-dollar agreement is entered into, there should be a resolution passed by the board of directors of the corporation authorizing it to enter into a split-dollar plan in consideration for the valuable services rendered in the past and to be rendered in the future by the employee in question.

INCOME TAX CONSEQUENCES OF SPLIT-DOLLAR PLANS

The income tax consequences to the employer and employee under a split-dollar life insurance plan were first dealt with by the Internal Revenue Service in a 1955 Revenue Ruling.[2] The Ruling involved a basic split-dollar insurance plan established by an employer and employee using the endorsement system. The conclusion of the Service was that such an arrangement should be regarded, for Federal income tax purposes, as though an interest-free loan was actually made by the employer to the employee in an amount equal to the cash surrender value of the policy. Based on this interpretation, the employee does not realize any income as a consequence of the plan. The mere making available to the employee of money without interest does not

---

[2] Rev. Rul. 55-713, 1955-2 CB 23.

result in taxable income to him. Since the employer is merely considered to be making loans to the employee, it receives no deduction for its contributions under the plan. This Ruling gave a tremendous boost to the popularity of split-dollar insurance plans.

The income tax free treatment accorded the employee under a split-dollar plan came to a halt when the Internal Revenue Service altered its position in a Revenue Ruling issued in 1964.[3] Since then, the Service has taken the position that a split-dollar arrangement, regardless of whether it utilizes the endorsement system or collateral assignment system, should not be treated in substance as a loan from employer to employee. This is because the employee is not expected to repay the funds provided by the employer except out of the death proceeds or cash value of the policy. Instead, the substance of the arrangement is as follows: The employer provides that portion of the premium which generates the investment element (cash value) in the life insurance contract. This should entitle the employer to the earnings accruing to the investment element. However, the effect of the arrangement to share premium costs is that the earnings on the investment element in the policy are applied to provide current life insurance protection to the employee from year to year, at no cost to him, to the extent that the earnings are sufficient to do so. Under this interpretation, the typical split-dollar plan results in a taxable economic benefit to the employee represented by the amount of the annual premium cost that he should bear and of which he is relieved. The Ruling states that the value of the benefit to be included annually in the employee's taxable income is an amount equal to the one year term cost of the life insurance protection which the employee is entitled to from year to year, less any portion of the premium provided by the employee. In arriving at the annual economic benefit to the employee, the one year term insurance rates contained in the Government's so-called P.S. 58 Rate Table may be used.[4] If the issuer of the insurance policy publishes rates for individual, initial issue, one year term policies available to all standard risks, such rates may be used in place of the P.S. 58 rates.[5]

Computing the economic benefit. An example of how the economic benefit to the employee is determined should be helpful. At this point the significance of any policy dividends that may be payable will be ignored. Assume that a $100,000 ordinary life policy with an annual premium of $2,800 is purchased under a basic split-dollar plan. In the year in question the annual increase in cash value, and thus the employer's contribution toward

---

[3]Rev. Rul. 64-328, 1964-2 CB 11.

[4]This table reflects one year term costs based upon Table 38, U.S. Life & Actuarial Tables, and 2½% interest. A copy of this table is contained in Rev. Rul. 55-747, 1955-2 CB 228.

[5]Rev. Rul. 66-110, 1966-1 CB 12.

the premium, is $2,600. The employee must, therefore, pay $200. Further assume that in the event the employee dies during the year, the portion of the death proceeds payable to the employer is $10,000 (its total premium contribution) with the remaining $90,000 of death proceeds payable to the insured employee's personal beneficiary. In order to determine the amount the employee must include in his taxable income as a result of the economic benefit he receives, the first step is to calculate the term cost of the insurance protection provided his personal beneficiary. If it is assumed that the employee's attained age is forty-two, then based on the P.S. 58 Rate Table, the term cost of providing insurance protection for him is $5.07 for each $1,000 of protection. Since $90,000 would be payable to his personal beneficiary in the event of the employee's death, the total cost of the insurance protection is $456. However, since the employee was required to contribute $200 toward the payment of the premium, the value of his economic benefit and the amount which he must include in his taxable income is $256 ($456-$200). Each year the amount that must be included in the employee's taxable income will vary because the input data will be different. Thanks to a grandfather clause contained in the 1964 Ruling, only policies purchased under split-dollar arrangements or utilized to establish such arrangements *after* November 13, 1964 will be treated as giving rise to a taxable economic benefit to the employee.

Income tax treatment of employer. In addition to applying the economic benefit doctrine to the employee in a split-dollar insurance plan, Revenue Ruling 64-328 also concludes that the employer should be treated as a beneficiary under the split-dollar policy. This results in no deduction being allowed the employer for its share of premium payments since premiums paid by an employer on insurance covering the life of an employee where the employer is directly or indirectly a beneficiary under the policy are not deductible.[6]

Although it is generally held that this precludes the employer from claiming any deduction under a split-dollar plan, a logical case might be made for allowing the employer to deduct an amount equal to the economic benefit provided the employee. The claim would be based on the reasoning of the Internal Revenue Service in Revenue Ruling 64-328. That is, the economic benefit to the employee does not stem from the employer's premium payments, which will be returned to it at some time in the future. Instead, it comes from the annual earnings on the cash value of the insurance policy to which the employer is entitled, but which are used to meet a portion of the cost of the life insurance protection provided the employee. This being the case, a deduction to the employer for the economic benefit to the employee would not be a deduction for premiums paid by the employer,

---

[6]I.R.C. Sec. 264(a)(1).

but for the earnings on the cash value that are used to pay for the employee's insurance protection. Up to this time, this theory has not been tested in the courts.

Income tax treatment of death proceeds. The income tax treatment of any death proceeds payable under a split-dollar plan will be governed by Internal Revenue Code Section 101(a).[7] Thus, in the absence of a transfer for value problem, both the employer and the personal beneficiary of the employee will receive their shares of the proceeds free of income tax.

INCOME TAX TREATMENT OF POLICY DIVIDENDS

In analyzing the income tax treatment of the employee under a split-dollar plan, we have so far concentrated on the economic benefit provided the employee through current insurance protection under the base policy. However, another source of possible economic benefit to the employee is policy dividends. The value of any policy dividends used to benefit the employee will also be includable in his taxable income. As with the economic benefit derived from the insurance protection provided by the base policy, the tax treatment of any additional benefits received by the employee on account of policy dividends under a split-dollar plan will be the same whether the endorsement system or the collateral assignment system is used.[8]

Dividends paid in cash or accumulated at interest. If policy dividends are paid in cash to the employee or accumulated at interest for the benefit of the employee, the dollar value of the annual dividend will be included as part of the employee's economic benefit under the plan. On the other hand, if dividends are paid in cash to the employer or left to accumulate at interest for the benefit of the employer, they will not be taken into account in arriving at the employee's economic benefit.

Dividends used to reduce premiums. Under the basic split-dollar plan, the employer is obligated to pay that portion of each annual premium equal to the annual increase in cash surrender value. The employee is required to pay the balance of each annual premium, if any. Thus, where dividends are used to reduce the premiums and the net premium due nevertheless exceeds the annual increase in cash surrender value, it is the portion of the premium the employee is obligated to pay which is being reduced by the dividend. In such case, the dollar value of the dividend will be includable as part of the economic benefit received by the employee under the plan. For example, assume that the gross annual premium for insurance purchased under a basic split-dollar plan is $2,800. Further assume that for the year in question the annual increase in cash surrender value is $2,300. Therefore, not taking dividends into account, the employee must pay $500 toward the premium.

---

[7]Rev. Rul. 64-328, 1964-2 CB 11.

[8]Rev. Rul. 66-110, 1966-1 CB 12.

However, assume that dividends are used to reduce premiums and that in the year in question a dividend of $400 is paid. Now the employee will have to pay out of pocket only $100. Thus, it is clear that in this example the entire dividend is used for the economic benefit of the employee. Note, however, when computing the net amount that must be included in the employee's taxable income for the year as a result of the split-dollar plan, the amount of the dividend which is included in his economic benefit will also be taken into account in determining the portion of the premium paid by the employee. Thus, in this example the employee will be credited with a $500 premium contribution as an offset when determining the net amount which he must include in his taxable income.

If, under a basic split-dollar plan, the sum of the annual increase in cash surrender value plus the annual dividend which is used to reduce premiums exceeds the gross premium, then only a portion of the dividend should be includable in the economic benefit provided the employee under the plan. For example, if the annual gross premium is $2,800, the annual increase in cash surrender value $2,300 and the annual dividend $900, only $500 of the annual dividend should be includible as part of the employee's economic benefit. This is because the employer was obligated to pay up to $2,300 toward the premium for the year in question with the employee paying the balance. In fact, because the $900 dividend was used to reduce premiums, only $1,900 remained to be paid. Thus, the dividend was used to reduce the employer's obligation by $400 and the employee's obligation by $500. Hence, the economic benefit derived by the employee as a result of the use of the $900 dividend to reduce premiums was $500.

Dividends used to purchase paid-up additions. Dividends may be used each year to purchase single premium insurance of the same type as the base policy. The premium rate will be based upon the insured's attained age at the time the dividend is applied toward the purchase of the additional insurance. The cost of purchasing additional insurance through the application of policy dividends is less than if a new single premium policy is purchased in the usual manner. The premium rate is reduced when dividends are used primarily in recognition of the fact that there are no sales commissions payable on such a purchase.

Under a split-dollar plan, the income tax consequences of using dividends to purchase paid-up additions will depend upon how they are utilized. The typical approach in most split-dollar plans is to treat the additional amounts of insurance in the same manner as the insurance under the base policy. That is, the employer will contribute an additional sum toward the base policy premium each year equal in amount to the cash surrender value of the paid-up additional insurance purchased in that year. Furthermore, the employer will be designated beneficiary for a portion of the death proceeds payable under the paid-up additional insurance equal to its cash surrender value. The employee will designate a personal beneficiary to receive that portion of the death proceeds in excess of the cash surrender value of the paid-up additions. If the split-dollar agreement is terminated prior to the insured employee's death, the cash surrender value of the paid-up additions will belong to the employer. It can readily be seen that this application of paid-up additions parallels the treatment accorded the base policy under a basic split-dollar plan. Where this is so, the tax treatment of the paid-up additions will follow that of the base policy. The one-year term cost of the insurance protection provided the insured employee each year (determined by use of the P.S. 58 Rate Table or the insurance company's own one-year term rate, if available) will determine the value of the economic benefit to the employee as a result of the dividend being so used.

Another approach is to provide in the split-dollar agreement that the insured employee is to be treated as owner of the cash value of the paid-up additional insurance and entitled to designate his personal beneficiary to receive any death benefit attributable to the additions. If this is done, the employer's premium contribution would continue to be equal to the annual increase in the cash value of the base policy with the insured employee contributing the balance of any premium due. Under these circumstances the insured employee receives all of the benefits of the paid-up additions. Therefore, the dollar value of the dividends used to purchase the paid-up additions would be includable as part of his taxable economic benefit under the plan.

Dividends used to purchase one-year term insurance. It has already been pointed out that in a basic split-dollar plan, the share of the death benefit payable to the insured employee's beneficiary decreases as the employer's total premium contributions increase each year. The application of dividends to purchase one-year term insurance each year in an amount equal to the cash value of the policy (the so-called fifth dividend option) enables the portion of the death benefit payable to the insured employee's beneficiary to remain at a relatively constant level, approximately equal to the face amount of the base policy. This is accomplished by providing in the split-dollar agreement that the insured employee has the right to designate a personal beneficiary to receive any death benefit payable under the one-year term insurance. Where this is done, the dollar value of any dividend used to purchase one-year term insurance will be includible as part of the economic benefit to the employee under the plan.

When dividends are used to purchase one year term insurance the expense loading is minimal, primarily because no sales commissions are payable. As a result, the economic benefit measured by the actual dollar value of the dividends applied to purchase one-year term insurance generally will be less than if measured by the P.S. 58 Rate Table or, if available, the published individual one-year term rates of the insurance company involved.

The tax treatment of any excess annual dividend not used to purchase one-year term insurance will depend upon the dividend option elected as the method of receipt.

Some life insurance policies that may be utilized to establish a split-dollar plan pay no dividend. Such a nonparticipating policy may be at a competitive disadvantage when compared with a participating (dividend paying) policy where the parties want a level death benefit to be payable to the insured employee's beneficiary.

To overcome the unavailability of the fifth dividend option, some insurance companies issuing nonparticipating contracts permit the policy owner to add an increasing term rider to the base policy. The insurance protection provided by the term rider increases each year to keep pace with the increasing cash value of the base policy. By having the proceeds of the term rider payable to the insured employee's beneficiary, the total death benefit received by her will approximate the face amount of the base policy. The result is similar to that obtained by using a participating policy and electing the one-year term dividend option. To be consistent with the income tax treatment accorded dividends used to purchase term insurance, it would appear that if the employer paid the cost, the dollar value of the annual premium for the term rider would be includible as part of the employee's economic benefit under the split-dollar plan where the proceeds from the term rider are payable to his personal beneficiary.

ESTATE TAX TREATMENT OF SPLIT-DOLLAR PLANS

Up to this time, the Revenue Rulings dealing with split-dollar plans do not treat their estate tax consequences. In the absence of specific guidance, any conclusions must be based on the general principles associated with the estate tax treatment of life insurance. The applicable provision of the Internal Revenue Code states that the proceeds of insurance on the life of a decedent will be includable in his gross estate for Federal estate tax purposes if the decedent, at the time of his death, possessed any of the incidents of ownership of the policy, exercisable either alone or in conjunction with any other person.[9]

Endorsement system. Under the usual endorsement system the employer will be the sole owner of the life insurance policy used to fund a split-dollar plan. However, to protect the insured employee's rights under the agreement, the ownership rights of the employer will be modified by an endorsement which provides that the designation of the insured employee's personal beneficiary to receive a portion of the proceeds cannot be changed without

---

[9] I.R.C. Sec. 2042(2).

the consent of the insured employee. Thus, an incident of ownership, the right to name the beneficiary for a portion of the proceeds, can be exercised by the insured employee in conjunction with the employer.

In general, when a decedent at the time of his death possessed an incident of ownership in an insurance policy on his life, even if it applies to only a portion of the proceeds, it appears that the full value of the insurance proceeds will be includible in his gross estate. However, where property owned by a decedent at the time of his death is subject to the payment of a debt for which neither the decedent himself nor his estate is personally liable, the value of such property for Federal estate tax purposes is its full value less the amount of the debt for which the property is security.[10] If this general estate tax rule is applied to the typical split-dollar plan, the amount includable in the insured employee's gross estate should be the full proceeds less that portion which must be paid to the employer in satisfaction of the debt to it under the split-dollar agreement. This seems to follow from the fact that in the typical split-dollar plan neither the insured employee nor his estate will be personally liable to the employer for the amount of premiums paid by it. Instead, the employer will be entitled to reimbursement only from the proceeds of the life insurance policy subject to the agreement.

Where the endorsement system is used, the insured employee may be able to keep the entire death proceeds out of his gross estate for Federal estate tax purposes if he has no incidents of ownership at the time of his death. One way to accomplish this, and still protect the insured employee's rights, is to modify the employer's ownership rights in the policy by an endorsement which provides that the designation of the insured employee's personal beneficiary to receive a portion of the proceeds cannot be changed without the consent of the *personal beneficiary*, rather than without the consent of

the insured employee. If a written split-dollar agreement is entered into which gives the employee the right to designate the beneficiary for a portion of the proceeds, the employee should also absolutely assign his right to the person who is originally designated as beneficiary. If these steps are taken, the insured employee will have no incidents of ownership in the split-dollar life insurance policy and no portion of the proceeds should be includable in his gross estate for Federal estate tax purposes.

Where an endorsement system split-dollar plan is instituted between a corporation and a majority stockholder-employee, the portion of the proceeds payable to a beneficiary other than the corporation may be includable in the gross estate of the insured majority stockholder-employee even where the necessary steps have been taken to eliminate the possession of any incidents of owership in the policy held directly by the insured. This result is based on a proposed estate tax regulation which attributes the incidents of

---

[10]Reg. Sec. 20.2053-7.

ownership possessed by a corporation in an insurance policy on the life of a majority stockholder to the majority stockholder to the extent the proceeds are not payable to or for the benefit of the corporation.[11] If this proposed regulation is applied to an endorsement system split-dollar plan insuring a majority stockholder, the portion of the proceeds payable to the personal beneficiary of the majority stockholder will be includible in his gross estate.

Collateral assignment system. When a split-dollar plan is arranged under the collateral assignment system, the insured employee is generally designated the owner of the life insurance policy. As such, he can exercise all of the incidents of ownership in the policy up to the time of his death. Therefore, the death proceeds should be includable in his gross estate for Federal estate tax purposes.[12] In determining the value of the death proceeds for Federal estate tax purposes the fact that a portion of the proceeds is liable for the payment of a debt to the employer, but neither the insured employee nor his estate is personally liable for the payment of such debt, leads to the conclusion that the estate tax value of the proceeds should be the full proceeds less the amount which must be payable to the employer in satisfaction of the debt owed to it.[13]

Where the collateral assignment system is used and the insured employee wants to keep the proceeds out of his gross estate for Federal estate tax purposes, the beneficiary for the insured employee's share of the proceeds should initially apply for and own the life insurance policy. The owner of the policy should then enter into the collateral assignment split-dollar agreement with the insured's employer. Under this arrangement, the insured employee has no incidents of ownership in the policy and presumably the proceeds should be excludable from his gross estate.

In some cases there may be restrictions on a corporation's authority to make what is in form an interest free loan to a third party, such as the employee's wife, who bears no direct relationship to the corporation. If this is so, the insured employee should initially apply for and own the insurance on his life. He should then enter into the collateral assignment split-dollar agreement with the corporation. The agreement should permit the employee to absolutely assign all his rights thereunder. Once this is accomplished, the insured employee can transfer ownership of the insurance on his life subject to the collateral assignment and absolutely assign his rights under the split-dollar agreement.

Where the collateral assignment system is used and all incidents of ownership in the life insurance policy held directly by the insured employee have been eliminated, the fact that he is also a majority stockholder of the

---

[11]Proposed Reg. Sec. 20.2042-1(c)(2).

[12]I.R.C. Sec. 2042(2).

[13]Reg. Sec. 20.2053-7.

employer corporation should *not* result in a portion of the proceeds being includable in his gross estate. Since the corporation has no incidents of ownership in the life insurance policy, none can be attributed to an insured majority stockholder.

Effect of premiums paid in contemplation of death on estate tax treatment. If a decedent makes a gift of property within three years of his death and in contemplation of death, the value of the property will be includable in his gross estate for Federal estate tax purposes.[14] Thus, if an insured makes a gift of a life insurance policy within three years of his death and in contemplation of his death, the proceeds will be includable in his gross estate.[15] Life insurance proceeds have also been held to be includible in the insured's gross estate where another person applied for and owned the insurance from its inception but the purchase was prompted by the insured's paying the initial and subsequent premiums. In this situation, where the insured died within three years of the purchase of the policy, the death proceeds were held includable in his gross estate even though he never owned the policy when it was found that he had made a gift of the premium dollars in contemplation of death.[16] However, where the insured dies more than three years after the policy is purchased, only the dollar value of any premiums paid by the insured during the three year period prior to his death and found to be gifts in contemplation of death will be includable in his gross estate.[17]

In a basic split-dollar plan, the contribution of the insured employee toward the cost of his insurance protection may stem from two sources. First, the employee may contribute a portion of the premium out of pocket. Second, in consideration for the services he performs, the employer bestows an economic benefit on the employee in the form of payment for a portion of the insurance protection provided the employee. Thus, where the insured employee has rid himself of all incidents of ownership under a split-dollar plan and ownership of the insurance benefit provided the employee is in the hands of a third party, the portion of any premiums paid out of pocket by the insured employee and the value of the economic benefit he receives from his employer may be looked upon as gifts of "premiums" from the insured

---

[14] I.R.C. Sec. 2035.

[15] Reg. Sec. 20.2042-1(a)(2).

[16] Rev. Rul. 71-497, 1971-45 IRB 16; *Bel v. U.S.*, 29 AFTR 2d (5th circuit 1971); *Detroit Bank & Trust Co. v. U.S.*, No. 71-1790 (6th circuit 1972). Upon remand to the District Court, that court decided the creation of the insurance Trust and the transfer of the premium to it was Life Motivated and consequently the policy proceeds were not includable in the deceased's gross estate.

[17] Rev. Rul. 71-497, 1971-45 IRB 16.

employee to the third party owner. If the insured dies within three years of the time he transfers his interest in a split-dollar policy to a third party, or within three years of the time a split-dollar arrangement was originally entered into with a third party, such "premium payments" may be held to have been gifts made in contemplation of death. The result may be inclusion of the proceeds payable to the third party in the insured employee's gross estate for Federal estate tax purposes.

The gift of the portion of the premiums paid out of pocket by the insured employee may be avoided by having the third party pay that amount out of her own funds. Unfortunately, there does not appear to be a ready solution for avoiding the conclusion that the economic benefit in the form of insurance protection provided the employee represents a gift to the third party owner. Nevertheless, even if such gifts are held to have been made in contemplation of death, once the initial three-year period has passed, only the dollar value of the economic benefit provided the insured employee during the last three years of his life, and not all or a portion of the death proceeds, should be includable in his gross estate.

VARIATIONS OF THE BASIC SPLIT-DOLLAR PLAN

Under a basic split-dollar plan the employer contributes an amount equal to the annual increase in cash value each year and the insured employee must contribute the balance of the annual premium due, if any. In the first few years of the plan the financial burden on the insured employee will be substantial. For example, typical figures for a $100,000 ordinary life policy purchased at age forty-five from a mutual life insurance company show that the annual premium will be about $3,250. At the end of the first policy year, the cash value will be about $400. Therefore, in the first year of the split-dollar plan the employee will have to contribute $2,850 toward the premium with the employer contributing only $400. Although the employee's out of pocket expense diminishes rapidly each year, the substantial initial outlay required of the employee is often a stumbling block to the establishment of a basic split-dollar plan as a fringe benefit for key employees.

Even where the employee to be benefited can afford the large initial out of pocket expense, there are other tax consequences of the basic split-dollar approach that he may want to avoid. As previously pointed out, the insured employee's out of pocket contribution toward the premium can be used to offset the economic benefit that he must include in his taxable income. However, where the employee's premium contribution exceeds the economic benefit he receives from the plan in a particular year, he is not allowed to carry over any excess contribution to a future year in which his taxable economic benefit exceeds his premium contribution.

Level contribution method. To eliminate the high initial out of pocket cost to the employee and to take greater advantage of the offset for employee contributions against his taxable economic benefit, the annual premium contributions that the employee and the employer have to make may be leveled over some specified number of years. For example, if the employee is age forty-five and the plan is intended to stay in force until he reaches age sixty-five, the sum of the contributions the employee would be called upon to make over the twenty-year period under a basic split-dollar plan may be divided by twenty to get an average annual contribution. If the gross annual premium for a $100,000 ordinary life policy at age forty-five is $3,250, total gross premiums over a twenty-year period will be $65,000. If the total cash value at the end of the twenty-year period is $55,000, the sum of the insured employee's premium contributions over this period should be $10,000 ($65,000 - 55,000). Dividing $10,000 by twenty years gives an average annual employee contribution of $500. The employer would then have to contribute $2,750 each year. By utilizing the level contribution method the premium contribution required of the employee in the first year would be reduced in this case from $2,850 to $500. The difference will eventually be paid by the employee, but the timing of the payment is spread over the twenty-year period. This enables the employee to make better use of his premium contributions as an offset against the taxable economic benefit he receives under the plan.

Where the level contribution method is used, the employer will be entitled to receive a portion of the death proceeds equal to its total premium contributions at the time the employee dies. In the event the plan terminates during the employee's lifetime, the employer should be entitled to receive from the policy an amount equal to its premium payments. However, the maximum lifetime value of the policy will be its cash surrender value. Under the level contribution method, if the plan is terminated at any time prior to the end of the period over which contributions are leveled, the employer's total premium contribution will be in excess of the cash surrender value of the policy. The income tax consequences resulting from this unsecured portion of the employer's premium contribution have not been dealt with specifically by any cases or rulings. One way of viewing the transaction is to consider the annual amount the employer contributes in excess of the increase in cash value for the year in question to be a nontaxable interest-free loan to the employee. This loan will be repaid in the later years of the plan when the employer will actually be contributing less than the annual increase in cash value. At the end of the level contributions period the total employer contribution should be equal to the total cash value. If the plan is terminated prior to the end of the level contribution period, the employer's total premium contributions will exceed the cash surrender value with the difference representing the loan to the employee. If this loan is not repaid by the employee it might be viewed as taxable income in the year the debt is forgiven.

Noncontributory method. In some cases an employer may be willing to pay the entire premium cost under a split-dollar plan. For instance, when the insured employee is also a stockholder of the employer corporation. Under this plan, the proceeds of the policy will be split between the employer and the employee, but the obligation to pay premiums will lie solely with the employer. At the insured employee's death, the employer will be entitled to receive a portion of the proceeds equal to the premiums it has paid, with any balance going to the employee's beneficiary. In the event the plan is terminated during the employee's lifetime, the amount the employer will be able to receive from the policy will be limited to its cash surrender value. In many cases this may be less than the total amount of premiums paid by the employer.

The income tax consequences to the employer of a noncontributory split-dollar plan have not been dealt with specifically by the Internal Revenue Service or the courts. One approach would be to apply the income tax guidelines that have been spelled out for a basic split-dollar plan. If this is done, the employee merely would include in his taxable income the economic benefit each year measured by the term cost of the insurance protection provided his personal beneficiary. Under this approach, the fact that the employer is paying the share of the premium which the employee would be called upon to pay in a basic split-dollar plan does not result in any additional taxable income to the employee. However, since the employee is not contributing toward the premiums, he will have no offset against his taxable economic benefit.

Another approach might be to treat the excess employer contribution each year over the annual increase in cash value as a nontaxable interest-free loan payable out of the proceeds of the policy at the termination of the plan. If the proceeds are insufficient to pay the loan, the employee would have to pay the difference out of pocket. If the employee may be called upon personally to repay the loan he may be entitled to treat it as his premium contribution for the purpose of offsetting his taxable economic benefit.

To avoid the possibility that the employee may have to reimburse the employer out of pocket if he terminates his employment prior to death, the split-dollar agreement can provide that the employer will not receive back its cost until the employee's death, even if that is after termination of employment. At termination of employment, rather than cashing in the policy, the employer can elect the reduced paid-up insurance nonforfeiture option. In most cases, the reduced death benefit will at least equal the total premiums paid by the employer. If this is done, the employer will be guaranteed that it will recover the full amount of its premium contributions at the death of the insured employee.

In lieu of electing reduced paid-up insurance when the insured employee terminates his employment, the split-dollar agreement may provide that in consideration for the services that the employee has already rendered and will render in the future, the employer agrees to pay premiums under the split-dollar arrangement up to the time of the employee's death even if that occurs after he has terminated employment.

The economic benefit provided the insured after he terminates his employment may be viewed as deferred compensation paid by the employer. If this is done, the employer will be fully secured as long as total premiums do not exceed the death proceeds. Although there is no specific law on the point, there appears to be no reason why the insured should not continue to be taxed under this arrangement after he is separated from employment in the same manner as he was while an employee.

As with other variations of split-dollar, under a noncontributory plan the employer probably would be denied a deduction for any portion of its premium contribution since it has a beneficial interest in the policy. To overcome this result, at least in part, a modification of the noncontributory split-dollar plan is sometimes used. Under the modified noncontributory plan the first step is to compute the economic benefit that the employee would have to include in his taxable income if the plan were totally noncontributory. Then the employer gives the employee a bonus equal in amount to this economic benefit. If the amount of the bonus is reasonable when taken together with the employee's other compensation, it should be deductible to the employer and taxable to the employee. The next step is to have the employee contribute the bonus toward the premium that is due, with the employer contributing the balance of the premium cost. The employee will then be entitled to apply his premium contribution to offset his economic benefit under the plan. This will eliminate any taxable income to him as a result of the plan. The overall income tax results for the employee will be the same as it would be if the employer has contributed the entire premium. This is because the bonus that the employee must include in his income will be equal to the economic benefit that the employee would have had to include in his income if he did not contribute toward the premium. Thus, without altering the employee's tax treatment the employer should be permitted to deduct the portion of its annual cost which takes the form of a bonus to the employee.

Before adopting a noncontributory split-dollar plan the parties should weigh carefully the possible tax consequences against the benefits derived from this arrangement.

USE OF AN IN FORCE POLICY

The high premium cost to the employee in the first few years under a basic split-dollar plan can be avoided if a policy that has been in force for a few years is used to fund the plan. For example, assume the employer has a key man policy in force on the life of the employee that he is willing to use under the split-dollar plan. If the policy has been in force five years the employer's premium contribution in the first year under the split-dollar plan will be an amount equal to the sixth year increase in cash value. This should be substantial enough to reduce the employee's premium contribution to a level he can afford. Where the employer already owns the policy, the endorsement system of split-dollar would normally be utilized.

ADVANTAGES OF SPLIT-DOLLAR TO THE EMPLOYER AND EMPLOYEE

A fringe benefit in the form of a split-dollar life insurance plan has many attractive features.

Advantages to employee. From the standpoint of the employee, it will enable him to acquire needed life insurance protection at a cost that is much lower than he would have to pay if he purchased the protection on his own. Under the split-dollar plan, the employee's cost can be measured by the sum of his premium contributions, if any, plus the increase in tax that he has to pay as a result of the economic benefit he receives under the plan. For example, if an employee enters into a noncontributory split-dollar plan at age forty-five, using the figures for a typical $100,000 ordinary life policy, the average annual cost to the employee over a twenty-year period will be approximately $440 per year if it is assumed that he is in a 32 percent top income tax bracket. In comparison a twenty-year nonparticipating level term policy with a face amount of $100,000 purchased at age forty-five will cost approximately $1,370 per year. In addition to the substantial savings in cost to the employee when compared with the personal purchase of a term policy, the split-dollar insurance policy may act as a hedge against future uninsurability and as a source of insurance protection beyond retirement age. This can be accomplished by providing in the split-dollar agreement that at its termination, the employee has the option to purchase the ordinary life contract used to fund the agreement for an amount equal to its cash value. In the event the employee cannot afford to purchase the policy out of his own funds, he may acquire the purchase money by making a policy loan. Any interest paid by the employee should be deductible if at least four of the first seven premiums that were due from the inception of the policy were paid without borrowing.[18] For the purpose of being able to claim the interest deduction it does not matter that the insured employee may not have been the owner of the policy during the first seven years of its existence.[19]

Advantages to employer. From the standpoint of the employer, a split-dollar insurance plan can be an extremely attractive fringe benefit. The

---

[18] I.R.C. Secs. 264(a) and 264(c).

[19] Rev. Rul. 71-309 IRB 1971-29, 83.

employer is free to discriminate among employees and choose only those upon whom it wants to bestow this additional benefit. Perhaps this will be only those key men whom the employer wants to tie closer to the firm. If it is a closely held corporation, the firm may want to enter into such arrangements with only the stockholder-employees.

The cost to the employer of a split-dollar plan is minimal. Since the employer will eventually receive back its investment, its cost may be measured by the loss of the potential income it could have earned, after taxes, if its premium contributions were invested in some other form for its own benefit. If the employer believes that this is too great a potential cost, it can arrange the split-dollar plan so as to be able to borrow the cash value of the policy and invest it in any way that it desires. If this is done, its cost will be fixed at the interest which must be paid on the policy loan. If the employer does not borrow any part of four of the first seven premiums, its interest payments should be deductible for Federal income tax purposes.[20]

Another advantage to the employer is the fact that control over the benefit provided the employee under a split-dollar plan remains in its hands. That is, the employer may be free to terminate the arrangement at any time and, at least in the basic split-dollar plan, receive from the policy an amount equal to its premium contributions.

OTHER USES OF SPLIT-DOLLAR INSURANCE PLANS

In the typical employer-employee split-dollar plan insurance is purchased on the life of the employee. However, where an employee is in need of insurance protection, not on his life, but on the life of someone else, the employer may nevertheless provide the employee with the insurance protection through the use of a split-dollar plan.

Sole proprietor buy-out. An individual who is the sole owner of a business, whether incorporated or not, may not have any family members to whom he wants to leave his business at his death. He may find it difficult to sell the business to an outsider at a decent price. In such a situation, it is not unusual for the business owner to seek out a key employee of the firm and offer to sell the business to him at the business owner's death. Although the employee may be anxious to accept the offer, one major stumbling block is often the lack of funds with which to make the purchase. An obvious solution would be insurance on the life of the employer owned by the employee. However, the employee may not be able to afford the premium payments. To solve this problem the employer may enter into a split-dollar insurance plan with the employee. In this case, the insurance will be on the life of the employer rather than the employee.

Either a basic split-dollar plan or one of its variations can be used. Since

---

[20]I.R.C. Sec. 264(c).

the arrangement is between employer and employee, the economic benefit measured by the term cost of the insurance protection provided the employee on the life of the employer will be taxable to the employee. However, the additional tax payable by the employee will be far less than the premiums he would have to pay if he purchased the insurance on his own.

Split-dollar in a cross-purchase buy-sell agreement. After weighing the factors involved, it is sometimes determined that it will be to the advantage of the stockholders of a closely held corporation to arrange their buy-sell agreement on a cross-purchase basis rather than in the form of a stock redemption plan.[21] One drawback to the use of a cross-purchase buy-sell agreement is that the stockholders are personally responsible for the payment of premiums on insurance used to fund the plan. However, the corporation can help to finance the purchase of the needed insurance through the use of a split-dollar plan.

Where a split-dollar plan is entered into for this purpose, the collateral assignment system is generally used. Each stockholder will apply for and own a policy on the life of his co-stockholder. Each stockholder then collaterally assigns the policy he owns on his co-stockholder's life to the corporation as security for the corporation's premium payments. Here also, either the basic split-dollar arrangement or one of its variations can be used. Since the split-dollar plan is between employer and employee, each stockholder-employee will be taxed on the economic benefit he receives as a result of the plan. This will be measured by the term cost of the insurance protection provided each stockholder-employee on the life of his co-stockholder.

If a split-dollar plan used to fund a cross-purchase buy-sell agreement is arranged under the endorsement system, it could result in a transfer for value problem. That is, a portion of the proceeds received by the surviving stockholder-employee may be taxable to him as ordinary income. The reason for this possibility is based on the mechanics of the endorsement system. Normally the corporation will apply for and own the life insurance. It then transfers the right to receive a portion of the proceeds of the policy on the life of each stockholder to his co-stockholder. This is a transfer for value (the consideration being services rendered to the corporation) to a co-stockholder of the insured. Such a transfer does not come within any of the exceptions to the transfer for value rule and would thus subject the proceeds to income taxation. There is a possibility that this transfer for value problem could be avoided if each stockholder-employee initially applied for the insurance on the life of his co-stockholder and then transferred ownership of the policy to the corporation, reserving the right to receive the portion of the proceeds in excess of the premiums paid by the corporation. This transfer comes within

---

[21] For a discussion of the factors involved in reaching this decision see page 309 of this text.

the exceptions to the transfer for value rule since it is a transfer to a corporation of which the insured is a stockholder.[22]

Where one of the parties to the cross-purchase buy-sell agreement is a majority stockholder-employee, the use of an endorsement system split-dollar plan to help fund the agreement could create a serious estate tax trap for him. This is because the incidents of ownership in the life insurance policy on his life possessed by the corporation may be attributed to the majority stockholder-insured to the extent that the proceeds of the policy are not payable to or for the benefit of the corporation.[23] In this case, a portion of the proceeds of the policy on his life is payable to the co-stockholder of the majority stockholder-insured and not for the benefit of the corporation. The result could be that the value of his stock in the corporation and the insurance proceeds received by his co-stockholder and used to purchase his stock will be both includible in his gross estate for Federal estate tax purposes. To avoid the possibility of this onerous result the collateral assignment system should be used.

Family split-dollar plan. It is not necessary to have an employer-employee relationship to take advantage of the benefits that can be provided by a split-dollar insurance plan. For example, a father may be concerned about the lack of insurance protection for his married daughter in the event that her husband should die. He may be willing to assist her husband financially in the purchase of insurance on his life but does not want to do so at the expense of the share of his estate which will eventually go to his wife and other children. In this circumstance, he can enter into a split-dollar plan with his son-in-law by the terms of which he will receive back from the proceeds an amount equal to the premiums that he has paid. His daughter will be protected by insurance on her husband's life at a minimal cost to them. Since this is not an employer-employee arrangement, there should be no taxable income charged to the son-in-law. However, the value of the economic benefit he receives as a result of the arrangement may be treated as a taxable gift from the father. In most cases, however, a gift tax will not be payable since the economic benefit will not exceed the $3,000 annual exclusion from the gift tax that is available to all donors for gifts of a present interest. There are obviously many other situations where the split-dollar concept can be put to good use between family members.

Other uses. The possible uses to which a split-dollar insurance plan can be put have by no means been exhausted. Any time one party has a need for insurance protection and another party can be found who is willing to assist in the purchase of the insurance needed, the elements are present for the adoption of a split-dollar insurance plan.

---

[22]I.R.C. Sec. 101(a)(2)(B).

[23]Proposed Reg. Sec. 20.2042-1(c)(2).

Index of Cases

A

Adams v. Jarvis, 239
Alexander v. Sims, 170 *n*
Alsworth v. Packard, 144
Altheimer v. Hunter, 50, 52
Anderson v. Droge, 134
Anglo-American Direct Tea Trading Co. v. Seward, 55
Archer, In re, 41
Aron v. Gillman, 205, 318, 329
Athol Mfg. Co. v. Commissioner, 111 *n*
Atlantic Oil Co. v. Patterson, 445 *n*
Auditore's Will, Matter of, 285
Austin v. Munro, 61

B

Bailey v. Smith, 318
Balafas v. Balafas, 169
Barrett v. W. A. Webster Lumber Co., 254
Bates Street Shirt Co. v. Waite, 291, 293, 399
Bauchle v. Smylie, 136, 150
Bell v. Hepworth, 158
Bensel et al., Executors, 384, 385, 387, 389
Billings' Appeal [106 Pa. 558], 31
Black v. Parker Manufacturing Co., 413
Blauvelt v. Citizens Trust Co., 415, 416
Block's Will, In re, 302, 305
Blodgett v. Silberman, 125, 126
Bloomingdale v. Bloomingdale, 263 *n*
Blut v. Katz, 144
Bogene Inc., 425
Bohnsack v. Detroit Trust Co., 316, 322
Borden's Estate, Matter of, 178
Borg v. International Silver Co., 355
Boston Safe Deposit and Trust Co., 242
Boulle v. Tompkins, 60
Bowen v. Lewis, 78
Bradford Robinson Printing Co., 451 *n*

Bringham v. M. and J. Corporation, 349 *n*
Brodrick v. Gore, 243, 392
Brooks v. U.S. Ct. of Apps., 424
Brown, Matter of, 296, 298
Buehrle v. Buehrle, 220
Burke, Harold J., 96
Burrall v. Bushwick R.R. Co., 259
Burwell v. Cawood, 50
Butcher v. Hepworth, 157
Butler v. Wright, 88

C

Cahill v. Haff, 131
Camden Land Co. v. Lewis, 292
Cardos v. Cristadoro, 320
Casale v. Comm., 448 *n*, 481 *n*,
Casey v. Hurley, 167
Chertow's Estate, In re, 76
City Bank Farmers Trust Co. v. Hewitt Realty Co., 260 *n*
Cochran v. Whitby (Estate of Soper), 313
Coe v. Winchester, 169, 177, 180, 185, 203, 315, 318
Colwell v. Garfield National Bank, 158
Commissioner v. Bensel, 384, 385, 386
Conant v. Blount, 64, 66, 85, 90
Conner v. Conner, 170 *n*
Conway, Succession of, 205
Cross v. Beguelin, 348 *n*
Cuppy v. Ward, 269 *n*

D

Dannat v. Jones, 60
Dartmouth College v. Woodward, 249
Delamater v. Hepworth, 157
Denawitz v. Milch, 149 *n*, 161
Dennis' Estate, Matter of [136 N.Y.S. (2d) 84], 30
Detroit Bank and Trust Co. v. U.S., 499 *n*
Dickman Lumber Co. v. U.S., 410 *n*

508

Subject Index

GLASSBORO STATE COLLEGE